H

SEXING THE BODY

BASIC
BOOKS

A MEMBER OF THE PERSEUS BOOKS GROUP

SEXING THE BODY

GENDER POLITICS *and the*
CONSTRUCTION *of* SEXUALITY

ANNE FAUSTO-STERLING

181.8980

Published by Basic Books,
A Member of the Perseus Books Group

Book design by Victoria Kuskowski

All uncredited illustrations are from the author's collection and are used with her permission.

First Edition

A CIP catalog record for this title is available from the Library of Congress.
ISBN 0-465-07713-7 (cloth)
ISBN 0-465-07714-5 (paper)

For the ever delightful and always stimulating Paula.

You excite my heart and my mind.

CONTENTS

PREFACE

In my previous book, *Myths of Gender: Biological Theories About Women and Men* (Basic Books, 1985), I exhorted scholars to examine the personal and political components of their scholarly viewpoints. Individual scientists are inclined to believe one or another claim about biology based in part on scientific evidence and in part on whether the claim confirms some aspect of life that seems personally familiar. As someone who has lived part of her life as an unabashed heterosexual, part as an unabashed lesbian, and part in transition, I am certainly open to theories of sexuality that allow for flexibility and the development of new behavior patterns, even in adulthood. I do not find it surprising, however, that someone who has always felt either heterosexual or homosexual might be more open to theories that posit a biologically determined sexuality that unfolds as one grows into adulthood.

Regardless of one's personal leanings, anyone who wants to make a general argument beyond his or her limited knowledge must gather evidence and put it together in a way that makes sense to others. I hope I have done that well enough to convince readers of the need for theories that allow for a good deal of human variation and that integrate the analytical powers of the biological and the social into the systematic analysis of human development.

For a book written for a general audience, this volume has an unusually large notes and bibliography section. That is because, in essence, I have written two books in one: a narrative accessible to a general audience and a scholarly work intended to advance discussion and arguments within academic circles. At times the scholarly discussion can become arcane or devolve into side issues that deflect attention from the main narrative. Furthermore, academics often demand detailed evidence in the form of quotes from original sources or detailed accounts of a particular experiment. One of the ways I have used the notes is to carry on the scholarly discussions without distracting the general reader. Although one need not do so to follow my general argument, I nevertheless urge everyone to read the notes, as they add both depth and diversity to the text.

Furthermore, *Sexing the Body* is a highly synthetic work, and thus most readers, be they academicians or members of a general audience, will be unfamiliar with—and quite possibly skeptical of—at least some of the areas on which I touch. For this reason as well, I chose to footnote heavily, indicating that claims I make even in passing have substantial backing in the academic literature. Then, too, readers intrigued with particular topics can use the notes and bibliography as a resource for further reading of their own. This, I fear, is the teacher in me. My biggest desire in writing this book is to stimulate discussion and reading on the part of my readers, so the rich and up-to-date bibliography draws on significant literatures in fields ranging from science studies to feminism to sexuality studies to human development to systems theory and biology.

I have also included a fair amount of artwork, and again this is unusual for a book of this type. Some of the illustrations consist of cartoons or humorous drawings describing events discussed in the text. I was inspired to take this route by others who have conveyed scientific ideas using cartoons. Many people think of science as a humorless profession, and feminists are always accused of lacking a sense of humor. But this feminist scientist finds humor everywhere. I hope that some of the illustrations encourage readers suspicious of the cultures of science and of feminism to see that it is possible to be deeply serious about one's profession while maintaining a sense of humor.

Biology itself is a very visual field, as a glance at current biology textbooks reveals. Some of my illustrations, then, are intended to convey information visually, rather than verbally. In this I am merely being true to my own academic tradition. At any rate, I encourage the reader to laugh if so moved, to study diagrams if he or she wishes, or to skip over the illustrations and focus on the text, if that is the reader's preferred mode.

ACKNOWLEDGMENTS

This book took more than six years to write. During that time I have had the consistent support of family and friends who put up with my obsession and my withdrawal from polite company whenever I focused on a new deadline. I thank all of them and each of them. Each of you (and you know who you are) provide the bedrock on which I stand.

When I needed to review and synthesize material from fields outside my own, I depended on the generosity of academics and independent scholars to read drafts and let me know when I had some basic concept wrong or had left out some essential work. Each of the people in the long list that follows has a busy schedule and writing projects of his or her own, yet took the time to read and comment on early versions of one or more chapters of this book or to help me formulate some of its ideas. There are those who shared with me early versions of their own work, bringing me quickly up to date. If I have omitted anyone, I apologize in advance. Of course, these scholars bear no responsibility for the final version.

Elizabeth Adkins-Regan, Pepe Amor y Vasquez, Mary Arnold, Evan Balaban, Marc Breedlove, Laura Briggs, Bill Byne, Cheryl Chase, Adele Clarke, Donald Dewesbury, Milton Diamond, Alice Dreger, Joseph Dumit, Julia Epstein, Leslie Feinberg, Thalia Field, Cynthia García-Coll, GISP 006, Elizabeth Grosz, Philip Gruppuso, Evelynn Hammonds, Sandra Harding, Ann Harrington, Bernice L. Hausman, Morgan Holmes, Gail Hornstein, Ruth Hubbard, Lily Kay, Suzanne Kessler, Ursula Klein, Hannah Landecker, James McIlwain, Cindy Meyers-Seifer, Diana Miller, John Modell, Susan Oyama, Katherine Park, Mary Poovey, Karen Romer, Hilary Rose, Steven Rose, Londa Schiebinger, Chandak Sengoopta, Roger Smith, Lynn Smitley, Linda Snelling, Peter Taylor, Douglas Wahlsten, Kim Wallen.

The participants in the listserve "Loveweb" have shared references and reprints, have been willing to argue and disagree with me, and in the process have helped me clarify my views. Struggle, intellectual and otherwise, can be the fire that forges better ideas.

The editors formerly or currently at Basic Books have played a major role in the final shaping and writing of the manuscript. I owe a special debt to Steven Fraser, Jo Ann Miller, and Libby Garland. Steve believed in the book at the start and offered insightful comments on several of the early chapters. Jo Ann and Libby produced thoughtful and detailed editing of the entire manuscript, which has immeasurably strengthened the book.

Portions of this book were written while I was on leave of absence from Brown University. I thank my colleagues for putting up with my disappearance and the Brown administration for facilitating my leaves. I thank the Brown administrative assistants and secretaries who helped me. I have had generous support from librarians in the Brown University library system. They helped me find even the most obscure sources and responded with promptness and support to my sometimes urgent requests. No scholar can ply her trade without the help of good librarians. Special thanks go to my research assistants: Veronica Gross, Vino Subramanian, Sonali Ruder, Miriam Reumann, and Erica Warp.

Portions of this book were written while I was in residence at the Rockefeller Foundation retreat in Bellagio, Italy. Other portions were written while I was supported by a fellowship from the American Council of Learned Societies, and still other portions while I was a Fellow of the Dibner Institute for the History of Science and Technology at the Massachusetts Institute of Technology. I thank everyone involved with these institutions for their support, both financial and practical.

Two talented illustrators, Diane DiMassa and Alyce Jacquet, have added immeasurably to the project. I thank them for their thoughtful work. Erica Warp stepped in at the last minute to contribute as well to the artwork.

Last but far from least, my life partner, Paula Vogel, has offered constant support. She has been enthusiastic about the project from the start. She read two drafts of every chapter and provided intellectual stimulation and emotional consistency without which I could not have completed the book. I dedicate *Sexing the Body* to her.

SEXING THE BODY

1

DUELING DUALISMS

Male or Female?

In the rush and excitement of leaving for the 1988 Olympics, Maria Patiño, Spain's top woman hurdler, forgot the requisite doctor's certificate stating, for the benefit of Olympic officials, what seemed patently obvious to anyone who looked at her: she was female. But the International Olympic Committee (IOC) had anticipated the possibility that some competitors would forget their certificates of femininity. Patiño had only to report to the "femininity control head office,"[1] scrape some cells off the side of her cheek, and all would be in order—or so she thought.

A few hours after the cheek scraping she got a call. Something was wrong. She went for a second examination, but the doctors were mum. Then, as she rode to the Olympic stadium to start her first race, track officials broke the news: she had failed the sex test. She may have looked like a woman, had a woman's strength, and never had reason to suspect that she wasn't a woman, but the examinations revealed that Patiño's cells sported a Y chromosome, and that her labia hid testes within. Furthermore, she had neither ovaries nor a uterus.[2] According to the IOC's definition, Patiño was not a woman. She was barred from competing on Spain's Olympic team.

Spanish athletic officials told Patiño to fake an injury and withdraw without publicizing the embarrassing facts. When she refused, the European press heard about it and the secret was out. Within months after returning to Spain, Patiño's life fell apart. Spanish officials stripped her of past titles and barred her from further competition. Her boyfriend deserted her. She was evicted from the national athletic residence, her scholarship was revoked, and suddenly she had to struggle to make a living. The national press had a field day at her expense. As she later said, "I was erased from the map, as if I had never existed. I gave twelve years to sports."[3]

Down but not out, Patiño spent thousands of dollars consulting doctors about her situation. They explained that she had been born with a condition called *androgen insensitivity*. This meant that, although she had a Y chromosome and her testes made plenty of testosterone, her cells couldn't detect this masculinizing hormone. As a result, her body had never developed male characteristics. But at puberty her testes produced estrogen (as do the testes of all men), which, because of her body's inability to respond to its testosterone, caused her breasts to grow, her waist to narrow, and her hips to widen. Despite a Y chromosome and testes, she had grown up as a female and developed a female form.

Patiño resolved to fight the IOC ruling. "I knew I was a woman," she insisted to one reporter, "in the eyes of medicine, God and most of all, in my own eyes."[4] She enlisted the help of Alison Carlson, a former Stanford University tennis player and biologist opposed to sex testing, and together they began to build a case. Patiño underwent examinations in which doctors "checked out her pelvic structures and shoulders to decide if she was feminine enough to compete."[5] After two and a half years the International Amateur Athletic Federation (IAAF) reinstated her, and by 1992 Patiño had rejoined the Spanish Olympic squad, going down in history as the first woman ever to challenge sex testing for female athletes. Despite the IAAF's flexibility, however, the IOC has remained adamant: even if looking for a Y chromosome wasn't the most scientific approach to sex testing, testing *must* be done.

The members of the International Olympic Committee remain convinced that a more scientifically advanced method of testing will be able to reveal the true sex of each athlete. But why is the IOC so worried about sex testing? In part, IOC rules reflect cold war political anxieties: during the 1968 Olympics, for instance, the IOC instituted "scientific" sex testing in response to rumors that some Eastern European competitors were trying to win glory for the Communist cause by cheating—having men masquerade as women to gain unfair advantage. The only known case of a man infiltrating women's competition occurred back in 1936 when Hermann Ratjen, a member of the Nazi Youth, entered the women's high-jump competition as "Dora." His maleness didn't translate into much of an advantage: he made it to the finals, but came in fourth, behind three women.

Although the IOC didn't require modern chromosome screening in the interest of international politics until 1968, it had long policed the sex of Olympic competitors in an effort to mollify those who feared that women's participation in sports threatened to turn them into manly creatures. In 1912, Pierre de Coubertin, founder of the modern Olympics (from which women were originally banned), argued that "women's sports are all against the law of nature."[6] If women were *by nature* not athletic competitors, then what was one to make of the sportswomen who pushed their way onto the Olympic scene? Olympic officials rushed to certify the femininity of the women they let through the door, because the very act of competing seemed to imply that they could not be true women.[7] In the context of gender politics, employing sex police made a great deal of sense.[8]

Sex or Gender?

Until 1968 female Olympic competitors were often asked to parade naked in front of a board of examiners. Breasts and a vagina were all one needed to certify one's femininity. But many women complained that this procedure was degrading. Partly because such complaints mounted, the IOC decided to make use of the modern "scientific" chromosome test. The problem, though, is that this test, and the more sophisticated polymerase chain reaction to detect small regions of DNA associated with testes development that the IOC uses today, cannot do the work the IOC wants it to do. A body's sex is simply too complex. There is no either/or. Rather, there are shades of difference. In chapters 2–4 I'll address how scientists, medical professionals, and the wider public have made sense of (or ought to make sense of) bodies that present themselves as neither entirely male nor entirely female. One of the major claims I make in this book is that labeling someone a man or a woman is a social decision. We may use scientific knowledge to help us make the decision, but only our beliefs about gender—not science—can define our sex. Furthermore, our beliefs about gender affect what kinds of knowledge scientists produce about sex in the first place.

Over the last few decades, the relation between *social expression* of masculinity and femininity and their *physical underpinnings* has been hotly debated in scientific and social arenas. In 1972 the sexologists John Money and Anke Ehrhardt popularized the idea that sex and gender are separate categories. *Sex*, they argued, refers to physical attributes and is anatomically and physiologically determined. *Gender* they saw as a psychological transformation of the self—the internal conviction that one is either male or female (gender identity) and the behavioral expressions of that conviction.[9]

Meanwhile, the second-wave feminists of the 1970s also argued that sex is distinct from gender—that social institutions, themselves designed to perpetuate gender inequality, produce most of the differences between men and women.[10] Feminists argued that although men's and women's bodies serve different reproductive functions, few other sex differences come with the territory, unchangeable by life's vicissitudes. If girls couldn't learn math as easily as boys, the problem wasn't built into their brains. The difficulty resulted from gender norms—different expectations and opportunities for boys and girls. Having a penis rather than a vagina is a sex difference. Boys performing better than girls on math exams is a gender difference. Presumably, the latter could be changed even if the former could not.

Money, Ehrhardt, and feminists set the terms so that *sex* represented the body's anatomy and physiological workings and *gender* represented social forces that molded behavior.[11] Feminists did not question the realm of physical sex; it was the psychological and cultural meanings of these differences—gender—that was at issue. But feminist definitions of sex and gender left open the possibility that male/female differences in cognitive function and behavior[12] could *result* from sex differences, and thus, in some circles, the matter of sex versus gender became a debate about how "hardwired" intelligence and a variety of behaviors are in the brain,[13] while in others there seemed no choice but to ignore many of the findings of contemporary neurobiology.

In ceding the territory of physical sex, feminists left themselves open to renewed attack on the grounds of biological difference.[14] Indeed, feminism has encountered massive resistance from the domains of biology, medicine, and significant components of social science. Despite many positive social changes, the 1970s optimism that women would achieve full economic and social equality once gender inequity was addressed in the social sphere has faded in the face of a seemingly recalcitrant inequality.[15] All of which has prompted feminist scholars, on the one hand, to question the notion of sex itself,[16] while on the other to deepen their inquiry into what we might mean by words such as *gender, culture,* and *experience.* The anthropologist Henrietta A. Moore, for example, argues against reducing accounts of gender, culture, and experience to their "linguistic and cognitive elements." In this book (especially in chapter 9) I argue, as does Moore, that "what is at issue is the embodied nature of identities and experience. Experience . . . is not individual and fixed, but irredeemably social and processual."[17]

Our bodies are too complex to provide clear-cut answers about sexual difference. The more we look for a simple physical basis for "sex," the more it becomes clear that "sex" is not a pure physical category. What bodily signals and functions we define as male or female come already entangled in our ideas about gender. Consider the problem facing the International Olympic Committee. Committee members want to decide definitively who is male and who is female. But how? If Pierre de Coubertin were still around, the answer would be simple: anybody who desired to compete could not, by definition, be a female. But those days are past. Could the IOC use muscle strength as some measure of sex? In some cases. But the strengths of men and women, especially highly trained athletes, overlap. (Remember that three women beat Hermann Ratjen's high jump). And although Maria Patiño fit a commonsense definition of femininity in terms of looks and strength, she also had testes and a Y chromosome. But why should these be the deciding factors?

The IOC may use chromosome or DNA tests or inspection of the breasts and genitals to ascertain the sex of a competitor, but doctors faced with uncertainty about a child's sex use different criteria. They focus primarily on reproductive abilities (in the case of a potential girl) or penis size (in the case of a prospective boy). If a child is born with two X chromosomes, oviducts, ovaries, and a uterus on the inside, but a penis and scrotum on the outside, for instance, is the child a boy or a girl? Most doctors declare the child a girl, despite the penis, because of her potential to give birth, and intervene using surgery and hormones to carry out the decision. Choosing which criteria to use in determining sex, and choosing to make the determination at all, are social decisions for which scientists can offer no absolute guidelines.

Real or Constructed?

I enter the debates about sex and gender as a biologist and a social activist.[18] Daily, my life weaves in and out of a web of conflict over the politics of sexuality and the making and using of knowledge about the biology of human behavior. The central tenet of this book is that truths about human sexuality created by scholars in general and by biologists in particular are one component of political, social, and moral struggles about our cultures and economies.[19] At the same time, components of our political, social, and moral struggles become, quite literally, embodied, incorporated into our very physiological being. My intent is to show how these mutually dependent claims work, in part by addressing such issues as how—through their daily lives, experiments, and medical practices—scientists create truths about sexuality; how our bodies incorporate and confirm these truths; and how these truths, sculpted by the social milieu in which biologists practice their trade, in turn refashion our cultural environment.

My take on the problem is idiosyncratic, and for good reason. Intellectually, I inhabit three seemingly incompatible worlds. In my home department I interact with molecular biologists, scientists who examine living beings from the perspective of the molecules from which they are built. They describe a microscopic world in which cause and effect remain mostly inside a single cell. Molecular biologists rarely think about interacting organs within an individual body, and even less often about how a body bounded by skin interacts with the world on the other side of the skin. Their vision of what makes an organism tick is decidedly bottom up, small to large, inside to outside.

I also interact with a virtual community—a group of scholars drawn together by a common interest in sexuality—and connected by something called a listserve. On a listserve, one can pose questions, think out loud, comment on relevant news items, argue about theories of human sexuality, and report the latest research findings. The comments are read by a group of people hooked together via electronic mail. My listserve (which I call "Loveweb") consists of a diverse group of scholars—psychologists, animal behaviorists, hormone biologists, sociologists, anthropologists, and philosophers. Although many points of view coexist in this group, the vocal majority favor body-based, biological explanations of human sexual behavior. Loveweb members have technical names for preferences they believe to be immutable. In addition to homosexual, heterosexual, and bisexual, for example, they speak of *hebephilia* (attracted primarily to pubescent girls), *ephebephilia* (aroused by young males in their late teens or early twenties), *pedophilia* (aroused by children), *gynephilia* (aroused by adult women), and *androphilia* (attracted to adult men). Many Loveweb members believe that we acquire our sexual essence before birth and that it unfolds as we grow and develop.[20]

Unlike molecular biologists and Loveweb members, feminist theorists view the body not as essence, but as a bare scaffolding on which discourse and performance build a completely acculturated being. Feminist theorists write persuasively and often imaginatively about the processes by which culture molds and effectively creates the body. Furthermore, they have an eye on politics (writ large), which neither molecular biologists nor Loveweb participants have. Most feminist scholars concern themselves with real-world power relationships. They have often come to their theoretical work because they want to understand (and change) social, political, and economic inequality. Unlike the inhabitants of my other two worlds, feminist theorists reject what Donna Haraway, a leading feminist theoretician, calls "the God-trick"—producing knowledge from above, from a place that denies the individual scholar's location in a real and troubled world. Instead, they understand that all scholarship adds threads to a web that positions racialized bodies, sexes, genders, and preferences in relationship to one another. New or differently spun threads change our relationships, change how we are in the world.[21]

Traveling among these varied intellectual worlds produces more than a little discomfort. When I lurk on Loveweb, I put up with gratuitous feminist-bashing aimed at some mythic feminist who derides biology and seems to have a patently stupid view of how the world works. When I attend feminist conferences, people howl in disbelief at the ideas debated on Loveweb. And the molecular biologists don't think much of either of the other worlds. The questions asked by feminists and Loveweb participants seem too complicated; studying sex in bacteria or yeast is the only way to go.

To my molecular biology, Loveweb, and feminist colleagues, then, I say the following: as a biologist, I believe in the material world. As a scientist, I believe in building specific knowledge by conducting experiments. But as a feminist Witness (in the Quaker sense of the word) and in recent years as a historian, I also believe that what we call "facts" about the living world are not universal truths. Rather, as Haraway writes, they "are rooted in specific histories, practices, languages and peoples."[22] Ever since the field of biology emerged in the United States and Europe at the start of the nineteenth century, it has been bound up in debates over sexual, racial, and national politics.[23] And as our social viewpoints have shifted, so has the science of the body.[24]

Many historians mark the seventeenth and eighteenth centuries as periods of great change in our concepts of sex and sexuality.[25] During this period a notion of legal equality replaced the feudal exercise of arbitrary and violent power given by divine right. As the historian Michel Foucault saw it, society still required some form of discipline. A growing capitalism needed new methods to control the "insertion of bodies into the machinery of production and the adjustment of the phenomena of population to economic processes."[26] Foucault divided this power over living bodies (*bio-power*) into two forms. The first centered on the individual body. The role of many science professionals (including the so-called human sciences—psychology, sociology, and economics) became to optimize and standardize the body's function.[27] In Europe and North America, Foucault's standardized body has, traditionally, been male and Caucasian. And although this book focuses on gender, I regularly discuss the ways in which the ideas of both race and gender emerge from underlying assumptions about the body's physical nature.[28] Understanding how race and gender work—together and independently—helps us learn more about how the social becomes embodied.

Foucault's second form of bio-power—"*a biopolitics of the population*"[29]— emerged during the early nineteenth century as pioneer social scientists began to develop the survey and statistical methods needed to supervise and manage "births and mortality, the level of health, life expectancy and longevity."[30] For Foucault, "discipline" had a double meaning. On the one hand, it implied a form of control or punishment; on the other, it referred to an academic body of knowledge—the discipline of history or biology. The disciplinary knowledge developed in the fields of embryology, endocrinology, surgery, psychology, and biochemistry have encouraged physicians to attempt to control the very gender of the body—including "its capacities, gestures, movements, location and behaviors."[31]

By helping the normal take precedence over the natural, physicians have also contributed to populational biopolitics. We have become, Foucault writes, "a society of normalization."[32] One important mid-twentieth-century sexologist went so far as to name the male and female models in his anatomy text Norma and Normman (sic).[33] Today we see the notion of pathology applied in many settings—from the sick, diseased, or different body,[34] to the single-parent family in the urban ghetto.[35] But imposing a gender norm is socially, not scientifically, driven. The lack of research into the normal distributions of genital anatomy, as well as many surgeons' lack of interest in using such data when they do exist (discussed in chapters 3 and 4), clearly illustrate this claim. From the viewpoint of medical practitioners, progress in the handling of intersexuality involves maintaining the normal. Accordingly, there ought to be only two boxes: male and female. The knowledge developed by the medical disciplines empowers doctors to maintain a mythology of the normal by changing the intersexual body to fit, as nearly as possible, into one or the other cubbyhole.

One person's medical progress, however, can be another's discipline and control. Intersexuals such as Maria Patiño have unruly—even heretical—bodies. They do not fall naturally into a binary classification; only a surgical shoehorn can put them there. But why should we care if a "woman" (defined as having breasts, a vagina, uterus, ovaries, and menstruation) has a "clitoris" large enough to penetrate the vagina of another woman? Why should we care if there are individuals whose "natural biological equipment" enables them to have sex "naturally" with both men and women? Why must we amputate or surgically hide that "offending shaft" found on an especially large clitoris? The answer: to maintain gender divisions, we must control those bodies that are so unruly as to blur the borders. Since intersexuals quite literally embody both sexes, they weaken claims about sexual difference.

This book reflects a shifting politics of science and of the body. I am deeply committed to the ideas of the modern movements of gay and women's liberation, which argue that the way we traditionally conceptualize gender and sexual identity narrows life's possibilities while perpetuating gender inequality. In order to shift the politics of the body, one must change the politics of science itself. Feminists (and others) who study how scientists create empirical knowledge have begun to reconceptualize the very nature of the scientific process.[36] As with other social arenas, such scholars understand practical, empirical knowledge to be imbued with the social and political issues of its time. I stand at the intersection of these several traditions. On the one hand, scientific and popular debates about intersexuals and homosexuals—bodies that defy the norms of our two-sex system—are deeply intertwined. On the other, beneath the debates about what these bodies mean and how to treat them lie struggles over the meaning of objectivity and the timeless nature of scientific knowledge.

Perhaps nowhere are these struggles more visible than in the biological accounts of what we would today call sexual orientation or sexual preference. Consider, for instance, a television newsmagazine segment about married women who "discovered," often in their forties, that they were lesbian. The show framed the discussion around the idea that a woman who has sex with men must be heterosexual, while a woman who falls in love with another woman must be lesbian.[37] On this show there seemed to be only these two possibilities. Even though the women interviewed had had active and satisfying sex lives with their husbands and produced and raised families, they knew that they must "be" lesbian the minute they found themselves attracted to a woman. Furthermore, they felt it likely that they must always have been lesbian without knowing it.

The show portrayed sexual identity as a fundamental reality: a woman is either inherently heterosexual or inherently lesbian. And the act of coming out as a lesbian can negate an entire lifetime of heterosexual activity! Put this way, the show's depiction of sexuality sounds absurdly oversimplified. And yet, it reflects some of our most deeply held beliefs—so deeply held, in fact, that a great deal of scientific research (on animals as well as humans) is designed around this dichotomous formulation (as I discuss in some detail in chapters 6–8).[38]

Many scholars mark the start of modern scientific studies of human homosexuality with the work of Alfred C. Kinsey and colleagues, first published in 1948. Their surveys of sexual behavior in men and women provided modern sex researchers with a set of categories useful for measuring and analyzing sexual behaviors.[39] For both men and women, they used a rating scale of o to 6, with o being 100 percent heterosexual, 6 being 100 percent homosexual. (An eighth category—"X"—was for individuals who experienced no erotic attractions or activities.) Although they designed a scale with discrete categories, Kinsey and co-workers stressed that "the reality includes individuals of every intermediate type, lying in a continuum between the two extremes and between each and every category on the scale."[40]

The Kinsey studies offered new categories defined in terms of sexual arousal—especially orgasm—rather than allowing terms such as *affection, marriage,* or *relationship* to contribute to definitions of human sexuality.[41] Sexuality remained an individual characteristic, not something produced within relationships in particular social settings. Exemplifying my claim that with the very act of measuring, scientists can change the social reality they set out to quantify, I note that today Kinsey's categories have taken on a life of their own. Not only do sophisticated gays and lesbians occasionally refer to themselves by a Kinsey number (such as in a personal ad that might begin "tall, muscular Kinsey 6 seeks . . . "), but many scientific studies use the Kinsey scale to define their study population.[42]

Although many social scientists understand the inadequacy of using the single word *homosexual* to describe same-sex desire, identity, and practice, the linear Kinsey scale still reigns supreme in scholarly work. In studies that search for genetic links to homosexuality, for example, the middle of the Kinsey scale disappears; researchers seek to compare the extreme ends of the spectrum in hopes of maximizing the chance that they will find something of interest.[43] Multidimensional models of homosexuality exist. Fritz Klein, for example, created a grid with seven variables (sexual attraction, sexual behavior, sexual fantasies, emotional preference, social preference, self-identification, hetero/homo lifestyle) superimposed on a time scale (past, present, future).[44] Nevertheless, one research team, reporting on 144 studies of sexual orientation published in the *Journal of Homosexuality* from 1974 to 1993, found that only 10 percent of these studies used a multidimensional scale to assess homosexuality. About 13 percent used a single scale, usually some version of the Kinsey numbers, while the rest used self-identification (33 percent), sexual preference (4 percent), behavior (9 percent), or, most shockingly for an academic publication, never clearly described their methods (31 percent).[45]

Just as these examples from contemporary sociology show that the categories used to define, measure, and analyze human sexual behavior change with time, so too has a recent explosion of scholarship on the social history of human sexuality shown that the social organization and expression of human sexuality are neither timeless nor universal. Historians are just beginning to pry loose information from the historical record, and any new overviews written are sure to differ,[46] but I offer a cartoon summary of some of this work in figure 1.1.

As historians gather information, they also argue about the nature of history itself. The historian David Halperin writes: "The real issue confronting any cultural historian of antiquity, and any critic of contemporary culture, is . . . how to recover the terms in which the experiences of individuals belonging to past societies were actually constituted."[47] The feminist historian Joan Scott makes a similar argument, suggesting that historians must not assume

FIGURE 1.1: A cartoon history of sex and gender. (Source: Diane DiMassa, for the author)

that the term *experience* contains a self-evident meaning. Instead, they must try to understand the workings of the complex and changing processes "by which identities are ascribed, resisted, or embraced and 'to note' which processes themselves are unremarked and indeed achieve their effect because they are not noticed."[48]

For example, in her book *The Woman Beneath the Skin,* the historian of science Barbara Duden describes coming upon an eight-volume medical text.

Written in the eighteenth century by a practicing physician, the books describe over 1,800 cases involving diseases of women. Duden found herself
unable to use twentieth-century medical terms to reconstruct what illnesses
these women had. Instead she noticed "bits and pieces of medical theories that
would have been circulating, combined with elements from popular culture;
self-evident bodily perceptions appear alongside things that struck [her] as
utterly improbable." Duden describes her intellectual anguish as she became
more and more determined to understand these eighteenth-century German
female bodies on their own terms:

> To gain access to the inner, invisible bodily existence of these ailing
> women, I had to venture across the boundary that separates . . . the inner
> body beneath the skin, from the world around it . . . the body and its
> environment have been consigned to opposing realms: on the one side are
> the body, nature, and biology, stable and unchanging phenomena; on the
> other side are the social environment and history, realms of constant
> change. With the drawing of this boundary the body was expelled from
> history.[49]

In contrast to Duden's anguish, many historians of sexuality have leaped enthusiastically into their new field, debating with one another as they dug into
their freshly discovered resources. They delighted in shocking the reader with
sentences such as: "The year 1992 marked the 100th anniversary of heterosexuality in America"[50] and "From 1700–1900 the citizens of London made
a transition from three sexes to four genders."[51] What do historians mean by
such statements? Their essential point is that for as far back as one can gather
historical evidence (from primitive artwork to the written word), humans
have engaged in a variety of sexual practices, but that this sexual activity is
bound to historical contexts. That is, sexual practices and societal understandings of them vary not only across cultures but over time as well.

The social scientist Mary McIntosh's 1968 article, "The Homosexual
Role," provided the touchstone that pushed scholars to consider sexuality as
a historical phenomenon.[52] Most Westerners, she pointed out, assumed that
people's sexuality could be classified two or three ways: homosexual, heterosexual, and bisexual.[53] McIntosh argued that this perspective wasn't very in-
formative. A static view of homosexuality as a timeless, physical trait, for
instance, didn't tell us much about why different cultures defined homosexuality differently, or why homosexuality seemed more acceptable in certain

times and places than in others.[54] An important corollary to McIntosh's insistence on a history of homosexuality is that heterosexuality, and indeed all forms of human sexuality, have a history.

Many scholars embraced McIntosh's challenge to give human sexual expression a past. But disagreement about the implications of this past abounds.[55] The authors of books such as *Gay American History* and *Surpassing the Love of Men* eagerly searched the past for role models that could offer psychological affirmation to members of the nascent gay liberation movement.[56] Just as with the initial impulses of the women's movement to find heroines worthy of emulation, early "gay" histories looked to the past in order to make a case for social change in the present. Homosexuality, they argued, has always been with us; we should finally bring it into the cultural mainstream.

The initial euphoria induced by these scholars' discovery of a gay past was soon complicated by heated debates about the meanings and functions of history. Were our contemporary categories of sexuality inappropriate for analyzing different times and places? If gay people, in the present-day sense, had always existed, did that mean that the condition is inherited in some portion of the population? Could the fact that historians found evidence of homosexuality in whatever era they studied be seen as evidence that homosexuality is a biologically determined trait? Or could history only show us how cultures organize sexual expression differently in particular times and places?[57] Some found the latter possibility liberating. They maintained that behaviors that might seem to be constant actually had totally different meanings in different times and places. Could the apparent fact that in ancient Greece, love between older and younger men was an expected component of the development of free male citizens mean that biology had nothing to do with human sexual expression?[58] If history helped prove that sexuality was a social construction, it could also show how we had arrived at our present arrangements and, most important, offer insights into how to achieve the social and political change for which the gay liberation movement was battling.

Many historians believe that our modern concepts of sex and desire first made their appearance in the nineteenth century. Some point symbolically to the year 1869, when a German legal reformer seeking to change antisodomy laws first publicly used the word *homosexuality*.[59] Merely coining a new term did not magically create twentieth-century categories of sexuality, but the moment does seem to mark the beginning of their gradual emergence. It was during those years that physicians began to publish case reports of homosexuality—the first in 1869 in a German publication specializing in psychiatric and nervous illness.[60] As the scientific literature grew, specialists emerged to collect and systematize the narratives. The now-classic works of Krafft-Ebing and Havelock Ellis completed the transfer of homosexual behaviors from publicly accessible activities to ones managed at least in part by medicine.[61]

The emerging definitions of homo- and heterosexuality were built on a two-sex model of masculinity and femininity.[62] The Victorians, for example, contrasted the sexually aggressive male with the sexually indifferent female. But this created a mystery. If only men felt active desire, how could two women develop a mutual sexual interest? The answer: one of the women had to be an *invert*, someone with markedly masculine attributes. This same logic applied to male homosexuals, who were seen as more effeminate than heterosexual men.[63] As we will see in chapter 8, these concepts linger in late-twentieth-century studies of homosexual behaviors in rodents. A lesbian rat is she who mounts; a gay male rat is he who responds to being mounted.[64]

In ancient Greece, males who engaged in same-sex acts changed, as they aged, from feminine to masculine roles.[65] In contrast, by the early part of the twentieth century, someone engaging in homosexual acts *was,* like the married lesbians on the TV news show, a homosexual, a person constitutionally disposed to homosexuality. Historians attribute the emergence of this new homosexual body to widespread social, demographic, and economic changes occurring in the nineteenth century. In America, many men and eventually some women who had in previous generations remained on the family farm found urban spaces in which to gather. Away from the family's eyes, they were freer to pursue their sexual interests. Men seeking same-sex interactions gathered in bars or in particular outdoor spots; as their presence became more obvious, so too did attempts to control their behavior. In response to police and moral reformers, self-consciousness about their sexual behaviors emerged—a budding sense of identity.[66]

This forming identity contributed to its own medical rendering. Men (and later women) who identified themselves as homosexual now sought medical help and understanding. And as medical reports proliferated, homosexuals used them to paint their own self-descriptions. "By helping to give large numbers of people an identity and a name, medicine also helped to shape these people's experience and change their behavior, creating not just a new disease, but a new species of person, 'the modern homosexual.' "[67]

Homosexuality may have been born in 1869, but the modern heterosexual required another decade of gestation. In Germany in 1880 the word *heterosexual* made its public debut in a work defending homosexuality.[68] In 1892, heterosexuality crossed the ocean to America, where, after some period of

debate, a consensus developed among medical men that "heterosexual referred to a normal 'other-sex' Eros. [The doctors] proclaimed a new heterosexual separatism—an erotic apartheid that forcefully segregated the sex normals from the sex perverts."[69]

Through the 1930s the concept of heterosexuality fought its way into the
public consciousness, and by World War II, heterosexuality seemed a permanent feature of the sexual landscape. Now, the concept has come under heavy
fire. Feminists daily challenge the two-sex model, while a strongly self-
identified gay and lesbian community demands the right to be thoroughly normal. Transsexuals, transgendered people, and, as we shall see in the next three
chapters, a blossoming organization of intersexuals all have formed social
movements to include diverse sexual beings under the umbrella of normality.

The historians whose work I've just recounted emphasize discontinuity.
They believe that looking "for general laws about sexuality and its historical
evolution will be defeated by the sheer variety of past thought and behavior."[70]
But some disagree. The historian John Boswell, for instance, applies Kinsey's
classification scheme to ancient Greece. How the Greeks interpreted the molle
(feminine man) or the tribade (masculine woman), in Boswell's view, did not
necessarily matter. The existence of these two categories, which Boswell
might consider to be Kinsey 6s, shows that homosexual bodies or essences
have existed across the centuries. Boswell acknowledges that humans organized and interpreted sexual behaviors differently in different historical eras.
But he suggests that a similar range of bodies predisposed to particular sexual
activities existed then and now. "Constructions and context shape the articulation of sexuality," he insists, "but they do not efface recognition of erotic
preference as a potential category."[71] Boswell regards sexuality as "real"
rather than "socially constructed." While Halperin sees desire as a product of
cultural norms, Boswell implies we are quite possibly born with particular
sexual inclinations wired into our bodies. Growth, development, and the acquisition of culture show us how to express our inborn desires, he argues, but
do not wholly create them.

Scholars have yet to resolve the debate about the implications of a history
of sexuality. The historian Robert Nye compares historians to anthropologists. Both groups catalogue "curious habits and beliefs" and try, Nye writes,
"to find in them some common pattern of resemblance."[72] But what we conclude about people's past experiences depends to a large extent on how much
we believe that our categories of analysis transcend time and place. Suppose
for a minute that we had a few time-traveling clones—genetically identical
humans living in ancient Greece, in seventeenth-century Europe, and in the

contemporary United States. Boswell would say that if a particular clone was homosexual in ancient Greece, he would also be homosexual in the seventeenth century or today (figure 1.2, Model A). The fact that gender structures differ in different times and places might shape the invert's defiance, but would not create it. Halperin, however, would argue that there is no guarantee that the modern clone of an ancient Greek heterosexual would also be heterosexual (figure 1.2, Model B). The identical body might express different forms of desire in different eras.

There is no way to decide whose interpretation is right. Despite surface similarities, we cannot know whether yesterday's *tribade* is today's butch or whether the middle-aged Greek male lover is today's pedophile.[73]

Nature or Nurture?

While historians have looked to the past for evidence of whether human sexuality is inborn or socially constructed, anthropologists have pursued the same questions in their studies of sexual behaviors, roles, and expressions found in contemporary cultures around the globe. Those examining data from a wide variety of non-Western cultures have discerned two general patterns.[74] Some cultures, like our own, define a permanent role for those who engage in same-sex coupling—"institutionalized homosexuality," in Mary McIntosh's terminology.[75]

In contrast are those societies in which all adolescent boys, as part of an expected growth process, engage in genital acts with older men. These associations may be brief and highly ritualized or may last for several years. Here oral-genital contact between two males does not signify a permanent condition or special category of being. What defines sexual expression in such cultures is not so much the sex of one's partner as the age and status of the person with whom one couples.[76]

Anthropologists study vastly differing peoples and cultures with two goals in mind. First, they want to understand human variation—the diverse ways in which human beings organize society in order to eat and reproduce. Second, many anthropologists look for human universals. Like historians, anthropologists are divided about what information drawn from any one culture can tell them about another, or whether underlying differences in the expression of sexuality matter more or less than apparent commonalities.[77] In the midst of such disagreements, anthropological data are, nevertheless, often deployed in arguments about the nature of human sexual behavior.[78]

The anthropologist Carol Vance writes that the field of anthropology today reflects two contradictory strains of thought. The first she refers to as the

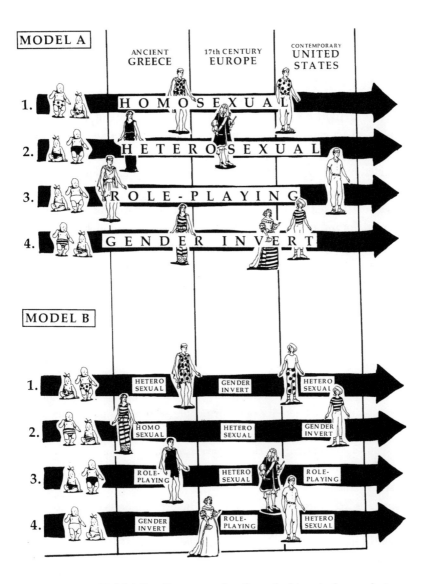

FIGURE 1.2: *Model A:* Reading *essentialism* from the historical record. A person with inborn homosexual tendencies would be homosexual, no matter what historical era. *Model B:* Reading *constructionism* from the historical record. A person of a particular genetic make-up might or might not become homosexual, depending on the culture and historical period in which he or she was raised.

(Source: Alyce Santoro, for the author)

"cultural influences model of sexuality," which, even as it emphasizes the importance of culture and learning in the molding of sexual behavior, nevertheless assumes "the bedrock of sexuality . . . to be universal and biologically determined; in the literature it appears as the 'sex drive' or 'impulse.'"[79] The second approach, Vance says, is to interpret sexuality entirely in terms of social construction. A moderate social constructionist might argue that the same physical act can carry different social meanings in different cultures,[80] while a more radical constructionist might argue that "sexual desire is itself constructed by culture and history from the energies and capacities of the body."[81]

Some social constructionists are interested in uncovering cross-cultural similarities. For instance, the anthropologist Gil Herdt, a moderate constructionist, catalogs four primary cultural approaches to the organization of human sexuality. *Age-structured homosexuality,* such as that found in ancient Greece, also appears in some modern cultures in which adolescent boys go through a developmental period in which they are isolated with older males and perform fellatio on a regular basis. Such acts are understood to be part of the normal process of becoming an adult heterosexual. In *gender-reversed homosexuality,* "same-sex activity involves a reversal of normative sex-role comportment: males dress and act as females, and females dress and behave as males."[82] Herdt used the concept of *role-specialized homosexuality* for cultures that sanction same-sex activity only for people who play a particular social role, such as a shaman. Role-specialized homosexuality contrasts sharply with our own cultural creation: *the modern gay movement.* To declare oneself "gay" in the United States is to adopt an identity and to join a social and sometimes political movement.

Many scholars embraced Herdt's work for providing new ways to think about the status of homosexuality in Europe and America. But although he has provided useful new typologies for the cross-cultural study of sexuality, others argue that Herdt carries with him assumptions that reflect his own culture.[83] The anthropologist Deborah Elliston, for instance, believes that using the term *homosexuality* to describe practices of semen exchange in Melanesian societies "imputes a Western model of sexuality . . . that relies on Western ideas about gender, erotics and personhood, and that ultimately obscures the meanings that hold for these practices in Melanesia." Elliston complains that Herdt's concept of age-structured sexuality obscures the composition of the category "sexual," and that it is precisely this category that requires clarification to begin with.[84]

When they turn their attention more generally to the relationships between gender and systems of social power, anthropologists face the same sorts of intellectual difficulties when studying "third" genders in other cultures. During the 1970s European and North American feminist activists hoped that anthropologists could provide empirical data to support their political arguments for gender equality. If, somewhere in the world, egalitarian societies existed, wouldn't that imply that our own social structures were not inevitable? Alternatively, what if women in every culture known to humankind had a subordinate status? Didn't such cross-cultural similarity mean, as more than one writer suggested, that women's secondary standing must be biologically ordained?[85]

When feminist anthropologists traveled around the world in search of cultures sporting the banner of equity, they did not return with happy tidings. Most thought, as the feminist anthropologist Sherry Ortner writes, "that men were in some way or other 'the first sex.'"[86] But critiques of these early cross-cultural analyses mounted, and in the 1990s some prominent feminist anthropologists reassessed the issue. The same problem encountered with collecting information by survey emerges in cross-cultural comparisons of social structures. Simply put, anthropologists must invent categories into which they can sort collected information. Inevitably, some of the invented categories involve the anthropologists' own unquestioned axioms of life, what some scholars call "incorrigible propositions." The idea that there are only two sexes is an incorrigible proposition,[87] and so too is the idea that anthropologists would know sexual equality when they saw it.

Ortner thinks that argument about the universality of sexual inequality has continued for more than two decades because anthropologists assumed that each society would be internally consistent, an expectation she now believes to be unreasonable: "no society or culture is totally consistent. Every society/culture has some axes of male prestige and some of female, some of gender equality, and some (sometimes many) axes of prestige that have nothing to do with gender. The problem in the past has been that all of us . . . were trying to pigeonhole each case." Now she argues instead that "the most interesting things about any given case is precisely the multiplicity of logics operating, of discourses being spoken, of practices of prestige and power in play."[88] If one attends to the dynamics, the contradictions, and minor themes, Ortner believes, it becomes possible to see both the currently dominant system *and* the potential for minor themes to become major ones.[89]

But feminists, too, have incorrigible propositions, and a central one has been that all cultures, as the Nigerian anthropologist Oyeronke Oyewumi writes, "organize their social world through a perception of human bodies" as male or female.[90] In taking European and North American feminists to task over this proposition, Oyewumi shows how the imposition of a system of

gender—in this case, through colonialism followed by scholarly imperial-
ism—can alter our understandings of ethnic and racial difference. In her own
detailed analysis of Yoruba culture, Oyewumi finds that relative age is a far
more significant social organizer. Yoruba pronouns, for example, do not indicate sex, but rather who is older or younger than the speaker. What they think
about how the world works shapes the knowledge that scholars produce about
the world. That knowledge, in turn, affects the world at work.

If Yoruba intellectuals had constructed the original scholarship on Yoruba-
land, Oyewumi thinks that "seniority would have been privileged over gender."[91] Seeing Yoruba society through the lens of seniority rather than that
of gender would have two important effects. First, if Euro-American scholars
learned about Nigeria from Yoruba anthropologists, our own belief systems about the universality of gender might change. Eventually, such knowledge might alter our own gender constructs. Second, the articulation of a
seniority-based vision of social organization among the Yoruba would, presumably, reinforce such social structures. Oyewumi finds, however, that African scholarship often imports European gender categories. And "by writing
about any society through a gendered perspective, scholars necessarily write
gender into that society. . . . Thus scholarship is implicated in the process of
gender-formation."[92]

Thus historians and anthropologists disagree about how to interpret human sexuality across cultures and history. Philosophers even dispute the validity of the words *homosexual* and *heterosexual*—the very terms of the argument.[93] But wherever they fall along the social constructionist spectrum,
most argue from the assumption that there is a fundamental split between
nature and culture, between "real bodies" and their cultural interpretations.
I take seriously the ideas of Foucault, Haraway, Scott, and others that our
bodily experiences are brought into being by our development in particular
cultures and historical periods. But especially as a biologist, I want to make
the argument more specific.[94] As we grow and develop, we literally, not just
"discursively" (that is, through language and cultural practices), construct
our bodies, incorporating experience into our very flesh. To understand this
claim, we must erode the distinctions between the physical and the social
body.

Dualisms Denied

"A devil, a born devil, on whose nature nurture can never stick." So Shakespeare's Prospero denounces Caliban in *The Tempest*. Clearly, questions of nature and nurture have troubled European culture for some time. Euro-

American ways of understanding how the world works depend heavily on the use of dualisms—pairs of opposing concepts, objects, or belief systems. This book focuses especially on three of these: sex/gender, nature/nurture, and real/constructed. We usually employ dualisms in some form of hierarchical argument. Prospero complains that nature controls Caliban's behavior and that his, Prospero's, "pains humanely taken" (to civilize Caliban) are to no avail. Human nurture cannot conquer the devil's nature. In the chapters that follow we will encounter relentless intellectual struggle over which element in any particular pair of dualisms should (or is believed to) dominate. But in virtually all cases, I argue that intellectual questions cannot be resolved nor social progress made by reverting to Prospero's complaint. Instead, as I consider discrete moments in the creation of biological knowledge about human sexuality, I look to cut through the Gordian knot of dualistic thought. I propose to modify Halperin's *bon mot* that "sexuality is not a somatic fact, it is a cultural effect,"[95] arguing instead that sexuality *is* a somatic fact *created by* a cultural effect. (See especially this book's final chapter.)

Why worry about using dualisms to parse the world? I agree with the philosopher Val Plumwood, who argues that their use makes invisible the interdependencies of each pair. This relationship enables sets of pairs to map onto each other. Consider an extract of Plumwood's list:

Reason	Nature
Male	Female
Mind	Body
Master	Slave
Freedom	Necessity (nature)
Human	Nature (nonhuman)
Civilized	Primitive
Production	Reproduction
Self	Other

In everyday use, the sets of associations on each side of the list often run together. "Culture," Plumwood writes, accumulates these dualisms as a store of weapons "which can be mined, refined and redeployed. Old oppressions stored as dualisms facilitate and break the path for new ones."[96] For this reason, even though my focus is on gender, I do not hesitate to point out occasions in which the constructs and ideology of race intersect with those of gender.

Ultimately, the sex/gender dualism limits feminist analysis. The term *gender*, placed in a dichotomy, necessarily excludes biology. As the feminist theorist Elizabeth Wilson writes: "Feminist critiques of the stomach or hormonal structure . . . have been rendered unthinkable."[97] (See chapters 6–8 herein for an attempt to remedy the hormone deficiency.) Such critiques remain unthinkable because of the real/constructed divide (sometimes formulated as a division between nature and culture), in which many map the knowledge of the real onto the domain of science (equating the constructed with the cultural). Dichotomous formulations from feminists and nonfeminists alike conspire to make a sociocultural analysis of the body seem impossible.

Some feminist theorists, especially during the last decade, have tried—with varying degrees of success—to create a nondualistic account of the body. Judith Butler, for example, tries to reclaim the material body for feminist thought. Why, she wonders, has the idea of materiality come to signify that which is irreducible, that which can support construction but cannot itself be constructed?[98] We have, Butler says (and I agree), to talk about the material body. There *are* hormones, genes, prostates, uteri, and other body parts and physiologies that we use to differentiate male from female, that become part of the ground from which varieties of sexual experience and desire emerge. Furthermore, variations in each of these aspects of physiology profoundly affect an individual's experience of gender and sexuality. But every time we try to return to the body as something that exists prior to socialization, prior to discourse about male and female, Butler writes, "we discover that matter is fully sedimented with discourses on sex and sexuality that prefigure and constrain the uses to which that term can be put."[99]

Western notions of matter and bodily materiality, Butler argues, have been constructed through a "gendered matrix." That classical philosophers associated femininity with materiality can be seen in the origins of the word itself. "Matter" derived from *mater* and *matrix,* referring to the womb and problems of reproduction. In both Greek and Latin, according to Butler, matter was not understood to be a blank slate awaiting the application of external meaning. "The matrix is a . . . formative principle which inaugurates and informs a development of some organism or object . . . for Aristotle, 'matter is potentiality, form actuality.' . . . In reproduction women are said to contribute the matter, men the form."[100] As Butler notes, the title of her book, *Bodies That Matter,* is a well-thought-out pun. To be material is to speak about the process of materialization. And if viewpoints about sex and sexuality are already embedded in our philosophical concepts of how matter forms into bodies, the matter of bodies cannot form a neutral, pre-existing ground from which to understand the origins of sexual difference.[101]

Since matter already contains notions of gender and sexuality, it cannot be a neutral recourse on which to build "scientific" or "objective" theories of sexual development and differentiation. At the same time, we have to acknowledge and use aspects of materiality "that pertain to the body." "The domains of biology, anatomy, physiology, hormonal and chemical composition, illness, age, weight, metabolism, life and death" cannot "be denied."[102] The critical theorist Bernice Hausman concretizes this point in her discussion of surgical technologies available for creating male-to-female versus female-to-male transsexual bodies. "The differences," she writes, "between vagina and penis are not merely ideological. Any attempt to engage and decode the semiotics of sex . . . must acknowledge that these physiological signifiers have functions in the real that will escape . . . their function in the symbolic system."[103]

To talk about human sexuality requires a notion of the material. Yet the idea of the material comes to us already tainted, containing within it pre-existing ideas about sexual difference. Butler suggests that we look at the body as a system that simultaneously produces and is produced by social meanings, just as any biological organism always results from the combined and simultaneous actions of nature and nurture.

Unlike Butler, the feminist philosopher Elizabeth Grosz allows some biological processes a status that pre-exists their meaning. She believes that biological instincts or drives provide a kind of raw material for the development of sexuality. But raw materials are never enough. They must be provided with a set of meanings, "a network of desires"[104] that organize the meanings and consciousness of the child's bodily functions. This claim becomes clear if one follows the stories of so-called wild children raised without human constraints or the inculcation of meaning. Such children acquire neither language nor sexual drive. While their bodies provided the raw materials, without a human social setting the clay could not be molded into recognizable psychic form. Without human sociality, human sexuality cannot develop.[105] Grosz tries to understand how human sociality and meaning that clearly originate outside the body end up incorporated into its physiological demeanor and both unconscious and conscious behaviors.

Some concrete examples will help illustrate. A tiny gray-haired woman, well into her ninth decade, peers into the mirror at her wrinkled face. "Who *is* that woman?" she wonders. Her mind's image of her body does not synchronize with the mirror's reflection. Her daughter, now in her mid-fifties, tries to remember that unless she thinks about using her leg muscles instead of her knee joint, going up and down the stairs will be painful. (Eventually she will acquire a new kinesic habit and dispense with conscious thought about the matter.) Both women are readjusting the visual and kinesic components of their body image, formed on the basis of past information, but always a bit out of date with the current physical body.[106] How do such readjustments occur,

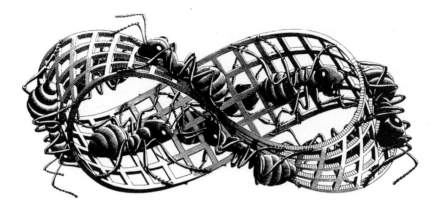

FIGURE 1.3: Möbius Strip II, by M. C. Escher. (© Cordon Art; reprinted with permission)

and how do our earliest body images form in the first place? Here we need the concept of the psyche, a place where two-way translations between the mind and the body take place—a United Nations, as it were, of bodies and experiences.[107]

In *Volatile Bodies*, Elizabeth Grosz considers how the body and the mind come into being together. To facilitate her project, she invokes the image of a Möbius strip as a metaphor for the psyche. The Möbius strip is a topological puzzle (figure 1.3), a flat ribbon twisted once and then attached end to end to form a circular twisted surface. One can trace the surface, for example, by imagining an ant walking along it. At the beginning of the circular journey, the ant is clearly on the outside. But as it traverses the twisted ribbon, without ever lifting its legs from the plane, it ends up on the inside surface. Grosz proposes that we think of the body—the brain, muscles, sex organs, hormones, and more—as composing the inside of the Möbius strip. Culture and experience would constitute the outside surface. But, as the image suggests, the inside and outside are continuous and one can move from one to the other without ever lifting one's feet off the ground.

As Grosz recounts, psychoanalysts and phenomenologists describe the body in terms of feelings.[108] The mind translates physiology into an interior sense of self. Oral sexuality, for example, is a physical feeling that a child and later an adult translates into psychosexual meaning. This translation takes place on the inside of the Möbius surface. But as one traces the surface toward the outside, one begins to speak in terms of connections to other bodies and objects—things that are clearly not-self. Grosz writes, "Instead of describing the oral drive in terms of what it feels like . . . orality can be understood in terms of what it does: creating linkages. The child's lips, for example, form connections . . . with the breast or bottle, possibly accompanied by the hand in conjunction with an ear, each system in perpetual motion and in mutual interrelation."[109]

Continuing with the Möbius analogy, Grosz envisions that bodies create psyches by using the libido as a marker pen to trace a path from biological processes to an interior structure of desire. It falls to a different arena of scholarship to study the "outside" of the strip, a more obviously social surface marked by "pedagogical, juridical, medical, and economic texts, laws, and practices" in order to "carve out a social subject . . . capable of labor, or production and manipulation, a subject capable of acting as a subject."[110] Thus Grosz also rejects a nature versus nurture model of human development. While acknowledging that we do not understand the range and limits of the body's pliability, she insists that we cannot merely "subtract the environment, culture, history" and end up with "nature or biology."[111]

Beyond Dualisms

Grosz postulates innate drives that become organized by physical experience into somatic feelings, which translate into what we call emotions. Taking the innate at face value, however, still leaves us with an unexplained residue of nature.[112] Humans are biological and thus in some sense natural beings *and* social and in some sense artificial—or, if you will, constructed entities. Can we devise a way of seeing ourselves, as we develop from fertilization to old age, as simultaneously natural and unnatural? During the past decade an exciting vision has emerged that I have loosely grouped under the rubric of developmental systems theory, or DST.[113] What do we gain by choosing DST as an analytic framework?

Developmental systems theorists deny that there are fundamentally two kinds of processes: one guided by genes, hormones, and brain cells (that is, nature), the other by the environment, experience, learning, or inchoate social forces (that is, nurture).[114] The pioneer systems theorist, philosopher Susan Oyama promises that DST: "gives more clarity, more coherence, more consistency and a different way to interpret data; in addition it offers the means for synthesizing the concepts and methods . . . of groups that have been working at cross-purposes, or at least talking past each other for decades." Nevertheless, developmental systems theory is no magic bullet. Many will resist its insights because, as Oyama explains, " it gives less . . . guidance on fundamental truth" and "fewer conclusions about what is inherently desirable, healthy, natural or inevitable."[115]

How, specifically, can DST help us break away from dualistic thought processes? Consider an example described by systems theorist Peter Taylor, a goat born with no front legs. During its lifetime it managed to hop around on its hind limbs. An anatomist who studied the goat after it died found that it had an S-shaped spine (as do humans), "thickened bones, modified muscle insertions, and other correlates of moving on two legs."[116] This (and every goat's) skeletal system developed as part of its manner of walking. Neither its genes nor its environment determined its anatomy. Only the ensemble had such power. Many developmental physiologists recognize this principle.[117] As one biologist writes, "enstructuring occurs during the enactment of individual life histories."[118]

A few years ago, when the neuroscientist Simon LeVay reported that the brain structures of gay and heterosexual men differed (and that this mirrored a more general sex difference between straight men and women), he became the center of a firestorm.[119] Although an instant hero among many gay males, he was at odds with a rather mixed group. On the one hand, feminists such as myself disliked his unquestioning use of gender dichotomies, which have in the past never worked to further equality for women. On the other, members of the Christian right hated his work because they believe that homosexuality is a sin that individuals can choose to reject.[120] LeVay's, and later geneticist Dean Hamer's, work suggested to them that homosexuality was inborn or innate.[121] The language of the public debate soon became polarized. Each side contrasted words such as *genetic, biological, inborn, innate,* and *unchanging* with *environmental, acquired, constructed,* and *choice.*[122]

The ease with which such debates evoke the nature/nurture divide is a consequence of the poverty of a nonsystems approach.[123] Politically, the nature/nurture framework holds enormous dangers. Although some hope that a belief in the nature side of things will lead to greater tolerance, past history suggests that the opposite is also possible. Even the scientific architects of the nature argument recognize the dangers.[124] In an extraordinary passage in the pages of *Science,* Dean Hamer and his collaborators indicated their concern: "It would be fundamentally unethical to use such information to try to assess or alter a person's current or future sexual orientation. Rather, scientists, educators, policy-makers and the public should work together to ensure that such research is used to benefit all members of society."[125]

The feminist psychologist and critical theorist Elisabeth Wilson uses the hubbub over LeVay's work to make some important points about systems theory.[126] Many feminist, queer, and critical theorists work by deliberately displacing biology, hence opening the body to social and cultural shaping.[127] This, however, is the wrong move to make. Wilson writes: "What may be

politically and critically contentious in LeVay's hypothesis is not the conjunction neurology-sexuality per se, but the particular manner in which such a
conjunction is enacted."[128] An effective political response, she continues,
doesn't have to separate the study of sexuality from the neurosciences. Instead, Wilson, who wants us to develop a theory of mind and body—an account of psyche that joins libido to body—suggests that feminists incorporate
into their worldview an account of how the brain works that is, broadly speaking, called connectionism.

The old-fashioned approach to understanding the brain was anatomical.
Function could be located in particular parts of the brain. Ultimately function
and anatomy were one. This idea underlies the corpus callosum debate (see
chapter 5), for example, as well as the uproar over LeVay's work. Many scientists believe that a structural difference represents the brain location for measured behavioral differences. In contrast, connectionist models[129] argue that
function emerges from the complexity and strength of many neural connections acting at once.[130] The system has some important characteristics: the
responses are often nonlinear, the networks can be "trained" to respond in
particular ways, the nature of the response is not easily predictable, and information is not located anywhere—rather, it is the net result of the many
different connections and their differing strengths.[131]

The tenets of some connectionist theory provide interesting starting
points for understanding human sexual development. Because connectionist
networks, for example, are usually nonlinear, small changes can produce large
effects. One implication for studying sexuality: we could easily be looking in
the wrong places and on the wrong scale for aspects of the environment that
shape human development.[132] Furthermore, a single behavior may have many
underlying causes, events that happen at different times in development. I
suspect that our labels of homosexual, heterosexual, bisexual, and transgender are really not good categories at all, and are best understood only in terms
of unique developmental events[133] affecting particular individuals. Thus, I
agree with those connectionists who argue that "the developmental process
itself lies at the heart of knowledge acquisition. Development is a process
of emergence."[134]

In most public and most scientific discussions, sex and nature are thought
to be real, while gender and culture are seen as constructed.[135] But these are
false dichotomies. I start, in chapters 2–4, with the most visible, exterior
markers of gender—the genitalia—to illustrate how sex is, literally, constructed. Surgeons remove parts and use plastic to create "appropriate" genitalia for people born with body parts that are not easily identifiable as male or
female. Physicians believe that their expertise enables them to "hear" nature

telling them the truth about what sex such patients ought to be. Alas, their truths come from the social arena and are reinforced, in part, by the medical tradition of rendering intersexual births invisible.

Our bodies, as well as the world we live in, are certainly made of materials. And we often use scientific investigation to understand the nature of those materials. But such scientific investigation involves a process of knowledge construction. I illustrate this in some detail in chapter 5, which moves us into the body's interior—the less visible anatomy of the brain. Here I focus on a single scientific controversy: Do men and women have differently shaped corpus callosums (a specific region of the brain)? In this chapter, I show how scientists construct arguments by choosing particular experimental approaches and tools. The entire shape of the debate is socially constrained, and the particular tools chosen to conduct the controversy (for example, a particular form of statistical analysis or using brains from cadavers rather than Magnetic Resonance Image brain scans) have their own historical and technical limitations.[136]

Under appropriate circumstances, however, even the corpus callosum is visible to the naked eye. What happens, then, when we delve even more deeply—into the body's invisible chemistry? In chapters 6 and 7, I show how in the period from 1900 to 1940 scientists carved up nature in a particular fashion, creating the category of sex hormones. The hormones themselves became markers of sexual difference. Now, the finding of a sex hormone or its receptor in any part of the body (for example, on bone cells) renders that previously gender-neutral body part sexual. But if one looks, as I do, historically, one can see that steroid hormones need not have been divided into sex and nonsex categories.[137] They could, for example, have been considered to be growth hormones affecting a wide swath of tissues, including reproductive organs.

Scientists now agree about the chemical structure of the steroid molecules they labeled as sex hormones, even though they are not visible to the naked eye. In chapter 8, I focus in part on how scientists used the newly minted concept of the sex hormone to deepen understanding of genital development in rodents, and in part on their application of knowledge about sex hormones to something even less tangible than body chemistry: sex-related behavior. But, to paraphrase the Bard, the course of true science never did run smooth. Experiments and models depicting the role of hormones in the development of sexual behaviors on rodents formed an eerie parallel with cultural debates about the roles and abilities of men and women. It seems hard to avoid the view that our very real, scientific understandings of hormones, brain development, and sexual behavior are, nevertheless, constructed in and bear the marks of specific historical and social contexts.

This book, then, examines the construction of sexuality, starting with structures visible on the body's exterior surface and ending with behaviors and motivations—that is with activities and forces that are patently invisible—inferred only from their outcome, but presumed to be located deep within the body's interior.[138] But behaviors are generally social activities, expressed in interaction with distinctly separate objects and beings. Thus, as we move from genitalia on the outside to the invisible psyche, we find ourselves suddenly walking along the surface of a Möbius strip back toward, and beyond, the body's exterior. In the book's final chapter, I outline research approaches that can potentially show us how we move from outside to inside and back out again, without ever lifting our feet from the strip's surface.

"THAT SEXE WHICH PREVAILETH"

The Sexual Continuum

*I*N 1843 LEVI SUYDAM, A TWENTY-THREE-YEAR-OLD RESIDENT OF SALIS-
bury, Connecticut, asked the town's board of selectmen to allow him to vote
as a Whig in a hotly contested local election. The request raised a flurry of
objections from the opposition party, for a reason that must be rare in the
annals of American democracy: it was said that Suydam was "more female
than male," and thus (since only men had the right to vote) should not be
allowed to cast a ballot. The selectmen brought in a physician, one Dr. William Barry, to examine Suydam and settle the matter. Presumably, upon en-
countering a phallus and testicles, the good doctor declared the prospective
voter male. With Suydam safely in their column, the Whigs won the election
by a majority of one.

A few days later, however, Barry discovered that Suydam menstruated regularly and had a vaginal opening. Suydam had the narrow shoulders and broad
hips characteristic of a female build, but occasionally "he" felt physical attractions to the "opposite" sex (by which "he" meant women). Furthermore,
"his feminine propensities, such as fondness for gay colors, for pieces of calico, comparing and placing them together and an aversion for bodily labor,
and an inability to perform the same, were remarked by many."[1] (Note that
this nineteenth-century doctor did not distinguish between "sex" and "gender." Thus he considered a fondness for piecing together swatches of calico
just as telling as anatomy and physiology.) No one has yet discovered whether
Suydam lost the right to vote.[2] Whatever the outcome, the story conveys both
the political weight our culture places on ascertaining a person's correct
"sex" and the deep confusion that arises when it can't be easily determined.

European and American culture is deeply devoted to the idea that there
are only two sexes. Even our language refuses other possibilities; thus to write

about Levi Suydam (and elsewhere in this book) I have had to invent conventions—s/he and h/er to denote individuals who are clearly neither/both male and female or who are, perhaps, both at once. Nor is the linguistic convenience an idle fancy. Whether one falls into the category of man or woman matters in concrete ways. For Suydam—and still today for women in some parts of the world—it meant the right to vote. It might mean being subject to the military draft and to various laws concerning the family and marriage. In many parts of the United States, for example, two individuals legally registered as men cannot have sexual relations without breaking antisodomy laws.[3]

But if the state and legal system has an interest in maintaining only two sexes, our collective biological bodies do not. While male and female stand on the extreme ends of a biological continuum, there are many other bodies, bodies such as Suydam's, that evidently mix together anatomical components conventionally attributed to both males and females. The implications of my argument for a sexual continuum are profound. If nature really offers us more than two sexes, then it follows that our current notions of masculinity and femininity are cultural conceits. Reconceptualizing the category of "sex" challenges cherished aspects of European and American social organization.

Indeed, we have begun to insist on the male-female dichotomy at increasingly early ages, making the two-sex system more deeply a part of how we imagine human life and giving it the appearance of being both inborn and natural. Nowadays, months before the child leaves the comfort of the womb, amniocentesis and ultrasound identify a fetus's sex. Parents can decorate the baby's room in gender-appropriate style, sports wallpaper—in blue—for the little boy, flowered designs—in pink—for the little girl. Researchers have nearly completed development of technology that can choose the sex of a child at the moment of fertilization.[4] Moreover, modern surgical techniques help maintain the two-sex system. Today children who are born "either/or—neither/both"[5]—a fairly common phenomenon—usually disappear from view because doctors "correct" them right away with surgery. In the past, however, intersexuals (or hermaphrodites, as they were called until recently)* were culturally acknowledged (see figure 2.1).

How did the birth and acknowledged presence of hermaphrodites shape ideas about gender in the past? How did, modern medical treatments of intersexuality develop? How has a political movement of intersexuals and their supporters emerged to push for increased openness to more fluid sexual iden-

---

* Members of the present-day Intersexual Movement eschew the use of the word hermaphrodite. I will try to use it when it is historically proper. Since the word intersexual is a modern one, I will not use it when writing about the past.

FIGURE 2.1: Sleeping hermaphrodite, Roman second century B.C.
(Erich Lessing, from Art Resource; reprinted with permission)

tities, and how successful have their challenges been? What follows is a most literal tale of social construction—the story of the emergence of strict surgical enforcement of a two-party system of sex and the possibility, as we move into the twenty-first century, of the evolution of a multiparty arrangement.

Hermaphrodite History

Intersexuality is old news. The word *hermaphrodite* comes from a Greek term that combined the names Hermes (son of Zeus and variously known as the messenger of the gods, patron of music, controller of dreams, and protector of livestock) and Aphrodite (the Greek goddess of sexual love and beauty). There are at least two Greek myths about the origins of the first hermaphrodite. In one, Aphrodite and Hermes produce a child so thoroughly endowed with the attributes of each parent that, unable to decide its sex for sure, they name it Hermaphroditos. In the other, their child is an astonishingly beautiful male with whom a water nymph falls in love. Overcome by desire, she so deeply intertwines her body with his that they become joined as one.

If the figure of the hermaphrodite has seemed odd enough to prompt speculation about its peculiar origins, it has also struck some as the embodiment of a human past that predated dualistic sexual division. Early biblical interpreters thought that Adam began his existence as a hermaphrodite and that he divided into two individuals, male and female, only after falling from grace. Plato wrote that there were originally three sexes—male, female, and hermaphrodite—but that the third sex became lost over time.[6]

Different cultures have confronted real-life intersexuals in different ways. Jewish religious texts such as the Talmud and the Tosefta list extensive regulations for people of mixed sex, regulating modes of inheritance and of social conduct. The Tosefta, for example, forbids hermaphrodites from inheriting their fathers' estates (like daughters), from secluding themselves with women (like sons), and from shaving (like men). When they menstruate they must be isolated from men (like women); they are disqualified from serving as witnesses or as priests (like women); but the laws of pederasty apply to them. While Judaic law provided a means for integrating hermaphrodites into mainstream culture, Romans were not so kind. In Romulus's time intersexes were believed to be a portent of a crisis of the state and were often killed. Later, however, in Pliny's era, hermaphrodites became eligible for marriage.[7]

In tracking the history of medical analyses of intersexuality, one learns more generally how the social history of gender itself has varied, first in Europe and later in America, which inherited European medical traditions. In the process we can learn that there is nothing natural or inevitable about current medical treatment of intersexuals. Early medical practitioners, who understood sex and gender to fall along a continuum and not into the discrete categories we use today, were not fazed by hermaphrodites. Sexual difference, they thought, involved quantitative variation. Women were cool, men hot, masculine women or feminine men warm. Moreover, human variation did not, physicians of this era believed, stop at the number three. Parents could produce boys with different degrees of manliness and girls with varying amounts of womanliness.

In the premodern era, several views of the biology of intersexuality competed. Aristotle (384–322 B.C.), for example, categorized hermaphrodites as a type of twin. He believed that complete twinning occurred when the mother contributed enough matter at conception to create two entire embryos. In the case of intersexuals, there was more than enough matter to create one but not quite enough for two. The excess matter, he thought, became extra genitalia. Aristotle did not believe that genitalia defined the sex of the baby, however. Rather, the heat of the heart determined maleness or femaleness. He argued that underneath their confusing anatomy, hermaphrodites truly belonged to one of only two possible sexes. The highly influential Galen, in the first century A.D., disagreed, arguing that hermaphrodites belonged to an intermediate sex. He believed that sex emerged from the opposition of male and female principles in the maternal and paternal seeds in combination with interactions between the left and right sides of the uterus. From the overlaying of varying degrees of dominance between male and female seed on top of the several potential positions of the fetus in the womb, a grid containing from three to seven cells emerged. Depending upon where on the grid an embryo fell, it could range from entirely male, through various intermediate states, to entirely female. Thus, thinkers in the Galenic tradition believed no stable biological divide separated male from female.[8]

Physicians in the Middle Ages continued to hold to the classical theory of a sexual continuum, even while they increasingly argued for sharper divisions of sexual variation. Medieval medical texts espoused the classical idea that the relative heat on the right side of the uterus produced males, the cooler fetus developing on the left side of the womb became a female, and fetuses developing more toward the middle became manly women or womanly men.[9] The notion of a continuum of heat coexisted with the idea that the uterus consisted of seven discrete chambers. The three cells to the right housed males, the three to the left females, while the central chamber produced hermaphrodites.[10]

A willingness to find a place for hermaphrodites in scientific theory, however, did not translate into social acceptance. Historically, hermaphrodites were often regarded as rebellious, disruptive, or even fraudulent. Hildegard of Bingen, a famous German abbess and visionary mystic (1098–1179) condemned any confusion of male and female identity. As the historian Joan Cadden has noted, Hildegard chose to place her denunciation "between an assertion that women should not say mass and a warning against sexual perversions. . . . A disorder of either sex or sex roles is a disorder in the social fabric . . . and in the religious order."[11] Such stern disapproval was unusual for her time. Despite widespread uncertainty about their proper social roles, disapproval of hermaphrodites remained relatively mild. Medieval medical and scientific texts complained of negative personality traits—lustfulness in the masculine femalelike hermaphrodite and deceitfulness in the feminine malelike individual,[12] but outright condemnation seems to have been infrequent.

Biologists and physicians of that era did not have the social prestige and authority of today's professionals and were not the only ones in a position to define and regulate the hermaphrodite. In Renaissance Europe, scientific and medical texts often propounded contradictory theories about the production of hermaphrodites. These theories could not fix gender as something real and stable within the body. Rather, physicians' stories competed both with medicine and with those elaborated by the Church, the legal profession, and politicians. To further complicate matters, different European nations had different ideas about the origins, dangers, civil rights, and duties of hermaphrodites.[13]

For example, in France, in 1601, the case of Marie/Marin le Marcis engendered great controversy. "Marie" had lived as a woman for twenty-one
years before deciding to put on men's clothing and registering to marry the
woman with whom s/he cohabited. "Marin" was arrested, and after having
gone through harrowing sentences—first being condemned to burn at the
stake, then having the penalty "reduced" to death by strangling (and we
thought *our* death row was bad!!)—s/he eventually was set free on the condition that s/he wear women's clothing until the age of twenty-five. Under
French law Marie/Marin had committed two crimes: sodomy and cross-
dressing.

English law, in contrast, did not specifically forbid cross-gender dressing.
But it did look askance at those who donned the attire of a social class to which
they did not belong. In a 1746 English case, Mary Hamilton married another
woman after assuming the name "Dr. Charles Hamilton." The legal authorities were sure she had done something wrong, but they couldn't quite put
their finger on what it was. Eventually they convicted her of vagrancy, reasoning that she was an unusually ballsy but nonetheless common cheat.[14]

During the Renaissance, there was no central clearinghouse for the handling of hermaphrodites. While in some cases physicians or the state inter-
vened, in others the Church took the lead. For instance, in Piedra, Italy, in
1601, the same year of Marie/Marin's arrest, a young soldier named Daniel
Burghammer shocked his regiment when he gave birth to a healthy baby girl.
After his alarmed wife called in his army captain, he confessed to being half
male and half female. Christened as a male, he had served as a soldier for seven
years while also a practicing blacksmith. The baby's father, Burghammer said,
was a Spanish soldier. Uncertain of what to do, the captain called in Church
authorities, who decided to go ahead and christen the baby, whom they named
Elizabeth. After she was weaned—Burghammer nursed the child with his
female breast—several towns competed for the right to adopt her. The
Church declared the child's birth a miracle, but granted Burghammer's wife
a divorce, suggesting that it found Burghammer's ability to give birth incompatible with role of husband.[15]

The stories of Marie/Marin, Mary Hamilton, and Daniel Burghammer
illustrate a simple point. Different countries and different legal and religious
systems viewed intersexuality in different ways. The Italians seemed relatively
nonplussed by the blurring of gender borders, the French rigidly regulated it,
while the English, although finding it distasteful, worried more about class
transgressions. Nevertheless, all over Europe the sharp distinction between
male and female was at the core of systems of law and politics. The rights of
inheritance, forms of judicial punishment, and the right to vote and partici-

pate in the political system were all determined in part by sex. And those who fell in between? Legal experts acknowledged that hermaphrodites existed but insisted they position themselves within this gendered system. Sir Edward Coke, famed jurist of early modern England wrote "an Hermaphrodite may purchase according to that sexe which prevaileth."[16] Similarly, in the first half of the seventeenth century, French hermaphrodites could serve as witnesses in the court and even marry, providing that they did so in the role assigned to them by "the sex which dominates their personality."[17]

The individual him/herself shared with medical and legal experts the right to decide which sex prevailed but, once having made a choice, was expected to stick with it. The penalty for reneging could be severe. At stake was the maintenance of the social order and the rights of man (meant literally). Thus, although it was clear that some people straddled the male-female divide, the social and legal structures remained fixed around a two-sex system.[18]

The Making of the Modern Intersexual

As biology emerged as an organized discipline during the late eighteenth and early nineteenth centuries, it gradually acquired greater authority over the disposition of ambiguous bodies.[19] Nineteenth-century scientists developed a clear sense of the statistical aspects of natural variation,[20] but along with such knowledge came the authority to declare that certain bodies were abnormal and in need of correction.[21] The biologist Isidore Geoffroy Saint-Hilaire played a particularly central role in recasting scientific ideas about sexual difference. He founded a new science, which he dubbed *teratology,* for the study and classification of unusual births. Saint-Hilaire and other like-minded biologists set out to study all anatomical anomalies, and they established two important principles that began to guide medical approaches to natural variation. First, Saint-Hilaire argued that "Nature is one whole"[22]—that is, that even unusual or what had been called "monstrous" births were still part of nature. Second, drawing on newly developed statistical concepts, he proclaimed that hermaphrodites and other birth anomalies resulted from abnormal embryonic development. To understand their genesis, he argued, one must understand normal development. Studying abnormal variations could in turn illuminate normal processes. Saint-Hilaire believed that unlocking the origins of hermaphrodites would lead to an understanding of the development of sexual difference more generally. This scientific transposition of the old mythic fascination with hermaphrodites has remained, to this day, a guiding principle of scientific investigation into the biological underpinnings of sex/

gender roles and behaviors of nonintersexuals. (See chapters 3 and 4 for a discussion of the modern literature.)

Saint-Hilaire's writings were not only of importance to the scientific community, they served a new social function as well. Whereas in previous centuries, unusual bodies were treated as unnatural and freakish, the new field of teratology offered a natural explanation for the birth of people with extraordinary bodies.[23] At the same time, however, it redefined such bodies as pathological, as unhealthy conditions to be cured using increased medical knowledge. Ironically, then, scientific understanding was used as a tool to obliterate precisely the wonders it illuminated. By the middle of the twentieth century, medical technology had "advanced" to a point where it could make bodies that had once been objects of awe and astonishment disappear from view, all in the name of "correcting nature's mistakes."[24]

The hermaphrodite vanishing act relied heavily on the standard scientific technique of classification.[25] Saint-Hilaire divided the body into "sex segments," three on the left and three on the right. He named these zones the "profound portion," which contained ovaries, testicles, or related structures; the "middle portion," which contained internal sex structures such as the uterus and seminal vesicles; and the "external portion," which included the external genitalia.[26] If all six segments were wholly male, he decreed, so too was the body. If all six were female, the body was clearly female. But when a mixture of male and female appeared in any of the six zones, a hermaphrodite resulted. Thus, Saint-Hilaire's system continued to recognize the legitimacy of sexual variety but subdivided hermaphrodites into different types, laying the groundwork for future scientists to establish a difference between "true" and "false" hermaphrodites. Since the "true" hermaphrodites were very rare, eventually a classification system arose that made intersexuality virtually invisible.

In the late 1830s, a physician named James Young Simpson, building on Saint-Hilaire's approach, proposed to classify hermaphrodites as either "spurious" or "true." In spurious hermaphrodites, he wrote, "the genital organs and general sexual configuration of one sex approach, from imperfect or abnormal development, to those of the opposite," while in true hermaphrodites "there actually coexist upon the body of the same individual more or fewer of the genital organs."[27] In Simpson's view, "genital organs" included not only ovaries or testes (the gonads) but also structures such as the uterus or seminal vesicles. Thus, a true hermaphrodite might have testes and a uterus, or ovaries and seminal vesicles.

Simpson's theory presaged what the historian Alice Dreger has dubbed the Age of Gonads. The honor of offering definitive powers to the gonads fell to a

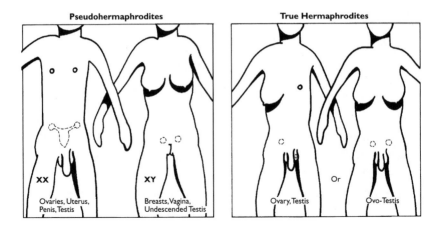

FIGURE 2.2: "Pseudo-hermaphrodites" have either ovaries or testes combined with the "opposite" genitalia. "True hermaphrodites" have an ovary and a testis, or a combined gonad, called an ovo-testis.
(Source: Alyce Santoro, for the author)

German physician named Theodor Albrecht Klebs, who published his ideas in 1876. Like Simpson, Klebs contrasted "true" with what he called "pseudo"-hermaphrodites. He restricted the term *true hermaphrodite* to someone who had both ovarian and testicular tissue in h/her body. All others with mixed anatomies—persons with both a penis and ovaries, or a uterus and a mustache, or testes and a vagina—no longer, in Klebs's system, qualified as true hermaphrodites. But if they were not hermaphrodites, what were they? Klebs believed that under each of these confusing surfaces lurked a body either truly male or truly female. Gonads, he insisted, were the sole defining factor in biological sex. A body with two ovaries, no matter how many masculine features it might have, was female. No matter if a pair of testes were nonfunctional and the person possessing them had a vagina and breast, testes made a body male. The net result of this reasoning, as Dreger has noted, was that "significantly fewer people counted as 'truly' both male and female."[28] Medical science was working its magic: hermaphrodites were beginning to disappear.

Once the gonads became the decisive factor (figure 2.2), it required more than common sense to identify an individual's true sex. The tools of science—in the form of a microscope and new methods of preparing tissue for microscopic examination—became essential.[29] Rapidly, images of the hermaphrodite's body disappeared from medical journals, replaced by abstract photographs of thinly sliced and carefully colored bits of gonadal tissue. Moreover,

as Alice Dreger points out, the primitive state of surgical techniques, especially the lack of anesthesia and antisepsis, at the end of the nineteenth century
meant that doctors could obtain gonadal tissue samples only after death or
castration: "Small in number, dead, impotent—what a sorry lot the true hermaphrodites had become!"[30] People of mixed sex all but disappeared, not
because they had become rarer, but because scientific methods classified them
out of existence.

At the turn of the century (1896, to be exact), the British physicians
George F. Blackler and William P. Lawrence wrote a paper examining earlier
claims of true hermaphroditism. They found that only three out of twenty-
eight previously published case studies complied with the new standards. In
Orwellian fashion, they cleansed past medical records of accounts of hermaphroditism, claiming they did not meet modern scientific standards,[31]
while few new cases met the strict criterion of microscopic verification of the
presence of both male and female gonadal tissue.

Arguing About Sex and Gender

Under the mantle of scientific advancement, the ideological work of science
was imperceptible to turn-of-the-century scientists, just as the ideological
work of requiring Polymerase Chain Reaction Sex Tests of women athletes
is, apparently, to the I.O.C. (See chapter 1.) Nineteenth-century theories of
intersexuality—the classification systems of Saint-Hilaire, Simpson, Klebs,
Blackler, and Lawrence—fit into a much broader group of biological ideas
about difference. Scientists and medical men insisted that the bodies of males
and females, of whites and people of color, Jews and Gentiles, and middle-
class and laboring men differed deeply. In an era that argued politically for
individual rights on the basis of human equality, scientists defined some bodies
as better and more deserving of rights than others.

If this seems paradoxical, from another point of view it makes good sense.
Political theories that declared that "all men are created equal" threatened to
do more than provide justification for colonies to overthrow monarchies and
establish independent republics. They threatened to undermine the logic behind fundamental social and economic institutions such as marriage, slavery,
or the limiting of the right to vote to white men with property. Not surprisingly, then, the science of physical difference was often invoked to invalidate
claims for social and political emancipation.[32]

In the nineteenth century, for example, women active in the movement to
abolish slavery in the United States, soon began to insist on their right to speak
in public,[33] and by mid-century women in both the United States and England

were demanding better educational opportunities and economic rights and the right to vote. Their actions met fierce resistance from scientific experts.[34] Some doctors argued that permitting women to obtain college degrees would ruin their health, leading to sterility and ultimately the degeneration of the (white, middle-class) human race. Educated women angrily organized counterattacks and slowly gained the right to advanced education and the vote.[35]

Such social struggles had profound implications for the scientific categorization of intersexuality. More than ever, politics necessitated two and only two sexes. The issue had gone beyond particular legal rights such as the right to vote. What if, while thinking she was a man, a woman engaged in some activity women were thought to be incapable of doing? Suppose she did well at it? What would happen to the idea that women's natural incapacities dictated social inequity? As the battles for social equality between the sexes heated up in the early twentieth century, physicians developed stricter and more exclusive definitions of hermaphroditism. The more social radicals blasted away at the separations between masculine and feminine spheres, the more physicians insisted on the absolute division between male and female.

Intersexuals Under Medical Surveillance

Until the early nineteenth century, the primary arbiters of intersexual status had been lawyers and judges, who, although they might consult doctors or priests on particular cases, generally followed their own understanding of sexual difference. By the dawn of the twentieth century, physicians were recognized as the chief regulators of sexual intermediacy.[36] Although the legal standard—that there were but two sexes and that a hermaphrodite had to identify with the sex prevailing in h/her body—remained, by the 1930s medical practitioners had developed a new angle: the surgical and hormonal suppression of intersexuality. The Age of Gonads gave way to the even less flexible Age of Conversion, in which medical practitioners found it imperative to catch mixed-sex people at birth and convert them, by any means necessary, to either male or female (figure 2.3).

But patients, troubling and troublesome patients, continued to place themselves squarely in the path of such oversimplification. Even during the Age of Gonads, medical men sometimes based their assessment of sexual identity on the overall shape of the body and the inclination of the patient—the gonads be damned. In 1915, the British physician William Blair Bell publicly suggested that sometimes the body was too mixed up to let the gonads alone dictate treatment. The new technologies of anesthesia and asepsis made it possible for small tissue samples (biopsies) to be taken from the gonads of

FIGURE 2.3: A cartoon history of intersexuality. (Source: Diane DiMassa, for the author)

living patients. Bell encountered a patient who had a mixture of external traits—a mustache, breasts, an elongated clitoris, a deep voice, and no menstrual period—and whose biopsy revealed that the gonad was an ovo-testis (a mixture of egg-producing and sperm-producing tissues).

Faced with a living and breathing true hermaphrodite Bell reverted to the older legal approach, writing that "predominating feminine characteristics have decided the sex adopted." He emphasized that one need not rely wholly

on the gonads to decide which sex a patient must choose, but that "the posses-
sion of a [single] sex is a necessity of our social order, for hermaphrodites as
well as for normal subjects."[37] Bell did not abandon, however, the concepts of
true and pseudo-hermaphroditism. Indeed, most physicians practicing today
take this distinction for granted. But faced with the insistent complexity of
actual bodies and personalities, Bell urged that each case be dealt with flexibly,
taking into account the many different signs presented by the body and behaviors of the intersexual patient.

But this returned doctors to an old problem: Which signs were to count?
Consider a case reported in 1924 by Hugh Hampton Young, "the Father of
American Urology."[38] Young operated on a young man with a malformed pe-
nis,[39] an undescended testis, and a painful mass in the groin. The mass turned
out to be an ovary connected to an underdeveloped uterus and oviducts.
Young pondered the problem:

> A normal-looking young man with masculine instincts [athletic, hetero-
> sexual] was found to have a . . . functioning ovary in the left groin. What
> was the character of the scrotal sac on the right side? If these were also
> undoubtedly female, should they be allowed to remain outside in the scro-
> tum? If a male, should the patient be allowed to continue life with a func-
> tioning ovary and tube in the abdomen on the left side? If the organs of
> either side should be extirpated, which should they be?[40]

The young man turned out to have a testis, and Young snagged the ovary. As his
experience grew, Young increasingly based his judgment calls on his patients'
psychological and social situations, using sophisticated understandings of the
body more as a guide to the range of physical possibilities than as a necessary
indicator of sex.

In 1937, Young, by then a professor of urology at Johns Hopkins University, published *Genital Abnormalities, Hermaphroditism and Related Adrenal Diseases*, a book remarkable for its erudition, scientific insight, and open-
mindedness. In it he further systematized the classification of intersexes
(maintaining Blackler and Lawrence's definition of true hermaphroditism)
and drew together a wealth of carefully documented case histories, both his
own and others', in order to demonstrate and study the medical treatment of
these "accidents of birth." He did not judge the people he described, several
of whom lived as "practicing hermaphrodites"—that is, they had sexual experiences as both men and women.[41] Nor did he attempt to coerce any of
them into treatment.

One of Young's cases involved a hermaphrodite named Emma who grew up as a female. With both a large clitoris (one or two inches in length) and a vagina, s/he could have "normal" heterosexual sex with both men and women. As a teenager s/he had sex with a number of girls to whom she was deeply attracted, but at age nineteen s/he married a man with whom s/he experienced little sexual pleasure (although, according to Emma, he didn't have any complaints). During this and subsequent marriages, Emma kept girl-friends on the side, frequently having pleasurable sex with them. Young described h/her as appearing "to be quite content and even happy." In conversa-tion, Dr. Young elicited Emma's occasional wish to be a man. Although he assured her that it would be a relatively simple matter, s/he replied, "Would you have to remove that vagina? I don't know about that because that's my meal ticket. If you did that I would have to quit my husband and go to work, so I think I'll keep it and stay as I am. My husband supports me well, and even though I don't have any sexual pleasure with him, I do have lots with my girlfriend." Without further comment or evidence of disappointment, Young proceeded to the next "interesting example of another practicing hermaph-rodite."[42]

His case summary mentions nothing about financial motivations, saying only that Emma refused a sex fix because she "dreaded necessary opera-tions,"[43] but Emma was not alone in allowing economic and social considera-tions to influence her choice of sex. Usually this meant that young hermaphro-dites, when offered some choice, opted to become male. Consider the case of Margaret, born in 1915 and raised as a girl until the age of 14. When her voice began to deepen into a man's, and her malformed penis grew and began to take on adult functions, Margaret demanded permission to live as a man. With the help of psychologists (who later published a report on the case) and a change of address, he abandoned his "ultrafeminine" attire of a "green satin dress with flared skirt, red velvet hat with rhinestone trimming, slippers with bows, hair bobbed with ends brought down over his cheeks." He became, instead, a short-haired, baseball- and football-playing teenager whom his new classmates called Big James. James had his own thoughts about the advantages of being a man. He told his half-sister: "It is easier to be a man. You get more money (wages) and you don't have to be married. If you're a girl and you don't get married people make fun of you."[44]

Although Dr. Young illuminated the subject of intersexuality with a great deal of wisdom and consideration for his patients, his work was part of the process that led both to a new invisibility and a harshly rigid approach to the treatment of intersexual bodies. In addition to being a thoughtful collection of case studies, Young's book is an extended treatise on the most modern methods—both surgical and hormonal—of treating those who sought help.

Although less judgmental and controlling of patients and their parents than his successors, he nevertheless supplied the next generation of physicians with the scientific and technical bedrock on which they based their practices.

As was true in the nineteenth century, increased knowledge of the biological origins of sexual complexity facilitated the elimination of their signs. Deepening understandings of the physiological bases of intersexuality combined with improvements in surgical technology, especially since 1950, began to enable physicians to catch most intersexuals at the moment of birth.[45] The motive for their conversion was genuinely humanitarian: a wish to enable individuals to fit in and to function both physically and psychologically as healthy human beings. But behind the wish lay unexamined assumptions: first, that there should be only two sexes; second, that only heterosexuality was normal; and third, that particular gender roles defined the psychologically healthy man and woman.[46] These same assumptions continue to provide the rationale for the modern "medical management" of intersexual births.

OF GENDER AND GENITALS:

THE USE AND ABUSE OF THE MODERN INTERSEXUAL

XD

Confronting the Intersex Newborn

THE DOCTORS

A CHILD IS BORN IN A LARGE METROPOLITAN HOSPITAL IN THE UNITED States or Western Europe. The attending physician, realizing that the newborn's genitalia are either/or, neither/both, consults a pediatric endocrinologist (children's hormone specialist) and a surgeon. They declare a state of medical emergency.[1] According to current treatment standards, there is no time to waste in quiet reflection or open-ended consultations with the parents. No time for the new parents to consult those who have previously given birth to mixed-sex babies or to talk with adult intersexuals. Before twenty-four hours pass, the child must leave the hospital "as a sex," and the parents must feel certain of the decision.

Why this rush to judgment? How can we feel so certain within just twenty-four hours that we have made the right assignment of sex to a newborn?[2] Once such decisions are made, how are they carried out and how do they affect the child's future?

Since the 1950s, psychologists, sexologists, and other researchers have battled over theories about the origins of sexual difference, especially gender identity, gender roles, and sexual orientation. Much is at stake in these debates. Our conceptions of the nature of gender difference shape, even as they reflect, the ways we structure our social system and polity; they also shape and reflect our understanding of our physical bodies. Nowhere is this clearer than in the debates over the structure (and restructuring) of bodies that exhibit sexual ambiguity.

Oddly, the contemporary practice of "fixing" intersex babies immediately after birth emerged from some surprisingly flexible theories of gender. In the 1940s, Albert Ellis studied eighty-four cases of mixed births and concluded that "while the *power* of the human sex drive may possibly be largely dependent on physiological factors . . . the *direction* of this drive does not seem to be directly dependent on constitutional elements."[3] In other words, in the development of masculinity, femininity, and inclinations toward homo- or heterosexuality, nurture matters a great deal more than nature. A decade later, the Johns Hopkins psychologist John Money and his colleagues, the psychiatrists John and Joan Hampson, took up the study of intersexuals, whom, Money realized, would "provide invaluable material for the comparative study of bodily form and physiology, rearing, and psychosexual orientation."[4] Agreeing with Ellis's earlier assessment, Money and his colleagues used their own studies to state in the extreme what these days seems extraordinary for its complete denial of the notion of natural inclination. They concluded that gonads, hormones, and chromosomes did not automatically determine a child's gender role: "From the sum total of hermaphroditic evidence, the conclusion that emerges is that sexual behavior and orientation as male or female does not have an innate, instinctive basis."[5]

Did they then conclude that the categories "male" and "female" had no biological basis or necessity? Absolutely not. These scientists studied hermaphrodites to prove that nature mattered hardly at all. But they never questioned the fundamental assumption that there are only two sexes, because their goal in studying intersexuals was to find out more about "normal" development.[6] Intersexuality, in Money's view, resulted from fundamentally abnormal processes. Their patients required medical treatment because they *ought* to have become either a male or a female. The goal of treatment was to assure proper psychosexual development by assigning the young mixed-sex child to the proper gender and then doing whatever was necessary to assure that the child and h/her parents believed in the sex assignment.[7]

By 1969, when Christopher Dewhurst (Professor of Obstetrics and Gynecology in London at the Queen Charlotte Maternity Hospital and the Chelsea Hospital for Women) and Ronald R. Gordon (Consultant Pediatrician and Lecturer in Child Health at Sheffield University) wrote their treatise on *The Intersexual Disorders*, medical and surgical approaches to intersexuality neared a state of hitherto unattained uniformity. It seems hardly surprising that this coalescence of medical views occurred during the era that witnessed what Betty Friedan dubbed "the feminine mystique"—the post–World War II ideal of the suburban family structured around strictly divided gender roles. That people failed to conform fully to this ideal can be gleaned from the near hysterical tone of Dewhurst and Gordon's book, which contrasts markedly with the calm and reason of Young's founding treatise.

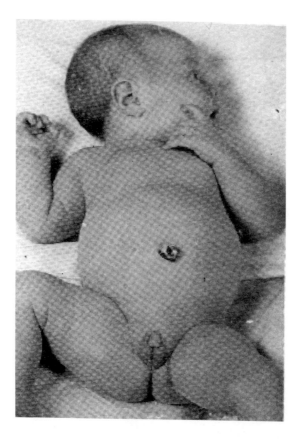

FIGURE 3.1: A six-day old XX child with masculinized external genitalia. (Original photo by Lawson Wilkins in Young 1961 [figure 23.1, p. 1405]; reprinted with permission, Williams and Wilkins)

Dewhurst and Gordon open their book with a description of a newborn intersexual child, accompanied by a close-up photograph of the baby's genitals. They employ the rhetoric of tragedy: "One can only attempt to imagine the anguish of the parents. That a newborn should have a deformity . . . (affecting) so fundamental an issue as the very sex of the child . . . is a tragic event which immediately conjures up visions of a hopeless psychological misfit doomed to live always as a sexual freak in loneliness and frustration."

They warn that freakhood will, indeed, be the baby's fate should the case be improperly managed, "but fortunately, with correct management the outlook is infinitely better than the poor parents—emotionally stunned by the event—or indeed anyone without special knowledge could ever imagine."

Luckily for the child, whose sweet little genitalia we are invited to examine intimately (figure 3.1), "the problem was faced promptly and efficiently by the local pediatrician." Ultimately, readers learn, the parents received assurance that despite appearances, the baby was "really" a female whose external genitalia had become masculinized by unusually high levels of androgen present during fetal life. She could, they were told, have normal sexual relations (after surgery to open the vaginal passageway and shorten the clitoris) and even be able to bear children.[8]

Dewhurst and Gordon contrast this happy outcome with that of incorrect treatment or neglect through medical ignorance. They describe a fifty-year-old who had lived h/her life as a woman, again treating the reader to an intimate close-up of the patient's genitalia,[9] which shows a large phallic-like clitoris, no scrotum, and separate urethral and vaginal openings. S/he had worried as a teenager about her genitals and lack of breasts and menstruation, the doctors report, but had adjusted to "her unfortunate state." Nevertheless, at age fifty-two the doubts returned to "torment" h/her. After diagnosing h/her as a male pseudo-hermaphrodite, doomed to the female sex assignment in which she had lived unhappily, Dewhurst and Gordon noted that the case illustrated "the kind of tragedy which can result from incorrect management."[10] Their book, in contrast, is meant to provide the reader (presumably other medical personnel) with lessons in correct management.

Today, despite the general consensus that intersexual children must be corrected immediately, medical practice in these cases varies enormously. No national or international standards govern the types of intervention that may be used. Many medical schools teach the specific procedures discussed in this book, but individual surgeons make decisions based on their own beliefs and what was current practice when they were in training—which may or may not concur with the approaches published in cutting-edge medical journals. Whatever treatment they choose, however, physicians who decide how to manage intersexuality act out of, and perpetuate, deeply held beliefs about male and female sexuality, gender roles, and the (im)proper place of homosexuality in normal development.

THE PARENTS

When a mixed-sex child is born, somebody (sometimes the surgeon, sometimes a pediatric endocrinologist, more rarely a trained sex education counselor) explains the situation to the parents.[11] A "normal" boy, they say, may be born with a penis (defined as a phallus that has a urethral tube [through which urine flows] running lengthwise through its center and opening at the tip). This boy also has one X and one Y chromosome (XY), two testes

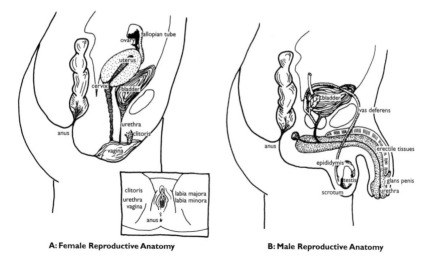

A: Female Reproductive Anatomy   B: Male Reproductive Anatomy

FIGURE 3.2: *A*: Female reproductive anatomy. *B*: Male reproductive anatomy. (Source: Alyce Santoro, for the author)

descended into scrotal sacs, and a variety of tubing, which in the sexually mature male transports sperm and other components of the seminal fluid to the outside world (figure 3.2B).

Just as often, the child has a clitoris (a phallus that does not have a urethra) which, like a penis, contains ample supplies of blood and nerves. Physical stimulation can cause both to become erect and to undergo a series of contractions that we call orgasm.[12] In a "normal" girl the urethra opens near the vagina, a large canal surrounded at its opening by two sets of fleshy lips. The canal walls connect on the inside to the cervix, which in turn opens up into the uterus. Attached to the uterus are oviducts, which, after puberty, transport egg cells from the nearby pair of ovaries toward the uterus and beyond (figure 3.2A). If this child also has two X chromosomes (XX), we say she is female.

The doctors will also explain to the parents that male and female embryos develop by progressive divergence from a common starting point (figure 3.3). The embryonic gonad makes a choice early in development to follow a male or female pathway, and later in development the phallus ends up as either a clitoris or a penis. Similarly, the embryonic urogenital swellings either remain open to become vaginal labia or fuse to become a scrotum. Finally, all embryos contain structures destined to become the uterus and fallopian tubes and ones with the potential to become the epididymis and vas deferens (both are tubular structures involved with transporting sperm from the testes to the body's

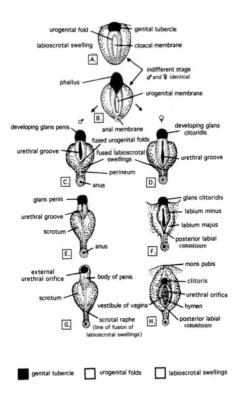

FIGURE 3.3: The development of external genitalia from the embryonic period through birth. (Source: Redrawn by Alyce Santoro from Moore 1977, p. 241, with permission from W. B. Saunders)

exterior). When the sex is chosen, the appropriate structures develop and the rest degenerate.

So far, so good. The doctors have simply recounted some basics of embryology. Now comes the tricky part: what to tell the parents of a child whose development has not proceeded along the classic path. Generally doctors inform parents that the infant has a "birth defect of unfinished genitalia," and that it may take a little time before they'll know whether the child is a boy or a girl.[13] The doctors can and will, they assure the parents, identify the "true" sex that lies underneath the surface confusion. Once they do, their hormonal and surgical treatments can complete nature's intention.[14]

Modern medical practitioners still use the nineteenth-century categories of "true" and "male pseudo" or "female pseudo" hermaphrodites.[15] Since most intersexuals fall into the pseudo category, doctors believe that an intersexual child is "really" a boy or a girl. Money, and others trained in his approach, specifically ban the word *hermaphrodite* from use in conversation with the parents. Instead, doctors use more specific medical terminology—such as "sex chromosome anomalies," "gonadal anomalies," and "external organ anomalies"[16] —that indicate that intersex children are just unusual in some aspect of their physiology, *not* that they constitute a category other than male or female.

The most common types of intersexuality are congenital adrenal hyperplasia (CAH), androgen insensitivity syndrome (AIS), gonadal dysgenesis, hypospadias, and unusual chromosome compositions such as XXY (Klinefelter Syndrome) or XO (Turner Syndrome) (see table 3.1). So-called true hermaphrodites have a combination of ovaries and testes. Sometimes an individual has a male side and a female side. In other cases the ovary and testis grow together in the same organ, forming what biologists call an ovo-testis.[17] Not infrequently, at least one of the gonads functions quite well (the ovary more often than the testis),[18] producing either sperm or eggs and functional levels of the so-called sex hormones—androgens or estrogens. In theory, it might be possible for a hermaphrodite to give birth to h/her own child, but there is no recorded case of that occurring. In practice, the external genitalia and accompanying genital ducts are so mixed that only after exploratory surgery is it possible to know what parts are present and what is attached to what.[19]

Parents of intersexuals often ask how frequently children like theirs are born and whether there are any parents of similar children with whom they might confer. Doctors, because they generally view intersex births as urgent cases, are unaware of available resources themselves, and because the medical research is scanty, often simply tell parents that the condition is extremely rare and therefore there is nobody in similar circumstances with whom they can consult. Both answers are far from the truth. I will return to the question of support groups for intersexuals and their parents in the next chapter. Here I address the question of frequency.

How often are intersex babies born? Together with a group of Brown University undergraduates, I scoured the medical literature for frequency estimates of various categories of intersexuality.[20] For some categories, usually the rarest, we found only anecdotal evidence. But for most, numbers exist. The figure we ended up with—1.7 percent of all births (see table 3.2) — should be taken as an order-of-magnitude estimate rather than a precise count.[21]

Even if we've overestimated by a factor of two, that still means a lot of intersexual children are born each year. At the rate of 1.7 percent, for example, a city of 300,000 would have 5,100 people with varying degrees of intersexual development. Compare this with albinism, another relatively uncommon human trait but one that most readers can probably recall having seen.

TABLE 3.1 *Some Common Types of Intersexuality*

NAME	CAUSE	BASIC CLINICAL FEATURES
Congenital Adrenal Hyperplasia (CAH)	Genetically inherited malfunction of one or more of six enzymes involved in making steroid hormones	In XX children, can cause mild to severe masculinization of genitalia at birth or later; if untreated, can cause masculinization at puberty and early puberty. Some forms drastically disrupt salt metabolism and are life-threatening if not treated with cortisone.
Androgen Insensitivity Syndrome (AIS)	Genetically inherited change in the cell surface receptor for testosterone	XY children born with highly feminized genitalia. The body is "blind" to the presence of testosterone, since cells cannot capture it and use it to move development in a male direction. At puberty these children develop breasts and a feminine body shape.
Gonadal Dysgenesis	Various causes, not all genetic; a catch-all category	Refers to individuals (mostly XY) whose gonads do not develop properly. Clinical features are heterogeneous.
Hypospadias	Various causes, including alterations in testosterone metabolism[a]	The urethra does not run to the tip of the penis. In mild forms, the opening is just shy of the tip; in moderate forms, it is along the shaft; and in severe forms, it may open at the base of the penis.
Turner Syndrome	Females lacking a second X chromosome. (XO)[b]	A form of gonadal dysgenesis in females. Ovaries do not develop; stature is short; lack of secondary sex characteristics; treatment includes estrogen and growth hormone.
Klinefelter Syndrome	Males with an extra X chromosome (XXY)[c]	A form of gonadal dysgenesis causing infertility; after puberty there is often breast enlargement; treatments include testosterone therapy.

a. Aaronson et al. 1997.

b. The story is, of course, more complicated. For some recent studies, see Jacobs, Dalton, et al. 1997; Boman et al. 1998.

c. There are a great many chromosomal variations classified as Klinefelter (Conte and Grumbach 1989).

TABLE 3.2 *Frequencies of Various Causes of Nondimorphic Sexual Development*

CAUSE	ESTIMATED FREQUENCY/ 100 LIVE BIRTHS
Non-XX or non-XY (except Turner's or Klinefelter's)	0.0639
Turner Syndrome	0.0369
Klinefelter Syndrome	0.0922
Androgen Insensitivity Syndrome	0.0076
Partial Androgen Insensitivity Syndrome	0.00076
Classic CAH (omitting very high-frequency population)	0.00779
Late-onset CAH	1.5
Vaginal agenesis	0.0169
True hermaphrodites	0.0012
Idiopathic	0.0009
TOTAL	1.728

Albino births occur much less frequently than intersexual births—in only about 1 in 20,000 babies.[22]

The figure of 1.7 percent is an average from a wide variety of different populations; the number is not uniform throughout the world. Many forms of intersexuality result from an altered genetic state, and in some populations, the genes involved with intersexuality are very frequent. Consider, for example, the gene for congenital adrenal hyperplasia (CAH). When present in two doses (that is, when an individual is homozygous for the gene), it causes XX females to be born with masculinized external genitalia (although their internal reproductive organs are those of a potentially fertile woman) (see table 3.1). The frequency of the gene for CAH varies widely around the world. One study found that 3.5 per thousand Yupik Eskimos born had a double dose of the CAH gene. In contrast, only 0.005/1,000 New Zealanders express the trait. The frequency of a related genetic change that leaves the genitalia unaffected but can cause premature pubic hair growth in children and symptoms such as unusual hair growth and male pattern baldness in young women, also varies widely around the world. These altered genes result in symptoms in 3/1,000 Italians. Among Ashkenazic Jews, the number rises to 37/1,000.[23]

Furthermore, the incidence of intersexuality may be on the rise. There has already been one medical report of the birth of a child with both an ovary and testes to a mother who conceived via in vitro fertilization. It seems that two embryos, one XX and one XY, fused after three were implanted into her uterus. Save for the ovary, the resulting fetus was a normal, healthy boy, formed from the fusion of an XX and an XY embryo![24] There is also concern that the presence of environmental pollutants that mimic estrogen have begun to cause widespread increases in the incidence of intersex forms such as hypospadias.[25]

But if our technology has contributed to shifts in our sexual makeup, it nevertheless also provides the tools to negate those changes. Until very recently, the specter of intersexuality has spurred us to police bodies of indeterminate sex. Rather than force us to admit the social nature of our ideas about sexual difference, our ever more sophisticated medical technology has allowed us, by its attempts to render such bodies male or female, to insist that people are either naturally male or female. Such insistence occurs even though intersexual births occur with remarkably high frequency and may be on the increase. The paradoxes inherent in such reasoning, however, continue to haunt mainstream medicine, surfacing over and over in both scholarly debates and grassroots activism around sexual identities.

"Fixing" Intersexuals

THE PRENATAL FIX

To produce gender-normal children, some medical scientists have turned to prenatal therapy. Biotechnology has already changed the human race. We have, for example, used amniocentesis and selective abortion to lower the frequency of Down Syndrome births, and in some parts of the world we have even altered the sex ratio by selectively aborting female fetuses,[26] and now both the sonogram and amniotic testing of pregnant women can detect signs of the baby's gender as well as a wide variety of developmental problems.[27] Most types of intersexuality cannot be changed by prenatal interventions, but one of the most frequent kinds—CAH—can. Is this a good thing? How might the elimination of a major cause of genital ambiguity affect our understanding of "that which qualifies a body for life within the domain of cultural intelligibility"?[28]

The genes that cause CAH are well characterized, and several approaches to detecting their presence in the embryo now exist.[29] A woman who suspects she may be pregnant with a CAH baby (if she or someone in her family carries CAH) can undergo treatment and then get tested. I put it in that order, because to prevent masculinization of an XX-CAH child's genitalia, treatment (with a steroid called dexamethasone) must begin as early as four weeks after conception.[30] The earliest methods for diagnosis, however, can't be used until the ninth week.[31] For every eight fetuses treated for CAH, only one will actually turn out to be an XX child with masculinized genitals[32]. If it turns out that the fetus is a male (physicians are not worried about fetal masculinization—you can never, apparently be *too* masculine)[33] or does not have CAH, treatment can be discontinued.[34] If, however, the fetus is XX and is affected by CAH, the mother and fetus continue dexamethasone treatment for the duration of the pregnancy.[35]

It might sound like a good idea, but the data are slim. One study compared seven untreated CAH girls (born with masculinized genitals) with their prenatally treated sisters. Three were born with completely female genitals, while four were only mildly masculinized compared with their siblings.[36] Another study of five CAH girls reported considerably more feminine genital development.[37] In medicine, however, everything has a price. The diagnostic tests[38] stand a 1 to 2 percent chance of inducing miscarriage, and the treatment produces side effects in both mother and child: mothers may retain fluids, gain a lot of extra weight, develop hypertension and diabetes, have increased and permanent scarring along abdominal stretch lines, grow extra facial hair, and become more emotional. "The effect on fetal 'metabolism' is not known,"[39] but one recent study reports negative effects such as failure to thrive and delayed psychomotor development. Another research group found that prenatal dexamethasone treatment may cause a variety of behavioral problems, including increased shyness, less sociability, and greater emotionality.[40]

Today many still do not advocate such treatment because "the safety of this experimental therapy has not been established in rigorously controlled trials."[41] On the other hand, prenatal diagnosis allows physicians to recognize the metabolic alterations and begin treatment at birth. Early and continuous treatment can prevent possible salt-wasting crises (which endanger the child's life) and address other CAH-related problems, such as premature growth stoppage and extremely early puberty. This also benefits XY CAH kids, since they still have the metabolic problems, even if their genitals are fine. Finally, genital surgery on XX CAH children can be eliminated or minimized.

Parents have given prenatal therapy mixed reviews. In one study of 176 pregnancies, 101 parents accepted prenatal treatment after being apprised of the pros and cons, while seventy-five refused the treatment. Fifteen of the seventy-five had CAH fetuses (eight XX and seven XY), and parents chose to abort three of the untreated XX fetuses.[42] In another study, researchers surveyed 38 mothers' attitudes after experiencing treatment. Although each woman had severe side effects and was concerned about the possible short- and long-term effects of dexamethasone on her child and herself, each said she would do it again to avoid giving birth to a girl with masculine genitals.[43]

Prenatal *diagnosis* seems warranted because it can prepare physicians and parents alike for the birth of a child whose chronic medical problems will demand early hormonal treatment. Whether prenatal *therapy* is ready for prime time is another question. To put it starkly: Are seven unnecessary treatments, with their attendant side effects worth one less virilized girl child? If you believe that virilization requires extensive reconstructive surgery in order to avoid damage to the child's mental health, the answer will probably be yes.[44] If, however, you believe that many of the surgeries on CAH children are unnecessary, then the answer might well be no. Perhaps compromises are possible. If one could lessen the side effects of dexamethasone treatment by limiting it to the period of initial genital formation, this would probably alleviate the most severe genital problems, such as fusion of the labia, but might not halt clitoral enlargement. Surgeries involving fused labia and reconstruction of the urogenital sinus are complex, not always successful, and essential if the affected individual wants to bear children. All other things being equal, it would seem best to avoid such surgery. As I argue in the rest of this chapter and the next, however, downsizing an overgrown clitoris is simply not necessary.

THE SURGICAL FIX

If there has been no prenatal "fix" and an intersex child is born, doctors must decide, as they would put it, nature's intention. Was the newborn infant "supposed" to have been a boy or a girl? Dr. Patricia Donahoe, Professor of Surgery at Harvard Medical School and a highly accomplished researcher in the fields of embryology and surgery, has developed a rapid procedure for choosing an ambiguous newborn's gender assignment. First she ascertains whether the newborn has two X chromosomes (is chromatin-positive) and then whether the child has symmetrically placed gonads. She places a chromatin-positive child with symmetrical gonads in the female pseudo-hermaphrodite box. In contrast, she is likely to classify an XX child with asymmetrical gonads as a true hermaphrodite, since the asymmetry most commonly reflects the presence of a testis on one side and an ovary on the other.

Children with one X chromosome (chromatin-negative) can also be divided into two groups: one with symmetrical and one with asymmetrical gonads. Babies with gonadal symmetry who are chromatin-negative fall into the male pseudo-hermaphrodite cubbyhole, while gonadally asymmetrical chromatin-negatives receive the label mixed-gonadal dysgenesis, a catchall category containing individuals whose potentially male gonads have some form of abnormal development.[45] This stepwise decision tree, which uses the permutations derived from the symmetry of gonads and the presence or absence of a second X, enables the physician to categorize the intersexual newborn fast. A more thorough and accurate assessment of the individual's specific situation can take weeks or months.

Enough is known about each of the four categories (true, male pseudo, female pseudo, and gonadal dysgenesis) to predict with considerable, although not complete, accuracy how the genitalia will develop as the child grows and whether the child will develop masculine or feminine traits at puberty. Given such knowledge, medical managers employ the following rule: "Genetic females should always be raised as females, preserving reproductive potential, regardless of how severely the patients are virilized. In the genetic male, however, the gender of assignment is based on the infant's anatomy, predominantly the size of the phallus."[46]

Doctors insist on two functional assessments of the adequacy of phallus size. Young boys should be able to pee standing up and thus to "feel normal" during little-boy peeing contests; adult men, meanwhile, need a penis big enough for vaginal penetration during sexual intercourse.[47] How big must the organ be to fulfill these central functions and thus fit the definition of *penis?* In one study of 100 newborn males, penises ranged in length from 2.9 to 4.5 centimeters (1.25 to 1.75 inches).[48] Donahoe and her co-workers express concern about a phallus of 2.0 centimeters, while one less than 1.5 centimeters long and 0.7 centimeters wide results in a female gender assignment.[49]

In fact, doctors are not sure what to count as a normal penis. In an "ideal" penis, for example, the urethra opens at the very tip of the glans. Suburethral openings are often thought of as a pathology designated with the medical term *hypospadias.* In a recent study, however, a group of urologists examined the location of the urethral opening in 500 men hospitalized for problems unrelated to hypospadias. Judged by the ideal penis, only 55 percent of the men were normal.[50] The rest had varying degrees of mild hypospadias, in which the urethra opened near, but not at, the penis tip. Many never knew that they had been urinating from the wrong place their entire lives! The authors of this study conclude:

> Pediatric urologists should be aware of the observed "normal distribu-
> tion" of meatal [urethral] positions . . . since the aim of reconstructive

surgery should be to restore the individual to normal. However, pure es-
thetic surgery would try to surpass the normal . . . this is the case in many
patients with hypospadias in whom the surgeon attempts to place the meatus in a position where it would not be found in 45% of so-called normal men.[51]

The worries in male gender choice are more social than medical.[52] Physical
health is usually not an issue, although some intersexed babies might have
problems with urinary tract infection, which, if very severe, can lead to kidney damage. Rather, early genital surgery has a set of psychological goals. Can
the surgery convince parents, caretakers, and peers—and, through them, the
child him/herself—that the intersexual is really a male? Most intersexual
males are infertile, so what counts especially is how the penis functions in
social interactions—whether it "looks right" to other boys, whether it can
"perform satisfactorily" in intercourse. It is not what the sex organ does for
the body to which it is attached that defines the body as male. It is what it does
vis-à-vis other bodies.[53] Even our ideas about how large a baby's penis needs
to be to guarantee maleness are fairly arbitrary. Perhaps unintentionally, Donahoe drove home the social nature of the decision-making process when she
commented that "phallus size at birth has not been reliably correlated with
size and function at puberty."[54] Thus, doctors may choose to remove a small
penis at birth and create a girl child, even though that penis may have grown
to "normal" size at puberty.[55]

Deciding whether to call a child a boy or a girl, then, employs social definitions of the essential components of gender. Such definitions, as the social
psychologist Suzanne Kessler observes in her book *Lessons from the Intersexed,*
are primarily cultural, not biological.[56] Consider, for instance, problems
caused by introducing European and American medical approaches into cultures with different systems of gender. A group of physicians from Saudi Arabia recently reported on several cases of XX intersex children with congenital
adrenal hyperplasia (CAH), a genetically inherited malfunction of the enzymes that aid in making steroid hormones. Despite having two X chromosomes, some CAH children are born with highly masculinized genitalia and
are initially identified as males. In the United States and Europe such children,
because they have the potential to bear children later in life, are usually raised
as girls. Saudi doctors trained in this European tradition recommended such
a course of action to the Saudi parents of CAH XX children. A number of
parents, however, refused to accept the recommendation that their child, initially identified as a son, be raised instead as a daughter. Nor would they accept
feminizing surgery for their child. As the reporting physicians write, "female

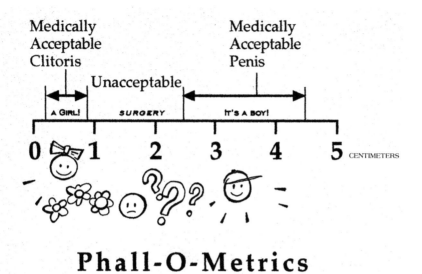

Phall-O-Metrics

FIGURE 3.4: Phall-o-Metrics. The ruler numbers indicate centimeters (not to scale). (Source: Alyce Santoro, for the author)

upbringing was resisted on social grounds. . . . This was essentially an expression of local community attitudes with . . . the preference for male offspring."[57]

If labeling intersex children as boys is tightly linked to cultural conceptions of the maleness and "proper penile function," labeling such children as girls is a process even more tangled in social definitions of gender. Congenital adrenal hyperplasia (CAH) is one of the most common causes of intersexuality in XX children. CAH kids have the potential to become fertile females in adulthood. Doctors often follow Donahoe's rule that reproductive function be preserved, although Kessler reports one case of a physician choosing to reassign as male a potentially reproductive genetic female infant rather than remove a well-formed penis.[58] In principle, however, the size rule predominates in male assignment. One reason is purely technical. Surgeons aren't very good at creating the big, strong penis they require men to have. If making a boy is hard, making a girl, the medical literature implies, is easy. Females don't need anything built; they just need excess maleness subtracted. As one surgeon well known in this field quipped, "you can make a hole but you can't build a pole."[59]

As a teaching tool in their struggle to change the medical practice of infant genital surgery, members of the Intersexual Rights Movement have designed a "phall-o-meter" (shown in figure 3.4), a small ruler that depicts the permis-

TABLE 3.3 *Recent History of Clitoral Surgery*

TYPE OF SURGERY	# OF PUBLISHED REPORTS	YEARS OF PUBLICATION	TOTAL # OF PATIENTS REPORTED ON
Clitorectomy	7	1955–1974	124
Clitoral Reduction	8	1961–1993	51
Clitoral Recession	7	1974–1992	92
Comparative Papers	2	1974, 1982	93[a]

Source: Extracted from data found in Rosenwald et al. 1958; Money 1961; Randolf and Hung 1970; Randolf et al. 1981; Donahoe and Hendren 1984; Hampson 1955; Hampson and Money 1955; Gross et al. 1966; Lattimer 1961; Mininberg 1982; Rajfer et al. 1982; van der Kamp et al. 1992; Ehrhardt et al. 1968; Allen et al. 1982; Azziz et al. 1986; Newman et al. 1992b; Mulaikal et al. 1987; Kumar et al. 1974; and Hendren and Crawford 1969.

a. May include previously reported data.

sible ranges of phallus size for males and females at birth. It provides a graphic summary of the reasoning behind the decision-making process for assigning gender. If the clitoris is "too big" to belong to a girl, doctors will want to downsize it,[60] but in contrast to the penis, doctors have rarely used precise clitoral measurements in deciding the gender of a newborn child. Such measurements, however, do exist. Since 1980, we have known that the average clitoral size of newborn girls is 0.345 centimeters.[61] More recent studies show that clitoral length at birth ranges from 0.2 to 0.85 centimeters.[62] One surgeon prominent in the field of sex reassignment surgery, when interviewed in 1994, seemed unaware that such information existed. He also thought the measurements irrelevant, arguing that for females "overall appearance" counts rather than size.[63] Thus, despite published medical information showing a range of clitoral size at birth, doctors may use only their personal impressions to decide that a baby's clitoris is "too big" to belong to a girl and must be downsized, even in cases where the child is not intersexual by any definition.[64] Physicians' ideas about the appropriate size and look of female genitals thus sometimes leads to unnecessary and sexually damaging genital surgery.[65]

Consider, for example, infants whose genitalia lie in that phallic limbo: bigger than 0.85 but smaller than 2.0 centimeters long (see figure 3.4). A systematic review of the clinical literature on clitoral surgery from 1950 to the present reveals that although doctors have been consistent over the years in assigning such infants to become female, they have radically shifted their ideas about female sexuality and, consequently, their notions of appropriate surgical treatment for female-intersex babies (see table 3.3). In the early days of surgical treatment, doctors performed complete clitorectomies on children assigned to be females (the procedure is illustrated in figure 3.5), reasoning that female orgasm was vaginal rather than clitoral.[66]

During the 1960s, physicians slowly began to acknowledge the clitoral basis of female orgasm, although even today some surgeons maintain that the clitoris is unnecessary for female orgasm.[67] In the sixties, then, physicians turned to the procedures still used in some form today. In the operation known as a clitoral reduction, the surgeon cuts the shaft of the elongated phallus and sews the glans plus preserved nerves back onto the stump (figure 3.6). In the less frequently used clitoral recession, the surgeon hides the clitoral shaft (referred to by one group of surgeons as "the offending shaft")[68] under a fold of skin so that only the glans remains visible (figure 3.7). Depending upon their anatomy at birth, some female-assigned children face additional surgery: vaginal construction or expansion and labio-scrotal reduction.

Intersex children assigned to become boys also face extensive surgery. There are over 300 surgical "treatments" described in the medical literature for hypospadias, the opening of the urethra at some point along the shaft of

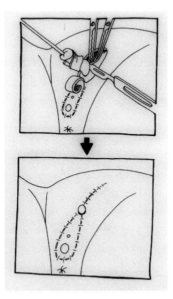

FIGURE 3.5: Removing the clitoris (clitorectomy).

(Source: Alyce Santoro, for the author)

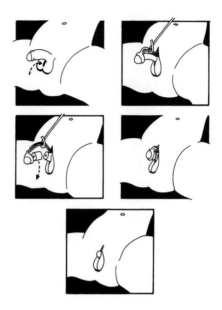

FIGURE 3.6: Reducing the clitoris (clitoral reduction).
(Source: Alyce Santoro, for the author)

the penis rather than at its tip (necessitating that the child urinate sitting down). Some of these operations address penile chordee, the binding of the penis to the body by tissue, which causes it to curve and have difficulty becoming erect—a condition that often results from intersexual development.[69] Except for the most minor forms of hypospadias all involve extensive suturing and, on occasion, skin transplants. A male-assigned child may receive as many as three operations on the penis during the first couple of years of life, and even more by the time puberty hits. In the most severe cases, multiple operations can lead to densely scarred and immobile penises, a situation one physician has dubbed "hypospadias cripple."[70]

No consensus has formed about which technique consistently results in the lowest complication rates and necessitates the fewest operations. The enormous surgical literature on hypospadias is inconclusive. Every year dozens of new papers appear describing new surgical techniques, each supposed to give better results than the dozens of preceding techniques.[71] Many of the surgical reports focus on special techniques for what the surgeons call "secondary operations"—that is, surgery designed to repair previously failed surgeries.[72] There are many reasons for the sprawling literature on hypospadias. The condition *is* highly variable and thus calls for widely varied treatments. But a re-

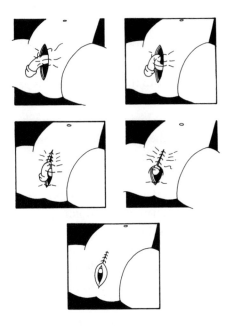

FIGURE 3.7: Hiding the clitoris (clitoral recession).

(Source: Alyce Santoro, for the author)

view of the literature also suggests that surgeons take particular pleasure in pioneering new approaches to penile repair. Even medical professionals have remarked on this obsession with penis-building. As one prominent urologist who has a technique for hypospadias named after himself writes: "Each hypospadias surgeon has his fetishes."[73]

THE PSYCHOLOGICAL FIX

Although influential researchers such as John Money and John and Joan Hampson believed that gender identity formation during early childhood is extraordinarily malleable, they also thought that gender ambiguity later in life was pathological. How, then, was an intersex infant to make the transition from the open-ended possibilities present at birth to the fixed gender identity the medical establishment deemed necessary for psychological health? Because a child's psychological schema developed in concert with his or her body image, Money and the Hampsons insisted, early genital surgery was imperative. A child's body parts had to match his or her assigned sex. While such anatomical clarity was important for the young child,[74] Money, the Hampsons, and those who followed their lead argued, it was even more important for the child's parents. As Peter Pan might have said, "they had to believe" in their child's gender identity for that identity to become real. Hampson and Hampson write: "In working with hermaphroditic children and their parents, it has become clear that the establishment of a child's psychosexual orientation begins not so much with the child as with his parents."[75]

Ironically, in their extensive discussions about what *not* to tell parents, medical practitioners reveal the logical bind they face when they try to explain to patients and parents that the gender they have assigned—and often performed surgery to create—is not arbitrarily chosen, rather, it is natural and somehow inherent to the patient's body all along. Thus developed a tradition of gender doublespeak. Medical manuals and original research articles almost unanimously recommend that parents and children not receive a full explanation of an infant's sexual status. Instead of saying that an infant is a mixture of male and female, physicians are to allege that the intersex child is clearly either male or female, but that embryonic development has been incomplete. One physician writes: "every effort should be made to discourage the concept that the child is part male and part female. . . .This is often best handled by explaining that 'the gonads were incompletely developed . . . and therefore required removal.' All efforts should be made to discourage any feeling of sexual ambiguity."[76]

A recent medical publication cautions that in counseling parents of intersexual children, doctors must "prevent contradictory or confusing information from adding to the uncertainty of the parents. . . . If the external genitalia of the child are unclear, the parents are only informed that the cause will be investigated."[77] This group of Dutch physicians and psychologists often treat androgen-insensitive (see table 3.1) children. AIS children have an X and an Y chromosome and active testes, but because their cells are insensitive to testosterone, they cannot develop masculine secondary sex characteristics and often respond at puberty to their own testicular estrogen by developing a voluptuous female figure. Such children are generally raised as girls, both because of their feminine body structure and because past experience has shown that AIS children usually develop a female gender identity. Often the AIS child's testes are removed but, caution the Dutch researchers, "we speak only about gonads, not testicles. If the gonad contains ovarian and testicular tissue we say that the gonad is not entirely developed in a female direction."[78]

Other physicians are aware that they must reckon with their patients' knowledge and curiosity. Because "sex chromatin testing may be done in high school biology courses and the media coverage of sexual medicine is increasingly detailed," writes one group of researchers, "one dare not assume that an adolescent can be spared knowledge about his or her gonadal or chromosomal status." But they also suggest that an XY intersex raised as a girl never be told that she once had testes that were removed, emphasizing that nuanced scientific understanding of anatomical sex is incompatible with a patient's need for clear-cut gender identity. An intersex child assigned to become a girl, for instance, should understand any surgery she has undergone not as an operation that changed her into a girl, but as a procedure that removed parts that didn't belong to her as a girl. "By convention the gonad is recorded as a testis," these physicians write, "but in the patient's own formulation it is best regarded as an imperfect organ . . . not suited to life as a female, and hence removed."[79]

Others believe that even this limited degree of openness is counterproductive. One surgeon suggests that "accurate patho-physiological explanations are not appropriate and medical honesty at any price is of no benefit to the patient. For instance, there is nothing to be gained by telling genetic males raised as females about the maleness of their chromosomes or gonads."[80] In their suggestions for withholding information about patients' bodies and their own decisions in shaping them, medical practitioners unintentionally reveal their anxieties that a full disclosure of the facts about intersex bodies would threaten individuals'—and by extension society's—adherence to a strict male-female model. I do not suggest a conspiracy; rather, doctors' own deep conviction that all people are either male or female renders them blind to such logical binds.

Being coy about the truth in what doctors consider the interest of psychological health, however, can be at odds with sound medical practice. Consider the controversy over the early removal of testes in AIS children. The reason generally given is that the testes can become cancerous. However, the cancer rates for testes of AIS patients don't increase until after puberty. And although the androgen-insensitive body cannot respond to androgens made by the testes, it can and at puberty does respond to testicular estrogen production. Natural feminization may well be better than artificially induced feminization, especially with regard to the dangers of developing osteoporosis. So why don't doctors delay removal of the testes until just after puberty? One reason is surely that doctors might then have to tell a truer story to the AIS patient, something they are extremely reluctant to do.[81]

Kessler describes just such a case. A child received surgery when s/he was too young to remember or fully understand the import of the changes in h/her anatomy. When s/he reached puberty, doctors told her that she needed to take estrogen pills for some time to come, explaining that her ovaries hadn't been normal "and had been removed." Apparently wishing to convince h/her that her femininity was authentic despite her inability to have children, the doctor explained that her "uterus won't develop but [she] could adopt children." Another physician on the treatment team approved of his colleague's explanation. "He's stating the truth, and if you don't state the truth . . . then you're in trouble later." Given that the girl never had a uterus or ovaries, however, this was, as Kessler points out, "a strange version of 'the truth.'"[82]

In recent years patients have had more than a little to say about such half-truths and outright lies, and I will consider their viewpoints in the next chapter. For now, I turn from the treatment protocols developed with an eye toward keeping intersexuality within the bounds of a two-sex gender system, to experimental studies conducted by physicians and psychologists on human intersexuals. In the long tradition established by Saint-Hilaire, such investigations use intersexuality to reflect on the "normal" development of masculinity and femininity.

The Uses of Intersexuality

BECOMING MALE/BECOMING FEMALE

The underlying assumptions of the surgical approach to intersex babies have not gone uncontested. Not everyone believes that sexual identity is fundamentally malleable. By far the most dramatic of these debates has been an almost thirty-year battle between John Money and another psychologist, Milton Diamond. In the 1950s Money, together with his collaborators, the Hampsons, argued that the sex assignment and sex of rearing predicted a hermaphrodite's adult gender role and sexual orientation more accurately than did any aspect of h/her biological sex: "Theoretically, our findings indicate [that] neither a purely hereditary nor a purely environmental doctrine of the origins of gender role . . . is adequate. On the one hand it is evident that gender role and orientation is not determined in some automatic, innate, instinctive fashion by physical agents like chromosomes. On the other hand it is also evident that the sex of assignment and rearing does not automatically and mechanistically determine gender role and orientation."[83]

But were Money's claims applicable to the majority of sexually unambiguous children? Had he and his colleagues—via the study of intersex children—arrived at a general, possibly even universal, theory of psychosexual development? Money believed he had, and to prove it he pointed to the case of an unambiguously male child named John, who lost his penis at about seven months of age after a circumcision accident. Reasoning from his studies on intersexuals, Money counseled that the child be raised as a girl and surgically altered to fit her new status in life. A particularly compelling component of this case was the fact that there was a control: Joan (as she was renamed) had an identical twin brother. This case, Money hoped, would clinch his argument about the importance of sex of rearing. If Joan developed a female gender identity, while her genetically identical brother continued down the road to adult masculinity, then environmental forces clearly trumped genetic makeup.

The family ultimately agreed to the sex change, and by the time the child reached her second year she had had feminizing surgery and her testicles had been removed. With great delight, Money quoted Joan's mother to the effect that Joan had grown to love wearing dresses, that she hated being dirty, and that "she just loves to have her hair set."[84] Money concluded that his case demonstrated that "gender dimorphic patterns of rearing have an extraordinary influence on shaping a child's psychosexual differentiation and the ultimate outcome of a female or male gender identity." In a particularly enthusiastic moment, he wrote: "To use the Pygmalion allegory, one may begin with the same clay and fashion a god or a goddess."[85]

Money's account of psychosexual development rapidly gained favor as the most progressive, most liberal, most up-to-date point of view around.[86] But not everyone thought it made sense. In 1965 Milton Diamond, at the time a young Ph.D., decided to take on Money and the Hampsons. He did so at the suggestion and with the help of mentors who came from a rather different tradition in the field of psychology.[87] Diamond's advisers proposed a new paradigm for understanding the development of sexual behaviors: hormones, not environment, they argued, were the decisive factor.[88] Early in development, these chemical messengers acted directly to organize the brain; hormones produced at puberty could activate the hormonally organized brain to produce sex-specific behaviors such as mating and mothering.[89] Although these theories were based on studies of rodents, Diamond drew heavily on them to attack Money's work.[90]

Diamond argued that Money and his colleagues, were essentially suggesting that humans are sexually neutral at birth. He challenged their interpretations of their data, arguing "that the very same data may not be inconsistent with more classical notions of inherent sexuality at birth." Diamond agreed that Money and his colleagues had shown that "hermaphroditic individuals . . . find it possible to assume sexual roles opposite to their genetic sex, morphological sex, etc." But he disagreed with their broader conclusions, arguing, "to assume that a sex role is exclusively or even mainly a very elaborate, culturally fostered deception . . . and that it is not also reinforced by taboos and potent defense mechanisms superimposed on a *biological prepotency or prenatal organization and potentiation* seems unjustified and from the present data

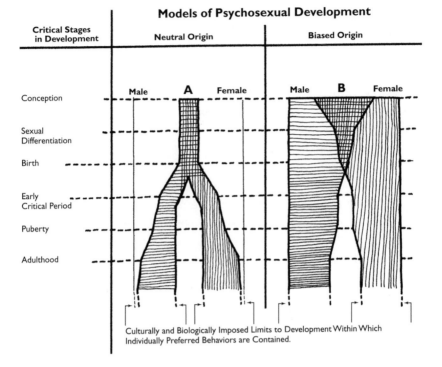

FIGURE 3.8: Models of psychosexual development. (Redrawn and interpreted from Diamond 1965. Source: Alyce Santoro for the author)

unsubstantiated."[91] In other words, Diamond argued that even if Money and his colleagues might be correctly interpreting intersexual development, their work shed no light on what he called "normals."[92]

Diamond also pointed out that the John/Joan case was the *sole* example of "normal" prenatal hormone exposure being overcome by rearing. In opposition to the Money and Hampson theory of gender neutrality molded by environment into gender identity,[93] Diamond posed his own model of "psychosexual predisposition." He suggested that male and female embryos each begin with partially overlapping but relatively broad potential for psychosexual development. As both pre- and postnatal development proceeds, however, there appear "limits and restrictions in the form of culturally and biologically acceptable sexual outlets within the total capability"[94] (figure 3.8).

Only one other scholar dared to challenge Money.[95] In 1970 Dr. Bernard Zuger, a practicing psychiatrist, found several clinical case studies in which adolescent or adult intersexuals rejected their sex of rearing and insisted on changing sex. These individuals seemed to be listening to some inner voice that said that everyone in authority surrounding h/her was wrong. Doctors and parents might have insisted that they were female, removed their testes, injected them with estrogen, and surgically provided them with a vagina, but still, they *knew* they were really males. Zuger concluded: "The data from hermaphrodites purporting to show that sex of rearing overrides contradictions of chromosomes, gonads, hormones, internal and external genitalia in gender role determination are found unsupportable on methodological and clinical grounds. Conclusions drawn from the data as to the adoption of such assigned gender role and the psychological hazard of changing it after very early childhood are shown not to be in agreement with other similar data found in the literature."[96]

Money was furious. When Zuger's paper appeared, he published a rebuttal in the journal *Psychosomatic Medicine*, fuming, "What really worries me, even terrifies me, about Dr. Zuger's paper, however, is more than a matter of theory alone . . . it will be used by inexperienced and/or dogmatic physicians and surgeons as a justification to *impose* an erroneous sex reassignment on a child . . . omitting a psychological evaluation as irrelevant—to the ultimate ruination of the patient's life."[97] In his 1972 book with Anke Ehrhardt, Money lashed out again: "it thus appears that the prejudices of physicians skew today's hermaphroditic sex reassignment statistics in favor of change from girl to boy, and in male rather than female hermaphrodites. It would not be necessary to belabor this point except that some writers still do not understand it."[98]

But Diamond pursued Money with a determination worthy of Inspector Javert in *Les Misérables*. Throughout the 1960s and 70s he published at least five more papers contesting Money's views. In a 1982 publication, he recounted how psychology and women's studies texts had taken up John/Joan "to support the contention that sex roles and sexual identity are basically learned." Even *Time* magazine was propagating Money's social constructionist doctrine. But Diamond reiterated his view that "nature sets limits to sexual identity and partner preference and that it is within these limits that social forces interact and gender roles are formulated, a biosocial-interaction theory."[99] (Note that by 1982 the terms of the debate had shifted. Diamond now spoke of *sexual* rather than *gender* identity, and a new term, *partner preference,* slipped in. I will return to partner preference—the origins of homosexuality—later.)

Diamond did not write this article just to gripe. He had big news. In 1980 the BBC produced a TV documentary on the John/Joan case. At first the producers planned to feature Money and his views while using Diamond for an oppositional backdrop. But the BBC reporters had found that by 1976 Joan, then thirteen years old, was not well adjusted. She walked like a boy, felt that boys had better lives, wanted to be a mechanic, and peed standing up. The psychiatrists then caring for the child thought she was "having considerable difficulty in adjusting as a female" and suspected she would not succeed in remaining one. When the journalists told Money of these findings, he refused to talk further with them, and they broadcast the psychiatrists' findings of John's discontent without additional input from Money. Diamond learned of all this from the BBC production team, but the film did not air in the United States. In an attempt to bring the facts to light in John's country of origin, Diamond, in 1982, published a secondhand account of the documentary in the hopes of discrediting Money's sex/gender theory once and for all.[100]

The paper did not make the splash Diamond had wanted. But he did not give up. He started advertising in the *American Psychiatric Association Journal*, asking the psychiatrists who had taken over John/Joan's case to contact him so that they could get the truth out in the open. But John's psychiatrist, Keith Sigmundson, who said he "was shit-scared of John Money . . . I didn't know what he would do to my career,"[101] let years go by before he finally responded and told Diamond what no other professionals had known: in 1980 Joan had had her breasts removed, later had a penis reconstructed, and was married and living with a woman and serving as her children's father. Finally, Diamond and Sigmundsen made front-page news when they published the update on John/Joan, whom they now referred to as Joan/John.[102]

Diamond and Sigmundson used the failure of John's sex reassignment to dispute two basic ideas: that individuals are psychosexually neutral at birth, and that healthy psychosexual development is intimately related to the appearance of the genitals. Using the compelling details of the updated story, in which John/Joan/John's mother now recounted his/her consistent rejection of and rebellion against attempts to socialize him as a girl, Diamond argued that far from being sexually neutral, the brain was in fact prenatally gendered. "The evidence seems overwhelming," he wrote, "that *normal* humans are not psychosexually neutral at birth but are, in keeping with their mammalian heritage, predisposed and biased to interact with environmental, familial and social forces in either a male or a female mode."[103]

Since the Diamond/Sigmundson exposé, similar reports of rejection of sex reassignments and of the successful rearing as males of children born with malformed penises have received wide attention.[104] Diamond and a few others have gained a foothold (although some still harbor doubts)[105] in calling for new treatment paradigms—above all, postponing immediate and irreversible surgery and providing counseling instead. "With this management," Diamond reasons, "a male's predisposition to act as a boy and his actual behavior will be reinforced in daily interactions and on all sexual levels and his fertility will be preserved."[106]

The debate, however, is not over. In 1998 a group of Canadian psychiatrists and psychologists published a follow-up of another case of sex reassignment following *ablatio penis* (as accidental loss of the penis is so delicately called in the medical literature). This child was reassigned at seven months (much earlier than John/Joan, who was almost two years old when reassigned). In 1998 the unnamed patient was twenty-six years old and living as a woman. She had had love affairs with men, but had left her most recent boyfriend and now lives as a lesbian. She works in a blue-collar job "practiced almost exclusively by men." The authors note "a strong history of behavioral masculinity during childhood and a predominance of sexual attraction to females in fantasy." Yet they do not argue that the sex assignment was entirely unsuccessful. Rather, they insist that gender *identity* in this case *was* successfully changed by rearing, even if gender role and sexual orientation were not. "Perhaps," they conclude, "gender role and sexual orientation are more strongly influenced by biologic factors than is gender identity formation."[107]

Their theories have sparked intense debate. Some sexologists, for example, argue strongly that this paper by Susan Bradley and her colleagues actually provides evidence for rather than against Diamond's position. And the conversations have become even more nuanced as adult intersexuals have begun to contribute their viewpoints. Not incidentally, they also suggest more complex interpretations of the case studies than offered by academics or practicing physicians.[108] Even John Money, who has refused to discuss the case, has adopted a more intricate position. In a comment on another case of *ablatio penis,* in which a dog attacked a child, he concedes that with both early and late sex reassignment, "the long term outcome is less than perfect." He acknowledges that boys reassigned as girls often become lesbian, something he views as a negative because of the associated social stigma. Without ever citing Diamond or alluding to the debate, he concedes: "There is, as yet, no unanimously endorsed set of guidelines for the treatment of genital trauma and mutilation in infancy, and no provision for a statistical depository of outcome data."[109]

DEFINING HETEROSEXUALITY:
A HEALTHY INTERSEXUAL IS A STRAIGHT INTERSEXUAL!

A specter is haunting medicine—the specter of homosexuality. What seems to be a recent focus on the connection between gender and sexual orientation only makes more explicit concerns that have long motivated scientific discussions of gender and intersexuality. It is impossible to understand the continuing arguments over the treatment of intersexuals without putting them in the historical context of highly charged debates over homosexuality. In the 1950s, as one historian writes, "The media and government propaganda associated homosexuals and other 'sex psychopaths' with communists as the most dangerous nonconformists—invisible enemies who could live next door and who threatened the security and safety of children, women, the family, and the nation."[110] Joseph McCarthy and Richard Nixon saw homosexual Communists under every pumpkin leaf. When doctors chose to assign a definitive sex to an ambiguously sexed child, then, it was not enough that the child become psychologically male or female. For the treatment to count as successful, the child had to become heterosexual. The Hampsons, who understood homosexuality as a psychopathology, a "disorder of psychologic sex," stressed that properly treated intersex children posed no threat of homosexuality.[111] They advised medical practitioners that parents of intersexual children "need to be told that their child is not destined to grow up with abnormal and perverse desires, for they get hermaphroditism and homosexuality hopelessly confused."[112]

One can hardly blame the parents for feeling confused. If intersexuality blurred the distinction between male and female, then it followed that it blurred the line dividing hetero- from homosexual. Might one, in the course of treating an intersexual, end up creating a homosexual? It all came down to how you defined sex. Consider an AIS child born with an X and a Y chromosome in each cell, testes and ambiguous but primarily female-appearing external genitalia. Because her cells are insensitive to the testosterone her testes produce, she will be raised as a girl. At puberty her testes will make estrogen, which will transform her body into that of a young woman. She falls in love with a young man. She still has testes and an XY chromosome composition. Is she homosexual or heterosexual?

Money and his followers would say she is blessedly heterosexual. Money's logic would be that this person, raised as a female, has a female gender identity.[113] In the complex trek from anatomical sex to social gender, her male sex chromosomes and gonads have been ruled unimportant because her hormonal and assigned sex are female. As long as she is attracted to men, she is safely heterosexual. We have chosen, medically and culturally, to accept this kind of person as a straight woman, a definition she probably accepts as well.[114]

Money and his collaborators developed their treatment programs for intersexuality in the 1950s, when homosexuality was defined as a mental pathology. Even so, Money himself is quite clear that the designation "homosexual" is a cultural choice, not a natural fact. In discussing matched pairs of hermaphrodites, some raised as girls and others as boys, he and Ehrhardt write that such "cases represent what is, to all intents and purposes, experimentally planned and iatrogenically induced homosexuality. But *homosexuality in these cases must be qualified as homosexuality on the criterion of genetic sex, gonadal sex, or fetal hormonal sex.* Post surgically, it is no longer homosexuality on the criterion of the external sex organs nor of the sex of replacement hormonal puberty."[115]

More recently, the gay liberation movement has inspired a change in views that has helped medical practitioners see, to some extent, that their theories are compatible with a more tolerant view of sexual orientation. Diamond, who in 1965 spoke of "effeminacy and other sexual deviations," today writes that "it is our understanding of natural diversity that a wide offering of sex types and associated origins should be anticipated." "Certainly," he continues, "the full gamut of heterosexual, homosexual, bisexual and even celibate options . . . must be offered and candidly discussed."[116] Diamond continues to argue that nature is the arbiter of sexuality, but now, he believes, nature permits more than two normal types of sexuality. Today, he (and others) read from nature a story of diversity. Of course, nature has not changed since the 1950s. Rather, we have changed our scientific narratives to conform to our cultural transformations.

SAVING SEX: THE INTERSEXUAL AS NATURE'S EXPERIMENT

Money's prescriptions for managing intersexuality paint him, and those who agree with him, into an ideological corner. On the one hand, they believe that intersexuals inhabit bodies whose sexual development has gone awry. On the other hand, they argue that sexual development is so malleable that if one starts with a young enough child, bodies and sexual identities can be changed almost at will. But if bodily sex is so malleable, why bother maintaining the concept?[117]

Scientists struggling with this dilemma focus on intersexuals not only as patients in need of medical attention, but also as a kind of natural experiment. In particular, since the 1970s, intersexuals have been central to the scientific search for hormonal causes of behavioral differences between the sexes. Deliberate manipulations of hormones during development, performed with impunity on rats and monkeys, cannot be done on humans. But when nature provides us with an experiment, it seems natural enough to study her offering.

Building upon extensive animal research (see chapter 8) showing that gonodal hormones influence behavioral development, investigators have used intersexuals to examine three widely believed in sex differences:[118] differences in sexual desire,[119] differences in play in children, and differences in cognition, especially spatial abilities.[120] Analyzing this body of work shows how intersexuals, seen as deviations from the norm who need to be "fixed" in order to preserve a two-gender system, are also studied to prove how "natural" the system is to begin with.

Consider, for example, the attempts of modern psychologists to understand the biological origins of lesbianism by studying female intersexuality caused by hyperactive adrenal glands (CAH). CAH girls are born with masculinized genitalia because their overactive adrenal glands have, during fetal development, produced large amounts of masculinizing hormone (androgen). When discovered at birth, the overproduction of androgen is stopped by treatment with cortisone and the genitals are "feminized" by surgery.

Even though to date there is no direct evidence to show that, in human embryos, hormones affect brain and genital development during the same time period,[121] scientists wondered if the excess prenatal androgen also affected brain development. If the fetal brain were masculinized, permanently altered by exposure to testosterone, would that "cause" CAH girls to have more masculine interests and sexual desires? The question itself suggests a particular theory of the lesbian as fallen woman. As the psychoanalysts Maggie Magee and Diana Miller write, "A woman who makes her emotional and intimate life with another woman is seen as having 'fallen' from the path of true feminine development, expressing masculine not feminine identification and desires."[122] Applying this concept to CAH girls seemed to make sense. Their "extra" androgen production had caused them to fall from the path of true female development. Studying CAH girls, then, might provide support for the hypothesis that hormones, gone awry, lie at the heart of homosexual development.[123]

From 1968 to the present, approximately a dozen (the number continues to grow) studies have looked for evidence of unusual masculinity in CAH girls. Were they more aggressive and active as children? Did they prefer boys' toys? Were they less interested in play rehearsal of mothering and, the ultimate question, did they become lesbians or harbor homosexual thoughts and desires?[124] In the gender system that frames this research, girls who like boys' toys, climb trees, don't like dolls, and think about having careers are also likely to be prone to homosexuality. Sexual attraction to women is understood to be merely a male-typical form of object choice, no different in principle from liking football or erector sets. Girls with masculine interests, then, may reflect an entire suite of behaviors, of which adult homosexuality is but a postpubertal example.[125]

Recently Magee and Miller analyzed ten studies of CAH girls and women. Although Money and colleagues originally reported that CAH girls were more active than controls (higher energy expenditure, more aggressive, more rough-and-tumble play),[126] more recent work, Miller and Magee conclude, does not bear them out.[127] Furthermore, none of the studies found increased dominance assertion in CAH girls.[128] A few publications report that CAH girls are less interested than control girls (often unaffected siblings) in doll play and other forms of "rehearsal" for motherhood. Inexplicably, however, one research group found that CAH girls spent more time playing with and caring for their pets, while other researchers found that CAH patients did not wish to have their own children and more often preferred the idea of a career to staying at home.[129] All in all, the results provide little support for a role for prenatal hormones in the production of gender differences.

Magee and Miller find special fault with the ten studies of lesbianism in CAH women. These, they point out, contain no common concept of female homosexuality. Definitions range from "lesbian identity, to homosexual relationships, to homosexual experience, to same-sex fantasies" and dreams.[130] Although several studies report increases in homosexual thoughts or fantasies, none found exclusively homosexual CAH females. One of the research groups concluded that "prenatal hormone effects do not determine the sexual orientation of an individual,"[131] others cling to the idea that "early exposure to androgens may have a masculinizing influence on sexual orientation in women."[132]

Thus, a critical look at the studies of masculine development in CAH girls reveals a weak, problem-ridden literature. Why, then, do such studies continue to appear? I believe these highly skilled, well-trained scientists,[133] return again and again to drink from the well of intersexuality because they are so deeply immersed in their own theory of gender that other ways of collecting and interpreting data become impossible to see. They are fish who swim beautifully in their own oceans but cannot conceptualize walking on solid ground.[134]

Wrap-Up: Reading Nature Is a Sociocultural Act

All choices, whether to treat with chemicals, perform surgeries, or let genitally mixed bodies alone, have consequences beyond the immediate medical realm. What might the phrase "social construction" mean in the material world of bodies with differing genitals and differing behavior patterns? The feminist philosopher Judith Butler suggests that "bodies . . . only live within the productive constraints of certain highly gendered regulatory schemas."[135] The medical approaches to intersexual bodies provide a literal example. Bodies in the "normal" range are culturally intelligible as males or females, but the rules for living as male or female are strict.[136] No oversized clits or undersized penises allowed. No masculine women or effeminate men need apply. Currently, such bodies are, as Butler writes, "unthinkable, abject, unlivable."[137] By their very existence they call into question our system of gender. Surgeons, psychologists, and endocrinologists, through their surgical skills, try to make good facsimiles of culturally intelligible bodies. If we choose to eliminate mixed-genital births through prenatal treatments (both those currently available and those that may become available in the future), we are also choosing to go with our current system of cultural intelligibility. If we choose, over a period of time, to let mixed-gender bodies and altered patterns of gender-related behavior become visible, we will have, willy-nilly, chosen to change the rules of cultural intelligibility.

The dialectic of medical argument is to be read neither as evil technological conspiracy nor as story of sexual open-mindedness illumined by the light of modern scientific knowledge. Like the hermaphrodite h/herself, it is neither and both. Knowledge about the embryology and endocrinology of sexual development, gained during the nineteenth and twentieth centuries, enables us to understand that human males and females all begin life with the same structures; complete maleness and complete femaleness represent the extreme ends of a spectrum of possible body types. That these extreme ends are the most frequent has lent credence to the idea that they are not only natural (that is, produced by nature) but normal (that is, they represent both a statistical and a social ideal). Knowledge of biological variation, however, allows us to conceptualize the less frequent middle spaces as natural, although statistically unusual.

Paradoxically, theories of medical treatment of intersexuality undermine beliefs about the biological inevitability of contemporary sex roles. Theorists such as Money suggest that under certain circumstances the body is irrelevant for the creation of conventional masculinity and femininity. Chromosomes emerge as the least important factor, the internal organs—including the gonads—as the next least important. The external genitalia and secondary sex characteristics obtain status for their ability to visually signal to all concerned that one should behave in certain gender-appropriate ways. In this view the society in which the child is reared, not mysterious inner bodily signals, decides which behaviors are appropriate for males and which for females.

Real-life medical practitioners, however, concerned with convincing parents, grandparents, and nosy neighbors about gender choices made for intersex infants, develop a language that reinforces the idea that lurking inside the mixed-sex child is a real male or female body. Thus they also encourage the idea that children are actually born with gender and contradict the idea that gender is a cultural construction. The same contradiction emerges when psychologists appeal to prenatal hormones to explain supposedly higher frequencies of lesbianism and other desires deemed inappropriate for a psychologically healthy female.

Within these contradictory practices and views there is room for maneuver. Scientific and medical understandings of multiple human sexes bring with them both the means to disrupt and the tools to reinforce dominant beliefs about sex and gender. Sometimes feminist analyses of science and technology present these enterprises as monolithic behemoths against which all resistance is powerless. Feminist accounts of reproductive technology have been particularly susceptible to this view, but recently the philosopher Jana Sawicki has provided a more empowering analysis. She writes: "although new reproductive technologies" can sustain the status quo for "existing power relations," technology also offers new possibilities for disruption and resistance."[138] Not only is this also the case for the medical management of intersexuality, I suggest it is always the case. Feminists must become comfortable enough with technology to ferret out the points of resistance.

Our theories of sex and gender are knitted into the medical management of intersexuality. Whether a child should be raised as a boy or girl, and subjected to surgical alterations and various hormonal regimes, depends on what we think about a variety of matters. How important is penis size? What forms of heterosexual lovemaking are "normal"? Is it more important to have a sexually sensitive clitoris—even if larger and more penile than the statistical norm—than it is to have a clitoris that visually resembles the common type? The web of knowledge is intricate and the threads always linked together. Thus we derive theories of sex and gender (at least those that claim to be scientific or "nature-based") in part from studying intersexual children brought into the management system. When needed we can, as well, appeal to animal studies, although those too are produced within a social system of sex and gender beliefs (see chapter 8).

This does not mean, however, that we are forever stuck—or blessed, depending upon your point of view—with our current account of gender. Gender systems change. As they transform, they produce different accounts of nature. Now, at the dawn of a new century, it is possible to witness such change in the making. We are moving from an era of sexual dimorphism to one of variety beyond the number two. We inhabit a moment in history when we have the theoretical understanding and practical power to ask a question unheard of before in our culture: "Should there be only two sexes?"

SHOULD THERE BE ONLY TWO SEXES?

———— Xⅅ ————

Hermaphroditic Heresies

IN 1993 I PUBLISHED A MODEST PROPOSAL SUGGESTING THAT WE RE-
place our two-sex system with a five-sex one.[1] In addition to males and females, I argued, we should also accept the categories herms (named after
"true" hermaphrodites), merms (named after male "pseudo-hermaphrodites"), and ferms (named after female "pseudo-hermaphrodites"). I'd intended to be provocative, but I had also been writing tongue in cheek, and so
was surprised by the extent of the controversy the article unleashed. Right-
wing Christians somehow connected my idea of five sexes to the United Nations–sponsored 4th World Conference on Women, to be held in Beijing two
year later, apparently seeing some sort of global conspiracy at work. "It is
maddening," says the text of a *New York Times* advertisement paid for by the
Catholic League for Religious and Civil Rights,[2] "to listen to discussions of
'five genders' when every sane person knows there are but two sexes, both of
which are rooted in nature."[3]

John Money was also horrified by my article, although for different reasons. In a new edition of his guide for those who counsel intersexual children
and their families, he wrote: "In the 1970's nurturists . . . became . . . 'social
constructionists.' They align themselves against biology and medicine. . . .
They consider all sex differences as artifacts of social construction. In cases of
birth defects of the sex organs, they attack all medical and surgical interventions as unjustified meddling designed to force babies into fixed social molds
of male and female. . . . One writer has gone even to the extreme of proposing that there are five sexes . . . (Fausto-Sterling)."[4] Meanwhile, those battling against the constraints of our sex/gender system were delighted by the
article. The science fiction writer Melissa Scott wrote a novel entitled *Shadow
Man*, which includes nine types of sexual preference and several genders, in-

cluding fems (people with testes, XY chromosomes, and some aspects of female genitalia), herms (people with ovaries and testes), and mems (people with XX chromosomes and some aspects of male genitalia).[5] Others used the idea of five sexes as a starting point for their own multi-gendered theories.[6]

Clearly I had struck a nerve. The fact that so many people could get riled up by my proposal to revamp our sex/gender system suggested that change (and resistance to it) might be in the offing. Indeed, a lot *has* changed since 1993, and I like to think that my article was one important stimulus. Intersexuals have materialized before our very eyes, like beings beamed up onto the Starship Enterprise. They have become political organizers lobbying physicians and politicians to change treatment practices. More generally, the debate over our cultural conceptions of gender has escalated, and the boundaries separating masculine and feminine seem harder than ever to define.[7] Some find the changes under way deeply disturbing; others find them liberating.

I, of course, am committed to challenging ideas about the male/female divide. In chorus with a growing organization of adult intersexuals, a small group of scholars, and a small but growing cadre of medical practitioners,[8] I argue that medical management of intersexual births needs to change. *First,* let there be no unnecessary infant surgery (by *necessary* I mean to save the infant's life or significantly improve h/her physical well-being). *Second,* let physicians assign a provisional sex (male or female) to the infant (based on existing knowledge of the probability of a particular gender identity formation—penis size be damned!). *Third,* let the medical care team provide full information and long-term counseling to the parents and to the child. However well-intentioned, the methods for managing intersexuality, so entrenched since the 1950s, have done serious harm.

First, Do No Harm

Stop infant genital surgery. We protest the practices of genital mutilation in other cultures, but tolerate them at home.[9] Some of my medical colleagues are apparently so scandalized by my thoughts on intersexuality that they refuse to discuss them with me.[10] Perhaps they think that I am sacrificing the well-being of unfortunate children on the altar of gender politics. How could I possibly consider using a poor intersexual child as a battering ram to assault the fortress of gender inequality? From the point of view of caring medical practitioners, this critique makes some sense. In the midst of daily medical crises that require rapid and highly pragmatic solutions, it is hard to step back, survey the broad picture, and ask whether another response is possible. Nevertheless, one reason I am convinced that my proposal is neither unethical nor implausible is that the medical "cure" for intersexuality frequently does more damage than good.

As we have seen, infant genital surgery is cosmetic surgery performed to achieve a social result—reshaping a sexually ambiguous body so that it conforms to our two-sex system. This social imperative is so strong that doctors have come to accept it as a medical imperative, despite strong evidence that early genital surgery doesn't work: it causes extensive scarring, requires multiple surgeries, and often obliterates the possibility of orgasm. In many of the case reports of clitoral surgery, the only criteria for success are cosmetic, rather than later sexual function. Table 4.1 summarizes information from nine clinical reports on the results of reduction clitoroplasties (see figure 3.6) on eighty-eight patients.[11] The inadequacy of the evaluations is glaringly obvious. Two of nine reports never state the criteria for success; four emphasize cosmetic criteria; only one considers psychological health or does long-term follow-up. Intersexual activists have increasingly revealed the complex and painful stories behind these anonymous numbers, challenging the medical establishment's most cherished beliefs and practices regarding intersexual children.[12]

Cheryl Chase, the charismatic founder of the Intersexual Society of North America (ISNA), has played a particularly important role in this battle. She has chosen to go public with her own story, reaching out to other intersexuals and to the medical profession. At age thirty-six, Chase operated a successful small business that sent her traveling all over the world.[13] Were she not eager to share her past, there would be no way of knowing, by simply meeting her, about her medical history. Born with ovo-testes but internal and external genitalia that were female, the only external sign of her difference was an enlarged clitoris. Her parents raised her as a boy until she was eighteen months old. Then, at the advice of physicians, she underwent complete clitorectomy (see figure 3.5). Her parents changed her name, threw away all her boy's clothes, destroyed all photos of Cheryl as a boy and raised her as girl.

When she was older, doctors operated again, this time to remove the testicular portion of her gonads. She was told that she had a hernia operation. Her medical records confirm her personal recollections that during the annual check-ups that followed, the doctor never spoke directly to her. Nor did her mother ever follow up on a psychiatric referral noted in the case records. Still, at age eighteen, Chase knew something had happened. She sought to learn the contents of her medical records. But a doctor who agreed to help changed her mind after reading the records and refused to tell Chase of their contents. Finally, at the age of twenty-three, she got another doctor to tell her that she had been diagnosed as a true hermaphrodite and surgically "corrected" to be female.[14]

For fourteen years Chase buried this information somewhere in her subconscious. Then, while living abroad, she fell into a suicidal depression. She returned home, began therapy, and struggled to come to terms with her past. In her quest to find out whether she can ever hope to become orgasmic without having a clitoris, she has consulted concerned sex therapists and anatomists. The lack of help from intersex specialists has dismayed her. "When I began to search them out," she writes, "I expected to find some help. I thought that these doctors would have excellent connections to therapists skilled in dealing with histories like mine. They have none, nor do they have any sympathy."[15]

Although Chase despairs of gaining full sexual function, she has dedicated her life to changing the practice of early genital surgery. She hopes that others may not be denied the possibility of the full range of sexual pleasure that she sees as a human birthright. In pursuing this goal, she does not advocate putting kids in the front line of a gender war. Rather, she suggests they grow up as either social males or females; then, as adolescents or adults, they can make up their own minds about surgery—with the full knowledge of the risks to continued sexual function. They may also reject their assigned gender identity, and if they do, they will not be missing critical parts of their anatomy because of premature surgery.

Chase has become a savvy political organizer. Although she started her battle single-handedly, her troops increase daily. "When I established ISNA in 1993, no such politicized groups existed. . . . Since ISNA has been on the scene, other groups with a more resistant stance vis-à-vis the medical establishment have begun to appear. . . . In 1996, another mother who had rejected medical pressure to assign her intersex infant as a female . . . formed the Hermaphroditic Education and Listening Post (Help)."[16] Although many of the newer groups are less explicitly political, some nevertheless appreciate ISNA's more radical approach.[17] And Chase continues to build coalitions among various organizations of intersexuals, academics, and practicing physicians and psychologists. Slowly, Chase and others have begun to change medical practice in the United States.[18]

Still, these activists face strong opposition. Chase was clitorectomized in the early 1960s. I have had physicians tell me that both the surgery she received and the lack of information offered her were typical then, but not now. While surgical styles have changed (with no evidence that they are any better),[19] clitorectomy still does occur on occasion.[20] So does the practice of lying to

TABLE 4.1 *Outcomes of Reduction Clitoroplasty*

# OF SUBJECTS	AGE AT FIRST SURGERY	AGE AT EVALUATION	CRITERIA FOR SUCCESS	RESULTS	COMMENTS	SOURCE
14	2 mos.–15 yrs.	Immediately post-op	Not stated	1 "good," 1 "unsatisfactory," and 12 "excellent" (p. 225)	3 cases involved females with "idiopathic enlargement"; no painkillers used on infants and young children	a
18	< 6 mos. to 38 yrs.	Not stated	Cosmetic, social, and preservation of function	Unclear	Virtually no data offered	b
7	< 16 yrs.	Not stated	Cosmetic, possibility of sexual function	1 out of 2 adolescents reported "satisfactory sexual gratification" (p. 225)	Invoke work of Masters and Johnson to dispute earlier views that clitorectomy doesn't affect sexual function and argue against the earlier operation	c
11	Varied but no specifics	Unknown	Cosmetic, reports on sexual satisfaction (2 patients)	"Cosmetically satisfactory" (p. 355)	8-yr.-old with previous clitoral recession relieved of pain from sexual arousal by reduction; 2 sexually active females reported "the same pleasant clitoral sensations postoperatively" (p. 355)	d
3	Infants	Not stated	Not stated	Reports on a ventral approach that does less damage to clitoral nerves	"It is difficult to evaluate clinically whether the sensory function of the external genitalia has been left undisturbed" (p. 341)	e

10	Infants	Not stated	Cosmetic and function	"Excellent" (but no data)	Apparently this reports only on immediate post-op condition; no long-term follow-up	f
9	< 1 year	< 1 year	Cosmetic but no specifics	No follow-up or detailed description	Recommends early intervention	g
10	0.5–5 yrs.	median of 20.8 years	Psychological health and physical normality; independent evaluations via psychological, gynecological, and physical evaluations	"Neither the anatomical aspect nor the functionality of the external genitalia was satisfactory" (p. 48); patients mostly psychologically masculine or intermediate between masculine & feminine	Recommends continuous treatment (psychological and counseling) by an interdisciplinary team throughout childhood; each child averaged 3 genital surgeries (range: 1–6)	h
6	3–13 months	6–42 months	Cosmetic, esp. success in hiding the glans from view	"All patients achieved a pleasing cosmetic result" (p. 652)	Favors reduction clitoroplasty over recession	i
6	Not stated	15–30	Orgasm	"All . . . referred orgasm during intercourse"	Favors clitoroplasty	j
6	6 mos.–14 yrs.	Not stated	Not stated	4/6 required 2nd surgery	Results listed simply as "satisfactory"	k

a. Randolf and Hung 1970. b. Kumar et al. 1974. c. Fonkalsrun et al. 1977. d. Mininberg 1982. e. Rajfer et al. 1982. f. Oesterling et al. 1987.
g. Sharp et al. 1987. h. Van der Kamp et al. 1992. i. Bellinger 1993. j. Costa et al. 1997. k. Joseph 1997.

patients and withholding medical information even after they have reached the age of majority. Consider Angela Moreno's more recent tale. In 1985, when she was twelve years old, her clitoris grew to a length of 1.5 inches. Having nothing to compare this to, she thought she was normal. But her mother noticed and with alarm hauled her off to a doctor who told her she had ovarian cancer and needed a hysterectomy. Her parents told her that no matter what, she would still be their little girl. When she awoke from surgery, however, her clitoris was gone. Not until she was twenty-three did she find out she was XY and had had testes, not ovaries. She never had cancer.[21] Today Moreno has become an ISNA activist and credits ISNA with helping her heal psychologically from the damage done by lies and surgery. She dreams of teaching in a Montessori school and perhaps adopting a child. She writes: "If I had to label myself man or woman, I'd say, a different kind of woman. . . . I'm not a case of one sex or the other, nor am I some combination of the two. I was born uniquely hermaphroditic—and from the bottom of my heart, I wish I'd been allowed to stay that way."[22]

Outspoken adult patients have begun to protest the practice of lying to children about their intersexuality. While in the past only a few professional voices advocated a more literal version of truth-telling,[23] new voices—those of the patients themselves—have recently begun to demand full disclosure. In 1994 a woman with AIS published her story anonymously in the *British Journal of Medicine*.[24]

She had never been told the full truth. The facts of her case had dribbled out—a slip of tongue by a nurse here, an inadvertent remark by a doctor there. And as a teenager she did something the treatment manuals rarely seem to bargain for. Smart and curious, she went to a medical library and did some detective work. What she discovered was not comforting. When she finally pieced together the full picture, she felt humiliated, sad, and betrayed. She experienced deep suicidal feelings. It took her years to resolve enough of the issues to feel better about herself. She advises physicians dealing with intersex children that full truth-telling combined with a frank discussion of ideas about gender identity is the best medical practice.

This woman's story struck a chord with those who had had similar experiences. A woman who had been born without a vagina wrote a letter to the journal's editor echoing the sentiments of the anonymously published piece:

> neither I nor my parents were offered any psychological support. . . . Unless parents can talk openly with a professional counselor (not a doctor) and are given information—on what and when to tell their child, contacts with other sufferers, sources of counseling or psychotherapy . . . they will

become imprisoned by their own feelings . . . [failure to take such action] could be far more damaging than truth disclosure in a caring, supportive environment.[25]

Indeed, all the newly formed organizations of adult intersexuals[26] say the same thing: "Tell us the whole story. Don't insult our intelligence with lies. When speaking to children develop staged, age-appropriate information. But lying never works and it can destroy the relationship between patient and parents and patient and physician".[27]

In one sense it is hardly surprising that clitoral surgery continues today alongside unsubstantiated claims that it does not affect sexual function.[28] The anatomy and physiology of the clitoris are still poorly understood.[29] In the medical literature, this structure has gone through long periods—including the present—of underrepresentation. Current medical illustrations, for example, fail to portray the structure's variability,[30] or even its complete, complex structure.[31] Indeed, in medical texts (with the exception of women's self-help books), the clitoris was more completely represented and labeled at the turn of the last century than it is today. If doctors are unaware of genital variation and know little about clitoral function, how can they know whether the cosmetic appearance or functional physiology following surgery is "satisfactory"?

SCARRING AND PAIN

Personal accounts from intersexuals who have experienced genital surgery breathe life into some otherwise dry facts. Foremost among these is that long-term studies of genital surgery are scarce as hen's teeth.[32] Nevertheless, the medical literature is rife with evidence of the negative effects of such surgery. In a survey of the existing medical articles, a colleague, Bo Laurent, and I noted mentions of scarring, which can cause insensitivity, and of multiple surgeries, which usually leave the genital area more heavily scarred than a single operation. We also found five mentions of residual pain in the clitoris or clitoral stump.[33] Particularly striking was a report noting that ten of sixteen patients with clitoral recessions had clitoral hypersensitivity.[34]

Vaginoplasty, the general term for a variety of techniques to enlarge, reshape, or construct vaginas *de novo*, also carries dangers such as "dense scarring and vaginal stenosis"[35] (the obstruction or narrowing of a passage, duct, or canal). Laurent and I found ten different mentions of scarring associated with vaginal surgery. Stenosis is the most commonly listed complication.[36] One cause of this narrowing of the vaginal or introital opening is scar tissue. Thus one surgical team lists keeping the vagina free of an annular scar as a *goal*.[37] In our literature review we found that vaginoplasties, especially when performed in infancy,[38] resulted in frequencies of vaginal stenosis as high as 80 to 85 percent.[39]

Multiple genital surgeries can have negative psychological as well as physical effects. One group of physicians concedes that the trauma of such surgery might partly cancel out its intended benefits: "if the child believes she is physically abused by medical personnel, with excessive and painful attention focused on the genitalia, the psychological adjustment may be less favorable."[40] Personal accounts from intersexuals confirm the downside of their medical treatments. Many intersexual adults report that repeated genital examinations, often with photographs and a parade of medical students and interns, constitute one of their most painful childhood memories. Joan/John, for instance, has described his yearly visits to the Johns Hopkins clinic as "abusive".[41]

Others concur. An intersexual man pointed out to me that one method of measuring penile growth and function in intersex boys involved the doctor masturbating the boy to achieve erection. Young girls who receive vaginal surgery suffer similarly invasive practices. When an infant or toddler is operated on, parents are taught to insert a dildo so that the newly built vagina won't close.[42] Medicine's focus on creating the proper genitals, meant to prevent psychological suffering, clearly contributes to it.[43]

MULTIPLE SURGERIES

The statistics tell the story. Although the medical literature exudes confidence about the feasibility of genital makeovers, the procedures are complex and risky. From 30 to 80 percent of children receiving genital surgery undergo more than one operation. It is not uncommon for a child to endure from three to five such procedures. One review of vaginoplasties done at Johns Hopkins University Hospital between 1970 and 1990 found that twenty-two out of twenty-eight (78.5 percent) of girls with early vaginoplasties required further surgery. Of these, seventeen had already had two surgeries, and five had already had three.[44] Another study reported that achieving successful clitoral recessions "required a second procedure in a number of children, a third in several patients and a glansplasty in others." (Glansplasty involves cutting and reshaping the phallic tip, or glans.) They also reported multiple operations following initial early vaginoplasties.[45, 46]

There are fairly good data on vaginoplasty, one of the more common surgeries performed on intersexuals. Laurent and I summarized the information from 314 patients and offer it in table 4.2. The table suggests the spotty nature of medical evaluation. Researchers gave specific criteria for evaluating an operation's success for only 218 patients. For adults (about 220 patients), one standard criterion was the ability to have vaginal intercourse. What emerges from these studies is that even on their own terms, these surgeries are rarely successful and often risky. *First*, there are relatively high frequencies of postoperative complications leading to additional surgeries. At times the multiple surgeries cause significant scarring. *Second*, several authors emphasize the need for psychological reinforcement to allow patients to accept the operation. *Third*, overall success rates can be very disappointing. One study found that although out of eighty patients, 65 percent had "satisfactory" vaginal openings, 23 percent of these didn't have sexual intercourse.[47] When initial surgeries did not succeed, many patients refused additional operations. Thus, in those studies of vaginoplasty for which evaluation of surgical success includes clear criteria and reporting, the surgery has a high failure rate.

Studies of hypospadias surgery reveal good news, bad news, and news of uncertain valence. The good news is that adult men who have undergone hypospadias surgery reached important sexual milestones—for example, age of first intercourse—at the same age as men in control groups (who had undergone inguinal, but not genital, surgery as children). Nor did they differ from control groups in sexual behavior or functioning. The bad news is that these men were more timid about seeking sexual contact, possibly because they had more negative feelings about their genital appearance. Furthermore, the greater the number of operations men had, the higher their level of sexual inhibition.[48] Surgery was least successful for men with severe hypospadias, who could often have normal erections but found that problems such as spraying during urination and ejaculation persisted.[49]

And the news of uncertain valence? It all depends on whether you think strict adherence to prescribed gender role signifies psychological health. One study, for example, found that boys who had been hospitalized more often for hypospadias-related problems showed higher levels of "cross-gender" behavior.[50] For intersex management teams, such as one that aims explicitly "to prevent the development of cross-gender identification in children born with . . . ambiguous genitalia," such results might signify failure.[51] On the other hand, practitioners have found that even when they follow Money's management principles to the T, as many as 13 percent of all intersex kids—not just boys with hypospadias—end up straying from the treatment's strict gender demands. This distresses psychologists who adhere to the two-party system.[52] But to those of us who believe gender is quite varied anyway, gender variability among intersexual children does not constitute bad news.

TABLE 4.2 *Evaluation of Vaginoplasty*

# OF SUBJECTS	AGE AT SURGERY	AGE AT EVALUATION	CRITERIA FOR SUCCESS	RESULTS	COMMENTS	SOURCE
7	Infants	Not given	Not given	"Satisfactory" (no stated criteria)	Says clitorectomy desirable with advanced degree of masculinization	a
42	< 1 yr. to >2 yrs.	>16	Comfortable vaginal penetration	· Initial surgery: 34% success · Success after 3 procedures: 62%	Significant patient failure to follow through on surgical options; higher success rates with older patients	b
23	Not given	15–37 yrs.	Coital activity; report of orgasm	· 15 with frequent activity (1x/day–2x/wk) · 5 "decreased frequencies" · 13 orgasmic during vaginal penetration · 9 orgasmic during manual stimulation by partner · 50% require vaginal lubricant	"The single most important factor determining success was the psychological adjustment of the patient as it existed before knowledge of the anomaly" (p. 546)	c
23	Average 1.84–5.5 yrs.	Not given	Not given	· 15 (the younger population) had serious post-op complications including stenosis and vaginal agenesis · 8 older patients listed as adequate	Recommends delaying "definitive vaginoplasty until . . . puberty, rather than provoke dense scarring and vaginal stenosis following an aggressive procedure at an earlier age"	d

80	Not given	18–70 yrs.	Questionnaires reporting on sexual activity, marital status	• 65% had satisfactory introitus and vagina • 23% of those with adequate introitus had no sexual activity, compared with 64% of those with inadequate introitus	Suggests greater emphasis on adequate surgical correction and "greater use of psychoendocrine services . . . to allow the patients to accept vaginoplasty" (p. 182)	e
14 (?)	Not given	Adult	Not given	• 2/4 with thigh flap operation: problems with vaginal size • 8/14 with pull-through operations: severe stenosis requiring 2nd operations • 3 have uncomfortable hair growth in introitus	Discusses pros and cons of various vaginoplasty techniques; does not comment on best age for the surgery, but apparently performed on infants	f
13	Before puberty	11–22 years	Not given	• Stenosis requiring additional surgery in 10/13 cases • 3/13 had successful intercourse	• Lack of success "discouraging" (p. 601) • "as a rule the introitus that has been revised early undergoes scarring" (p. 601) • "it is unwise to attempt introital reconstruction until after puberty" (p. 601)	g

(continued)

TABLE 4.2 *(Continued)*

# OF SUBJECTS	AGE AT SURGERY	AGE AT EVALUATION	CRITERIA FOR SUCCESS	RESULTS	COMMENTS	SOURCE
45	3 to > 15 yrs.	Not stated	Position of the posterior border of the vaginal opening; suppleness of the sutures and lack of inflammation and stenosis; quality of the vaginal opening; absence of hypertrophy of surrounding muscles	• 16/45 cases required additional operations after puberty • 6/12 favorable cases said they had satisfactory sexual intercourse	Corrective surgery has partly reached its goals in enabling sex reassignment at an early age	h
28	3 wks. to 5 yrs.	18–25 yrs.	Successful vaginal penetration	• 6/28 required only 1 surgery • 22/28 required 3–4 surgeries	Discusses anatomical factors leading to need for multiple surgeries, but continues to favor early surgery	i
23	Not given	14–38 yrs.	Penetration without pain or bleeding; orgasm	• With postsurgical dilation, 7/8 satisfactory • without dilation, 4/8 unsatisfactory • 7 had no sexual activity	Concludes that childhood vaginoplasty followed by adult dilation produces good results; also presents data on clitorectomy vs. clitoroplasty	j

| 38 | All but 1 between 15 and 30 yrs. | Not stated | Lubrication; vaginal length or diameter; fertility; lack of psychological problems | • Lack of vaginal lubrication: 6/38
• vaginal size too small: 5/38
• infertile: 10/38
• psychological problems: 3/38
• lack of counseling: 12/38
• of 23 sexually active, 18 had satisfactory intercourse | k |

a. Hendren and Crawford 1969.   b. Azziz et al. 1986.   c. Hecker and McGuire 1977.   d. Allen et al. 1982.   e. Mulaikal et al. 1987.   f. Newman et al. 1992a.   g. Sotiropoulos et al. 1976.   h. Nihoul-Fekete 1981; Nihoul-Fekete et al. 1982.   i. Bailez et al. 1992.   j. Costa et al. 1997.   k. Fliegner 1996.

The Right To Refuse

Modern management manuals devote a great deal of thought to how to get parents to go along with suggested treatments. Clearly it is a matter of great delicacy. And so it must be, because parents *can* be intractable. Sometimes they assert their own views about their child's sex and about the degree of surgical alteration they will permit. In the 1990s, Helena Harmon-Smith's son was born with both an ovary and a testis, and doctors wanted to turn him into a girl. Harmon-Smith refused. "He had parts I didn't have," she wrote, and "he is a beautiful child."[53] Harmon-Smith did not see the need for surgical intervention, but against her express instructions, a surgeon removed her son's gonads. In response she has become an activist, founding a support group for parents called Hermaphrodite Education and Listening Post (HELP).

Recently Harmon-Smith published instructions, in the form of Ten Commandments, for physicians who encounter the birth of an intersexual child. The Commandments include: Thou shalt "not make drastic decisions in the first year"; thou shalt "not isolate the family from information or support"; thou shalt "not isolate the patient in an intensive care unit" but shalt "allow the patient to stay on a regular ward."[54] Kessler suggests a new script to be used in announcing the birth of an XX child affected by CAH: Congratulations. "You have a beautiful baby girl. The size of her clitoris and her fused labia provided us with a clue to an underlying medical problem that we might need to treat. Although her clitoris is on the large size it is definitely a clitoris. . . . The important thing about a clitoris is how it functions, not how it looks. She's lucky. Her sexual partners will find it easy to locate her clitoris."[55]

Parental resistance is not new. In the 1930s Hugh Hampton Young described two cases in which parents refused to let doctors perform surgery on their intersexual children. Gussie, aged fifteen, had been raised as a girl. After admission to a hospital (the reason for hospitalization is unclear), Young learned (from performing a surgical examination under general anesthesia) that Gussie had a testis on one side, an enlarged clitoris/penis, a vagina, and an underdeveloped fallopian tube and uterus but no ovary. While the child was on the operating table, they decided to bring the testis down into the scrotum/enlarged labium. They then told the mother that the child was not a girl, but a boy, advised her to change h/her name to Gus and to have h/her return for further "normalizing" surgery.

The mother's response was outraged and swift: "She became greatly incensed, and asserted that her child was a girl, that she didn't want a boy, and that she would continue to bring up the patient as a girl."[56] Parental resistance put Young on the spot. He had already created a new body with an external testicle. Ought he to accommodate the mother's insistence that Gus remain Gussie? And if so, how? Should he offer to remove the penis and testicle, even though that would leave Gussie without any functioning gonad? Should he attempt to manipulate h/her hormonal productions? These questions remained unanswered; the child never returned to the hospital. In a similar case the parents refused to allow even exploratory surgery and, following an initial external examination of the child, never returned. Young was left to ponder the possibilities that lay beyond his control. "Should," he wondered, "this patient be allowed to grow up as a male . . . even if [surgery] shows the gonads to be female?"[57]

Young also discussed several cases of adult hermaphrodites who refused not only treatment but the chance to get a full "scientific" explanation of their "condition." George S., for example, raised as a girl, ran away from home at age fourteen, dressing and living as a man. Later s/he married as a man, but found it too hard to support a wife. So s/he emigrated from England to America , dressed again as a woman, and became some man's "mistress," although s/he also continued to be the male partner in intercourse with women. H/her fully developed breasts caused embarrassment and s/he asked Young to remove them. When Young refused to do so without operating to discover h/her "true" sex, the patient vanished. Another of Young's patients, Francies Benton, made h/her living as an exhibit in a circus freak show. The advertisement read "male and female in one. One body--two people" (see figure 4.1). Benton had no interest in changing h/her lifestyle, but sought Young's expertise to satisfy h/her curiosity and to provide medical testimony verifying the truth of h/her advertising claims.[58]

Dogma has it that without medical care, especially early surgical intervention, hermaphrodites are doomed to a life of misery. Yet there are few empirical investigations to back up this claim.[59] In fact, the studies gathered to build a case for medical treatment often do just the opposite. Francies Benton, for example, "had not worried over his condition, did not wish to be changed, and was enjoying life."[60] Claus Overzier, a physician at the Medical Clinic at the University of Mainz, Germany, reports that in the majority of cases the psychological behavior of patients agreed only with their sex of rearing and not with their body type. And in many of these cases, body type was not "smoothed over" to conform to sex of rearing. In only fifteen percent of his ninety-four cases were patients discontented with their legal sex; and in each of these it was a "female" who wished to become a "male". Even Dewhurst and Gordon, who are adamant about the importance of very early treatment, acknowledged great success in "changing the sex" of older patients. They reported on twenty cases of children reclassified into a different sex after the

FIGURE 4.1: Francies Benton, a "practicing hermaphrodite," and his/her advertising copy. (Reprinted with permission from Young 1937, pp. 144–45.)

supposedly critical period of eighteen months. They deemed all the reclassifications "successful," wondering whether sex "re-registration can be recommended more readily than has been suggested so far."[61] Rather than emphasize this positive finding, however, they stressed the practical difficulties involved with late sex changes.

Sometimes patients refuse treatment despite strikingly visible consequences, such as beard growth in females. Randolf et al. discuss one girl who "has adamantly refused further surgery in spite of the disfiguring prominence of her clitoris,"[62] while Van der Kamp et al. report that nine out of ten adult women who had undergone vaginal reconstruction felt that such operations should not be done until early adolescence.[63] Finally, Bailez et al. report on an individual's refusal of a fourth operation needed to achieve a vaginal opening suitable for intercourse.[64]

Intersexual children who grow up with genitalia that seem to contradict their assigned gender identities are not doomed to lives of misery. Laurent and I turned up more than eighty examples (published since 1950) of adolescents and adults who grew up with visibly anomalous genitalia (see tables 4.3 and 4.4). In only one case was an individual deemed potentially psychotic, but that was connected to a psychotic parent and not to sexual ambiguity. The case summaries make clear that children adjust to the presence of anomalous genitalia and manage to develop into functioning adults, many of whom marry and have active and apparently satisfying sex lives. Striking instances include men with small penises who have active marital sex lives without penetrative intercourse.[65] Even proponents of early intervention recognize that adjustment to unusual genitalia is possible. Hampson and Hampson, in presenting data on more than 250 postadolescent hermaphrodites, wrote: "The surprise is that so many ambiguous-looking patients were able, *appearance notwithstanding,* to grow up and achieve a rating of psychologically healthy, or perhaps only mildly non-healthy."[66]

The clinical literature is highly anecdotal. There exist no consistent or arguably scientific standards for evaluating the health and psychological well-being of the patients in question. But despite the lack of quantitative data, our survey reveals a great deal. Although they grew up with malformations such as small phalluses, sexual precocity, pubertal breast development, and periodic hematuria (blood in the urine; or in these cases menstrual blood), the majority of intersexual children raised as males assumed lifestyles characteristic of heterosexually active adult males. Fifty-five intersexual children grew up as females. Despite genital anomalies that included the presence of a penis, an enlarged clitoris, bifid scrota, and/or virilizing puberty, most assumed the roles and activities of heterosexually active females.

Two interesting differences appear between the group raised as males (RAM) and the one raised as females (RAF). First, only a minority of the RAF's chose to feminize their masculinized genitalia during adolescence or adulthood, while well over half of the RAM's elected surgery to masculinize their feminized bodies. Second, 16 percent of the RAF's decided as adolescents or adults to change their identities from female to male. Individuals who initiated such changes adjusted successfully—and often with expressed delight—to their new identities. In contrast, only 6 percent of the RAM's wished to change from male to female. In other words, males appear to be more anxious to change their feminized bodies than females are to change their masculinized ones. In a culture that prizes masculinity, this is hardly surprising. Again we see that it is possible to visualize the medical and biological only by peering through a cultural screen.[67]

Revisiting the Five Sexes

Those who defend current approaches to the management of intersexuality can, at best, offer a weak case for continuing the status quo. Many patients are scarred—both psychologically and physically—by a process heavy on sur-

TABLE 4·3 *Psychological Outcomes of Children Raised as Males with Unusual Genitalia*

DEVELOPMENTAL PATTERN (SAMPLE SIZE)	CHANGE IN ASSIGNED SEX	MEDICAL INTERVENTION	METHODS OF ASSESSMENT	OUTCOME	COMMENTS	SOURCE
XX intersex (1)	None; raised as male	Age 11: removal of 1 ovary; age 24: ovarian biopsy	Physical and hormonal only	A married male with a satisfactory sex life	Never told about his actual physical condition	a
Small penis, bifid scrotum, urinate at base of phallus; at puberty breast growth and identification of uterus, oviducts, and ovaries	Raised as male; reassigned female as teenager	Vaginal reconstruction at age 17; no clitoral surgery	Physical, hormonal, psychiatric interviews, and MMPI, Rorschach test	Married at age 20 and hoping to have child	As a child liked being a boy; received considerable sex ed from parents; mother encouraged her to be secret about genitals because of anatomical difference	b
Sexual precocity in genetic, gonadal, and hormonal male (1)	None; raised as male	Extensive family counseling	IQ; standard psychological tests; interviews	"Thoroughly adequate psychological adjustment" (p. 15)	Healthy family life	c
XX intersex; small hypospadic phallus; fused, empty labioscrotum (1)	None; raised as male	As teenager, breasts and female internal organs removed; hormone treatments; at age 25 plastic surgery on penis	Extensive interviews	Married male; "to the world at large . . . he passed as an ordinary male college graduate—one of the more stable and well-adjusted" (p. 317)	Only case study in a paper that summarizes a large number of studies but gives few specific details	d

CAH; small phallus with urethra running through it (1)	None; raised as male; hematuria at age 18 warranted medical workup	At age 18, removal of uterus and ovaries; hormonal treatment	Clinical report	"Attending college, majoring in music, and was interested in sports"; had sexual contacts with women (p. 157)	"At age 10 the patient noticed that his external genitalia were smaller than those of other boys his age, and, from that time on, took care not to expose himself before his school-mates" (p. 156)	e
CAH; penile urethra; phallus 5 cm long at age 21 (1)	None; raised as male; cyclic urethral bleeding	None	Physical only	A married male	No data given on psycho-logical status	f
CAH; pubic and axillary hair since age 5; men-struation at age 26; micropenis; penile urethra (1)	None; at age 35 expressed wish to be a woman	Adrenal surgery, which resulted in death of patient	Physical and casual observation	Normal intelligence; served in Army during WWII	During adolescence, attracted to male companions	g
Same physical develop-ment (1) (Younger brother of previous case)	None	Hormone treatment starting at age 25 (refused surgery due to death of brother)	Physical and casual observation	Married at age 22; had sexual inter-course regularly	Began menstruation at 22	h
CAH with microphallus (2)	None; raised as males	Ovaries, uterus removed at ages 12 and 31, respectively	Psychological, via interview	Both married; one with child via donor insemination; rate sex lives as good	Adapted to sexual activity other than vaginal intercourse	i

(continued)

TABLE 4.3 *(Continued)*

DEVELOPMENTAL PATTERN (SAMPLE SIZE)	CHANGE IN ASSIGNED SEX	MEDICAL INTERVENTION	METHODS OF ASSESSMENT	OUTCOME	COMMENTS	SOURCE
Intersex with small penis and developed breasts (1)	One; raised as male	At 15 yrs. surgical removal of ovary and uterus	None	Married to a woman, sought infertility counseling		k
Intersex; enlarged clitoris, menstruation; good breast development, no beard, pubic, or axillary hair (1)	None; raised as male	At age 20: removed ovary and uterus but left remaining ovo-testis	Physical and brief observation	Married as a male; worked as a farmer	"Comparatively quiet . . . preferred to work alone . . . had some inferiority complex" (p. 148)	l
Intersex raised as male (1)	None	Ovo-testis removed at age 29	Case report of interviews	Aware of genital abnormality since age 8; managed to hide it and was active in male sports such as football; worked in masculine occupations; married at age 26 to a genetic and social female	Breast development at age 15 led him to abandon competitive swimming and football	m
Abnormal genitalia, enlarged breasts, periodic hematuria (1)	None; raised as male	Surgery at age 21 to remove uterus and ovary	Conversations with patient	Patient behaved, worked as a male; had female sexual partners	Wanted to make him female; patient refused, preferring sex of rearing	n

Ambiguous genitalia, breasts (1)	None: raised as male	At age 15–16: mammoplasty, 3-stage repair of hypospadias, hysterectomy	Conversations with patient	Participated in sports with other boys; "social adaptation adequate throughout childhood" (p. 663)		o
Intersex raised as male (1)	None	As a young man: hysterectomy to stop menstruation and breast reduction	Case report	Patient "totally pleased" (p. 1,151), but he had to sit down to urinate	Patient managed to conceal from his family his need to sit down to urinate	p
Various causes: hormonal and secondary body morphology contradicted assigned sex (27)*	None; 4 raised as males; 23 raised as females	Uncertain	Psychological and physical	"4 ambivalent with respect to gender role" (p. 256)	All ambivalent cases reared as girls	q
Intersex: XX, XY mosaic: breasts and hematuria; unusual genitalia noted at birth (1)	None; raised as male	Diagnosis at age 14 included uterus and fallopian tubes, which were removed	Case report focused on chromosome composition	Psychological examiners recommended against sex change	No details of life outcome	r

(continued)

TABLE 4.3 (*Continued*)

DEVELOPMENTAL PATTERN (SAMPLE SIZE)	CHANGE IN ASSIGNED SEX	MEDICAL INTERVENTION	METHODS OF ASSESSMENT	OUTCOME	COMMENTS	SOURCE
12 adults raised as males with small penises	None	Some had had testes removed; others may have had surgery for hypospadias	Interviews	• 9 had sexual intercourse starting at ≈ 16 yrs. • All heterosexual males • 6 felt normal • 6 got teased	The best adjusted were those whose parents "emphasized the abnormalities or refused to discuss them, often telling the child to hide himself produced shy and anxious children" (p. 571); "a small penis does not preclude normal male role and a micropenis or microphallus alone should not dictate a female gender assignment in infancy" (p. 571)	s

* Also listed in table 4.4.   a. Glen 1957.   b. Norris and Keettel 1962.   c. Money and Hampson 1955.   d. Money 1955; Money et al. 1955b.
e. Peris 1960.   f. Maxted et al. 1965.   g. Madsen 1963.   h. Madsen 1963.   i. Van Seters and Slob 1988.   j. Van Seters and Slob 1988.
k. Ten Berge 1960.   l. Ben-lih and Kai 1953.   m. Capon 1955.   n. Ben-lih et al. 1959.   o. Hughes et al. 1958.   p. Jones and Wilkins 1961.
q. Money 1955.   r. Gilgenkrantz 1987.   s. Reilly and Woodhouse 1989.

gical prowess and light on explanation, psychological support, and full disclosure. We stand now at a fork in the road. To the right we can walk toward reaffirmation of the naturalness of the number 2 and continue to develop new medical technology, including gene "therapy" and new prenatal interventions to ensure the birth of only two sexes. To the left, we can hike up the hill of natural and cultural variability. Traditionally, in European and American culture we have defined two genders, each with a range of permissible behaviors; but things have begun to change. There are househusbands and women fighter pilots. There are feminine lesbians and gay men both buff and butch. Male to female and female to male transsexuals render the sex/gender divide virtually unintelligible.

All of which brings me back to the five sexes. I imagine a future in which our knowledge of the body has led to resistance against medical surveillance,[68] in which medical science has been placed at the service of gender variability, and genders have multiplied beyond currently fathomable limits. Suzanne Kessler suggests that "gender variability can . . . be seen . . . in a new way— as an expansion of what is meant by male and female."[69] Ultimately, perhaps, concepts of masculinity and femininity might overlap so completely as to render the very notion of gender difference irrelevant.

In the future, the hierarchical divisions between patient and doctor, parent and child, male and female, heterosexual and homosexual will dissolve. The critical voices of people discussed in this chapter all point to cracks in the monolith of current medical writings and practice. It is possible to envision a new ethic of medical treatment, one that permits ambiguity to thrive, rooted in a culture that has moved beyond gender hierarchies. In my utopia, an intersexual's major medical concerns would be the potentially life-threatening conditions that sometimes accompany intersex development, such as salt imbalance due to adrenal malfunction, higher frequencies of gonadal tumors, and hernias. Medical intervention aimed at synchronizing body image and gender identity would only rarely occur before the age of reason. Such technological intervention would be a cooperative venture among physician, patient, and gender advisers. As Kessler has noted, the unusual genitalia of intersexuals could be considered to be "intact" rather than "deformed"; surgery, seen now as a creative gesture (surgeons "create" a vagina), might be seen as destructive (tissue is destroyed and removed) and thus necessary only when life is at stake.[70]

Accepted treatment approaches damage both mind and body. And clearly, it is possible for healthy adults to emerge from a childhood in which genital anatomy does not completely match sex of rearing. But still, the good doctors

TABLE 4.4 *Psychological Outcomes of Children Raised as Females with Unusual Genitalia*

DEVELOPMENTAL PATTERN (SAMPLE SIZE)	CHANGE IN ASSIGNED SEX	MEDICAL INTERVENTION	METHODS OF ASSESSMENT	OUTCOME	COMMENTS	SOURCE
Raised as female with a penislike clitoris; menstruated at 13 (1)	None	Surgery in adulthood; clitoral amputation	Psychological, hormonal	States that patient was satisfied	Patient was primarily attracted to women but had a female gender identity; psychiatrist wanted to surgically turn her into a man (to prevent homosexuality?), but she refused	a
Sexual precocity in genetic, gonadal, and hormonal female (3)	None; raised as female	Extensive family counseling	IQ and standard psychological tests and interviews	2/3 well adjusted; 1 predicted to become psychotic	Unadjusted individual has psychotic father/poorly adjusted family	b
XY intersex; enlarged clitoris (2–3 cm); bifid scrotum; urinates through vagina (2 "sisters")	None; raised as female	None; examined at time of marriage because of urinary oddity	Physical, hormonal	Apparently healthy females who married	Both aware of physique at age 10 because of how they urinated. No mention of discomfort with large clitoris	c

XY intersex; small penis and vagina (1)	None; raised as female	As a married adult, penis removed and vagina dilated	None	Happily married but infertile		d
XY intersex; malformed external genitalia; no breast development (1)	None; raised as female	At age 21 testes removed, vagina enlarged, estrogen treated	Unknown	"Quite well adjusted in her role as a woman" (p. 43)		e
Testicular failure; ambiguous but feminized genitalia (3)	Sex change from female to male at ages 20–33		Conversations with physician	2: no information; 1: "patient most satisfied" (p. 1,214)	Calls for a "somewhat less rigid attitude" about when to do surgery (p. 1,216)	f
Normal male with severe perineal hypospadias, raised as female (1)	Sex reassigned at 14	Surgery to correct hypospadias	Psychological tests and interviews	Successful adjustment following a period of several months	"The Johns Hopkins team . . . [has] not provided convincing evidence" for view that early sex change is imperative (p. 1,217)	g
CAH females (7)	None; raised as female	None	Psychological and interviews	2 are married; "were entirely feminine in their outlook and ways" (p. 255)		h

(continued)

TABLE 4.4 *(Continued)*

DEVELOPMENTAL PATTERN (SAMPLE SIZE)	CHANGE IN ASSIGNED SEX	MEDICAL INTERVENTION	METHODS OF ASSESSMENT	OUTCOME	COMMENTS	SOURCE
Various causes: hormonal and secondary body morphology contradicted assigned sex (27)*	None; 4 raised as males, 23 as females	Uncertain	Psychological and physical	"4 ambivalent with respect to gender role" (p. 256)	All ambivalent cases reared as girls	i
Intersexes with penis, bifid scrotum, testes, and ovotestis (2)	None; raised as female	At age 26 and 24, surgery to reshape genitalia	Conversations with physicians; physical	Both married as women; "apparently normal girls" (p. 280)	One had no vaginal opening; husband had "intercourse" using space between perineum and legs; the other had no orgasms; both experienced postsurgical loss of libido	j
Penis-sized clitoris (1)	None; raised as female	At age 17, penile extirpation and vaginal dilation	None	Patient felt herself to be female	"She was, with some difficulty, persuaded to submit to surgical treatment" (p. 79)	k

Hypospadias; raised as female (1)	Changed from female to male at age 13	Several surgeries at patient's request to repair hypospadias	Extensive first-hand account of how he coped with the change	Married with 2 adopted children	Wishes he could have intercourse and biological children, but resigned; "I have a full and for the most part happy life" (p. 1,256)	l
Hypospadias; raised as female (1)	Changed from female to male at age 13	Surgical repair of hypospadias and exposure of hooded penis	Anecdotal	Successful marriage	Patient anxious to make the change, "had his own ideas . . . even to selection of a name and a decidedly masculine program of activities" (p. 490)	m
Intersex; raised as female (1)	None	Surgery at 18 to open vagina	Case report	Identified as male at birth but mother raised as female; oriented toward males and wished to marry	Early in her life the patient was told by her mother that "she was different from other boys and girls and that she should not let others see her genitalia" (p. 431)	n
Intersex, raised as male (1)	None	Repair of hypospadias at age 29	Case report	Married to genetic female; reported coitus twice weekly with orgasms for both partners	Small, curved penis "did not trouble the patient before he got married" (p. 332), and he only sought help because he could not ejaculate inside the vagina and he wanted to have children	o

(continued)

TABLE 4.4 *(Continued)*

DEVELOPMENTAL PATTERN (SAMPLE SIZE)	CHANGE IN ASSIGNED SEX	MEDICAL INTERVENTION	METHODS OF ASSESSMENT	OUTCOME	COMMENTS	SOURCE
XY intersex, raised as female (1)	At puberty became typically male and chose to change sex	Not clearly stated	Case report	"He was totally relieved by being told he was a male" (p. 1,151)	At age 22 married as a man	p
Incomplete AIS; 46 XY; raised as female with enlarged clitoris (1)	At age 33 had breasts removed	Breast removal in adulthood	Case report; hormonal, anatomical, and psychiatric testing	Individual had strongly male gender identity apparently from a very early age; sexual orientation to females	Male gender identity evident in early childhood	q

If not specified, surgery occurred at the time of change in sex of rearing.   * Also listed in table 4.3.   a. Nogales et al. 1956.   b. Hampson and Money 1955. c. Lubs et al. 1959.   d. Ten Berge 1960.   e. Jones 1957.   f. Dewhurst and Gordon 1963.   g. Berg 1963.   h. Money 1955.   i. Money, Hampson, et al. 1955. j. Witschi and Mengert 1942.   k. Laycock and Davies 1953.   l. Armstrong 1966.   m. Brown and Fryer 1957.   n. Brewer et al. 1952.   o. Zachariae 1955. p. Jones and Wilkins 1961.   q. Gooren and Cohen-Kettenis 1991.

are skeptical.[71] So too are many parents and potential parents. It is impossible not to personalize the argument. What if you had an intersexual child? Could you and your child become pioneers in a new management strategy? Where, in addition to the new intersexual rights activists, might you look for advice and inspiration?

The history of transsexualism offers food for thought. In European and American culture we understand transsexuals to be individuals who have been born with "good" male or "good" female bodies. Psychologically, however, they envision themselves as members of the "opposite" sex. A transsexual's drive to have his/her body conform with his/her psyche is so strong that many seek medical aid to transform their bodies hormonally and ultimately surgically, by removal of their gonads and transformation of their external genitalia. The demands of self-identified transsexuals have contributed to changing medical practices, forcing recognition and naming of the phenomenon. Just as the idea that homosexuality is an inborn, stable trait did not emerge until the end of the nineteenth century, the transsexual did not fully emerge as a special type of person until the middle of the twentieth. Winning the right to surgical and legal sex changes, however, exacted a price: the reinforcement of a two-gender system.[72] By requesting surgery to make their bodies match their gender, transsexuals enacted the logical extreme of the medical profession's philosophy that within an individual's body, sex, and gender must conform. Indeed, transsexuals had little choice but to view themselves within this framework if they wanted to obtain surgical help. To avoid creating a "lesbian" marriage, physicians in gender clinics demanded that married transsexuals divorce before their surgery. Afterwards, they could legally change their birth certificates to reflect their new status.

Within the past ten to twenty years, however, the edifice of transsexual dualism has developed large cracks. Some transsexual organizations have begun to support the concept of *transgenderism*, which constitutes a more radical re-visioning of sex and gender.[73] Whereas traditional transsexuals might describe a male transvestite—a man dressing in women's clothing—as a transsexual on the road to becoming a complete female, transgenderists accept "kinship among those with gender-variant identities. Transgenderism supplants the dichotomy of transsexual and transvestite with a concept of continuity." Earlier generations of transsexuals did not want to depart from gender norms, but rather to blend totally into their new gender role. Today, however, many argue that they need to come out as transsexuals, permanently assuming a transsexual identity that is neither male nor female in the traditional sense.[74]

Within the transgender community (which has its own political organizations and even its own electronic bulletin board on the Internet), gender variations abound. Some choose to become women while keeping their male genitals intact. Many who have undergone surgical transformation have taken up homosexual roles. For example, a male-to-female transsexual may come out as a lesbian (or a female-to-male as a gay male). Consider Jane, born a physiological male, now in her late thirties, living with her wife (whom she married when her name was still John). Jane takes hormones to feminize herself, but they have not yet interfered with her ability to have erections and intercourse as a man:

> From her perspective, Jane has a lesbian relationship with her wife (Mary). Yet she also uses her penis for pleasure. Mary does not identify herself as a lesbian, although she maintains love and attraction for Jane, whom she regards as the same person she fell in love with although this person has changed physically. Mary regards herself as heterosexual . . . although she defines sexual intimacy with her spouse Jane as somewhere between lesbian and heterosexual. [75]

Does acceptance of gender variation mean the concept of gender would disappear entirely? Not necessarily. The transgender theorist Martine Rothblatt proposes a chromatic system of gender that would differentiate among hundreds of different personality types. The permutations of her suggested seven levels each of aggression, nurturance, and eroticism could lead to 343 (7 x 7 x 7) shades of gender. A person with a mauve gender, for example, would be "a low-intensity nurturing person with a fair amount of eroticism but not much aggressiveness." [76] Some might find Rothblatt's system silly or unnecessarily complex. But her point is serious and begins to suggest ways we might raise intersex children in a culture that recognizes gender variation.

Is it so unreasonable to ask that we focus more clearly on variability and pay less attention to gender conformity? The problem with gender, as we now have it, is the violence—both real and metaphorical—we do by generalizing. No woman or man fits the universal gender stereotype. "It might be more useful," writes the sociologist Judith Lorber, ". . . to group patterns of behavior and only then look for identifying markers of the people likely to enact such behaviors." [77]

Were we in Europe and America to move to a multiple sex and gender role system (as it seems we might be doing), we would not be cultural pioneers. Several Native American cultures, for example, define a third gender, which may include people whom we would label as homosexual, transsexual, or intersexual but also people we would label as male or female.[78] Anthropologists have described other groups, such as the Hijras of India, that contain individuals whom we in the West would label intersexes, transsexuals, effeminate men, and eunuchs. As with the varied Native American categories, the Hijras vary in their origins and gender characteristics.[79] Anthropologists debate about how to interpret Native American gender systems. What is important, however, is that the existence of other systems suggests that ours is not inevitable.

I do not mean to romanticize other gender systems; they provide no guarantee of social equality. In several small villages in the Dominican Republic and among the Sambia, a people residing in the highlands of Papua, New Guinea, a genetic mutation causing a deficiency in the enzyme 5-α-reductase occurs with fairly high frequency.[80] At birth, XY children with 5-α-reductase deficiency have a tiny penis or clitoris, undescended testes, and a divided scrotum. They can be mistaken for girls, or their ambiguity may be noticed. In adolescence, however, naturally produced testosterone causes the penises of XY teenagers deficient in 5-α-reductase to grow; their testes descend, their vaginal lips fuse to form a scrotum, their bodies become hairy, bearded, and musclebound.[81]

And in both the Dominican Republic and New Guinea, DHT-deficient children—who in the United States are generally operated on immediately—are recognized as a third sex.[82] The Dominicans call it *guevedoche*, or "penis at twelve," while the Sambians use the word *kwolu-aatmwol*, which suggests a person's transformation "into a male thing."[83] In both cultures, the DHT-deficient child experiences ambivalent sex-role socialization. And in adulthood s/he most commonly—but not necessarily with complete success—self-identifies as a male. The anthropologist Gil Herdt writes that, at puberty, "the transformation may be from female—possibly ambiguously reared—to male-aspiring third sex, who is, in certain social scenes, categorized with adult males."[84]

While these cultures know that sometimes a third type of child is born, they nevertheless recognize only two gender roles. Herdt argues that the strong preference in these cultures for maleness, and the positions of freedom and power that males hold, make it easy to understand why in adulthood the *kwolu-aatmwol* and the *guevedoche* most frequently chose the male over the female role. Although Herdt's work provides us with a perspective outside our own cultural framework, only further studies will clarify how members of a third sex manage in cultures that acknowledge three categories of body but offer only a two-gender system.

Toward the End of Gender Tyranny: Getting There from Here

Simply recognizing a third category does not assure a flexible gender system. Such flexibility requires political and social struggle. In discussing my "five sexes" proposal Suzanne Kessler drives home this point with great effect:

> The limitation with Fausto-Sterling's proposal is that legitimizing other sets of genitals . . . still gives genitals primary signifying status and ignores the fact that in the everyday world gender attributions are made without access to genital inspection . . . what has primacy in everyday life is the gender that is performed, regardless of the flesh's configuration under the clothes.

Kessler argues that it would be better for intersexuals and their supporters to turn everyone's focus away from genitals and to dispense with claims to a separate intersexual identity. Instead, she suggests, men and women would come in a wider assortment. Some women would have large clitorises or fused labia, while some men would have "small penises or misshapen scrota—phenotypes with no particular clinical or identity meaning."[85] I think Kessler is right, and this is why I am no longer advocating using discrete categories such as herm, merm, and ferm, even tongue in cheek.

The intersexual or transgender person who presents a social gender— what Kessler calls "cultural genitals"—that conflicts with h/her physical genitals often risks h/her life. In a recent court case, a mother charged that her son, a transvestite, died because paramedics stopped treating him after discovering his male genitals. The jury awarded her $2.9 million in damages. While it is heartening that a jury found such behavior unacceptable, the case underscores the high risk of gender transgression.[86] "Transgender warriors," as Leslie Feinberg calls them, will continue to be in danger until we succeed in moving them onto the "acceptable" side of the imaginary line separating "normal, natural, holy" gender from the "abnormal, unnatural, sick [and] sinful."[87]

A person with ovaries, breasts, and a vagina, but whose "cultural genitals" are male also faces difficulties. In applying for a license or passport, for instance, one must indicate "M" or "F" in the gender box. Suppose such a person checks "F" on his or her license and then later uses the license for identification. The 1998 murder in Wyoming of homosexual Matthew Shepherd makes clear the possible dangers. A masculine-presenting female is in danger of violent attack if she does not "pass" as male. Similarly, she can get into legal trouble if stopped for a traffic violation or passport control, as the legal authority can accuse her of deception—masquerading as a male for possibly illegal purposes. In the 1950s, when police raided lesbian bars, they demanded that women be wearing three items of women's clothing in order to avoid arrest.[88] As Feinberg notes, we have not moved very far beyond that moment.

Given the discrimination and violence faced by those whose cultural and physical genitals don't match, legal protections are needed during the transition to a gender-diverse utopia. It would help to eliminate the "gender" category from licenses, passports, and the like. The transgender activist Leslie Feinberg writes: "Sex categories should be removed from all basic identification papers—from driver's licenses to passports—and since the right of each person to define their own sex is so basic, it should be eliminated from birth certificates as well."[89] Indeed, why are physical genitals necessary for identification? Surely attributes both more visible (such as height, build, and eye color) and less visible (fingerprints and DNA profiles) would be of greater use.

Transgender activists have written "An International Bill of Gender Rights" that includes (among ten gender rights) "the right to define gender identity, the right to control and change one's own body, the right to sexual expression and the right to form committed, loving relationships and enter into marital contracts."[90] The legal bases for such rights are being hammered out in the courts as I write, through the establishment of case law regarding sex discrimination and homosexual rights.[91]

Intersexuality, as we have seen, has long been at the center of debates over the connections among sex, gender, and legal and social status. A few years ago the Cornell University historian Mary Beth Norton sent me the transcripts of legal proceedings from the General Court of the Virginia Colony. In 1629, one Thomas Hall appeared in court claiming to be both a man and a woman. Because civil courts expected one's dress to signify one's sex, the examiner declared Thomas was a woman and ordered her to wear women's clothing. Later, a second examiner overruled the first, declaring Hall a man who should, therefore, wear men's clothing. In fact, Thomas Hall had been christened Thomasine and had worn women's clothing until age twenty-two, when he joined the army. Afterward s/he returned to women's clothing so that s/he could make a living sewing lace. The only references to Hall's anatomy say that he had a man's part as big as the top of his little finger, that he did not have the use of this part, and that—as Thomasine herself put it—she had "a peece of an hole." Finally, the Virginia Court, accepting Thomas(ine)'s gender duality, ordered that "it shall be published that the said Hall is a man *and* a woman, that all inhabitants around may take notice thereof and that he shall go clothed in man's apparel, only his head will be attired in a Coiffe with an apron before him."[92]

Today the legal status of operated intersexuals remains uncertain.[93] Over the years the rights of royal succession, differential treatment by social security or insurance laws, gendered labor laws, and voting limitations would all have been at stake in declaring an intersex legally male or female. Despite the lessening of such concerns, the State remains deeply interested in regulating marriage and the family. Consider the Australian case of an XX intersex born with an ovary and fallopian tube on the right side, a small penis, and a left testicle. Reared as a male, he sought surgery in adulthood to masculinize his penis and deal with his developed breasts. The physicians in charge of his case agreed he should remain a male, since this was his psychosexual orientation. He later married, but the Australian courts annulled the union. The ruling held that in a legal system that requires a person to be either one or the other, for the purpose of marriage, he could be neither male nor female (hence the need for the right to marry in the Bill of Gender Rights).[94]

As usual, the debates over intersexuality are inextricable from those over homosexuality; we cannot consider the challenges one poses to our gender system without considering the parallel challenge posed by the other. In considering the potential marriage of an intersexual, the legal and medical rules often focus on the question of homosexual marriage. In the case of *Corbett v. Corbett 1970,* April Ashley, a British transsexual, married one Mr. Corbett, who later asked the court to annul the marriage because April was really a man. April argued that she was a social female and thus eligible for marriage. The judge, however, ruled that the operation was pure artifact, imposed on a clearly male body. Not only had April Ashley been born a male, but her transforming surgery had not created a vagina large enough to permit penile penetration. Furthermore, sexual intercourse was "the institution on which the family is built, and in which the capacity for natural hetero-sexual intercourse is an essential element." "Marriage," the judge continued, "is a relationship which depends upon sex and not gender."[95]

An earlier British case had annulled a marriage between a man and a woman born without a vagina. The husband testified that he could not penetrate more than two inches into his wife's artificial vagina. Furthermore, he claimed even that channel was artificial, not the biological one due him as a true husband. The divorce commissioner agreed, citing a much earlier case in which the judge ruled, "I am of the opinion that no man ought to be reduced to this state of quasi-natural connexion."[96]

Both British judges declared marriage without the ability for vaginal-penile sex to be illegal, one even adding the criterion that two inches did not a penetration make. In other countries—and even in the several U.S. states that ban anal and oral contact between both same-sex and opposite-sex partners and those that restrict the ban to homosexual encounters[97]—engaging in certain types of sexual encounters can result in felony charges. Similarly, a Dutch physician discussed several cases of XX intersexuals, raised as males, who married females. Defining them as biological females (based on their two X chromosomes and ovaries), the physician called for a discussion of the legality of the marriages. Should they be dissolved "notwithstanding the fact that they are happy ones?" Should they "be recognized legally and ecclesiastically?"[98]

If cultural genitals counted for more than physical genitals, many of the dilemmas just described could be easily resolved. Since the mid-1960s the International Olympic Committee has demanded that all female athletes submit to a chromosome or DNA test, even though some scientists urge the elimination of sex testing.[99] Whether we are deciding who may compete in the women's high jump or whether we should record sex on a newborn's birth certificate, the judgment derives primarily from social conventions. Legally, the interest of the state in maintaining a two-gender system focuses on questions of marriage, family structure, and sexual practices. But the time is drawing near when even these state concerns will seem arcane to us.[100] Laws regulating consensual sexual behavior between adults had religious and moral origins. In the United States, at least, we are supposed to experience complete separation of church and state. As our legal system becomes further secularized (as I believe it will), it seems only a matter of time before the last laws regulating consensual bedroom behavior will become unconstitutional.[101] At that moment the final legal barriers to the emergence of a wide range of gender expression will disappear.

The court of the Virginia Colony required Thomas/Thomasine to signal h/her physical genitals by wearing a dual set of cultural genitals. Now, as then, physical genitals form a poor basis for deciding the rights and privileges of citizenship. Not only are they confusing; they are not even publicly visible. Rather, it is social gender that we see and read. In the future, hearing a birth announced as "boy" or "girl" might enable new parents to envision for their child an expanded range of possibilities, especially if their baby were among the few with unusual genitals. Perhaps we will come to view such children as especially blessed or lucky. It is not so far-fetched to think that some can become the most desirable of all possible mates, able to pleasure their partners in a variety of ways. One study of men with unusually small penises, for example, found them to be "characterized by an experimental attitude to positions and methods." Many of these men attributed "partner sexual satisfaction and the stability of their relationships to their need to make extra effort including non-penetrating techniques."[102]

My vision is utopian, but I believe in its possibility. All of the elements needed to make it come true already exist, at least in embryonic form. Necessary legal reforms are in reach, spurred forward by what one might call the "gender lobby": political organizations that work for women's rights, gay rights, and the rights of transgendered people. Medical practice has begun to change as a result of pressure from intersexual patients and their supporters. Public discussion about gender and homosexuality continues unabated with a general trend toward greater tolerance for gender multiplicity and ambiguity. The road will be bumpy, but the possibility of a more diverse and equitable future is ours if we choose to make it happen.

SEXING THE BRAIN:

HOW BIOLOGISTS MAKE A DIFFERENCE

The Callosum Colossus

SUPPOSE MY UTOPIAN VISION, AS DESCRIBED IN THE LAST CHAPTER, came to pass. Would all gender differences disappear? Would we award jobs, status, income, and social roles based only on individual differences in physique, intellect, and inclination? Perhaps. But some would argue that no matter how widely we opened the door, ineluctable differences between groups would remain. Scientists, such naysayers would argue, have proven that in addition to our genitalia, key anatomical differences between the male and female brain make gender an important marker of ability. To drive home their point, they might cite well-publicized claims that, compared to men's, the corpus callosum—the bundle of nerve fibers connecting the left and right brain hemispheres—in women's brains is larger or more bulbous. And *that,* they would exclaim, will limit forever the degree to which most women can become highly skilled mathematicians, engineers, and scientists. But not everybody believes in this difference in brain anatomy.

External anatomy seems simple. Does the baby's hand have five or six fingers? Just count them. Do boys have penises and girls vaginas (intersexuals notwithstanding)? Just look. Who could disagree about body parts? Scientists use the rhetoric of visibility to talk about gender differences in the brain, but moving from easily examined external structures to the anatomy of the interior is tricky. Relationships among gender, brain function, and anatomy are both hard to interpret and difficult to see, so scientists go to great lengths to convince each other and the general public that gender differences in brain anatomy are both visible and meaningful.[1] Some such claims provoke battles that can last for hundreds of years.[2] In coming to understand how and why these battles can last so long, I continue to insist that scientists do not simply read nature to find truths to apply in the social world. Instead, they use truths taken from our social relationships to structure, read, and interpret the natural.[3]

Medical "solutions" to intersexuality developed as scientific innovations, ranging from new methods of classification to new skills in microscopy, interacted with the preconception that there are only two genders. Scientific unanimity reigned in part because the social beliefs about male and female were not in dispute. But when the social arena forms a battleground, scientists have a hard time developing a consensus. In this chapter, I show how, as they move from difference on the body's surface to interior differences, scientists use their tools to debate about masculinity and femininity. For what professions are those with "masculine" or "feminine" brains most suited? Should special efforts be made to encourage women to become engineers? Is it "natural" for boys to have trouble learning to read? Are gay men more suited to feminine professions such as hairdressing or flower arranging because of a more feminine corpus callosum? These interlocking social questions sustain the debate about the anatomy of the corpus callosum.[4]

The winter of 1992 was a hard one. There was nothing to do but sit around and contemplate our collective corpus callosums. Or so it seemed; what else would explain the sudden spate of news articles about this large bundle of nerve fibers connecting the left and right brain hemispheres? *Newsweek* and *Time* magazines started the trend by running feature stories about gender differences and the brain.[5] Women, a *Time* illustration informed its readers, often had wider corpus callosums than men. This difference, suggested a caption to one of the glossy illustrations, could "possibly [provide] the basis for woman's intuition." The text of the article concedes that not all neurobiologists believe in this alleged brain difference. Meme Black, writing for *Elle*, was less cautious: that women have larger corpus callosums, she wrote, could explain why "girls are less apt than boys to gravitate toward fields like physics and engineering."[6]

Others agreed. A *Boston Globe* article about gender difference and the corpus callosum quoted Dr. Edith Kaplan, a psychiatrist and neurologist: "throughout life men's and women's brains are anatomically different, with women having a thicker corpus callosum. . . . Because of these interconnections," she suggests, women have stronger verbal skills and men stronger visuo-spatial ones.[7] Not to be outdone, *The New York Times* science editor Nicholas Wade wrote that definitive research that revealed callosal sex differences discredited "some feminist ideologues" who "assert that all minds are created equal and women would be just as good at math if they weren't discouraged in school." [8] (Imagine!)

Nor did the intrigue stop with questions about whether women's brains made them unsuitable for science careers. Rather, the media seemed prepared to believe that all physiological and social differences could ultimately be traced to differences in the form of one part of the brain. Follow the logic of a 1995 *Newsweek* cover story entitled "Why Men and Women Think Differently," suggesting that brain differences in the corpus callosum might explain why women think holistically (assuming they do), while men's right brains don't know what their left is doing (if that is, indeed, the case). "Women have better intuition," the author stated, "perhaps because they are in touch with the left brain's rationality and the right's emotions simultaneously."[9] To support this theory the article cited studies that found CAH girls to be more male-like than other girls in both play patterns and cognitive strengths, and suggested—in a stunning piece of circular reasoning—that such studies might indicate that sex hormones are responsible for differences in CC size.[10]

As if this sort of argument were not far-fetched enough, some pushed the CC determinism even further. In 1992, for instance, the psychologist Sandra Witelson mixed a different seasoning into the stew, publishing an article in which she argued that just as men and women differ in cognitive abilities and CC structure, so too did gay and straight men. (As usual, lesbians were nowhere to be found.) "It is as if, in some cognitive respects, [gay men] are neurologically a third sex," she wrote, adding that the brain differences may eventually help account for "the apparently greater prevalence and ability of homosexual men compared to heterosexual men in some professions."[11] She didn't elaborate on just which professions she meant, but by arguing that the form of the corpus callosum helps determine handedness, gender identity, cognitive patterns, and sexual preference, she effectively suggested that this one area of the brain plays a role in regulating almost every aspect of human behavior.[12]

These newspaper and magazine stories show us the corpus callosum hard at work, its sleeves rolled up, sweat pouring down its face, as it strives to provide researchers with a single anatomical control center, a physical origin for an array of physiological and social variations. Why does the CC have to work so hard? Why don't the facts just speak for themselves? In the late 1800s anatomists, who had previously always drawn male skeletons, suddenly developed an interest in female bone structure. Because the skeleton was seen to be the fundamental structure—the material essence of the body—finding sex differences would make clear that sexual identity penetrated "every muscle, vein and organ attached to and molded by the skeleton."[13] A controversy arose. One scientist—a woman—drew females with skulls proportionately smaller than those of males, while another—a male—painted women whose skulls were larger relative to the rest of their bodies than were those of males.

At first everyone favored the former drawings, but—after much back and forth—scientists conceded the accuracy of the latter. Nevertheless, scientists clung to the fact that women's brains were smaller in absolute size, thus proving that women were less intelligent.[14] Today we turn to the brain rather than the skeleton to locate the most fundamental sources of sexual difference.[15] But, despite the many recent insights of brain research, this organ remains a vast unknown, a perfect medium on which to project, even unwittingly, assumptions about gender.

The contemporary CC debate began in 1982 when the prestigious journal *Science* published a brief article by two physical anthropologists. The paper received instant notoriety when the talk-show host Phil Donahue inaccurately credited the authors with describing "an extra bundle of neurons that was missing in male brains."[16] The *Science* article reported that certain regions of the corpus callosum were larger in females than in males. Although admittedly preliminary (the study used nine males and five females), the authors boldly related their results to "possible gender differences in the degree of lateralization for visuospatial functions."[17] Here's the lay translation: some psychologists (but not all[18]) believe that men and women use their brains differently. Men, supposedly, make almost exclusive use of the left hemisphere when processing visuo-spatial information, while women allegedly use both hemispheres. In psycho-jargon, men are more lateralized for visuo-spatial tasks. Layered on top of this claim is another (also disputed), that greater lateralization implies greater skill capacity. Men often perform better on standardized spatial tasks, and many believe that this also explains their better performance in mathematics and science. If one buys this story *and* if one believes that the posited functional differences are inborn (resulting, for example, from anatomical differences, perhaps induced by hormones during fetal development), then one can argue that it makes no sense to develop a social policy calling for equal representation of men and women in fields such as engineering and physics. You can't, after all, squeeze blood out of a stone.

The psychologist Julian Stanley, who heads a national program for mathematically talented youth, recently reported that male twelfth graders got higher scores on Advanced Placement tests in physics. He believes the test scores imply that "few females will be found to reason as well mechanically as most males do. This could be a serious handicap in fields such as electrical engineering and mechanics. . . . Such discrepancies would . . . make it inadvisable to assert that there *should* be as many female as male electrical engineers." "It doesn't make sense," he continued, "to suppose that parity is a feasible goal until we find ways to increase such abilities among females."[19] Meanwhile, Stanley's colleague, Dr. Camilla Benbow, suggests with very little evidence[20] that sex differences in mathematics may emanate, at least in part, from inborn differences in brain lateralization.[21]

We see the corpus callosum employed here as part of what Donna Haraway calls "the technoscientific body." It is a node from which emanate "sticky threads" that traverse our gendered world, trapping bits and pieces like newly hung flypaper.[22] Callosal narratives become colossal, linking the underrepresentation of women in science with hormones, patterns of cognition, how best to educate boys and girls,[23] homosexuality, left versus righthandedness, and women's intuition.[24] The sticky threads do not restrict themselves to gender narratives, but glue themselves as well to stories about race and nationality. In the nineteenth and early twentieth centuries the CC itself was racially implicated. In the late twentieth century, styles of thinking (thought by many to be indirectly mediated by the CC[25]) are often racialized. Instead of learning that "Negroes" have smaller CC's than Caucasians,[26] we now hear that Native Americans or Asians (of every stripe) think more holistically than do Europeans. In discussions of the corpus callosum and its role in connecting left and right brain hemispheres, the slippery dualisms that Val Plumwood warned us against (see chapter 1) abound (table 5.1). The CC does not easily bear such weight, and therein lies the heart of this chapter. How have scientists turned the corpus callosum into an object of knowledge? Given this techno-scientific object's recalcitrance, what are the scientific weapons deployed in the battle to make the corpus callosum do gender's bidding?

Taming the Wild CC

Most claims about what the corpus callosum does are based on data about its size and shape. But how in the world can scientists produce accurate measurements of a structure as complex and irregularly shaped as the corpus callosum? Looked at from above, the CC resembles a raised topographical map (figure 5.1). A pair of ridges run oddly parallel for some distance, but diverge to the south. Flanking one ridge to the west and the other to the east lie plateaus, while a vast valley runs between the ridges. East-west striations traverse the entire territory. These striations—which represent millions of nerve fibers—constitute the corpus callosum.[27] As the ridges and valleys suggest, these fibers don't run along a flat, two-dimensional surface; instead they rise and fall. Moreover, as the edges of the map indicate, the fibers are not wholly separate from other parts of the brain, but instead connect to and entangle with them. As one pair of researchers writes: "the corpus callosum is shaped much like a bird with complicated wing formation. Further these wings co-mingle with the ascending white matter tracts . . . making the lat-

TABLE 5.1 *Nineteenth- and Twentieth-Century*
Left/Right Brain Dichotomies[a]

19TH CENTURY		20TH CENTURY	
LEFT	RIGHT	LEFT	RIGHT
Anterior	Posterior	Verbal	Visuo-spatial/ nonverbal
Humanness	Animality	Temporal	Simultaneous
Motor activity	Sensory activity	Digital	Analogic
Intelligence	Emotion/sensibility	Rational	Intuitive
White superiority	Nonwhite inferiority	Western thought	Eastern thought
Reason	Madness	Abstract	Concrete
Male	Female	Female	Male
Objective	Subjective	Objective	Subjective
Waking self	Subliminal self	Realistic	Impulsive
Life of relations	The organic life	Intellectual	Sensuous

a. Taken from Harrington 1985.

eral portion of the corpus callosum essentially impossible to define with certainty.[28]

Or one could imagine the CC as a bunch of transatlantic telephone cables. In the middle of the Atlantic (the valley on the map, which joins the left and right cerebral hemispheres), the cables are bundled. Sometimes the bundles bunch up into ridges; but as the cables splay out to homes and offices in North America and Europe, they lose their distinct form. Smaller bunches of wire veer off toward Scandinavia or the Low Countries, Italy or the Iberian Peninsula. These in turn subdivide, going to separate cities and ultimately to particular phone connections. At its connecting ends, the corpus callosum loses its structural definition, merging into the architecture of the cerebrum itself.

The "real" corpus callosum, then, is a structure that is difficult to separate from the rest of the brain, and so complex in its irregular three dimensions as to be unmeasurable. Thus, the neuroscientist who wants to study the CC must

ANTERIOR

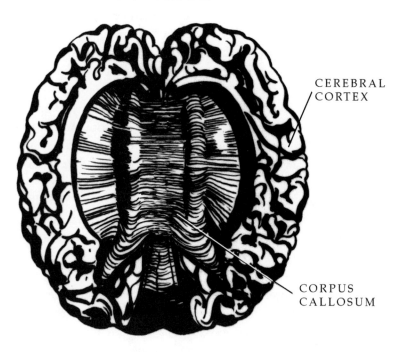

CEREBRAL
CORTEX

CORPUS
CALLOSUM

POSTERIOR

FIGURE 5.1: A three-dimensional rendering of the entire corpus callosum cleanly dissected from the rest of the brain. (Source: Alyce Santoro, for the author)

first tame it—turn it into a tractable, observable, discrete laboratory object. This challenge itself is nothing new. Pasteur had to bring his microbes into the laboratory before he could study them;[29] Morgan had to domesticate the fruit fly before he could create modern Mendelian genetics.[30] But it is crucial to remember that this process fundamentally alters the object of study. Does the alteration render the research invalid? Not necessarily. But the processes researchers use to gain access to their objects of study—processes often ignored in popular reporting of scientific studies—reveal a great deal about the assumptions behind the research.[31]

Scientists began to tame the CC before the turn of the century. Then, great hopes were pinned on using it to understand racial differences (with a little gender thrown in to boot). In 1906 Robert Bennet Bean, working in the anatomical laboratory at Johns Hopkins University, published a paper entitled "Some Racial Peculiarities of the Negro Brain."[32] Bean's methods seemed unassailable. He carefully divided the CC into subsections, paid careful attention to specimen preparation, provided the reader with large numbers of CC tracings,[33] made extensive use of charts and tables, and acquired a large study sample (103 American Negroes and 49 American Caucasians). So useful were his results that some of the participants in the late-twentieth-century debate not only refer to his work but have reanalyzed his data.[34] Indeed, despite some modernist flourishes (like the use of sophisticated statistics and computers), the methods used to measure the size and shape of the corpus callosum in cadavers has not changed during the ninety odd years since the publication of Bean's account. I do not want to tar modern scientists with the brush of earlier research that most now find racist. My point is that, once freed from the body and domesticated for laboratory observation, the CC can serve different masters. In a period of preoccupation with racial difference, the CC, for a time, was thought to hold the key to racial difference. Now, the very same structure serves at gender's beck and call.[35]

Bean's initial measurements confirmed earlier studies purporting to show that Negroes* have smaller frontal lobes but larger parietal lobes than Caucasians. Furthermore, he found that Negroes had larger left frontal but smaller left parietal lobes, while the left/right asymmetry was reversed for Caucasians. These differences he felt to be completely consistent with knowledge about racial characteristics. That the posterior portion of the Negro brain was large and the anterior small, Bean felt, seemed to explain the self-evident truth that Negroes exhibited "an undeveloped artistic power and taste . . . an instability of character incident to lack of self-control, especially in connection with the sexual relation." This of course contrasted with Caucasians who were clearly "dominant . . . and possessed primarily with determination, will power, self-control, self-government . . . and with a high development of the ethical and aesthetic faculties." Bean continues: "The one is subjective, the other objective; the one frontal, the other occipital or parietal; the one a great reasoner, the other emotional; the one domineering but having great self-control, the other meek and submissive, but violent and lacking self-control."[36] He found also that the anterior (*genu*) and posterior (*splenium*) ends of the corpus callosum were larger in men than in women. Nevertheless, he focused primarily on race. He reasoned that the middle portions (called the *body* and the *isthmus*) contained fibers responsible for motor activity, which he thought to be more similar between the races than other brain regions.[37]

---

* I use the word Negro because it is used in Bean's paper.

TABLE 5.2 *Bean's Results*

CAUCASIAN MALE > CAUCASIAN FEMALE > NEGRO MALE > NEGRO FEMALE	CAUCASIAN MALE > CAUCASIAN FEMALE > NEGRO MALE = NEGRO FEMALE	NEGRO MALE > NEGRO FEMALE > CAUCASIAN MALE > CAUCASIAN FEMALE	NEGRO MALE > NEGRO FEMALE = CAUCASIAN MALE > CAUCASIAN FEMALE
Total callosal area	Anterior/posterior half (ratio)	Splenium	Body/isthmus (ratio)
Area of anterior half			
Area of genu			
Area of isthmus			
Area of body			
Genu/splenium (ratio)			

Indeed, he found the greatest racial differences outside the motor areas. Prevailing beliefs about race led Bean to expect the splenium, which presumably contained fibers linking more posterior parts of the left and right brain halves—areas thought to be more responsible for the governance of primitive functions—to be larger in nonwhites than whites. And the measurements confirmed it. Similarly, he predicted that the genu, connecting the more anterior parts of the brain, would be larger in Caucasians, a prediction again confirmed by his numbers.[38]

Then, as now, such work stimulated both scientific and public challenges. In 1909 Dr. Franklin P. Mall, Chairman of the Anatomy Department at Johns Hopkins, disputed Bean's findings of racial and sexual differences in the brain.[39] Mall's objections have a familiar ring: extensive individual variation swamped group differences. No differences were great enough to be obvious on casual inspection, and Bean and others did not normalize their results by taking into account differences in brain weight. Furthermore, Mall thought his own measurements were more accurate because he used a better instrument, and he did his studies blind in order to eliminate "my own personal equation."[40] In conclusion, he wrote: "Arguments for difference due to race, sex and genius will henceforward need to be based upon new data, really scientifically treated and not on the older statements."[41] At the same time that

Mall engaged Bean in the scientific arena, Bean and the anthropologist Franz Boas tangoed in the popular media.[42] The social context may change, but the weapons of scientific battle can be transferred from one era to the next.

DEFINING THE CORPUS CALLOSUM

Scientists don't measure, divide, probe, dispute, and ogle the corpus callosum per se, but rather a slice taken at its center (figure 5.2). This is a two-dimensional representation of a mid-saggital section of the corpus callosum.[43] This being a bit of a mouthful, let's just call it CC. (From here on, I'll refer to the three-dimensional structure—that "bird with complicated wing formation"—as the 3-D CC.) There are several advantages to studying the two-dimensional version of the CC. First, the actual brain dissection is much easier. Instead of spending hours painstakingly dissecting the cerebral cortex and other brain tissues connected to the 3-D CC, researchers can obtain a whole brain, take a bead on the space separating left and right hemispheres, and make a cut. (It's rather like slicing a whole walnut down the middle and then measuring the cut surface.) The resulting half brain can be photographed at one of the cut faces. Then researchers can trace an outline of the cut CC surface onto paper and measure this outline by hand or computer. Second, because tissue preparation is easier, the object can be more handily standardized, thus assuring that when different laboratory groups compare results, they are talking about the same thing. Third, a two-dimensional object is far easier to measure than a three-dimensional one.[44]

But methodological questions remain about this postmortem (PM) technique. For example, to prepare the brains, one must pickle them (a process of preservation called fixation). Different laboratories use different fixation methods, and all methods result in some shape distortion and shrinkage. Thus, some doubt always exists about the relationship between living, functioning structure and the dead, preserved brain matter actually studied. (For example, one could imagine that a size difference between two groups could result from different quantities of connective tissue that might show different shrinkage responses to fixation.)[45]

Although researchers disagree about which techniques for obtaining brain samples cause the least distortion, they rarely acknowledge that their data, based on two-dimensional cross sections, might not apply to brains as they actually exist: three-dimensionally in people's heads. In part, this may be because researchers are more interested in the relative merits of the postmortem technique and techniques made possible by a new machine, the Magnetic Resonance Imager (MRI). Some hope that this advanced technology will allow a unified account of the CC to emerge.[46]

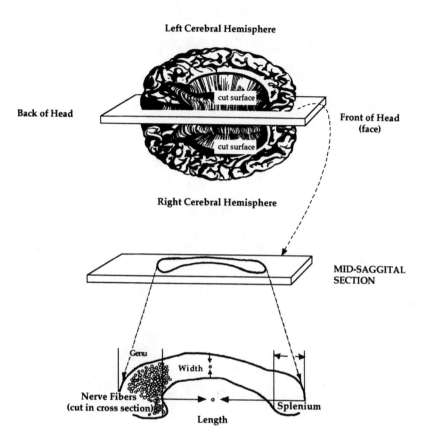

Left Cerebral Hemisphere

cut surface

Back of Head

Front of Head
(face)

cut surface

Right Cerebral Hemisphere

MID-SAGGITAL
SECTION

Genu

Width

Nerve Fibers
(cut in cross section)

Splenium

Length

FIGURE 5.2: The transformation of the 3-D corpus callosum to a version represented in only two dimensions. (Source: Alyce Santoro, for the author)

MRI's (figure 5.3) offer two major advantages. First, they come from living, healthy individuals; second, living, healthy individuals are more available than autopsied brains.[47] Hence larger samples, better matched for possibly confounding factors such as age and handedness, can be used. But there is no free lunch. The neuroscientists Sandra Witelson and Charles Goldsmith point out that the boundaries between the CC and adjacent structures appear less clearly in MRI's than PM's. Furthermore, the scans have a more limited spatial resolution, and the optical slices taken are often much thicker than the manual slices taken from postmortems.[48] Jeffrey Clarke and his colleagues note that "the contours of the CC's were less sharp in the MRI graphs than in the postmortem" while others cite difficulties in deciding just which of the many optical slices was the true mid-saggital slice.[49] Finally, studies using MRI's are

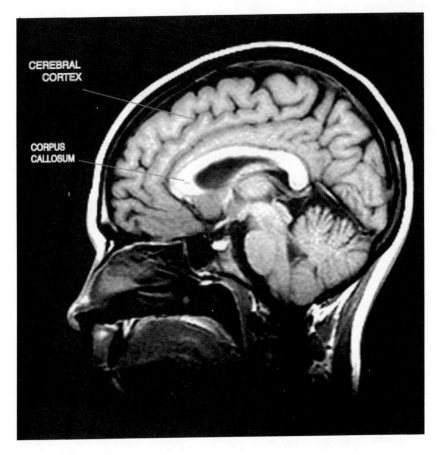

CEREBRAL CORTEX

CORPUS CALLOSUM

FIGURE 5.3: An MRI image of a mid-saggital section of a human head. The convolutions of the cerebral cortex and the corpus callosum are clearly visible. (Courtesy of Isabel Gautier)

hard to standardize with respect to brain weight or size. Thus, because, MRI's, like PM's, represent certain brain features, researchers using either technique study the brain at an interpretive remove.

TAMING BY MEASURING

Can scientists succeed in making measurements of the CC on which they all agree? Can they use their CC data to find differences between men and women or concur that there are none to be found? It would appear not. Here I look at thirty-four scientific papers, written between 1982 and 1997.[50] The authors use the latest techniques—computerized measurements, complex statistics, MRI's, and more—but still they disagree. In their efforts to convince one another (and the outside world) that the CC is or is not significant for questions of gender, these scientists work hard to come up with the right techniques, the best measurement, the approach so perfect as to make their claims unassailable.

Looking at table 5.3, one sees that almost nobody thought there were absolute size differences in the entire CC. Instead, scientists subdivided the two-dimensional CC (see figure 5.4). Researchers chose different segmentation methods and constructed different numbers of subdivisions. Most symbolized the arbitrary nature of the CC subsections by labeling them with letters or numbers. Others used names coined in an earlier time. Almost everyone, for example, defined the splenium as the CC's posterior one-fifth, but a few divided the CC into six[51] or seven parts[52] calling the most posterior segment the splenium. Each approach to subdividing the CC represented an attempt to tame it—to make it produce measurements the authors hoped would be objective and open to replication by others. Labeling choices gave the methods different valences. By labeling the subdivisions with only letters or numbers, some made visible the arbitrary nature of the method. Others assigned traditional anatomical names, leaving one with a feeling of reality—that there might be visible substructure to the CC (just as the pistons are visibly distinct within the gasoline engine).

To succeed in extracting information about the brain's workings, scientists *must* domesticate their object of study, and we see in table 5.3 and figure 5.4 the variety of approaches used to accomplish this end. Indeed, this aspect of making a difference is so deeply built into the daily laboratory routine that most lab workers lose sight of it. Once extracted and named, the splenium, isthmus, midbodies, genu, and rostrum all become biological things, structures seen as real, rather than the arbitrary subdivisions they actually are. Simplifying body parts in order to layer some conceptual order onto the daunting complexity of the living body is the daily bread of the working scientist. But there are consequences. When neuroanatomists transform a 3-D CC into a splenium or genu, they provide "public access to new structures rescued out of obscurity or chaos." The sociologist Michael Lynch calls such creations "hybrid object(s) that (are) demonstrably mathematical, natural and literary."[53] They are mathematical because they now appear in measurable form.[54] They are natural because they are, after all, derived from a natural object—the 3-D CC. But the corpus callosum, splenium, genu, isthmus, rostrum, and anterior and posterior midbodies, *as represented in the scientific paper*, are literary fictions.

There is nothing inherently wrong with this process. The difficulty arises when the transformed object—Lynch's tripartite hybrid—ends up being

TABLE 5.3 *Absolute Sex Differences in the Corpus Callosum: A Summary*

| | # OF STUDIES FINDING | | | | | |
Measurement taken (see figure 5.4)	ADULT FEMALE LARGER	ADULT MALE LARGER	ADULTS DON'T DIFFER	MALE CHILD LARGER[b]	CHILDREN DON'T DIFFER	NO FETAL DIFFERENCE[c]
Callosal area	0	1[a]	16[a]	1	2	2
Maximum splenial width	3	0	11	0	1	2
Callosal length	0	0	7	1	0	0
Area: division 1	0	1	7	0	1	0
Area: division 2	0	0	8	0	1	0
Area: division 3	0	2	7	0	1	0
Area: division 4	1	0	9[g]	0	1	0
Area: division 5 (splenium)	0[f]	0	17[g]	1[d]	2	0
Width 1	0	0	2	0	0	0
Width 2	0	0	2	0	0	0

Width 3	0	0	2	0	2	0
Width 4 (minimal splenial)	0	1	3[c]	0	0	1
Minimal callosal width	2	2	0	0	0	0
Maximum body width	0	0	2	0	0	0
Area of anterior 4/5ths	0	0	2	0	0	0

a. One of the findings showed a difference with one statistical test (ANOVA) but not with another (MANOVA).

b. There were no cases in which female children had larger parts.

c. In one case an absolute difference favoring female fetuses was found in splenial width but not area.

d. Depends on which statistical test is used.

e. Difference appeared in postmortem but not MRI's.

f. De Lacoste-Utamsing and Holloway (1982) say there is a difference, but then cite a statistical probability of p = 0.08, which is usually considered statistically insignificant.

g. Based on dividing the CC into 7 parts (the isthmus being the 6th and the splenium the 7th).

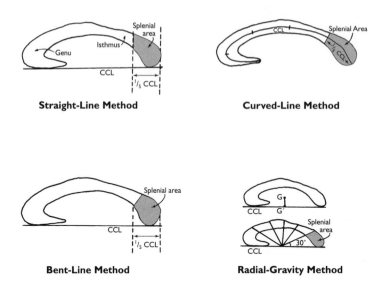

FIGURE 5.4: A sampling of methods used to subdivide the corpus callosum.
(Source: Alyce Santoro, for the author)

mistaken for the original. Once a scientist finds a difference, he or she tries to interpret its meaning. In the debate at hand, all of the interpretations have proceeded as if the measured object *was* the corpus callosum. Instead, interpretation ought to try to work by reversing the abstraction process; here, though, one runs into trouble. Far too little is known about the detailed anatomy of the intact, three-dimensional corpus callosum to accomplish such a task. One is left to assign meaning to a fictionalized abstraction,[55] and the space opened up for mischief becomes enormous.

THERE IS MEASURE IN ALL THINGS (CALLOSAL)

With all the subdivisions agreed upon, finally, students of the corpus callosum are in business. Now they can make dozens of measurements. From the undivided CC come dimensions of the total surface area, length, width, and any of these divided by brain volume or weight. From the subdivided CC come named or numbered parts: the anterior one-fifth becomes the genu, the posterior one-fifth the splenium, a narrower portion in the center the isthmus. Once researchers have created a measurable object out of the CC, what do they find?

The results summarized in tables 5.3, 5.4, and 5.5 reveal the following: no matter how they carve up the shape, only a few researchers find absolute sex differences in CC area. A small number report that males and females have differently shaped corpus callosums (females have a more bulb-shaped splenium, making the CC wider, according to these authors), even though the shape does not translate into a size (area or volume) difference. The few studies of fetuses and young children came up with no measurable sex differences; these results suggest that, if there is a gender difference in adult CC's, it appears only with age.[56] Finally, reports about sex differences in corpus callosum size during old age conflict, permitting no firm conclusions about gender differences in the elderly.[57]

Some researchers have suggested that, if there is a gender difference in the CC, it may be the opposite of what scientists have commonly assumed it would be. Men generally have larger brains and bodies than women. If it turns out that women and men have similar-sized CC's but women have smaller brains, then on a relative per volume or per weight basis, do women have *larger* CC's?[58] Following this logic, many researchers have compared the relative size of the whole and/or parts of the male and female corpus callosum. Table 5.4 summarizes these relative measures, and the decision is split: about half report a difference, while half do not.

Although most investigators interested in gender differences focus on the splenium—the more (or less) bulbous-shaped posterior end of the corpus callosum—others have turned their attention to a different segment of the CC named the isthmus (see figure 5.4). While those who measure the splenium have tended to look only for differences between men and women, those examining the isthmus believe this part of the brain is linked to several characteristics—not only gender, but also left- or right-handedness and sexual orientation. Some find that the area of the isthmus is smaller in right-handed than in non-right-handed males, but that women show no such difference.[59] I've tabulated these results in table 5.5. Here, too, there is little consensus. Some find a structural difference related to handedness in males but not females; some find no handedness-related differences; one paper even reports that one of the CC regions is larger in right-handed than in left-handed women, but smaller in left-handed than in right-handed men.[60]

What do scientists do with such diverse findings? One approach uses a special form of statistics called meta-analysis, which pools the data from many small studies to create a sample that behaves, mathematically, as if it were one large study. Katherine Bishop and Douglas Wahlsten, two psychologists, have published what seem to be the unequivocal results of such a meta-analysis. Their study of forty-nine different data sets found that men have slightly larger CC's than women (which they presume is because men are larger), but no significant gender differences in either absolute or relative size or shape of

TABLE 5.4 *Relative Sex Differences in the corpus Callosum: A Summary*

| | # OF STUDIES FINDING | | | | | |
	ADULT FEMALE LARGER	ADULT MALE LARGER	ADULTS DON'T DIFFER	MALE CHILD LARGER	CHILDREN DON'T DIFFER	NO FETAL DIFFERENCE
Measurement taken (see figure 5.4)						
Callosal area/brain weight or volume	7		8		2	
Area: division 1/brain weight or volume		1	2			
Area: division 2/brain weight or volume			2			
Area: division 3/brain weight or volume		1	1			
Area: division 4/brain weight or volume	1		2			
Splenial width or area/brain weight, volume, or length	3		5[c]			
Splenial area/callosal area or length	3		4			
Slenderness index (CC length/ideal thickness)[b]	2[d]		1[d]			1[d]

Bulbosity coefficient (average splenial width/average width of the adjacent region of the corpus callosum)[a]	2[d]
Bulbosity coefficient/total callosal area	1
Minimal width/total callosal area	1
Area 6 (of 7 ÷'s)/total callosal area	1

a. I've nicknamed this the "turkey-baster" coefficient, or TBC, because it is based on the idea that a bulbous splenium growing out of a narrow-necked CC gives a turkey-baster shape to the overall structure. See Allen, Richey et al. 1991.

b. Clarke et al. (1989) define the ideal thickness as the corpus callosum area divided by the length of the median line (calculated to bisect the mid-sagittal corpus callosum area).

c. I calculated one of these results from the data presented by Emory et al. 1991; 1 of the 5 is based on subdividing the CC into 4 parts.

d. Find a difference for postmortems but not MRI.

TABLE 5.5 *Hand Preference, Sex, and Corpus Callosum Size: A Summary*

	# OF STUDIES FINDING					
Measurement taken (*see figure 5.4*)	MALES ONLY: RIGHT < LEFT-HANDED[a]	MALES ONLY: RIGHT = LEFT-HANDED[a]	FEMALES ONLY: RIGHT = LEFT-HANDED[a]	FEMALES ONLY: RIGHT > LEFT-HANDED[a]	MALES & FEMALES COMBINED: RIGHT < LEFT-HANDED[a]	MALES & FEMALES COMBINED: RIGHT = LEFT-HANDED[a]
Total callosal area	2	3	6	0	1	4
Isthmus: area[b]	3	1	3	0	2[c]	1
Isthmus/total callosal area	1					
Anterior half[b]	1	1	2	0	1	1
Posterior half[b]	1	1	2	0	1	1
Region 2[b]	2	1	1	1	1	1
CC/brain						1
Splenium/brain						1

a. The definitions of handedness actually used are both more complex and subtler than just left vs. right.   b. For regionalization of CC in handedness studies, see figure 5.4.   c. LH males > females.

the CC as a whole or of the splenium. Bishop and Wahlsten recalculated the statistical significance of a finding of an absolute sex difference in splenial area each time they added a new study to their data base. When only a small number of studies with a cumulatively small sample size existed, the results suggested the existence of a sex difference in splenial area. As additional data (from newer studies) accumulated in the literature, however, the sex differences diminished. By the time ten studies had appeared, the absolute splenial sex difference had disappeared and nobody has successfully resurrected it.[61]

Researchers, however, continue to debate the existence of relative differences in CC structure. Bishop and Wahlsten found none, but when a different research team performed a second meta-analysis, they found not only that men have slightly larger brains and CC's than women, but that relative to overall brain size, women's CC's were bigger. This study did not contain enough data, however, to conclude that relative size of male and female spleniums differed.[62]

But these meta-analyses run into the same methodological issues experienced by individual studies. Is there a legitimate way to establish a relative difference? What factor should we divide by: brain weight, brain volume, total CC size? One research team has called the practice of simply dividing an area by total brain size "pseudostatistics."[63] (Them's fightin' words!) Another researcher countered that it is no wonder colleagues will attack the methodology behind any study that discovers gender differences, given that "one end of the political spectrum is invested in the conclusion that there are no differences."[64] We are left with no consensus.[65]

DOING BATTLE WITH NUMBERS

To the outsider coming to the dispute for the first time, the flurry of numbers and measures is bewildering. In displaying and analyzing their measurements, scientists call on two distinct intellectual traditions, both often labeled with the word *statistics*.[66] The first tradition—the amassing of numbers in large quantity to assess or measure a social problem—has its roots (still visible today) in eighteenth- and nineteenth-century practices of census takers and the building of actuarial tables by insurance companies.[67] This heritage has slowly mutated into the more recent methodology of significance testing, aimed at establishing differences between groups, even when individuals within a group show considerable variation. Most people assume that, because they are highly mathematical and involve complex ideas about probability, the statistical technologies of difference are socially neutral. Today's statistical tests, however, evolved from efforts to differentiate elements of human society, to make plain the differences between various social groups (rich and poor; the law-abiding and the criminal; the Caucasian and the Negro; male and female; the English and the Irish; the heterosexual and the homosexual—to name but a few).[68]

How are they applied to the problem of gender differences in the CC? The CC studies use both approaches. On the one hand, morphometrists make many measurements and arrange them in tables and graphs. On the other, they use statistical tests to correlate measurements with variables such as sex, sexual preference, handedness, and spatial and verbal abilities. Sophisticated statistical tools serve both rhetorical and analytical functions. Each CC study amasses hundreds of individual measurements. To make sense of what the philosopher Ian Hacking calls this "avalanche of numbers,"[69] biologists categorize and display them in readable fashion.[70] Only then can investigators "squeeze" information out of them. Does a structure change size with age or differ in people suffering from a particular disease? Do men and women or people of different races differ? The specialized research article, which presents numbers and extracts meaning from them, is really a defense of a particular interpretation of results. As part of his or her rhetorical strategy, the writer cites previous work (thus gathering allies), explains why his or her choice of method is more appropriate than that used by another lab with different outcome, and uses tables, graphs, and drawings to show the reader a particular result.[71]

But statistical tests are not just rhetorical flourishes. They are also powerful analytic tools used to interpret results that are not obvious from casual observation. There are two approaches to the statistical analysis of difference.[72] Sometimes distinctions between groups are obvious, and what is more interesting is the variation within a group. If, for example, we were to examine a group of 100 adult Saint Bernard dogs and 100 adult Chihuahuas, two things might strike us. First, all the Saint Bernards would be larger than all the Chihuahuas. A statistician might represent them as two nonoverlapping bell curves (figure 5.5A). We would have no trouble concluding that one breed of dog is larger and heavier than the other (that is, there is a group difference). Second, we might notice that not all Bernards are the same height and weight, and the Chihuahuas vary among themselves as well. We would place such Bernard or Chihuahua variants in different parts of their separate bell curves. We might pick one out of the lineup and want to know whether it was small for a Saint Bernard or large for a Chihuahua. To answer that question we would turn to statistical analyses to learn more about individual variation within each breed.

Sometimes, however, researchers turn to statistics when the distinction between groups is not so clear. Imagine a different exercise: the analysis of

FIGURE 5.5: *A*: Comparing Chihuahuas to Saint Bernards. *B*: Comparing huskies to German shepherds. (Source: Alyce Santoro, for the author)

100 huskies and 100 German shepherds. Is one breed larger than the other? Their bell curves overlap considerably, although the average height and weight differ somewhat (figure 5.5B). To solve this problem of "true difference," modern researchers usually employ one of two tactics. The first applies a fairly simple arithmetical test, now automated in computer programs. The test takes three factors into account: the size of the sample, the mean for each population, and the degree of variation around that mean. For example, if the mean weight for shepherds is 50 pounds, are most of the dogs close to that weight or do they range widely—say, from 30 to 80 pounds? This range of variation is called the standard deviation (SD). If there is a large SD, then the population varies a great deal.[73] Finally, the test calculates the probability that the two population means (that of the huskies and that of the shepherds) differ by chance.

Researchers don't have to group their data under separate bell curves to establish differences between populations. They can instead group all the data together, calculate how variable it is, and then analyze the causes of that variability. This process is called the analysis of variance (ANOVA). In our doggie example, researchers interested in the weight of huskies and German shepherds would pool the weights of all 200 dogs, and then calculate the total variability, from the smallest husky to the largest German shepherd.[74] Then they would use an ANOVA to partition the variation—a certain percent accounted for by breed difference, a certain percentage by age or brand of dog chow, and a certain percentage unaccounted for.

Tests for mean differences allow us to compare different groups. Is the difference in IQ between Asians and Caucasians real? Are males better at math than females? Alas, when it comes to socially applied decision making, the clarity of the Chihuahua versus the Saint Bernard is rare. Many of the CC studies use ANOVA. They calculate the variability of a population and then ask what percentage of that variability can, for example, be attributed to gender or handedness or age. With the widespread use of ANOVA's then, a new object of study has crept in. Now, rather than actually looking at CC size, we are analyzing the contributions of gender and other factors to the *variation* of CC size around an arithmetical mean. As scientists use statistics to tame the CC, they distance it yet further from its feral original.[75]

Convincing others of a difference in CC size would be easiest if the objects simply looked different. Indeed, in the CC dispute a first line of attack is to claim that the difference in shape between the splenia of male and female CC's is so great that it is obvious to the casual observer. To test this claim, researchers draw an outline of each of the 2-D CC's in their sample. They then give a mixture of the drawings, each labeled only with a code, to neutral observers, who sort the drawings into bulbous and slender categories. Finally, they decode the sorted drawings and see whether all or most of the bulbous file turn out to have come from women and the slenders from men. This approach does not yield a very impressive box score. Two groups claim a visually obvious sex difference; a third group also claims a sex difference, but males and females overlap so much that the researchers can only detect it using a statistical test for significant difference.[76] In contrast, five other research groups tried visual separation of male from female CC's but failed in the attempt.

When direct vision fails to separate male from female, the next step is to bring on the statistical tests. In addition to those who attempted to visually differentiate male from female CC's, nine other groups attempted only a statistical analysis of difference.[77] Two of these reported a sex difference in splenial shape, while seven found no statistical difference. This brings the box score for a sex difference in splenial shape to 5 for, 13 against. Even statistics can't discipline the object of study into neatly sorted categories. As Mall found in 1908, the CC seems to vary so much from one individual to the next that assigning meaningful differences to large groups is just not possible.

In 1991, after the CC debate had been raging for nine years, a neurobiologist colleague told me that a new publication had definitively settled the matter. And the news accounts—both in the popular and the scientific press—

suggested he was right. When I began to read the article by Laura Allen and her colleagues I was indeed impressed.[78] They used a large sample size (122 adults and 24 children), they controlled for possible age-related changes, and they used two different methods to subdivide the corpus callosum: the straight-line and the curved-line methods (see figure 5.4). Furthermore, the paper is packed with data. There are eight graphs and figures interspersed with three number-packed, subdivided tables, all of which attest to the thoroughness of their enterprise.[79] Presenting their data in such detail demonstrates their fearlessness. Readers need not trust the authors; they can look at their numbers for themselves, recalculating them in any fashion they wish. And what do the authors conclude about gender differences? "While we observed a dramatic sex difference in the *shape* of the corpus callosum, there was no conclusive evidence of sexual dimorphism in the area of the corpus callosum or its subdivisions."[80]

But despite their emphatic certainty, the study, I realized as I reread it, was less conclusive than it seemed. Let's look at it step by step. They used both visual inspection and direct measurement. From their visual (which they call subjective) data, they reach the following conclusion.

> Subjective classification of the posterior CC of all subjects by sex based on a more bulbous-shaped female splenium and a more tubular-shaped male splenium revealed a significant correlation between the observers' sex rating based on shape and the actual gender of the subject ($\chi^2 = 13.2603$; 1 df; contingency coefficient = 0.289; p<0.003). Specifically, 80 out of 122 (66 percent) of the adult's CC ($\chi^2 = 10.123$; 1 df; contingency coefficient = 0.283; p<0.0011) were correctly identified.[81]

First, we can extract the actual numbers: using splenial shape, their blind classifiers could correctly categorize as male or female 80 out of 122 tracings of adult 2-D CC's. Was that good enough to claim a visual difference, or might we expect the 80 out of 122 to occur by chance? To find out, the authors employ a chi-squared test (symbolized by the Greek letter χ^2). The well-known founder of modern statistics, Karl Pearson (and others) developed this test to analyze situations in which there was no unit of measurement (for example, inches or pounds). In this case the question is: Is the correlation between bulbous and female or slender and male good enough to warrant the conclusion of a visual difference? The take-home is in the figure p<0.0011. This means that the probability of 80 of 122 correct identifications happening solely by chance is one-tenth of 1 percent, well below the cutoff point of 5 percent (p<0.05) used in standard scientific practice.[82]

Well, 66 percent of the time observers could separate male from female
CC's just by eyeballing their shape. And the χ^2 test tells us how significant this
differentiation process is. Statistics don't lie. They do, however, divert our
attention from the study design. In this case, Allen et al. gave their CC tracings
to three different observers, who had no knowledge of the sex of the individual whose brain had generated the drawing. These blind operators divided the
drawings into two piles—bulbous or tubular, on the assumption that if the
difference were obvious, the pile of tubular shapes should mostly turn out to
have come from men and the bulbous from women. So far so good. Now
here comes the trick. The authors designated a subject's gender as correctly
classified if two out of the three blind observers did it right.

How does this work out numerically? The complex statistical passage
quoted above says that 66 percent of the time the observers got it right. This
could actually mean several things. There were 122 drawings of the corpus
callosum. Since three different observers looked at each drawing, that means
that there were 366 individual observations. In the best case (from the authors' point of view), all three observers always agreed about any individual
CC. This would mean that 244/366 (66 percent) of their individual observations accurately divined sex on the basis of shape. In the worst case, however,
for those measures that they counted as successful separations, only two out
of the 3 observers *ever* agreed about an individual brain. This would mean
that only 160/366 (44 percent) of the individual observations successfully
separated the CC drawings on the basis of sex. Allen et al. do not provide the
reader with the complete data, so their actual success remains uncertain. But
using a chi-squared test on their refined data convinces many that they have
finally found an answer that all can accept.

The data do not speak for themselves. The reader is presented with tables,
graphs, and drawings and are pushed through rigorous statistical trials, but
no clear answer emerges. The data still need more support, and for this scientists try next to interpret their results plausibly. They support their interpretations by linking them to previously constructed knowledge. Only when
their data are woven into this broader web of meaning can scientists finally
force the CC to speak clearly. Only then can "facts" about the corpus callosum emerge.[83]

WHEN IS A FACT A FACT?

Like all scholarship, Allen and her colleagues' study is necessarily embedded
in the context of an ongoing conversation about the broader subject matter
it explores—in this case, the corpus callosum. They must rely heavily on
preexisting work to establish the validity of their own. Allen and her col-

leagues note, for example, that even though the CC has a million or more nerve fibers running through it, this enormous number still represents only 2 percent of all the neurons in the cerebral cortex. They note evidence that fibers in the splenium may help transfer visual information from one brain hemisphere to the other. Another region—the isthmus—for which they find no sex difference (but for which others find a complex of differences between gay and straight and left- and right-handed men), carries fibers connecting left and right cortical regions involved with language function.

Allen and colleagues need to keep their discussion pithy. After all, they want to examine their findings, not review all that is known about the structure and function of the corpus callosum. Let's imagine this aspect of the production of facts about the corpus callosum as a macramé weaving. Here an artist uses knots as links in the creation of intricate, webbed patterns. The connecting threads secure individual knots within the larger structure, even though a single knot in the web may not be all that strong. My drawing of the CC weaving (figure 5.6) includes only contemporary disputes. But each knot also contains a fourth dimension—its social history.[84] To locate the knot labeled "corpus callosum gender differences," Allen et al. have spun out a thread and secured it to a second knot, labeled "structure and function of the corpus callosum." That tangle is, in turn, secured by a second web of research.

Speculation abounds about the CC's structure and function. Perhaps more nerve fibers permit faster information flow between left and right brain hemispheres; perhaps faster flow improves spatial or verbal function (or vice versa). Or perhaps larger (or smaller) CC segments slow the flow of electricity between brain halves, thus improving spatial or verbal abilities (or vice versa). But what, exactly, does the CC in general and the splenium in particular do? What kinds of cells course through the CC, where do they go, and how do they function?[85] The function/structure knot contains hundreds of papers produced by overlapping research communities, only some of which are interested in sex differences. One team of sociologists calls such groups "persuasive communities,"[86] whose language choices or use of techniques such as sophisticated statistics may condition how its members envision a problem.[87] Work on the structure and function of the corpus callosum links several persuasive communities. One locale, for example, compares the numbers of large and small neurons, some with an insulating coat of myelin, others lying naked in different regions of the CC. These cells perform different functions and thus provide clues to CC function.[88]

The structure/function node is dense.[89] An issue of the journal *Behavioural Brain Research* devoted entirely to work on the function of the corpus callosum illustrates the point. Some papers in the volume addressed findings and con-

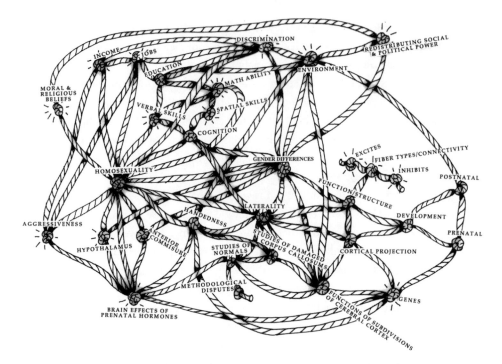

FIGURE 5.6: A macramé weaving of knots of knowledge in which the corpus callosum debate is embedded. (Source: Alyce Santoro, for the author)

troversies on hemispheric lateralization, speaking directly to the implications for CC function.[90] The laterality work in turn connects to studies of handedness, sex differences, and brain function.[91] These also interconnect with a literature that debates the interpretation of studies on humans with damaged CC's and compares results to studies that try to infer CC function from intact subjects.[92] One well-known aspect of lateralization is handedness—how shall we define it, what causes it (genes, environment, birth position?), what does it mean for brain functions, how does it affect CC structure (and how does CC structure affect handedness?), are there sex differences, and do homosexuals and heterosexuals differ? Handedness is a busy knot.[93]

All of these knots connect at some point with one labeled cognition.[94] Sometimes tests designed to measure verbal, spatial, or mathematical abilities reveal gender differences.[95] Both the reliability of such differences and their origin provide fodder for unending dispute.[96] Some link a belief in gender differences in cognition to the design of educational programs. One essayist, for example, drew a parallel between teaching mathematics to women and giving flying lessons to tortoises.[97] Elaborate and sometimes completely opposite theories connect cognitive sex differences with callosal structure. One, for example, suggests that higher mathematical ability derives from differing numbers of excitatory neurons in the CC, while another suggests that the inhibitory nature of the CC neuron is most important.[98]

The effects of hormones on brain development form an especially powerful knot in this macramé weaving (I will have a lot more to say about hormones in the next three chapters). Allen and her colleagues wonder whether sex differences in the corpus callosum might be induced by hormones, some other genetic cause, or the environment. After briefly considering the environmental hypothesis,[99] they write: "However, more striking have been the data indicating that nearly all sexually dimorphic structures examined thus far have been shown to be influenced by perinatal gonadal hormone levels."[100] This brief statement invokes a huge and complex literature about hormones, the brain, and behavior (some of which we have already considered in the context of intersexuality). Standing alone, the corpus callosum research may be weak. But with the vast army of hormone research to back it up, how could claims of a difference possibly fail? Even though there is no convincing evidence to link human corpus callosum development to hormones,[101] invoking the vast animal literature[102] stabilizes the shaky CC knot.[103]

Within each of the persuasive communities represented in figure 5.6 by knots on the macramé weaving, one finds scientists at work. They are devising new methods to test and substantiate their favored hypothesis or to refute a viewpoint they believe in error. They measure, use statistics, or invent new machines, trying to stabilize the fact they pursue. But in the end, few of the facts (excised, unsupported knots) about gender differences are particularly robust[104] (to use a word favored by scientists) and must, therefore, draw significant strength from their links to the weaving. These researchers work primarily on the science side of things, studying genes, development, parts of the brain, hormones, analyses of brain-damaged people, and more (figure 5.7A). This portion of the nexus appears to deal with more objective phenomena, the realm traditionally handed over to science.[105] On the cultural side of the macramé weaving (figure 5.7B) we find that webbed into the sex difference knot are some decidedly political items: cognition, homosexuality, environment, education, social and political power, moral and religious beliefs. Very rapidly we have skated along the strands from science to politics, from scientific disputes to political power struggles.[106]

Talking Heads: Do Facts Speak for Themselves?

Can we ever know whether there is a gender difference in the corpus callosum?[107] Well, it depends a bit on what we mean by *knowing*. The corpus callo-

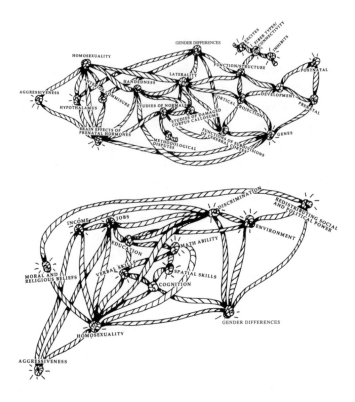

FIGURE 5.7A (*top*): The "science half" of the woven knowledge connections; 5.7B (*bottom*): The "culture half" of the woven knowledge connections.
(Source: Alyce Santoro, for the author)

sum is a highly variable bit of anatomy. Scientists go to great lengths to fix it in place for laboratory observation, but despite their efforts it won't hold still. It may or may not change, depending on the experience, handedness, health, age, and sex of the body it inhabits. Knowing, then, means finding a way to approach the CC so that it says the same thing to a wide array of investigators. I think the likelihood of this happening is small. Ultimately, the questions researchers take into their studies, the methodologies they employ, and their decisions about which additional persuasive communities to link their work to, all reflect cultural assumptions about the meanings of the subject under study—in this case, the meanings of masculinity and femininity.

A belief in biologically based difference is often linked to conservative social policy, although the association between political conservatism and biological determinism is by no means absolute.[108] I cannot predict on a priori grounds whether or not in the future we will come to believe in gender differences in the CC, or whether we will simply let the matter fall, unresolved, by the wayside. If we were to reach social agreement on the politics of gender in education, however, what we believe about CC structure wouldn't matter. We know now, for example that "training with spatial tasks will lead to improved achievement on spatial tests."[109] Let's further suppose that we could agree that schools "should provide training in spatial ability in order to equalize educational opportunities for boys and girls."[110]

If we were culturally unified around such a meaning of equal opportunity, the CC dispute might follow one of several possible paths. Scientists might decide that, given how little we still know about how the CC works, the question is premature and should be set aside until our approaches to tracing nervous function in the CC improve. Or they might decide that the difference does exist, but is not forever fixed at birth. Their research program might focus on which experiences influence such changes, and the information gained might be of use to educators devising training programs for spatial ability. Feminists would not object to such studies because the idea of inferiority and immutability would have been severed from the assertion of difference, and they could rest secure in our culture's commitment to a particular form of equal educational opportunity. Or we might decide that the data, after all, do not support a consistent anatomical group difference in the CC at any point in the life cycle. We might, instead, ask research questions about the sources of individual variability in CC anatomy. How might genetic variability interact with environmental stimulus to produce anatomical difference? Which stimuli are important for which genotypes? In other words, we might use developmental systems theory to frame our investigations of the corpus callosum. Choosing a scientific path acceptable to most, and littering that path with agreed-upon facts, is only possible once we have achieved social and cultural peace about gender equity. Such a view of fact formation does not deny the existence of a material, verifiable nature; nor does it hold that the material— in this case the brain and its CC—has no say in the matter.[111]

The CC is not voiceless. Scientists, for example, cannot arbitrarily decide that the structure is round rather than oblong. With regard to gender differences, however, let's just say that it mumbles. Scientists have employed their immense talents to try to get rid of background noise, to see if they can more clearly tune in the CC. But the corpus callosum is a pretty uncooperative medium for locating differences. That researchers continue to probe the corpus callosum in search of a definitive gender difference speaks to how entrenched their expectations about biological differences remain. As with intersexuality, however, I would argue that the real excitement of studies on the corpus callosum lies in what we can learn about the vastness of human variation and the ways in which the brain develops as part of a social system.

SEX GLANDS, HORMONES, AND GENDER CHEMISTRY

In Which Testosterone Taints the Fountain of Youth

IN A 1945 HOMAGE TO MEDICAL SCIENCE, THE FIFTY-FOUR-YEAR-OLD bacteriologist and popular science writer Paul de Kruif published a book entitled *The Male Hormone*, in which he revealed to the world a deeply personal fact: he was taking testosterone. Beginning in his late thirties, he explained, he had become aware of his declining virility. His energy had diminished and even worse, so had his courage and self-confidence. A mere five years earlier, when his old boss had retired, the prospect of a change in his work life had filled him with terror and hysteria. "That was before testosterone. That was a nice little symptom of my own male hormone hunger, of my stage of slipping, of losing my grip." But at age fifty-four, his confidence, he reported, was waxing strong. And he owed it all to testosterone: "I'll be faithful and remember to take my twenty or thirty milligrams a day of testosterone. I'm not ashamed that it's no longer made to its own degree by my own aging body. It's chemical crutches. It's borrowed manhood. It's borrowed time. But just the same, it's what makes bulls bulls." [1]

In the 1960s Dr. Robert A. Wilson claimed that estrogen could do for women what testosterone supposedly did for men. As estrogen declined during the menopause, women suffered a terrible fate. "The stigmata of Nature's defeminization" included "a general stiffness of muscles, a dowager's hump, and a vapid cow-like negative state." Postmenopausal women, he wrote in the *Journal of the American Geriatric Society*, existed but did not live. On the streets "they pass unnoticed and, in turn, notice little." [2] With support from Ayerst Pharmaceuticals he offered to cure the menopause—to this day, referred to as an estrogen deficiency disease—by giving women Premarin, Ayerst's brand name for estrogen. [3]

Today fascination with the healing properties of estrogen and testosterone continues unabated. Estrogen and a related hormone, progesterone, have become the most extensively used drugs in the history of medicine.[4] In the popular imagination, sex and hormones are linked as they were in de Kruif's and Wilson's day. "Yes," de Kruif wrote in 1945, "sex is chemical and the male sex chemical seemed to be the key not only to sex but to enterprise, courage and vigor."[5] In 1996, when testosterone made it onto the cover of *Newsweek*, the headline read: "Attention: aging men—testosterone and other hormone treatments offer new hope for staying youthful, sexy and strong."[6]

But in the age of unisex, testosterone treatment is not just for men. Women, especially postmenopausal ones (those same cow-like creatures whose lives Dr. Wilson lamented) can also benefit from a little of the old T-molecule. One proponent of giving testosterone to older women, Dr. John Studd (really!) of the Department of Obstetrics and Gynecology at Chelsea and Westminster Hospital in London, recently said of his testosterone-treated female patients: "They may have their lives transformed. Their energy, their sexual interest, the intensity and frequency of orgasm, their wish to be touched and have sexual contact—all improve."[7] What's more, it turns out that men need estrogen for normal development of everything from bone growth to fertility.[8]

Why, then, have hormones always been strongly associated with the idea of sex, when, in fact, "sex hormones" apparently affect organs throughout the entire body and are not specific to either gender? The brain, lungs, bones, blood vessels, intestine, and liver (to give a partial list) all use estrogen to maintain proper growth and development.[9] In broad outline, the widespread effects of estrogen and testosterone have been known for decades. One of the claims I make in this chapter and the next is that relentlessly, over this century, scientists have integrated the signs of gender—from genitalia, to the anatomy of gonads and brains, then to our very body chemistry—more thoroughly than ever into our bodies. In the case of the body's chemistry, researchers accomplished this feat by defining as sex hormones what are, in effect, multi-site chemical growth regulators, thus rendering their far-reaching, non-sexual roles in both male and female development nearly invisible. Now that the label of sex hormone seems attached with epoxy to these steroid molecules, any rediscovery of their role in tissues such as bones or intestines has a strange result. By virtue of the fact that so-called sex hormones affect their physiology, these organs, so clearly *not* involved in reproduction, come to be seen as sex organs. Chemicals infuse the body, from head to toe, with gender meanings.

Scientists did not integrate gender into the body's chemistry by conscious design. Indeed, they simply went about their business as talented working scientists. They investigated the hottest new research topics, found the financial and material resources to support their work, established fruitful collaborations between investigators with different backgrounds and training, and ultimately, signed international agreements to standardize the naming and experimental evaluation of the various chemical substances they purified and examined. But in this and the following chapter, as we watch scientists engage in each of these normal activities, we will also observe how, despite a lack of overt intention, scientific work on hormone biology was deeply linked to gender politics. I argue that we can understand the emergence of scientific accounts of sex hormones only if we see the scientific and the social as part of an inextricable system of ideas and practices—simultaneously social and scientific. To illustrate, I turn to a key scientific moment in the history of hormones, one in which scientists struggled to impose gender on the internal secretions of ovaries and testes.

The discovery of "sex hormones" is an extraordinary episode in the history of science.[10] By 1940, scientists had identified, purified, and named them. As they explored hormone science (endocrinology), however, researchers could make hormones intelligible only in terms of the struggles around gender and race that characterized their working environments. Each choice that scientists made about how to measure and name the molecules they studied naturalized cultural ideas about gender.[11] Each institution and persuasive community involved in hormone research brought to the table a social agenda about race and gender. Pharmaceutical companies, experimental biologists, physicians, agricultural biologists, and sex researchers intersected with feminists, advocates of homosexual rights, eugenicists, birth control advocates, psychologists, and charitable foundations. Each of these groups, which I will call social worlds, were linked by people, ideas, laboratories, research materials, and funding, and much more.[12] By examining how these worlds intersected, we can see the ways in which certain molecules became part of our system of gender—how gender became chemical.

Hormones! The Very Idea!

The gonads, people have long known, affect the body and psyche in myriad ways. For centuries, farmers have known that castration affects both the physique and behavior of farm animals. And although human castration was officially banned by the Vatican, in Europe the specialized singing voices of the castrati were heard in more than a few church choirs through the end of the nineteenth century. These castrated boys grew into tall and unusual shapes while their tremulous sopranos attained an odd, otherworldly quality.[13] During the last quarter of the nineteenth century, surgeons frequently removed the ovaries of women they deemed "insane, hysterical, unhappy, difficult for their husbands to control or disliked running a household."[14] But why such drastic measures seemed to work was less than certain. Most nineteenth-century physiologists postulated that the gonads communicated their effects through nervous connections.

Others, however, found evidence that the gonads acted via chemical secretions. In 1849 Arnold Adolf Berthold, Professor of Physiology at the University of Göttingen, "transformed languid capons into fighting roosters." First he created the capons by removing their testicles, then he implanted the disconnected gonads into the birds' body cavities. Because the implants were unconnected to the nervous system, he surmised that any effects they might have must be blood-borne. Berthold started with four birds: two received the testicular implants and two did not. In his inimitable style, de Kruif described the results: "While the two caponized birds . . . became fat pacifists, these other two . . . remained every inch roosters. They crowed. They battled. They chased hens enthusiastically. Their bright red combs and wattles kept on growing"[15] (figure 6.1).

Berthold's results languished until 1889, when the French physiologist Charles-Edouard Brown-Séquard reported to his colleagues at the Société de Biologie in Paris that he had injected himself with extracts made from crushed guinea pig and dog testicles. The results, he said, were spectacular. He experienced a renewed vigor and increased mental clarity. He also reported on female patients whose physical and mental health had improved after taking the filtered juice of guinea pig ovaries.[16] Although many physicians responded to Brown-Séquard's claims with more than a little skepticism, the idea of *organotherapy*—treatment with organ extracts—gained enormous popularity. While physiologists debated the truth of the claims, sales of "extracts of animal organs, gray matter, testicular extract," for the treatment of "locomotor ataxia, neurasthenia and other nervous diseases" were brisk in both Europe and the United States.[17] Within a decade, however, the new treatments fell into disrepute. Brown-Séquard admitted that the effects of his testicular injections were short-lived, probably the result of the power of suggestion. While gonadal extracts failed to live up to their promise, two other organ treatments did offer medical benefits: extracts made from the thyroid gland proved effective in the treatment of thyroid disorders, and adrenal extracts worked as vasoconstrictors.[18]

Despite such successes, research physiologists remained skeptical of the

FIGURE 6.1: Berthold's gonad transfer experiments. (Source: Alyce Santoro, for the author)

chemical message idea implicit in organotherapy.[19] Nineteenth-century physiologists' firm belief that the nervous system controlled bodily functions made
it difficult, at first, to recognize the significance of chemical messengers, the
products of internal organ secretions.

SEX HORMONES TAKE FORM AS GENDER CHANGES SHAPE

It wasn't until the turn of the last century that scientists began to examine
seriously the idea that chemical secretions regulated the body's physiology.
Although in the 1890s the British physiologist Edward Schäfer interpreted the
results of gonadectomy (the removal of either the testis or the ovary) in terms
of nervous function, over the next few years, he and his students began to
reevaluate.[20] In 1905 Ernest Henry Starling, Schäfer's successor as Professor
of Physiology at the University College in London, coined the word *hormone*
(from the Greek "I excite or arouse"). He defined hormones as chemicals that
"have to be carried from the organ where they are produced to the organ
which they affect, by means of the blood stream."[21]

British physiologists gave birth to and embraced the hormone concept during the years 1905 to 1908. Their scientific issue (especially the secretions

produced by the sex glands, the ovaries and testes) arrived during a period when the populace of the United States and many European nations had begun to reevaluate traditional constructions of gender and sexuality.[22] New debates opened up over the rights of homosexuals and women—while what historians have called a "crisis in masculinity" developed in both Europe and the United States.[23] At the same time, events such as the founding of the field of scientific sexology; Sigmund Freud's early years, as he moved from theories of neurology to the invention of psychoanalytic psychiatry; and the insistence, especially in the United States, of an experimental approach to the biological sciences developed in the context of these gender struggles.[24] The attempt to define and understand the role sex hormones played in human physiology was no exception. From the beginning, such research efforts both reflected and contributed to competing definitions of masculinity and femininity, thus helping to shape the implications of such definitions for the social and economic roles to be played by the men and women of the twentieth century.

What were some of the elements visible in the new debates about masculinity and femininity? The historian Chandak Sengoopta writes that turn-of-the-century Vienna experienced "a crisis of gender . . . a moment when the boundaries and norms of male and female shifted, disintegrated and seemed to intertwine."[25] In Central Europe this crisis also took on racial overtones, as social commentators debated the Jewish Question, depicting Jewish men as both effeminate *and* as sexual predators.[26] In this same period, the German physician and reformer Magnus Hirschfeld and his colleagues founded the Scientific-Humanitarian Committee, which repeatedly petitioned the Reichstag to repeal the national sodomy law.[27] Male homosexuals, they argued, were natural sexual variants, not criminals. Women's rights and the emergence of homosexuality were no less salient in England and the United States.[28] Table 6.1 lists two decades of events that wove together the social movements of feminism and homosexual activism with the emergence of the scientific study of sex and the idea of sex hormones.

The Biopolitics of Feminism and Homosexuality

At the turn of the century, social commentators tried to extract political lessons from scientific knowledge about human development.[29] In 1903, for example, a Viennese philosophy student named Otto Weininger published an influential book entitled *Sex and Character* that drew on the ideas of nineteenth-century embryology to develop a comprehensive theory of masculinity, femininity, and homosexuality. Weininger believed that even after their distinctive anatomies emerged, males and females each contained both male and female sex-determining substances (plasms) in their cells. The proportion of these

TABLE 6.1 *Thinking About Sex and Sexuality at the Turn of the Century*[a]

DATE	EVENT
1889	Geddes and Thomson publish *The Evolution of Sex*[b]
1892	Richard von Krafft-Ebing publishes *Psychopathia Sexualis, with especial reference to Contrary Sexual Instinct: A medico-legal study.*
1895	Oscar Wilde tried publicly for homosexual conduct[c]
1896	Havelock Ellis begins work on his *Studies in the Psychology of Sex*[d]
1897	Magnus Hirschfeld founds the Scientific-Humanitarian Committee
1898	Havelock Ellis's book *Sexual Inversion* seized and prosecuted for being lewd and scandalous
1903	Otto Weininger publishes *Sex and Character*, which elaborates a complex biological theory of sex[e]
1904	Endocrinologist Eugen Steinach studies the effects of sex hormones on animal behavior
1905	Swiss psychiatrist August Forel publishes *La Questionne Sexuelle*, advocating marriage for same-sex couples[f]

a. Based on information obtained from Wissenschaft 1999; see also Bullough 1994.
b. Geddes and Thomson 1895. This book provided a definitive account of biological variability in systems of sexual reproduction and accounted for the evolution of sex in terms that many still use today. The book focuses primarily on the nonhuman biological work, yet became a cornerstone for thinking about the evolution of sex in humans.
c. While "the sensational trial of Oscar Wilde in 1895 for homosexual conduct created wide public interest in sex inversion and called forth a considerable literature" (Aberle and Corner 1953, p. 5), then as now scientific interest in female homosexuality lagged behind (Havelock Ellis's work on homosexuality devoted no more than one-third of its pages to lesbianism, which it linked to prostitution). But during the first two decades of the twentieth century, lesbianism nevertheless became a public issue.
d. [The original U.S. publication date for Ellis was 1901. I quote from a 1928 edition.] Ellis's tomes on human sexuality set a high scientific standard for the period; he was dispassionate and nonjudgmental about the wide variation in human sexual behavior. For more on the origins of modern sexology, see Jackson 1987; Birken 1988; Irvine 1990a, 1990b; Bullough 1994; and Katz 1995.
e. Sengoopta 1992, 1996. For the influence of this book in England, see Porter and Hall 1995.
f. Forel 1905.

TABLE 6.1 *(continued)*

DATE	EVENT
1905	Sigmund Freud publishes *Three Essays on the Theory of Sex*
1906	American feminist Emma Goldman, an advocate of birth control and women's rights, founds the magazine *Mother Earth*
1907	German physician Iwan Bloch calls for the scientific study of sex[g]
1908	Magnus Hirschfeld edits the first issue of the *Journal of Sexology*
1909	Edward Carpenter publishes *The Intermediate Sex: A Study of Some Transitional Types in Men and Women*[h]
1910	British physiologist Francis Marshall publishes first comprehensive book on *The Physiology of Reproduction*[i]
1912	Ovarian hormones extracted using lipid solvents[j]
1913	British endocrinologist Walter Heape publishes *Sex Antagonism*[k]

g. Bloch defined 14 areas of sexological investigation, including sexual anatomy and physiology (hormones); the physiology of sexual performance; the psychology and evolution of sex; the comparative biology of sex; sexual hygiene; sexual politics, including legislation; sexual ethics; sexual ethnology; and sexual pathology.

h. Carpenter 1909. Carpenter (1844–1929) was himself a member of what he called the "intermediate sex." He believed in biological differences between the sexes, but thought that the existing social distance was harmful. For more on Carpenter, see Porter and Hall 1995, pp. 158–60.

i. Marshall 1910. This book established the forming field of reproductive biology by uniting in a single text contributions from embryology, anatomy, physiology, and gynecology. For more on Marshall, see Clarke 1990a, 1990b, 1998).

j. Corner 1965.

k. Heape 1913. Heape argued that men and women have fundamentally different evolutionary interests and that sex antagonism is a biological problem. In discussing what he calls "the unrest among women," he writes that "it is primarily a biological problem we are dealing with, that the violation of physiological principles has long preceded that of economic law, and that existing conditions cannot be clearly understood and satisfactorily dealt with until this fact is clearly recognized" (pp. 11–12). For additional discussion in relation to sex hormones, see Oudshoorn 1994 and Clarke 1998.

plasms differed from one individual to the next, thus explaining the wide range of masculinity and femininity observed among humans. Homosexual men had almost equal proportions of masculine and feminine plasms.[30] In England, Edward Carpenter published similar ideas: Nature, it might appear, in mixing elements which go to compose each individual, does not always keep her two groups of ingredients—which represent the sexes—properly apart . . . wisely, we must think—for if a severe distinction of elements were always maintained the two sexes would soon drift into far latitudes and absolutely cease to understand each other."[31] Weininger thought that women's drive for emancipation emanated from the masculine elements in their bodies. He linked this masculinity with lesbian desire, using talented women such as Sappho and Georges Sand to exemplify his claims. But even the most talented women still had a great deal of female plasm in their bodies, making full equality with men impossible. Thus built into this theory is the a priori assumption that all striving for public life, talent, and achievement by definition comes from masculine plasm. At best, women could achieve only partial manhood.[32]

In the United States, writers also described women's desire to vote as a biological phenomenon. James Weir, writing in the magazine *The American Naturalist*, used evolutionary arguments. Primitive societies, he noted, were matriarchies. Giving women the right to vote and hold public office would bring about a return to matriarchy. Women have this atavistic desire to vote for a simple reason. Feminists are virtually all *viragints*—domineering, aggressive, and psychologically abnormal women. They are evolutionary throwbacks. Some have "the feelings and desires of a man," but even the most masculine among them can function only by emotion, not logic. Weir saw "in the establishment of equal rights, the first step toward the abyss of immoral horrors so repugnant to our cultivated ethical tastes—the matriarchate."[33]

Of course not everyone, and especially not all scientists, opposed women's emancipation. But the social models of gender both fed and emerged from two sources of nineteenth-century biology: the embryological and the evolutionary. The idea that the public sphere was *by definition* masculine lay so deep in this period's metaphysical fabric that it did not seem surprising to argue that women who aspired to the Rights of Man had also, by definition, to be masculine.[34] Whether female masculinity was an evolutionary throwback or an embryological anomaly was a matter for debate.[35] But it was this context in which inherent sex difference—and female inferiority—was taken as a matter of unquestionable fact that shaped the scientific investigation of the internal secretions of ovaries and testes.

Enter Hormones, Center Stage

By 1915 three book-length treatises on reproduction, hormones, and the sexes had been published. *The Physiology of Reproduction*, by Francis H. A. Marshall, which appeared in 1910, summarized more than a decade of work and became the founding text of the new field of reproductive biology. Marshall, a university lecturer in agricultural physiology, studied the breeding cycles of farm animals and the effects of ovarian secretions on the health and physiology of reproductive organs such as the uterus. His work on what he sometimes called "generative physiology" (the physiology of reproduction) had far-reaching influence, not only forming the basis of new techniques in animal breeding but also shaping the theory and practice of the field of gynecology. Marshall hoped to draw together previously unrelated accounts of reproduction, and in doing so freely consulted and cited works of "zoology and anatomy, obstetrics and gynaecology, physiology and agriculture, anthropology and statistics."[36]

The Physiology of Reproduction examined every known aspect of generation: fertilization, reproductive anatomy, pregnancy, lactation, and, of special interest for the history of hormone research, chapters on "The Testicle and Ovary as Organs of Internal Secretion" and "The Factors Which Determine Sex." In the former section, Marshall massed scientific evidence, which had accumulated rapidly during the first decade of the twentieth-century, showing that ovaries and testes secreted "stuff" that influenced other organs in the body. The idea of sex hormones had, at this moment, taken its baby steps.[37]

Marshall's tone is dry and factual, his text filled with detailed descriptions of experiments reporting the effects of gonadal extracts on mammalian development. He seems entirely uninterested in the social implications of his work, yet he relies heavily on scholarship that was itself explicitly concerned with the connections between biology and gender. For example, without endorsing their social views, he notes the "special help" provided by Patrick Geddes and J. Arthur Thomson's 1889 book *The Evolution of Sex*, a compendium of sex in the animal world that sets up the active sperm and the sluggish egg as exemplars of essential biological truths about sex differences: "It is generally true that the males are more active, energetic, eager, passionate and variable; the females more passive, conservative, sluggish and stable. The more active males, with a consequently wider range of experience, may have bigger brains and more intelligence; but the females, especially as mothers, have indubitably a larger and more habitual share of the altruistic emotions."[38]

Despite the book's detached tone, Marshall did not entirely ignore the social metaphysics of gender. In discussing "Factors Which Determine Sex," he considered Weininger's ideas in some detail, noting the latter's thoughts on the biology of "the Sapphist and the virago to the most effeminate male." The general idea that animals—including humans—contain both masculine and feminine traits attracted Marshall. He was less sanguine that the sources of masculinity and femininity lay within individual cells, as Weininger hypothesized, suggesting instead that his "physiological mode of thought requires one to associate the characters of an organism with its particular metabolism,"[39] including, by implication, hormonal physiology. In a footnote Marshall explicitly linked the world of animal experiments on reproduction and hormones to the human social world studied by sexologists, citing key texts by Krafft-Ebing, Havelock Ellis, August Forel, and Iwan Bloch (see table 6.1).

If Marshall was coy about the social ramifications of reproductive biology, the biologist Walter Heape—a colleague, to whom he dedicated *The Physiology of Reproduction*—left no doubt about where he stood when he published his influential *Sex Antagonism* in 1913. Heape had conducted fundamental research in reproductive biology, studying the estrus cycle in mammals, proving that mating stimulated ovulation in rabbits, and more generally making a place for reproductive science within the field of agriculture.[40] By 1913, he was applying his knowledge of the animal world to the human condition.

Heape was disturbed by the social upheavals around him, particularly the dramatic and highly visible suffrage and labor movements. Women activists in the U.S. and Britain took to the streets in the early twentieth-century to protest their inferior social, economic, and political status. Women garment workers walked in picket lines across the U.S.,[41] and in 1909 a broad coalition of labor, older suffragists, organizations of black women activists,[42] and immigrant housewives pushed for enfranchisement in new and militant combinations.[43] The movement had broad appeal, as "women at both ends of the economic spectrum had new appetite for political organization."[44] Meanwhile, in England, suffragettes disrupted Parliament by unfurling banners from the galleries, smashing windows, and assaulting guards at 10 Downing Street.[45]

Heape began his book by attributing "the condition of unrest, which permeates society . . . to three sources. Racial antagonism, Class antagonism, and Sex antagonism."[46] These antagonisms, he felt, particularly sex antagonism, were rooted in the social mismanagement of biological difference. Men and women had fundamentally different generative roles. If woman lived "in accord with her physiological organization,"[47] he insisted, by attending to home and hearth and leaving public affairs to men (whose sexuality naturally rendered them more restless and outward-reaching), she would be able to avoid the evils of mental derangement, spinsterhood and its implied masculinity, and general ill health.[48] Interestingly, Heape acknowledged a certain measure of biological overlap between male and female bodies. But this didn't lead him to question his assumptions about the fundamental nature of sex difference. Rather, he saw the mix of sex characteristics in each body as a metaphor for how gender difference functioned in the body politic. Sex antagonism, he wrote, was present within "every individual of one sex . . . Thus both sexes are represented in every individual of each sex, and while the male qualities are most prominent in the man and the female qualities are most prominent in the woman, they each have qualities of the other sex more or less hidden away within them." Each individual, then, carried a mixture of dominant and subordinate factors that were, "in reality, though more or less feebly, antagonistic."[49]

It was the British gynecologist William Blair Bell who took the step of linking social sex differences to hormones. He thought that the internal secretions of individual organs ought not be considered in isolation, but rather as part of a whole-body system of interactions among the various endocrine organs. Whereas scientists had generally thought that "a woman was a woman because of her ovaries alone," Bell believed that *"femininity itself is dependent on all the internal secretions."* To support his theory, Bell noted the existence of women with testes and individuals with ovaries "who are not women in the strict sense of the word."[50] Bell's views helped dethrone the gonad as the sole determinant of sex, thus changing medical understanding and treatments of intersexuality.[51] They also completely recast scientific ideas about the nature and origins of "normal" sexuality.

Bell believed that women's ovaries and other endocrine glands inclined them toward "womanly" pursuits and sexuality; those women who were "unwomanly," he believed, were living contrary to the tendencies of their own bodies. Those he considered "nearest to nature" or "untouched by civilization" were women "who enjoy sexual intercourse, and who are, perhaps, somewhat promiscuous . . . yet their maternal instincts are strong." Women "touched by civilization" ranged from those who eschewed sexual desire but wanted maternity, and those who delighted in sexual pleasures but had no maternal instincts (and who were "not strictly speaking normal"), to women who wanted neither sex nor motherhood. These latter were "on the fringe of masculinity . . . usually flat-chested and plain . . . their metabolism is often for the most part masculine in character: indications of this are seen . . . in the aggressive character of the mind." Bell concluded that "the normal psychology of every woman is dependent on the state of her internal secretions, and that unless driven by force of circumstances—economic and social—she will have no inherent wish to leave her normal sphere of action."[52] As in so much of the endocrinological literature from this period, the social concern for women who wanted out of their "normal sphere of action" loomed large.

Heape and Bell spoke about sex antagonism in a social sense, and believed that internal secretions helped create masculine and feminine minds and bodies. The Viennese physician and physiologist Eugen Steinach, however, believed the hormones themselves displayed antagonism. As a physician and researcher in Prague, and then as Director of the Physiology Division of the Viennese Institute for Experimental Biology, he worked in the growing tradition of animal transplantation studies, transferring testes into female rats and guinea pigs, and ovaries into male rodents (of which more in a moment).[53] Steinach's interventionist style of experimentation embodied the spirit of a new, authoritative analytical approach that was sweeping both Europe and the United States.[54] Masculine and feminine bodies and behaviors, he felt, resulted from the activities of sex hormones, and his animal experiments provided evidence for the antagonistic nature of the sex hormones. In Steinach's hands, hormones themselves acquired masculine and feminine characteristics. Sex became chemical, and body chemistry became sexed. The drama of sex difference didn't just stem from internal secretions; it was already being played out in them.[55]

Steinach believed hormones patrolled the borders dividing male from female and homosexual from heterosexual. His research on rats and guinea pigs and the importation of his results into humans illustrate the complex ways in which gender belief systems become part of scientific knowledge. He began his career as an experimentalist in 1884, working on a variety of problems in physiology—none obviously related to sex. In 1894, however, he published a paper on the comparative anatomy of male sex organs, foreshadowing his experimental turn toward sexual physiology. Ten papers and sixteen years later, he returned to the physiology of sex. His article "The Development of Complete Functional and Somatic Masculinity in Mammals as a Particular Effect of Internal Secretion of the Testicle" marked the beginning of modern experiments on the role of hormones in sexual differentiation.[56]

Indeed, his entire life's work was premised on the unexamined idea that there must be a sharp "natural" distinction between maleness and femaleness. Despite the rather gender-bending experiments he performed, the highly anthropomorphic way he described his results speaks to how deeply his assumptions about sexual difference shaped his science. First, he concluded that the hormonal products of ovaries and testes, which he called the "puberty glands," had sex-specific effects. Testes produced substances so powerful that they could cause young female rats and guinea pigs to develop both the physical and psychical characters of males. He reasoned that hormonal effects on the psyche must work through changes in the brain in a process he dubbed the "erotization of the central nervous system."[57] Steinach thought that all mammals contained rudimentary structures (*Anlage*) for both sexes. Puberty gland secretions promoted the development of either ovaries, influencing feminine growth, or testes, for masculine. But this was only part of the story. He also believed that the sex glands actively inhibited the *Anlage* of the "opposite" sex. Thus, ovarian substances in the female not only produced feminine growth but inhibited masculine growth. Meanwhile, testicular secretions in the male inhibited feminine development. Steinach called this process of sex-specific growth inhibition "sex hormone antagonism."

What experimental evidence led Steinach to describe physical growth processes in such militaristic terms as "battles of the antagonistic actions of sex hormones" and "sharp antagonisms"?[58] He transplanted ovaries into newborn, castrated male rats and guinea pigs (see table 6.2). Over time, these males developed many feminine characteristics. Their bone and hair structure became typical of the well-groomed female rodent; they developed functional mammary glands, willingly suckled infants, and presented their rumps to male suitors in a suitably feminine manner. Ovaries, it seemed, produced a specifically feminizing substance. But there was more. First, ovarian transplants would not "take" in the male body unless the testes were removed. Second, Steinach compared the growth of the penis in males with ovarian transplants to males that had been castrated but received no implants. Remarkably, to him, the penis seemed to shrink under the influence of the female puberty gland, until it was smaller than a penis from plain old castrates. Finally, Steinach observed, the feminized, castrated males were even smaller than their unoperated sisters. The ovarian implants had not only prevented them from growing into larger, heavier males; they seemed actually to have inhibited their growth (see figure 6.2).

Although at first Steinach referred to these last processes simply as "inhibitions,"[59] he soon began to describe them with the stronger language of the battle between the sexes. Did his initial data demand such strong language? It would seem not. In a 1912 study on rats, when he first reported the data on penile shrinkage, for example, he found no such effect on the prostate or seminal vesicles—facts that Steinach explained by noting how small these organs already were at the time of ovarian implant. In 1913, however, he described seminal vesicle shrinkage—above and beyond the level of control castrates—in castrated guinea pigs with ovarian transplants.[60] Thus, the data on organ development were weak and contradictory. Nor does reciprocal inhibition obviously show why feminized males were smaller than their intact sisters; one can imagine other explanations for the fact that gonadal implants

TABLE 6.2 *Steinach's Experiments*

EXPERIMENT	ANIMAL	RESULTS	CONCLUSION	YEAR
Ovaries transplanted into young, male castrates	R, GP	· Transplant only "takes" in castrated males · ovary does not promote growth of penis, prostate, and other secondary characteristics · ovary causes penis to shrink (R but not GP) · ovary stimulates mammary growth (GP) · implanted males smaller and have more "feminine" hair structure (R & GP) · implanted males show female mating reflexes, maternal responses, and lack of masculine mating or aggressive impulses	· Sex hormone antagonism · since testis does not promote such growth,[a] ovary and testis secrete different substances · ovary inhibits male development · secretes female-specific substance · ovary inhibits male growth (size, hair quality) · hormones cause an "eroticization of the central nervous system"	1912[b]
Testes transplanted into spayed female	R, GP	· Mammaries and uterus remain undeveloped · indifferent anlage develop in a masculine direction · body and hair type more masculine · implanted females more aggressive, make sexual advances to females in heat	· Testis implants inhibit female characteristics · testis promotes male development · testis masculinizes growth patterns · hormones cause an "eroticization of the central nervous system" (p. 723)	1913[c]
Simultaneous transplant of ovaries and testes into castrated juvenile males	GP	· Many masculine secondary sex characteristics develop · functioning mammary glands develop	· Growth-inhibiting influences of ovary cannot assert self in presence of testes · ovaries can influence the development of female anlage and testes the development of male anlage	1913[d]

R = rats   GP = Guinea Pigs   a. Steinach 1910.   b. Steinach 1912.   c. Steinach 1913.   This paper also mentions the feminizing effects of X ray–induced ovarian hypertrophy in females later reported with Holznecht (1916), which is the nearest Steinach ever comes to examining the effects of ovaries in females.   d. Steinach 1913.

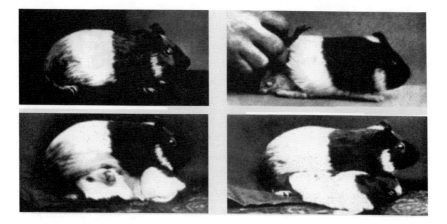

FIGURE 6.2A: Feminized nursing male guinea pig. *Left to right:* full profile of the animal;
demonstration of its male sex characters; feeding a young guinea-pig; feeding two young guinea pigs.

FIGURE 6.2B: Masculinization series: *Left to right:* masculinized sister,
castrated sister, normal sister, normal brother?

wouldn't "take" in the presence of their "opposite" number. For example, perhaps testes stimulated the activity of some other gland, thus producing an environment unfavorable to ovarian growth (and vice versa).[61]

Steinach's language of conflict not only reflected preexisting ideas about the natural relationship between male and female; it also set up an analytical framework that shaped his ongoing research interests and experimental designs. What would happen, he wondered, if both gonads were transplanted into a neutered host and "under equal and indeed equally unfavorable . . . conditions forced to battle it out"?[62] In some cases the ovary and testis blended into a single "ovo-testis" and when Steinach examined these tissues under the microscope he had "the impression that a battle raged between the two tissues."[63] When he turned to secondary sex characters, he found that bisexual animals, created via double transplants, looked like super-males: larger and stronger than their normal brothers. Steinach concluded that the growth-inhibiting influence of the female puberty gland, so evident in earlier experiments, could not assert itself with a male gland in place. That did not mean, however, that the testes neutralized the ovaries (this was not a rock-paper-scissors scenario). The bisexual animals had strong and masculine builds, but they also grew "strong, long, ready-to-suckle teats."[64] Steinach concluded that in his double transplants, all signs of the cross-gender inhibitory actions of the gonads had disappeared. The testis promoted male development, the ovaries promoted female organs, and "the inhibiting forces were unable to assert themselves."[65]

His data are compatible with the conclusions, but they do not point toward them indisputably. Philosophers call this *underdetermination*, and it is a common aspect of scientific fact-making. The organism's response to particular experimental interventions limits the permissible conclusions, but often not uniquely. Hence, scientists have several plausible interpretations from which to choose. Both the final choice and its reception beyond the boundaries of a single laboratory depend in part on nonexperimental, social factors.

Describing the interaction between ovarian and testicular secretions as antagonism (as opposed to inhibition), for instance, was scientifically plausible. At the same time, however, it also superimposed on the chemical processes of guinea pig and rat gonads a political story about human sex antagonism that paralleled contemporary social struggles. Physiological functions became political allegory—which, ironically, made them more rather than less credible, because they seemed so compatible with what people already "knew" about the nature of sex difference.

Or consider the choice to do double transplants.[66] Why did he not spend more time detailing the growth effects of male and female secretions in male and female bodies, choosing to learn more about what the hormones did in their "natural" locations? Part of the answer certainly lies in his commitment to the new experimental methods that demanded that normal processes be disrupted in order to learn about underlying events. But beyond that, having accepted the language of hormone antagonism, and working in a milieu in which both female masculinity and male femininity threatened social stability, the double-transplant experiments seemed both obvious and urgent. They spoke to the politics of the day. That Steinach's interests were shaped by political debates is made clearest, perhaps, by his focus on homosexuality.[67] In his animal studies, he believed he had found evidence that cross-transplantation of testes or ovaries led to altered sexual behavior. His animal research provided him with a foundation for a detailed theory of human homosexuality. Those with "periodic attacks of the homosexual drive," he argued, had gonads that alternated between the production of male and female hormones. In contrast, "constant homosexuals" developed opposite sexual organs when, at puberty, their male-hormone-producing tissue degenerated.[68] To confirm his theories, Steinach searched for "female tissue" in the testes of male homosexuals, and found both testicular atrophy and the presence of cells that he called F-cells, which he believed synthesized the female hormone.

Then he performed the ultimate test of his ideas. In collaboration with the Viennese surgeon R. Lichtenstern, he removed one testicle from each of seven homosexual men, implanting in its place testicles from heterosexuals.[69] (The implanted testis had been removed for medical reasons—for example they were unilaterally undescended. This left the heterosexual patient with one working testicle.) At first they euphorically reported success: the appearance of sexual interest in the "opposite" sex. As time went on, however, the failure of the operations became evident, and after 1923 no further operations were done.[70] Steinach's choice of experiments and choice of interpretation were influenced in part by the scientific traditions of the time and in part, of course, by the responses of the organisms under study, but also by the social milieu in which he lived, which defined male and female, homosexual and heterosexual, as oppositional categories—definitions that seemed both borne out and in need of scientific bolstering, given the political upheavals of the day.

Still, social milieus do not uniquely determine scientific facts. Indeed, in the United States and England, significant scientific opposition to the idea of sex-hormone antagonism emerged.[71] By 1915 British physiologists, representing the emerging field of endocrinology, and American geneticists seemed to have reached an impasse. The geneticists felt that chromosomes defined or controlled the development of sex. The endocrinologists, believed that hormones defined the man (or the woman). An American embryologist, Frank Rattray Lillie (1870–1947) broke the logjam with his work on freemartins, the sterile, masculinized female co-twin of a male calf. In 1914, the manager of Lillie's private farm sent him a pair of dead twin fetal calves, still enveloped in their fetal membranes.[72] One was a normal male, but the other's body seemed to mix together male and female parts. Intrigued, he continued to study the question, obtaining more material from the Chicago stockyards.[73] Fifty-five twin pairs later, Lillie concluded, in a now classic 1917 publication, that the freemartin was a genetic female whose development had been altered by hormones from her twin brother, following the commingling of the circulatory systems after the fusion of their initially separate placentas.[74] He thus demonstrated how the genetic view of sex worked in concert with the hormonal view. Genes started the sex determination ball rolling, but hormones did the follow-through work.

The naturally occurring freemartin in many ways resembled Steinach's gonad-implanted animals a fact that Lillie recognized immediately.[75] Lillie, though, was reticent about allowing his calves to speak about the nature of male and female hormones. He wondered, for example, why only the female twins were affected. Why didn't female secretions feminize the male, as they did in Steinach's rodents? Lillie proposed two possibilities. Perhaps there was "a certain natural dominance of male over female hormones," or, alternatively, the timing of male and female development differed.[76] If the testis began to function earlier in development than the ovary, perhaps in these unusual twins the male gonad secreted a hormone that transformed the potential ovary into a testis before it ever had the chance to make female hormones. Careful anatomical studies supported the timing hypothesis. "Hence," Lillie concluded, "there can be no conflict of hormones."[77] Finally, Lillie felt unable to conclude much about the nature of male hormone activity. Initially, it suppressed ovarian development; but did the later appearance of masculine characters such as an enlarged phallus or the growth of sperm-transport systems result from mere absence of ovarian tissue or from the positive stimulation offered by male hormones? He remained unsure.[78]

Such uncertainty prompted Lillie to "mildly suggest" to his protégé, Carl R. Moore, that he repeat Steinach's work.[79] Moore agreed, performing reciprocal transplants—ovaries into castrated juvenile male rats and testes into spayed juvenile females. Immediately, he encountered gender trouble. "It is unfortunate that the distinguishing somatic characters of the male and female rat are not more sharply marked," he wrote. "Steinach has placed considerable emphasis upon these weight and body-length relations of his feminized males and masculinized females as being indicative of maleness and femaleness. It is the opinion of this writer, however, that such slight differences . . . are but poor criteria of maleness and femaleness."[80] After further critical comments, Moore rejected weight and length as satisfactory measures of rat gender. Similarly, he found hair structure, skeletal differences, fat deposits, and mammary glands too variable to indicate gender reliably.[81]

But although Moore rejected Steinach's account of physical gender markers in rats, he argued that certain behaviors indicated clear links between hormones and sex differences. Feminized male rats (castrated with ovary transplants), he found, wanted to mother. They positioned themselves to allow newborns to suckle (even though they had no teats!) and aggressively defended the pups against intruders. Normal males and masculinized females showed no interest in the babies. Masculinized females did, however, show unusual behaviors of their own—they tried to mate with normal females— mounting and licking themselves between mounts, as would an intact male.

But even with behavioral markers, Moore observed, gender differences were not always obvious. "Steinach has described the docility of the normal female rat (does not fight, is easily handled, not so apt to bite or to resist handling, etc.) but here again the variations are too great to be of any practical value. Many females of this colony are decidely [sic] more pugnacious than males. In several cases, these, after repeated handling, would bite, scratch, and resemble any other than a meek and mild-tempered female of the colony."[82]

Moore pushed the issue.[83] In a series of papers emerging over a decade, he systematically dismantled Steinach's work (see table 6.3). Steinach had insisted that male rats and guinea pigs were much larger than females, and that castrated females grew larger than their normal sisters (see figure 6.2) if they had implanted testes. In contrast, castrated males with ovarian implants seemed actually to shrink, becoming smaller than even their normal sisters. Moore argued differently. He cited already published work showing that merely removing the ovaries caused female rats to grow larger. In his own experiments on rats, a sex difference in size remained even after gonad removal, suggesting that gonads had nothing to do with the fact that male rats were larger. His results with guinea pigs increased his skepticism. While early in development the growth rate of male and female differed, one year after birth males and females were the same size, and as time progressed females became the larger sex. Spayed females grew at the same rate as intact ones, and only the male showed an effect from castration—becoming smaller than intact males, spayed females, and intact females. Moore concluded his 1922 article with a direct jab at Steinach:

> Striking as may be the influence of the internal secretions of the sex glands on some characters in certain animal forms, it appears difficult and often impossible to discover characters in ordinary laboratory animals that are of sufficient difference and constancy in the two sexes to be capable of analysis by experimental procedure. And many of the characters cited in the literature supposedly offering a demonstration of the power of sexual secretions to effect modifications in the opposite sex fall to the ground if subjected to critical analysis. In the writer's opinion the character of weight reactions in guinea pigs belong to this group.[84]

Steinach, meanwhile, stood by his theories. He wrote that Moore misunderstood his work and that his opposition was "meaningless." In a last, dramatic experiment, he took advantage of advances in hormone chemistry (discussed in the next chapter), injecting ovarian and placental extracts containing active female hormone into young male rats (rather than using the

TABLE 6.3 *Moore's Transplantation Experiments*

EXPERIMENT	ANIMAL	RESULTS	CONCLUSION	SOURCE
Testis graft into spayed female (F); ovary graft into castrated male (M)	Rat	• Weight and hair quality very variable • M's with ovaries show maternal behavior • F's with testes show no maternal behavior • aggression present in normal M's and F's • F's with testes try to mate as M's	• Unreliable markers of sex differences • ovaries feminize male parental behavior • testes masculinize female parental behavior • aggression is a poor marker for sex differences • testes masculinize female mating behaviors	a
Compares growth in castrated M's and spayed F's over 180 days	Rat	• Castrated M's always weigh more than spayed F's	• Sex difference in size not related to gonadal secretions	b
Graft ovaries into M's with one intact testis and testes into F's with intact ovaries	Rat	• In grafted ovaries, follicles develop normally, but do not ovulate • in grafted testes, sperm-forming cells degenerate but not the Sertoli cells	• Both results dispute Steinach's claim that grafts succeed only when host gonad is removed—a cornerstone of his claim for hormone antagonism	c
Graft ovaries into M's with one intact testis and testes into F's with intact ovaries	Rat	• In grafted ovaries, follicles develop normally, but do not ovulate • in grafted testes, sperm-forming cells degenerate but not the Sertoli cells • male and implanted ovary develops normal penis, prostrate, and psychical characters (becomes a breeding male)	• Disputes Steinach's inability to graft ovaries in M's with testis intact • ignores result; not clear (to AFS) that the testis grafts truly succeeded • "presence of a normal testicle does not prevent . . . growth . . . of an ovary grafted into a male rat" (p. 167) • "there is no indication of an antagonism between the ovary or testis" (p. 169)	d

TABLE 6.3 *(continued)*

EXPERIMENT	ANIMAL	RESULTS	CONCLUSION	SOURCE
Castrated and spayed M's and F's; implanted ovaries and testes in "opposite sex"	Guinea pig	• Castration/spaying causes loss of sex drive • M with ovary graft shows mammary growth but no sign of psychical femininity • F with testis is aggressive, tried to mate with F in heat • F with testis: clitoris grows to resemble a penis	• Notes behavioral variability • "somatic modifying power of the ovary is unquestionable" (p. 384) • psychical behavior changed in a male direction • there are positive modifying effects of gonads, but no hormone antagonism	e
Castrated or spayed animals and compared growth curves	Guinea pig	• Unoperated M's, F's, and spayed F's reach same size within a year • castrated males remain smaller	• Long-term, spaying does not affect weight • castration causes a relative loss in weight compared to normal male • "the relative weight of a gp is worthless as an indication of its sexual condition" (p. 309)	f

a. Moore 1919. b. Moore 1919. c. Moore 1920. d. Moore 1921b. Moore summarizes this paper at its beginning: "It may be stated in advance that in the case of the white rat there is no evidence of an antagonism existing between the adult sex glands" (p. 131). e. Moore 1921c. f. Moore 1922. Moore cannot hide his feeling that Steinach is a bad experimenter: "Without further discussion of the above point, it should be clearly demonstrated to the reader that such a comparison of weights of two or three animals, chosen at random, is absolutely unreliable as evidence of their sexual nature. As the writer pointed out previously, the same criticism applies to rats" (p. 293).

less certain organ transplants). The result: an inhibition of the development of testicular growth, as well as the seminal vesicles, prostate, and penis, confirmed his view that female hormones antagonized male development.[85]

But in 1932 Moore and his collaborator, Dorothy Price, had repeated the experiment and gone him one better. First, they concluded that "contrary to Steinach . . . oestrin [the factor extracted from ovaries] is without effect upon the male accessories. It neither stimulates nor depresses them." Steinach's dismissal was merely the appetizer, however, to the main course: a new vision of hormone function. The debate with Steinach over hormone antagonism, they wrote, "forced us to extend our interpretations to link gonad hormone action with the activity of the hypophysis."[86] Moore and Price set forth several principles: (1) in their proper location, hormones stimulate the growth of reproductive accessories, but have no effects on organs of the opposite sex; (2) pituitary (hypophysis) secretions stimulate the gonads to make their own hormones; but (3) "gonads have no *direct* effect on the gonads of either the same, or the opposite, sex;" and (4) gonadal hormones from either sex depress pituitary activity, diminishing the amount of sex-stimulating substance flowing through the organism.[87] In short, Moore and Price demoted the gonads, making them one of several sets of players in a more complex system in which power was decentered. Gonads and pituitaries controlled one another's activities by a feedback system analogous to that of a thermostat.[88]

What should we make of this moment in hormone history? Did Moore's "good science" simply win out over Steinach's sloppy work?[89] Or does this dispute about the chemical sexing of the body reveal a more complex relationship between scientific and social knowledge? Certainly Moore relied more broadly on previously published work, provided more data, and seemed prepared to rule out what he called "the personal equation" by attending to problems of variability.[90] He clearly felt that Steinach chose his data to fit his theory, rather than building a theory from neutrally collected information. But Moore, although following a path that ultimately led to what we believe today to be the "right" answer, had his own unexplained experimental lapses. For example, he directly contradicted Steinach by showing that he could implant an ovary into a rat that retained its own testis. But when he extended this work to guinea pigs, he used only castrated or spayed animals to host his implants. Why? Did the guinea pig experiments work less well when he left the host's gonad intact? Or perhaps this experimental choice reflected Moore's lower level of interest in questions of sexual intermediacy and homosexuality.[91]

Or consider his results with testicular implants. These may not have provided a real test of Steinach's work. Steinach reported that his testicular implants contained a lot of interstitial cell growth (now known to be the source of testosterone production).[92] Moore's implants grew poorly, and seemed not to produce much in the way of interstitial cell growth. In fact, it is not clear that his testicular grafts were physiologically active, yet he concluded that they had no masculinizing effects. It seems possible, however, that the experiment simply failed. Without successful testicular grafts, there could be no test of this aspect of Steinach's work.

Right or wrong, the idea of sex antagonism, when imported into the arena of hormone biology, stimulated an enormously productive debate.[93] Moore and Price ultimately created an account that integrated elements of a "separate but equal" status with a sexually nonspecific role for gonadal hormones as powerful growth regulators. On the one hand, they argued that testis hormone (still unnamed in 1932) had promoted the growth of male accessory glands but had no direct effects on female parts. Similarly, the ovarian hormone (named oestrin under circumstances described in the following chapter) stimulated certain aspects of female growth but had no direct effects on male differentiation. On the other hand, both hormones could inhibit the pituitary in either sex, thereby indirectly suppressing gonadal hormone production. Moore and Price offered no socially redolent phrase (analogous to "hormone antagonism") to describe their theory, although they acknowledged that their work would be of interest to those concerned with intersexuality and hermaphrodites. Perhaps they came from a more cautious scientific tradition;[94] perhaps the crises of gender, class, and race had begun to wane by the time Moore and Price reached their conclusions.[95] Although answering such questions is a matter for future historical investigation, here I argue that reading gender into and from bodies is a more complex matter than merely allowing the body to speak the truth.

Although defeated by hormone biologists, the idea of hormone antagonism did not die. Steinach, himself, never abandoned it.[96] The medical endocrinologist and sexologist Harry Benjamin, who pioneered the idea of surgery as a cure for transsexualism,[97] praised the idea of sex hormone antagonism in Steinach's obituary. "Opposition to this theory of the physiological antagonism of sex hormones still exists," he wrote, "but remains unconvincing in view of many corroborating experiments."[98] Others also continued to subscribe to Steinach's model. In 1945, our pal de Kruif would refer to sex antagonism as a "chemical war between the male and female hormones . . . a chemical miniature of the well-known human war between men and women."[99] A scientific fact, once established, may sometimes be disproved in one field, remain a "fact" in others, and have a further life in the popular mind.

DO SEX HORMONES REALLY EXIST?
(GENDER BECOMES CHEMICAL)

Getting Ready for the Deluge

CARL MOORE'S AND DOROTHY PRICE'S WORK DID NOT END CONFUSION about the biological nature of masculinity and femininity, nor about the hormones themselves. During the decade preceding World War I, scientific insights accumulated slowly, but in the postwar era a new phase of research on hormones—later called the "endocrinological gold rush" and the "golden age of endocrinology"[1]—was made possible by interlocking networks of new scientific and political institutions in the United States and England. Once again, the social worlds that provided the context for scientific work are an essential part of the story; in particular, understanding the social context helps us see how our gendered notions about hormones have come to be.

World War I badly disrupted European science. Furthermore, physiologists and biochemists were immersed in the study of proteins. The chemicals used to extract and test proteins, however, did not work on gonadal hormones, which, as events would have it, belonged to a class of molecules called steroids—derivatives of cholesterol—(see figure 7.1). It was not until 1914 that organic chemists identified steroids and found ways to extract them from biological material (although biochemists had hit upon lipid extraction of gonad factors a couple of years earlier).[2] Gonadal hormones had been defined as chemical messengers, but before 1914 nobody knew how to study them as isolated chemical compounds. Instead, as we've seen, their presence could be surmised only through a complex combination of surgery and implantation. One skeptical scientist wrote that researchers in this early period relied on the testing of "ill-defined extracts on hysterical women and cachexic girls." By the end of World War I, "The social and scientific hopes of a medical endocrinology of human sex function and dysfunction had not been fulfilled."[3]

Despite the slow accumulation of scientific information about hormones,

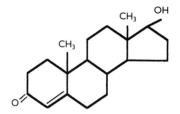

TESTOSTERONE

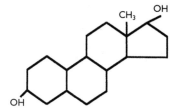

ESTRADIOL

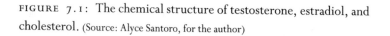
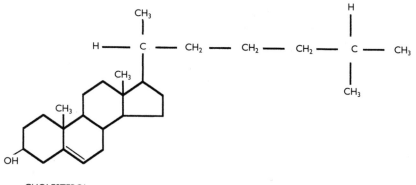

CHOLESTEROL

FIGURE 7.1: The chemical structure of testosterone, estradiol, and cholesterol. (Source: Alyce Santoro, for the author)

important changes were afoot. Alliances, intrigue, and melodrama began to link the work of biologists such as Frank Lillie with that of psychologists such as Robert Yerkes, philanthropists such as John D. Rockefeller, Jr., and several stripes of social reformer. These included women who sported the newly minted moniker "feminist,"[4] and (with some double casting) eugenicists, sexologists, and physicians. Hormones, represented on paper as neutral chemical formulae, became major players in modern gender politics.

The early twentieth century was an era of profound crossover between social and scientific knowledge, research and application. The new business managerial class looked to scientific wisdom to help make its workers and complex industrial production processes as efficient as possible;[5] social reformers looked to scientific studies for guidance in managing a host of social ills. Indeed, this was the era in which the social sciences—psychology, sociology, and economics—came into their own, applying scientific techniques to the human condition. Practitioners of the so-called hard sciences, meanwhile, also saw themselves as experts with something to say about social matters, devising scientific solutions for problems ranging from prostitution, divorce, and homosexuality to poverty, inequality, and crime.[6]

The intertwining biographies of the era's most passionate social reformers with those of its most prominent scientific researchers point to the complex connections between social and scientific agendas. Consider, for instance, the role that science and scientists played in the lives of some early-twentieth-century feminists and as they formulated their ideas about gender.[7] As a young woman, Olive Schreiner, the South African feminist and novelist, had a love affair with Havelock Ellis, one of sexology's founding fathers. His influence can be found in her well-known 1911 treatise, *Women and Labor,* in which Schreiner argued that economic freedom for women would lead to greater heterosexual attraction and intimacy.[8] Nor was Schreiner the only feminist Ellis affected. From 1913 to 1915 the birth control activist Margaret Sanger sought him out and became his lover, after traveling to Europe to avoid U.S. prosecution for sending birth control literature through the mail, and for defending an attempt to blow up the Rockefeller estate in Tarrytown, New York.[9] Like Schreiner, and like anarchists and free-love advocates such as Emma Goldman, Sanger promoted birth control by openly linking sexual and economic oppression. And like Goldman, Sanger risked imprisonment by defying the U.S. Comstock Laws that banned as obscene the distribution of birth control information and devices.[10]

Birth control, especially, was a cornerstone of feminist politics. One activist of the period wrote: "Birth control is an elementary essential in all aspects of feminism. Whether we are the special followers of Alice Paul, or Ruth Law or Ellen Key, or Olive Schreiner, we must all be followers of Margaret Sanger."[11] And Margaret Sanger strove mightily to influence the research paths of hormone biologists, hoping that their science could provide salvation for the millions of women forced to give birth too many times under terrible circumstances. Indeed, over the years she secured more than a little institutional funding for scientists willing to take on aspects of her research agenda. Part of the story of sex hormones developed in this chapter involves a struggle

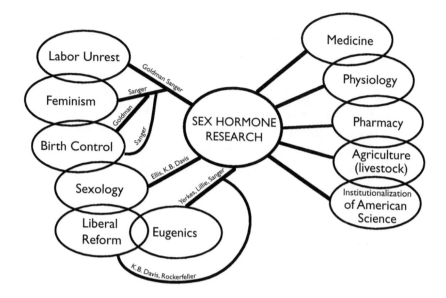

FIGURE 7.2: Personal and institutional social worlds. (Source: Alyce Santoro, for the author)

between scientists and political activists to secure one another's help while holding on to their specific goals—either promoting birth control or further-ing "pure" knowledge about sex hormones.

But even more than the personal channels between activists and scientists, unprecedented partnerships between philanthropist social reformers, social scientists, and government-fostered institutions made possible the develop-ment of new scientific knowledge about gender and hormones (see figure 7.2). In 1910, John D. Rockefeller, Jr., served as a member of a New York City grand jury investigating the "white slave trade."[12] Deeply affected by the deliberations, he organized and privately funded the Bureau of Social Hygiene (BSH). Over the following thirty years the BSH gave nearly six million dollars for the "study, amelioration, and prevention of those social conditions, crimes and diseases which adversely affect the well-being of society, with special ref-erence to prostitution and the evils associated therewith."[13] Among the many enterprises supported under the bureau's aegis was the Laboratory of Social Hygiene for the study of female offenders, designed and run by the feminist penologist and social worker Katherine Bement Davis (1860–1935).[14]

Davis had received a Ph.D. in political science from the University of Chi-cago. Her sociology professors there included Thorstein Veblen and George Vincent, who himself later headed the Rockefeller Foundation.[15] In 1901 she became Superintendent for Women at the newly opened Bedford Hills Reformatory for Women in New York State. There her pioneering work on female sex offenders drew Rockefeller's attention. In 1912 he bought land next to the reformatory and established the Laboratory of Social Hygiene. He called Davis "the cleverest woman I have ever met."[16] By 1917 she had become general secretary and a member of the board of directors of the Bureau of Social Hygiene. Her interests extended beyond the problems of criminality, and she used her influence to extend the BSH's work to include "normal" people, public health and hygiene, and a great deal of basic biological research into the physiology and function of sex hormones.[17]

But still, the scaffolding that supported the explosion of hormone research during the 1920s was not quite in place. In 1920 the psychologist Earl F. Zinn, a staff member for Dr. Davis's Bureau of Social Hygiene, proposed an extraordinary new effort to understand human sexuality.[18] His request for financial support to the National Research Council—the new research arm of the National Academy of Sciences—came directly to the attention of pioneer psychologist Robert M. Yerkes.[19] In October 1921, Yerkes convened a group of distinguished anthropologists, embryologists, physiologists, and psychologists, who encouraged the NRC to undertake a broad program in sex research. Attendees noted that "the impulses and activities associated with sex behavior and reproduction are fundamentally important for the welfare of the individual, the family, the community, the race."[20] With this urging and complete outside funding from the Bureau of Social Hygiene, the NRC's Committee for Research in Problems of Sex (CRPS) came into existence.

The new committee's scientific advisory committee contained Yerkes, the physiologist Walter B. Cannon, Frank R. Lillie, Katherine B. Davis, and a psychiatrist named Thomas W. Salmon. They were "a little group of earnest people . . . facing a vast realm of ignorance and half-knowledge, scarcely knowing even where or how to begin."[21] Their initial mission was to "understand sex in its many phases." The strategy was to launch "a systematic attack from the angles of all related sciences."[22] Within a year, however, Lillie had hijacked the committee, turning it away from a multidisciplinary approach and toward the study of basic biology.[23] Lillie listed the following topics for study, in order of importance: genetic aspects of sex determination, the physiology of sex and reproduction, the psychobiology of sex in animals, and, finally, human sexuality, including individual, anthropological, and psychosocial aspects. During its first twenty-five years, CRPS funded much of the major research in hormone biology, the anthropology of sexual behavior, animal psychology, and, later, the famed Kinsey studies. Yerkes chaired the committee for its entire time, while Lillie remained a member until 1937.

Lillie and Yerkes turned CRPS toward the support of research on hormone biology, arguing that basic biology was fundamental to the understanding of the complex problems that had originally stimulated Rockefeller to fund the BSH and CRPS. These two scientists, however, were no ivory tower nerds, unaware of or uninfluenced by the major social trends of their time. Indeed, they both shaped and were shaped by prevailing concerns about sexual politics and human sexuality. As head of the Marine Biological Laboratory in Woods Hole, Massachusetts, and Chairman of the Department of Zoology at the University of Chicago (from 1910 to 1931), Lillie was already a major player in the development of American biology. His work on freemartins placed him in the center of the emerging field of reproductive biology, and he planned to organize biological research at the University Chicago around the fields of embryology and sex research. Lillie intended to unify the various disciplinary strands in his department under a tent of social utility.

In particular, he strongly supported the eugenics movement, which he believed provided a scientific approach to the management of human social ills. Eugenicists warned that the nation's "racial stock" was endangered by the vast influx of Eastern European immigrants and by the continued presence in the population of former slaves and their descendants. To limit the burden placed on the white middle class by poverty and crime, believed to result from the "weak heredity" of immigrants and darker-skinned peoples, eugenicists advocated controlling the reproduction of the so-called unfit and promoted child-bearing among those thought to represent strong racial stock. A member of the Eugenics Education Society of Chicago, the general committee of the Second International Eugenics Congress (1923), and the advisory council of the Eugenics Committee of the United States, Lillie explained his views to the University of Chicago student newspaper: if "our civilization is not to go the way of historical civilizations, a halt must be called to the social conditions that place biological success, the leaving of descendants, in conflict with economic success, which invites the best intellects and extinguishes their families." In his plans to build an Institute of Genetic Biology Lillie elaborated on this theme: "We are at a turning point in the history of human society . . . the populations press on their borders everywhere, and also, unfortunately, the best stock biologically is not everywhere the most rapidly breeding stock. The political and social problems involved are fundamentally problems of genetic biology."[24]

Lillie's eugenics concerns allied him directly with two other activists in the eugenics movement, Margaret Sanger and Robert Yerkes. By the late teens, Sanger had traded in her radical feminist persona for a more conservative image. Sanger's (and the birth control movement's) waning interest in women's rights paralleled their increased rhetoric touting the value of birth control for lowering the birthrate among those seen to be of lesser social value. "More children from the fit, less from the unfit—that is the chief issue of birth control," Sanger wrote in 1919. Eugenicists wrote regularly for the American Birth Control League's magazine, the *Birth Control Review*, while during the 1920s only 4.9 percent of its articles focused on feminist issues.[25]

Like Lillie, Yerkes was a trained scientist. He had received his Ph.D. in psychology from Harvard in 1902, and for the next ten to fifteen years worked on organisms ranging from invertebrates such as earthworms and fiddler crabs to creatures with warm blood and backbones—including mice, monkeys, and humans. At Harvard, Yerkes crossed paths with Hugo Munsterberg, one of the early founders of industrial psychology, who promoted the idea of a natural hierarchy of merit. In a democracy such as the United States, this meant that social differences must come from inherent biological ones. Yerkes wrote: "in the United States of America, *within limits set by age, sex, and race*, persons are equal under the law and may claim their rights as citizens."[26]

In this early period of his work, Yerkes concentrated on measuring those limits. The future of mankind, he felt, "rests in no small measure upon the development of the various biological and social sciences . . . . We must learn to measure skillfully every form and aspect of behavior."[27] In the early twentieth century, when psychology was struggling for scientific respectability, Yerkes worked hard to demonstrate what the emerging discipline could offer.[28] When World War I came along, he seized the opportunity, convincing the army that it needed psychologists to rank the abilities of all soldiers for further sorting and task assignment. With Lewis M. Terman[29] and H. H. Goddard, two other proponents of mental testing, Yerkes turned the IQ test into an instrument that could be applied en masse, even to the many illiterate army recruits. By war's end, Yerkes had amassed IQ data on 1.75 million men and shown that the tests could be applied to large institutions. In 1919 the Rockefeller Foundation awarded him a grant to develop a standard National Intelligence Test. It sold five hundred thousand copies in its first year.[30]

CRPS, led by Lillie and Yerkes, was not the only organization focusing attention and money on the problems of hormone biology. Starting in the 1920s, Margaret Sanger and other birth control advocates actively began to recruit research scientists to their cause, in the hope that they could create a technological solution to the personal and social misery brought on by unwanted pregnancies.[31] Sanger enrolled her scientific supporters through the Birth Control Clinical Research Bureau (which she founded in 1923). Among the members of her professional advisory board were Leon J. Cole, a professor of genetics at the University of Wisconsin, who had close associations with

Lillie because of their mutual interest in freemartin research. The freemartin connection also extended to the British researcher F. A. E. Crew, whom Sanger had enlisted to try to develop a safe, effective spermicide.[32] Because the mailing of contraceptive information in the United States was illegal, the spermicide research went on in England, but not without the support of yet another private American agency—the Committee on Maternal Health, which obtained funds from the Bureau of Social Hygiene and funneled them to Crew.[33] From time to time, Sanger also directly received Rockefeller money for specific projects and conferences.

Thus the personal, institutional, research, financial, and ultimately political interests of the actors promoting and carrying out research in hormone biology overlapped in intricate ways. During the 1920s, with the backing of this strengthened research apparatus, scientists finally brought the elusive gonadal secretions under their control. Chemists used abstract notation to describe them as steroid molecules (see figure 7.1). They could classify them as alcohols, ketones, or acids. Yet as it became clearer that hormones played multiple roles in all human bodies, theories linking sex and hormones became more confusing, because the assumptions that hormones were "gendered" were already deeply ingrained. Today, it seems hard to see how asocial chemicals contain gender. But if we follow the hormone story from the 1920s until 1940, we can watch as gender became incorporated into these powerful chemicals that daily work their physiological wonders within our bodies.

As this high-powered, well-funded research infrastructure fell into place, the optimism became palpable. "The future belongs to the physiologist," wrote one physician. Endocrinology opened the door to "the chemistry of the soul."[34] Indeed, between 1920 and 1940 hormone researchers enjoyed a heyday. They learned how to distill active factors from testes and ovaries. They devised ways to measure the biological activity of the extracted chemicals, and ultimately, produced pure crystals of steroid hormones and gave them names reflecting their structures and biological functions. Meanwhile, biochemists deduced precise chemical structures and formulae to describe the crystallized hormone molecules. As hormone researchers took each step toward isolation, measurement, and naming, they made scientific decisions that continue to affect our ideas about male and female bodies. Those judgments, understood as "the biological truth about chemical sex," were, however, based on preexisting cultural ideas about gender. But the process of arriving at these decisions was neither obvious nor free from conflict. Indeed, by looking at how scientists struggled to reconcile experimental data with what they felt certain to be true about gender difference, we can learn more about how hormones acquired sex.

In 1939 CRPS supported the publication of the second edition of a book entitled *Sex and Internal Secretions*.[35] The volume represented much of what had been accomplished since the National Research Council, with Rockefeller support, began funding hormone research in 1923. True to Frank Lillie's program, most of this scientific book of 1,000-plus pages covered findings on the chemistry and biology of hormones, describing magnificent feats of discovery.

The collective efforts of hormone researchers seemed potentially to offer some radical ways to think about human sex. Lillie recognized as much.[36] "There is," he wrote in his introductory comments, "no such biological entity as sex. What exists in nature is a dimorphism . . . into male and female individuals . . . in any given species we recognize a male form and a female form, whether these characters be classed as of biological, or psychological or social orders. *Sex is not a force that produces these contrasts.* It is merely a name for our total impression of the differences." Sounding like today's social constructionists, Lillie reflected: "It is difficult to divest ourselves of the pre-scientific anthropomorphism . . . and we have been particularly slow in the field of the scientific study of sex-characteristics in divesting ourselves not only of the terminology but also of the influence of such ideas."[37]

Lillie, however, could not follow his own advice. Ultimately he and his colleagues proved unable to abandon the notion that hormones are linked essentially to maleness and femaleness. Even as he noted that every individual contained the "rudiments of all sex characters, whether male or female" and reiterated Moore's arguments against the concept of hormone antagonism, Lillie wrote of unique male and female hormones: "As there are two sets of sex characters, so there are two sex hormones, the male hormone . . . and the female."[38] Chapter after chapter in the 1939 edition of *Sex and Internal Secretions* discusses the surprising findings of "male" hormones in female bodies and vice versa, but Lillie never saw this hormonal cross-dressing as a challenge to his underlying notion of a biologically distinct male and female.

Today we still contend with the legacy of what Lillie called "pre-scientific anthropomorphism." When I searched a computer database of major newspapers from February 1998 to February 1999, I found 300 articles mentioning estrogen and 693 discussing testosterone.[39] Even more astonishing than the number of articles was the diversity of topics. Articles on estrogen covered subjects ranging from heart disease, Alzheimer's, nutrition, pain tolerance, immunity, and birth control to bone growth and cancer. Articles on testosterone covered behaviors such as asking directions (will he or won't he?), cooperation, aggression, hugging, and "female road rage," as well as a diverse range of medical topics including cancer, bone growth, heart disease, female impotence, contraception, and fertility. A quick perusal of recent scientific publications shows that, in addition to my newspaper list, researchers have learned that testosterone and estrogen affect brain, blood cell formation, the circulatory system, the liver, lipid and carbohydrate metabolism, gastrointestinal function, and gall bladder, muscle, and kidney activities.[40] Yet despite the fact that both hormones seem to pop up in all types of bodies, producing all sorts of different effects, many reporters and researchers continue to consider estrogen the female hormone and testosterone the male hormone.

Do all of these different organ systems deserve to be seen as sex characters by virtue of the fact that they are affected by chemicals that we have labeled sex hormones? Would it not make as much sense to follow the lead of one current research group, which suggests that these are "not simply sex steroid[s]?"[41] Why not redefine these molecules as the ubiquitous and powerful growth hormones they are? Indeed, why were these hormones not seen in this light from the very beginning? By 1939, scientists knew of the myriad effects of steroid hormones. But the scientists who first learned how to measure and name the testis and ovarian factors entwined gender so intricately into their conceptual framework that we still have not managed to pull them apart.

Purifying

In 1920, the male hormone turned boys into men, and the female hormone made women out of the girls. Feminists had won a major political victory in gaining the right to vote, and America had rid her shores of many foreign radicals. But out of this apparent calm, a new unrest soon broke loose. While feminism struggled to maintain its newfound identity, women's roles continued to change and sex hormones started to multiply.[42]

Three interrelated scientific questions took center-stage in the new research centers established in the 1920s. Which cells in the ovary or testis produced the substance or substances responsible for the sorts of effects Steinach, Moore, and others had observed? How could one chemically extract active hormones from these tissues? And finally, once one produced an active extract, could it be purified? In 1923, the biologists Edgar Allen and Edward A. Doisy, working at the Washington University Medical School in Saint Louis, announced the localization, extraction, and partial purification of an ovarian hormone.[43] Just six years earlier Charles Stockard and George Papanicolaou (for whom the Pap smear is named) had developed an easy method to monitor the estrus cycle of the rodent.[44] Allen and Doisy now used the technique to assess the potency of extracts obtained from ovarian follicle fluid removed from hog ovaries.[45] By injecting their extracts into spayed animals, they could try to induce changes in vaginal cells typical of rodents in estrus.

FIGURE 7.3: Pregnant women's urine has high concentrations of female hormone. (Source: Alyce Santoro, for the author)

First they showed that only substances from the fluid surrounding the oocyte in the ovary (called the follicular fluid) affected the estrus cycle. Not only did the spayed animals exhibit a change on the cellular level; they also changed behaviorally. Allen and Doisy noted that the animals displayed "typical mating instincts, the spayed females taking the initiative in courtship." Having established a reliable method to test for hormone activity—called a bioassay, because the test relies on the measurable response of a living organism—Allen and Doisy also tested extracts marketed by pharmaceutical companies. These turned out to have no bio-activity, justifying what they called a "well-founded skepticism concerning commercial preparations."[46]

Allen and Doisy had made a great start. They had a reliable bioassay. They had shown that the ovarian factor came from the liquid that filled the ovarian follicles (rather than, for example, the corpus luteum—another visible structure in the ovary). But purification was another story. Progress was slow at first because the raw material was available in only limited quantities and at "staggering" costs. About 1,000 hog ovaries yielded 100 cubic centimeters (about a fifth of a pint) of follicular fluid, at the cost of approximately $1.00 per milligram of hormone.[47] Then, in 1927, two German gynecologists discovered that urine from pregnant women has extremely high concentrations of the female hormone,[48] and the race was on, first to gain access to enough of that suddenly valuable commodity (figure 7.3) and then to isolate and purify

FIGURE 7.4: Men's urine has high concentrations of male hormone. (Source: Alyce Santoro, for the author)

the hormone. By 1929, two groups (Doisy's in St. Louis and Butenandt's in Göttingen)[49] had succeeded in crystallizing the urinary hormone and analyzing its chemical structure. But was it really the same as the hormone made in the ovaries? The final proof came in 1936, when Doisy and his colleagues used four tons of sow ovaries to produce a few crystallized milligrams of chemically identical molecules.[50] The urinary hormone and the ovarian factor were one and the same.

The isolation of the male hormone followed a similar track. First, scientists developed a method of assaying an extract's strength—the number of centimeters of regrowth over a specified time period of a cockscomb after castration (expressed in International Capon Units—ICU's for short). Then they had to search for an inexpensive hormone source. Again, they found it in cheap and ubiquitous pee. In 1931, Butenandt isolated 50 milligrams of male hormone from 25,000 liters of men's urine collected from Berlin's police barracks (figure 7.4).

Scientists had found male hormones in testes and men's urine, and female hormones in ovaries and the urine of pregnant women. So far so good; everything seemed to be where it belonged. But at the same time, other research was threatening to unravel Steinach's (and Lillie's) formulation that each hormone belonged to and acted in its respective sex, defining it biologically and psychologically. To begin with, it turned out that the male and female hormones came in several molecular varieties. There wasn't a single substance, but a family of chemically related compounds with similar, but not identical, biological properties. The two hormones became many.[51] Even more bewildering, there were scattered reports of female sex hormones isolated from males. In 1928, nine such reports appeared. The gynecologist Robert Frank wrote that he found this news "disconcerting" and "anomalous,"[52] while an editorial in the *Journal of the American Medical Association* called the report of female hormone bioactivity in "the testes and urine of normal men" "somewhat disquieting."[53] So convinced was the editorial writer of the unlikelihood of such a finding that he (I presume the pronoun is correct) questioned the validity of vaginal smear tests, which had become the standard of measurement in most of the laboratories working in female hormone purification.[54]

But the shock of finding female hormone in the testes and urine of "normal men" paled in comparison to another finding, published in 1934. In an article variously described by other scientists as "surprising," "anomalous," "curious," "unexpected," and "paradoxical,"[55] the German scientist Bernhard Zondek described his discovery of the "mass excretion of oestrogenic hormone in the urine of the stallion"—that cherished mythic symbol of virility.[56] In short order, others found female hormones where they ought not to be. In 1935, thirty-five such scientific reports appeared, followed the next year by another forty-four. The first report of male hormones in females appeared in 1931, and by 1939 had been confirmed by at least fourteen additional publications.[57]

Actually, the first report of cross-sex hormone action had appeared as early as 1921, when Zellner reported that testes transplanted into castrated female rabbits could cause uterine growth. But the full import of such work became apparent only when the hormones of one sex turned up in the bodies of the other. Not only did contrary sex hormones appear unexpectedly in the wrong sex: they also seemed able to affect tissue development in their opposite number! By the mid-1930s it was clear that male hormones could affect female development and vice versa. The anatomists Warren Nelson and Charles Merckel, for example, noted the "amazing effect" of an androgen in females. Administration of this "male" hormone stimulated mammary growth, enlargement of the uterus, "a striking enlargement of the clitoris," and "periods of prolonged estrus."[58]

At first, scientists tried to fit their findings into the old dualistic scheme. For a while they referred to the cross-sex hormones as heterosexual hormones. What did heterosexual hormones do? Nothing, some suggested. They're just nutritional by-products with no connection to the gonads. (So suggested Robert T. Frank, who claimed that "all ordinary foodstuffs contain female sex hormone. An average-sized potato contains at least 2 M. U. [mouse units].")[59] The further discovery that the adrenal glands could make hetero-sexual hormones provided brief relief for those who found their existence anxiety-provoking. At least the gonads themselves still functioned along strict gender lines, since cross-sex hormones did not originate with them![60] As an alternative to the nutritional hypothesis, Frank found the presence of female hormone in the bile "of great theoretical interest and is of importance in explaining the occurrence of [*sic*] female sex hormone reaction in the blood of males and in the urines [*sic*] of males."[61]

Finally, some argued that the heterosexual hormones indicated a diseased state. Although the men from whom estrogen was extracted appeared to be normal, they might, perhaps, be "latent hermaphrodites."[62] But given how widespread the findings were, that position was hard to maintain. All of which led to a crisis of definition: if hormones could not be defined as male and female by virtue of their unique presence in either a male or a female body, then how could scientists define them in a manner that would prove translat-able among different research laboratories as well as the pharmaceutical companies that wished to develop new medicines from these powerful bio-chemicals?

Measuring

Traditionally, scientists address such crises, which often plague new and rap-idly expanding fields, by agreeing to standardize. If only everyone used the same method of measurement, if only everyone quantified their products in the same manner, and if only all could agree on what to call these proliferating substances that had somehow escaped the boundaries of the bodies to which they were supposed to belong—then finally, scientists hoped, they could straighten out what had become a messy situation. In the 1930s, standardiza-tion became central to the agenda of sex hormone experts.

During the first three decades of the twentieth century, scientists had used a bewildering variety of methods to test for the presence of female hormones. Generally speaking, they removed the ovaries from test animals and then in-jected or implanted test substances or tissue parts and looked for the restora-tion of some missing function. But what missing function were they to look for, and how accurately could it be measured? Gynecologists focused on the organ dearest to their hearts—the uterus— measuring the impact of test substances on the increase in uterine weight in test animals following ovariec-tomy. Laboratory scientists, however, used a much wider variety of tests. They measured muscular activity, basal metabolism, blood levels of calcium and sugar, the feather coloration of domestic fowl, and the growth of mammary glands and the vulva.[63] Not to be outdone, psychologists used a variety of behaviors to assess the presence of hormonal activity: maternal nest building, sexual vigor and drive, and maternal behavior toward newborn pups.[64]

The question of how to measure and standardize the presence and strength of the female hormone was not merely academic. Many of the early research reports on measurement and standardization explicitly addressed the question of pharmaceutical preparations.[65] Drug companies, leaping on the opportunities presented by the advances in hormone research, began hawking preparations made from male or female sex glands. Especially popular was the idea that testicular hormones could slow or even reverse the aging process. One report on the extraction and measurement of testicular hormones attacked the use of preparations in humans, writing: "Thus far there is no indication that this product can be of any value in restoring 'vigor' to the aged or neurasthenic. However, if there is an indication for its use and if the dosage in man is comparable to that found in the capon, the daily injection equivalent for a 150 pound man would have to be an amount equivalent to at least 5 pounds of bulls' testes tissue or 2 gallons of normal male urine."[66]

This initial scientific skepticism had little impact on the hormone market. As late as 1939, companies such as Squibb, Hoffman-LaRoche, Parke-Davis, Ciba, and Bayer were marketing approximately sixty different ovarian preparations of doubtful activity.[67] Mindful of the debacle in 1899, in which the scientist Edouard Brown-Séquard (see chapter 6) had insisted that testicular extracts made him feel younger and more vigorous, only to withdraw his claims a few years later, gynecologists wanted to make sure such preparations had genuine therapeutic value.[68] So too did the pharmaceutical companies that funded basic research aimed at standardizing hormone preparations.[69] Finally, in 1932, an international group of gynecologists and physiologists met under the auspices of the Health Organization of the League of Nations to develop a standard measure and definition of the female sex hormone.

As one of the participants, A. S. Parkes, later noted, "the proceedings were unexpectedly smooth."[70] Participants in the First Conference on Standardization of Sex Hormones, held in London, agreed, for instance, that the term "specific oestrus-producing activity" is to be understood as the power of producing, in the adult female animal completely deprived of its ovaries, an accurately recognizable degree of the changes characteristic of normal oestrus. For the present, the only such change regarded by the Conference as providing a suitable basis for quantitative determination of activity in comparison with the standard preparation is the series of changes in the cellular contents of the vaginal secretion of the rat or mouse.[71] Amusingly, the tradition of using mice in America and rats in Europe led to two standard units: the M.U.(mouse unit) and the R.U. (rat unit).

Despite this agreement, the standardization conference did not satisfy everyone. By narrowing the definition of the female hormone to its actions in the estrus cycle, conference members had rendered less visible the hormone's other physiological effects. Dutch scientists, who had played a key role in the processes of identification and hormone purification, criticized what they called the "unitary school" of sex endocrinology.[72] A 1938 publication by Korenchevsky and Hall at the Lister Institute of London underscored their point. Estrogens could stunt growth, produce fat depositions, accelerate the degeneration of the thymus gland, and decrease kidney weight, the authors pointed out. These were, then, "not merely sex hormones, but . . . hormones also possessing manifold important effects on non-sexual organs."[73] Was it biologically correct to define the female hormone solely in terms of the mammalian estrus cycle? Didn't that divert attention from the many nonsexual roles in the body? Indeed, given that "sex hormones are not sex specific,"[74] could they legitimately continue to call these hormones sex hormones? Did sex hormones really exist?

The establishment of a standard measure and definition of the male sex hormone followed a similar pattern. Again, a wide variety of effects from substances injected after castration presented themselves as potential standards for the male sex hormone. The growth of the cockscomb as the standard unit of measure emerged victorious over other contenders—changes in the weight of the prostate, seminal vesicle, and penis to the size of the comb of the fowl, the horns of the stag, the crest of the male salamander, or the production of mating plumage in certain birds. The Second International Conference on Standardization of Sex Hormones, which took place in London in 1935, recognized the need for a mammalian assay, but concluded that an acceptable one did not exist. It was therefore "agreed that the International Standard for the male hormone activity should consist of crystalline androsterone and the unit of activity was defined as 0.1 mgm [*sic*]. This weight is approximately the daily dose required to give an easily measurable response in the comb of the capon after 5 days."[75] As with the female hormone, "all functions and processes that were unrelated to sexual characteristics and reproduction were dropped."[76]

Defining the female hormone in terms of the physiology of the estrus cycle, and the male hormone in terms of a secondary sex characteristic less central to the drama of reproduction, did not necessarily represent what we might call today "the best science." For both the male and the female hormones, more than one potentially accurate, easy-to-use assay contended for the role of standard-bearer. For example, the male Brown Leghorn chicken has black, round-tipped breast feathers, while its saddle feathers are orange, long, and pointed. The female Leghorn has salmon, round-tipped breast feathers and round-tipped, brown saddle feathers. Injecting female hormone into plucked capons produced the growth of new salmon-colored breast or brown saddle feathers. The experiments on this dimorphism "suggest that the production of brown pigments in the breast feather of the Brown Leghorn capon might be used as an indicator for the female hormone."[77] The test was easy, did not involve killing any of the test animals, and took only three days. In apparent contrast, the rat estrus assay required great care because of individual variability—a fact noted at the time it was chosen as the standard measure.[78]

In the case of the male hormone, a test based on prostate and seminal vesicle growth in castrated rats stood out as an alternative to the comb growth test. Korenchevsky and his colleagues distrusted the comb growth test for a number of reasons. They were especially disturbed that the urine of both pregnant and "normal" women stimulated comb growth to the same degree as did urine from men. "The specificity of the comb test, therefore, becomes doubtful" and should be "replaced by a test on the sexual and other organs of mammals."[79] On the other hand, Thomas F. Gallagher and Fred Koch, who developed the comb test, thought the mammalian assays had not proven their mettle. "We know of no studies," they wrote, "in which animal variability has been established by means of mammalian tests. Our opinion is that the mammalian tests thus far devised will be found to be either more time-consuming or less accurate or both."[80]

Thus, the choice of a measurement that distanced animal masculinity from reproduction, linked animal femininity directly to the cycle of generation, and made less visible the effects of these hormones on nonreproductive organs in both males and females was not inevitable. Nature did not *require* that these particular tests become the standard of measurement. Choices for particular measures were probably not made because of the gender views—either conscious or subconscious—of the main players. That would be far too simplistic an explanation. Being present at the conference may have carried a big advantage. Neither Korenchevsky nor Gustavson were present at either of the international standardization conferences, while Doisy and Koch, whose assay systems were chosen, were conference participants. At any rate, the hypothesis that gender ideology *caused* the particular assay choices would require more in-depth research to confirm or deny. Nevertheless, the choices made, for whatever reasons—rivalries, publication priority, convenience—have profoundly influenced our understanding of the biological nature of masculinity and femininity. These decisions shaped the sexing of the sex hormones. The normal processes of science—the drive to standardize, analyze, and accurately measure—gave us particular sex hormones at the same time that they proscribed the possible truths about how the body works, about how the body *does* gender.

From the moment the process of measuring male or female hormones was standardized, a set of molecules of a known chemical composition and structure officially became sex hormones. From that time on, any physiological activity those hormones had were, by definition, sexual, even though the "male" or "female" hormones affected tissues such as bones, nerves, blood, liver, kidneys, and heart (all of which was known at the time). That hormones had such wide-reaching effects didn't change the association of hormones with sex. Instead, these non-reproductive tissues became sexual by virtue of their interaction with sex hormones. The scientific definitions of standard mouse, rat, and comb units seemed to echo on a molecular level the notion of human makeup that Sigmund Freud had insisted on: sex was at the very center of our beings.

Naming

If choosing how to standardize hormonal measurements was crucial in consolidating their identities as sexual substances, so too was choosing what to call them. It was no random act of scientific purity to name male hormones "androgens," female hormones "estrogens," the hormone isolated first from urine collected in a police barracks (but later identified as the culprit found in the testes) "testosterone" (chemically speaking—a ketone steroid from the testis), and the hormone first crystallized from the urine of pregnant women (and later shown to exist in hog ovaries) "estrogen" or, more rarely, estrone (chemically speaking, a ketone related to estrus). Rather, these names became the standards only after considerable debate. They both reflected and shaped ideas about the biology of gender in the twentieth century.

During the early days of sex hormone research, investigators showed remarkable restraint. They did not name or define. Referring only to the "male hormone" and the "female hormone," or occasionally their tissue of origin (as in the "ovarian hormone"), they patiently awaited further clarification.[81] By 1929, a number of contender names for the female hormone had been floated. The words *ovarin, oophorin, biovar, protovar, folliculin, feminin, gynacin,* and *luteovar* all referred to site of origin. In contrast, *sistomensin* (making the menses subside), *agomensin* (stimulating the menses), *estrous hormone,* and *menoformon* (causing the menses) all referred to proposed or demonstrated biolog-

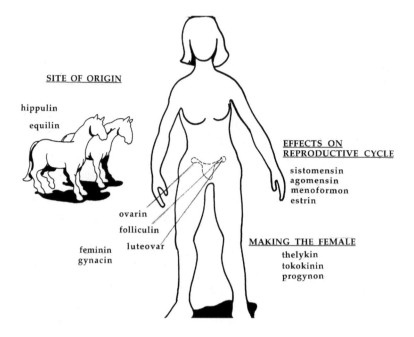

FIGURE 7.5: Naming the female hormone. (Source: Alyce Santoro, for the author)

ical actions. Some researchers preferred Greek constructs, hence the words *thelykin* (thelys = the feminine: kineo = I set going), *theelin, theeol,* and for the male hormone, *androkynin. Tokokinins* signified "the procreative hormone (Zeugungshormon) applicable to both male and female" (see figure 7.5). But the definitive moment had not arrived. Frank, for example, felt that "the term female sex hormone covers all needs until we know more about the substance itself. The term is applicable to any substance which either increases or actually establishes feminine characteristics and feminineness."[82]

In the early 1930s the terms male and female hormone began to loosen their grip. In 1931, the author of a research paper referred to an "ambosexual" hormone (one having actions in both sexes); in 1933, a researcher noted the "*so-called* female sex hormone." In 1937, the *Quarterly Cumulative Index Medicus* introduced the terms *androgens* (to build a man) and *estrogens* (to create estrus) to its subject index, and within a few years these words had taken hold.[83] But not without some jockeying and debate. Two interrelated problems emerged: what to call the male and female hormones (of which it was then known there were clearly several), and how to refer to their contrary locations and actions (female hormones in stallion urine).

Using the word *estrus* (meaning "gadfly," "crazy," "wild," "insane") as the root on which biochemists built female hormone names happened over drinks "in a place of refreshment near University College," when the endocrinologist A. S. Parkes and friends coined the term *estrin*.[84] One of the participants in this brainstorming session found the choice "a happy thought which gave us a satisfactory general term and a philologically manageable stem upon which to base all the new nouns and adjectives that physiologists and organic chemists soon needed."[85] In 1935, the Sex Hormone Committee of the Health Organization of the League Nations chose the name "estradiol" for the substance isolated from sow ovaries, thus linking the concept of estrus with the terminology of the organic chemist.

By 1936, scientists had crystallized at least seven estrogenic molecules. The Council on Pharmacy and Chemistry of the American Medical Association wrestled with what to call them. With Doisy on the committee, there was a lot of sympathy for calling the female hormone *theelin*, the word he had coined. But it turned out that Parke, Davis and Company had already marketed their purified estrin under the "theelin" trademark, thus making the word unavailable for general use. That made using the root *estrus* the next best choice. Unfortunately, Parke, Davis and Company had also trademarked the word *estrogen*, but on request from the Council on Pharmacy and Chemistry, the company gave up its proprietary rights to the name, and the Council adopted the word as a generic term.[86] The Council accepted the common names *estrone, estriol, estradiol, equilin*, and *equilenin* (the latter two being chemicals found in mare's urine). They also retained the names *theelin, theeol*, and *dihydrotheelin* as synonyms for *estrone, estriol,* and *estradiol*.[87]

The die had been cast, although for a few more years people would continue to suggest modifications. Parkes, for instance, with an ever-growing awareness of the diverse biological effects of the female hormone complex, proposed a new term, which would make the naming system for male and female hormones parallel. "One hesitates to advocate the use of new words," he wrote, "but obvious anomalies are becoming evident in the description of certain activities of the sex hormones." The terms *androgenic* and *estrogenic*, he remarked, had been introduced to "promote clear thinking and precision of expression . . . but it is now evident that [the terms] are inadequate." The word *estrogenic*, he argued, should apply only and literally to substances that produce changes in the estrus cycle. Noting that the ability of estrogen to feminize bird plumage, for example, could hardly be called estrogenic, in the literal meaning of the word, Parkes proposed that *gynoecogenic* be "used as a general term to describe activity which results in the production of the attributes of femaleness."[88] But his proposal came too late. The nonparallel nomenclature—*androgens* for the male hormone group, *estrogens* for the collection of female hormones—took hold. Eventually, terms with the root *thelys*, which denoted not the reproductive cycle but the more general concept of the feminine, dropped from common usage, and thus the ideal of female hormones became inextricably linked to the idea of female reproduction.

Naming the male hormone group, meanwhile, had been fairly simple. A review of androgen biochemistry did not even note the naming question, although the companion article on the biochemistry of estrogenic compounds devoted four pages to nomenclature.[89] With only one exception, the male hormone name simply combined the Greek root for *man* ("andrus") with the technical naming systems of the biochemist. Only for the molecule we now call testosterone (and its derivatives) did the more specific term, *testis*, provide the etymological building block.

By the mid-1930s then, scientists had crystallized the hormones, agreed on the best way to measure them, and named them. Only one problem remained. If androgens made men and estrogens produced a distinctly female mating frenzy, then how ought these hormones to be categorized when they not only showed up in the wrong body but seemed to have physiological effects as well? Korenchevsky and co-workers referred to such hormones as "bisexual" and proposed to group both androgens and estrogens according to this property. Only one hormone (progesterone—from the corpus luteum) could they envision as purely male or female. They designated a second group as "partially bisexual," some with chiefly male properties, others with predominantly female ones. Finally, they proposed the existence of "true bisexual hormones," ones that cause a return to "the normal condition of all the atrophied sex organs . . . to the same degree in both male and female rats."[90] Testosterone belonged to this group.

In 1938 Parkes suggested a different tack. He disliked the term *bisexual* because it implied "having sexual feeling for both sexes" and proposed instead the term *ambisexual*, which could, he felt, "be applied with perfect propriety to substances . . . which exhibit activities pertaining to both sexes."[91] These fine distinctions never took hold. Even today the classification question dogs the steps of biologists, especially those interested in correlating hormones with particular sexual behaviors.

Gender Meanings

We can see from this story of hormone discovery that the interchanges between social and scientific gender are complex and usually indirect. Scientists struggled with nomenclature, classification, and measurement for a variety of reasons. In scientific culture, accuracy and precision have high moral status, and as good scientists, using the highest standards of their trade, endocrinologists wanted to get it right. Yet in terms of nomenclature, only Parkes seems to have come up with the "correct" proposal, and his views fell by the way-side. One reason for this (but not the only one) is that in the struggle to get it right, "it" was a loaded term—denoting a variety of social understandings of what it meant in the years 1920 to 1940 to be male or female.

Whatever "it" was defined both biological and social normality. For example, Eugen Steinach proposed that hormones kept underlying bisexual potentials from appearing, abnormally, in the wrong body.[92] Males made only male hormones that antagonized or suppressed female development even in the presence of female hormone. Females made female hormones that antagonized or suppressed male development even in the presence of male hormones. Each sex normally had its own sphere. Steinach's views influenced more than a decade of hormone researchers, including Lillie. But as it became clear that the body regulates hormones through complex and balanced cycles that involve feedback with the pituitary gland,[93] the notion of direct hormone antagonism gave way, even though scientists such as Lillie held on to the notion of separate spheres.[94]

Because of their loyalty to a two-gender system, some scientists resisted the implications of new experiments that produced increasingly contradictory evidence about the uniqueness of male and female hormones. Frank, for example, puzzling at his ability to isolate female hormone from "the bodies of males whose masculine characteristics and ability to impregnate females is unquestioned," finally decided that the answer lay in contrary hormones found in the bile.[95] Others suggested that the finding of adrenal sex hormones could "save" the hypothesis of separate sex-hormonal spheres. In a retrospective piece, one of the Dutch biochemists wrote: "By proposing the hypothesis of an extra-gonadal source to explain the presence of female sex hormones in male bodies, scientists could avoid the necessity to attribute secretion of male sex hormones to the ovary."[96]

But scientists are a diverse lot, and not everyone responded to the new results by trying to fit them into the dominant gender system. Parkes, for example, acknowledged the finding of androgen and estrogen production by the adrenal glands as "a final blow to any clear-cut idea of sexuality."[97] Others wondered about the very concept of sex. In a review of the 1932 edition of *Sex and Internal Secretions* (which summarized the first ten years of advances funded by the Committee for Research in Problems of Sex), the British endocrinologist F. A. E. Crew went even further, asking "Is sex imaginary? . . . . It is the case," he wrote, "that the philosophical basis of modern sex research has always been extraordinarily poor, and it can be said that the American workers have done more than the rest of us in destroying the faith in the existence of the very thing that we attempt to analyze." Nevertheless, Crew believed that science would ultimately define sex, "the object of its searchings," instead of vice versa. "If in a decade so much has been disclosed," he wrote, "what shall we not know after a century of intelligent and industrious work?"[98] Despite growing scientific evidence to the contrary, sex *must* exist.

Scientists struggled to understand the role of hormones in constructing sex difference, in a cultural milieu awash with changes in the meaning and structure of gender systems. In 1926, Gertrude Ederle stunned the world by becoming the first woman to swim the English Channel, besting the preexisting men's record in the process. Two years later, Amelia Earhart became the first woman to fly across the Atlantic. While the symbols were dramatic, far-reaching changes proceeded a bit more doggedly. From 1900 to 1930, gainful employment of married women outside the home doubled, but only to about 12 percent, and in the decade following the passage of the 19th Amendment, feminist efforts to infiltrate all corners of the labor market remained an uphill struggle.

But while resistance to complete economic equality persisted, during the period from 1920 to 1940, a major reconceptualization of the family, gender, and human sexuality took place. For example, in Kinsey's famous survey, only 14 percent of women born before 1900 admitted to premarital intercourse before the age of twenty-five; for those born in the first decade of the twentieth century, the percentage rose to 36.[99] Feminism, the growing popularity of Freudian psychology, the new field of sexology, and the increasing knowledge about sex hormones and internal secretions all "swelled a tide of scorn for 'Victorian' sexual morality."[100]

Diversity in scientific voices paralleled diversity within feminism itself. For example, some feminists argued that women could labor in any field on a par with men; others thought that their special reproductive differences made them deserving of protective legislation governing their hours and the degrees of danger in which their jobs might place them.[101] By the end of the 1930s feminists faced a dilemma of their own rhetorical making (one, I might add, with which contemporary feminism also struggles): if women and men were complete equals, then organizing as members of one or the other sex made little sense. If, on the other hand, they were truly different, then just how far might one push the demand for equality? In 1940, Eleanor Roosevelt summed up the problem with precision: "women must become more conscious of themselves as women and of their ability to function as a group. At the same time they must try to wipe from men's consciousness the need to consider them as a group or as women in their everyday activities, especially as workers in industry or the professions."[102]

Amid such gender turmoil, it was never possible to resolve the identity of the sex hormones. In 1936, John Freud, a Dutch biochemist working on hormone structure, suggested abandoning the entire concept of sex hormones. Estrogen and its relatives acted as "growth-promoters to the smooth muscle, stratified epithelium and some glandular epithelia of ectodermal origin."[103] Envisioning hormones as catalysts would make it "easier to imagine the manifold activities of each hormonal substance." He imagined that "the empirical concept of sex hormones will disappear and a part of biology will definitely pass into the property of biochemistry."[104]

While we should honor (albeit with some feminist hindsight) the intellectual heritage of hormone research, starting with Berthold's experiments on gonad implants in capons, the time has come to jettison both the organizing metaphor of the sex hormone and the specific terms *androgen* and *estrogen*. What could we put in their stead? Our bodies make several dozen different, but closely related and chemically interconvertible, molecules belonging to the chemical group we call steroids. Often, these molecules reach their destination via the circulatory system, but sometimes cells make them right at the site of use. Hence, it is usually appropriate to call them hormones (given the definition that a hormone is a substance that travels through the bloodstream to interact with an organ some distance from its place of origin). So, for starters, let's agree to call them *steroid hormones* and nothing else. (I'm willing to keep their technical biochemical designations, provided we remember the etymological limits of the naming system.)

A variety of organs can synthesize steroid hormones, and an even wider variety can respond to their presence. Under the right circumstances these hormones can dramatically affect sexual development at both the anatomical and the behavioral level. They are present in different quantities and often affect the same tissues differently in conventional males and females. At the cellular level, however, they can best be conceptualized as hormones that govern the processes of cell growth, cell differentiation, cell physiology, and programmed cell death. They are, in short, powerful growth hormones affecting most, if not all, of the body's organ systems.

Retraining ourselves to conceptualize steroid hormones in these terms provides us with important opportunities. The theoretical near-unity achieved by hormone biologists at the end of the 1930s is dead. If any possibility exists for obtaining a meaningful, all-encompassing theory of action and physiological effect of these cholesterol-based molecules, we must leave the sex paradigm behind. Second, if we are to understand the physiological components of sexual development, and of mating-related animal behaviors, we must be willing to break out of the sex hormone straitjacket, looking at the steroids as one of a number of components important to the creation of male, female, masculinity, and femininity. Not only will we then start to see non-steroid, physiological constituents of such development, but we will become able to conceptualize the ways in which environment, experience, anatomy, and physiology result in the behavior patterns that we find interesting or important to study.

One of the lessons of this chapter is that social belief systems weave themselves into the daily practice of science in ways that are often invisible to the working scientist. To the extent that scientists proceed without seeing the social components of their work, they labor with partial sight. In the case of sex hormones, I suggest that widening our scientific vision would change our understanding of gender. But of course, such changes can occur only as our social systems of gender change. Gender and science form a system that operates as a single unit—for better and for worse.

THE RODENT'S TALE

Using Hormones to Sex the Brain

BY THE 1940S, HORMONE BIOLOGISTS, BIOCHEMISTS, AND REPRODUC-
tive endocrinologists had identified, crystallized, named, and classified a host
of new hormones. They had also outlined the roles of hormones—both gonadal and pituitary—in the control of the reproductive cycle, leaving researchers poised to look more seriously at the possibility that hormones regulated human behavior. The study of the chemical physiology of behavior came
into its own, beginning in the late 1930s, as the old institutional and funding
coalitions that had facilitated and directed the blossoming of hormone biology
experienced a sea change.[1]

Until 1933, the Rockefeller Foundation had funneled its support of sex
research through the social service-oriented Bureau of Social Hygiene, but
then the Foundation took over direct funding of the Committee for Research
in Problems of Sex (CRPS).[2] The transfer marked a transition from the development of national science in direct service to social change to one in which
the scientists themselves developed research agenda, which appeared, at least
on the surface, to be motivated solely by the ideal of knowledge for knowledge's sake.[3] As early as 1928, CRPS had signaled this change in its new five-
year plan. "Modern science," CRPS committee members had written, "particularly experimental medicine, has shown that the greatest benefits to mankind have come from fundamental researches, the implications of which could
not be foreseen. . . . Pressing social and medical problems" would most likely
only be solved by first obtaining a scientific understanding of human sexuality.[4]

The Rockefeller Foundation took over the Committee for Research in
Problems of Sex just as the conservative engineer Warren Weaver became
the full-time director of Rockefeller's Division of Natural Sciences. Weaver

consolidated a growing movement among biologists who argued that the next round of great advances would come from the application of the laws of physical science to biology. He began his tenure by enthusiastically emphasizing the close relationship between psychobiology and his arena in the natural sciences:

> Can man gain intelligent control of his own power? Can we develop so sound and extensive a genetics that we can hope to breed, in the future, superior men? Can we obtain enough knowledge of physiology and psychobiology of sex so that man can bring this pervasive . . . highly dangerous aspect of life under rational control? Can we unravel the tangled problem of the endocrine glands, and develop, before it is too late, a therapy for the whole hideous range of mental and physical disorders which result from glandular disturbances? . . . Can we, in short, create a new science of Man?[5]

Soon, however, Weaver's interest in psychobiology waned, while his focus on the newly named area of molecular biology waxed. Between 1934 and 1938, support for those fields of endocrine and reproductive biology with practical or clinical application declined, and in 1937 an official division of labor between the natural and the medical sciences became part of the Foundation's formal structure. Endocrinology and sex biology left Weaver's purview, enabling him to concentrate on the development of genetics, cell physiology, and biochemistry.[6]

By the 1940s, relatively little CRPS funding went to research in basic hormone biology. "Although much . . . remained to be learned about the relation of the hormones to sex behavior, it seemed that emphasis need no longer be placed upon the hormones themselves."[7] More and more, the committee funded research into the relationships among the hormones, the nervous system, and behavior. While Terman's work on masculinity, femininity, and the family continued to receive funding until after World War II, Yerkes and his heir-apparent, C. R. Carpenter, had turned to the study of dominance and sexual hierarchies in semiwild primate populations.[8] At the same time new voices—including that of the young Frank A. Beach, who was to become dean of the next generation of animal psychologists—appeared on the scene, a stage now set to apply the insights of science to the complexities of animal behavior. This new crop of researchers worked originally in the fields of embryology, comparative animal psychology, and ethology.[9] They could see the power of the new research tools—purified hormone preparations, using surgery to remove particular endocrine organs—and had at least a general idea of which organs made which hormones.[10] In the beginning, they studied a variety of species, but as time passed, the laboratory rodent—especially the rat and the guinea pig—emerged as premier models with which to explore hormones and sex-related behaviors in mammals.[11]

How did scientific experiments on hormones and behavior shape rodent masculinity and femininity from 1940 to the present? Often, culturally promoted ideas about human masculinity and femininity seemed to parallel the rat experiments. But I claim neither that culture functioned as puppeteer to the science, nor that our social structures were mere marionettes animated by the nature of bodies under study or scientists' findings about hormones. Instead, I see a fertile field of co-production—what the literary critic Susan Squier calls a "a thick and busy trading zone of boundary crossing and relationship."[12]

In this chapter I follow the journey of the masculine and feminine rodent as it scurries through Scienceville. Just as I argued that different medical approaches to intersexuality lead to differently embodied gender in humans, here I suggest that we can do a different, and I believe better, job of envisioning the manly—and not-so-manly—rat and, by extension, a different and better job of envisioning human sexuality without falling into the nature/nurture abyss.

If Hormones Make the Man, What Makes the Woman?

Harry Truman ended World War II by dropping two atomic bombs. As the cold war grew, American kids learned how to protect themselves from the A-bomb: duck and cover. Some parents built bomb shelters and debated the ethics of turning away or even shooting their less visionary neighbors when the time came. Gender politics became bound up with the new language of national security. As several historians have shown, this was an era in which stable domestic arrangements—that is, "traditional" family structures—were equated with and thought to guarantee domestic (and national) stability.

The equation of sexual order and nuclear containment worked both ways. Communist atomic power was regarded as a direct threat to the stability of American families. In 1951, the Harvard physician Charles Walter Clarke warned that atomic attack would destroy the normal social supports for family and community life, opening "the potential for sexual chaos." Health professionals, he suggested, should stockpile an ample supply of penicillin to treat a postatomic epidemic of venereal disease, while preparing for "a vigorous repression of prostitution, and measures to discourage promiscuity, drunkenness and disorder."[13]

Sexual chaos even seemed to threaten national security from within. In 1948, for example, Guy Gabrielson, national chairman of the Republican party, wrote that "sexual perverts" had "infiltrated the government" and were "perhaps as dangerous as the actual Communists."[14] Not only were homosexuals weak willed, unmanly, and thus vulnerable to Communist infiltration and threats, but their lifestyle (to coin a more modern usage) mocked the traditional family, weakening it in the same way that Communists, who urged that political loyalties supersede blood ties, sought to undermine capitalist civilizations. Furthermore, the American male was having a masculinity crisis—a bad hair day writ large. As the historian Arthur Schlesinger, Jr., wrote at the time, the symptoms included an alarming merging of gender roles both at home and at work. A fascination with homosexuality, "that incarnation of sexual ambiguity," and with "the changing of sex—the Christine Jorgenson phenomenon—" expressed "a deeper tension about the problem of sexual identity."[15]

Postwar ideologues insisted that national security depended on women and men taking up their appropriate domestic roles. Women, many suggested, were naturally suited to roles as wives and mothers. In language that closely resembled the words used by contemporary biologists to describe female differentiation in the embryo, a 1957 *Ladies' Home Journal* article entitled "Is College Education Wasted on Women?" made the point clearly. College was a good place for women to look for husbands, but "certainly the happiest women have never found the secret of their happiness in books or lectures. They do the right thing instinctively."[16]

In contrast, and also in language that bore a striking resemblance to contemporary writings about the biology of male development, men apparently needed substantial support and reassurance in order to fulfill their natural roles as breadwinners and husbands. Postwar propagandists fretted about the feminizing effects of a new and growing sector of the economy—the white-collar worker, the organization and advertising man—who sat at a desk all day, physically inactive and under great stress. One typical magazine article urged women to build up their mates' sense of manliness, to consider that men who "spend their lives behind a big mahogany desk, or . . . in a lesser job," need to "escape the doubts the best of them entertain about themselves."[17] They want a woman who can reassure them of their own masculinity by choosing them despite being attractive enough to interest other men.

But the era's experts also emphasized that what men did in the domestic realm was crucial to maintaining their masculinity and building a manly next generation.[18] Paternal intervention in child rearing was essential if one was to avoid raising a sissy boy. A 1950 article in *Better Homes and Gardens* began, "Are we staking our future on a crop of sissies? . . . You have a horror of seeing your son a pantywaist, but he won't get red-blooded and self reliance [*sic*] if you leave the whole job of making a he-man of him to his mother."[19] A mother could "instinctively" raise a daughter, but her innate response to protect her son from harm interfered with his developing independence and manliness.[20] Fatherhood itself became a new badge of manliness, even though parenting was not thought to come as naturally to men as to women. Men, the popular wisdom went, had to attend classes on marriage and the family to learn from the experts how to do it right.

Despite the widespread ideology of sexual and gender role conformity that prevailed in films, magazines, government policies, and school curricula, the decade we tend to remember as the "Leave It to Beaver" era saw its share of challenges to mainstream notions of gender. The publication of the Kinsey reports, for example, challenged accepted views of American sexual behavior, by suggesting that homosexual encounters, premarital sex, and masturbation were widespread and biologically normal.[21] With the 1953 founding of *Playboy* magazine, Hugh Hefner created a cultural space for the philandering yet highly masculine bachelor and a model of sorts for the sexually liberated woman. And, during the late 1950s, the Beat Generation challenged conventional definitions of masculinity at the same time that underground homosexual rights movements slowly emerged from obscurity.

Scientists who studied animal sexuality in this era, then, worked with complex cultural stock. On the one hand, they could formulate their metaphors and theories in terms of mainstream accounts of gender. On the other, the very existence of countercurrents that challenged such standard viewpoints made it possible for some scientists to envision new ideas about animal sexuality. Consider studies on the development in fetuses of anatomical differences between males and females. In 1969, the French embryologist Alfred Jost summarized the conclusions of his previous twenty years of work in this field: "Becoming a male is a prolonged, uneasy and risky adventure; it is a kind of struggle against inherent trends toward femaleness."[22] All males, be they rats, guinea pigs, or humans, had to strive against an inner femininity. Just as the advice magazines of the 1950s had warned, the danger of sissydom lurked beneath the masculine surface. How did Jost come to this conclusion, which closely echoed the gender anxieties of the period? How did this conclusion, gained from careful studies of male and female embryos, translate into research on the relationship between hormones and masculine and feminine behaviors?

When, in 1947, the thirty-two-year-old Jost initiated a series of publications describing his experiments on the development of male and female anatomy in rabbits and rats, he entered into a debate about whether androgens and estrogens were equal-opportunity hormones.[23] Researchers in the previous decade had agreed that injecting testosterone or other androgens into developing females masculinized their internal ducts and external genitalia. More controversial was the question of whether estrogens exerted a parallel effect on male embryos. Eugen Steinach's earlier models of male and female hormonal physiology framed the discussion. The Scottish researcher B. P. Wiesner, for example, found that estrogens (he still called them *thelykinins*) injected into newborn male rats (whose external genitals are poorly developed at birth) inhibited penile growth, producing feminized males. He believed, however, that the estrogen inhibited the testis rather than acting directly on the genitalia. He thus rejected a di-hormonic theory that animals acquired masculinity and femininity through the action of equal but opposite-acting hormonal systems. Wiesner wrote: "[the mono-hormonic theory] recognizes the absolute dominance of male hormone in developmental processes and it describes the conditions under which female differentiation may occur as the *absence of any*, rather than the presence of a *specific, sex hormone.*"[24]

In contrast, researchers at Northwestern University Medical School's Department of Physiology and Pharmacology argued that testosterone and estrogen played comparable roles in male and female development. In one set of experiments R. R. Greene and his associates injected high concentrations of estrogenic hormones into pregnant rats. Males born to the treated females had "external genitalia of the female type and three to six pairs of well-developed nipples." Their testes did not descend toward the scrotum, but remained in a position more typical of ovaries. Furthermore, the male duct system did not grow properly, the prostate did not develop, and these rats had partial development of the upper vagina, uterus, and oviduct. Finally, Greene and co-workers noted a paradoxical effect of estrogen injection: some of the female embryos found in injected pregnant mothers emerged with masculine anatomical characters. So the estrogen feminized male fetuses but masculinized female ones. Greene and colleagues found "the available facts more compatible with the di-hormonic theory."[25] Indeed, taken on their own, the results of hormone-injection experiments in mice and rats seemed to indicate that the active effects of estrogens and androgens appeared virtually parallel (see table 8.1)

In an attempt to resolve the mono- versus di-hormonic debate, Jost chose an innovative experimental technique. Operating on rabbit fetuses still inside the mother, he eliminated the embryonic gonad. Both technically difficult and physiologically more "normal" than injecting large doses of purified hormones, his approach produced information about the roles played by the em-

TABLE 8.1 *Summary of Androgen and Estrogen Effects on Early Fetal Development*

	ANDROGEN EFFECTS ON FEMALE FETAL DEVELOPMENT		ESTROGEN EFFECTS ON MALE FETAL DEVELOPMENT	
ANATOMICAL STRUCTURE	RAT	MOUSE	RAT	MOUSE
Gonad position	Masculinized	Masculinized	Feminized	Feminized
Female internal genitalia	No effect	No effect	Stimulated	Stimulated
Male internal genitalia	Stimulated	Stimulated	Inhibited	Inhibited
External genitalia	Masculinized	Masculinized	Feminized	Feminized

Source: Adapted from Greene et al. 1940b, tables 3 and 4, pp. 333–34.

bryo's own gonadal hormones. He tried four different types of experiments: fetal castration (removal of either the testes or the ovaries), fetal parabiosis (the joining together of the circulatory systems of two developing embryos), grafting embryonic testes or ovaries onto an embryo of the "opposite" sex, and hormone injection.[26]

Jost's techniques were new to those who studied mammals, and his success with these demanding surgeries drew attention to his work. The castrations, performed between nineteen and twenty-three days of fetal development, produced striking results. In castrated male embryos, developing masculine structures such as the epididymis (a duct that, when mature, carries sperm from the testes to the outside during ejaculation) disintegrated, while the structures forming the oviducts, uterus, and part of the cervix developed as if the embryo were female rather than male. Furthermore, the fetally castrated male rabbit developed a vagina and a clitoris rather than a penis and scrotum. In contrast, removing the ovary of a fetal female did not obviously affect the course of sexual development. Oviducts, uterus, cervix, and vagina all differentiated in near normal fashion, although if the castration was performed early enough, these organs did not grow to full size.

What struck Jost especially was that without a fetal testis, the male duct system degenerated, while even in male embryos the female system developed. What made these two duct systems behave so differently? Since males had no ovaries, those structures could not be responsible for supporting continued female development. Wondering whether maternal estrogen or perhaps estrogen made by the male's adrenals might cause female duct development, Jost performed additional experiments, concluding finally that "*a crystal of androgen could counteract the absence of testicles and assure development of masculine somatic characteristics.*"[27]

Putting the whole story together, Jost concluded, first, that the female duct system developed without stimulation from the embryonic ovary. Hence, female structures could differentiate in both castrated males and females. The testes, he theorized, made some substance that inhibited female duct development. The fact that female ducts developed even in castrated male embryos implanted with testosterone led him to postulate that two substances must be involved. One, testosterone, stimulated development of male ducts and genitalia. The other, at the time merely postulated but later identified as a proteinlike hormone called Mullerian Inhibiting Substance (MIS), caused the female ducts to degenerate.[28] The fetal testis normally makes both chemicals.

Cautiously and in some detail, Jost discussed the implications of his results for mono- and di-hormonic theories of sexual development. First, he noted that the male and female duct systems, originally present in both sexes, had rather different developmental potentials. No matter the genetic sex of the embryo, for example, the female ducts could develop if not inhibited by a testicular secretion, while the male ducts degenerated unless grown in the presence of testosterone. Did these results lend support to Wiesner's monohormonal theory? Jost reminded his readers that when the ovaries were removed at an early stage, the female duct system did not grow to a normal size. Thus, it was "probable that the ovary also produces a morphogenetic secretion, but that it, without a doubt, plays a more limited role than the testicular secretion." Furthermore, the fact that ovarian action did not cause the breakdown of the male duct system did not prove that the ovaries played no role. There could, Jost suggested, be some sort of double assurance—that is, some other source of hormone could be called into action in the ovaries' absence. He suggested that future experiments focus on the role of the ovary, on the physiology of the fetal ovary, and on castrations performed at earlier stages of development.[29]

Despite the skills and insights that led him to challenge his colleagues' theories, Jost failed to notice that his theory adopted wholesale the metaphor of female lack and male presence. From the 1950s through the mid-1960s he referred to females as the neutral or anhormonal sex type. They became females, according to him, because they *lacked* testes, while the testes played the principal role in separating male from female development. By the early 1970s, Jost described male development as a heroic feat, a successful traverse of a road fraught with danger. The testes *imposed* masculinity with the help of a tiny yet powerful Y chromosome. The male embryo struggled against the inherent push toward femininity.[30]

Both the rhetorical and theoretical structures of Jost's work, and of other scientific investigations into hormones more generally, seemed to mirror ongoing social debates about gender. Di-hormonic ideas were compatible with a vision in which the sexes occupied separate spheres. Scientists understood each sex as formed through active and specifically controlled processes. Di-hormonic theories thus understood both male and female development as processes that needed accounting for; the parallel notion of maleness and femaleness might seem more readily to suggest male and female equivalence. In contrast, mono-hormonic theories emphasized the perilous nature of masculine development, using language suggesting the dangers to men of underlying femininity: "Masculine characteristics of the body have to be imposed in males . . . against a basic feminine trend of the mammalian body." Females, in contrast, represented the natural starting template. In Jost's theory, then, masculinity, in the body biologic as in the body politic, required aggressive action to maintain itself.[31]

The longstanding notion that femaleness represented a bodily absence, while a physical presence defined maleness, in combination with postwar insistence on the need for men to build their masculinity and women to follow passively their natural inclinations, partly explains why Jost and others accepted an underproven hypothesis.[32] The unexamined rhetoric of female absence also helps account for the fact that neither Jost nor others performed extensive, detailed experiments to find out just what *did* govern female development if, as the fetal castration data suggested, the fetal ovary played a minor role.[33] If female development was a state of nature, only male development required explanation, and the phrase "sexual differentiation" really meant "male differentiation."[34]

Jost's model of the female as the product of an absence persists even today. These days scientists study the genes involved with driving the development of the ovary or testis itself.[35] But until recently, the idea that females "just happen" has been a staple of even the most sophisticated scientific thought. The author of one scientific article, discussing the importance of particular genes for the development of an ovary or testis after the sperm has delivered either a second X or a Y chromosome to the egg,[36] writes: "In the *presence* of a Y chromosome . . . the gonads . . . form as testes. . . . In the *absence* of testes female . . . genitalia develop. . . . Sex determination can thus be equated with determination of testis formation."[37] "In the human . . . the female is the *constitutive* sex and the male the *induced* sex. Therefore sex determination can be considered the equivalent of being determined as male," writes another scientist.[38] "The female developmental pathway," says a third, "has often been referred to as the default pathway."[39]

The scientific model of sexual development that won out over others is the one that borrowed most from, and best fit with, conservative notions that characterized femaleness by passivity and lack, but it has done more than just bolster conservative viewpoints. Indeed, the idea that all embryos start as female, that the "natural ground state" is feminine and maleness a mere afterthought, has delighted some feminists. The feminist science writer Natalie Angier, for instance, writes that "from a biological perspective women are not the runners-up; women are the original article. We are Chapter 1, lead paragraph, descendants of the true founding citizen of Eden."[40] Just as the metaphor of a female ground state has cultural purchase in the arena of gender politics, it has opened doors to important scientific insights. Evolutionarily, for example, the idea suggests that females preceded males onto this earth, that the male is derived from the female—Adam's Rib in reverse. This idea has fueled fascinating research on topics that include the evolution of the Y chromosome and the varieties of sexual systems found in the animal world.[41]

But the metaphor giveth and the metaphor taketh away. Think of the dualisms the default metaphor generates. If the female plan is natural, does that equate females with nature, thus implying that culture is masculine? And if femininity can contaminate or undermine masculinity, then does "maintaining masculinity require *suppression* of the feminine"?[42]

When Jost wrote that "Becoming a male is a prolonged, uneasy, and risky adventure; it is a kind of struggle against inherent trends toward femaleness," he constructed a narrative, in which the adventure, the risk, and the heroic accomplishment all belong to the male. Building on Jost's narrative, many current chronicles of primary sex determination have little to say about female development. For years the phrase "sex determination" has been "considered the equivalent of being determined as male."[43] Accepting such a viewpoint, I argue here and elsewhere, has stimulated a great deal of research into the mechanisms (genetic and hormonal) of male development, but few have doggedly pursued the mechanism of female development.[44] In a 1986 review, the geneticists Eva Eicher and Linda L. Washburn criticized research on sex determination for "presenting the induction of testicular tissue as an active . . . event while presenting the induction of ovarian tissue as a passive (automatic) event. Certainly the induction of ovarian tissue is as much an active, genetically directed developmental process as is the induction of testicular tissue. . . . Almost nothing has been written about genes involved in the induction of ovarian tissue from the undifferentiated gonad."[45] Only in the 1990s did theories of female development begin to emerge.[46]

The lack of scientific attention to female development is not due simply to the power of the presence/absence metaphor. Indeed, other metaphors— especially narratives about master genes and switches[47]—*and* the animals themselves also account for the scientific history of male and female development. For example, when one sex researcher looked for active effects of estrogen on female guinea pig development, he found that estrogen injections caused the test animals to abort, making it difficult to follow up on this line of research.[48] He decided that it was more prudent for his career to pursue a line of research more likely to give publishable results in a reasonable period of time.

Like most scientists working on mammalian steroid hormones, Jost hoped that his work would apply, both practically and theoretically, to humans. Almost from the beginning, he interacted with medical scientists concerned with human development. In 1949, following up on contacts provided by his brother, Dr. Marc Jost, Alfred Jost visited Johns Hopkins University. There he met Dr. Lawson Wilkins, a pioneer in the study of human intersexuality (see chapters 2–4). An intense afternoon of discussion of Wilkins's clinical cases convinced him of Jost's mono-hormonic account of mammalian sexual development, a viewpoint he applied immediately in his forthcoming book on sexual malformation in humans. In turn, Jost noted how important the approval of this senior, renowned clinician was to the younger experimental scientist (Jost was thirty-three, Wilkins fifty-five, at the time of the encounter).[49]

The Nerve of It All: From Bisexual to Heterosexual

Jost's default model of sexual development influenced far more than the study of genitalia and sex-related anatomy. By the late 1950s, scientists had imported the idea into the study of behavior. They theorized that testosterone primed the male brain, readying it for sex-related activities such as mounting, intercourse, and territorial defense. The female brain developed gender in testosterone's absence. The idea seemed to map perfectly onto Jost's account of anatomical development. But behavior was a more slippery subject than anatomy. Despite the confusions presented by intersexuality—in humans or in animals—anatomical development remained a reasonably clear-cut way to measure hormonal effects. There were testes or ovaries, an epididymis or a fallopian tube, a scrotum or vaginal lips. But research on sexual behavior moved beyond questions of anatomy to questions of masculinity, femininity, homosexuality, bisexuality, and heterosexuality.

BISEXUALITY

From the 1930s through the 1950s, the Committee for Research in Problems of Sex turned its support to studies of sexual behavior in animals and humans. Frank Ambrose Beach emerged as a young scientist in the 1930s and, by the mid-1940s, had articulated a detailed theory of animal sexuality. As an undergraduate Beach had abandoned all hope of understanding human psychology, deciding that "white rats were simpler," although he still wanted to solve basic problems in psychology. For his Ph.D. he damaged specific areas of the brain's cerebral cortex to see if he could perturb maternal behavior in rats. From there to the study of hormones and sexual behavior was a short jump. During and just after World War II, Beach and other students of animal psychology accomplished three tasks.[50] They detailed behaviors that they could quantify and designate as masculine or feminine; they developed some sense of behavioral differences among different species and among individuals of the same species; and they studied the effects of estrogen, progesterone, and testosterone on adult sexual behaviors. In synthesizing the results of such experiments, they articulated a vision of the origins of animal masculinity and femininity, one that many researchers eagerly applied to humans.

In this discussion I highlight three aspects of Beach's work. First, he insisted on the diversity of animal behavior—within each sex, within each species, and among different species and genera. Second, he took what we would today call a systems approach to animal behavior, emphasizing the interactions among the varied physiological systems within each body, as well as the social context eliciting or permitting particular behaviors. Third, he was an outspoken liberal on the topic of human sexual diversity. In looking at his career and ideas, we can once again see clearly how the social and the scientific form part of a single fabric.

In a remarkably prolific four-year period, Beach reported in at least fourteen scientific papers on the results of his research on rat sexuality. Not surprisingly, he found sex differences in the control of male and female mating behaviors. When a female rat feels amorous, she characteristically darts, hops, and vibrates her ears. When the male mounts her, she flattens her back, raises her rump, moves her tail to one side, and permits copulation (see figure 8.1). The rump raising and presenting are a reflex action also inducible when an experimenter strokes a female rat's back. The technical name for this response

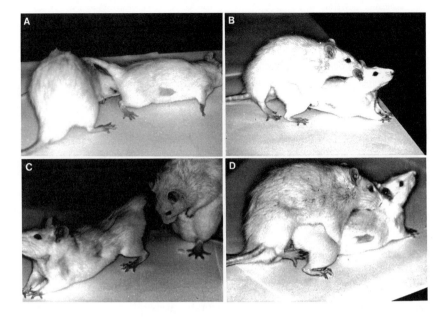

FIGURE 8.1: Mating and lordosis in the laboratory rat. *A*: The male investigates to determine whether the female is in estrus. *B*: If she is in estrus, the male mounts and clasps his forepaws around her hindquarters. This tactile stimulation causes her to move her tail to one side and arch her back (lordosis). *C*: The male dismounts and grooms himself. *D*: After several mounts, the male ejaculates. (Photos courtesy of Julie Bakker)

is *lordosis*. A willing male smells and licks the female's genitals, and, if she permits, mounts her, introduces his penis (intromission), and thrusts deeply. He may repeat this behavior as many as 10 times before ejaculating. After each intromission, he rapidly withdraws and licks his genitals. To the experimental psychologist, each of these separate actions provides an opportunity to subdivide mating into parts that may be counted and analyzed for the possible influences of hormones, environment, and life experience.[51] For each sex, the suite of behaviors defines masculinity or femininity with regard to mating.[52] But just as noteworthy as differences between the sexes were the striking individual differences within each sex, among laboratory strains of the same species, and among rodent species. Neurologically, Beach argued, all animals have a bisexual potential. What, he wanted to know, were the factors that lead to particular sexual expressions, be they heterosexual matings, male-male mountings, male lordosis, female-female or female-male mountings?

Beach and other animal sex researchers had to defend both the importance and the propriety of their work. During the 1940s and 50s, psychoanalytic "environmental" theories of human development were far more popular than biological interpretations of behavior. Especially during the 1950s, human psychology had been strongly marked by psychoanalysis.[53] To comparative animal psychologists, however, Freud seemed frustratingly ungrounded in quantitative, experimental biology. Animal psychology had developed in the United States following the lead of John B. Watson and others,[54] while in Europe ethologists such as Konrad Lorenz dramatized the concepts of ethology with experiments on imprinting in birds. His famous photographs of baby ducks and geese following him around as if he were their parent, because he was the first moving object they saw upon hatching, captured the imagination of many in the United States. In general, students of both human and animal psychology had stressed the importance of experience and learning combined with the idea of instinctive, inborn drives (hunger, sexual desire, and so on) in the shaping of behavior. Now endocrinologists and physiologists hoped to swing the pendulum back toward biology.[55] Furthermore, sex itself was not a topic for polite company.[56] Such an unfavorable atmosphere may explain why Beach opened his major 1942 paper on the attack. "Students of animal behavior," he wrote, "have often speculated upon the nature of sexual excitement, and schools of psychological thought have been founded upon ambiguous concepts of the human 'sex drive.'" Beach intended to put the discussion on a scientific footing and to offer a "phylogenetic interpretation of human behavior."[57]

Beach provided a multilayered, sexually diverse model of animal behavior. Many vertebrates, he noted, were born with the nerve-muscle circuits (motor patterns) needed to solicit and execute the sex act fully formed. Male rats, for example, did not normally mate until they were thirty-five to eighty days old. But testosterone injection at much younger ages elicited a full range of adult behavior. Evidence for innate motor patterns did not, however, extend to the great apes. Here, it seemed, practice and experience were central to the ability to copulate, a fact of particular importance for Beach's "phylogenetic interpretation of human sex life."

Being born with the basic circuitry, however, was not enough—especially since Beach thought the motor patterns for both masculine and feminine mating responses were present in each sex. How did one pattern come to dominate in a particular individual? Perhaps an answer could be found by analyzing the components of sexual arousal. Beach emphasized a holistic approach to such analysis.[58] Arousal, for example, resulted from the particular constitution of the individual rat,[59] the potency of stimulus objects, and the animal's prior experience. Just as individual males varied in their interest in mating, particular females differed in their receptivity. Both mattered if a mating were to take place. An indifferent female and a less than enthusiastic male might fail to get it on. But couple a low-energy male with a highly receptive female, and sparks flew.[60]

Beach analyzed the inclinations of the mating couple. Prior experience mattered. Males segregated for long periods with other males were far less likely to mate than ones raised in isolation or with females. The senses mattered. The receptive female presented males with a veritable cornucopia of stimuli—movement, body postures, ear vibrations, smell, taste, touch—that all contributed to getting the male excited enough to mate. Rob a male of one of his five senses and he would still mate. But knock out more than one, and he pretty much lost interest.[61] Although it was not clear how,[62] the brain—Beach suspected the cerebral cortex—was also necessary for mating. And last, but not least, hormones mattered. Hormones could increase an animal's general excitability by increasing its sensitivity to stimulating signals (all that odor, ear-wiggling, and hopping about).

Both testosterone and estrogen had sexually nonspecific effects. Injecting inexperienced male rats with testosterone, for example, got them so excited that they tried to mate with nonreceptive females, young males, and even guinea pigs![63] Injecting testosterone into female rats also increased their general excitability, as well as their tendency to exhibit both male and female mating patterns. But even untampered-with female rats would sometimes execute male mating patterns—mounting and thrusting on other animals, both male and female.[64] Estrogen could also induce male mating patterns in both sexes and, of course, derived its name from its ability to produce estrus in female rodents. Beach insisted on "the absence of a perfect correlation between the hormonal condition of the animal and the character of the overt behavior." Even rats were not mere slaves to their hormone levels. "Psychic factors" mattered, albeit not to the same degree as for humans.[65]

In his 1942 review article, Beach used a diagram to unify the pieces of the puzzle: the sensory inputs, the role of the central nervous system, and the function of hormones (figure 8.2). He hypothesized a Central Excitatory Mechanism (C.E.M.), a group of nerve cells that received incoming information from sense receptors and sent outgoing signals to the neural circuits that executed the male and female mating patterns. Different incoming receptors stimulated different numbers of nerve cells in the C.E.M. Thus, smell might be more important than vision. But the effects in the central mechanism added up.[66] Smell alone might not increase excitation to the point where a signal left the center and stimulated mounting or lordosis. Or it might be enough to stimulate mounting, but not intromission. But additional stimulation from other sense receptors could put the excitation level over the top. Hormones,

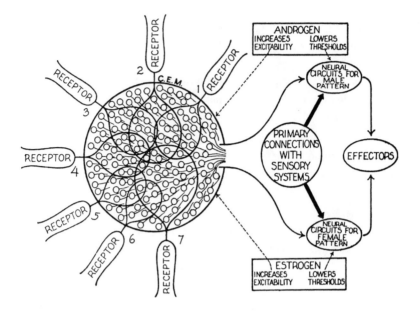

FIGURE 8.2: Beach's model of the mechanisms by which hormones affect behavior. (Beach 1942b, p. 189; reprinted with permission)

in Beach's scheme, played three roles. First, they could act directly on the C.E.M. to stimulate the level of sexual excitement. Second, they could lower the threshold needed to stimulate the circuits governing the male or female behavior patterns. Third, they could directly affect the senses. Beach suspected, for example, that testosterone increased the tactile sensitivity of the penis.[67] The penis's touch receptors would send more intense signals back to the C.E.M., further stimulating the rat's sexual excitement.

In Beach's scheme, males and females differed quantitatively but not qualitatively. Androgen could stimulate female mounting and thrusting, for example, but not as easily as it could in a male. A female with especially sensitive sense receptors, for example, might need less androgen or estrogen to reach a state of sexual excitement than one with less sensitive or fewer receptors. Beach's hypothesis accounted nicely for individual variability within each sex, as well as for the fact that both sexes could, under some conditions, display both masculine and feminine mating patterns and, finally, that both androgen and estrogen could induce either of these patterns in either sex.

Beach did much of his early work at the American Museum of Natural History in New York, but by 1946 his growing reputation led Yale University to hire him as a member of its Department of Psychology. From that position of authority, he actively promoted his ideas about animal sexuality. In 1948,

Beach delivered the prestigious Harvey Lecture in New York. Emphasizing the similarity of males and females, he noted: "The physiological mechanisms for feminine sexual behavior are found in all males and those for masculine behavior exist in all females. . . . Human homosexuality reflects the essentially bisexual character of our mammalian inheritance."[68] Human societies may condemn the immorality of homosexual behavior, Beach wrote, but one could not appeal to nature as a justification: our mammalian ancestry proved homosexuality to be quite natural.

Beach's animal research intertwined with the broader social discussions of human sexuality. He did most of his work on animal bisexuality just before and during World War II. Just after the war, he began to apply his ideas to humans, at a moment, he wrote, when "public attitudes toward open discussion and scientific exploration of problems relating to sex had become remarkably lenient, if not enlightened."[69] The importance of his work seemed greatly strengthened by Kinsey's findings of extensive bisexual behavior in men and women. In 1946, Beach acknowledged access to Kinsey's as yet unpublished results,[70] but since Beach knew Kinsey and was one of his interviewers,[71] it is likely that he had been thinking about the work on humans since the early 1940s.[72] In turn, Kinsey repeatedly cited Beach's animal studies in order to locate human behavior within the panoply of normal mammalian biology.[73] The war itself made homosexuality more visible.[74] At the same time, Beach did experiments on rats that suggested a remarkable range of sexual behaviors, and he interviewed humans about their sexual behaviors. At least through the early 1950s Beach's views remained compatible with elements of the national discussion.[75]

HETEROSEXUALITY

As the cold war ideology that praised heterosexuality and ranted about the homosexual menace came to dominate the national scene during the 1950s, more restrictive readings of animal sexuality gained visibility and strength. By 1959, a new rodent emerged that was distinctly heterosexual and far more bound by gender roles than were Beach's rats. A new theory implied that individual variation resulted from early hormone exposure;[76] it also made little attempt to develop the kind of integrated account of behavior so evident in Beach's work. Instead, biologists divorced life experience from biological explanations of behavior, leaving it as a kind of embarrassing little sister—always mentioned, but never really included in the big kids' game. And, finally, as researchers applied Jost's account of genital development to animal behavior, femininity became an absence, masculinity a struggle.

One key figure through whom we can trace this progression is William C.

Young, who obtained his Ph.D. at the University of Chicago for work on sperm transport (from the testis to the outside world). During the 1930s and 1940s, with CRPS funding, Young focused on mating behaviors in the guinea pig.[77] His motto was, "Observe, measure, and record!" and he did just that.[78] He noted the cyclic nature of the female's mating responses, detailed exactly when during the estrus cycle particular behaviors came and went, and figured out the relationship between cyclical changes in estrogen and progesterone and the waxing and waning of the female mating response. Like the rat, the female guinea pig exhibited lordosis when in heat, "frequently . . . accompanied by a guttural vocalization and by the pursuit and mounting of other females and even males."[79]

Even though the females went "through the motions of copulation except that they do not afterwards roll dorsally and clean their genitalia," Young and his colleagues displayed a certain ambivalence about this untoward female behavior.[80] On the one hand, they described such mounting as a normal part of the female sex drive.[81] On the other, they labeled it "homosexual behavior by normal females."[82] In one set of experiments, Young and colleagues found that a combination of estrogen and progesterone induced female mounting. Testosterone—much to their surprise—had little effect.[83]

Young's 1941 review of research on mating behavior in female mammals covered much of the same territory as Beach's 1942 synthesis. Young hesitated, however, to posit overarching theories about such complex behavior. "Endocrine, neural, genetic, ontogenetic, nutritional, environmental, psychological, pathological and age factors . . . and doubtless others" all combined to produce mating behaviors. Figuring out the part played by any particular factor seemed nearly impossible. "Nevertheless . . . some starting point must be chosen . . . the ovarian hormones have been selected, not because they are necessarily the exclusive limiting factor, but because they are the means to the induction of heat by experimental procedures and the means by which the role of the other factors can be elucidated." Hormones, in other words, were "the hook," the entry point to the understanding of sexual behaviors.[84]

During the first part of his career, Young worked mostly on female guinea pigs, but in 1950 he and his colleagues turned their attention to males. First they carefully described and measured five aspects of male mating behavior: nuzzling, sniffing, nibbling, mounting, intromission, and ejaculation.[85] Time and again they observed individual variation in male behavior. Some males had high sex drives, while others seemed hardly interested in mating. Did the low-drive males have less circulating testosterone? No. When these researchers castrated high- and low-drive individuals and then injected them each with the same concentration of testosterone, the differences remained. The guinea pig who had been an enthusiastic stud before castration returned full throttle when given back his missing hormones. But the originally lackluster fellow retained his disinterest even when given high levels of testosterone. Because the amount of circulating hormone didn't explain the differences, Young postulated that in different animals the tissues mediating sexual behavior must differ in their ability to respond to the hormone.[86]

How, though, did these mediating tissues come to differ from one male to the next? For several years, Young and his students studied both genetic and experiential factors. Genetic differences between inbred and outbred animals told some of the story. And early social experiences mattered a lot. In some experiments they separated newborns from their siblings—housing them only with their mothers for the first ten to twenty-five days of life and thereafter rearing them in total isolation. In an inbred strain in which the males always have a low sex drive, isolation after twenty-five days of nursing caused drastic drops in sexual performance. In stud strains, weaning at ten days followed by isolation severely depressed the mating response. The conclusion: "Contact with other animals has an organizing action on the development of the copulatory pattern of the male guinea pig."[87]

By the late 1950s, Young and his co-workers had completed exhaustive studies of male and female mating behaviors. In the many experiments Young, Beach, and others had performed since the 1930s, hormones seemed to behave much as Beach had postulated. In one way or another, they could stimulate the expression of potentials "previously organized or determined by genetical and experiential factors."[88] But other experiments suggested that hormone exposure early in development might have long-term effects on behavior, effects not evident until animals reached maturity. The discrepancy between such data and Beach's theory was unresolved. Young and his colleagues decided to reopen the question of long-term hormonal effects and in doing so started a new chapter in the history of the manly rat.

In 1959, when cold war rhetoric about homosexuality, communism, and the family was at its peak, Young and his three younger colleagues published their now classic paper "Organizing Action of Prenatally Administered Testosterone Proprionate on the Tissues Mediating Mating Behavior in the Guinea Pig" (hereafter referred to as Young's 1959 paper). The stakes were high, and they knew it. A finding that prenatal exposure to androgens or estrogens had "an organizing action that would be reflected by the character of adult sexual behavior" might mean that a whole range of adult behaviors could be traced largely to prebirth hormonal chemistry. It would also suggest a parallel between the importance of hormones for behavior and their importance for anatomical development. Finally, positive results would "direct attention to a possible origin of behavioral differences between the sexes which is *ipso facto* important for psychologic and psychiatric theory."[89]

This last comment, which referred to John and Joan Hampson's work on the development of sexual difference in humans, carried a subtle but important signal. Remember (from chapter 3) that during the 1950s the Hampsons and John Money had studied the development of human intersexuals raised as either males or females. Unlike Beach, who clearly accepted human homosexuality as part of a natural range of sexual behavior, the Hampsons considered homosexuality and transvestism to be abnormal.[90] By citing their work, Phoenix et al. implied their disagreement with Beach's view of underlying bisexuality, while at the same time suggesting that the guinea pig studies might lead to the finding of a biological basis for homosexuality.[91]

The publication of Young's 1959 paper shaped the study of hormones and sexual behavior for decades to come. The writers proposed a theory—the organizational/activational (O/A) model of hormone activity—that relegated Beach's 1942 synthesis to the back drawers of history. What did Young and his colleagues find? What was their initial statement of the O/A model? How did the heterosexual rodent—the manly guinea pig or the feminine rat—replace the bisexual animal as the center of attention?

Young and his colleagues suggested that pre- or perinatal hormones *organized* central nervous tissue so that at puberty hormones could *activate* specific behaviors. They injected pregnant guinea pigs with testosterone.[92] The injected mothers produced female intersexes (which researchers called *hermaphrodites* in the article). All of the testosterone-exposed offspring had internal anatomical signs of masculinization. Some also developed masculinized external genitalia. When these females grew up, they took longer to come into heat after stimulation by injections of estrogen and progesterone. Their lordosis responses were much weaker than unexposed controls, and "the low gutteral growl which is so characteristically a part of the pattern of lordosis in normal females was commonly, and in some individuals always, lacking." They also vigorously mounted other guinea pigs when injected with testosterone. Except for the growl emitted by the female during lordosis, quantity, not quality, distinguished feminine from masculine. In one experiment, for example, 89 percent of control females came into estrus after spaying and hormone injection, compared with 65 percent of the prenatally treated females with normal external genitalia, 22 percent of externally masculinized females, and 38 percent of castrated males (a second type of control group).[93] A lack of estrus, longer latency to achieve estrus, shorter length of heat, shorter lordotic response, and mounting in the absence of estrogen/progesterone injection all signaled a decrease in femininity and an increase in masculinity. Masculinity and femininity became mutually exclusive. An increase in one implied a decrease in the other.

Young and his colleagues began by studying masculinized female guinea pigs, but soon turned to the feminization of males. Following Jost's presence/absence logic, they reasoned that if adding testosterone imposed masculinity, removing it should permit underlying femininity to emerge. They castrated young rats or rabbits "prior to completion of the organizing action of the androgen," and in adulthood injected a mixture of estrogen and progesterone in an effort to elicit "feminine behavior in response to mounting by intact males." They found that males castrated before the age of ten days showed a higher frequency of feminine behavior, defined in rats as estrus and lordosis, ear wiggling, darting, and crouching. Castration affected male lordosis more dramatically than the wiggling, darting, and crouching, suggesting that not all aspects of rat femininity were similarly organized.[94]

What made Young's 1959 paper special was not the particular results; he and other colleagues had published similar findings a full nineteen years earlier, and Beach was getting similar data in dogs.[95] Rather, it was the scientists' explanation of their findings that proved important. Did exposing embryos to sex hormones, these authors wondered, affect the neural substrates underlying sexual behavior, substrates they assumed were found in "central nervous tissues"?[96] If so, might fetal hormones permanently fix an individual's behavioral potential as either masculine or feminine? The authors drew heavily on Jost's work describing how, in the embryo, testosterone promoted the differentiation of male genitalia, while Mullerian Inhibiting Substance caused the female parts to disintegrate. In adulthood, the ovaries or testes, the uterus or epididymis, all responded to the hormones of puberty. This second response was functional, rather than developmental. Young and colleagues thought that something similar must happen to "the neural tissues mediating mating behavior." In the embryo, such tissue differentiated, or "organized" in "the direction of either masculinization or feminization,"[97] while in the adult, hormones "activated" the previously organized tissues.

The ideas developed in the 1959 paper extended Jost's account of hormones and anatomy to behavior. Prenatal testosterone "heightened" the "responsiveness" to adult testosterone, while simultaneously suppressing the ability "to display the feminine components" after estrogen/progesterone treatment. Testosterone, the researchers theorized, played a dual role. First, it heightened masculinity by increasing the frequency of mounting behavior. Second, it suppressed femininity by decreasing the frequency and duration of lordosis. Estrogen and progesterone played roles in the adult as hormonal activators. The unstated implication: feminine behavior underlay all development. Testosterone suppressed it and imposed masculine capabilities on an underlying feminine system.[98]

Young's group drew further on the anatomical analogy to refute Beach and others' earlier claims of adult bisexuality. "These investigators stressed the increased responsiveness of their masculinized guinea pigs and mice" to injected androgens, seeming "to regard the change as the expression of an inherent bisexuality. . . . The existence of bisexuality is assumed. We suggest, however, that this adult bisexuality is unequal in the neural tissues as it is in the . . . genital tissues."[99] Even though it was possible to elicit cross-gender behavior in adults, it was hard to do so. Again drawing the analogy with genital anatomy, they noted that both males and females contained vestiges of organs present in the embryo, that such organs could respond to adult hormones, but that the responses of the vestige and the fully formed organ were rarely identical. By extending the anatomical model of hormone action to behavior, the authors acknowledged the widespread existence of cross-gendered behaviors but downgraded their importance, paving the way for a biological account of male and female as heterosexual.[100]

Boldly, they proposed that their findings might extend well beyond the highly stylized reproductive behaviors on which they had gathered data.[101] Rejecting the psychologists' arguments about "shaping behavior by manipulating the external environment," they proposed that all behavior patterns had underlying biological causes. In this instance, they had demonstrated that testosterone "acts on the central nervous tissues in which patterns of sexual behavior are organized."[102]

Spreading the Word

Young's 1959 paper electrified scientists interested in hormones and behavior. By the mid-1960s the research literature was filled with articles validating the O/A hypothesis in rats, hamsters, mice, and monkeys. The hypothesis had become a theory and then a concept.[103] And as a concept, it extended well beyond coital behaviors. As the years passed, scientists applied it to nest building, maternal care, aggression, open field activity, running in an exercise wheel, play fighting, development of a sweet tooth (adult female rats like sweets more than their male counterparts do), conditioned taste avoidance, maze learning, and brain asymmetries.[104] The fact that the O/A hypothesis built on Jost's already accepted accounts of anatomical development, the theory's apparently widespread applicability, and its socially acceptable focus on heterosexual development were all key factors contributing to its rapid acceptance.[105]

Young's ideas not only set the research agenda in his own field. During the 1960s, he led the way in a major shift in theories of behavior. Whereas earlier he and other researchers had emphasized the importance of individual (genetic) variability, physiological complexity, *and* environment in the development of sexual behaviors, now social and biological scientists took up his call to focus on the hormonal causes of gendered behavior. Young himself played a key role in arguing that research into the importance of hormones for the development of animal mating behaviors shed light on the human condition.

One can see this shift in Young's thinking and its application to humans in his 1961 comprehensive review of "The Hormones and Mating Behavior." Although he here recounts earlier experiments demonstrating individual variability in rat and guinea pig behavior, as well as work demonstrating the importance of experience in the development of sexual behaviors, he seemed more impressed with the dramatic findings that prenatal hormones also influenced mating behaviors. He reemphasized the potentially long arm of the O/A theory, suggesting that it would apply to a variety of nonreproductive behaviors for which sex differences had been found. And, while acknowledging the widespread belief in "psychological factors" in the development of human sexual behaviors, he nevertheless envisioned a sweeping change: if, as he predicted, prenatal hormones turned out to affect a multitude of behaviors, it would "bond . . . the work of experimental embryologists . . . and the work of the psychologists and psychiatrists" who needed to understand the development of neural tissues.[106]

Near the end of his life (he died in 1965), as his former students and postdocs became prominent, Young endorsed the reorganization of disciplinary boundaries that encompassed the study of animal and human behavior. In 1964, in a lead article in *Science,* the official journal of the American Association for the Advancement of Science, Young, Charles Phoenix, and Robert Goy wrote: "Without discounting the influence of psychologic factors, which we know is great, or the need for carefully recorded observations of behaviors, we expect that, increasingly, the materials and techniques used will be those of the neurologist and biochemist." Indeed, by the end of the 1960s, knowledge about the development of sexually dimorphic behaviors had shifted significantly. Individual genetic differences and the importance of social interactions (even for rodents) became less visible.[107] Hardly anyone mentioned the fact that males that had been prenatally "organized" by testosterone still needed postnatal organization in the form of social contact. As a result, male and female rodent behaviors, as well as those of humans, for whom they served as a model, emerged as more stereotyped than they had previously seemed, and as more rigidly determined by prenatal hormonal environments.

This happened despite efforts by many prominent researchers to stave off single-factor models of development. Speaking at an interdisciplinary conference that included experts on human development, Charles Phoenix "hoped that the concept of the organizing action of prenatal androgen will not give rise to time-worn arguments of heredity versus environment or be conceived of as a fatalistic theory that renders useless the need for studying the effect of the environment on the development of normal sexual behavior." But the developers of the O/A theory were unable to integrate their findings on early hormone effects with their findings on environmental determinants of sexual behavior. In fact, their working model of development got in the way. It has the same difficulties as the sex/gender account of human bodies. Development and experience, nature and nurture, are never separate, but always co-produce one another. Thus Phoenix's concluding sentence in this passage only reinstates the problem he wished he and others could avoid: "What is suggested here is a mechanism whereby the information encoded in genetic material is translated into morphology and, ultimately, behavior." In this sentence, the body comes first, then experience may be imposed upon it. With such a model it is never possible to escape "the time-worn arguments of heredity versus environment."[108]

While the O/A theory grew deep roots during the 1960s, by the mid-1970s accepted definitions of rodent masculinity and femininity had come under fire—both from Frank Beach and from some of his students, among whom were those inspired by the newly emerged women's liberation movement.[109] The role of estrogen in establishing both masculine and feminine behaviors again became a topic for debate, and the possibility emerged that masculinity and femininity ran in parallel, rather than oppositional lines.[110] As founding editor of the new journal *Hormones and Behavior*, which rapidly became the premier location for publishing articles on hormones and sexual behavior and at conferences, Beach attacked the O/A theory.[111] Immediate responses in print or in explicit experimental deed were sparse, and he himself fell nearly silent about it afterward—as if the tide were too strong and the personal ties to those who disagreed too dear for even such a renowned scientist to swim against.[112]

Beach continued, however, to believe in a bisexual model of adult development. Reminding readers that untreated adult females would not only mount other animals but would thrust and show a pattern of intromission, he concluded that "the female rat's nervous system is capable of mediating all of the masculine responses with the noteworthy exception of ejaculation."[113] If one wanted to understand the relationships between hormones and behavior, he concluded it would be better to study the immediate factors leading to a particular behavior than to construct what he called "imaginary brain mechanisms." Nevertheless, by the 1970s Beach had qualified what had been learned about "a basic bisexuality of the brain." He agreed with Young that in genetic males the suite of masculine behaviors was easier to activate than the female repertoire, while the converse held for females. In addition, in both sexes the female repertoire was more sensitive to estrogen stimulation, while the male behavioral suite responded more easily to androgen.[114] For Beach, a "basic bisexuality" did not mean a lack of sex differences.

While Beach published a few more papers critical of experimental procedures used to study prenatal sex hormone effects,[115] others examined the effects of hormones on genital development more carefully.[116] A report that neonatal androgen produced measurable anatomical differences in the brain's hypothalamus, however, seemed to confirm the organizational hypothesis.[117] Still, matters were more complex than originally envisioned. A summary of a work session intended to produce a state-of-the-art account of hormones and sex differences concluded: "despite such evidence against complete determinative influence of peripheral structures, the expression of adequate sexual behavior clearly is partly dependent upon adequate peripheral structures. When observed, suppression of behavior must be carefully interpreted and assurances provided" before concluding that the central nervous system is the only culprit.[118]

Eventually Beach accepted the evidence that prenatal hormones could permanently affect brain development. Nevertheless, he continued to remind anyone who would listen that the hormone/behavior interaction was complex, depending on genetic makeup, an individual's current emotional and physical condition, and personal history.[119] By 1981, the psychologist Harvey Feder, one of the new generation of hormone researchers, found that drawing analogies with Jost's anatomical studies was "no longer helpful . . . and may even be counterproductive."[120] In the decade since Beach's critique, evidence had accumulated showing prenatal hormonal effects on brain anatomy. But the relationship between anatomical effects and behavior remained (and still remain) unclear.[121] Beach was right that the basic wiring for suppressed behaviors exists into adulthood; Young was right that they need special circumstances to be called into play. Despite the fact that some of Beach's criticisms had not withstood the test of time, problems continued to arise for the O/A.

Many of them had, in one way or another, to do with how best to conceptualize and experiment on gender differences. In the 1970s the long arm of the women's movement moved into the rat lab.

LIBERATING THE FEMALE RAT

Beach was a minority voice in a sexually conservative era, but increasingly, scientists could not avoid hearing the political and social arguments voiced by people such as Betty Friedan, whose 1963 best-selling book *The Feminine Mystique* exploded the suburban family idyll. As Friedan founded the National Organization for Women (in 1966), other movements for social change—civil rights, the antiwar movement, and, with the Stonewall Riot of 1969, the gay liberation movement—gained national visibility.[122] By the time of the publication of Money and Ehrhardt's *Man and Woman, Boy and Girl*, in 1972, a groundbreaking work about the biology of sexual development, the women's liberation movement was clearly a force to be dealt with. Money and Ehrhardt figured that would satisfy no one. "The advocates of male supremacy like to quote the findings of Chapter 6" that claimed that fetal hormones affect brain development, "while neglecting the findings of Chapters 7 and 8," which discuss the importance of the environment in the formation of gender identity. "The advocates of women's liberation, by contrast, attend chiefly to Chapters 7 and 8 and neglect Chapter 6."[123]

And in 1974 the psychologist Richard Doty published an article entitled "A Cry for the Liberation of the Female Rodent: Courtship and Copulation in Rodentia" (see figure 8.3). Doty, who had done his postdoctoral studies under Frank Beach's supervision, noted that females per se were understudied. During the 1960s, only 20 percent of the articles on rat copulation published in the *Journal of Comparative and Physiological Psychology* focused on females. Another 68 percent studied males alone, while 12 percent examined both.[124] Doty also critiqued the standard system for measuring sexual behavior in the laboratory, a critique made consequential because such measurements lay at the heart of experiments supporting the O/A theory.[125]

In developing the best ways to observe male sexual behavior, most scientists tried to keep the behavior of the test female constant. They usually put male rats in a small observation cage and permitted them time to sniff it out and become accustomed to their surroundings. Once the male rat was comfy, the scientist introduced the female. The male rat might mount her a few times while she arched her back in the lordosis posture, permitting intromission and ejaculation. Experienced males come to know the procedure very well, becoming so excited, one rat runner wrote, "that when eventually the female

FIGURE 8.3: Liberating the female rat. (Source: Alyce Santoro, for the author)

is introduced, the male will no longer inspect whether or not she is in estrous," but just attempts to mount.[126] Even today, most researchers try to minimize female variability, often using circular test chambers so that the females have no corners to back into to prevent mounting. Hormone studies usually employ sexually experienced males, because in inexperienced ones the precopulatory behaviors, including mounting, depend on the female's soliciting behavior.[127] (I can't stop myself from thinking of this observation as the rodent variation on the tradition of having older women initiate young men into sexual adulthood.)

In fact, when experimenters introduced female choice, funny things began to happen. Doty noted experiments in which females had to *want* to mate—a desire expressed by pressing a bar to gain access to a stud male. In such situations females paced their sexual contacts (and thus those of the males) in a manner that perhaps more accurately reflected behavior in the wild. Varying the test situation also affected the results of experiments with pre- or perinatal hormone exposure. The psychologist Roger Gorski described experiments in which he first allowed a female rat that had been treated perinatally with androgens to become accustomed to her test area. According to the O/A theory, prenatal androgen treatment ought to have suppressed female lordosis—the measurement of her femininity. Indeed, this is what happened when the androgen-treated female was simply dropped into a test arena containing a waiting male. But when Gorski introduced the test male only after letting the female check out her new cage for a couple of hours, he found that "most females exhibited a very high LQ" (Lordosis Quotient, a standard measure arrived at by taking the number of male mounts that induce lordosis and dividing it by the total number of mounts). The permanent organizing effects of

androgen on the female brain seemed to have disappeared.[128] His result, Gorski noted, showed that the masculinization of androgen-treated females is
context-dependent.[129]

That the effects of prenatal hormone treatment were contingent on the
experimental test situation was not the only discovery that challenged the
O/A theory during the 1970s. Some researchers, led by Frank Beach, challenged the prevailing model of rodent masculinity and femininity. Beach suggested understanding female heterosexual mating behaviors as consisting of
three components: *attractivity* (how much she attracted males), *proceptivity*
(how attracted the female was to a particular male and whether she solicited
mating responses from him), and *receptivity* (a female's passive willingness to
mate).[130] In the standard laboratory setup, experimenters usually measured
only the passive, receptive component of female behavior. But some experiments suggested that prenatal hormones could affect receptive behaviors
without altering proceptive or attractive ones.[131] Thus, Beach argued, any
good theory relating hormones to behavior ought to take account of such complexity.[132]

A second, equally important theoretical challenge researchers posed to
the O/A theory revolved around an even broader question: What relationship
existed between masculinity and femininity? If an animal (or person) were
extremely masculine (by whatever measure), did that mean he or she would,
by definition, be *un*feminine? Or were masculinity and femininity separate
entities, able to vary independently of each other? (Remember Beach's early
experiments showing that lordotic males also sired offspring.) How could
some individuals be masculine and feminine at the same time?

Young's 1959 paper had implied that masculinity and femininity were
graded, mutually exclusive responses. The more feminine a guinea pig, the
less masculine she was. The psychobiologist Richard Whalen, another of
Beach's students, found that for rats, the situation was not so straightforward.
Under the right circumstances, he could produce males or females that both
mounted *and* exhibited high frequencies of lordosis. In other words, masculine and feminine were not mutually exclusive responses, but rather had what
scientists called an "orthogonal" relationship[133] (see figure 8.4). Later,
Whalen and Frank Johnson complicated matters by manipulating the hormone doses and times of stimulation in order to show that masculinization
itself had at least three independent physiological components.[134] Whalen
proposed an orthogonal model of rat sexuality in which, he argued, masculinity and femininity varied independently of each other. The same animal could
be both highly masculine *and* highly feminine, highly feminine but not at all
masculine (or vice versa), or might score low on both scales.

A. Linear Model

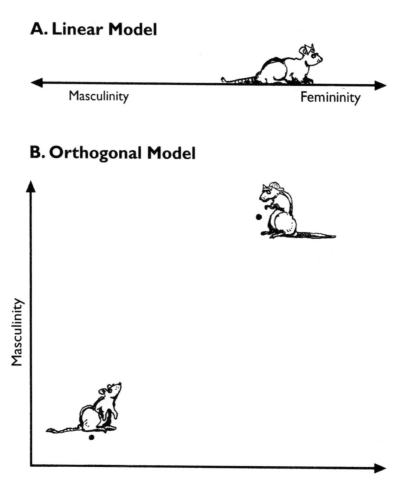

Masculinity   Femininity

B. Orthogonal Model

Masculinity

Femininity

FIGURE 8.4: *A*: A linear model of masculinity and femininity. As an animal becomes more feminine, it must also become less masculine. *B*: An orthogonal model of masculinity and femininity. The animal in the upper-right-hand corner shows many feminine *and* many masculine traits. The animal in the lower-left-hand corner shows only a few feminine or a few masculine traits. (Source: Alyce Santoro, for the author)

While Beach's and his students' work echoed feminist insistence that passivity did not define femininity and that masculine and feminine behaviors showed significant overlap, other researchers seemed to be drawing from the same pool of ideas. For example, Whalen published his orthogonal model the same year that the psychologist Sandra Bem popularized the idea of androgyny by designing a scale to measure their independent variations in humans. The fact that neither was aware of the other's work at the time suggests that the concept of independent masculinity and femininity was "in the air," although the precise route bringing the idea to Whalen and Bem remains difficult to pin down.[135]

Following Whalen's lead, scientists modified their terminology. *Defeminization* came to mean the suppression of female-typical behavior (such as lordosis) in genetic females, while *masculinization* applied to the enhancement of male-typical behaviors in genetic females. Parallel terminology applied to genetic males, for which *demasculinizing* treatments decreased the frequency of male typical behaviors, while *feminizing* ones increased female-typical behaviors. Using these words had the unexpected effect of "encourag[ing] questions about spontaneous bisexuality that might be overlooked with a different theoretical framework."[136]

The climate of the 1970s, with its focus on human androgyny, the clamor of the women's movement, and the nascent gay rights movement, helped make visible certain problems with the way scientists envisioned the biology of rodent sex. Even at the biochemical level, it turned out, sexual distinctions were far from clear-cut. In fact, during the 1970s biochemists realized that testosterone, that most masculine of molecules, usually exerted its influence on brain development only after it had been transformed (through a biochemical process called *aromatization*) into estrogen! The scientists who discovered the phenomenon, which again made it difficult to conceptualize these steroid hormones as specific sex hormones, echoed the 1930s reactions to the finding of estrogenic activity in stallion urine: they called aromatization paradoxical or surprising. Nevertheless, attention had returned to the role of estrogen in sexual development.[137]

THE GAY RAT

Throughout the 1980s social scientists turned to biology to explain human sexual practices, while biologists found their own research paradigms influenced by new social acceptance and definitions of human sexual diversity. In 1981, researchers Alan Bell, Martin Weinberg, and Sue Hammersmith published a study called *Sexual Preference: Its Development in Men and Women*. They had interviewed hundreds of homosexuals, obtaining information on past histories, family lives, and relationships with their mothers, fathers, siblings, and others. No single factor, however, stood out as the cause of homosexuality. Although they did not study biological components to homosexuality, the authors devoted a short chapter to the question of biology, noting that prenatal hormones could affect brain development.[138] Similarly, medical researchers interested in human endocrinology and gender development both followed and contributed to the work on hormones and animal development, often interacting with the rodent researchers at symposia.[139] Those more closely connected to the world of neuroendocrinology had been pursuing the theory of prenatal hormone effects using human intersexuality—especially CAH girls and AIS males—as the human experimental analogs to androgenized or castrated rats and guinea pigs.

As new and more complicated accounts of human homosexuality began to take shape in public debate, researchers working on animal behaviors suddenly began to reevaluate their own experiments on rodent sexuality. When Beach insisted in the 1940s that rodents were inherently bisexual, he meant that females had the potential to behave like males during mating. That meant that they might pursue and mount another animal, no matter the sex. Similarly a male had the potential to exhibit a more typically feminine repertoire, including ear wiggling and lordosis. Since a male that exhibited lordosis might also mount vigorously and sire offspring, and a female that mounted might also mate and bear young, Beach conceptualized the underlying system as bisexual.[140] At the time, Kinsey warned that applying the terms *homosexual* and *bisexual* to animals was "unfortunate," leading clinicians to badly misinterpret the animal experiments.[141] Indeed, over the decades, Kinsey's concerns have been borne out. Studies of animal and human sexuality have been hopelessly confused with each other.

During the 1980s, medical researchers, proposing with some vigor the idea that human homosexuality resulted from prenatal exposure to the wrong quantity or quality of hormone, often assumed that the case had already been made for animals. But the growth of the gay rights movement contributed new terms to the national discussion. While the nature of gay life became more visible, deep fissures appeared in the animal work. Consider, for example, the idea that a male rat that exhibits lordosis when mounted by another animal performs a homosexual act, while at the same time, the mounting male behaves heterosexually. The analogy to humans would suggest that only one member of a male-male couple is homosexual, but usually we understand that when two men have sex, both are homosexual.[142] The analogy holds for female rats—only the mounting female was seen as homosexual or bisexual. While this view of human female-female couples was typical during the

1920s, by the 1980s we believed both members of same sex-couples to be equally gay. Soon scientists hotly debated the wisdom of applying animal models to humans.[143]

During the 1980s, the terms *sexual orientation* and *sexual preference* became common stand-ins for the word *homosexual*. They seemed somehow more polite, more benign, and by avoiding the loaded term *homosexual*, they served the gay rights movement well. Rhetorically, it became possible to campaign against discrimination based on sexual orientation or preference. But these phrases embodied new concepts that in turn caused scientists to regroup. By the end of the '80s experimental psychologist Elizabeth Adkins-Regan argued the importance of applying "sexual preference or orientation" to animal studies. She noted that most of the studies on hormones and reproductive behaviors in rodents simply did not test for sexual orientation or preference because the test animals were never offered a choice.[144] Furthermore, choice tests themselves needed to distinguish between social and sexual preference. Animals living in all-female or all-male groups and mating only during breeding season, for example, might well prefer same-sex sociality, even though their mating preferences were strictly heterosexual.

As cultural consciousness about human homosexuality changed, so too did the rat experiments. My own survey of articles appearing in the journal *Hormones and Behavior* between 1978 and 1998 shows that the first article using *sexual preference* in its title appeared in 1983. The next showed up in 1987, and between then and 1998 another sixteen articles studying choice, preference, or orientation (in animals) appeared. To remedy the problem of studying rodent preference using an experimental design that offered the animals no choice, a group of Dutch animal behaviorists devised a new test system specifically for the study of sexual orientation in rats. They divided an open field cage into three compartments. In the middle compartment, the test animal roams freely and can choose to sit near (or sometimes to enter) one of two compartments, the first of which contains a sexually active male, the second a female in heat. Test animals choose to spend time with one or the other so-called stimulus animals, or can choose solitude. Should a male spend more time with a female, he would be heterosexual, while more time spent hanging out with the male stimulus would indicate homosexuality. In this setup, rats can also express bisexual or asexual choices. In the 1940s, rodents were "bisexual." In the (gay) 1990s, rodents have "preferences" and "orientations." Whether they mount or show lordosis is a separate story.[145] Once again, we see that experiment and culture co-produce scientific knowledge,[146] while such hybrid knowledge in turn shapes social debates about human homosexuality.[147]

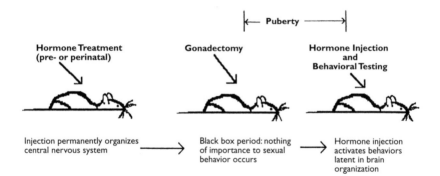

FIGURE 8.5: Overview of the design and interpretation of experiments leading to the organizational/activational theory of hormones and behavior.

UNDERSTANDING RAT SEX

Instead of trying, impossibly, to divorce ourselves from culture, claiming, somehow, that we scientists can create value-free knowledge, suppose we embraced our cultural locations? Suppose we strove to create stories about rodent sexuality that look at everything from genes to culture (rat culture, that is) as part of an indivisible system that produces adult behavior. Such a narrative would resemble "Dungeons and Dragons" more than "Little Red Riding Hood." The elements of such a narrative already exist in the scientific literature. What remains is to draw them together.

In broad outline the O/A theory goes like this. During the pre- (guinea pigs) or peri- (rats) natal period, hormones (usually testosterone, but some believe estrogen will do the trick) permanently affect brain development. Somehow (although it is still not at all clear how),[148] neural structures in the brain become dedicated to future behaviors such as mounting or lordosis (see figure 8.5). Puberty hits, activates the previously organized neural pathways, and the behavior becomes visible. Beach, Young, and the many fine animal behaviorists who have followed in their footsteps have all known that this picture is static and oversimplified, and fails to integrate the developing animal into its environment. Why haven't they proposed more dynamic accounts of rodent sex?

The experiments exist. It is the will and the theory that are missing. As long as one insists that in the interaction between nature and nurture, at some early moment in development nature starts it all, while only later does nurture tinker, a resolution is impossible. Often scientists talk in terms of "predispositions": natural inclinations that experience and social interactions can modify, but with greater or lesser difficulty. One thoughtful review of the

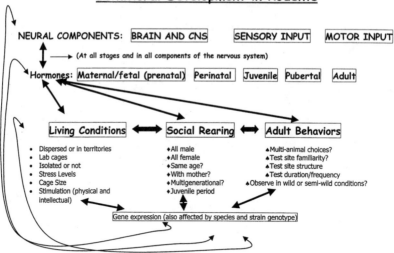

FIGURE 8.6: An enriched account of behavioral development in rodents.

interactions of social and hormonal influences on sex differences in rhesus monkeys concludes that nature needs nurture and that nurture needs nature.[149] That's almost right, but still the nature/nurture dualism persists. What I suggest is that we switch our vision (sort of like putting on 3-D glasses), so that we see nature and nurture as an indivisible, dynamic system. Such a systems approach to developmental psychology is not new, merely underreported.[150]

Animals develop in an environment. In utero, that environment includes the mother's physiology. A mother's body chemistry results from her behavior. What does she eat? Does she encounter stress? How do her hormones respond to such experiences?[151] Life experience before birth may also depend on how many wombmates an animal has, and even on whether it is sandwiched in between opposite-sex siblings.[152] Furthermore, the fetus's own movements and spontaneous neural responses can affect its development.[153] But that's only the beginning. Rodents have lots of brothers and sisters, and the number and type of sibling affects their behavior after birth.[154] So too does their interaction with their mothers. The entire life cycle, from before birth through weaning and juvenile play into puberty and adulthood, provides opportunities for experiences key to the development of the rodent sexual response (see figure 8.6).

How might life experiences and hormones co-produce adult behavior?

Some concrete examples illustrate. In one of the classic O/A papers, Harris and Levine reported that hormone-treated females have smaller, rounder, and otherwise abnormal vaginal openings;[155] others found that all the female rats exposed perinatally to androgen had closed vaginas, and most (91 percent) had enlarged clitorises.[156] Furthermore, testosterone-exposed females were larger than unexposed females.[157] Such physical differences could easily lead to different learning experiences. Larger females may learn to mount more often, and those with enlarged genitalia may find certain forms of sexual activity to be exceptionally pleasurable. De Jonge, for example, provides evidence that progesterone affects a female rat's mating interest only if a sexual reward is available. A closed vagina may make a female less receptive to mounting attempts, resulting in fewer juvenile learning experiences and lowered adult lordosis. Carefully timed chemical treatments, however, can produce an animal with normal-looking external genitalia, but exhibiting altered behavior. Therefore, changes in behavior do not result only from altered genitalia.[158]

Beach, Young, and many others have provided abundant evidence for the importance of social interactions in the development of mating behaviors. Animals bred in isolation are sexually incompetent,[159] and just having a roommate is not enough. The *kind* of companion matters, too. What components of upbringing contribute to developing sexual behaviors? In one set of experiments, 15 percent of normal male rats raised in isolation exhibited lordosis; if raised with females of the same age, however, half of the males exhibited lordosis; and if raised with males, 30 percent exhibited lordosis.[160] The reasons for such differences are unknown; but behaviors such as lordosis, the development of which involve perinatal hormones, also depend heavily on the circumstances of upbringing.[161]

What about the five senses? Testosterone affects more than just the genitalia and the brain. For example, male and female rat pups smell different. This testosterone-dependent difference induces mother rats to lick their male offspring more frequently and vigorously, especially in the anogenital region. The licking, in turn, affects adult male sexual behavior. Males raised by mothers whose nasal passages had been blocked (and who thus licked them less) took longer to ejaculate and had a longer refractory period between ejaculations. The psychologist Celia Moore and her colleagues also report that males raised by mothers that licked less had fewer spinal motor neurons in a region of the spinal cord associated with ejaculatory behavior. In other words, the development of a part of the central nervous system (a specific region of the spinal cord) is influenced by maternal behavior. Here the effect of testosterone is only indirect (on pup odor that stimulates licking).[162]

Young male rats also spend more time grooming their genitalia than do females, and this additional stimulation speeds up the journey to puberty. Similarly, female mice mature more quickly if they stay in the vicinity of certain puberty-enhancing odors.[163] In other words, an individual rat's own growth depends in part on his or her behavior. Nature and nurture are not separate here. Salt and water balance, pup leg extension, and urine release— each of which differs in male and female pups—all affect licking behavior. The brain, it seems, is one among several elements affected by early hormone exposure. Some elements are anatomical, some physiological, some behavioral, and some social. They all form part of a unitary system.[164]

Hormone treatment also affects muscle and nerve development outside the brain. For example, male rats have a set of three muscles, needed for erection and ejaculation, attached to the penis. Nerve cells growing out of the lower spinal cord connect to these muscles. The muscles and nerves accumulate androgen that the muscles require for sexual function. In female rats, one of these muscles degenerates shortly after birth unless it receives androgen during a particular period.[165] We don't know whether testosterone-mediated changes in female mounting behavior might be related to the presence of this muscle, but we do understand that how much sex a male rat has affects the size of the motor neurons that innervate these muscles. In this example, "differences in sexual behavior cause, rather than are caused by, differences in brain structure."[166]

And what about rat multiculturalism? Again, Beach, Young, and others showed years ago that different genetic strains exhibit different patterns of sexual activity.[167] An adequate model of sexual behavior must include individual genetic differences and incorporate the effects of an extensive period of maternal interaction, as well as experience gained from littermate, cagemate, and partner interaction. In recent years only the studies of de Jonge and her colleagues and of Moore have analyzed hormonal effects on behavior in this more complex framework, but even their work still takes place in a severely oversimplified environment: the laboratory. There is no guarantee that hormonal effects on mating behavior, proven in restricted laboratory situations, have much explanatory power in natural populations.[168]

The O/A pretty much ignores possible hormone effects from shortly after birth until puberty. Whether or not hormones are important between birth and puberty varies with the species. In some, ovarian hormones may affect the development of sex-related behaviors more or less continuously until puberty. Measures of feminine mating behaviors were higher in both female and castrated male rats that had ovaries implanted at various times prior to puberty. Implanted animals also had smaller body weights at puberty, a result proportional to the length of time the ovary had been implanted.[169] Furthermore, secretions during postnatal development can change the response of adult female rats to estrogen.[170]

Although many mammals have an initial discrete testosterone-sensitive period, some do not. Pigs, for example, respond to testosterone from birth until puberty, and the effects of injected hormones on behavior progress with time. Since juvenile pigs frequently engage in sexual play in both male-male and male-female combinations, it seems especially possible that experience and hormone co-produce adult behaviors.[171] In rats, both masculine copulatory responses and an increased orientation toward other females can result either from specific sexual experience during adulthood or from hormonal treatments during puberty or early adolescence.[172] In short, the fact that varying levels of specific hormones circulate during the course of an individual's life span affecting nervous system anatomy and function warrants a life-span approach to understanding the role of hormones in the development of sex differences in neural structure. A life cycle, systems account of animal development does not ignore the weeks between birth and puberty, and a more complete theory opens new experimental vistas, ones less visible under the O/A regime.[173]

In an article on the sexual differentiation of the nervous system, the neuroanatomist C. Dominique Toran-Allerand writes: "It is generally believed that testicular androgens exert an inductive, or organizational influence in the developing CNS [central nervous system] during restricted (critical), late fetal or early postnatal periods of neural differentiation, at which time the tissue is sufficiently plastic to respond *permanently* and *irreversibly* to these hormones"[174] In their 1959 paper, Young and colleagues concluded their experiments after testing treated guinea pigs twice, once at six to nine months and again at one year of age. Guinea pigs, however, can live as long as eight years. Yet there are no lifelong longitudinal studies of guinea pig mating behaviors under different hormonal and experiential situations. This is true as well for virtually all the other rodents studied in similar fashion, although the claim of permanence may be more accurate for animals such as mice, which normally live for only one to two years.[175]

Behaviors that show up in the months immediately following puberty may change with subsequent life experience. For instance, perinatally androgenized female rats, under certain circumstances, will show a lowered frequency or intensity of lordosis. Extensive testing, however, can overcome such changes.[176] Similarly, testosterone can typically activate mounting in developmentally normal female rats.[177] As one reviewer states, "the essential 'wiring' for these behaviors persists. . . . In this sense Beach was correct in questioning the idea that perinatal steroids change the essential structure of the nervous system."[178]

The notion of permanence faces other troubles as well. Activating effects were originally thought to be transitory, lasting from a few hours to a few days. In contrast, permanent organization events are supposed to last a lifetime. In practice, this has meant several months to about a year. But how does one classify hormonal effects on the brain that last for weeks rather than days or months? A variety of such cases exists for both songbirds and mammals. In these examples, particular brain structures respond to hormone increases, even in adulthood, by growth and to hormone reduction by shrinkage.[179] If the brain can respond to hormonal stimuli with anatomical changes that can endure for weeks or even months, then the door opens wide for theories in which experience can play a significant role. Even rodents engage in extensive periods of social play, activities that influence the development of the nervous system and future behaviors. It is at least plausible that play activities alter hormone levels and that the developing brain can respond to such changes.[180] Hormonal systems, after all, respond exquisitely to experience, be it in the form of nutrition, stress, or sexual activity (to name but a few possibilities). Thus, not only does the distinction between organizational and activational effects blur, so too does the dividing line between so-called biologically and socially shaped behaviors.

Humans are learners, and proudly so. We are, arguably, the most mentally complex of all animals (no offense meant to the great apes, who might argue with us if they could speak). It seems ironic, therefore, that our most prominent and influential accounts of the development of sexual behaviors in advanced mammals omit learning and experience. Because the control of hormone synthesis differs between primates and other species,[181] a case can be made that studies on the hormonal basis of sexual behaviors in nonprimates tell us little, if anything, about primates, including humans.[182] As I turn in the final chapter to theories of human sexuality, I make a broader claim: that the theories we have derived from rodent experimentation are inadequate even for rodents.

GENDER SYSTEMS:

TOWARD A THEORY OF HUMAN SEXUALITY

Portrait of the Scientist as a Young Girl

Consider a child born in the summer of 1944. Later she became a scientist. Does a portrait of her at age two (figure 9.1)—one hand holding a water-filled test tube up to the light, the other grasping a measuring cup— give evidence of the early expression of an inborn inclination to measure and analyze, of her genes leading her down the road to the research laboratory? Or is it testimony to her feminist mother's determination to find nontraditional toys for her young daughter? As the child grew, her mother began to write children's books about nature, and the young girl and her brother (who also became a scientist) learned on their walks through the woods to spot mosses, ferns, mushrooms, and insect homes.[1] When she was in graduate school, her father wrote a biography of Rachel Carson.[2] Science genes or environment? A logical argument can be made for each interpretation, and there is no way to prove whether either answer is right.[3]

For many who would think about this girl's life path, gender is not far from the surface. Her early interest in frogs and snakes marked her as a tomboy, a label some social scientists today interpret as an early sign of untoward masculinity.[4] When she was eleven, her friends at summer camp wrote her epitaph—"In memory of Anne, who liked bugs better than boys" —perhaps foreshadowing a future homosexuality. But that summer she developed a painful crush on one of the young male camp counselors, and by the time she was twenty-two she would marry for love and lust. Only years later would that epitaph for an eleven-year-old seem prophetic.

This young girl didn't like dolls, kept pet snakes and frogs, and grew up first with heterosexual interests and later developed homosexual ones. How are we to interpret her life, or any life? Speculating about genes for analytical personalities or homosexuality may make for good party chitchat or provide

FIGURE 9.1: A budding scientist? (Source: Philip Sterling)

solace for those eager to explain why someone turned out "that way." But partitioning genes from environment, nature from nurture, is a scientific dead end, a bad way of thinking about human development. Instead, I suggest we heed the words of the philosophers John Dewey and Arthur Bentley, who half a century ago "asserted the right to see together . . . much that is talked about conventionally as if it were composed of irreconcilable spheres."[5]

In this book I have shown how medical and scientific knowledge about anatomy and physiology acquires gender. I started at the outside, with genital gender, and moved inward, from the brain to body chemistry and ultimately to something quite intangible: behavior (in rodents). It turns out, however, that we cannot understand the underlying physiology of behavior without considering an animal's social history and contemporary environment. True to the image of the Möbius strip, when we reached a level of analysis that involved chemistry (and, by implication, genes)—that is, when we were at the most interior moment in our journey—we had, suddenly, to consider the most exterior of factors: What was the animal's social history? What was the architecture of the test apparatus? Why did specific genetic strains respond to hormone stimuli only under certain conditions? And while the driving question on the exterior surface of the Möbius strip is, "How does knowledge about the body acquire gender?" the active question on the inside surface is, "How do gender and sexuality become somatic facts?" How, in other words, does the social become material? Answering this inside question would require a book-length essay, so in this concluding chapter I offer but a framework for future research.

Successful investigations of the process of gender embodiment must use three basic principles. First, nature/nurture is indivisible. Second, organisms—human and otherwise—are active processes, moving targets, from fertilization until death.[6] Third, no single academic or clinical discipline provides us with the true or best way to understand human sexuality. The insights of many, from feminist critical theorists to molecular biologists, are essential to the understanding of the social nature of physiological function.

"R" Genes Us?

We live in a genocentric world.[7] The "genes 'r' us" habit is so deeply imbued in our thought processes that it seems impossible to think otherwise. We think of our genes as a blueprint for development, linear information that need only be read out of the book of life. We go to movies in which the major premise is that a DNA sequence isolated from a fossilized mosquito is all we need to create *Tyrannosaurus rex*. (The nicety, clearly found in *Jurassic Park*, that the

DNA needed an egg to become a *T. rex* is lost in the shuffle).[8] And we hear almost daily on the news that the project to sequence human DNA molecules has led us from the genes for breast cancer and diabetes to Parkinson's and more. Present-day students of human genetics can do the rest, "discovering" genes for alcoholism, shyness, and—yes—homosexuality.[9]

Even when scientists are themselves cautious about imbuing all power to the gene, popular renditions of new scientific findings dispense with linguistic subtlety. When Dean Hamer and his colleagues published evidence that some male homosexuals possessed the same region of DNA located on the X chromosome, for instance, they used fairly cautious language. Phrases such as "the role of genetics in male homosexual orientation," "genetically influenced," or "a locus related to sexual orientation" abound in the paper.[10] Such caution did not, however, extend to other pages in the same issue of *Science*, the journal in which the Hamer group's report appeared. In the Research News section of the same issue, the headline ran: "Evidence for Homosexuality Gene: A genetic analysis . . . has uncovered a region on the X chromosome that appears to contain a gene or genes for homosexuality."[11] Two years later, coverage in a more popular venue, *The Providence Journal,* had, on the same page, headlines referring to "gay gene" research and "schizophrenia gene search."[12]

But what does it mean to speak of gay genes or genes for some other complex behavior? Do such phrases, or Hamer and colleagues' more circumspect language advance our understanding of human sexuality? I think that the language not only fails to illuminate the issues at hand; it gives us intellectual cataracts.[13]

A brief review of basic genetic physiology demonstrates why: genetic function can be understood only in the context of that developmental system we call the cell. Most protein sequence information in a cell can be found in DNA located in the cell's nucleus. The DNA itself is a large molecule composed of linked chemicals called bases.[14] Genetic information is not continuous in the DNA molecule. A stretch that codes for part of a protein (called an *exon*) may be linked to a noncoding region (called an *intron*). Before a gene's information can be used in protein construction, the cell must make an RNA caste for both the coding and noncoding regions of the DNA. Then enzymes snip out the introns and stitch the exons together into a linear sequence containing the template for a specific protein. Making the protein requires the coordinated activity of additional special types of RNA molecules and many different proteins.

In shorthand, we sometimes say that genes make proteins; but it is precisely such shorthand that gets us into trouble. Naked DNA cannot make a protein. It needs many other molecules—special RNAs to carry the amino acid to the ribosome and secure it, like a vise, so that other proteins can link it to its next neighbor. Proteins also help transport the DNA's message out of the nucleus and into the cytoplasm, help the DNA unwind so that other molecules can interpret its message in the first place and cut and splice the RNA template. In short, DNA or genes don't make gene products. Complex cells do. Put pure DNA in a test tube and it will sit there, inert, pretty much forever. Put DNA in a cell and it may do any number of things, depending in large part on the present and recent past histories of the cell in question.[15] In other words, a gene's actions, or lack thereof, depend on the microcosm in which it finds itself.[16] New work, suggesting that as many as 8,000 genes can be expressed in a developmentally stimulated cell, shows just how complex that microcosm can be.[17]

Development, to paraphrase the philosopher Alfred North Whitehead, is a moving target. As an organism emerges from a single fertilized egg cell, it builds on what has gone before. By analogy, consider how a forest grows back in an empty, unmowed field. At first annuals, grasses, and woody shrubs appear, then a few years later scattered cedars, willows, hawthornes, and locusts. These trees need full sun to grow, so as they get larger, they create so much shade that their own seedlings cannot survive. But the white poplar does well under the conditions created by the cedar and its companions. Eventually, the poplar and other trees create a cool, leaf-covered forest floor on which the seedlings of hemlock, spruce, red maple, and oak thrive. Finally these create conditions for hemlock, beech, and sugar maple to grow. These new trees, in turn, create a microclimate under which their own seedlings thrive, and a stable constellation of trees, called a climax forest, finally develops. The regularity of such a succession of growth does not result from some ecological program found in the genes of cedar, hawthorne, and willow trees, "rather it arises via a historical cascade of complex stochastic [random processes that can be studied statistically] interactions between various" living organisms.[18]

The work of M. C. Escher offers a helpful analogy. In the early 1940s he produced a series of woodcuts designed to divide a plane into interlocking figures. Two features of these images help us see how developmental systems theory applies to cells and development (see figure 9.2). First, as one stares at the image, the birds jump into view, then the fish swim up. Both are always there, but how one focuses at a particular moment makes one animal more visible than the other. Second, each line simultaneously delineates the outline of both a fish and a bird. If Escher were to change the shape of the bird, the

FIGURE 9.2: Symmetry drawing E34B, by M. C. Escher. (© Cordon Art, reprinted with permission)

fish would change shape as well. Thus it is with a systems account of cellular physiology. Genes (or cells or organisms) and environment are like the fish and the bird. Change one change all. See one see all.

Socializing the Cell

NERVE CELLS AND BRAINS

Genes, then, function as part of a complex cell with its own important history. Cells, in turn, operate as large, intimately connected groups that form coherent organs within a complex, functionally integrated body. It is at this level, when we look at cells and organs within the body, that we can begin to glimpse how events outside the body become incorporated into our very flesh.

Just after the turn of the twentieth century in the Bengal Province of India, the Reverend J. A. Singh "rescued" two children (whom he named Amala and

Kamala), girls succored since infancy by a pack of wolves.[19] The two girls could run faster on all four limbs than other humans could on two. They were profoundly nocturnal, craved raw meat and carrion, and could communicate so well with growling dogs at feeding time that the dogs allowed the girls to eat from the same bowls. Clearly these children's bodies—from their skeletal structure to their nervous systems—had been profoundly changed by growing up with nonhuman animals.

Observations of wild children dramatize what has become increasingly clear to neuroscientists, especially in the past twenty years: brains and nervous systems are plastic. Overall anatomy—as well as the less visible physical connections among nerve cells, target organs, and the brain—change not only just after birth but even into the adult years. Recently, even the dogma that no new cells appear in the adult brain has gone the way of the dodo.[20] Anatomical change often results when the body's nervous system responds to, and incorporates, external messages and experiences.

Examples abound in which a social interaction causes a physical change in the nervous system.[21] Two types of studies seem especially relevant to a framework for understanding human sexuality. One concerns the development and plasticity of nerve cells and their interconnections in the central and peripheral nervous systems.[22] The other addresses changes in nerve cell receptors that potentially can bind transmitters such as serotonin or steroid hormones such as estrogens and androgens, which can in turn activate the protein synthetic machinery of a particular set of cells.[23] These examples show how nervous systems and behaviors develop as part of social systems.

Scientists sometimes disrupt such systems by interfering with the genetic function of one or another component. Analytically, this is akin to removing a spark plug to see whether and how it interferes with the running of an internal combustion engine. For example, scientists have created mice that lack the gene for serotonin receptors and have observed their distorted behaviors.[24] But although such experiments provide important information about how cells function and communicate, they cannot explain how mice develop particular behaviors in particular social settings.[25]

How might social experience affect the neurophysiology of gender? The comparative neurobiologists G. Ehret and colleagues offer an example in their study of paternal behavior in male mice. Males that never have contact with young pups will not retrieve them in the spirit of good fathering (when they inch too far from the nest), but even a few hours or a day spent in the company of baby rats will evoke ongoing paternal pup retrieval. Ehret and colleagues found that early exposure to pups correlated with increased estrogen receptor binding in a number of areas of the brain and decreased binding in one area.[26]

In other words, parenting experience may have changed the hormonal physiology of the father's brain as well as the mouse's ability to care for his pups.

The fact that human brains are also plastic, a concept that recently has begun to make it into the mass media,[27] makes it possible to imagine mechanisms by which gendered experience could become gendered soma. Environmental signals stimulate the growth of new brain cells or cause old ones to make new connections.[28] At birth the human brain is quite incomplete. Many of the connections between nerve cells and other parts of the body are tentative, requiring at least a little external stimulation to become permanent. In some brain regions, unused neural connections disintegrate throughout the first twelve years of life.[29] Thus, early physical and cognitive experience shape the brain's structure.[30] Even muscular movements before birth play a role in brain development.

One way the brain "hardens" a neural connection is by producing a fatty sheath, called myelin, around the individual nerve fibers. At birth the human brain is incompletely myelinated. Although major myelination continues through the first decade of life, the brain is not completely fixed even then. There is an additional twofold increase in myelinization between the first and second decades of life, and an additional 60 percent between the fourth and sixth decades,[31] making plausible the idea that the body can incorporate gender-related experiences throughout life.

Finally (for this discussion at least),[32] large groups of cells can change their patterns of connectivity—or *architecture*, as brain scientists call it. For years neuroanatomists have performed experiments to find out what segment of the brain responds when they stimulate an exterior part of the body. Touching the face provokes certain cortical nerves to fire, touching the hand and individual fingers affects different nerves, the feet still other nerve cells. Textbooks often summarize such experiments with a cartoon of a misshapen body (called a *homunculus*) superimposed on the brain cortex. Scientists used to think that after early childhood, the shape of the homunculus did not change. But following a series of experiments with other primates, this viewpoint has changed dramatically.[33]

One recent study compared the representation on the cerebral cortex of the fingers of the left hand of stringed instrument players to age- and gender-matched controls who had no experience with stringed instruments. String players constantly move the second through fifth digits of the left hand. The left hand homunculus was visibly larger for digits two through five compared to both non-string players and to the musicians' own right hands.[34] Or consider people who, blind from a young age, have become accomplished Braille readers.[35] Not surprisingly, they have enlarged the hand representation for their Braille-reading fingers. But their brains have made an even more amazing readjustment. They have recruited a region of the cortex that sighted people use to process visual information (the so-called visual cortex) and instead use it to process tactile sensations.[36]

For both musicians and those blind from birth, cortical reorganization probably takes place during childhood, a fact that confirms something we already know: children have enormous learning capacities. Such studies extend our ideas about learning, however, by showing that the material anatomic connections in the brain respond to external influences. Such knowledge wreaks havoc with both attempts to maintain a distinction between mind and body and attempts to offer up the body as a precursor to behavior. Instead they back up an insistence that the environment and the body co-produce behavior and that it is inappropriate to try to make one component prior to the other.[37]

The studies on Braille users and musicians show brain plasticity in the young, but can adult brain anatomy change as well? The answer comes from the study of a phenomenon that has long fascinated students of the human brain, from neurosurgeons to phenomenologists: the mystery of the phantom limb. Amputees often feel that the missing part is still present. At first the phantom seems to the patient to be shaped like the missing part. With time, however, the perceived shape changes; in contrast to a real limb, a phantom part feels lighter and hollow. Like a ghost, the phantom limb seems able to penetrate a solid object.[38]

Someone who has lost a hand may "feel" the missing hand following light stimulation of the lips; a light touch to the face may make someone who has lost an arm "feel" the missing limb, a phenomenon called *referred sensation*. A series of recent studies tries to explain such sensations with the finding that nerves in the region of the homunculus previously devoted to the now-missing limb are "taken over" by adjacent areas—in the example given, the cortical field connecting exterior stimuli to the face. The size of the homunculus for the intact hand also increases, presumably in response to increased use demanded by the loss of one hand.[39] Although remapping of the brain's cortex probably doesn't explain all phantom limb phenomena,[40] it does provide a dramatic instance of how adult brain anatomy responds to new circumstances.[41]

How might all this apply to the development of sexual difference and human sexual expression? Answers developed to date have been impossibly vague, in part because we have been thinking too much about individual components and not enough about developmental systems. Paul Arnstein, a practicing nurse concerned with understanding physiological links between learning and chronic pain, writes that: "The true nature of the central nervous system has eluded investigators because of its fully integrated, constantly changing structure and a symphony of chemical mediators. Each sensation, thought, feeling, movement and social interaction changes the structure and function of the brain. The mere presence of another living organism can have profound effects on the mind and body."[42] We will begin to understand how gender and sexuality enter the body only when we learn how to study the symphony and its audience together.

SEXUAL ANATOMY AND REPRODUCTION

During our lives, the brain changes as part of a dynamic developmental system that includes everything from nerve cells to interpersonal interactions. In principle, we can apply similar concepts to gonads and genitals. The gonads and genitals developed during fetal development continue to grow and change shape during childhood, affected by such things as nutrition, health status, and random accidents. At puberty anatomic sex expands to include not only genital differentiation but also secondary sex characteristics, which in turn depend not only on nutrition and general health but also on levels of physical activity. For example, women who train for long-distance events lose body fat, and below a certain fat-to-protein ratio, the menstrual cycle shuts down. Thus, gonadal structure and function respond to exercise and nutrition levels, and of course they also change during the life cycle.

Not only does sexual physiology change with age—so, too, does sexual anatomy. I don't mean that a penis drops off or an ovary dissolves, but that one's physique, one's anatomical function, and how one experiences one's sexual body change over time. We take for granted that the bodies of a newborn, a twenty-year-old, and an eighty-year-old differ. Yet we persist in a static vision of anatomical sex. The changes that occur throughout the life cycle all happen as part of a biocultural system in which cells and culture mutually construct each other. For example, competitive athletics leads both athletes, and a larger public who emulate them, to reshape bodies through a process that is at once natural and artificial. Natural, because changing patterns of diet and exercise change our physiology and anatomy. Artificial, because cultural practices help us decide what look to aim for and how best to achieve it. Furthermore, disease, accident, or surgery—from the transformations undergone by surgical transsexuals, to the array of procedures (applied to secondary sexual characteristics) that include breast reduction or enlargement and penile enlargement—can modify our anatomic sex. We think of anatomy as constant, but it isn't; neither, then, are those aspects of human sexuality that derive from our body's structure, function, and inward and outward image.

Reproduction also changes throughout the life cycle. As we grow, we move from a period of reproductive immaturity into one during which procreation is possible. We may or may not actually have children (or actually be fertile, for that matter), and when and how we choose to do so will profoundly affect the experience. Motherhood at twenty and at forty, in a heterosexual couple, as a single parent, or in a lesbian partnership is not a singular, biological experience. It will differ emotionally and physiologically according to one's age, social circumstance, general health, and financial resources. The body and the circumstances in which it reproduces are not separable entities. Here again something that we often think of as static changes across the life cycle and can be understood only in terms of a biocultural system.[43]

In their book *Rethinking Innateness*, the psychologist Jeffrey Elman and his colleagues ask why animals with complex social lives go through long periods of postnatal immaturity, which would seem to present big dangers: "vulnerability, dependence, consumption of parental and social resources." "Of all primates," they note, "humans take the longest to mature."[44] Their answer: long periods of development allow more time for the environment (historical, cultural, and physical) to shape the developing organism. Indeed, development within a social system is the sine qua non of human sexual complexity. Form and behavior emerge only via a dynamic system of development. Our psyches connect the outside to the inside (and vice versa) because our multiyear development occurs integrated within a social system.[45]

Thank Heaven for Little Girls—and Little Boys, Too

THE PROCESS OF GENDER

"All this cell, brain, and organ development stuff is fascinating," a frustrated parent might say to me. "But I still want to know why my little boy rushes around shooting imaginary laser guns, while my little girl prefers jump rope." Many Loveweb participants raise similar challenges, citing studies showing that gender differences appear at an early age—surely, they believe, an argument for inborn difference. How can I reconcile the observations of countless parents and the multitude of studies by sociologists and developmental psychologists with a systems approach to gender acquisition? Here I fit together already existing pieces of the puzzle.

"Gender," argue some sociologists, "is a situated accomplishment . . . not merely an individual attribute but something accomplished in interaction with others."[46] Both children and adults learn through direct feedback from

others to "do gender."[47] Classmates, parents, teachers, and even strangers on
the street evaluate how a child dresses. A boy who wears pants conforms to
social norms, while one who dons a skirt does not. And he hears about it
right away! Gender, then, is never merely individual, but involves interactions
between small groups of people. Gender involves institutional rules. If a gay
man made up as a woman walks down the street, he soon learns that he has
deviated from a gender norm. The same man in a gay bar will receive compli-
ments as he partakes in a subculture that plays by a different set of guidelines.
Furthermore, we "do gender" as part of "doing difference." We establish
identities that include race and class as well as gender, and we do gender
differently depending upon our location in racial and class hierarchies.[48]

In America and Europe, boys and girls begin to behave differently during
the preschool years. By middle school each group thinks the other has "coo-
ties," but during the years of hormonal hell, they return to each other for sex
and socializing. As adults they live and work in overlapping but gender-divided
institutions, and as old people they are separated once more, this time by the
differential death rates for men and women. Developmental psychologists,
sociologists, and systems theorists have some tantalizing findings about how
children acquire gender, although obtaining similar information for the rest
of the life cycle remains for future scholars.[49]

Traditionally, psychology has offered three approaches to understanding
gender development: Freudian psychodynamics, social learning, and cognitive development. For Freud, the child's own awareness of his or her genitals
produces erotic fantasies, which in turn lead to identification with a suitable
adult figure and the development of an appropriate gender role.[50] Social learning proponents focus on adult awareness of an infant's genitals, which leads to
differential reinforcement, the offer of gender-appropriate models, and thus
the development of gender role and identity.[51] Cognitive theory also starts
with others' awareness of a child's genitals. This leads to labeling and thence to
gender identity and finally to the acquisition of an appropriate gender role.[52]
Feminist social scientists have used each of these paradigms to produce information about the development of sexual difference. A primary goal in the past
has been to produce better accounts of female development, since in their
original forms all three theories primarily produced narratives about how
boys became men. More recently, however, a number of feminist voices have
begun to challenge the very structure of the field, calling for more complex
accounts of difference *and* a return to the study of male-female similarities.[53]
Here I depend especially on the work of cognitive and social learning researchers. Regardless of the particular approach, the goal remains that of understanding the development of the self: "behavior, experience, and identifi-

cations, including sexual desire and object choice, [that] are relatively stable or fixed or that, at least, . . . [are] a basic or primary 'core' of identity."[54]

Gender and sexuality often appear to us as universal features of human existence. Need such apparent universality mean that human sexuality and gender are inborn and only superficially shaped by social experience? We can see that this is the wrong way to ask the question by looking at the development of another apparently universal human behavior: smiling.[55] Newborns have a simple smile: the face relaxes while the sides of the mouth stretch outward and up. An identical "smile" has been seen in fetuses as young as twenty-six weeks of gestation. This suggests that, initially, a basic set of neural connections develops that enables a developing human to "smile" as a reflex, even in utero. In the newborn, smiling occurs spontaneously in rapid eye movement (REM) sleep states, but at first does not function as a mode of emotional expression.

By two weeks after birth, smiles begin to appear infrequently when the baby is awake, and more body parts are recruited into the event. The lips curl up farther, "cheek muscles contract, and the skin around the eyes wrinkles." Three-month-old babies smile much more frequently when awake, and they do so in nonrandom bursts, in response to stimuli in the environment. By the time an infant is from half a year to two years old, smiling blends with a wide variety of other facial expressions—surprise, anger, excitement. Furthermore, the facial expressions have become both more complex and individually varied. Accompanying the smile may be "nose wrinkles, jaw drops, blinks, blows, and brow raises that served to communicate affects from pleasure to mischief."[56] Thus, over two years, smiling changes in shape (and all that shape implies in terms of muscle and nerve recruitment), timing, and connection to other expressive actions. A smile is not a smile is not a smile (to butcher Gertrude Stein a bit).

At the same time that the muscles and nerves that govern smiling develop and become more complex, so too do the functions and social contexts that elicit smiling. While at birth, drowsiness and a decrease in sensory input elicits smiling, soon infants respond by smiling at familiar voices and sounds, and less regularly to touch. By six weeks, a baby smiles mostly while awake, in response to visual cues. By three to six months, a baby is more likely to smile at its mother than at inanimate objects, and by the end of the first year "smiling serves a variety of communicative functions, including the intent to flirt or do mischief."[57] At first blush, smiling seems to be a simple reflexive response, but over time it changes in complex ways—in terms of the nerves and muscles involved, but also in terms of what social situations elicit smiling and how the child uses smiling as part of a complex system of communication—

with other humans. Thus a physiological response becomes "socialized" not only in terms of intentional use but also in terms of the actual body parts (which nerves and muscles are used and what stimulates them) themselves.

Looking at the smile response as a developmental system enables us to exchange meaningless claims such as that "smiling is inborn and genetic" for carefully designed experimental studies "that systematically vary the conditions . . . which . . . may influence the form, timing and function of smiling" over different parts of the life cycle.[58] The psychologist Alan Fogel and his colleagues have used their studies of the smile response to develop what they call a dynamic systems perspective on emotion.[59] First they argue that emotions are relational rather than individual. Young infants, for example, smile in response to other people or objects. Second, they view emotions as self-organizing, stable systems. But stability does not imply permanence. Thus visual induction of the smiling response is stable in infants for three to four months, but is eventually replaced by a new stable system involving a variety of forms of physical interactions with its mother (or other caretaker).[60]

Little if any of the work on dynamic developmental systems has made its way into the study of human sexual development, but its applicability seems obvious. First, we need to stop looking for universal causes of sexual behavior and gender acquisition and instead learn more about (and from) individual difference. Second, we need to think harder about how to study sex and gender as part of a developmental system. Third, we need to become more imaginative and specific about we mean by the word *environment*. At the moment I think we are pretty clueless about the environmental components of human sexual development, but the idea provided by Fogel and others—that behaviors go through periods of instability (when they are more easily changed) and stability (when they seem fixed)—is helpful.

We do have some starting points. Since the mid-1980s, several groups of developmental psychologists have asked a set of interrelated questions about gender: What do children know about sex (the body parts), and when do they know it? Does such knowledge correlate with or affect gender-related behaviors such as differing patterns of play? A story outline has begun to emerge.[61] Psychologists have introduced the concept of a schema or schematic processing, which enable children to use rudimentary knowledge to make choices about "appropriate" play, peers, and behaviors. According to this line of thought, children adopt particular sex roles as they integrate their own sense of self with their developing gender schema, a process—like the developing smile—that takes several years. It is a reasonable (and testable) guess that during this time certain forms of bodily gender expression (such as "throwing like a girl") develop stability. But—also like the developing smile—stability need not suggest permanence, as observing top girl Little Leaguers would make quite clear.

Anybody who has observed a young child as he or she learns about the world has seen schema in operation. I remember, for example, when my toddler niece pointed at a clock with a schematic outline of an owl's face. "Owl," she proudly pronounced. I recall being amazed that she could recognize such a featureless representation when her storybooks all showed detailed drawings of these nocturnal birds. But she had internalized an owl schema, which enabled her to recognize this bird on the basis of minimal information. Beverly Fagot and her colleagues studied gender schema in children ranging in age from 1.75 to 3.25 years. They gave the kids a "gender task"—to correctly classify pictures of adults and children as "mommy," "daddy," "boy," or "girl." The younger children (those averaging about two years old) could not pass the test—that is, they apparently had no working concept of gender. The older children, however, (those averaging about 2.5 years), correctly classified both adults and children. Furthermore, those children who had developed boy-girl labels behaved differently from those who had not. The older kids, for example, preferred same-sex play groups, and girls who passed the labeling test were less aggressive.[62]

Fagot and Leinbach also observed 1.5-year-old kids at home. At this age they could neither pass gender-labeling tests nor engage in sex-typed play. By the time the children were 2.25 years old about half, called early labelers, could accurately label boys and girls. Two differences emerged between the early and late labelers. First, "parents of future early labelers gave more positive and negative responses to sex-typed toy play" and, by 2.25 years, "early labelers showed more traditional sex-typed behavior than late labelers."[63] By age 4, early and late labelers did not differ in preference for sex-stereotyped play. The early labelers maintained a greater awareness of sex stereotypes, however. Fagot and colleagues conclude that "the child's construction of a gender schema reflects back the behavioral, cognitive, and affective dimensions of the familial environment."[64]

I used to ride my bike to grade school, ruminating as I traveled the suburban New York landscape. For a time one problem in particular held my attention. I knew that boys had short hair, girls had long hair, and babies were born bald. How, I puzzled, did adults have the awesome power to declare immediately the sex of a newborn? I knew about genitalia, of course. I had an older brother, and we bathed together until I was four or five. Occasionally, also, I caught a glimpse of my father in the altogether. But I never connected such information to my puzzlement with birth announcements. Then, one day when I was about ten years old, biking home from school, the answer just popped into my head. "So *that's* how they know," I thought. As I look back now, through feminist theory-fogged scrim, I realize that as a child, gender had been clear on my horizon many years before sex became visible.[65]

I was not alone in my confusion, just a bit slow to resolve it. In America, at least, small children seem to base their initial, rudimentary gender schema on cultural markers of gender, not knowledge of genital differences. In one study, the psychologist Sandra Bem showed 3-, 4- and 5-year-olds photographs of either a naked boy or a naked girl and then of the same child dressed either in girls' or boys' clothing. Children younger than three had a hard time labeling the naked children as a boy or a girl, but successfully used social clues—clothes and hairstyles—to classify the dressed ones.[66] About 40 percent of the 3-, 4- and 5-year-old children accurately identified sex in all the photos once they had knowledge of genitalia. The rest, however, had not yet acquired a notion of sex constancy—that is, they used gender signals such as hairstyle and clothing to decide who was a boy and who was a girl. This also meant that some of these children believed that they could become the opposite sex by dressing as one. Their own gender identity was not yet fixed.

Children's understanding of anatomical constancy didn't seem to affect sex role preferences. Instead, early gender schema proved critical. "First, children learned to label the sexes, and only later did they show strong sex-typed toy and peer preferences and knowledge about sex differences in toys and clothing." Even though children did not need a concept of sex stability to develop sex-stereotyped preferences, having such knowledge strengthened the level of such preferences. It may be that "children who can label the sexes but do not understand anatomical stability are not yet confident that they will always remain in one gender group."[67] In keeping with the above findings, older children (aged 6 to 10 years) make more extreme stereotypic gender judgments than do younger ones. Not surprisingly, they first learn to associate characteristics relevant to their own sex and only later stabilize their expectations of the other sex (see figure 9.3).[68]

FROM INDIVIDUALS TO INSTITUTIONS AND BACK AGAIN

By the time children become accomplished members of the grade and middle school social scenes, they know that they are either a boy or a girl, and they expect to remain so. How do gender-aware children "do gender"? In her important study, *Gender Play: Girls and Boys in School*, the sociologist Barrie Thorne builds an essential methodological framework for studying older children. She became increasingly unhappy, she writes, "with the frameworks of 'gender socialization' and 'gender development'" in use for work on gender in children's lives. Thorne complains that traditional ideas about gender so-

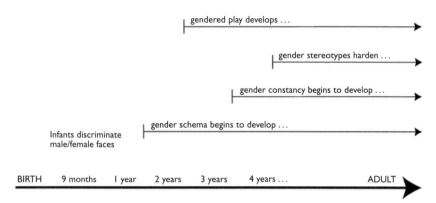

FIGURE 9.3: Stages in the development of gender specificity. (Source: Erica Warp, for the author)

cialization presume a one-way interaction from strong (the powerful adult) to weak (the passive, accepting child), and that even when granting some agency to children, social scientists have defined them as recipients, bodies acted upon by adults and the surrounding culture. Adults have "the status of full social actors," while children are "incomplete, adults-in-the-making." Thorne argues that social scientists would do better to see "children not as the next generation's adults, but as social actors in a range of institutions." Finally, and most important, traditional frameworks of gender socialization focus on the unfolding of individuals. In her work, Thorne chose to begin instead with "group life—with social relations, the organization and meanings of social situations, the collective practices through which children and adults create and recreate gender in their daily interactions"—that is, with a system and its process.[69]

By focusing on how social context and daily practice—of both children and adults—generate meaning, Thorne moves away from the question "Are girls and boys different?" and asks instead how children actively create and challenge gender structures and meanings.[70] She urges us to turn gender into a complex of concepts having to do with both individual and social structure. Furthermore, she finds it important to understand that "gender relations are not fixed . . . but vary by context" (including race, class, and ethnicity). As a feminist, Thorne's goal is to promote equity in education and beyond. Applying her approaches to the study of boys and girls, she feels, can help accomplish such ends. In a similar vein, the psychologist Cynthia García-Coll and her colleagues propose to integrate studies of gender in children with studies of race, ethnicity, and social class.[71]

Dynamic systems theorists such as Alan Fogel suggest, in principle, how gender can move from outside to inside the body, while developmental psychologists and sociologists such as Thorne, Fagot, Bem, Garcia-Coll, and others show how institutional gender, as well as attributes such as race and social class, might become part of individual systems of behavior. Indeed, gender is represented both within social institutions and within individuals. The sociologist Judith Lorber provides a European-American roadmap for such distinctions (see table 9.1). The institutional components of gender feed back on individual aspects; individuals interpret sexual physiology in the context of institutional and individual gender. The subjective sexual self always emerges in this complex system of gender. Lorber argues (and I agree), that "as a social institution, gender is a process of creating distinguishable social statuses for the assignment of rights and responsibilities. . . . As a *process*, gender creates the social differences that define 'woman' and 'man.' . . . Gendered patterns of interaction acquire additional layers of gendered sexuality, parenting, and work behaviors in childhood, adolescence and adulthood."[72] Thus Lorber, as well as other feminist sociologists and psychologists,[73] points out that concern with our subjective selves is not "merely" about human psychology and physiology. Rather, gendered individuals exist in social institutions strongly marked by a variety of power inequities.[74]

Although Lorber correlates institutional with individual gender, it was not her goal to show how the individual physically imbibes the institutional. But the work of sociologists and historians can provide helpful roadmaps for future work.[75] Consider the work of survey sociologists such as Kinsey and others who have followed in his footsteps. Surveying populations to learn more about human sexuality is a tricky business. On the one hand, population surveys provide us with information about gender and sexuality that can be very important in the formulation of policy issues ranging from poverty to public health.[76] On the other hand, when we create the categories that enable us to count, we bring into being new types of people.[77]

Consider the seemingly simple question: How many homosexual men and women are there in the United States? To answer it, we must first decide who is homosexual and who is heterosexual. Do we base our decision on identity? If so, we would count only those who will say, at least to themselves, "I am a homosexual" or "I am a heterosexual." Or should we count men who consider themselves fully heterosexual, but who once or twice a year get drunk, go to a gay bar, and have sex with several men— later indicating that since their urge to have such sex is so easily satisfied by such irregular encounters, they see no need to tell their wives or to apply the label "homosexual"?[78] Should we create a separate category for bisexuals, and how shall we define the true bisexual?[79] Is a man who in his early adolescence experimented once or twice

TABLE 9.1 *Lorber's Subdivision of Gender*

AS A *SOCIAL INSTITUTION*, GENDER IS COMPOSED OF:	FOR AN *INDIVIDUAL*, GENDER IS COMPOSED OF:
Gender statuses: socially recognized genders and expectations for their enactment behaviorally, gesturally, linguistically, emotionally, and physically	*Sex category:* individual assigned prenatally, at birth, or following reconstructive surgery
Gendered division of labor	*Gender identity:* the individual's sense of gendered self as a worker and family member
Gendered kinship: the family rights and responsibilities for each gender status	*Gendered marital and procreative status:* fulfillment or nonfulfillment of allowed or disallowed mating, impregnation, childbearing, and/or kinship roles
Gendered sexual scripts: the normative patterns of sexual desire and sexual behavior as prescribed for different gender statuses	*Gendered sexual orientation:* socially and individually patterned sexual desires, feelings, practices, and identifications
Gendered personalities: combinations of traits patterned by gendered behavioral norms for different gender statuses	*Gendered personality:* internalized patterns of socially normative emotions as organized by family structure and parenting
Gendered social control: the formal and informal approval and reward of conforming behavior and stigmatization and medicalization of nonconforming behavior	*Gendered processes:* "doing gender"—the social practices of learning and enacting gender-appropriate behaviors, i.e., of developing a gender identity
Gender ideology: the justification of gender statuses, often by invoking arguments about natural (biological) difference	*Gender beliefs:* incorporation of, or resistance to, gender ideology
Gender imagery: the cultural representations of gender in symbolic language and artistic productions	*Gender display:* presentation of self as a kind of gendered person through dress, cosmetics, adornments, and permanent and reversible body markers

Source: Adapted from Lorber 1994, pp. 30–31.

with another male but ever since has had sex only with women bisexual? Are people who are homosexual in prison but not on the street bisexual?[80]

By answering such questions, survey sociologists create the categories by which we organize sexual experience. As sociologists create "objective" information about human sexuality, they provide individually useful categories. The "Kinsey 6," for example, is now part of the national culture and contributes to the structuring of the psyche of some individuals, while the man who gets drunk and has homosexual sex once a year need not conceptualize himself as a homosexual because he does not have a "preference" or an "orientation" toward men.[81] None of this is to suggest that survey sociologists should close up shop. Indeed, the information they create is deeply important. But we should always hold in view the fact that surveys necessarily incorporate past ideas about gender and sexuality while at the same time creating new categories that are bound to carry both institutional and individual weight.

Historians as well as sociologists contribute to both the structure and understanding of institutional and individual gender. The psychologist George Elder, Jr., writes: "Human lives are socially embedded in specific historical times and places that shape their content, pattern, and direction. . . . Types of historical change are experienced differentially by people of different ages and roles."[82] The historian Jeffrey Weeks applies this idea to the study of human sexuality by suggesting that we study five aspects of the social production of systems of sexual expression.[83] *Kinship and family* systems and *economic and social changes* (such as urbanization, the increasing economic independence of women, and the growth of a consumer economy)[84] both organize and contribute to changing forms of human sexual expression. So, too, do new types of *social regulation*, which may be expressed through religion or the law. What Weeks calls *the political moment*, that is, "the political context in which decisions are made—to legislate or not, to prosecute or ignore—can be important in promoting shifts in the sexual regime," also profoundly contributes to individual sexual expression.[85] Finally, Weeks invokes what he calls *cultures of resistance*. Stonewall, for example, where the symbolic founding event of the gay rights movement took place, was, after all, a bar where gay men gathered for social rather than political purposes. Although, ultimately, self-identified homosexuals took to conventional political means—voting, lobbying, and political action committees—the prior existence of private spaces in which a gay subculture developed enabled such activities by making visible the potential allies with whom one might join to exact political change, while at the same time modifying individual embodiment of what came to be known as gay sexuality.[86]

Understanding the history of technology is also key to understanding the individual embodiment of contemporary gender systems. Think, for example, about the category of the transsexual. In the nineteenth century transsexuals did not exist. To be sure, men passed as women, and vice versa.[87] But the modern-day transsexual, a person who uses surgery and hormones to transform his or her birth genitals, could not have existed without the necessary medical technology.[88] The transsexual emerged as an identity or type of human, when, in exchange for medical recognition and access to hormones and surgery, transsexuals convinced their doctors that they had become the most stereotypical members of their sex-to-be.[89] Only then would physicians agree to create a medical category that transsexuals could apply in order to obtain surgical treatment.

Russian Dolls

Is there some easy way to envision the double-sided process that connects the production of gendered knowledge about the body on the one surface to the materialization of gender within the body on the other?[90] While no metaphor is perfect, Russian nesting dolls have always fascinated me. As I take apart each outer doll, I wait expectantly to see if there is yet a smaller one within. As the dolls get tinier and tinier, I marvel at the delicacy of the craft that produces successively smaller dolls. But displaying them is a dilemma. Should I leave each doll separate but visible, lined up in an ever-diminishing row? Such a display is pleasing, because it shows each component of the largest doll, but dissatisfying, because each individual doll, while visible, is empty. The complexity of the nesting is gone and, with it, the pleasure, craft, and beauty of the assembled structure. Understanding the system of nesting dolls comes not from seeing each separate doll, but from the process of assembly and disassembly.

I find the Russian nesting doll useful for envisioning the various layers of human sexuality, from the cellular to the social and historical (figure 9.4).[91] Academics can take the system apart for display or to study one of the dolls in more detail. But an individual doll is hollow. Only the complete assembly makes sense. Unlike its wooden counterpart, the human nesting doll changes shape with time. Change can happen in any of the layers, but since the entire assembly has to fit together, altering one of the component dolls requires the interlinked system—from the cellular to the institutional—to change.

While social and comparative historians write about the past to help us understand why we frame the present in particular ways (the outermost doll),

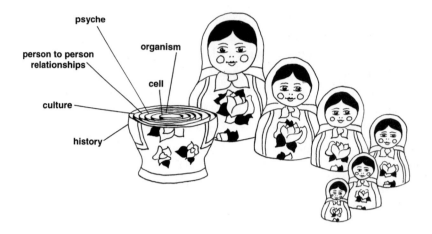

FIGURE 9.4: The organism as represented by a system of Russian stacking dolls. (Source: Erica Warp, for the author)

analysts of popular culture, literary critics, anthropologists, and some sociologists tell us about our current culture (the second largest doll). They analyze our aggregate behaviors, think about how individuals and institutions interact, and chronicle social change. Other sociologists and psychologists think about individual relationships and individual development (the third largest doll), while some psychologists write about the mind or psyche (the fourth doll in). As the location (or, as some would prefer, activity) that links events that occur outside the body to those that occur inside the organism (the second smallest doll),[92] the mind plays an important and peculiar function. The brain is a key organ in the transfer of information from outside the body in and back again, and neuroscientists of many stripes try not only to understand how the brain works as an integrated organ but also how its individual cells function. Indeed, cells compare the final, tiny doll found within the organism.[93] In different organs, cells specialize for a variety of functions. They also work as systems, their history and immediate surroundings stimulating signals for particular genes—to contribute (or not) to cellular activities.

Using Russian nesting dolls as a framework suggests that history, culture, relationships, psyche, organism, and cell are each appropriate locations from which to study the formation and meanings of sexuality and gender. Developmental systems theory, whether applied to the assembled doll or to its subunits, provides the scaffolding for thought and experiment. Assembling the smaller dolls into a single large one requires the integration of knowledge derived from very different levels of biological and social organization. The cell, the individual, groups of individuals organized in families, peer groups, cultures, and nations and their histories all provide sources of knowledge about human sexuality. We cannot understand it well unless we consider all of these components. To accomplish such a task, scholars would do well to work in interdisciplinary groups. And while it is not reasonable, for example, to ask all biologists to become proficient in feminist theory or all feminist theorists to be proficient in cell biology, it *is* reasonable to ask each group of scholars to understand the limitations of knowledge obtained from working within a single discipline. Only nonhierarchical, multidisciplinary teams can devise more complete (or what Sandra Harding calls "less false")[94] knowledge about human sexuality.

I do not naively believe that tomorrow everyone will rush out and join interdisciplinary research teams while revising their belief systems about the nature of scientific knowledge. But public controversies about sex differences and sexuality will continue to break out. Can homosexuals change? Were we born that way? Can girls do high-level mathematics and compete well in the physical sciences? Whenever these or related quandaries boil to the surface, I hope that readers can return to this book to find new and better ways to conceptualize the problems at hand.

The feminist theorist Donna Haraway has written that biology is politics by other means.[95] This book provides an extended argument for the truth of that claim. We will, I am sure, continue to fight our politics through arguments about biology. I want us never, in the process, to lose sight of the fact that our debates about the body's biology are always simultaneously moral, ethical, and political debates about social and political equality and the possibilities for change. Nothing less is at stake.

NOTES

Chapter 1: Dueling Dualisms

1. Hanley 1983.

2. My description of these events is based on the following reports: de la Chapelle 1986; Simpson 1986; Carlson 1991; Anderson 1992; Grady 1992; Le Fanu 1992; Vines 1992; Wavell and Alderson 1992.

3. Quoted in Carlson 1991 p. 27.

4. Ibid.

The technical name for Patiño's condition is Androgen Insensitivity Syn-drome. It is one of a number of conditions that leads to bodies having mixtures of male and female parts. Today we call such bodies *intersexes*.

5. Quoted in Vines 1992, p. 41.

6. Ibid., p. 42.

7. The contradiction plagued women's athletics at all levels. See, for ex-ample, Verbrugge 1997.

8. The Olympics specifically, and women's sport in general, have built all sorts of gender difference into the heart of its practice. Barring women from certain events or having different rules for the men's and women's games pro-vide obvious examples. For a detailed discussion of gender and sport, see Cahn 1994. For other examples of how gender itself contributes to the con-struction of different male and female bodies in sports, see Lorber 1993 and Zita 1992.

9. Money and Ehrhardt define "gender role" as "everything that a person says and does to indicate to others or to the self the degree that one is either male, or female, or ambivalent."

They define "gender identity" as "the sameness, unity, and persistence of one's individuality as male, female, or ambivalent. . . . Gender identity is the private experience of gender role, and gender role is the public experience of gender identity" (Money and Ehrhardt 1972, p. 4. For a discussion of Money's separation of "sex" from "gender," see Hausman 1995.

Money and Ehrhardt distinguish between chromosomal sex, fetal gonadal sex, fetal hormonal sex, genital dimorphism, brain dimorphism, the response of adults to the infant's gender, body image, juvenile gender identity, pubertal hormonal sex, pubertal eroticism, pubertal morphology, and adult gender identity. All of these factors, they believe, work together to define a person's adult gender identity.

10. See, for example, Rubin 1975. Rubin also questions the biological basis of homosexuality and heterosexuality. Note that feminist definitions of gender applied to institutions as well as personal or psychological differences.

11. The sex/gender dichotomy often became a synonym for debates about nature versus nurture, or mind versus body. For a discussion of how to use debated dichotomies as an aid to understanding the intertwining of social and scientific belief systems see, Figlio 1976.

12. Many scientists and their popularizers claim that men are more competitive, more aggressive or assertive, are more sexual, more prone to infidelity and more. See, for example Pool 1994 and Wright 1994. For a critique of such claims, see Fausto-Sterling 1992, 1997 a,b.

13. For feminists this debate is very problematic because it pits the authority of science, especially biology, against the authority of social science— and in any battle of this sort, social science is bound to lose. Science in our culture brings with it all the trappings of special access to the truth: the claim of objectivity.

14. Spelman labeled feminist fear of the body "somatophobia." See, Spelman 1988. Recently a colleague commented to me that I seem scared of biological theories of behavior. This puzzled him because at the same time he could see that I am devoted to biological studies as one way of gaining interesting and useful information about the world. He was right. Like many feminists, I have good reason to be scared of bringing biology into the picture. It is not only my knowledge of centuries of arguments in which the body has been used to justify power inequities. I have also encountered such arguments at a personal level throughout my life. In grade school, a teacher told me that women could be nurses but not doctors (after I had announced my intention to become the latter). When, as a young Assistant Professor, I joined the faculty at Brown, a Full Professor in the History Department told me kindly, but with great authority, that history showed that there had never been any women geniuses in either the sciences or the field of letters. We were, it seemed, born to be mediocre. To cap it off, when I returned from scientific meetings, emotionally shaken by my inability to break into the all-male conclaves, where the true scientific exchanges occurred (chatting at the socials and at meals), I read that "men in groups" was a natural outcome of male bonding that had evolved from prehistoric hunting behaviors. Nothing, really, was to be done about it.

I now understand that I experienced the political power of science. This "power is exercised less visibly, less conspicuously (than overt state or institutional power), and *not on but through* the dominant institutional structures, priorities, practices and languages of the sciences" (Harding 1992, p. 567, emphasis in the original). Thus it is no wonder that I and other feminists were (and are) suspicious of grounding the development of the psyche in some bodily essence. We responded to what came to be called "essentialism." A century ago and today, feminist essentialists argue that women *are* naturally different—and that such difference forms the basis for either social equality or superiority. For entrée into the extensive feminist debates about essentialism, see J. R. Martin 1994 and Bohan 1997.

15. For a discussion of this recalcitrance in terms of gender schema in adulthood, see Valian 1998a, 1998b.

16. See chapters 1–4 herein; also Feinberg 1996; Kessler and McKenna 1978; Haraway 1989, 1997; Hausman 1995; Rothblatt 1995; Burke 1996; and Dreger 1998b.

One recent sociological account of problems of embodiment considers that "'the cutting edge' of contemporary social theorising around the body may in fact be located within feminism itself" (Williams and Bendelow 1998, p. 130).

17. Moore 1994, pp. 2–3.

18. My social activism has included participation in organizations working for civil rights for all people, regardless of race, gender, or sexual orientation. I have also worked on traditionally feminist issues such as shelters for battered women, reproductive rights, and equal access for women in the academy.

19. I am actually willing to broaden this claim to include *all* scientific knowledge, but in this book I make the argument only for biology—the scientific endeavor I best understand. For extended arguments on the topic, see Latour 1987 and Shapin 1994.

20. Some would point to the fact that people express very unpopular sexualities despite strong contrary social pressure, even the threat of bodily harm. Clearly, they say, nothing in the environment encouraged the development of such behavior, but the body will out. Others argue that there must be some prenatally determined disposition that, in interaction with unknown environmental factors, leads to a strongly held, often immutable adult sexuality. Members of this latter group, probably the majority of Loveweb members, call themselves *interactionists*. But their version of interactionism (meaning that the body and the environment interact to produce behavior patterns) calls for a large dose of body and only a little sprinkling of environment. "The real issue," one of the staunchest and most articulate interactionists writes, "is how the body generates behavior" ("Lovenet" discussion).

21. Scholarship is not the sole agent of change; it combines with other agents, including traditional means such as voting and forming consumer preference blocks.

22. Haraway 1997, p. 217. See also Foucault 1970; Gould 1981; Schiebinger 1993 a,b.

23. See, for example, Stocking 1987, 1988; Russett 1989 ; Poovey 1995.

24. The historian Lorraine Daston notes that the idea of nature or the natural invoked in debates about the body changed between the eighteenth and nineteenth centuries: "Early modern nature was incapable of 'hard facts.' . . . Modern nature abounded in bitter revelations about the illusions of ethics and social reform, for nature was ruthlessly amoral" (Daston 1992, p. 222).

25. During this time, Foucault maintains, the change from Feudalism to Capitalism required a new concept of the body. Feudal lords applied their power directly. Peasants and serfs obeyed because God and their sovereign told them to (except, of course, when they revolted, as they did from time to time). The punishment for disobedience was, to the modern eye, violent and brutal: drawing and quartering. For a stunning description of this brutality, see the opening chapters of Foucault 1979.

26. Foucault 1978, p. 141.

27. These efforts created "an *anatomo-politics of the human body*" (Foucault 1978 p. 139; emphasis in the original).

28. Because some of the arguments about sex and gender represent the old nature/nurture arguments in modern drag, their resolution (or, as I argue for, their dissolution) is relevant to debates about racial difference. For a discussion of race in terms of modern biological knowledge, see Marks 1994.

29. Foucault 1978, p. 139; emphasis in the original.

30. Ibid. In chapter 5 I discuss how the rise of statistics enables twentieth-century scientists to make claims about sex differences in the human brain.

31. Sawicki 1991, p. 67; see also McNay 1993 for specific discussions of Foucault in a feminist context.

32. Foucault 1980, p. 107.

33. Quoted in Moore and Clarke 1995, p. 271.

34. Illustrating the anatomo-politics of the human body.

35. Exemplifying the biopolitics of the population.

36. Harding 1992, 1995; Haraway 1997; Longino 1990; Rose 1994; Nelson and Nelson 1996.

37. See also Strock 1998.

38. Furthermore, the theories derived from such research deeply affect how people live their lives. Recently, for example, a movement to turn homosexuals into "straight" people has garnered a lot of publicity. It matters a lot to individual homosexuals if they and others think they can change or if they believe their homosexual desire is permanent and unchangeable (Leland and Miller 1998; Duberman 1991).

For further discussion on this point, see Zita 1992.

For a detailed analysis of bisexuality, see Garber 1995 and Epstein 1991.

The sociologist Bruno Latour argues that once a scientific finding becomes so thoroughly accepted that we dignify it by calling it a fact, placing it without question in textbooks and scientific dictionaries, it moves out of view, behind a veil that he refers to as a black box (Latour 1987). Place a fact in a Latourian black box and people stop looking at it. Nobody asks whether, at the time of its origin, it functioned ideologically in the social or political arena or whether it embodied particular cultural practices or ways of seeing the world.

39. Kinsey et al., 1948; Kinsey et al., 1953.

Kinsey's Eight Categories. 0: "all psychologic responses and all overt sexual activities directed towards persons of the opposite sex." 1: "psychosexual responses and/or overt experience are almost entirely toward individuals of the opposite sex." 2: "the preponderance of their psychosexual responses and/or overt experiences are heterosexual, although they respond rather differently to homosexual stimuli." 3: Individuals who "stand midway on the heterosexual-homosexual scale." 4: Individuals whose "psychologic responses are more often directed toward other individuals of their own sex." 5: "almost entirely homosexual in their psychologic responses and/or their overt activities." 6: "exclusively homosexual." X: "do not respond erotically to either heterosexual or homosexual stimuli and do not have overt physical contacts" (Kinsey et al. 1953, pp. 471–72).

40. When they looked at accumulated homosexual encounters, from adolescence through age forty, they reported that homosexual responses had reached 28 percent for women and almost 50 percent for men. When they asked about interactions that led to orgasm, the numbers were still high: 13 percent for women and 37 percent for men (ibid., p. 471). Kinsey did not endorse the notion of homosexuality as a natural category. His system, emphatically, did not carve nature at the joints.

41. He did, of course, study these other aspects of human sexual existence, but they were not explicitly part of the 0–6 scale and Kinsey's complexity and subtlety of analysis were often lost in subsequent discussions. As recently as 1989, some researchers complained about the adequacy of the Kinsey scale and proposed more complex grid-like models. One created a grid with seven variables down (sexual attraction, sexual behavior, sexual fantasies, emotional preference, social preference, self-identification, hetero/homo lifestyle) and a time scale (past, present, future) across (Klein 1990).

42. See, for example, Bailey et al. 1993; Whitam et al. 1993; Hamer et al. 1993; and Pattatucci and Hamer 1995.

From the very beginning Kinsey fell under both political and scientific attack. He lost his funding after certain members of Congress became outraged. Scientists, especially statisticians, attacked his methodology. Kinsey had obtained data from an impressively large number of men and women, but he had collected his overwhelmingly middle class, white, Midwestern population using what sociologists now call a snowball sample. Starting with students as one source, he had branched out to their friends and family, their friends' friends and family, and so on. As word of the study spread (for example, through his public speaking engagements), he picked up more people, some volunteering after hearing him speak. Although he actively sought out people from different environments, there seems little doubt that he selected a segment of the population who was especially willing, and in some cases even eager, to talk about sex. Might this have accounted for the high frequencies of homosexual encounters in his reports?

On the positive side, Kinsey and a small number of highly trained co-workers (in a fashion true to the racism and sexism of the period, Kinsey's interviewers had to be male, white, and WASP) conducted all of the interviews. Rather than use preset questionnaires, they followed a memorized procedure and had the leeway to pursue lines of questioning in order to be sure they had gotten complete answers. More modern survey approaches have exchanged this more flexible, but also more idiosyncratic, interview process for a level of standardization that permits using less highly trained interview personnel. It is very hard to know whether important data are lost as a result. I owe this point to James Weinrich (personal communication) (Brecher and Brecher 1986; Irvine 1990a, b).

43. This is a necessary feature of doing molecular linkage studies (for any multifactorial trait) because the power of resolution is so low. (See Larder and Scherk 1994.) If the trait is not narrowed enormously, it is impossible to find statistically significant association. But narrowing the trait makes it inappropriate to generalize a finding to the general population (Pattatucci 1998).

44. For the grid model, see Klein 1990. For one version of an orthogonal model, see Weinrich 1987.

45. Chung and Katayama 1996.

In the most important recent survey of human sexual practices in the United States, Edward O. Laumann, John H. Gagnon, Robert T. Michael, and Stuart Michaels categorized their results along three axes: same-sex sexual behavior, desire, and identity (Laumann, Gagnow, et al. 1994). For example, Laumann and colleagues found that 59 percent of women with at least some homosexual interest expressed same-sex desire but no other behaviors, and 15 percent reported that they had same-sex desire, behaviors, *and* self-identity as lesbian. Thirteen percent reported same-sex behaviors (sexual interactions) but without strong homosexual desire and without identifying as lesbian. Although the precise distributions for men differed, the same general conclusion held. There is a "high degree of variability in the way that differing elements of homosexuality are distributed in the population. This variability relates to the way that homosexuality is organized as a set of behaviors and practices and experience subjectively, and it raises provocative questions about the definition of *homosexuality*" (Laumann Gagnow et al. 1994, p. 300). The sample size for these studies was 3,432, age range 18 to 59. There were discrepancies in the data, which the authors note and discuss. Among them:

22 percent of women report being forced into some sexual act, but only 3 percent of men say they have force women into sex. Men say they have more sex partners than women do, so who are the men having all that sex with? See Cotton 1994; see also Reiss 1995.

46. I often hear from my biology colleagues that our compatriots in other fields have an easier time than we because scientific knowledge changes continuously while other fields are static. Hence we need constantly to revise our courses, while a historian or Shakespearean scholar can legitimately give the same old lecture, year after year. In fact, nothing could be further from the truth. The field of literature changes all the time as new theories of analysis and new philosophies of language become part of the academic's tools. And an English professor who does not regularly update her lectures or develop new courses to reflect the changing field receives just as much criticism as the biochemistry professor who reads his lectures directly from the textbook. My colleagues' attitudes represent an attempt at boundary maintenance—a method of trying to make scientific work special. The entire thrust of current analyses of science, however, suggests that it is not so different after all. For an overview of work in the social studies of science, see Hess 1997.

47. Halperin 1990, pp. 28–29.

48. Scott 1993, p. 408.

49. Duden 1991, pp. v, vi.

50. Katz 1995.

51. Trumbach 1991a.

52. McIntosh 1968.

53. In philosophy the question of how to categorize human sexuality is usually discussed in terms of "natural kinds." The philosopher John Dupré writes more generally about the difficulties of biological classification of any sort: "There is no God-given, unique way to classify the innumerable and diverse products of the evolutionary process. There are many plausible and defensible ways of doing so, and the best way of doing so will depend on both the purposes of the classification and the peculiarities of the organisms in question" (Dupré 1993, p. 57). For other discussions of natural kinds with regard to classifying human sexuality, see Stein 1999 and Hacking 1992 and 1995.

Even now many of us spend idle moments speculating about whether So and so is "really" straight or "really" a queer just as we "might question whether a certain pain indicated cancer" (McIntosh 1968, p. 182).

54. Only through time travel, Latour argues, can one understand the social construction of a particular scientific fact. Interested parties must journey back to a period just before the fact in question appeared on Earth and follow along as citizens of an earlier time participated in its "discovery," argued about its reality, and finally agreed to place it in the dark box of facticity (see

note 38). Thus we cannot understand modern scientific formulations of the structure of human sexuality without traveling back in time to their point of origin.

55. There is now a rich and growing literature on the history of sexuality. For an overview of ideas about masculinity and femininity, see Foucault 1990 and Laqueur 1990. For studies of sexuality in Rome and in early Christendom, see Boswell 1990 and Brooten 1996. For up-to-date scholarship on the Middle Ages and the Renaissance, see Trumbach 1998 and 1987; Bray 1982; Huussen 1987; and Rey 1987). For changing expressions of sexuality in the eighteenth and nineteenth centuries, see Park 1990; Jones and Stallybrass 1991; Trumbach 1991a, b; Faderman 1982; and Vicinus 1989. For additional historical accounts, see Boswell 1995; Bray 1982; Bullough and Brundage 1996; Cadden 1993; Culianu 1991; Dubois and Gordon 1983; Gallagher and Laqueur 1987; Groneman 1994; Jordanova 1980 and 1989; Kinsman 1987; Laqueur 1992; and Mort 1987. For looks at how ideas about health and disease have been linked to our definitions of sex, gender, and morality, see Moscucci 1990; Murray 1991; Padgug 1979; Payer 1993; Porter and Mikuláš 1994; Porter and Hall 1995; Rosario 1997; Smart 1992; and Trumbach 1987 and 1989.

56. Katz 1976 and Faderman 1982.

57. Halwani 1998 provides one example of the ongoing nature of this debate.

58. Sometimes touted as the seat of modern democracy, Athens was, in fact, ruled by a small group of elite male citizens. Others—slaves, women, foreigners, and children—had subordinate status. This political structure provided the scaffolding for sex and gender. There were, for example, no specific prohibitions against men having sex with one another. What really mattered was what *kind* of sex one had. A citizen could have sex with a boy or a male slave so long as he actively penetrated and the other passively received. This sort of sex did not violate the political structure or bring into question the masculinity of the active partner. On the other hand, penetrative sex between citizens of equal status "was virtually inconceivable" (Halperin 1990, p. 31). The sex act declared one's social and political standing. "Sex between social superior and social inferior was a miniature drama of polarization which served to measure and define the social distance between them" (idem, p. 32). Position mattered. In the pattern that emerges from analyzing the variety of sex acts depicted in drawings on Greek vases, male citizens always penetrated women or male slaves from the rear. (No, the missionary position is neither universal nor "natural"!) But in the much-touted relationships between older men and their younger male citizen protégés, sex (without penetration) happened face to face (Keller 1985). Weinrich 1987 distinguishes among three forms of homosexuality identified either in different cultures or

in previous historical eras: inversion homosexuality, age-structured homosexuality, and role-playing homosexuality. See also Herdt 1990a and 1994a, b.

59. Katz 1990 and 1995. Other authors (Kinsman 1987) note the written use of the word in 1869 by the Hungarian K. M. Benkert. Something must have been in the air.

60. Hansen 1992 and 1989. French, Italian, and American accounts followed soon after.

61. Ellis 1913. A number of historians point out that the medical profession's involvement in defining types of human sexuality was only part of the story. For a variety of more nuanced accounts see Krafft-Ebing 1892; Chauncey 1985 and 1994; Hansen 1989 and 1992; D'Emilio 1983 and 1993; D'Emilio and Freedman 1988; and Minton 1996. Duggan writes: "turn-of-the-century sexologists, far from creating or producing new lesbian identities, drew their 'cases' from women's own stories and newspaper retellings of them as well as from French fiction and pornography as 'empirical' bases for their theories" (Duggan 1993, p. 809).

62. In earlier periods male and female sexuality was understood to lie along a continuum from hot to cold (Laqueur 1990).

63. The true invert of this period cross-dressed and, when possible, took up appropriately masculine work. Ellis, writing in 1928, described the inverted lesbian: "The brusque, energetic movements, the attitude of the arms, the direct speech, . . . the masculine straightforwardness and sense of honor . . . will all suggest the underlying psychic abnormality to a keen observer . . . there frequently a pronounced taste for smoking cigarettes . . . but also a decided tolerance for cigars. There is also a dislike and sometimes incapacity for needlework and other domestic occupations, while there is often some capacity for athletics." Ellis 1928, p. 250. No single book made this point more clearly while affecting the lives of thousands of lesbians well into the 1970s than Hall 1928. See also chapter 8 of Silverman 1992.

64. Although the notion of the invert strongly influenced turn-of-the century sex experts (who became known as sexologists), the idea was unstable, changing as strict sex roles weakened and men and women began more often to appear in the same public spaces. Ellis and then Freud began to note that in men one might separate masculine behaviors and roles from same-sex desire. Thus object choice (or what we today often call sexual preference) grew in importance as a category for classifying sexuality. A similar division came more slowly to women, perhaps not fully emerging until the feminist revolution of the 1970s smashed rigid sex roles into bits. For more on the history of sexology, see Birken 1988; Irvine 1990a,b; Bullough 1994; Robinson 1976; and Milletti 1994.

For a fascinating description of this transformation from the point of view of lesbians themselves, see Kennedy and Davis 1993.

65. Although male-male sex did not bother them, the Greeks recognized the existence of *molles*, unmasculine men who wanted to be penetrated, and *tribades*, women who, although engaging in sex with men, preferred other women. They considered both groups mentally troubled. But the abnormality lay not in same-sex desire. Rather, what worried Greek physicians was that *molles* and *tribades* were *gender* deviants. They either mysteriously wished to surrender male power by becoming a passive sex partner, or, intolerably, they tried, by becoming the active partner, to assume male political status. Both the *molle* and the *tribade* differed from normal folk by having too much of a good thing. They were understood to be oversexed. (*Molles* apparently developed the desire to be penetrated because taking the active role did not offer sufficient sexual release.) David Halperin writes: "these gender-deviants desire sexual pleasure just as most people do, but they have such strong and intense desires that they are driven to devise some unusual and disreputable . . . means of gratifying them" (Halperin 1990, p. 23).

66. The historian Bert Hansen writes: "A tentative sense of identity facilitated further interaction . . . which then facilitated the formation of a homosexual identity for more individuals" (Hansen 1992, p. 109).

67. Ibid., p. 125. See also Minton 1996.

The historian George Chauncey provides impressive evidence for a large and fairly open and accepted social world for urban gay men during the first third of this century. He argues that, in contrast to that period, gay culture encountered a great period of repression from the 1930s through the 1950s (Chauncey 1994). Allan Bérubé (1990) documents the participation of gay men and women in World War II. He suggests that the modern gay movement forms one of the ultimate legacies of their struggles in the armed services. For a fascinating oral history of the postwar gay rights movement, see Marcus 1992. Additional essays on the postwar period may be found in Escoffier et al. 1995. For discussions of historiographical problems in writing histories of sexuality, see Weeks 1981a, b and Duggan 1990.

68. Its English language entrée occurred in 1889 with the English translation of Krafft-Ebing's *Psychopathia Sexualis*.

69. Katz 1990 p. 16.

Today the concept of heterosexual appears to us as inexorably natural. But the first 30 years of the twentieth century had passed before it solidified on American shores. In 1901 neither the terms *heterosexual* nor *homosexual* appeared in the *Oxford English Dictionary*. During the teens and 20s novelists, playwrights, and sex educators fought censorship and public disapproval to make a public space for the erotic heterosexual. Only in 1939 did the word *heterosexual* finally emerge from the medical demi-monde to achieve that honor of all honors, publication in the *New York Times*. From there to Broadway, as a lyric in the musical *Pal Joey*, took another decade.

Katz 1990. The full *Pal Joey* lyric is quoted on p. 20; for a more detailed account of the history of the modern concept of heterosexuality, see Katz 1995. In 1929 the sex educator Mary Ware Dennett was convicted of sending obscene material—a sex education pamphlet for children—through the mails. Her criminal writings declared the joys of sexual passion (of course, within the confines of love and marriage). The author Margaret Jackson argues that the development of the field of sexology undermined feminists of the period "by declaring that those aspects of male sexuality and heterosexuality were in fact *natural*, and by constructing a 'scientific' model of sexuality on that basis" (Jackson 1987, p. 55). For further discussion of feminism, sexology, and sexuality in this period, see Jeffreys 1985.

70. Nye 1998, p. 4.

71. Boswell 1990, pp. 22, 26.

72. Nye 1998, p. 4.

73. As, for example, James Weinrich suggests (Weinrich 1987).

74. Not all anthropologists agree on the exact number of patterns; some cite as many as six patterns. As with many of the ideas discussed in this chapter, the academy is still in flux as new data pour in and new approaches to analyzing old data proliferate.

75. McIntosh 1968.

76. In the years since McIntosh's essay, books' worth of scholarship on the topic have been published. See, for example, Dynes and Donaldson 1992a, 1992b, and Murray 1992.

77. For reviews of cross-cultural studies of human sexuality, see Davis and Whitten 1987; Weston 1993; and Morris 1995.

78. See, for example, how Weinrich uses the notion of human universals to infer the biological basis of behavioral traits (Weinrich 1987).

79. Vance 1991, p. 878.

80. Note that such a definition permits Boswell to be a mild social constructionist while still believing that homosexual desire is inborn, transhistorical, and cross-cultural. Indeed, the phrase *social construction* does not refer to a unified body of thought. The meaning of the phrase has changed with time; more modern "constructionists" are generally more sophisticated than early ones. For a detailed discussion of the different forms of constructionism and essentialism, see Halley 1994.

81. Vance 1991, p. 878. Halperin certainly falls into this more radical constructionist category.

82. Herdt 1990a, p. 222.

83. A careful reading of Herdt's account of Melanesian societies reveals three underlying (Western) assumptions: that homosexuality is a lifelong practice, that it is an "identity," and that these definitions of homosexuality may be found worldwide.

84. Elliston 1995, p. 849.

Ibid., p. 852.

Anthropologists have similar disagreements about the implications of Native American practices that scholars refer to as "Berdache"—a variety of practices involving culturally sanctioned cross-gender roles and behaviors. Some argue that the existence of Berdache proves that the assumption of cross-gender roles and behaviors is a universal expression of inborn sexuality, but others find this to be an ahistorical, simplistic view of practices that have varied greatly across North American cultures and history. Carolyn Epple, who has been studying contemporary Navajo *nádleehí* (the Navajo word for "Berdache") observes, for instance, that Navajo definitions of *nádleehí* vary from case to case. Such variation makes sense because the Navajo worldview she studies "seems to place more emphasis on situation-based definitions than on fixed categories." Epple is very careful to qualify phrases such as the "Navajo Worldview" by indicating that she is talking about the one her informants discuss. There is no singular worldview, because it changes historically and regionally, and is better understood as a complex of overlapping belief systems. This contrasts with Euro-American assumptions that homosexuality is a fixed or natural kind.

(For discussions of natural kinds, see Dupré 1993; Koertge 1990; and Hacking 1992 and 1995.) Moreover, Epple points out, the Navajos don't necessarily regard *nádleehí* as gender transgression. The Navajo Epple studies conceptualize everyone as both male and female. Thus they would not describe a man with a woman's mannerisms as feminine. "Given that both male and female are ever-present," Epple observes, "a gender valuation of 'masculine' *versus* 'feminine' will generally reflect the perspective of the observer, and not some absolute value" (Epple 1998, p. 32). For additional critiques of the "Berdache" concept, see Jacobs et al. 1997.

85. See, for example, Goldberg 1973 and Wilson 1978.

86. Ortner 1996.

87. Although they didn't invent the concept, Kessler and McKenna use the idea to excellent effect in their analysis of cross-cultural studies of gender systems (Kessler and McKenna 1978).

88. Ortner 1996, p. 146.

89. Ortner writes: "Hegemonies are powerful, and our first job is to understand how they work. But hegemonies are not eternal. There will always be (for both better and worse) arenas of power and authority that lie outside the hegemony and that may serve as both images of and points of leverage for alternative arrangements" (ibid., p. 172).

90. Oyewumi 1998, p. 1053. See also Oyewumi 1997.

91. Oyewumi 1998, p. 1061.

92. Oyewumi 1997, p. xv. Oyewumi notes that gender divisions are especially visible in African state institutions, which were derived originally from colonial formations—that is, they represent the transformed impositions of colonialism, including the gender beliefs of the colonizers.

93. Stein 1998. For a full treatment of Stein's ideas, see Stein 1999.

Much of contemporary biological, psychological, and anthropological research uses homosexuality as real or natural categories. Some examples include Whitam et al. 1993; Bailey and Pillard 1991; Bailey et al. 1993; and Buhrich et al. 1991.

94. One other feminist biologist, Lynda Birke, has moved in the same direction, but because her book is forthcoming, and I have only read an early outline and the advanced publicity, I cannot cite it more specifically (Birke 1999).

95. Halperin 1993, p. 416.

96. Plumwood 1993, p. 43.

Plumwood also argues that dualisms "result from a certain kind of denied dependency on a subordinated other." The denial, combined with a relationship of domination and subordination, shape the identity of each side of the dualism" (ibid., p. 41). Bruno Latour uses a different framework to make a similar point—that nature and culture have been artificially divided in order to create modern scientific practice. See Latour 1993.

97. Wilson 1998, p. 55.

98. In her words, she "wants to ask how and why 'materiality' has become a sign of irreducibility, that is, how is it that the materiality of sex is understood as that which only bears cultural constructions and, therefore, cannot be a construction" (Butler 1993, p. 28).

99. Ibid., p. 29.

100. Ibid., p. 31.

101. For other examples of sedimented meanings in science, see Schiebinger 1993a, on Linnaeus's choice of the breast as the word to designate the class mammalia, and Jordanova 1989 on Durkheim's account of women in his 1897 book *Suicide*.

102. Butler 1993, p. 66.

103. Hausman 1995, p. 69.

104. Grosz 1994, p. 55.

105. Singh 1942; Gesell and Singh 1941; Candland 1993; and Malson and Itard 1972.

106. "The body image cannot be simply and unequivocally identified with the sensations provided by a purely anatomical body. The body image is as much a function of the subject's psychology and sociohistorical context as its anatomy" (Grosz 1994, p. 79). See also Bordo 1993.

107. The philosopher Iris Young considers a similar set of problems in her book and essay of the same title (Young 1990).

108. Phenomenology is a field that studies the body as an active participant in the creation of self. Young writes: "Merleau-Ponty reorients the entire tradition of that questioning by locating subjectivity not in mind or consciousness but in the *body*. Merleau-Ponty gives to the lived body the ontological

status that Sartre . . . attribute(s) to consciousness alone" (Young 1990), p. 147.

Grosz relies heavily on a rereading of Freud, on the neurophysiologist Paul Schilder (Schilder 1950), and on the phenomenologist Maurice Merleau-Ponty (Merleau-Ponty 1962).

109. Grosz 1994. p. 116.

110. Ibid., p. 117. The scholars to whom Grosz turns to understand the processes of external inscription and subject formation include Michel Foucault, Friedrich Nietzsche, Alphonso Lingis, Gilles Deleuze, and Felix Guattari.

111. For continuing discussion of the positions Grosz develops, see Grosz 1995; Young 1990; and Williams and Bendelow 1998.

112. I suspect that Grosz understands this, but has chosen the ill-defined starting point of a "drive" (hunger, thirst, etc.) because she needed to begin her analysis somewhere. In fact, she mentored Elisabeth Wilson, whose work provides part of the theoretical basis needed to dissect the notion of drive itself.

113. In discussing developmental systems theory, I do a lot of "lumping." I have found new ways of thinking about organismic (including human) development among thinkers working in a number of different disciplines. They have not always read each other, but I discern common threads that link them. At the risk of doing one or more of them an injustice, I will refer to them under the rubric of developmental systems theorists. The disciplinary backgrounds out of which this work comes include: *Philosophy*: Dupré 1993; Hacking 1992 and 1995; Oyama 1985, 1989, 1992a, 1992b, 1993; and Plumwood 1993. *Biology:* Ho et al. 1987; Ho and Fox 1988; Rose 1998; Habib et al. 1991; Gray 1992; Griffiths and Gray 1994a, 1994b; Gray 1997; Goodwin and Saunders 1989; Held 1994; Levins and Lewontin 1985; Lewontin et al. 1984; Lewontin 1992; Keller and Ahouse 1997; Ingber 1998; Johnstone and Gottlieb 1990; and Cohen and Stewart 1994. *Feminist Theory*: Butler 1993; Grosz 1994; Wilson 1998; and Haraway 1997. *Psychology and Sociology*: Fogel and Thelen 1987; Fogel et al. 1997; Lorber 1993 and 1994; Thorne 1993; Garcia-Coll et al. 1997); Johnston 1987; and Hendriks-Jansen 1996. *Law*: Halley 1994. *Science Studies*: Taylor 1995, 1997, 1998a, and 1998b; Barad 1996.

114. Many social scientists and some geneticists view organisms as resulting from the addition of genes and environment. They study organisms by looking at their variability and ask what proportion of the variability can be attributed to genes and what proportion to environment. A third term, which they designate as a gene-environment interaction, may be added to the equation of the simple sums if genetic and environmental cause don't account for all of the variance. This approach has been roundly criticized on more than one occasion. Sometimes such scientists call themselves interactionists, because they accept that both genes and environment are involved. Their critics

note that this approach to the analysis of variance portrays genes and environment as separately measurable entities. Some of these critics also refer to themselves as interactionists because they consider it impossible to separate the genetic from the environmental. I prefer to use the idea of a developmental system because of this confusion of terminology and because the idea of a system entails the concept of mutual interdependence of its parts. For critiques of the partitioning of variance, see Lewontin 1974; Roubertoux and Carlier 1978; and Wahlsten 1990 and 1994.

115. Oyama 1985, p. 9. The revised and expanded edition of Oyama's book is due out in the year 2000 (Duke University Press).

116. Taylor 1998a, p. 24.

117. For references on this point, see Alberch 1989, p. 44. As another example, an embryo needs to move in the womb to integrate nerve, muscle, and skeletal development. Mallard ducklings still in the shell must hear themselves quack in order to respond to maternal quacks. (Wood ducks need to hear their siblings quack in order to develop the ability to recognize Mom.) (Gottlieb 1997).

118. Ho 1989, p. 34. Alberch makes a similar point, writing, "it is impossible to state that form determines function or vice versa since they are interconnected at the level of the generative process" (Alberch 1989, p. 44).

119. LeVay's results still await confirmation and in the meantime have been subject to intense scrutiny (LeVay 1991). See Fausto-Sterling 1992a and 1992b; Byne and Parsons 1993; and Byne 1995. I do not read anything into the current lack of confirmation other than that it is a difficult study to do because of the relative scarcity of autopsy material from individuals with a known sexual history. A confirmation of his results will not help us understand very much about the development or maintenance of homosexuality unless we place the information into a developmental system. Standing alone, his findings can prove neither nature nor nurture.

120. I was horrified to start getting mailings and phone calls from right-wing Christian organizations that assumed my public argument with LeVay meant I was sympathetic to their homophobic agenda.

121. Bailey and Pillard 1991; Bailey et al. 1993; Hamer et al. 1993.

122. In a detailed and brilliant analysis of the problems posed by the nature/nurture, essential/constructed, biology/environment dichotomies, the lawyer Janet Halley calls for the development of common ground from which to struggle for personal, political, and social equality (Halley 1994).

123. Oyama 1985.

124. LeVay 1996.

125. Extraordinary, because it is not customary to use a strictly scientific report to discuss the potential social implications of one's work. Hamer et al. 1993, p. 326.

126. Wilson is more interested in the philosophical nature of the attacks

on LeVay's work than in the technical critiques. She willingly grants the validity of many of these, as, indeed, does LeVay himself (see LeVay 1996). For the technical critiques see Fausto-Sterling 1992a and 1992b; and Byne and Parsons 1993.

127. Wilson includes me in the list of feminists who had a knee-jerk antibiologist response to LeVay. While I don't think that I have ever thought of human sexuality in terms that discard the body, it is true that I have been wary of putting many such thoughts into print because I was caught in the grip of the essentialist/antiessentialist dualism. The history of essentialist ideology in the oppression of women, homosexuals, and people of color has been an enormous counterweight in my thinking. Only now that I see how systems theory provides a way out of this dilemma am I willing to commit myself to discussing these questions on the printed page.

128. Wilson 1998, p. 203.

129. I will discuss here some of those connectionists who apply their ideas to brain function or who model brain function using computer models of neural networks.

130. The psychologist Esther Thelen writes: "A view now is that multimodal information is bound together frequently and in multiple sites along the processing stream and that there is no single localized area in the brain where perceptual binding occurs" (Thelen 1995, p. 89).

Connectionists postulate processing elements called *nodes*, or *units* (which might, for example, be nerve cells). The nodes have many connections that enable them both to receive and send signals to other nodes. Different connections have different weights or strengths. Some nodes receive signals while others send them. Between these two types of nodes lie one or more layers that transform signals as they are sent. The transformations happen according to basic rules. One type is a 1:1 (i.e., linear) transmission, another is a threshold (i.e., above a certain level of input, a new response is activated). It is the nonlinear responses of neural network models that most resemble actual human behavior and that have excited the imagination of cognitive psychologists.

131. I have cobbled together this primitive account of a complex field from three sources: Wilson 1998; Pinker 1997; and Elman et al. 1996.

132. This has recently been shown to be the case for studies of mouse behavior. Three groups of researchers on different parts of the North American continent took genetically identical strains of mice and attempted to get them to exhibit the same behavior. To do this, they standardized the experiments in every way they could think of—same time of day, same apparatus, same testing protocol, etc.—but they got markedly different results. There were clearly laboratory-specific environmental effects on behavior in these mice, but the experimentalists cannot figure out what environmental cues are

important. They urge caution and multiple-site testing before concluding that a genetic defect affects a behavior (Crabbe et al. 1999).

133. When researchers ask identical twins to solve puzzles, the twins come up with answers that are more alike than those of paired strangers. But if monitored using PET scans, while working on the puzzles, the twins' brains do not show identical function. "Those identical twins with their identical genes never have identical brains. Every measure differs." This result is explicable with a developmental systems account of behavior, but less so with an account that suggests that genes "program" behavior (Sapolsky 1997, p. 42).

134. Elman et al. 1996, p. 359. See also Fischer 1990.

135. Joan Fujimura writes: "Just because something is constructed does not mean that it is not real"(Fujimura 1997, p. 4). Haraway writes: "The bodies are perfectly 'real.' Nothing about corporealization is 'merely fiction.' But corporealization is tropic and historically specific at every layer of its tissues" (Haraway 1997, p. 142).

136. Haraway envisions objects such as the corpus callosum as nodes out of which grow "sticky threads" that "lead to every nook and cranny of the world" (see the last two chapters of this book for concrete examples). Biologists, doctors, psychologists, and sociologists all employ a "knot of knowledge-making practices," including "commerce, popular culture, social struggles . . . bodily histories . . . inherited narratives, new stories," neurobiology, genetics, and the theory of evolution to construct beliefs about human sexuality (Haraway 1997, p. 129). She refers to the construction process as material-semiotic practice and the objects themselves as material-semiotic objects. She uses this complex phrase very specifically to bypass the real/constructed divide. Human bodies are real (i.e., material) but they interact only via language—the use of signs (verbal and otherwise). Hence the word *semiotic*.

137. This is a good example of Dupré's argument that there is no fixed way to divide up nature (Dupré 1993) and of Latour's plea to look at science in action (Latour 1987).

138. Connectionists, of course, do not believe that behaviors and motivations have a permanent location in the brain; instead, they view behavior as the result of a dynamic process.

Chapter 2: *"That Sexe Which Prevaileth"*

1. Quoted in Epstein 1990. Epstein and Janet Golden found the Suydam story and made it available to other scholars.

2. A fact-checker for *The Sciences* called Suydam's town in Connecticut to verify the story. The town official asked to keep the family name quiet, appar-

ently because relatives still live in the area and the story still bothers some local residents.

3. Halley 1991.

4. Kolata 1998a.

5. I owe this phrase to Epstein 1990.

6. Young 1937 has a full and highly readable review of hermaphrodites from antiquity to the present.

7. Ibid.

8. This discussion comes from Epstein 1990; Epstein 1991; Jones and Stallybrass 1991; Cadden 1993; and Park 1990.

9. My account of sex determination and the meanings of gender in the Middle Ages comes from Cadden 1993.

10. In one variation of this idea the uterus had five chambers, with the middle one, again, producing the hermaphrodite.

11. Cadden 1993, p.213.

12. Ibid., p. 214.

13. Jones and Stallybrass 1991.

14. Ibid.; Daston and Park 1985.

15. Matthews 1959, pp. 247–48. I am indebted to a colleague, Professor Pepe Amor y Vasquez, for bringing this incident to my attention.

16. Quoted in Jones and Stallybrass 1991, p. 105.

17. Quoted in Ibid., p. 90.

18. Several historians note that concerns about homosexuality enhanced the felt need for social regulation of hermaphrodites. In fact, homosexuality itself was sometimes represented as a form of hermaphroditism. Thus intersexuality, although relatively rare, fell (and falls) into a broader category of sexual variation of concern to physicians as well as religious and legal authorities. See discussions in Epstein 1990; Park 1990; Epstein 1991; and Dreger 1998a, b.

19. Coleman 1971 and Nyhart 1995.

20. Foucault 1970; Porter 1986; and Poovey 1995. For more on the social origins of statistics, see chapter 5 of this book.

21. Daston 1992.

22. Quoted in Dreger 1988b, p. 33.

23. On earlier treatments of "monstrous births," see Daston and Parks 1998; for a modern scientist's evaluation of St.-Hilaire, see Morrin 1996.

24. These comments are inspired by Thomson 1996 and Dreger 1998b. For a discussion of how modern reproductive and genetic technology has pushed us even further in the direction of eliminating wondrous bodies, see Hubbard 1990.

25. For a discussion of the social function of classification and of how social ideology produces particular systems of classification, see Schiebinger 1993b; and Dreger 1998b.

26. Dreger 1998b.

27. Quoted in Ibid., p. 143.

28. Dreger 1998b, p. 146.

29. The microscope was not new, although it underwent continued improvement in the nineteenth century. Just as important was the development of techniques to slice tissues into very thin strips and to stain the tissue to make them distinct under microscopic examination (Nyhart 1995).

30. Dreger 1998b, p. 150.

31. For current estimates using this "modern" system, see Blackless et al. 1999.

32. For well-documented examples of the uses of the science of physical difference, see Russett 1989.

33. Sterling 1991.

34. Newman 1985.

35. Clarke 1873; Howe 1874; for the century-long struggle of women to enter science themselves, see Rossiter 1982 and 1995.

36. Historian Dreger based her book on over 300 cases in the medical literature in Britain and France.

37. Quoted in Dreger 1998b, pp. 161, 1.

38. Newsom 1994.

39. The man suffered from hypospadias, a failure of the urethra to run to the tip of the penis. Men with hypospadias have difficulties with urination.

40. Quoted in Hausman 1995, p. 80.

41. Practicing hermaphrodites differ from bisexuals. Bisexuals are completely male or completely female but not completely heterosexual. A *practicing hermaphrodite,* as Young used the term, meant a person who used his male parts to take the male role in sex with a woman and her female parts to take the female role in sex with a man.

42. Young, 1937, pp. 140, 142.

43. Ibid., p. 139.

44. Dicks and Childers 1934, pp. 508, 510.

45. The latest medical writings speculate about the future use of gene therapy in utero; in theory, such treatments could prevent many of the more common forms of intersexuality. See Donahoe et al. 1991.

46. Evidence for this lack of self-reflection on the part of the medical community may be found in Kessler 1990.

Chapter 3: Of Gender and Genitals: The Use and Abuse of the Modern Intersexual

1. An instructional tape for surgical trainees produced by the American College of Surgeons opens with the surgeon Richard S. Hurwitz saying, "The finding of ambiguous genitalia in the newborn is a medical and social emer-

gency." The following are typical quotes from medical articles on intersexual-ity: "Ambiguous sex in the newborn infant is a medical emergency" (New and Levine 1981, p. 61); "Although it is now well-accepted that ambiguity of the genitalia is a medical emergency, this was not the case a decade ago" (Lobe, et al. 1987, p. 651); "Gender assignment is a neonatal surgical emer-gency" (Pintér and Kosztolányi, 1990 p. 111). One surgeon called "the child with ambiguous genitalia a neonatal surgical emergency"(Canty 1977, p. 272). The goal of one surgeon is to make a gender assignment within twenty-four hours and "send the child out as a sex" (Lee 1994, p. 30). Rink and Adams (1998) write: "One of the more devastating problems that can befall new parents is the finding that their child has ambiguous genitalia. This is truly an emergency necessitating a team approach by the neonatologist, endo-crinologist, geneticist, and pediatric urologist" (p. 212). See also: Adkins 1999.

2. One physician believes that "after stillbirth, genital anomaly is the most serious problem with a baby, as it threatens the whole fabric of the per-sonality and life of the person." Apparently things like mental retardation, severe physical impairment necessitating lifelong dependence and life-threat-ening illness pale before having a baby with mixed genitalia (Hutson 1992 p. 239). The American College of Surgeons implies that the consequences of a little girl being born with an extremely large clitoris are alarming enough that surgery must be done even if there is serious risk from administering anesthesia. Dr. Richard Hurwitz notes that most genital surgeries are per-formed after six months to minimize anesthesia risks; "if the clitoris is very large, however, it may need to be taken care of earlier for social reasons" (ACS-1613: "Surgical Reconstruction of Ambiguous Genitalia in Female Children," 1994).

3. Ellis 1945; emphasis in the original.

4. Money 1952, p. 8. See also Money and Hampson 1955; Money et al. 1955a; Money 1955; Money et al. 1955b, Money et al. 1956; Money 1956; Money et al. 1957; Hampson and Money 1955; Hampson 1955; and Hampson and Hampson 1961.

5. Money et al. 1955a, p. 308.

6. More recently, in the foreword to Money 1994, Louis Gooren, M.D., wrote, "normalcy in sex is a basic human demand. Male and female created he them" (p. ix).

7. Kessler notes the following unexamined assumptions in Money's work: (1) genitals are naturally dimorphic, and genital categories are not socially constructed; (2) genitals that are not dimorphic can and should be altered by surgery; (3) gender is necessarily dichotomous because genitals are naturally dimorphic; (4) dimorphic genitals are the essential markers of gender dichot-omy; and (5) physicians and psychologists have legitimate authority to define the relationship between gender and genitals (Kessler 1998, p. 7). In this de-

tailed yet accessible book, Kessler systematically dissects each of these unacknowledged assumptions.

8. Dewhurst and Gordon 1963, p. 1.

9. This seems to be a convention of the genre; the reader sees the most intimate photographs, shots that would be viewed as pornographic if set in *Hustler* rather than a medical book. Indeed, in researching this book, I often found gaping holes in medical texts where photographs of intersexuals and/or their genitalia had been razored out by a previous reader. Interestingly, we always see the "before" shot, designed to illustrate sexual ambiguity, but less often the "after," in which one is to presume that all traces of difference have been eliminated. Thus the reader can judge "nature's" caprice but not the physician's handiwork. Figure 3.1 is a rare photograph of a whole infant.

10. Dewhurst and Gordon 1963, p. 3. The reader never learns what the "woman" has done in the thirty years since her "limited adjustment" to the time of outbreak of new torment. It is unclear whether she married, or how she earned her living.

11. This narrative is based on my readings of case histories, physician training manuals, interviews, and journal articles.

12. Orgasm, of course, is a whole-body experience, not restricted to the penis or clitoris, but most modern sexologists agree that the phallus is the origin point for this pleasurable physiological response.

13. Baker 1981, p. 262. According to Baker, the first three minutes of doctor-parent interaction are critical.

14. For full documentation and a much more detailed account of the standard script that physicians offer to the parents of intersex children, see Kessler 1998.

15. I believe the distinction between true and pseudo-hermaphroditism should be dropped and the general term *intersexuality* substituted. The authors of one medical text reviewing disorders of sexual development now use four major categories: disorders of gonadal differentiation, female pseudo-hermaphroditism, male pseudo-hermaphroditism, and unclassified forms of abnormal sexual development. They have demoted the term *true hermaphroditism* to a subcategory under the heading of "disorders of gonadal differentiation" Conte and Grumbach 1989, p. 1,814; table reprinted with permission).

I. Disorders of Gonadal Differentiation

A. Seminiferous tubule dysgenesis and its variants (Klinefelter Syndrome)

B. Syndrome of gonadal dysgenesis and its variants (Turner Syndrome)

C. Familial and sporadic XX and XY gonadal dysgenesis and their variants

D. True hermaphroditism

II. Female Pseudo-hermaphroditism

A. Congenital virilizing adrenal hyperplasia

B. Androgens and synthetic progestins transferred from maternal circulation

C. Malformations of intestinal and urinary tract (nonadrenal form of female pseudo-hermaphroditism)

D. Other teratologic factors

III. Male Pseudo-hermaphroditism

A. Testicular unresponsiveness of hCG and LH (Leydig cell agenesis or hypoplasia)

B. Inborn errors of testosterone biosynthesis

1. Errors affecting synthesis of both corticosteroids and testosterone (variants of congenital adrenal hyperplasia)

a. Cholesterol side chain cleavage deficiency (congenital lipoid adrenal hyperplasia)

b. 3-β-hydroxysteroid debydrogenase deficiency

c. 17-alpha-hydroxylase deficiency

2. Errors primarily affecting testosterone biosynthesis

a. 17,20-lyase deficiency

b. 17-alpha-hydroxysteroid oxidoreductase deficiency

C. Defects in androgen-dependent target tissues

1. End-organ resistance to androgenic hormones (androgen receptor defects)

a. Syndrome of complete androgen resistance and its variants (testicular feminization)

b. Syndrome of partial androgen resistance (Reifenstein Syndrome)

c. Androgen resistance in infertile men

2. Inborn errors in testosterone metabolism by peripheral tissues

a. 5 2-alpha-reductase deficiency—male pseudohermaphrodism with normal virilization at puberty (familial perineal hypospadias with ambiguous development of urogenital sinus and male puberty)

D. Dysgenetic male pseudohermaphroditism

1. X chromatin-negative variants of the syndrome of gonadal dysgenesis (e.g., XO/XY, XYp-)

2. Incomplete form of familial XY gonadal dysgenesis

3. Associated with degenerative renal disease

4. Vanishing testes syndrome (embryonic testicular regression)

E. Defects in synthesis, secretion, or response to mullerian duct inhibitory factor:

Female genital ducts in otherwise normal men—*uteri herniae inguinale*; persistent mullerian duct syndrome

F. Maternal ingestion of progestins

IV. Unclassified Forms of Abnormal Sexual Development

A. In males

1. Hypospadias

2. Ambiguous external genitalia in XY males with multiple congenital anomalies

B. In females

1. Absence or anomalous development of the vagina, uterus, and fallopian tubes (Rokitansky Syndrome)

16. Money 1968.

17. I have distilled the information presented here from the following sources: Gross and Meeker 1955; Jones and Wilkins 1961; Overzier 1963; and Guinet and Decourt 1969.

18. Federman 1967, p. 61.

19. Each of the three categories of intersex may in turn be subdivided. The medical researchers Paul Guinet and Jacques Decourt separated ninety-eight well-described cases of true hermaphroditism into four major types. Members of the first group (16 percent of the cases) exhibited "very advanced feminine differentiation" (Guinet and Decourt 1969, p. 588). They had separate openings for the vagina and urethra and a cleft vulva defined by both the large and small vaginal lips. At puberty they developed breasts and usually menstruated. Their oversized and sexually alert clitoris, which at puberty sometimes threatened to grow into a penis, usually impelled members of this group to seek medical attention. In fact, even through the 1960s some intersexes raised as girls first drew medical attention because they frequently masturbated, an activity deemed unseemly for the female. Members of Group II (15 percent) also had breasts, menstruation, and a feminine body type. But their vaginal lips fused to form a partial scrotum. Their phallus (a structure found in the fetus that most frequently becomes either a clitoris or a penis) was from 1.5 to 2.8 inches long, but they urinated through a urethra located in or around the vagina. Most often, true hermaphrodites (55 percent) appear in a more masculine physique. The urethra runs either through or near the phallus, which looks more like a penis than a clitoris. Any menstrual blood exits periodically during urination (a phenomenon known as *hematuria*, or bloody urine). The vagina (without labia), which opens above a normal-looking scrotum, is often too shallow to permit heterosexual intercourse. Despite the relatively male appearance of the genitalia, however, breasts appear at puberty, as is true for the last group (13 percent), whose phallus and scrotum are completely normal and who have only a vestigial vagina.

Internally, virtually all true hermaphrodites have a uterus and at least one oviduct in various combinations with sperm transport ducts. The data on chromosomal composition are not completely reliable, but it seems that most often true hermaphrodites have two X chromosomes. Quite rarely they are XY, and occasionally they contain mixtures of XX and XY tissue (or other more bizarre groupings of X and Y chromosomes) (Federman 1967). These data are unreliable in that it is virtually impossible with limited tissue sampling to eliminate the possibility of genetic mixtures—i.e., mosaics. The most up-to-date work in this arena uses molecular approaches, which can demonstrate the presence or absence of particular genes that are too tiny to see under the microscope. Even here, however, the problem of tissue sampling remains. See, for example, Fechner et al. 1994 and Kuhnle et al. 1994.

20. Blackless et al. in press, see the list in note 15.

21. The many technical reasons for this can be found in Blackless et al. in press.

22. As with any genetic trait, different populations have different gene frequencies. Thus my account of albinism is true for the United States but not necessarily for some parts of the world where the albinism gene is more common. The estimate of intersexual births "requiring" surgery comes close to the frequency of cystic fibrosis—1 in 2,500 sufferers—in Caucasian populations.

23. New et al. 1989, pp. 1,888, 1,896; Blackless et al. 1999.

24. Such so-called chimeric embryos are commonly produced by scientists studying development in model organisms such as mice. In this case, of course, the chimera was an accident. But given the increase in the number of in vitro fertilizations, such events are bound to happen again (Strain et al. 1998).

25. On environmental estrogens, see Cheek and McLachlan 1998; Clark et al. 1998; Dolk et al. 1998; Golden et al. 1998; Landrigan et al. 1998; Olsen et al. 1998; Santti et al. 1998; Skakkebaek et al. 1998; and Tyler et al. 1998.

26. The increasing interest among academics in the notion of the cyborg—part human, part machine—attests to such changes. Humans have pacemakers, artificial hearts, estrogen implants, plastic surgery, and more. Haraway 1991 provides the groundbreaking volume. See also Downey and Dumit 1997.

27. Learning about a child's chromosomes or genitalia sometimes initiates a process of gender definition well before birth. Rapp insists that we listen to the diversity of women's voices and not assume that we will always be the passive victims of new reproductive technologies (Rapp 1997).

28. Butler 1993, p. 2.

29. Speiser et al. 1992; Laue and Rennert 1995; Wilson et al. 1995; Wedell 1998; and Kalaitzoglou and New 1993.

30. Laue and Rennert 1995, p. 131 and New 1998.

31. The earliest method involves testing a tissue sample taken from the chorion, one of the protective membranes surrounding the fetus.

32. Laue and Rennert 1995, p. 131.

33. Unexpectedly, and for reasons not yet understood, some XY children with CAH have partially feminized genitalia (Pang 1994).

34. See the treatment protocol flow diagrams in Karaviti et al. 1992; Mercado et al. 1995; and New 1998.

35. More than a few uncertainties about timing still exist. One study reports the birth of a genitally female child, even though dexamethasone treatment did not begin until sixteen weeks of development (Quercia et al. 1998).

36. Mercado et al. 1995.

37. Lajicl et al. 1998.

38. The tests are either sampling of the chorion or the better-known amniocentesis.

39. Pang 1994, pp. 165–66.

40. Trautman et al. 1995.

41. Seckl and Miller 1997, p. 1,077. These authors also write: "The ethics of needlessly subjecting 7 of 8 fetuses at risk for CAH to an experimental therapy with unknown long-term consequences remain unresolved, and the long-term safety and outcome have not been established. Therefore, such prenatal treatment remains an experimental therapy" (p. 1,078).

42. Mercado et al. 1995.

43. Trautman et al. 1996.

44. See, for example, Speiser and New 1994 a, b.

45. Donahoe et al. 1991.

46. Ibid., p. 527.

47. Lee 1994, p. 58.

48. Flatau et al. 1975. Recently, standards have been published for penis size in premature infants. Does this mean we will start to see genital surgery on premature infants? See Tuladhar et al. 1998. The concern is that a micropenis unrelated to the prematurity be recognized right away so that treatment or sex reassignment will not be delayed.

49. Donahoe et al. 1991.

50. I owe this phrase to Leonore Tiefer, who has written persuasively about the normalization of demands for certain types of sexual function. The upsurge of demand for Viagra suggests that the idealization of penile function does not reflect the norm of daily life (Tiefer 1994a and 1994b).

51. These authors note that theirs is the first study of the normal distribution of the urethral opening and should form a basis for deciding whether hypospadias surgery is needed (Fichtner et al. 1995).

52. The assertion comes from the American Council of Surgery, training tape ACS-1613: "Surgical Reconstruction of Ambiguous Genitalia in Female Children" (1994).

53. Newman et al. 1992a, write that what matters "is the presence of a . . . phallus sufficient in size to function as a male urinary conduit, to offer a satisfactory appearance when compared to peers, and to function satisfactorily for sexual activity" (p. 646); see also Kupfer et al. 1992, esp. p. 328.

54. Donahoe and Lee 1988, p. 233.

55. Obsession with organ size is not universal. The Greeks thought the smaller penis to be more manly and sexy.

56. Kessler 1998.

57. Sripathi et al. 1997, pp. 786–87. A commentator on this example wrote: "It has to be accepted that attitudes towards sex of rearing and in par-

ticular toward feminizing genitoplasties in late-diagnosed patients with CAH
in the Middle East is going to be very different from those in Europe" (Frank
1997, p. 789). See also Ozbey 1998; and Abdullah et al. 1991.

58. Kessler 1990, pp. 18–19.

59. Hendricks 1993, p. 15. For more on the attitudes of some surgeons,
see Miller 1993.

60. See, for example, the discussions of clitoral size in Kumar et al. 1974.

61. Riley and Rosenbloom 1980.

62. Oberfield et al. 1989; see also Sane and Pescovitz 1992.

63. Lee 1994, p. 59.

64. Doctors refer to such cases as "idiopathic clitoromegaly"—that is,
the clitoris is enlarged for unknown reasons.

65. Gross et al. 1966.

66. Fausto-Sterling 1993c.

67. See Dr. Milton T. Edgerton's discussion in Sagehashi 1993, p. 956;
Masters and Johnson 1966. In a 1994 telephone interview, Dr. Judson Randolf
told me he developed the less drastic operation for clitoral recession after one
of his surgical nurses questioned the need for complete clitorectomy.

68. Randolf and Hung 1970, p. 230.

69. Smith 1997.

70. Stecker et al. 1981, p. 539.

71. The following is a sample of the most recent publications on hypospadias: Abu-Arafeh et al. 1998; Andrews et al. 1998; Asopa 1998; Caldamone et al. 1998; De Grazia et al. 1998; Devesa et al. 1998; Dolk 1998; Dolk
et al. 1998; Duel et al. 1998; Fichtner et al. 1998; Figueroa and Fitzpatrick
1998; Gittes et al. 1998; Hayashi, Maruyama, et al. 1998; Hayashi, Mogami,
et al. 1998; Hoebeke et al. 1997; Johnson and Coleman 1998; Kojima et al.
1998; Kropfl et al. 1998; Lindgren et al. 1998; Njinou et al. 1998; Nonomura
et al. 1998; Perovic 1998; Perovic and Djordjevic 1998; Perovic, Djordjevic,
et al. 1998; Perovic, Vukadinovic, et al. 1998; Piro et al. 1998; Retik and
Borer 1998; Rosenbloom 1998; Rushton and Belman 1998; Snodgrass et al.
1998; Titley and Bracka 1998; Tuladhar et al. 1998; Vandersteen and Husmann 1998; and Yavuzer et al. 1998. A multiyear search of Medline using the
entry word *hypospadias* located well over 2,000 medical publications on the
topic. For an accurate defense of hypospodias surgery see Glassberg, 1999.

72. See, for example, Duckett and Snyder 1992; Gearhart and Borland
1992; Koyanagi et al. 1994; Andrews et al. 1998; Duel et al. 1998; Hayashi,
Mogami, et al. 1998; Retik and Borer 1998; Vandersteen and Husmann 1998;
Issa and Gearhart 1989; Jayanthi et al. 1994; Teague et al. 1994; and Ehrlich
and Alter 1996.

73. Duckett 1996, p. 134.

74. Hampson and Hampson write: "body appearance does have an important, indirect bearing on the development of psychologic functioning, in-

cluding that which we term gender role or psychosexual orientation" Hampson and Hampson 1961, p. 1,415.

75. Ibid. , p. 1,417.

76. Peris 1960, p. 165.

77. Slijper et al. 1994, pp. 10–11.

78. Ibid., p. 14.

79. Lee et al. 1980, pp. 161–62.

80. Forest 1981, p. 149.

81. For an argument against early gonadectomy, see Diamond and Sigmundson 1997a.

82. Kessler 1990, p. 23.

83. They wrote: "the sex of assignment and rearing is consistently and conspicuously a more reliable prognosticator of a hermaphrodite's gender role and orientation than is the chromosomal sex, gonadal sex, the hormonal sex, the accessory internal reproductive morphology, or the ambiguous morphology of the external genitalia" (Money et al 1957, pp. 333–34).

84. This is at odds with the mother's statements thirty years later, when she confirmed John's memories of trying to rip off his frilly dresses. Memory and interpretation of a third party often pose difficulties in evaluating the utility of evidence from case studies.

85. Money and Ehrhardt 1972, pp. 144–45, p. 152. Money said he wanted to root out the nineteenth- and early-twentieth-century "tyranny of the gonads" (Dreger 1998b), which he felt often led to a sex assignment that was psychologically unwarranted. This rhetoric, however, does not really ring true, since physicians such as W. H. Young, whose work Money had to have known, had long since let go of using gonads alone to assign sex. Perhaps Money simply wanted to bring this work to a larger and still benighted audience of practitioners out in the boondocks. Perhaps, too, he was merely riding a larger wave of 1950s neo-Freudian psychology that emphasized the importance of a "proper family" and role models provided by a bread-earning dad and a stay-at-home mom. It will require more historical work to figure out exactly what Money's ideological commitments were and how they shaped his studies.

86. It is not clear why such a seemingly radical viewpoint gained such complete control of the medical discourse, making it impossible until very recently to challenge Money and his colleagues' approach to the treatment of intersex. Kessler writes: "Unlike the media, my interest in this case is not whether it supports a biological or a social theory of gender development but why gender theorists (including McKenna and myself) were too eager to embrace Money's theory of gender plasticity. Why also did it become the only theory taught to parents of intersexed infants?" (Kessler 1998, p. 7).

87. In the acknowledgment of his paper, Diamond writes, "I am indebted to Robert W. Goy, who originally suggested the writing of this paper, and

to Drs. William C. Young, Charles H. Phoenix, and Arnold A. Gerall for enlightening discussion of the theories and problems involved in a presentation of this type" (Diamond 1965, p. 169) Zucker writes: "Thus in a wonderfully dialectical manner, while Money and his colleagues were emphasizing the importance of psychosocial factors on aspects of psychosexual differentiation in humans, a method, a paradigm, and a theory of biological factors on psychosexual differentiation in lower animals were also being articulated" (Zucker 1996, p. 151).

88. Later, Robert W. Goy extended this approach to studies of rhesus monkeys. This paradigm is articulated in its most influential form in Phoenix et al. 1959. I discuss the paradigm and this paper in detail in chapter 8.

89. The history of this organizational/activational theory in rodents is another story (see chapter 8 of this book), and the extent of its applicability to primates is still a matter of contention (see Bleier 1984 and Byne 1995).

90. Diamond 1965.

91. Ibid., pp. 148, 150; emphasis added.

92. Diamond wrote: "although humans *can adjust* to an erroneously imposed gender role, (a) it does not mean that prenatal factors are not normally influential, and (b) that they do so with difficulty if not prenatally and biologically disposed." He also argued that humans share a common vertebrate heritage and should thus be expected to have developmental systems similar to other animals (Diamond 1965, p. 150; emphasis in original).

93. Diamond's characterization of Money's theory seems inaccurate to me. His depicts a psychosexually undifferentiated child whose gender identity seems to develop only in response to environmental upbringing. At first, it seems, there is complete choice about gender identity, but after a critical period in early childhood in which choice becomes restricted, new learning experiences would "enlarge and direct sexual development" (idem, p. 168). Money's actual position shifted with time, and even in his early publications he did not always support the idea of complete neutrality at birth. In order to distinguish clearly his own model, Diamond chose the most extreme version of Money's sometimes inconsistent ideas. On this point, see also Zucker 1996.

94. Diamond 1965, p. 168.

95. His work was published, followed by Money's negative review of the paper (Zuger 1970; Money 1970). There was also a brief, unanswered paper in the *British Medical Journal* published in 1966. It also provides a rare firsthand account of how delighted the child was to change from female to male at age thirteen, and his later successful development and marriage (Armstrong 1966).

96. Zuger 1970, p. 461.

97. Money includes Diamond in his list of negative examples (Money 1970, p. 464).

98. Money and Ehrhardt 1972, p. 154. Money and Ehrhardt here cite both Zuger and Diamond as negative examples.

99. Diamond 1982, p. 183.

100. Ibid. p. 184.

101. Quoted in Colapinto 1997, p. 92.

102. Angier 1997b. Even in 1997, Money's viewpoint was so widely accepted that Diamond and Sigmundson could not, at first, get their paper published (Diamond, personal communication 1998).

103. Diamond and Sigmundson 1997b, p. 303; emphasis added. See also 1997a and Reiner 1997. In this passage Diamond has a hard time following his own advice to avoid using terms such as *normal* vs. *mal-developed*, see paragraph 3, p. 1,046.

104. See, for example, Gilbert et al. 1993; Meyer-Bahlburg et al. 1996; Reiner 1996; Diamond 1997b; Reiner 1997a, b.; Phornputkul et al. in press; Van Wyk 1999; Bin-Abbas et al. 1999.

105. Cf. Diamond and Sigmundson 1997a and 1997b with Meyer-Bahlburg et al. 1996; Zucker 1996; and Bradley et al. 1998.

106. Diamond and Sigmundson 1997b, p. 304. See also: Lee and Grup-puso 1999, and Chase 1999.

107. Bradley et al. 1998, pp. 6–8 of printout of electronic article.

108. Here are some of their comments: "I find it interesting that the authors . . . do not investigate the possible effects of 'negative nurture' . . . which seem to leap right off the page: while John had a well-adjusted male twin and a supportive, loving father, Bradley's patient had an alcoholic father who left when she was 3–4 . . . followed by an alcoholic stepfather. No wonder she denied ever feeling that she had wanted to be male," "At 26 I was— ostensibly—happily, heterosexually married to a man; had a team of doctors shown up to ask me how I was, that is most certainly what I would have told them. Two years later I was divorced and pursuing further corrective surgery to normalize [to make more male-like] my genitalia" to make me more attractive to females. "I have been living as a male since March of 1998." Several others commented that at twenty-six their gender identities were not yet "finished." Indeed, a concept one finds throughout this debate is that there is but one true stable identity that individuals must find and live with. A sad case is one who never even knows his or her true identity ("I'm sure he's transsexual but he doesn't know it").

Finally, intersexual commentators about both papers argued that "what is read as rejection of being regendered could also be the rejection of a traumatic situation vis-à-vis being intimately studied." Despite the trauma of hospitalization, surgery, and frequent genital exams, "the papers mentioned remained focused on the question of gender identity order/disorder rather than questions of personal bodily integrity and violation." Only a few scholars in this field have raised the general question of how any surgical trauma early in development might affect later behavior and development. During this on-line debate, some of the sexologists politely thanked the intersexual corre-spondents for their thoughts, but none took on their substantive points. To do so would have made it even more difficult to interpret and thus enter medical case studies in the service of particular theories of gender formation.

109. Money 1998, pp. 113–14.

110. Bérubé 1990, p. 258.

111. Hampson and Hampson 1961, p. 1,425. Money et al. 1956, p. 49, list three treated hermaphrodites as "mildly unhealthy" because they "had homosexual desires and inclinations."

112. Money et al. 1955b, pp. 291–92. "It is important," one group writes, "that the parents have plenty of opportunity to express . . . their fears for the future, such as . . . fear for an abnormal sexual nature. Parents will feel reassured when they know that their daughter can develop heterosexually just like other children and that male characteristics are impossible" (Slijper et al. 1994, pp. 14–15). Note here, too, how lesbianism is associated with maleness. See also Dittmann et al. 1992, who write: "In our clinical experi-ence many parents—some from the day of diagnosis on—are deeply con-cerned about the psychosexual development and sexual orientation of their CAH daughters. Thus we recommend . . . all these aspects of psychosexual development, sexual behavior and sexual orientation should be considered and included in the clinical and psychosocial care of CAH patients and their families" (p. 164). I, of course, agree that such matters must be part of the counseling and sex education offered to intersex families. My point here is that responsibility for concerns about homosexuality are attributed to the family, whereas the treatment team always presents itself as being liberally open-minded on such matters. Never have I come across a therapist or physician who, in the literature on intersexuals has written something like: "I used to think homosexuality was an unhealthy outcome but now I realize it is not. I have, therefore, changed my treatment approach and analysis in the follow-ing ways."

113. See Money and Ehrhardt 1972, chapters 7 and 8, for a comparison of matched pairs of intersexuals who, according to the authors, develop different gender identities depending upon the sex of rearing. This type of case study comparison is rhetorically enormously powerful.

114. All of which lends credence to Suzanne Kessler and Wendy McKen-na's argument that gender is socially constructed and *sex* a misleading term. They write that "the 2-bodied system is not a given—that people are respon-sible for it" Kessler and McKenna personal communication, 1998, see also Kessler and McKenna 1978; Kessler 1998. This does not mean, as some skep-tics might suggest, that people make bodies. It means they make the system that categorizes them, and a system of just two bodies is not the only possible

system. As I discuss in the following chapter, a greater tolerance for sexual diversity may well lead to an era in which we no longer think of there being merely two sexes.

115. Money and Ehrhardt 1972, p. 235. Emphasis added. Money and Dalèry (1976) write: "a formula for creating the perfect female homosexual . . . on the criteria of chromosomal and gonadal sex is to take a chromosomal and gonadal female fetus and to flood the system with masculinizing hormone during the . . . period when the external genitals . . . are being differentiated. Then assign the baby as a boy at birth" (p. 369). Note that in Money's view, the perfect female homosexual has a penis and a masculinized brain! Kessler describes these situations in the following manner: "In what sense could a woman with a vagina who is sexually gratified by being penetrated by a 'woman' with a large clitoris (that looks and functions like a penis) be said to be a lesbian? If gendered bodies fall into disarray, sexual orientation will follow. Defining sexual orientation according to attraction to people with the same or different genitals, as is done now, will no longer make sense" Kessler 1998, p. 125.

116. Diamond 1965, p. 158; Diamond and Sigmundson 1997a, pp. 1,046–1,048. But see also some occasional slips, such as his use of the word *normal* here: "The evidence seems overwhelming that normal humans are not psychosexually neutral at birth but are, in keeping with their mammalian heritage, predisposed and biased to interact with environmental, familial and social forces in either a male or a female mode" (idem, p. 303).

117. Kessler and McKenna 1978. They write: "We will use gender, rather than sex, even when referring to those aspects of being a woman (girl) or man (boy) that have traditionally been viewed as biological. This will serve to emphasize our position that the element of social construction is primary in all aspects of being female or male, particularly when the term we use seems awkward (e.g., gender chromosomes)" (p. 7).

118. Whether these differences really exist, when during development they might appear and how we can fairly measure them is not under discussion here. (See Fausto-Sterling 1992b).

Even where we agree on the existence of such differences, the question of their origin remains. Will we rely primarily on a biological model of difference, in which gender is layered over a preexisting bodily foundation, which we call sex?

119. How, specifically, does this cash out in our ideas about masculinity, femininity, and sexual desire? To understand contemporary medical studies we must start, as is so often the case, with the Victorians. Men, our queenly forebears asserted, had active sexual desire, while women were passionless to the point of asexuality. Women's inborn passivity, wrote the German sexologist Richard von Krafft-Ebing, "lies in her sexual organization [nature/sex], and is not founded merely on the dictates of good breeding (nurture/gender)"

(quoted in Katz 1995, p. 31). In this system of thought a woman who had strong sexual desire, especially if she desired another woman, had, by definition, become masculine. To be a lesbian meant to invert the sexual order, to be a psychological and emotional man in a woman's body. (Money and Dalèry 1976, p. 369). During the first quarter of the twentieth century, at least when writing about sex in marriage, sexologists such as Havelock Ellis acknowledged that women experienced sexual passion. Nevertheless, he and others applied the concept of the invert to women who behaved like men: they were aggressive, might smoke cigars, dressed like men, and took other women as love objects. The passive woman in a lesbian relationship did not appear to be lesbian. For a more detailed discussion of these points, see Chauncey 1989 and Jackson 1987. As Radclyffe Hall melodramatically displayed in her novel *The Well of Loneliness* (1928), the "passive" partner could as easily run off with a man. Some major theorists of male homosexuality also held firmly to a model of complete gender inversion. The German reformer and homosexual rights advocate Magnus Hirschfeld, for example, considered the male invert to be hermaphroditic in both mind and body. He searched not only for behavioral clues but for intermediate body types. For a time he teamed up with the hormone researcher Eugen Steinach, who delighted him by claiming to have found special cells in the testes of male homosexuals. These cells, they believed, were responsible for producing hormones that feminized the invert in body and mind. Steinach's hormone research is important in the construction of knowledge about supposed male and female hormones. I discuss his work in more detail in chapter 6. For a fascinating account of the collaboration between Hirschfeld and Steinach, see Sengoopta 1998.

120. Much of what follows could certainly be applied to work on differences in spatial ability, but to avoid repetition of the principle point I will not discuss this work in detail. Some key references are Hines 1990; Hines and Collaer 1993; Sinforiani et al. 1994; and Hampson et al. 1998. Hines and Collaer suggest that any relationship between prenatal testosterone levels and increased spatial abilities could be secondary to hormone-influenced differences in play patterns. They also find that data supporting the idea that sex differences in mathematics are caused by prenatal androgen exposure "are weak" (p. 19).

121. Abramovich et al 1987.

122. Magee and Miller 1997, p. 19. See also Fuss 1993 and Magid 1993. There is an alternate theory of male homosexuality as hypermasculinity (Sengoopta 1998). According to some, such hypermasculinity explains why gay men in the modern U.S. are so sexually active. By analogy, lesbians may overexpress female sexuality, seen as a lack of sexual desire. This viewpoint has been used to explain so-called lesbian bed death (Symons 1979).

123. In contrast, lowered androgen exposure and even severe penile hypospadias were not seen to "interfere with the development of gender-typical

masculine behavior" in XY children (Sandberg and Meyer-Bahlburg 1995, p. 693).

124. In an earlier work I critiqued many of these studies, as did Ruth Bleier (Fausto-Sterling 1992; Bleier 1984). A small number of very recent studies have responded to the critiques by including in their experimental design blind assessments of behavior or by trying to find appropriate controls—e.g., other children suffering from non–sex-related chronic illness. But on the whole, the design of all these studies leaves much to be desired. I do not plan to rehash the experimental problems here so much as I want to show how our gender system has dictated the design of these studies and limited the interpretations of the data.

125. It could be otherwise. For example, there are orthogonal models of masculinity and femininity suggesting that masculinity and femininity are independent traits. Researchers using an orthogonal model might still study CAH girls. But they would look for different behaviors and use differently structured questionnaires (Constantinople 1973). Spence writes: "The multidimensional nature of sex-role and other gender-related phenomena is also beginning to be recognized. Although gender identity may be essentially dimorphic, the general statement that masculine and feminine attributes and behaviors cannot or do not coexist has been effectively refuted" (Spence 1984). See also Bem 1993. Still other researchers might decide to use CAH girls to investigate the long-term effects of chronic illness and repeated surgeries on gender-related play, rehearsal for adulthood, and postpubertal love object choice. Interesting effects of hormones could still emerge if they chose to compare hormonally caused chronic illness with other types.

126. Psychologists have often used the term *tomboyism* to define masculinity in CAH children. The imprecision of that term, perhaps after years of feminist critique, seems to have led recent writers to replace it with more specifically defined behavioral measures.

127. One set of studies distinguishes between the severe "salt-wasting" form of CAH, in which there do seem to be activity differences in affected girls, and the "simple-virilizing" form, for which masculine behavior is less pronounced. Many early studies did not distinguish between these two forms of the disease, which may well result in different behavior patterns. Explaining the behavioral differences presents the standard conundrum between biological and social possibilities. (See Dittmann et al. 1990a and 1990b).

128. Magee and Miller 1997, p. 83; Hines and Collaer 1993, p. 10.

129. Magee and Miller 1997. The pet care finding is from Leveroni and Berenbaum 1998. They offer several possible explanations—for example, that "CAH girls may spend more time with pets because they are less interested in infants but not less nurturant overall than controls" (p. 335). This would imply that testosterone interferes with the development of interest in infants, but that some general character called nurturance, which could get

directed everywhere but to children, existed independently of high androgen levels.

130. Magee and Miller 1997, p. 87.

131. Dittmann et al. 1992, p. 164.

132. Hines and Collaer 1993, p. 12.

133. In other words, they do "good science" by most measures (grants, publication, peer review, promotions). The science looks funny only if one acknowledges the possibility of other logical systems.

134. Consider a single study by the psychologists Sheri Berenbaum and Melissa Hines: Boys like to play with construction sets and trucks, but girls prefer dolls, dollhouses, and toy kitchen equipment. Many psychologists have found such average sex differences in studies of play preferences in young children. (Obviously the particular toys are culturally specific. However, sex differences in play preferences are culturally widespread, albeit differently expressed in different cultures). See also Maccoby, E., 1998. But how do such preferences come about? Berenbaum and Hines agree that children learn preferences from other children; but, they suggest, such learning cannot tell the entire story. "We present evidence that these sex-typed toy preferences are also related to prenatal or neonatal hormones (androgens)" (Berenbaum and Hines 1992, p. 203). Citing myriad animal studies showing the influence of hormones on the brain and behavior, they note that CAH girls present "a unique opportunity to study hormonal influences on human sex-typed behavior" (p. 203). In their introduction, the authors take note of the design deficiencies of previous work and vow in this study to do better. Specifically, they note four major problems (many of which both Bleier and I have raised as well (Bleier 1984, Fausto-Sterling 1992b). Previous studies (a) assessed behavior from interviews rather than direct observation, (b) were not done blind, i.e., those who assessed the data knew whether they were dealing with experimental or control subjects, (c) assessed behaviors as present or absent rather than as part of a continuum, and (d) often treated masculine and feminine behaviors as the far ends of a single continuum, rather than considering that they could both exist in the same individual.

They kept their vow. Compared to earlier studies, this one was, indeed, well done. One key difference (to which I will return shortly) was that Berenbaum and Hines considered the severity of CAH in the girls they observed. They looked, for example, at the age at diagnosis and the degree of genital virilization. They videotaped play sessions in which both boys and girls had access to male- and female-preferred toys as well as some gender-neutral options (toys preferred equally by both sexes). Neutral toys included books, game boards, and jigsaw puzzles). Finally, they had videotapes rated by two separate raters, neither of whom knew the status or identity of the children whose play choices they counted.

Berenbaum and Hines's major positive finding was that, compared to un-affected girl relatives, the CAH girls chose boys' toys more often and played with them longer—as often and as long as did the boys. They also played less with girls' toys, but not significantly so. They suggest this small effect size for CAH versus control in time spent with girls' toys may be an experimental artifact (p. 204). Finally, and it is their treatment of this last point that I want to examine, "the amount of time spent playing with sex-typed toys was not significantly related to any disease characteristic" (pp. 204–05), including the degree of virilization. They do not give specific data on possible correlations with time of diagnosis, but this too would be important information. (I sus-pect their sample size was too small to say anything one way or another.) But this information might be of interest if one assumes that the longer a child goes untreated, the longer will have been her exposure to unusual levels of androgen, hence the greater the likelihood of seeing a hormone effect— if, indeed, such exists. Furthermore, postnatal hormone exposure could be quite interesting to study because in theory, it would afford scientists the chance to look at how hormones and experience might co-produce some be-havior patterns. This makes special sense for humans because so much critical brain development occurs after birth. But the framework of the animal re-search used by these investigators makes it much less likely that they will think to ask such questions, which really require a different frame of reference and research program. There are other animal behavior traditions that would logi-cally lead, to such types of questions. I will discuss these at some length in the last chapter of this book. See also Gottlieb 1997.

Why should it matter if the degree to which CAH girls prefer boys' toys correlates significantly with how virilized their genitalia are? Remember that they want to compare their work to a vast literature on animal development. In this experimental terrain, researchers know when in the developmental process they inject test hormones and at what concentrations. To define criti-cal developmental periods, they vary the time of injection and inject different amounts of hormone to show a dose response (the higher the dose, the greater the effect). Such experimental fine-tuning is impossible in human studies. For how long and at which developmental stages were these girls exposed to high androgen levels? We don't know. What hormone levels were they exposed to? We don't know. Such information, in the long run, is critical to interpreting the results of studies on CAH girls, but it is for all intents and purposes un-available. Hence the need to fall back on arguments from the animal literature and allusions to "our common vertebrate heritage" (Diamond and Sigmund-son 1997b) and to rely on imperfect but important internal controls.

One such control is the degree of virilization. The fetal testis begins to secrete androgens eight weeks after fertilization and continues at high levels even as their production begins to drop off during the second and into the third trimester. Under their influence the internal and external genitals develop (see figure 3.1). Usually, the overall shaping of a boy's external organs occurs during weeks 9 to 12 of embryonic development, but growth and fine-tuning continues until birth and beyond. The genitalia, of course, grow slowly throughout childhood and more dramatically at puberty. Although the timing I describe is the statistical norm, it is not the only known developmental pathway. In one well-studied genetic variation, called 5-alpha-reductase deficiency, males are born with very feminine-looking genitals. But at puberty, the clitoris enlarges into a penis and the vaginal lips fuse to form a scrotum into which their testes descend. Given that fetal testosterone is present even in the third trimester (see graph on p. 292 of O'Rahilly and Müller 1996), possible effects on brain development could occur over a broad period of time, during which the central nervous system is developing apace.

CAH girls, of course, don't have testes. It is their adrenal glands that masculinize their genitalia, but the timing of these events is uncertain. The lack of information on this point is in stunning contrast to the impressive detail available on the molecular aspects of the CAH family of enzyme malfunction. Dr. Maria New and her colleagues write: "Adrenocortical cell differentiation occurs early in embryogenesis, with the formation of a provisional fetal zone, active for the remainder of gestation, that involutes after birth. Although *the schedule of evolving steroid synthesis in the fetal and adult (permanent) zones has not been completely elucidated*, it is clear that genital development in the fetus takes place under the influence of active adrenal steroid biosynthesis" (New et al. 1989, p. 1,887; emphasis added). In other words, there are two sources of adrenal hormones: the fetal adrenal cortex, which develops toward the end of the second month of development, and the permanent, which develops late in fetal development. The fetal adrenal cortex regresses and disappears by one year after birth. O'Rahilly and Müller 1996 write: "The functions of the fetal cortex are not entirely clear, but its enormous size is believed to be associated with a similarly great capacity for steroid production" (pp. 324–25). In the extreme it is possible the CAH girls experience elevated androgens from eight weeks after fertilization until some time after birth—a different pattern of exposure than XY boys experience. Interfering with fetal adrenal androgen production during the first trimester can allow female genitals to develop, but there is a lot of variability in the anatomical effects of CAH (Mercado et al. 1995, Speiser and New 1994a, b). If the level of adrenal androgen overproduction is low, or if overproduction starts late in development, CAH girls will presumably have more feminized genitals. If hormone concentrations are extremely high or start very early in development, the genitalia may become highly masculinized. Suppose in Berenbaum and Hines's study the degree of virilization *had* correlated with the degree of boy toy preference. An embryologist (such as myself) would argue that the result supported an argument that "early hormone exposure in females has a masculinizing effect on sex-typed toy preferences" (Berenbaum and Hines 1992). Why? Because if increased virilization measures heightened or prolonged androgen levels, and if andro-gen levels change behavior in an incremental fashion, then the more androgen (up to a point), the more of the measured behavior. What does it mean that they found no such correlation?

Here we arrive at the crux of the matter. For meaning to emerge from a set of data requires a frame of vision. My embryologist's frame of vision led me to understand the degree of virilization as a possible measure of how much androgen exposure a particular CAH girl had experienced. But Berenbaum and Hines did not use the degree of virilization as a control for hormone dose. For them a positive correlation would have provided evidence *against*, not *for*, their hypothesis. This is because some have suggested that parents might treat girls with penises differently than ones without penises. Or the children themselves might react to a more male-like body image. (I confess, in fact, that I am one of those who raised these possibilities. I did so from my other frame of reference—that of a feminist activist. This framework, I remind the reader, leads me to extreme skepticism toward theories focusing on the biological causes of behavior, especially sexual and racial differences that seem, always, to end up in the middle of discussions of social equality [Fausto-Sterling 1992]). As I write (mid-December 1998), for example, a discussion rages on Loveweb about the meaning of equal opportunity. Quoting anony-mously (and with changed names) from one of the participants, a highly re-spected researcher in the field of hormones and behavior: "John says he has no interest in eliminating sex differences. Susan says neither does she, but wants only equality of opportunity. The implication is that the existence of sex differences does not necessarily lead to inequality of opportunity. I suspect there are some on this list who would argue that as long as sex differences exist, equality of opportunity cannot be achieved. Does this latter view reflect a belief that all sex differences are socially constructed and therefore embody inequality of opportunity? Thus my question. Do sex differences have to be eliminated to achieve equality of opportunity between the sexes? For exam-ple, will equal opportunity exist only when males and females can both ges-tate babies?"

If parental behavior or altered body image were the key, the changed be-haviors might not result from the direct effects of hormones on the brain. Since there was no correlation, Berenbaum and Hines reasoned, there must be no difference in how parents socialized CAH girls and their unaffected relatives. (They did assess parental attitudes using a questionnaire, but felt their methods on this point left uncertainty. They noted that direct observa-tion of parent-child interaction, using blind assessments, would give more reliable information.) Thus they could safely conclude that androgens affect the developing male's brain, leading him to prefer trucks and building blocks as a toddler. Hines and Collaer 1993 further consider this question. Again they use the lack of virilization to refute interpretations based on nurture cues, arguing instead for a direct effect of androgen on the developing brain. They do worry more about what the lack of correlation might mean in terms of the embryo: "In humans," androgen levels are elevated in developing males compared to developing females from approximately week 8–24 of gestation and again from approximately the first to the sixth month of infancy. Because genital development occurs before brain development, one speculation would be that degree of genital virilization among CAH girls reflects the time of onset of the disorder, whereas behavioral changes reflect the degree of androgen elevation during later periods. If so, behavioral and physical virilization would correlate. Alternatively, the lack of a clear correspondence could relate to differences in enzymes needed to produce active hormones" (Hines and Collaer 1993, pp. 7–8). They also quote the single study (Goy et al. 1988) from primates (rhesus monkeys) in which one androgen-influenced behavior (rough play) is independent of the degree of virilization; others, such as mounting, correlate with levels of virilization. In this study the authors also found that mother rhesus monkeys inspected male genitals and masculinized female genitals a lot more often than they did unaffected female genitals. Furthermore, in this study, prenatal androgenization cannot produce a "pure" male behavioral response in masculinized females. Why? Possibly the androgen treatments weren't at the critical period of brain development. Or possibly behavioral development is more complex and includes effects from postnatal behavioral interactions. Note also how misleading is the title of Goy et al.'s paper: "Behavioral masculinization is independent of genital masculinization in prenatally female Rhesus monkeys." Why not "*Some* behavioral masculinization is independent"? Such a title would more accurately represent the contents of the paper. My biologist self is wrestling also with the validity of extrapolating studies on CAH children to unaffected male development. This is because the timing of hormone exposure is probably different. In most XY fetuses, testes make the hormones between months two and six with levels tapering off thereafter. In CAH fetuses, however, adrenal androgen production may begin during the latter third of the first trimester and continue until treatment begins (after birth). In one case hormone exposure is episodic, and in the other it is tonic. Brain development is continuous from the third week of development (and possibly until we die!). I have never seen a hypothesis about what region of the brain is suspected of being responsible for play, nurturing, and other childhood behaviors. Thus it is impossible to know which periods of development might be critical in terms of hormone/brain interaction. It surprises me that even in the primate studies, the question of what is happening in brain development during the period of experimental hormone injection is not discussed. Later, others suggest, he or his CAH female counterpart may become more aggressive (Berenbaum and Resnick 1997), develop better spatial abilities (Hampson et al. 1998), be less interested in taking care of babies (Leveroni and Berenbaum 1998), and desire women as sex and love objects. For additional discussion of female object choice in CAH women, see Zucker et al. 1996.

135. Butler 1993, p. xi. For a related analysis of hermaphrodites at the limits of subjectivity, see Grosz 1966.

136. In this analysis, a man or a woman would be someone whose chromosomes, fetal gonads and hormones, fetal, child, and adult genitals, adult gonads, and sexual orientation were each and all culturally intelligible as either male or female. When one or more of these components of gender differ from the others (as with intersexuals), they become uninterpretable bodies—i.e., culturally unintelligible.

137. Butler 1993, p. xi.

138. Sawicki 1991, p. 88. Lesbians using these technologies to create "natural" biological families is one good example.

Chapter 4: Should There Be Only Two Sexes?

1. Fausto-Sterling 1993a. The piece was reprinted on the Op-Ed page of the *New York Times* under the title "How Many Sexes Are There?" Fausto-Sterling 1994.

2. This is the same organization that tried to close down the Off Broadway play "Corpus Christi" (by Terence McNally) during the fall season of 1998 in New York City.

3. Rights 1995 Section 4, p. 11. The syndicated columnist E. Thomas McClanahan took up the attack as well. "What the heck," he wrote, "why settle for five genders? Why not press for an even dozen?" (McClanahan 1995 p. B6). Pat Buchanan also joined the chorus: "They say there aren't two sexes, there are five genders. . . . I tell you this: God created man and woman—I don't care what Bella Abzug says" (quoted in *The Advocate,* October 31, 1995). Columnist Marilyn vos Savant writes: "There are men and there are women—no matter how they're constructed . . . and that's that" (vos Savant 1996 p. 6).

4. Money 1994.

5. Scott's novel won the Lambda Literary Award in 1995. She specifically acknowledged my work on her web site.

6. See, for example, Rothblatt 1995; Burke 1996; and Diamond 1996.

7. Spence has been writing for some time about the impossibility of these terms. See, e.g., Spence 1984 and 1985.

8. For activists working for change see the Intersex Society of North

America (http://www.isna.org) and Chase 1998a,b; and Harmon-Smith 1998. For academics in addition to myself, see Kessler 1990; Dreger 1993; Diamond and Sigmundson 1997a,b; Dreger 1998b; Kessler 1998; Preves 1998; Kipnis and Diamond 1998; Dreger 1998c. For physicians who are moving toward (or embracing) the new paradigm see Schober 1998; Wilson and Reiner 1998; and Phornphutkul et al. 1999. More cautiously, Meyer-Bahlburg suggests modest changes in medical practice, including giving more thought to gender assignment (an "optimal gender policy"), elimination of nonconsensual surgery for mild degrees of genital abnormalities, and provision of more support services for intersex persons and their parents. He also calls for obtaining more data on long-term outcomes (Meyer-Bahlburg 1998).

9. See comments by Chase (1998a and 1998b). Chase has repeatedly tried to get the attention of mainstream American feminists through venues like *Ms.* Magazine and the academic journal *Signs,* but has been unable to stir their interest in the question of genital surgery on American newborns. It seems it is much more comfortable to confront the practices of other cultures than it is our own. The surgeon Justine Schober writes: "To this date, no studies of clitoral surgery address the long term results of erotic sexual sensitivity" (Schober 1998, p.550). Costa et al. 1997 report that of eight clitorectomized patients, two reported no orgasm during intercourse. Some who report orgasm find it much diminished compared to before surgery. Others find it so difficult to achieve that it becomes not worth the trouble.

10. Thankfully, some physicians are open to new ideas. Mine have struck a chord with one local pediatric endocrinologist, and we have presented a case and the new thinking about how to manage intersexual births in a Grand Rounds. The surgeon discussed here did not attend, but one other surgeon did.

One local surgeon, although a colleague in the Brown Medical School, has never acknowledged my many communications. These included copies of publications such *as Hermaphrodites with Attitude* and *Alias* (a newsletter of the AIS Support Group), as well as drafts of my own writing, for which I solicited feedback. After reading an article in an in-house newsletter delineating the "standard" surgical approaches to intersexuality, Cheryl Chase and I wrote asking for a chance to present the emerging alternative thinking on the topic. The surgeon replied (to Chase, with only a *cc* rather than direct address to me) that the publication was limited to members of the Department of Pediatrics. "We do not wish our publication to become a forum for expression of ideas, be they medical or otherwise," the letter read.

11. In a much earlier study, Money reported on the effects of clitorectomy. He located seventeen adult women who had had such surgery as adults. Twelve of these lived as women, were older than sixteen when they discussed their erotic responses, and could report on their postoperative sensations.

Three of the twelve apparently did not cooperate ("no data on orgasm were disclosed," p. 294). In four cases, "the data indicated the patient to be inexperienced in orgasm." In five cases, the women seemed to have experienced orgasm. The language of this report makes it unclear what the "before" and "after" surgery experiences were really like: "The point of these data on orgasm and clitorectomy is not, however, that some clitorectomized patients did not experience orgasm. On the contrary, the point is that the capacity for orgasm proved compatible with clitorectomy and surgical feminization of the genitalia in some, if not all, of these patients" (p. 294). This paper, giving confusing information about twelve patients, was an important citation for those who claimed that clitoral surgery did not damage sexual function (Money 1961).

12. In this chapter I discuss only evaluations of genital surgery. Some forms of intersexuality involve chromosomal and/or hormonal changes without affecting visible genital components. While these conditions receive medical attention, especially hormonal treatments, surgery is never involved because there are many fewer doubts about gender assignment. In the vast majority of these cases, the children involved have mental and emotional functions within a normal range. This is not to say that they encounter no difficulties because of their differences—only that the difficulties are surmountable. For recent literature on Turner Syndrome and other gender chromosome anomalies, see: Raboch et al. 1987; McCauley and Urquiza 1988; Sylven et al. 1993; Bender et al. 1995; Cunniff et al. 1995; Toublanc et al. 1997; and Boman et al. 1998.

13. Many of these details were conveyed to me by personal communication, but Chase's story is now widely documented. See, for example, Chase 1998a.

14. Chase's story of doctors refusing to tell her the truth even once she had reached adulthood are repeated over and over in the stories of hundreds of adult intersexuals. These may be found scattered in newsletters, media interviews, and academic books and articles, many of which I cite in this chapter. The sociologist Sharon Preves has interviewed forty adult intersexuals and is beginning to publish her results. In one article she recounts Flora's experience of visiting a genetic counselor at age twenty-four, who said, "I'm obliged to tell you that certain details of your condition have not been divulged to you, but I cannot tell you what they are because they would upset you too much" (Preves 1999, p. 37).

15. Cheryl Chase to Anne Fausto-Sterling (personal correspondence, 1993).

16. Chase 1998, p. 200. For more on HELP, see Harmon and Smith 1998 and visit their web site: http://www.help@jaxnet.com. Their address is P.O. Box 26292, Jacksonville, FL 32226.

17. Chase uses the following quote from an AIS support group newsletter. "Our first impression of ISNA was that they were perhaps a bit too angry and militant to gain the support of the medical profession. However, we have to say that, having read [political analyses of intersexuality by ISNA, Kessler, Fausto-Sterling, and Holmes], we feel that the feminist concepts relating to the patriarchal treatment of intersexuality are extremely interesting and do make a lot of sense" (Chase 1998, p. 200).

18. The intersexual rights movement has become international. For an example of "coming out" in Germany, see Tolmein and Bergling 1999. For other foreign organizations, consult the ISNA web page: http://www.isna.org.

19. For example, the surgeon John Gearhart and colleagues published a paper in which they measured nerve responses during phallic reconstruction. In their six-case study, they were able to monitor nerve responses in the phallus even after surgery. They wrote: "Our study clearly shows that modern techniques of genital reconstruction allow for preservation of nerve conduction in the dorsal neurovascular bundle and may permit normal sexual function in adulthood" (Gearhart et al. 1995, p. 486). (Note that their study was done on infants, and not enough time has elapsed for adult follow-up studies.) Both in a private letter and a letter to the *Journal of Urology* (Chase 1995), Cheryl Chase disputed the implications of their research with case studies of her own, collected from ISNA members. She cited the absence or diminishment of orgasm in adults whose nervous transmission was normal. Gearhart and colleagues responded by calling for long-term follow-up studies. In another article, Chase points out how surgical techniques are constructed as moving targets. Criticism can always be deflected by claiming that newer techniques have solved the problem. Given that it can take decades for some of the problems to emerge, this is indeed a dilemma (Chase 1998a; Kipnis and Diamond 1998).

20. Costa et al. 1997 and Velidedeoglu et al. 1997 list clitorectomy and clitoral recession as alternatives to clitoroplasty, coldly noting that "clitorectomy results in loss of a sensate clitoris" (p. 215).

21. The cancer story is not unusual. A number of adult intersexuals recount how, during their teen years, they believed they were dying of cancer. Moreno's story is recounted in Moreno 1998.

22. Ibid., p. 208. This sentiment is echoed by yet another ISNA activist, Morgan Holmes, a vibrant woman in her late twenties. To prevent a miscarriage, doctors had treated her mother with progestin, a masculinizing hormone, and Morgan was born with an enlarged clitoris. When she was seven, doctors performed a clitoral reduction. As with Cheryl Chase, no one talked about the operation, but Holmes remembers it. Although the surgery did not render her inorgasmic, her sexual function was severely affected. Like Chase,

Holmes chose to go public. In her Master's thesis, analyzing her own case in the context of feminist theories on the construction and meanings of gender, she writes passionately about lost possibilities:

> "I like to imagine, if my body had been left intact and my clitoris had grown at the same rate as the rest of my body, what would my lesbian relationships have been like? What would my current heterosexual relationship be like? What if—as a woman—I could assume a penetrative role . . . with both women and men? When the doctors initially assured my father that I would grow up to have 'normal sexual function,' they did not mean that they could guarantee that my amputated clitoris would be sensitive or that I would be able to achieve orgasm . . . What was being guaranteed was that I would not grow up to confuse the issue of who (man) fucks whom (woman). These possibilities . . . were negated in a reasonably simple two-hour operation. All the things I might have grown up to do, all the possibilities went down the hall with my clitoris to the pathology department. Me and my remains went to the recovery room and have not yet emerged" (Holmes 1994, p. 53).

23. Baker 1981; Elias and Annas 1988; Goodall 1991.

24. Anonymous 1994a.

25. Anonymous 1994b.

26. The fastest way to locate these organizations and the rich support and information they provide is via the Internet. The web address is http://www.isna.org. ISNA stands for Intersex Society of North America and their mailing address is: PO Box 3070, Ann Arbor, MI 48106-3070.

27. One woman writes: "When I discovered I had AIS the pieces finally fit together. But what fell apart was my relationship with both my family and physicians. It was not learning about chromosomes or testes that caused enduring trauma, it was discovering that I had been told lies. I avoided all medical care for the next 18 years. I have severe osteoporosis as a result of a lack of medical attention. This is what lies produce" (Groveman 1996, p. 1,829). This issue of the *Canadian Medical Association Journal* contains several letters with similar sentiments written by AIS women outraged that the CMAJ had awarded second prize in a medical student essay contest on medical ethics to an essay defending the ethics of lying to AIS patients. The essay was published in an earlier issue (Natarajan 1996). For many more stories see the issues of ISNA's (see previous note) newsletter, "Hermaphrodites with Attitude," the newsletter of ALIAS, an AIS support group (email aissg@aol.com), the journal *Chrysalis* 2:5 (fall 1997/winter 1998), and Moreno 1998. For further discussion of ethical decision making, see Rossiter and Diehl 1998 and Catlin 1998.

28. Meyer-Bahlburg writes: "Although current surgical procedures of clitoral recession, if done well, appear to preserve the glans clitoris and its in-
nervation, we are still in need of controlled long-term follow-up studies that
assess in detail the quality of clitoral functioning in adults who have undergone
such procedures [clitoral surgery] in infancy or childhood" (Meyer-Bahlburg
1998, p. 12).

29. The most recent full-length book on the clitoris is old, by medical
standards—dating from 1976 (Lowry and Lowry 1976). For a roadmap of
changing conventions in clitoral representations, see Moore and Clarke 1995.
A rare anatomical study of the clitoris concludes that "current anatomical
descriptions of female human urethral and genital anatomy are inaccurate"
(O'Connell et al. 1998, p. 1,892). For a more complete drawing of the clitoris
based on these recent findings, see Williamson and Nowak 1998. Furthermore, new aspects of female genital anatomy and physiology continue to be
described. See Kellogg and Parra 1991 and Ingelman-Sundberg 1997.

Perhaps the best and least known text depicting female sexual anatomy is
Dickinson 1949. Dickinson is remarkable because he draws the variability,
often in composite drawings, which give a vibrant sense of anatomical variation. Unfortunately, his drawings have been ignored in the more standard
anatomical texts. For attempts to standardize clitoral size in newborns, see
Tagatz et al. 1979; Callegari et al. 1987; Oberfield et al. 1989; and Phillip et
al. 1996.

30. Failure to attend to genital variability, especially in children, has made
it difficult to use anatomical markers to document sexual abuse in children.
Here we seem to be caught in a vicious circle. Our taboos on acknowledging
infantile and immature genitalia mean that we really haven't looked at them
very systematically. This means that we have no "objective" way to document
the very thing we fear: sexual abuse of children. It also leaves us ill-equipped
to have sensible conversations with intersex children and their parents about
their own anatomical differences. See, for example, McCann et al. 1990; Berenson et al. 1991; Berenson et al. 1992; Emans 1992; and Gardner 1992.

31. See, for example, a new, computerized image reproduced on p. 288
of Moore and Clarke 1995. This image labels only the glans and some nerves.
The shaft is barely visible and the crura are unlabeled. Compare this to feminist publications such as *Our Bodies, Ourselves*. Modern anatomy CD's for popular use barely mention the clitoris and show no labeled pictures of it (see, for
example, Bodyworks by Softkey).

32. Newman et al. 1992b (p. 182) write: "Long term results of operations that eliminate erectile tissue are yet to be systematically evaluated."

33. Newman et al. (1992b) mention one of nine patients with pain with
orgasm; p. 8 following clitoral recession. Randolf et al. (1981) write: "A second effort at recession is worthwhile and can be satisfactorily accomplished in
spite of old scar" (p. 884). Lattimer (1961), in his description of the recession

operation, refers to "the midline scar," which ends up hidden from view in the folds of the labia majora. Allen et al. (1982) cite 4/8 clitoral recessions complaining of painful erections. Nihoul-Fekete (1981) says that clitorectomy leaves painful stumps; about recession clitoroplasty, she writes: "Clitoral sensitivity is retained, except in cases where postoperative necrosis resulted from excessive dissection of the vascular pedicles" (p. 255).

34. Nihoul-Fekete et al. 1982.

35. Allen et al. 1982, p. 354.

36. Newman et al. (1992b) write that patients who underwent extensive vaginal and clitoral surgery have "sexual function ranging from satisfactory to poor" (p. 650). Allen et al. (1982) write that they limited vaginoplasties in infants, waiting until puberty for the full operation "rather than provoke dense scarring and vaginal stenosis following an aggressive procedure at an earlier age" (p. 354). Nihoul-Fekete (1981) mentions as a goal keeping the vagina free of an annular scar; on vaginoplasties: "Complications arise from poor healing with resultant stenosis of the vaginal opening" (p. 256). Dewhurst and Gordon (1969) write that if the fused labial folds are divided before bowel and bladder continence is achieved, "it may be followed by imperfect healing and perhaps scarring later" (p. 41).

37. Nihoul-Fekete 1981.

38. A debate continues over whether it is best to perform these early in childhood or wait until adolescence or adulthood. As with hypospadias surgery (see previous chapter), there are many varieties of surgery for vaginal reconstruction. For a brief history of them, see Schober 1998.

39. On stenosis or vaginal narrowing: 3 out of 10 moderate to severe introital stenosis; 5 out of 10 moderate to severe vaginal stenosis (van der Kamp et al. 1992). Operations before 1975—of 33: 8 vaginal stenosis, 3 small vaginal orifice, 1 labial adhesions; 1 penile fibrosis. Of 25 post 1975: 3 vaginal stenosis, 1 labial adhesions (Lobe et al. 1987); 8 out of 14 with vaginal pullthrough type vaginoplasties developed severe stenosis (Newman et al. 1992b); 8 out of 13 early vaginoplasties: stenosis caused by scarring (p. 601) (Sotiropoulos et al. 1976). Migeon says that girls with vaginal operations "have scar tissue from surgery. They experience difficult penetration. These girls suffer" (in Hendricks 1993). Nihoul-Fekete et al. (1982) report 10/16 clitoral recessions in which postpubertal patients reported hypersensitivity of the clitoris.

40. Bailez et al. 1992, p. 681.

41. Colapinto 1997.

42. One recent evaluation of the psychological health of intersex children found: "dilating the vagina at a younger age appeared to lead to severe psychological problems because it was experienced as a violation of the body integrity" (Slijper et al. 1998) p. 132.

43. Colapinto 1997; Money and Lamacz 1987.

44. Bailez et al. 1992.

45. Newman et al. 1992a, p. 651. The data from Allen et al.—that seven of their eight patients required more than one surgery to complete clitoroplasty—suggests that multiple operations may be the rule rather than the exception (Allen et al. 1982). Innes-Williams 1981, p. 243.

46. Additional data on multiple surgeries follow: Randolf et al. 1981: 8 out of 37 required second operations to make clitoral recession "work." Lobe et al. 1987: 13 out of 58 patients required more than two operations; it seems likely from their discussion that many more of the 58 required two operations, but the data are not given. Allen et al (1982): 7 out of 8 clitoroplasties needed additional surgery. Van der Kamp et al. (1982): 8 out of 10 patients required two or more surgeries. Sotiropoulos et al. 1976: 8 out of 13 early vaginoplasties required second operations. Jones and Wilkins (1961): 40 percent of patients required second surgery with vaginoplasties. Nihoul-Fekete et al. (1982) report 33 percent of their early vaginoplasties required later additional surgery. Newman et al. (1992a): 2 out of 9 required second recession operations; 1/9 required second vaginoplasty. Azziz et al. (1986): 30/78 repeat (second and third times) surgeries for vaginoplasties; success of vaginoplasties was only 34.3 percent when done on children younger than four years of age. Innes-Williams (1981) writing about operations for hypospadias: recommends for intersexes two operations and says that poor technique or poor wound healing can mean further (third or more) surgery. See also Alizai et al. 1999.

The number of surgeries can rise to as high as 20. In one study of 73 hypospadias patients the mean number of operations was 3.2, while the range ran from 1 to 20. See reports by Mureau, Slijper et al. 1995a, 1995b, 1995c.

47. Mulaikal et al. 1987.

48. The psychological results of hypospadias surgery may differ in different cultures. A series of studies done in the Netherlands, for example, where male circumcision is uncommon, found that dissatisfaction with genital appearance resulted in part from the circumcised appearance following hypospadias surgery (Mureau, Slijper et al. 1995a, 1995b, 1995c; Mureau 1997; Mureau et al. 1997). For an earlier study, see Eberle et al. (1993), who found persistent cases of sexual ambiguity (seen as a bad thing) in 11 percent of their hypospadias patients. Duckett found "this study most disturbing for those of us who offer an optimistic outlook for our patients with hypospadias" (Duckett 1993, p. 1,477).

49. Miller and Grant 1997. For more on the effects of hypospadias, see Kessler 1998, pp. 70–73.

50. Sandberg and Meyer-Bahlburg 1995. See also Berg and Berg 1983, who report increased uncertainty about gender identity and masculinity but no increase in homosexuality among men with hypospadias.

51. Slijper et al. 1998, p. 127.

52. Ibid.

53. Harmon-Smith, personal communication. For more on HELP and other support groups, consult the ISNA Web page: http://www.isna.org.

54. Harmon-Smith 1998. The full commandments are:

1) DO NOT tell the family to not name "the child"! Doing so only isolates them, and makes them begin to see their baby as an "abnormality."

2) DO encourage the family to call their child by a nickname (Honey, Cutie, Sweetie, or even "little one") or by a non-gender-specific name.

3) DO NOT refer to the patient as "the child." Doing so makes parents begin to see their child as an object, not a person.

4) DO call the patient by nickname/name chosen by the parents. It may be uncomfortable at first but will help the parents greatly. Example: "How is your little sweetie doing today?"

5) DO NOT isolate the patient in a NICU. This scares the parents and makes them feel something is very wrong with their child. It isolates the family and prevents siblings, aunts, uncles and even grandparents from visiting and it starts a process within the family of treating the new member differently.

6) DO allow the patient to stay on a regular ward. Admit patients to the children's wing, perhaps in a single room. Then visitors are allowed, and bonding within the family can begin.

7) DO connect the family with an information or support group. There are many available: National Organization for Rare Disorders (NORD); Parent to Parent; HELP; AIS support group; Intersex Society of North America; even March of Dimes or Easter Seals.

8) DO NOT isolate the family from information or support. Do not assume they will not understand or will be more upset if they learn about other disorders or related problems. Let the parents decide what information they want or need. Encourage them to seek out who can give them information and share experiences.

9) DO encourage the family to see a counselor or therapist. Do not only refer them to a genetic counselor; they will need emotional support as well as genetic information. Refer them to a family counselor, therapist or social worker familiar with family crisis intervention/therapy.

10) DO NOT make drastic decisions in the first year. The parents need time to adjust to this individual child. They will need to understand the condition and what their specific child needs. Allow them time to get over being presented with new information and ideas. Let them understand that their child is not a condition that must conform to a set schedule but

an individual. DO NOT schedule the first surgery before the patient even leaves the hospital. This will foster fear in the parents that this is life threatening and they have an abnormal or damaged child.

55. Kessler 1998, p. 129.

56. Young 1937, p. 154. For a more recent example, see several cases of parental refusal of sex reassignment following traumatic injury to their sons' penises in Gilbert et al. 1993.

57. Young 1937, p. 158.

58. Recently academics have begun to analyze the phenomenon of displaying extraordinary bodies as a form of public entertainment. For an entree into this literature, see Thomson 1996.

59. Kessler 1990.

60. Young 1937, p. 146.

61. Dewhurst and Gordon 1963, p. 77.

62. Randolf et al. 1981, p. 885.

63. Van der Kamp et al. 1992.

64. Bailez et al. 1992, p. 886. "A number of mothers reported their husbands were actually opposed to surgery," and they cite one patient whose surgery was postponed because the family wanted the child to participate in the decision-making process (Hendricks 1993). Migeon reports on others who stop taking medication that prevents virilization. Jones and Wilkins (1961) report a patient who accepted hysterectomy and mastectomy but refused genital operations, even though he had to pee sitting down. Azziz et al. (1986) report on sixteen patients requiring repeat operations to achieve goal of comfortable intercourse, five never followed through on having them. Lubs et al. (1959) talk of a sixteen-year-old patient with genital abnormalities: "The family felt she should not be subject to further examination and would permit no studies to be carried out" (p. 1,113). Van Seters and Slob (1988) describe a case of micropenis in which the father refused surgery until the boy was old enough to decide for himself. Hurtig et al. (1983) discuss noncompliance with taking antimasculinizing drugs in two of four patients they studied. Hampson (1955) mentions a few parents who have refused recommendations of sex change surgery, "assured by their own thoroughgoing conviction of the boyness of their son or the girlness of their daughter" (p. 267). Beheshti et al. (1983) mention two cases in which parents refused gender reassignment.

65. Van Seters and Slob (1988). For more on the ability of children with micropenises, raised as males to adjust to the male sexual role, see Reilly and Woodhouse 1989.

66. Hampson and Hampson 1961, pp. 1,428–29; emphasis added.

67. Because of the small sample size, these numbers do not reach statistical significance, it could be random chance that the numbers came out this way. I expand upon my prejudice to the contrary in this paragraph.

68. Actually, this moment is already here, as the agendas of ISNA and other organizations attest.

69. Kessler 1998, p. 131.

70. Ibid., p. 40

71. Despite medical skepticism, ISNA's message is making inroads. A recent article from a nursing journal discussed ISNA's viewpoint and noted that "it is important to help parents focus on their infant as a whole rather than on the infant's condition. The nurse can emphasize a child's features that are unrelated to gender, such as 'what beautiful eyes the baby has,' or 'your baby has a nose just like daddy's'" (Parker 1998, p. 22). See also the editorial in the same issue (Haller 1998).

72. There is a significant and fascinating literature on transsexuality. See, for instance, Hausman 1992 and 1995; Bloom 1994; Bollin 1994; and Devor 1997.

73. Major work on transgender theory and practice includes Feinberg 1996 and 1998; Ekins and King 1997; Bornstein 1994 and Atkins 1998. Also, browse issues of the journal *Chrysalis: The Journal of Transgressive Gender Identities*.

74. Bolin 1994, pp. 461, 473.

75. Ibid., p. 484.

76. Rothblatt 1995, p. 115.

77. Lorber 1993, p. 571.

78. See also the discussion in chapter 1. Also, Herdt 1994a,b; Besnier 1994; Roscoe 1991 and 1994; Diedrich 1994; and Snarch 1992.

79. An ascetic sect, the Hijras are invested with the divine powers of the goddess; they dance and perform at the birth of male children and at marriages, and also serve the goddess at her temple (Nanda 1986, 1989, and 1994).

80. Without the enzyme, the body cannot transform the hormone testosterone into a related form—dihydrotestosterone (DHT). In the embryo, DHT mediates the formation of the male external genitalia.

81. For a thorough recent review of the biology, see Quigley et al. 1995 and Griffin and Wilson 1989.

82. This form of androgen insensitivity is often misdiagnosed, and irreparable surgery, such as removal of the testes, is performed. When the potential difficulties go "unmanaged" until puberty, more satisfactory options are available for an affected individual. See the discussion on p. 1,929 of Griffin and Wilson 1989, and a case discussed in Holmes et al. 1992.

In Fausto-Sterling 1992, I discuss the appropriation of events in the small villages of the Dominican Republic for an argument raging in the United States over whether innate biology or sex of rearing determines gender role and preference. The debate parallels the Joan/John dispute and the study of gender role acquisition in CAH girls discussed in chapter 3.

83. Herdt and Davidson 1988; Herdt 1990b and 1994a, b.

84. Herdt 1994, p. 429.

85. Kessler 1998, p. 90.

86. Press 1998.

87. Rubin 1984, p. 282.

88. Kennedy and Davis 1993.

89. Feinberg 1996, p. 125.

90. For a complete statement of the International Bill of Gender Rights, see pp. 165–169 of Feinberg 1996.

91. For a thorough and thoughtful treatment of the legal issues (which by extrapolation might apply to intersexuals), see Case 1995. For a discussion of how legal decisions construct the heterosexual and homosexual subject, see Halley 1991, 1993, and 1994.

92. In Norton 1996, pp. 187–88.

93. As sex reassignment surgery became more common in the 1950s, doctors worried about their personal liability. Even though physicians obtained parental approval, could a child—upon reaching the age of majority—sue the surgeon "for charges ranging from malpractice to assault and battery or even mayhem"? Despite "this disagreeable quirk in the law," the worried physician writing this passage felt he ought not shrink from "handling these unfortunate children . . . in whatever way seems . . . to be most suitable and humane" (Gross and Meeker 1955, p. 321).

In 1957, Dr. E. C. Hamblen, reiterating the fear of lawsuit, sought the aid of a law clinic at Duke University. One suggested solution, which never saw the light of day, was to set up state boards or commissions "on sex assignment or reassignment, comparable to boards of eugenics which authorize sterilization." Hamblen hoped such action could protect a physician whose position he feared "might be precarious, indeed, if legal action subsequently resulted in a jury trial" (Hamblen 1957, p. 1,240). After this early flurry of self-concern, the medical literature falls silent on the question of the patient's right to sue. Perhaps doctors have relied both on their near certainty that current medical approaches to intersexuality are both morally and medically correct and on the realization that the vast majority of their patients would never choose to go public about such intimate matters. In the post–Lorena Bobbit era, however, it seems only a matter of time until some medical professional confronts the civil claims of a genitally altered intersexual.

94. O'Donovan 1985. For an up-to-date review of the legal status of the intersexual, see Greenberg 1999.

95. O'Donovan 1985, p. 15; Ormrod 1992.

96. Edwards 1959, p. 118.

97. Halley 1991.

98. Ten Berge 1960, p. 118.

99. See de la Chapelle 1986; Ferguson-Smith et al. 1992; Holden 1992; Kolata 1992; Serrat and Garcia de Herreros 1993; Unsigned 1993.

100. I never would have guessed, when I first drafted this chapter in 1993, that in 1998 homosexual marriages would be on the ballots in two states. Although it lost in both cases, clearly the issue is now open to discussion. I believe it is a matter of time before the debate will be joined again, with different results.

101. Rhode Island repealed its antisodomy law in 1998, the same year that a similar law was found unconstitutional in the state of Georgia.

102. Reilly and Woodhouse 1989, p. 571; see also Woodhouse 1994.

Chapter 5: Sexing the Brain: How Biologists Make a Difference

1. For a general discussion of the problems of visibility and observation in science, see Hacking 1983.

2. Arguments about body structure are not new. In the nineteenth century some well-known biologists poured lead shot into empty skulls and then held forth on which group of people (males or females, blacks or whites) had larger skulls. The idea was that the larger skulls held larger brains and that the larger the brain, the smarter the person. See Gould 1981 and Russett 1989. Although the claims that there are racial differences in brain structure are made less frequently, they do occasionally appear in scientific journals. See Fausto-Sterling 1993 and Horowitz 1995. The question of the reality and meaning of brain size differences has been the subject of debate for almost two centuries. The mode of analysis I develop in this chapter is easily applicable to claims of racial and ethnic differences in brain structure.

3. The natural world, of course, does have input into the conversation. Some natural "facts" are more visible, more easily agreed-upon than others. There is no scientific disagreement, for example, that the brains of cats and the brains of humans look different. But there are also no commissions to promote a national dialogue about cats. On the other hand, there is disagreement—both social and scientific—about the nature of animal intelligence and how human and animal minds may or may not differ. So if scientists attempted to locate a brain center for a humanlike cognitive process in the cat, disagreement would be inevitable because there is no consensus on the nature of animal cognition itself.

4. Often, when a research system is too complex to give satisfying answers, scientists abandon it and turn to "doable" problems. The most famous example in my own field involves Thomas Hunt Morgan, who made fruit flies into a model organism and who developed Mendelian genetics. Morgan started life as an embryologist, but found embryos so complex that he de-

spaired of finding answers. Initially he was skeptical of both genetics and evolution, but when, almost by accident, he began finding consistent and inter-
pretable results that others generalized beyond the fruit fly, his research path
became clear. For more on this history, see Allen 1975 and 1978 and Kohler
1994. For more on the concept of "doability," see Fujimura 1987 and Mitman
and Fausto-Sterling 1992. Several neuroscientists who read and commented
on the first draft of this chapter pointed out that a goodly number of people in
the field think that research on callosal size should be dropped because the
CC is so intractable. But the field of neuroscience is nothing if not diverse and
subdivided into different workgroups with different understandings of what
constitutes "the best" form of research. So for others, whose work I examine
here, the beat goes on. In the case of the corpus callosum, the collective failure to move on is one sure sign that a lot more is at stake than the reputations
of a few neuroscientists.

5. Gelman 1992; Gorman 1992.

6. Black 1992, p. 162.

7. Foreman 1994.

8. Wade 1944.

9. Begley 1995, pp. 51–52. Elsewhere I offer a different take on the *Newsweek* article: Fausto-Sterling 1997.

10. The author does present the alternate "social" explanation, and in
that sense does not take sides in the debate. Begley writes: "Is it farfetched to
wonder whether parts of girls' brains grow or shrink, while parts of boys'
expand or shrivel, because they were told not to worry their pretty heads
about math, or because they started amassing Legos from birth?" (Begley
1995, p. 54).

11. (Unsigned 1992). This is an idea that more than a few sexologists take
quite seriously. During the winter/spring of 1998, the Listserve of professional sexologists, "Loveweb" (a pseudonym), had an extended and heated
debate about if and why gay men gravitate to certain professions. In this debate
the question of differences in spatial abilities and brain structure figured
prominently.

12. Witelson 1991b; McCormick et al. 1990.

13. Schiebinger 1992, p. 114.

14. Schiebinger 1992.

15. Questions about the localization of function within the brain and
brain asymmetry changed throughout the century. In the first half of the nineteenth century, the belief that faculties of the mind were located in particular
parts of the brain met a resistance that stemmed from an association of the idea
of localization with social change movements and from a struggle between
theology and the emerging field of experimental biology. The localizers fell
into a political camp that advocated social reforms, such as doing away with
the monarchy and the death penalty and broadening the right to vote. The

antilocalizers cheered the coronation of Charles X and advocated the death penalty for blasphemers (Harrington 1987). The French neurologist and anthropologist Paul Broca finally settled the matter by correlating the loss of language ability in brain-damaged patients with a particular region (Broca's area) of the frontal lobe of the cerebral cortex and concluding that, at least for language, the brain hemispheres were asymmetrical. Broca's conclusions threatened "deeply rooted aesthetic and philosophical beliefs. . . . If it were established that the brain was functionally lopsided, this would make a mockery of the classical equation between symmetry . . . and notions of health and human physical perfection . . . .It might even undermine all recent efforts to bring logic and lawfulness to the study of the cortex, raising the spectre of retrograde movement toward the implicitly theological view of the cerebral cortex as an organ beyond all scientific classification" (Harrington 1987, p. 53).

Broca and other French neurologists, then, faced the specter of being dragged backward in time, away from an era of middle-class democracy and into a discourse that linked symmetry, a lack of localized brain functions, religion, and monarchy. Broca compromised by proposing that there were no *innate* cerebral asymmetries; instead, the brain grew unevenly during childhood. Broca's ideas about development during childhood rested, in turn, on a set of beliefs about racial brain differences that were also thought to emerge during childhood. See Gould 1981; Harrington 1987; and Russett 1989. Thus, asymmetry not only separated humans from animals; among humans, it divided the "advanced from the primitive races" (Harrington 1987, p. 66). Broca effected a major change. Whereas in the first half of the nineteenth century, perfectibility had been linked to symmetry, before long the ideas of perfectibility and asymmetry became linked. Soon it grew obvious that women (dubbed *Homo parietalis,* in contrast to white men, who became known as *Homo frontalis*; Fausto-Sterling 1992), small children, and the working classes all had more symmetrical brains. By the end of the century, the list of the imperfect had grown to include madmen and criminals (who as a group tended toward higher frequencies of left-handedness and ambidexterity, both of which correlate with lessened asymmetry). Broca advanced a new scientific view by separating it from an older set of political belief systems to which it had been linked, and attaching it to a new constellation. His one area of overlap (innate symmetry but developmental asymmetry) provided continuity and acceptability; once the new scientific belief system became strong enough it flourished, generating offspring of its own.

16. Donahue suggested that the difference could account for "women's intuition" (Donahue 1985).

17. De Lacoste-Utamsing and Holloway 1982, p. 1431.

18. Efron 1990; Fausto-Sterling 1992b.

19. Stanley 1993, pp. 128 (emphasis in the original), 136.

20. An entire issue of the journal *Brain and Cognition* (26 [1994]) is devoted to a critique of a theory by Geschwind and Behan on which Bendbow relies for her claims about innate skill differences in males and females.

21. Benbow and Lubinski 1993. The debate about a biological basis for possible differences in mathematics ability, possibly lodged in the corpus callosum, continues. For a more recent exchange on this topic, see Benbow and Lubinski 1997 versus Hyde 1997.

22. Haraway 1997, p. 129. The technoscientific objects that Haraway mentions are "fetus, chip/computer, gene, race, ecosystem, brain." She doesn't discuss the corpus callosum, but she does pay a lot of attention to the intersections between race and gender. Indeed, the paths traveled by the sticky race and the sticky gender thread cross many times, and entangle themselves more than once when they meet up in the CC.

23. Other aspects of education and child development are also grabbed up by these sticky threads. One paper, for example, claims a correlation between dyslexia and an altered corpus callosum structure (Hynd et al. 1995). This sticky node includes a host of issues in the diagnosis and treatment of learning disabilities, which reach far beyond the scope of this book.

24. One recent link involves theories of mental illness (Blakeslee 1999).

25. But see Efron 1990.

26. This claim was made by Bean (1906), who also wrote in the September 1906 issue of *Century Magazine* that: "The Caucasian and the negro [*sic*] are fundamentally opposite extremes in evolution. Having demonstrated that the negro and the Caucasian are widely different in characteristics, due to a deficiency of gray matter and connecting fibers in the negro brain . . . we are forced to conclude that is is [*sic*] useless to try to elevate the negro by education or otherwise." Quoted in Baker 1994, p. 210.

27. Allen et al. 1991.

28. Rauch and Jinkins 1994, p. 68.

29. Latour 1988; Latour 1983.

30. Kohler 1994.

31. For additional and varied discussion of how natural objects become laboratory tools, see the several articles in Clarke and Fujimura 1992.

32. Bean 1906.

33. Which look identical to tracings made by modern scientists. See, for example, Clarke et al. 1989 and Byne et al. 1988.

34. This is remarkable in a scientific world in which few publications are referred to ten years after their initial appearance.

35. I believe the two-dimensional CC is what might, in semiotic jargon, be called a free-floating signifier.

36. Bean 1906, p. 377. If you didn't know the context, might you not think this was a description of gender, rather than racial difference?

37. Ibid., p. 386.

38. In 1999 it is the splenium, now linked to cognitive functions, that is supposed to be larger in females.

39. Mall mentored an important woman anatomist, Florence Rena Sabine (1871–1953). For a brief biography, see Ogilvie 1986.

40. Mall 1909, p. 9.

41. Ibid., p. 32. Thirteen of the papers I summarize in tables 5.3 to 5.5 refer to Bean and/or Mall. Five that report sex differences and four that find no difference quote only Bean. None quote Mall alone, although his paper stood for decades as the defining work. Three groups that find their own sex difference quote both Mall and Bean, while one that reports no difference cites the earlier controversy.

42. See note 26 and Baker 1994.

43. For additional discussion of how maps, atlases, and other representations of the brain came to stand for the invisible brain "and all the forms of invisible work and failure hidden" therein (p. 224), see Star 1992.

44. Rauch and Jinkins (1994) write: "Measurements of the entire corpus callosum in three dimensions would also be a complex undertaking, since the corpus callosum is shaped much like a bird with complicated wing formation. Further these wings co-mingle with the ascending white matter tracts . . . making the lateral portion of the corpus callosum essentially impossible to define with certainty" (p. 68).

Even this domesticated CC presents problems, because it never separates entirely from the rest of the brain. Some of the research groups are careful to point this out: "The boundary of the CC is unequivocal dorsally but not ventrally. As in monkeys the splenium and adjacent part of the body cannot be macroscopically demarcated from the dorsal hippocampal commisure, which was therefore included to an unknown extent in our CC correction . . . the limit between the CC and the septum pellucidum was at times difficult to determine by inspection only" (Clarke et al. 1989, p. 217). This level of difficulty, however, experimenters feel they can live with, since the main body of the domestic CC is clear enough.

45. One scientific problem involves interpreting the huge variability found among men and among women. Elster et al. (1990) write: "As seen from our own data and that of others, callosal measurements vary nearly as much within sex as they do between sexes" (p. 325). See also Byne et al. 1988. A second question concerns the best method of looking at the corpus callosum. In the current dispute, investigators have used variations on two major methods. The first involves postmortem measurements on brains preserved from patients who have died from illnesses not affecting the brain. The revealed, two-dimensional surface of this CC cross-section then becomes the object of a variety of measurements. The alternate method is to use live volunteers who have agreed to have their heads examined by a magnetic resonance imager (MRI). This machine uses the body's natural chemical activity to visu-

alize the brain. The machine creates images on a TV screen of optical "slices" of the brain. Just as one might slice a loaf of bread, the machine begins at the outer surface, pictures the first thin slice, then proceeds toward the center, offering up visual slices. The visible outlines of the corpus callosum become the two-dimensional structure that the scientist then measures. The authors of a recent paper write:

> studies using autopsy or cadaver material also tend to have low sample sizes. While there are advantages in using postmortem material, such as direct measurement and the ability to measure brain weight, the paucity of specimens makes for questionable statistical conclusions. Other problems associated with the use of embalmed postmortem material are the changes resulting from formalin fixation. . . . Studies using magnetic resonance images have benefited from larger sample sizes. MRI studies using a slice thickness of 7–10 mm have been criticized, as the partial volume effect may lead to inaccurate results. [Constant and Ruther 1996, p. 99]

A third technical problem concerns the concept of "allometry." See, for example, Fairbairn 1997. For allometry debates applied to the problems of CC comparison, see Going and Dixson (1990), p. 166, who write:

> It is well known that the brains of men are larger and heavier than those of women. This presents a difficulty for studies of sexual dimorphism, in that real differences between the brains of men and women may be obscured, or spurious differences created, by this difference in size. The question arises whether it is proper to attempt correction for brain weight. Correction reflects the theoretical model of relationships between brain weight and the quantities under consideration, and the model may not be correct. Corrected data must therefore be interpreted with caution, even scepticism.

Contrast this point of view with Holloway, who finds relative differences to be of great interest (Holloway 1998; see also Peters 1988).

46. The modern dispute about CC gender differences began with measures of corpus callosums from brains obtained at autopsy (PM) (de Lacoste-Utamsing and Holloway 1982). As subsequent reports differed both from the original and from each other, a debate about method also emerged. Postmortem studies had smaller sample sizes, for example. For fifteen studies using MRI's the average sample size was 86.3 (range 10–122), while for fifteen studies using postmortems the sample size averaged 44.2 (range 14–70). The studies surveyed are listed in note 50.

47. Various forms of brain scans are gaining public recognition as a supposedly objective way to read the brain. Of course, MRI's and the especially

popular PET scans are constructed images. For more on brain scans, see Dumit 1997, 1999a and 1999b.

48. Witelson and Goldsmith 1991; Witelson 1989.

49. Clark et al. 1989, p. 217; Byne et al. 1988. Witelson points out that "study of the concordance between direct postmortem and MR measurement of callosal size remains to be done" (Witelson 1989, p. 821).

Using different technoscientific objects can lead to different results. I tallied up whether or not a research group had found sex or handedness differences in whole or part of the corpus callosum (either absolute or relative area differences). When MRI was the choice of method, seven research groups found a sex difference, while fourteen found no difference. In contrast, eight publications using postmortems reported sex differences, while seven did not. Is there something about using PM's (smaller sample size, nature of the object produced?) that makes it more likely for one to find a sex difference? (I used the studies listed in the following note.)

50. The papers are: Witelson 1985, 1989, and 1991a; Witelson and Goldsmith 1991; Demeter et al. 1988; Hines et al. 1992; Cowell et al. 1993; Holloway et al. 1993; de Lacoste-Utamsing and Holloway 1982; de Lacoste et al. 1986; Oppenheim et al. 1987; O'Kusky et al. 1988; Weiss et al. 1989; Habib et al. 1991; Johnson et al. 1944; Bell and Variend 1985; Holloway and de Lacoste 1986; Kertesz et al. 1987; Byne et al. 1988; Clarke et al. 1989; Allen et al. 1991; Emory et al. 1991; Aboitiz, Scheibel et al. 1992b; Clarke and Zaidel 1994; Rauch and Jinkins 1994; Going and Dixson 1990; Steinmetz et al. 1992; Reinarz et al. 1988; Denenberg et al. 1991; Prokop et al. 1990; Elster et al. 1990; Steinmetz et al. 1995; Constant and Ruther 1996.

51. Habib et al. 1991.

52. Witelson 1989.

53. Lynch 1990, p. 171.

54. "Starting," Lynch writes, "with an initially recalcitrant specimen, scientists work methodically to expose, work with, and perfect the specimen's surface appearances to be congruent with graphic representation and mathematical analysis" (Lynch 1990, p. 170).

55. For a discussion of other aspects of simplification in scientific work, see Star 1983. For more on the construction of research objects within social networks, see Balmer 1996 and Miettinen 1998.

56. If CC differences appear during childhood, they may, presumably, be affected by developmental experiences. In other words, differences in adult brain anatomy, may, in fact, have been produced by social differences in the first place. See, for example, Aboitiz et al. 1996 and Ferrario et al. 1996.

57. There is an ongoing dispute about how the CC changes with age and whether male and female CC's age differently. The principles culled from this aspect of the argument don't differ from those developed in this chapter, so I have chosen not to plumb the depths of the aging argument. See, for example,

Salat et al. 1996. How men and women age and the problems of old age are yet other social bits picked up by the sticky CC threads.

58. Holloway et al. 1993; Holloway 1998.

59. The explanation offered for this relationship between sex and handedness is that men's brains are more lateralized than women's (at least for certain cognitive functions). But in general, left-handers are less lateralized than right-handers. If one assumes that a larger CC area implies less lateralization, but that women, regardless of handedness, are already less lateralized, then adding handedness into the picture won't matter for them, but it will make a measurable difference for men.

60. Cowell et al. 1993.

61. Bishop and Wahlsten 1997. See also a detailed discussion by Byne (1995), who reaches conclusions similar to mine and Bishop and Wahlsten's.

Meta-analysis is, itself, a controversial process. Debate continues over how to evaluate conflicting results in the scientific literature. Some find the bean-counting method seen in my tables 5.3 to 5.5 most appropriate, others meta-analysis (Mann 1994). For a technical account of the effects of meta-analysis on research standards in psychology, see Schmidt 1992; for more on meta-analysis, see Hunt 1997.

62. Driesen and Raz 1995. They also concluded that left-handers have larger CC's than right-handers.

63. Fitch and Denenberg 1998. They argue that one cannot use relative values to compare different groups unless there is a proven correlation within each group. They use IQ to illustrate their point. "On average there is no sex difference between men and women on IQ tests. However, female brains are smaller than male brains, and weigh less." If one made a ratio of IQ to brain weight, women would be significantly smarter "per unit brain" than men. "The reason we do not use such a statistic is that research has established that there is no within-group correlation between IQ and brain size" ("within-group" means comparing women with smaller brains to women with larger brains). With regard to CC, they conclude: "the procedure of dividing brain size into CC area as a 'correction factor' is incorrect, and, because the female brain is typically smaller, can lead to false results suggesting a larger 'relative' CC in females" (p. 326).

Aboitiz (1998) argues that correction for brain size might be appropriate if one had a better idea of how function and size correlate. Holloway (1998) takes serious exception to the case against relative measurements: "Physical anthropologists . . . routinely use ratio data . . . we do so because an extremely interesting set of facts emerges: the relative size of the brain . . . does show sexually dimorphic differences, and they vary considerably within the mammalia" (p. 334). Wahlsten and Bishop (1998) also argue against the wanton use of ratios, although they believe such use can be legitimate under certain circumstances, ones not met in the CC studies.

64. Halpern (1998), p. 331. This asymmetric analysis of a scientific dispute suggests that one side (the feminists, in this case) has political investments that impair their ability to impartially evaluate a literature, while the other side can clearly hear the truth that nature speaks because they have no political investment. Halpern implies that one explanation of a failure to find sex differences is sloppy work, perhaps resulting from political commitments rather than a commitment to finding truths about the natural world. This argument against feminism takes the same form as Gould's analysis of Morton's work on racial differences in brain size (Gould 1981). Whichever side one is on (God's or the bad guy's) in these disputes, such asymmetric arguments paint one into a corner. Halpern offers a more balanced view (Halpern 1997).

65. Driesen and Raz (1995) suggest that researchers could improve the situation by improved reporting on the nature of their sample and even more measurements and different statistical tests. Bishop and Wahlsten (1997) argue that "it would be unwise to engage in further research on this topic unless a large enough sample is used in a single study" (p. 593). They think a minimum sample size would have to include 300 of each group—for a total of 600 brains! This sample size could accommodate the enormous variation within members of the same gender.

66. I found the concept of hypertext useful in incorporating the history of statistics into an analysis of the CC wars. Hypertext are those words or pictures that an internet surfer can signal in order to be transported to a whole new screen of information or activities. Haraway's description of hypertext is also helpful:

> In hypertext readers are led through, and can construct for themselves and interactively with others, webs of connections held together by heterogeneous sorts of glues. Pathways through the web are not predetermined but show their tendentiousness, their purposes, their strengths, and their peculiarities. Engaging in the epistemological and political game of hypertext commits its users to search for relationships in a funguslike mangrove or aspen forest where before there seemed to be neat exclusions and genetically distinct, single-trunk trees. [Haraway 1997, p. 231]

67. For examples of the literature on the social history of statistics connections between statistics, gender, race, and the social construction of scientific knowledge, see Porter 1986, 1992, 1995, and 1997; Porter and Mikuláš 1994; Porter and Hall 1995; Hacking 1982, 1990, and 1991; Wise 1995; and Poovey 1993.

As I write, the news is full of a politically charged battle over how to collect numbers for the year 2000 census. See, for example, Wright 1999.

68. The history of statistics as a technology of social management is poorly

known even among scientists who use statistical procedures to ensure mathematical objectivity. For the interested reader, therefore, I've included several endnotes on the origins of statistics. Once again, we find that scientific arguments, this time about numbers, are also social arguments.

Head measurements are a longtime favorite. At the turn of the century, criminologists measured as many parameters of the heads of criminals as they could think of (Lombroso and Ferrero 1895). Similarly, Quetelet presented dozens of tables about criminality, and Lombroso's little volume is packed with numbers. One table compared prostitutes, peasants, educated women, thieves, poisoners, assassins, infanticides, and normal women by measuring the following aspects of the cranium and face: anteroposterior diameter, transverse diameter, horizontal circumference, longitudinal curve, transverse curve, index of cephalon, anterior semicircumference, minimal frontal diamter, diameter of cheekbones, diameter of jaws, and height of forehead (Lombroso and Ferrero 1895, pp. 60–61).

69. Between 1820 and 1850, Europe experienced a great numerical explosion. From 1820 to 1840, "the rate of increase in the printing of numbers appears to be exponential whereas the rate of increase in the printing of words was merely linear" (Hacking 1982, p. 282). The increasing number of published statistical reports covered a growing diversity of measured things. Consider, for example, *A Treatise on Man and the Development of His Faculties*, by the Belgian astronomer-turned-statistician M. A. Quetelet. Originally published in Paris in 1835, the *Treatise* contains hundreds of numerical tables. Quetelet enumerated—that is he counted and categorized—"the development of the physical properties of man . . . development of stature weight, strength, &c., . . . development of the moral and intellectual qualities of man . . . [and] of the properties of average man, of the social system . . . and of the ultimate progress of our knowledge of the law of human development" (Quetelet 1842, table of contents). In the fourteen-page section on "The Development of the Propensity to Crime" alone, Quetelet included twenty-five statistical tables listing the numbers of people committing crimes in a particular year, their educational level compared to whether the crime was against property or people, the influence of climate and season on crime, the disposition of legal cases by city and town, crimes in different countries, sex differences in the types of crime, age of the criminal, motive for the crime, and much, much more. England, France, and Belgium all experienced a grand period of statistical gathering. Governments needed information about a changing populace. Was the birthrate high enough? What was the state of the working classes (and how likely were they to revolt)? How healthy were army recruits? The social and political questions of the time dictated the types of information sought and their tabular presentation. By the time of the French Revolution, statistics was not regarded as an arm of pure and applied mathematics, free from social import and content, but rather had come "to be conceived in

France and England as the empirical arm of political economy" (Porter 1986, p. 27).

70. Statistical tabulations required the creation of categories, a process the philosopher Ian Hacking calls subversive: "Enumeration demands *kinds* of things or people to count. Counting is hungry for categories. Many of the categories we now use to describe people are byproducts of the needs of enumeration" (Hacking 1982, p. 280; emphasis in original)—just as the application of measurement to the human body (morphometry) requires the creation of subdivisions such as the 2-D CC, the splenium, the genu, or the isthmus. As the historian Joan Scott writes: "Statistical reports are neither totally neutral collections of fact nor simply ideological impositions. Rather they are ways of establishing the authority of certain visions of social order, of organizing perceptions of 'experience'" (Scott 1988, p. 115). See also Poovey 1993.

In the first half of the nineteenth century, Quetelet formulated a way to characterize populations. For Quetelet, a group of individuals seemed chaotic, but as a *population*, they behaved according to measurable social laws. He believed so strongly in statistical laws that he devoted himself to creating a composite human: the average man whom he viewed as a moral ideal. He examined many facets of the average man: How had he been described by the literary world and in the fine arts? What physical and anatomical measures did anatomy and medicine offer? (Stigler 1986). Moreover, Quetelet standardized racial, sexual, and national types, which he believed enabled scientists to compare intelligence across the races. Caucasians, he felt, came out ahead. See Quetelet 1842, p. 98.

Quetelet equated deviation from a statistical norm with abnormality in the social, medical, or moral sense. Crime and social chaos resulted from the great disparity between the very wealthy and the very poor, while middle-income people who lived moderate lives were bound to live longer than those on the extreme. "The progress of civilization, the gradual triumph of mind, was equivalent to a narrowing of the limits within which the 'social body' oscillated" (Porter 1986, p. 103). Deviation from the mean represented a mistake or error.

71. The sociologist Bruno Latour uses metaphor to transform the drab-looking scientific text—filled with graphs, tables, and statistical testing—into a thrilling epic. Note that the hero here is the result—in this case—a finding of sex differences:

> What is going to happen to the hero? Is it going to resist this new ordeal? . . . Is the reader convinced? Not yet. Ah ha, here is a new test . . . Imagine the cheering crows and the boos. . . . The more we get into the niceties of the scientific literature, the more extraordinary it becomes. It is now real opera. Crowds of people are mobilized by the references; from offstage hundreds of accessories are brought in [e.g.. statistical tests and

analyses]. Imaginary readers . . . are not asked only to believe the author
but to spell out what sort of tortures, ordeals and trials the heroes should
undergo before being recognized as such. The text unfolds the dramatic
story of these trials. . . . At the end, the readers, ashamed of their former
doubts, have to accept the author's claim. These operas unfold thousands
of times on the pages of *Nature*. [Latour 1987, p. 53]

72. Statistics can be seen as a specialized technology of difference. Statistical analyses and the establishment of population means (which often became
norms) became an essential part of the field of psychology in the twentieth
century. Only then was a "normal" psychological subject established—built
by heavy reliance on population aggregates. For a full treatment of the role of
statistics in the narrowing of "epistemic access to the variety of psychological
realities," see Danziger 1990, p. 197. Danziger's history is especially important in analyzing lateralization studies, which are often used to demonstrate
the psychological relevance of CC studies.

73. During the second half of the nineteenth century, statisticians reinter-
preted the bell curve as representing mere variability rather than a distribution of error around an average, ideal type, as Quetelet thought. Eventually,
scientists renamed *standard error*, calling it *standard deviation* instead. Charles
Darwin's first cousin, Sir Francis Galton, did not extol the virtues of the median (see Porter 1986, p. 129). In contrast to earlier scientists, who focused
on improving humankind through improving environmental conditions, Galton wanted to use knowledge about the exceptional variant in order to use
evolution (selective breeding) to improve upon the bodies making up a population. To this end, he invented a new field of study and a social movement:
eugenics. In his book *Hereditary Genius: An Inquiry into Its Laws and Consequences*,
he wrote a prescription for improving the health of English society: "I propose
. . . that a man's natural abilities are derived by inheritance. . . . Consequently, as it is easy . . . to obtain by careful selection a permanent breed of
dog . . . gifted with peculiar powers . . . , so it would be quite practicable
to produce a highly-gifted race of men by judicious marriages during several
consecutive generations"(Galton 1892, p. 1). Dismissing the possibility that
variations in human ability resulted primarily from differences in training and
opportunity, he wrote: "I have no patience with the hypothesis that babies
are born pretty much alike, and that the sole agencies in creating differences
between boy and boy, and man and man, are steady application and moral
effort" (Galton 1892, p. 12). As evidence, he noted that despite the wider
educational opportunities available in America (compared with the more
rigid class system of Great Britain), England still produced more great writers, artists, and philosophers: "The higher kind of books . . . read in America
are principally the work of Englishmen. . . . If the hindrances to the rise of
genius were removed from English society as completely as they have been

removed from that of America, we should not become materially richer in highly eminent men"(Galton 1892. p. 36). Galton feared for the future of English civilization, but hoped that if he could figure out how to predict the inheritance of mental characteristics and devise a breeding program, higher civilizations could be saved. Galton and his students oversaw a gradual transition from Quetelet's concept of probable error to that of a standard deviation—free from any implication of natural error and providing the raw material with which eugenic programs could work. Similarly, Quetelet's law of error became a normal distribution. The same old bell curve, once seen to conceptualize nature's difficulties in making perfect copies of its essential template, became in Galton's hands a representation of nature's virtue in producing a wide and varying range of individuals.

Galton chose statistics as the best method for predicting the relationship between a parental trait—say, height or intelligence—and the same trait in offspring. He devised the concept of a correlation coefficient—a number that would express the relationship between two variables. His concept of correlation developed because his eugenic concerns "made possible a more general treatment of numerical variability" (Mackenzie 1981; Porter 1986). Subsequent developers of statistics, especially Karl Pearson (who invented the chi square and contingency tests) and R. A. Fisher (who invented the analysis of variance tests often used today), were also devotees of eugenics and, as with Galton, their concerns about human heredity drove their statistical discoveries. See Mackenzie 1981 for a fascinating discussion of the political implications of the chi-squared test and the way Fisher's concerns with eugenics led him to significantly narrow the scope of evolutionary theory. The field of modern biology has been importantly shaped by the eugenic commitments of a large number of biologists working in the first third of the twentieth century.

74. The process does not involve drawing such a curve; the information can be dealt with entirely through numbers. I invoke the curve here to help the reader visualize what is being done.

75. For a discussion of the limitations of the uses of ANOVA, see Lewontin 1974 and Wahlsten 1990. Lewontin writes: "What has happened in attempting to solve the problem of the analysis of causes by using the analysis of variation is that a totally different object has been substituted. . . . The new object of study, the deviation of phenotypic value from the mean, is not the same as the phenotypic value itself" (p. 403).

76. This test takes into account sample size, the degree of variation around the male mean, and the degree of variation around the female mean. Many of the workers in this dispute acknowledge the wide variability for both sexes in CC shape.

77. Both means testing and ANOVAs were used by various groups.

78. Allen et al. 1991.

79. Latour (1990) calls these graphs, tables, and drawings "inscriptions,"

and comments on their place in the scientific paper: because "the dissenter [in this case that would be me—the highly skeptical reader] can always escape and try out another interpretation . . . much energy and time is devoted by scientists to *corner* him and surround him with ever more dramatic visual effects. Although *in principle* any interpretation can be opposed to any text and image, *in practice* this is far from being the case; the cost of dissenting increases with each new collection, each new labeling, each new redrawing" (p. 42; emphasis in the original).

80. Allen et al. 1991, p. 933; emphasis in the original.

81. Ibid., p. 937.

82. In the first quarter of this century, Pearson developed the X^2 method to establish the validity of a correlation between two or more qualitative variables. But other methods also contested for this privilege. See Mackenzie 1981, pp. 153–183 for an analysis of a dispute between Pearson and his student G. Udny Rule over the best way to analyze such data. Rule studied social policy requiring a yes or no answer. Did, for example, a vaccine against a particular disease save lives during an epidemic? Rule invented a statistic—which he called Q—which could tell him whether there was a relationship between treatment and survival. Pearson not only wanted a yes or no answer, he wanted to study the strength or degree of any association. The motivation for this "strength of correlation" approach came directly from his wish to develop a practical program of eugenics—"to alter the relative fertility of the good and the bad stocks in the community" (Mackenzie 1981, p. 173). Pearson needed a mathematical theory in which knowledge of a person's ancestry could enable him to predict an individual's abilities, personality, and social propensities. In the 1890s, when Pearson first began working on problems of descent, there was no accepted way to study the heredity of unmeasurable characteristics such as color or mental ability. Pearson needed to extend the theory of correlation to measure the strength of inheritance of traits that had no units of measurement. Pearson solved his problem by collecting data on intelligence—based on teachers' estimates of a child's abilities—from over 4,000 pairs of siblings in the schools. He then asked: If one brother was rated highly intelligent, what was the likelihood that the other one would as well? His method of calculating correlation for these conditions convinced him that human character traits were strongly inherited. "We inherit," he wrote "our parents' tempers, our parents' conscientiousness, shyness and ability, even as we inherit their stature, forearm and span" (quoted in Mackenzie, p. 172). Rule criticized Pearson for making an unverifiable assumption—that the numbers used to calculate the X^2 were distributed in a bell-shaped curve. Pearson attacked Rule's Q because it could not measure the strength of correlation. Their positions were unreconcilable because they had designed their tests to accomplish different goals. The controversy between Rule and Pearson never really ended. Today both methods are used. According to Macken-

zie, Rule's Q is most popular among sociologists, while Pearson's correlation coefficient is more in vogue among psychometricians. For additional analysis of the issues raised by this dispute, see Gigerenzer et al. 1989.

83. This is not an attack on Allen et al. Indeed, this is one of the strongest papers in the CC collection. Rather, I use them to illustrate the tactics scientists use to stabilize and draw meaning from the CC.

84. That is, the type of story I explicated when discussing nineteenth-century disputes on brain laterality (see notes 68–73 and 82 on the social history of statistics).

A related and helpful theoretical approach would be to think of the CC as a boundary object, in this case a standardized form that "inhabits several intersecting social worlds and satisf[ies] the informational requirement of each" (Star and Griesemer 1989, p. 393). Boundary objects can take on different meanings in each social world, but they must be easily recognizable and thus provide a way to translate among different groups. The social worlds in this case can be read from figure 5.6. They include research areas with overlapping but differing foci, as well as social and political groupings—educational reformers, feminists, gay rights activists, and the like.

85. For some current theories of CC function, see Hellige et al. (1998), who suggest that larger CC size may reflect a greater functional isolation of the two hemispheres. Moffat et al. (1998) suggest that males (there were no females in this study) whose speech and handedness functions are located in different brain hemispheres may require increased interhemispheric communication and thus a larger CC. (Note the difference with the previous citation.) Nikolaenko and Egorov (1998) note that there is no commonly accepted model of brain asymmetry. They present a thesis in which the CC is the key to integrating dynamically interacting brain hemispheres. The nerve fibers that course through the CC certainly have different functions, some excitatory and others inhibitory. Some types of CC activity will surely inhibit information flow, and other types will enhance it. The level of subtlety needed to understand the mechanisms involved in brain cognition and their relationship to CC function are not currently available. See, for example, Yazgan et al. (1995), who write: "The corpus callosum is composed of fibres with excitatory and inhibitory functional effects, the proportions and distributions of which are unknown in the CC's of these particular subjects" (p. 776). The same may be said of all the subjects in all the human CC studies. For an extended treatment of hemispheric asymmetry, see Hellige 1993.

86. Allen et al. 1994. O'Rand (1989) applies the idea of a thought collective to beliefs about brain morphology and cognitive abilities. Star (1992) writes that a conclusion about the function of a particular region of the brain "is really a report about the collective work of a community of scientists, patients, journal publishers, monkeys, electrode manufacturers, and so on, over a period of some 100 years" (pp. 207–208).

87. Cohn (1987) discusses how entering into a linguistically defined community—in her case, defense intellectuals—imposes a particular mode of thought. To communicate within the community, one must use their language. But in choosing their language, one gives up other ways of seeing the world. See also Hornstein 1988.

88. See, for example, Aboitiz et al. 1992. Nobody knows whether size differences in CC subdivisions result from denser packing of neurons, a change in the relative proportions of differently sized neurons, or a reduction in the number of many different kinds of neurons. For attempts to answer some of these questions, see Aboitiz et al. 1992 and 1998a,b. In animals, researchers identify and trace individual nerve fibers from their origins in the cerebral cortex to their passage through the CC after injecting a dye in the cortex. Individual nerve fibers absorb the dye and conduct it along their axons. (An *axon* is the long end of a nerve fiber that conducts electrical impulses from the cell's point of origin to its connection to another nerve cell or a muscle cell.) When researchers later isolate the CC, they can find the dye and see which part of the CC contains axons originating from the region of the cerebrum they injected. In one study of this sort on rats, researchers confirmed that the splenium was comprised in part of axons originating in the visual cortex (the region of the brain involved with enabling vision). Some of the axons running through the CC were coated with an insulating substance called myelin, while others were bare nerve fibers. There were no sex differences in overall area of the CC or of the splenium. The total density of unmyelinated axons (number of fibers per mm^2 in certain subdivisions of the splenium) differed in male and female rats (female>male). Male rats, however, had the advantage in myelinated axons. Simply counting axons of all types buried the more subtle differences. The size of both fiber types was the same in males and females (Kim et al. 1996). This level of detail—currently unattainable in humans—is what is minimally necessary to relate functional consequences to structural differences. In humans, very careful dissection has revealed some of the general topographical features of connections between particular regions of the human cerebral cortex and particular regions of the corpus callosum (de Lacoste et al. 1985; Velut et al. 1998).

89. For a single volume that shows the density and diversity of this node, see Davidson and Hugdahl 1995. There are literally thousands of research articles on handedness, brain asymmetry, and cognitive function. This is one definition of node density. By *diverse*, I mean the range of questions (or number of subnodes) subsumed within this knot. Articles in the Davidson volume cover the following topics: hormonal influences on brain structure and function, brain anatomy, theories of visual processing, theories of aural processing, discussions of handedness, theories of learning, links to other medical questions such as sudden cardiac death, links to emotional aspects of behavior,

evolution of brain asymmetry, development of brain asymmetry, learning disabilities, and psychopathology.

90. See, for example, Bryden and Bulman-Fleming 1994 and Hellige et al. 1998.

91. Note the paper title of Goldberg et al. 1994. For an evaluation of methods used in laterality studies, see Voyer 1998.

92. See, for example, Bisiacchi et al. 1994; Corballis 1994; and Johnson et al. 1996.

93. For an up-to-date view of the debate about handedness, laterality, cognition, lateralization, sex differences, and much more, see Bryden et al. 1994 and the papers that reply to all, found in vol. 26 (1994) of *Brain and Cognition*. See also Hall and Kimura 1995.

94. For a recent study, see Davatzikos and Resnick 1998.

95. Whether one finds differences in performance on specialized tests of particular cognitive tasks may well depend on what sample one uses (e.g., a large general sample versus a sample of gifted children) and when and how one does the test. Although many previously reported differences have begun to diminish or even disappear, a few are stable with time. This does not, of course, mean that they are biological in origin, only that if they are social, they have not been modified by social change in the past twenty to thirty years. The number of different types of tests on which sex differences continue to appear and are of the same magnitude as they were twenty-five years ago is now small. The social import of any such differences, of course, remains in hot dispute. For discussions of meta-analyses of studies of gender differences in cognition see Voyer et al. 1995; Halpern 1997; Richardson 1997; and Hyde and McKinley 1997. For a discussion of the meaning and interpretation of differences on cognitive tasks, see Crawford and Chaffin 1997 and Caplan and Caplan 1997.

96. Fausto-Sterling 1992; Uecker and Obrzut 1994; Voyer et al. 1995; Hyde and McKinley 1997.

97. Gowan 1985.

98. Some of these conflicting theories are discussed in Clarke and Zaidel 1994.

To get a taste of the varying viewpoints and research on gifted children and the incorporation of findings on the corpus callosum, see Bock and Ackrill 1993.

99. Evidence that the human CC continues to develop into at least the third decade of life is reviewed by Schlaug et al. 1995. The implication of postnatal development is that environment (in this case, musical training) can influence brain anatomy. These researchers report that musicians who began their musical training before the age of seven had larger anterior CC size than controls. They find their results to be "compatible with plastic changes of

components of the CC during a maturation period within the first decade of life, similar to those observed in animal studies" (p. 1047). Note the invocation of animal studies.

100. Allen et al. 1991, p. 940.

101. Some scientific papers, however, explicitly raise the possibility. Cowell et al. (1993) link laterality, hormones, and sex differences in the frontal lobe while Hines (1990) floats the idea of hormonal effects on the human corpus callosum.

102. Halpern (1998) writes: "For obvious ethical reasons, experimental manipulations of hormones that are expected to alter the brain are conducted with nonhuman mammals. . . . Researchers assume that the effects in humans will be similar . . . but not identical. . . . Conclusions . . . are corroborated with data from . . . naturally occurring abnormalities . . . such as girls with congenital adrenal hyperplasia" (p. 330). Note how the hormone nodule always links back at some point to intersexuality. A similar approach to drawing strength from association with other arenas may be found in Wisniewski (1998).

103. Sociologist Susan Leigh Star and the psychologist Gail Hornstein describe this as a shell game that has played itself out in earlier disputes about the brain when "uncertainties from one line of work were 'answered' in the public construction of the theory by drawing on results from another domain. In triangulating results across domains, accountability to the anomalies in any single domain was never required" (Hornstein and Star 1994, p. 430).

104. Efron (1990) has written an extensive critique of the concept of hemispheric lateralization and of the experimental methods, such as the use of tachistoscopes and dichotic listening devices, which support claims of lateralization. Uecker and Obrzut (1994) question the interpretation of right-hemisphere male superiority for spatial tasks. Chiarello (1980) suggests there is no conclusive evidence that the CC is needed for lateralization of certain functions. Clarke and Lufkin (1993) find that variations in callosal size do not contribute to individual differences in hemispheric specialization. Jäncke et al. (1992) critique interpretations of dichotic listening tests for cerebral lateralization. Gitterman and Sies (1992) discuss nonbiological determinants of language organization in the brain, while Trope et al. (1992) question the generalizability of the analytic/holistic distinction between left and right brain hemispheres.

105. Writing about the skeleton debate, the historian Londa Schiebinger notes: "Since the Enlightenment, science has stirred hearts and minds with its promise of a 'neutral' and privileged viewpoint, above and beyond the rough and tumble of political life" (Schiebinger 1992, p. 114).

106. Latour considers objects of knowledge to be hybrids. Reading his account of the history of natural and political science as efforts to stabilize the

nature/nurture dichotomy by denying the hybrid nature of scientific facts was an illuminating experience for me (Latour 1993).

107. I have not exhausted the analysis. I don't consider, for example, the institutional resources available to different research groups. Allen et al., for example, work at UCLA and have access to a large collection of MRI's taken for other medical purposes. The researchers skeptical of sex differences, such as Byne et al. (1988), did not have institutional access to such a large database. Allen et al. can swamp out Byne and colleagues' finding of no difference by the sheer size of their database. Ruth Bleier's (she is the leader of the research group of Byne et al.) personal history as a political radical and feminist leads her to be more marginal in terms of her access to databanks. It is likely that, politically or otherwise, marginal people always have a harder time mobilizing counter data and getting their mobilized data heard.

Nor have I produced a detailed analysis of conventional rhetoric. For example, Allen et al. use the word *dramatic* to describe the sex difference in splenial shape, when in fact they had to use a rather tortured process to render the difference visible. The use of emphatic words is, of course, part of the rhetoric of calling attention to a particular finding.

108. This point really becomes clear when we think about homosexuality. In the early part of the century and currently, many liberal thinkers were/are genetic determinists. They believe(d) that homosexuality is "genetic," and that one social implication is that gay people should have equal civil rights. Religious conservatives, on the other hand, argue that homosexuality is a "choice" and that, since it is also a sin, homosexuals should choose to become straight. They use the ability to choose to argue against equal civil rights. Sandwiched in between, in the middle of the century, are the practices of Nazi Germany. Nazis believed that homosexuality is "genetic," but saw that as an argument for extermination.

109. Halpern 1997, p. 1,098.

110. Hyde and McKinley 1997, p. 49. What is meant by this goal is often unclear. Many conceptualize equal opportunity to mean no more than the absence of overt discrimination. Hyde's view is that it should involve active efforts to level the cognitive playing field. Furthermore, my argument assumes that when they appear, group differences in cognition are small enough that the right combination of skills training and encouragement could eliminate them. I am aware of the counterargument—that it would take extreme measures (cost too much, push girls too hard against their "natural" inclinations, etc.) to equalize group differences, or that perhaps equalizing group differences in cognition by training and remediation is simply not possible. (Currently, we offer remedial reading and verbal training. These are areas where group differences favoring girls often appear.) A further assumption underlying this argument is that known group differences in cognition actu-

ally account for subsequent professional achievement. My own view is that this is probably not a good assumption. I suspect that unacknowledged gender schema do a better job of explaining such difference. (See Valian 1998a,b for a full statement of this argument.)

111. I know from experience that some will read my position as antimaterialist regardless of my protestations, but reaffirming my materialist belief system is worth a shot.

Chapter 6: Sex Glands, Hormones, and Gender Chemistry

1. De Kruif 1945, pp. 225–26. De Kruif received his Ph.D. from the University of Michigan in 1916. Until the early 1920s he taught and practiced science in a university setting. His first book, *Our Medicine Men*, apparently got him fired from the Rockefeller Institute and he thereafter devoted himself to science writing. He provided Sinclair Lewis with the background for Lewis's classic *Arrowsmith* (1925). (See Kunitz and Haycraft 1942 for further biographical detail.) In a sense he contributed to the writing of this book, since his *Microbe Hunters* (1926) was among the many books my parents kept in our household as part of an ultimately successful plan to encourage both my brother and me to become scientists ourselves.

2. Quoted in Fausto-Sterling 1992b, pp.110–11.

3. See Wilson 1966.

4. Oudshoorn 1994, p. 9. Progesterone has been added to the estrogen pill to prevent possible increases in uterine cancer caused by estrogen alone.

5. De Kruif 1945, pp. 86–87. Frank Lillie stated the same case in more sober fashion when he referred to testosterone as "the specific internal secretion of the testis" and estrogen as the "specific internal secretion of the cortex of the ovary." He added: "As there are two sets of sex characters, so there are two sex hormones, the male hormone controlling the 'dependent' male characters, and the female determining the 'dependent' female characters" (Lillie 1939, pp. 6, 11).

6. Cowley 1996, p. 68.

7. Angier 1994, p. C13. See also *Star-Telegram* 1999; France 1999.

8. Sharpe 1997; Hess et al. 1997.

9. Angier 1997a.

10. For a beautifully detailed history of reproductive science in the twentieth century, see Clarke 1998.

11. Again, I use the idea that most scientific choices are underdetermined—that is, the actual data do not completely mandate a particular choice between competing theories, thus enabling the sociocultural valence of a particular theory to contribute to its attractiveness. See, for example, Potter 1989.

12. I am indebted to Adele Clarke for pointing me to the sociological

literature on social worlds. Sociologists use a "social worlds view" as a method of analyzing work organization, but here and in the following chapter I look instead at the implications for the production of scientific knowledge of studying the intersection of different social worlds. See Strauss 1978; Gerson 1983; Clarke 1990a; and Garrety 1997. Gerson defines social worlds as "activities carried out in common with respect to a particular subject or area of concern" (p. 359).

13. For more on castrati, see Heriot 1975. The eerie, tremulous voice of the last castrato known to have sung at the Vatican may be heard on the CD "Alessandro Moreschi: The Last Castrato, Complete Vatican Recordings" (Pavilion Records LTD, Pearl Opal CD 9823). Moreschi died in 1922. The original recordings are at the Yale University Collection of Historical Sound Recording.

14. Ehrenreich and English 1973; Dally 1991. From 1872 to 1906, 150,000 women had their ovaries removed. Among the crusaders who finally ended the practice of ovary removal was America's first woman doctor, Elizabeth Blackwell.

15. De Kruif 1945, pp. 53, 54. See also Berthold's original publication (Berthold 1849).

16. Corner 1965.

17. Borell 1976, p. 319.

18. Borell 1985.

19. Even in 1923, in their publication of what came to be seen as the definitive demonstration of a hormone produced by the ovarian follicles, Edgar Allen and Edward A. Doisey expressed skepticism: "There appears to be no conclusive evidence of either a definite localization of the hypothetic hormone or of the specific effect claimed for the commercial ovarian extracts in wide clinical use. The recent reviews of Frank and of Novak may be cited to illustrate the well founded skepticism concerning the activity of commercial preparations" (Allen and Doisey 1923, pp. 819–20).

Practicing gynecologists continued to push the point. Two Viennese practitioners, for example, reported that implanted ovaries could prevent the degeneration of the uterus, which otherwise followed removal of the female gonads.

20. The reevaluation resulted from new experimental approaches and the success of thyroid and adrenal extracts for treatment of certain forms of disease.

21. Quoted in Borell 1985, p. 11. By 1907, Schäfer had also come around. In an address to the Pharmaceutical Society of Edinburgh he argued that "It might be . . . supposed that this arrested development of . . . accessory organs [i.e., degeneration of the uterus] is the result of the cutting off of nervous influences, which are carried by the testicular and ovarian nerves." But, he went on, "the only rational explanation . . . is contained in the assumption

that the grafted organ produces . . . an internal secretion, which by virtue of the hormones it contains . . . can materially influence the development and structure of distant parts." Quoted in Borell 1985, pp. 13–14. See also Borell 1978.

22. See Noble 1977; Sengoopta 1992, 1996, and 1998; Porter and Hall 1995; Cott 1987.

23. On Europe, see Chauncey 1985, 1989, and 1994; D'Emilio and Freedman 1988; Sengoopta 1992. For an excellent Web site with information on the history of sexology, see *http://www.rki.de/GESUND/ARCHIV/TES-THOM2.HTM*, which is part of the Web site of the Robert Koch Institute in Germany.

For a discussion of the crisis and its relationship to American biology, see Pauly 1988, p. 126. For additional discussion of the construction of ideologies of masculinity in this period, see Halberstam 1998. See also Dubbert 1980.

24. Pauly 1987; Lunbeck 1994; Benson et al. 1991; Rainger et al. 1988; Noble 1977; Fitzpatrick 1990. For information on the origins of Rockefeller and Carnegie philanthropy, see chapter 1 of Corner 1964.

25. Sengoopta 1996, p. 466. For an account of the German women's movement in this period see Thönnessen 1969. The crisis in masculinity was international. See Chauncey 1989, p. 103.

26. Sengoopta 1996; Gilman 1994.

27. Sengoopta 1998.

28. On England, see Porter and Hall 1995. On the United States, see D'Emilio and Freedman 1988 and Chauncey 1989.

29. Nineteenth-century embryologists believed that, although they started from a common point, male embryos were more complex and better developed, while female differentiation was "only of a trivial kind." Oscar Hertwig, quoted in Sengoopta 1992, p. 261.

30. Sengoopta 1992, 1996. See also Anderson 1996.

31. Carpenter 1909, pp. 16–17. The reproductive biologist Walter Heape suggested in 1913 that Carpenter's worst fears of antagonism between the sexes had, in fact, been realized. Weininger published an algebraic formula to explain sexual attractions. He was not a fan of feminism and believed women to be by nature inferior to men. Carpenter was on the other side of the political fence, and he and his supporters derided the formulaic nature of Weininger's work. Nevertheless, their biological theories were not so different. See Porter and Hall 1995.

32. Sengoopta 1996.

33. Weir 1895, pp. 820, 825. Note that Weir's biological theory differs from Weininger's, but his metaphysics of gender is the same.

Other biologists, psychologists, and physicians also used the accusation of lesbianism to attack feminism. Dr. John Meagher, for example, wrote "the driving force in many agitators and militant women who are always after their rights, is often an unsatisfied sex impulse, with a homosexual aim. Married women with a completely satisfied libido rarely take an active interest in militant movements." Quoted in Cott 1987, p. 159.

34. In a Catch-22, pointing to talented women did not help anyone arguing that women and men have the same capabilities, since the counterargument would be that it was the male elements in their bodies that generated the talent.

35. For more on female masculinity in this period see, Halberstam 1998.

36. Marshall 1910, p. 1. For more on Marshall and the significance of his text, see Borell 1985 and Clarke 1998.

37. As late as 1907, a great deal of scientific debate existed about just what the ovaries did. Did they affect the uterus? Were they responsible for menstrual cycles? Did they work via nervous connections? See Marshall's experiments and literature review in Marshall and Jolly 1907.

38. Geddes and Thomson 1895, pp. 270–71. Geddes and Thomson also influenced sexual politics in America. One early sociologist based his Ph.D. thesis on their theories of metabolic differences between the sexes (Thomas 1907); Jane Addams turned their ideas to feminist use by insisting that modern civilization needed feminine skills with which nature had endowed women. For a discussion of the American scene, see Rosenberg 1982, pp. 36–43.

Marshall also turned to the latest hot science, citing, for example, the up and coming Thomas Hunt Morgan as an important source, thus showing that while he relied on those who had gone before, he was also forward-looking. Morgan founded the modern field of Mendelian genetics. He was among a small group of scientists who put American science on a modern footing. See Maienschein 1991.

39. Marshall 1910, pp. 655, 657.

40. Heape 1913. For more on Heape's role from a sociological point of view, see Clarke 1998.

41. Between 1905 and 1915, in U.S. cities large and small, more than 100,000 female garment workers went on strike. "Wage-earning women—most of them Jewish and Catholic immigrants—filled the streets of cities on picket lines, packed union halls, and marched in parades, asking for economic justice . . . for an end to deadly sweatshop conditions . . . and some hours of leisure" (Cott 1987, p. 23). The famous cry of the women strikers "Give Us Bread, But Give Us Roses" was revived and honored by feminists in the 1970s. The implication was that for women the issue was not merely economic; it was about their social and sexual status as well.

42. Ida Wells Barnett's anti-lynching campaign ran from 1918 to 1927. See Sterling 1979.

43. My local favorite is that in Providence, Rhode Island, in 1910 Jewish immigrant housewives "declared war against the kosher butchers." Quoted in Cott 1987, p. 31.

44. Cott 1987, p. 32.

45. Even sending them to jail did no good. From prison they staged hunger strikes, which brought on the specter of forced feeding. This only further insulted Victorian mores, which put a premium on treating women like ladies, something hard to square with stuffing a feeding tube down an unwilling throat.

46. Heape 1913, p. 1. Heape originally trained as an embryologist. Hence the ideas of nineteenth-century embryology—that female development was less significant or difficult than male development— would have been familiar to him. He was also on the cusp of the new endocrinology, and thus did not incorporate it fully into his theories of gender. See Marshall 1929.

47. Heape 1914, p. 210.

48. Heape borrows from Geddes and Thomson here: "The Male and the Female individual may be compared in various ways with the spermatozoa and ovum. The Male is active and roaming, he hunts for his partner and is an expender of energy; the Female is passive, sedentary, one who waits for her partner and is a conserver of energy" (Heape 1913, p. 49).

49. Heape 1914, p. 101, 102. (This passage continues with a diatribe about why women should not try to overdevelop their masculine parts. It contains the usual: too much education, independence, public visibility, will lead to sterility, insanity, etc.)

50. Bell 1916, p. 4; emphasis in the original.

51. See Dreger 1998, pp. 158–66.

52. Bell writes: "The mental condition of a woman is dependent on her metabolism; and the metabolism itself is under the influence of the internal secretions" (Bell 1916, p. 118). Other quotes in paragraph from pp. 120, 128, 129. Bell traces scientific views of woman as being driven by her uterus (van Helmont: *Propter solum uterum mulier est quod est*), to her ovaries (Virchow: *Propter ovarium solum mulier est quod est*), and finally to Bell's new modification (*Propter secretiones internas totas mulier est quod est*) (p. 129). See also Porter and Hall 1995.

53. For a summary of transplantation experiments done from the late 1800s until 1907, see Marshall and Jolly 1907.

54. Allen 1975; Maienschein 1991; Sengoopta 1998.

55. Hall 1976; Sengoopta 1998. Steinach also provoked considerable controversy with his Steinach Operation: in reality, nothing more than a vasectomy, which he claimed could rejuvenate aging men. It was an enormously popular operation, undergone by Sigmund Freud, W. B. Yeats, and many others. The historian Chandak Sengoopta describes the history of this moment: "The history of research on aging and its prevention, therefore, is not simply

a story of quackery. Nor, of course, does it fit the stereotype of science as a purely rational activity. It is more realistic (and rewarding) to view it as a very human phenomenon, in which the fear of old age and death interacted with the modernist faith in science to open a strange but not necessarily irrational field of research" (Sengoopta 1993, p. 65). See also Kammerer 1923.

56. For a list of his bibliography with titles and summaries in English, see Steinach 1940. This list may also be found on the World Wide Web: *http://www.rki.de/GESUND/ARCHIV/TESTHOM2.HTM.*

57. He repeated this phrase in many of his publications. But an early example of its use may be found in Steinach 1910, p. 566.

58. Steinach 1913a, p. 311. (*"Bekämpfung der antagonistischen Wirkung der Sexualhormone"* and *"schroffe Antagonismus."*)

59. Steinach 1912, 1913a.

60. Perhaps he found differences in guinea pigs because their organs were more developed at the time of implantation, and thus he could measure ovary-induced shrinkage. Nevertheless, at the time, ovarian effects differed in rats and guinea pigs. What requires explanation is why Steinach went for an overarching theory of hormone antagonism based on data that were still fuzzy. (Today, hormone researchers are aware that the timing of sexual development is very different in rats and guinea pigs, and could easily explain the differences in Steinach's results.)

61. The Danish scientist Knut Sand explained his own similar results as "a kind of immunity of the normal organism from the heterological gland." "These phenomena do not, I think, point so much to a real antagonism" (Sand 1919, p. 263). He offered a more detailed account of how this immunity might work. Steinach disputed Sand and, later, so did Moore. In an autobiography, written at the end of his life, Steinach cited Sand more favorably, but totally snubbed Moore.

62. "I asked myself the question whether and within which borders this harsh antagonism of sex hormones could be influenced, e.g., could be weakened, and in my experiments I started from the assumptions that there should be a substantial difference if a gonad is transplanted into an animal which is also affected by its normal puberty glands, thus having its homologous hormones flow through it, or if the masculine and feminine gonads are put together in a previously neutered organism and from there, under equal and indeed equally unfavorable conditions of function and existence forced to battle it out. The results of the experiments to be described confirm the correctness of this assumption." [Steinach 1913, p. 311; my translation]

63. Ibid., p. 320.

64. Ibid., p. 322.

65. Steinach 1940, p. 84.

66. At the time, nobody knew whether the gonads produced only one or several substances. Or that gonadal secretions were controlled, in turn, by

the activity of the hypophysis (the neurosecretory portion of the pituitary). Indeed, the results were confusing, and Steinach never explained why sex antagonism seemed to disappear under these circumstances.

67. Steinach (1913b) also elaborates on the importance of this work for theories of human sexuality. He engages in dialogue with theorists of human sexuality such as Albert Möll, Richard von Krafft-Ebing, Sigmund Freud, Iwan Bloch, and Magnus Hirschfeld. His suggestion that homosexuality can be attributed to secretions of female cells in the testes led to human transplants, mentioned earlier in this chapter.

68. Quoted in Herrn 1995, p. 45.

69. The German sexologist and pioneer for homosexual rights, Magnus Hirschfeld, took to Steinach's ideas like a duck to water. Hirschfeld had already placed the biological responsibility for homosexuality at the doorstep of hormones that he named andrin and gynäcin. He wanted to confirm Steinach's ideas by examining testicular tissue from homosexual men, but it was Steinach with Lichtenstern who performed the ultimate experiment (Herrn 1995, p. 45).

The donors in these experiments were "normal" men with undescended testes that required removal (Sengoopta 1998).

70. Herrn 1995. Additional material on Steinach may be found in Steinach 1940; Benjamin 1945; Schutte and Herman 1975; Schmidt 1984; and Sengoopta 1992, 1993, 1996, and 1998.

71. An editorial in *The Lancet*, for example, described Steinach's experiments and wrote: "Around these findings the theory has been constructed that the products of internal testicular and ovarian secretion—that is, the specific reproductive hormones of the two sexes—are sharply antagonistic to one another. The conclusions want more evidence to back them" (anonymous 1917).

72. Lillie became an important member of a new generation of American-trained biologists devoted to the experimental life. He received his Ph.D. at the University of Chicago under the tutelage of C. O. Whitman, who founded the Zoology Department there. By the time he began his freemartin work, Lillie had become chairman of the same department, as well as a key figure at the Wood's Hole Marine labs, through which many of the key players in embryology and genetics passed in this period.

Although from a modest middle-class home himself, Lillie had married Frances Crane, sister of Chicago plumbing magnate Charles R. Crane. The Lillies' great wealth not only put Lillie in the social circles of the ruling elite—including the Rockefellers, who funded the vast majority of his life's work—but it enabled him to use his own private (by marriage) fortune to build new laboratory space (the Whitman lab) at the University of Chicago. He chaired the Zoology Department there from 1910 to 1931, when he became Dean of Biological Sciences before retiring in 1936. As head of the Marine Biological Institute at Wood's Hole, he also obtained donations from his brother-in-law to build additional laboratory space (Crane Laboratory).

73. See Oudshoorn 1994 and Clarke 1998 for discussions of the importance of access to research materials in the history of sex hormone research. Kohler (1994), for example, shows how the very nature of genetic knowledge was shaped by scientists' interaction with the fruit fly, as they trained it from a somewhat unruly wild fly to become a domestic collaborator in the laboratory.

74. See Clarke 1991 and Mitman 1992 for a discussion of Lillie's freemartin work. See also Lillie 1916, 1917.

75. Lillie 1917, p. 415. See also Hall 1976.

76. Lillie 1917, p. 404.

77. Ibid., p. 415. In this classic paper, Lillie republished (with citation) the previously published data of his student, Ms. C. J. Davies. The genesis of freemartins continued to be debated for decades, and is still unresolved. Although most of Lillie's conclusions still offer a "best fit," there is no perfect fit (Price 1972).

78. Lillie 1917. Lillie writes "how much of the subsequent events is due to mere absence of the ovarian tissue, and how much to positive action of male sex-hormones is more or less problematical" (p. 418).

79. Price 1974, p. 393. Moore would later succeed Lillie as chair of the department at Chicago. For a biographical sketch of Moore, see Price 1974.

80. Moore 1919, p. 141. Moore describes in this passage the problem of variability and group difference discussed in chapter 5. He also cites work published between 1909 and 1913 showing that early spaying of a female causes her to grow larger. Thus "a spayed female with grafted testis would increase in weight above the normal for females not because of the testis but because of the absence of the ovary" (p. 142). We have no way of knowing whether Steinach read these papers to which Moore refers, and if so how he might have integrated them into his own conclusions.

81. Steinach's dramatic results on mammary development came from guinea pigs, because male rats do not have primordial teats able to respond to ovary implants. Moore suggests that his differences with Steinach could have resulted from their using different strains of rat. Steinach notes that he bred his guinea pigs "in such a manner as to produce animals of much the same type" (Steinach 1940, p. 62). It seems likely that Steinach also bred his rats to be more uniform. Perhaps he simply did not have as much variability in his colonies as did Moore. Here is another important aspect of the story. If we breed test animals to exaggerate differences we expect, then find the physiological causes of such differences, how much can we extrapolate back to more variable populations? For more on the history of rat colonies, see Clause 1993.

82. Moore 1919, p. 151. In a later paper he reemphasized this point "I

wish again to emphasize the absolute unreliability of closely graded indications of psychical behavior of rats and guinea pigs as an indication of their
sexual nature" (Moore 1920, p. 181).

83. Moore also chased after Steinach's theories on aging (see note 55). See
Price 1974 for a discussion of this work.

84. Moore 1922, p. 309.

85. Steinach and Kun 1926, p. 817.

86. Moore and Price 1932, pp. 19, 23.

87. Ibid., p. 19.

88. This understanding had been presaged in earlier publications, but it is
the 1932 paper that provides the detailed experimental support. See Moore
1921a,b,c and Moore and Price 1930. By this time Moore's work was supported by grants from the Committee on Research in Problems of Sex (discussed later in this chapter and in chapter 7).

89. In this discussion I am following one important tradition of modern
science studies by taking the "loser" in a scientific dispute seriously. For more
on this approach, see Hess 1997, pp. 86–88.

90. Moore wrote: "Many difficulties are involved in an intelligent anaylsis
[*sic*] of the psychical nature of animals and there is a very great danger of the
personal equation influencing an interpretation" (1921, p. 385).

91. For the moment this is a hypothesis, but further historical work on
Moore could provide evidence for or against it. Clarke quotes Moore as writing that "we are beginning to think that sex is very much less stable than we
had previously considered it" (Clarke 1993, p. 396).

92. According to the historian Chandak Sengoopta, Steinach believed
these cells were the source of the male hormone and was attacked for years
by influential scientists for this belief (personal communication, 1999).

93. When the social co-produces the biological, it is not necessarily to ill
effect (although I have spent important years of my life discussing cases for
which the effect is horrifying). I consider the argument about sex hormone
antagonism productive because it stimulated new experiments and, ultimately, an account of hormone physiology that accommodated more of the
experimental results. Nor have I really told the entire story, because I have
not offered a detailed social interpretation of Moore and Price. To do so would
be beyond the scope of this book.

94. I'm drawing on Jonathan Harwood's framework of styles of scientific
thought, which he applied to German geneticists in this same period. Did
Moore and Steinach have different "thought styles," leading them in different
scientific directions and to different modes of experimentation? See Harwood 1993.

95. At least one popular science book explicitly discussed Moore's experiments, including his conclusions that the hormones did not exhibit sex antagonism (Dorsey 1925). This book provides an apparently neutral account of

human biology, with virtually none of the social hysteria evident in earlier books, such as those by Heape and Bell.

96. Steinach 1940.

97. In Hausman 1995.

98. Benjamin 1945, p. 433. The obituary is more than a little hagiographic. Benjamin writes in the final paragraph: "When Steinach approached the 'dangerous' problem of sex physiology, all the sex taboos and prejudices of his day were arrayed against him," just as "in the times of Copernicus and Galileo, of Darwin, Haeckel and Freud" (p. 442).

99. De Kruif 1945, p. 116.

Chapter 7: Do Sex Hormones Really Exist?
(Gender Becomes Chemical)

1. Parkes 1966, p. 72; quoted in idem, 1966, p. xx.

2. Corner 1965.

3. Quoted in Hall 1976, p. 83, 84. The discussion in this paragraph is based on Hall's article. Physicians dealt with "a myriad of complaints and abnormalities that defied classification as failures or over-activity of the gonadal chemical messengers" (p. 83).

4. Cott 1987; Rosenberg 1982.

5. Noble 1977.

6. See, for example, Pauly's discussion of the Wood's Hole biological research laboratories as a summer resort providing scientists with a haven from the heartless city (Pauly 1988).

7. In February 1914, a group of women that included the journalist Mary Heaton Vorse, the psychologist Leta Stetter Hollingworth, the anthropologist Elsie Clews Parsons, and the socialist trade unionist Rose Pastor Stokes sponsored the first "feminist mass meeting" with the title "What is feminism?" As another group member, Elizabeth Gurley Flynn, the famed socialist and organizer for the Industrial Workers of the World, put it, they wanted to see "the women of the future, big spirited, intellectually alert, devoid of the old femininity" (quoted in Cott 1987, p. 38). For more on Parsons and Hollingworth, see Rosenberg 1982.

8. Schreiner 1911. (My father, Philip Sterling, gave me a copy of Schreiner's book, when I was a young woman. It was his way of helping me to understand the economic basis of women's inequality.)

9. She avoided charges of obscenity and incitement to murder and assassination (Paul 1995). The latter seems especially ironic in view of her later funding relationship with the Rockefeller Foundation.

10. Goldman served many months in jail for distributing birth control information to impoverished women on New York's Lower East Side and elsewhere around the country. While she espoused true equality between man

and woman, Sanger promoted a different version of feminism, emphasizing the right to choose motherhood. Both her view of motherhood and her vision of the sacredness of women's erotic desire grew out of her belief in the "absolute, elemental, inner urge of womanhood" (quoted in Cott 1987, p. 48).

11. Ibid. Alice Paul (1885–1977) was an American feminist who fought for passage of the nineteenth Amendment (women's suffrage). Ellen Key (1849–1926) was a Swedish social feminist. Ruth Law was a popular and pioneering aviatrix with strong feminist sympathies.

12. The "white slave trade" referred to organized crime rings that recruited young white women and forced them into a life of prostitution.

13. Quoted in Aberle and Corner 1953, p. 4.

14. For more on the relationship between Rockefeller and Davis, see Bullough 1988 and Fitzpatrick 1990. For more on the Rockefeller Foundation and the scientific study of social problems, see Kay 1993. Davis herself writes, "The Laboratory of Social Hygiene was established as one of the activities of the Bureau [of Social Hygiene] . . . the women at the State Reformatory . . . have led lives of sexual irregularity" (Introduction to Weidensall 1916).

15. While head of the Rockefeller Foundation, Vincent encouraged the development of the National Research Council, which only two years later created, with Rockefeller funding, the Committee for Research in Problems of Sex, the major funding vehicle for hormone biology research until 1940. See Noble 1977.

16. Lewis 1971, p. 440.

17. In 1929, Davis's own study, *Factors in the Sex Life of 2200 Women*, appeared. In it she recounted the results of her studies on middle-class women. No topic, from masturbation to the high frequencies of homosexuality, to the sexual mores of everyday married life, seemed too delicate to tackle. Her frank, scientifically detached approach symbolized the transition to the scientific study of sex and sexuality.

18. Earl F. Zinn, recent graduate of Clark University, where he studied with the noted psychologist G. Stanley Hall, apparently came up with his ideas in a discussion with Max J. Exner, member of the professional staff of the YMCA and director of that organization's Sex Education Committee. He had also authored a research study of the sexual behavior of college men (Exner 1915).

19. The NRC was organized to help prepare the nation for World War I. It was funded by the Engineering Foundation, which promoted scientific research for industry, and before the war's end it sought to shift its work to meet the scientific needs of postwar industry. See Haraway 1989 and Noble 1977. See also note 15 on George Vincent and Katherine B. Davis.

While Yerkes was enthusiastic about the idea, the NRC's Division of Anthropology and Psychology was not. Nor could he at first persuade the Division of Medical Sciences. But Yerkes persisted, finally convincing his colleagues to call a conference to discuss the matter.

20. Aberle and Corner 1953, pp. 12–13.

21. Ibid., p. 18.

22. Quoted in Clarke 1998, p. 96.

23. The full story of the hijacking can be found in Clarke 1998. Lillie took advantage of an intellectual and strategic vacuum. He articulated his own vision, which looked good in the absence of any competition. Indeed, it was good, but much more limited than the initial vision for CRPS. He and Yerkes benefited mightily by the hijacking, for CRPS supported the research and that of their intellectual offspring (e.g., Moore and Price) for years to come.

24. Mitman (1992) suggests that part of Lillie's motivation derived from his fears about his own social status: "Although born of a modest family, Lillie's marriage to Frances Crane transported him across class lines into the social circles of the wealthy elite. He had much to gain in his espousal of the notion that the lower echelons of society not breed like rabbits, for they were the very class that threatened to undermine his own social lot" (pp. 98, 99). His wife militantly supported workers' strikes, keeping company with well-known feminists such as Jane Addams. He carefully refrained from comment when his wife was arrested while protesting against "industrial slavery in America." The American conflicts of the era came right into his home. For a brief discussion, see Manning 1983, pp. 59–61.

25. Quoted in Gordon 1976, p. 281. Statistic in idem. In truth, eugenic concerns had been a part of the birth control movement from the beginning. Paul writes that unexpired subscriptions of the *American Journal of Eugenics* were completed with subscriptions to Goldman's *Mother Earth* (Paul 1995, p. 92). Both socialists and conservatives agreed that engineering healthy births was a legitimate social concern, not just a matter of individual choice. Nevertheless, Sanger did ally herself with the more conservative wing of the eugenics movement, and at the same time she narrowed her feminist concerns in a manner most distressing to more radical feminists.

For more on the eugenics movement see Kevles 1985 and Paul 1995 and 1998.

26. Quoted in Haraway 1989, p. 69; emphasis added.

27. Quoted in Gould 1981, p. 193.

28. In 1916, Harvard denied tenure to Yerkes, apparently because the administration considered the field of psychology unworthy (Kevles 1985).

29. After working with Yerkes on IQ testing, Lewis Terman and his graduate student Catherine Cox Miles turned their attention to the measurement of masculinity and femininity. With funding from the Committee for Research in Problems of Sex, they constructed scales of masculinity and femininity that they felt to be quantifiable and consistent. Contemporary social values

make the Terman/Miles tests seem impossibly out-of-date. For instance, one gained femininity points if one found "dirty ears, smoking, bad manners, bad smells . . . words like 'belly' or 'guts' and the sight of dirty clothes disgusting." One scored as more masculine if one disliked tall women, mannish women, or "women cleverer than you are" (Lewin 1984). Another of Terman's students, Edward K. Strong, applied the concepts of relative masculinity and femininity to vocational interest. Farmers and engineers he found to have masculine interests, while "writers, lawyers, and ministers are essentially feminine." "Are the differences," he wondered, "in interests of engineers and lawyers to be found in differences in hormone secretions?" E. Lowell Kelly, another of Terman's students, tested the idea that homosexuality represented an inversion of male and female by comparing the Terman-Miles test scores of eleventh grade boys, "passive" male homosexuals, "active" male homosexuals, women "inverts," and "superior women college athletes." Kelly found no correlation between the degree of inversion of his subjects and their masculinity or femininity, but Terman urged him not to publish these results until he had become more professionally established. In the end, the "data were no match for the conviction that feminine women and homosexual men 'must' have a lot in common" (Lewin 1984, p. 166).

30. Gould 1981 and Kevles 1985 and 1968 document the stories of the development of mental testing and eugenics in considerable detail and offer detailed critiques of the administration, results, and conclusions drawn from these tests. Kevles writes: "Intelligence testers examined ever more paupers, drunkards, delinquents, and prostitutes. Business firms incorporated mental tests in their personnel procedures . . . and a number of colleges and universities began to use intelligence-test results in the admissions process" (Kevles 1985, p. 82). Yerkes's army intelligence tests provided new ammunition for the eugenics movement. Confirming already strongly held beliefs, those who analyzed Yerkes's data concluded that the average mental age of the white American adult was just above that of the moron (a specific scientific category, not just an epithet hurled by eight-year olds). Southern Europeans and American Negroes scored even lower. This new "scientific" information became part of the eugenicists' rallying cry. They predicted the doom of white civilization, attributing the declining intelligence level to "the unconstrained breeding of the poor and feeble-minded, the spread of Negro blood through miscegenation and the swamping of an intelligent native stock by the immigrating dregs of southern and eastern Europe" (Gould 1981, p. 196).

31. Borell 1978, p. 52.

32. Borell 1978 and 1987; Clarke 1991.

33. Katz (1995) notes a certain irony in the censorship and repression of birth control and other sex-related research in this period because, as he argues, much of the research worked to establish a new role and definition for the concept of heterosexuality—one in which the heterosexual became nor-

mal, while all other forms of sexuality became abnormal or perverse (see esp. p. 92).

34. Berman 1921, pp. 21–22.

35. Allen et al. 1939.

36. Others have discussed Lillie's comments as well. See Oudshoorn 1994 and Clarke 1998.

37. Lillie 1939, p. 3; emphasis added.

38. Ibid., pp. 10, 11.

39. I used a database called Lexis-Nexis—Academic Universe, widely available at universities and research libraries.

40. For effects on bone growth, see Jilka et al. 1992; Slootweg et al. 1992; Weisman et al. 1993; Ribot and Tremollieres 1995; Wishart et al. 1995; Hoshino et al. 1996; and Gasperino 1995. For effects on the immune system, see Whitacre et al. 1999.

A recent article in *Discover* magazine began: "Estrogen is more than a sex hormone. It boosts the brainpower of rats" (Richardson 1994). Indeed, the proliferation of steroid effects on brain cells *is* startling. One or another hormone affects the development of the cerebellum, the hippocampus, a number of centers within the hypothalamus, the midbrain, and the cerebral cortex. In fact, the cerebral cortex, not the gonads, is the major site of estrogen synthesis in the male zebra finch (Schlinger and Arnold 1991; Arai et al. 1994; Brown et al. 1994; Litteria 1994; MacLusky et al. 1994; McEwen et al. 1994; Pennisi 1997; Koenig et al. 1995; Wood and Newman 1995; Tsuruo et al. 1996; and Amandusson et al. 1995). For effects on blood cell formation, see Williams-Ashman and Reddi 1971 and Besa 1994; on the circulatory system, see Sitruk-Ware 1995; on the liver, see Tessitore et al. 1995; Gustafsson 1994; on lipid and carbohydrate metabolism, see Renard et al. 1993; Fu and Hornick 1995; Haffner and Valdez 1995; and Larosa 1995; on gastrointestinal functions, see Chen et al. 1995; on the gallbladder, see Karkare et al. 1995; on muscle activities, see Bardin and Catterall 1981 and Martin 1993; on kidney activities, see Sakemi et al. 1995.

41. Koenig et al. 1995, p. 1,500.

42. For a thorough discussion of the popularization of sex hormones as part of the discourse of sexuality in the 1920s, see Rechter 1997. For more on the continued changes in sexuality in the 1920s in America, see also D'Emilio and Freedman 1988. On the biochemistry of androgens and estrogens, see Doisy 1939 and Koch 1939.

43. Allen and Doisey 1923. Allen was a major recipient of CRPS funds from 1923 until 1940.

44. Stockard and Papanicolaou 1917. The method involved using a cotton swab to remove cells from the vagina, and looking at the cells under the microscope. The type of cell changes during the estrous cycle in a manner that is reliable and quantifiable.

45. In this period, hormone research depended on ready access to large quantities of hormone-containing material. Those researchers who worked near slaughterhouses—e.g., in Chicago or St. Louis—had a big advantage. Later, when hormones were found in animal and human urine, those who could command large quantities of the urine became key brokers. For a fascinating discussion of the role of access to research material in the purification of sex hormones, see Oudshoorn 1994 and Clarke 1995.

46. Allen and Doisey 1923, pp. 820, 821. The marketing of hormone potions had become something of an embarrassment to the medical community. One reason to put the study of organ extracts on an arguably scientific basis was to defend the professional honor and status of the medical community (Unsigned 1921a and 1921b).

47. Frank 1929, p. 135.

48. Ascheim and Zondek 1927.

49. Both groups also had the support of major pharmaceutical companies (Oudshoorn 1994).

50. Parkes 1966b; Doisy 1939, writes: "one of the major events upon which the isolation of the hormone depended was the discovery of material existing in the urine of pregnant women" (p. 848).

In 1928, progesterone, a second ovarian hormone, was identified. By the mid-1930s it too had been purified. (For simplicity sake, I am leaving progesterone, the menstrual cycle, and its connection to the brain and pituitary hormones [FSH and LH] out of the story.)

51. See the articles in section C: "Biochemistry and Assay of Gonadal Hormones" of Allen et al. 1939.

52. Frank 1929, p. 114.

53. Note the use of the word *normal*. Presumably female hormones in male bodies could produce abnormalities (such as homosexuality?).

54. The editorial states: "This raises, of course, the question of specificity and whether the vaginal reactions so largely used in the laboratory study of these hormones in recent years are really reliable criteria of ovarian hormone action" (Unsigned 1928, p. 1,195).

55. See Oudshoorn 1994, p. 26.

56. Zondek 1934. Thirty-two years later, Zondek vividly recalled his astonishment. Throughout his life he remained unable to understand why all that female hormone did not feminize the stallion. See Finkelstein 1966, p. 11.

57. Oudshoorn 1990. See, for example, Womack and Koch 1932. By 1937, it was clear that the ovary itself was the site of testosterone production in the female (Hill 1937a and 1937b).

58. Nelson and Merckel 1937, p. 825. Klein and Parkes (1937) found the effects of testosterone in females mimicked the activity of progesterone, a result they found "unexpected" (p. 577) and "anomalous" (p. 579). See also Deanesly and Parkes 1936.

59. Frank and Goldberger 1931, p. 381.

Oudshoorn (1994) provides the basis for much of my discussion in this paragraph. See also Parkes 1966a,b.

60. Parkes 1966a,b.

61. Frank 1929, p. 197.

62. Parkes 1966b, p. xxvi.

63. This account is based on Frank 1929; Allen et al. 1939 and Oudshoorn 1994.

64. See also Stone 1939.

65. Chemistry 1928; Laqueur and de Jongh 1928.

66. Koch 1931b, p. 939.

67. Pratt 1939.

68. Frank (1929) writes: "Assay and biological standardization of the water-soluble commercial extracts now placed upon the market show a woeful lack of potency and rapid deterioration of the products. Unpleasant local reactions may arise at the site of injection. The prices of these pharmaceutical preparations are prohibitive. Consequently I warn against their general use until better products are at our disposal" (p. 297).

69. While CRPS funded most of the U.S. work, pharmaceutical companies often provided researchers with purified hormone preparations (Korenchevsky et al. 1932, p. 2,097). For example, thank "Messrs Schering Ltd for kindly supplying this preparation." Squibb gave a fellowship to F. C. Koch for 1925–26 (see Koch 1931, p. 322) and Deanesly and Parkes (1936) note their debt to "Messrs. Ciba for supplies of the substances referred to above" (p. 258).

70. Parkes 1966b, p. xxii.

71. Dale 1932, p. 122. At the conference it was also decided that a central standard sample would be kept by Dr. Guy Marrian at the University College in London in sealed ampoules filled with dry nitrogen. They set a minimum number of twenty animals, which had to be used in any valid test, and they standardized the solvents and method of administration of test substances.

72. Oudshoorn 1994, p. 47.

73. Korenchevsky and Hall 1938, p. 998. Additional non-reproductive effects are noted in Evans 1939.

74. David et al. 1934, p. 1,366.

75. Gustavson 1939, pp. 877–78. See also Gautier 1935.

76. Oudshoorn 1994, p. 53. See also Koch 1939, pp. 830–34.

77. Juhn et al. 1931, p. 395.

78. Kahnt and Doisy proposed a complex series of steps to make the estrus assay work reliably. First, they had to check potential test rats for several weeks and choose only those with normal cycles. Second, they had to check for two weeks after removing the ovaries and discard any animals that still showed signs of internal hormone production. Third, they primed their test

animals with injections of two rat units of hormone. Fourth, they tested each animal one week later with another injection; any that failed to respond were discarded as test animals. Fifth, another week later, they injected an amount of hormone too small to produce a result. If there was a response anyway, those animals were also discarded. Finally, they recommended using "a sufficient number of animals. If 75 per cent of the animals . . . give a + reaction, consider that the amount injected contained one R. U." (Kahnt and Doisy 1928, pp. 767–68). The League of Nations conference also noted the importance of using a large sample size.

79. Korenchevsky et al. 1932, p. 2,103.

80. Gallagher and Koch 1931, p. 319.

81. In one of the early articles on isolation of the testicular hormone, the authors wrote: "It is our feeling that until more is known of the chemical nature of the hormone, no name should be given to the extract. As yet, any name would be valueless and not at all descriptive" (Gallagher and Koch 1929, p. 500).

82. Frank 1929, p. 128. The list of terms comes from Frank's discussion on pp. 127–28.

83. In earlier work I comment on the imbalance between the terms *androgens* and *estrogens*; this discussion focuses on the particular historical moment in which the imbalance took hold. See Fausto-Sterling 1987 and 1989. The information on the Index Medicus comes from Oudshoorn 1990, p. 183, *n.* 66.

84. Parkes 1966b, p. xxiii. Parkes tells a similar story about the naming of the hormone progesterone. The 1961 edition of *Stedman's Medical Dictionary* defines an androgen as an agent "which makes a man" and an estrogen as one which "begets mad desire."

85. Corner 1965, p. xv.

86. "The Council desires to express its appreciation to Parke, Davis and Company, for its action in this matter as well as in the case of the name 'estrone'" (Chemistry 1936, p. 1,223).

87. Doisy 1939, p. 859.

88. Parkes 1938, p. 36. This would have provided an exact parallel to the term *androgenic*.

89. Koch 1939.

90. Korenschevsky et al. 1937. This group also found many of these hormones to cooperate in producing their effects (Korenchevsky and Hall 1937).

91. Parkes 1938, p. 36.

92. Because the embryo was bisexual and even adults retained a bit of that bisexual potential. "Even men whose instinct is normally heterosexual," he wrote, "may contain in their organisms minute vestigia of a female character even though under normal conditions they never come to functional expression" (Steinach 1940, p. 91).

93. While most readers are probably aware that such cycles regulate the menstrual cycle, they may be less aware that feedback loops involving the same pituitary hormones also regulate sperm formation in males.

94. In 1939, he wrote: "Moore seems to remove the necessity of assuming any antagonism in the simultaneous action of the two hormones, by showing that each operates independently within its own field" (Lillie 1939, p. 58).

95. Frank 1929, p. 120.

96. Quoted in Oudshoorn 1994, p. 28.

97. Parkes 1966b, p. xxvii. .

98. Crew 1933, p. 251.

99. See Cott 1987, p. 149. Davis (1929) offers a more detailed discussion of women's sexual practices.

100. Cott 1987, p. 150.

101. Cott (1987) documents a real split in the labor movement over this issue. It was a split that replayed itself among late twentieth-century feminists during their battle over the Equal Rights Amendment and the elimination of protective work legislation.

102. Quoted in ibid.

103. David et al. 1934, p. 1,366.

104. Quoted in Oudshoorn 1990.

Chapter 8: The Rodent's Tale

1. Milton Diamond, Elizabeth Adkins-Regan, William Byne, Donald Dewesbury, Marc Breedlove, and, indirectly, Kim Wallen—all of whom study the role of hormones in behavior and/or study the comparative psychology of animals—took time to comment on an earlier draft of this chapter. Their critiques were generous and of enormous help. I am very grateful for their efforts. Their commitment to helping me "get it right," even when I occasionally stepped on their toes, represents the spirit of open, scientific inquiry at its best. Of course, I am solely responsible for the final outcome.

2. Aberle and Corner 1953. Borell (1987) lists the transfer date as 1931. See also the discussion in Clarke 1998.

3. Borell (1987) quotes a BSH memorandum explaining the transfer: "It had been felt by the Bureau for some time that this would be an advantageous move, inasmuch as the Foundation, through its biological experts, could furnish an advisory control which the Bureau could not supply; and the Foundation also inclined to the view that the administration of this program and the evaluation of the results of the researches conducted are more clearly in the field of the present research programs of the natural sciences and medical sciences of the Foundation than in the program of the Bureau" (p. 79).

4. Quoted in Borell 1987, p. 79. Borell notes that this new independence of scientific researchers resulted in the abandonment of the search for an easy-

to-use spermicide contraceptive, which had anyway "never summoned the interest of scientists as the contraceptive pill was to do" (p. 85). The contraceptive pill was in the end developed (with Sanger's support and funding) at a private foundation founded by Gregory Pincus after he was denied tenure at Harvard following intense controversy over his early work on artificial parthenogenesis in mammals. See also Clarke 1990a and b.

5. Quoted in Kohler 1976, p. 291.

6. For the story of how these events led to the modern-day fields of molecular biology, see Kohler 1976; Kay 1993; and Abir-Am 1982.

7. Aberle and Corner 1953, p. 100.

8. Aberle and Corner (1953) list Terman's last CRPS grant for the preparation of a "report on the marital adjustment of intellectually superior subjects" (p. 129). For the path from Yerkes to Carpenter to modern primatology as a model for human sex behavior and social organization, see Haraway 1989.

9. For a brief history of the latter two fields in the United States, see Dewsbury 1989.

10. Many received funds from the Rockefeller Foundation both independently and via the Committee for Research in Problems of Sex. Before 1938, 25 percent of grants from CRPS funded behavioral research, with most of the rest addressing the basic physiology of sex and reproduction. From 1938 to 1947, however, 45 percent of CRPS's grants went for research into sex-related behavior, with a major focus on the role of hormones. For a complete list for this period, see Aberle and Corner 1953.

11. There is a large parallel literature on primates, work that hormone researchers have always felt to be particularly applicable to humans. Some of the concepts developed with rodents do not hold up well in primates. But the primate work is expensive and difficult, because of the long lives of the animals, the need for breeding colonies, and the growing recognition that primate behavior, even more than rodent behavior, needs naturalistic settings if one wants to draw conclusions about "normal" development. There is also an influential literature on birds, one of the few groups for which the relationship between hormones and certain aspects of brain development is fairly clear. See Schlinger 1998. For a current and extensive review of the work on vertebrates, see Cooke et al. 1998.

12. Squier 1999, p. 14 of electronic printout.

13. Quoted in May 1988, p. 93.

14. Quoted in D'Emilio 1983, p. 41. For a deeper discussion of the intertwining of anticommunism, homosexual repression, emphasis on a narrowly defined family structure, and the staking out of clear cultural definitions of masculinity and femininity, see May 1988 and 1995, Breines 1992, and Ehrenreich 1983. See D'Emilio 1983, Ehrenreich 1983, and Reumann 1998 for discussion of the enormous secondary literature on homosexuality and gender in the postwar period.

15. Schlesinger 1958, p. 63. Women, wrote Arthur Schlesinger, Jr., "seem an expanding, aggressive force, seizing new domains like a conquering army, while men, more and more on the defensive, are hardly able to hold their own and gratefully accept assignments from their new rulers. A recent book bears the stark and melancholy title *The Decline of the American Male*" (p. 63).

16. Quoted in May 1988, p. 140.

17. Quoted in May 1988, p. 66.

18. In the 1930s, masculinity did not require special attention. The field of andrology emerged as an independent discipline in the 1970s. See, for example, Bain et al. 1978. Niemi (1987) notes that the idea of andrology appeared as early as 1891, but that the first societies and journals didn't coalesce until the 1970s.

19. Quoted in May 1988, p. 147.

20. This idea resurfaces from time to time. In response to the increase in single mothers, Robert Bly described his vision of the "deep masculine"— something sons imbibed bodily from their fathers and that single mothers, no matter how well meaning, could never give (Bly 1992).

21. See D'Emilio 1983. For a thorough and illuminating discussion of the Kinsey reports and the national discussion of sex and sexuality, see Reumann 1998.

22. Quoted in Elger et al. 1974, p. 66, from remarks made at a 1969 workshop conference on "Integration of Endocrine and Non-endocrine Mechanisms in the Hypothalamus."

I have limited this entire discussion to mammals; there are significant differences found in other vertebrates.

23. Jost 1947, 1946a, 1946b, and 1946c.

24. Wiesner 1935, p. 32; emphasis in original.

25. Greene et al. 1940b, pp. 328, 450.

26. These experiments all addressed the question of secondary sex determination—i.e., the development of the gonadal duct system and external genitalia. Jost did not examine primary sex determination— i.e., the differentiation of the gonad as either a testis or an ovary.

From his first publication through the 1970s, Jost also actively promoted his work—publishing many times, often in review articles or in symposium proceedings, so that his original data, while supplemented steadily by new results, also received ongoing attention.

27. Jost 1946c, p. 301; his emphasis, my translation. Later experimenters identified two culprits. Embryonic testosterone encouraged differentiation of the male duct system and masculine external genitalia, while a new hormone—a proteinlike structure dubbed Mullerian Inhibiting Substance (MIS for short)—induced degeneration of the embryonic female duct system. The embryonic male testis makes both fetal testosterone and MIS. Jost tried re-

moving only one testis; under those circumstances male development continued apace, while the female duct system degenerated as it normally would in
an unoperated male fetus. From this and other experiments he concluded that
the testis secreted one or more factors that caused male duct differentiatied
and female duct degeneration. Jost also grafted testes onto female embryos or
ovaries into males, but the grafted tissue did not affect the embryos' development, a failure he attributed to the fact that he had to use older embryos,
which he presumed had already passed through the stage during which development was plastic. However, the androgen-supplemented embryos still
differed from normal males because they had at least some uterine development, although the vaginal region was "more or less inhibited." Jost never
reported testing the possible actions of estrogen on the development of either
castrated male or castrated female embryos, although it is possible that he
tried such tests but that the estrogen caused the embryos to abort.

28. MIS is currently an object of great research interest because it has
been identified as an important and ubiquitous growth factor—transforming
growth factor-β. Gustafson and Donahoe (1994) review the work on MIS
molecular biology (pp. 509–16).

29. Jost 1946c, p. 307; my translation. Jost soon extended his studies examining male and female duct tissue grown in in vitro tissue culture. This
work, however, did not eliminate the possibility of hormonal effects on female
development. As he, himself, pointed out, his culture system was not "anhormonal." In 1951, Jost wrote that the action of trace estrogens contained in
the serum used as his culture medium "cannot be neglected *a priori*. We must
ultimately return to the use of a synthetic hormone-free medium" (Jost and
Bozic 1951, p. 650); see also Jost and Bergerard 1949. But by 1953 his interpretation had begun to change. Acknowledging that female development
might be affected by maternal hormones produced in the placenta or the
mother's gonads, or by nonovarian fetal hormones (e.g., the adrenal glands),
and reminding his readers that he had provided evidence of some ovarian activity, he nevertheless felt "that maternal or extragonadal gynogenic substances can hardly account for the feminization of the gonadectomized fetus"
(Jost 1953, p. 387). This, he concluded, despite again acknowledging earlier
reports that estrogens could feminize male fetal development (Greene et al.
1940a, 1940b; Raynaud 1947. Jost (1953) wrote that "the interpretation of
this experiment was not evident" (p. 417).

30. Jost's rhetoric changed with time. In 1954, he wrote "the foetal testis
plays the principle role" in normal sexual development (implication: females
become female because they *lack* a testis) (Jost 1954, p. 246). In 1960, he
wrote: "the anhormonal (sex in mammals) is feminine and the testis prevents
males from differentiating as females" (Jost 1960, p. 59). By 1965 he was
saying that female mammals are "the neutral sex type" (Jost 1960, p. 59). In
1969, "becoming a male is a prolonged, uneasy, and risky adventure; it is a

kind of struggle against inherent trends toward femaleness" (Jost 1965, p. 612). Finally, in 1973, Jost wrote: "masculine characteristics . . . have to be imposed in males by the fetal testicular hormones against a basic feminine trend of the mammalian body. Female organogenesis results from the mere absence of testes, the presence or absence of ovaries being unimportant" (Jost et al. 1973, p. 41).

When computer terminology entered the language in the 1980s, researchers updated Jost's description of an inherent trend toward femaleness into a metaphor of female development as a "default pathway." The earliest use I can find of the phrase "default sex" to describe female development is 1978. The editors of the journal *Trends in Neuroscience* use the term in the introduction to Döhler 1978.

31. Jost et al. 1973. Jost was French, and I have not looked at the specifics of such discussions in France after World War II. But his ideas were known and discussed internationally and gained rapid acceptance in the United States. The production of scientific knowledge not only involves doing experiments and interpreting results, but being in the right place at the right time for a particular result and interpretation to be culturally intelligible. For more on this issue, see Latour 1987.

The mono-hormonic theories also echo nineteenth-century views of women, children, and nonwhites as being closer to nature. All races and sexes developed identically up to a point, but only white males continued developing into true adulthood. For a full treatment of these nineteenth-century views, see Russett 1989 and also Herschberger 1948.

32. Aristotle wrote: "The female is a female by virtue of a *lack* of certain qualities. We should regard the female nature as afflicted with a natural defectiveness." St. Thomas thought that women were imperfect men, incidental beings. In the oedipal drama of becoming (à la Freud), the female psyche must accommodate to the absence of a penis, while the male psyche must adjust to the fear of its loss and thus a return to some basal female state (quoted in de Beauvoir 1949, p. xxii).

Additional explanations for the acceptance of the female = absence, male = presence theory may include the difficulty of the necessary experiments, the time needed to fill in difficult-to-get details, which could be obtained only by diverting attention from easier and more immediately productive (in terms of publications) experiments. One component of scientific success is the ability to balance a forward-moving program against the importance of digging into a recalcitrant problem.

Some of the unresolved experimental results included: (1) the possibility that Jost's castrations were not done early enough to detect an effect of removing the fetal ovary; (2) that injected estrogens could feminize male development and stimulate the growth of female organs; (3) while Jost tried substituting injected testosterone for the removed testis, he never performed parallel experiments for the removed ovary; (4) he did not work to identify possible nonovarian sources of estrogen or other nonestrogenic differentiative factors that might govern female differentiation; (5) Jost knew that the fetal ovary made estrogen from an early point, but did not seem to worry about the function of the estrogen.

The possibility that estrogen, from either the mother or the fetal ovary, might play a role in secondary sex determination is still not completely resolved. Certainly in some vertebrates it "is thought to play a major role in the gonadal differentiation," (di Clemente et al. 1992, p. 726); see also (Reyes et al. 1974. George et al. (1978) found that the embryonic rabbit ovary begins to make large quantities of estrogen at exactly the same time as the fetal testis begins to make testosterone. They suggest further studies to clarify the function of this fetal estrogen (Ammini et al. 1994; Kalloo et al. 1993). These latter authors find that: "The presence of estrogen receptors suggests that maternal estrogen may play a direct role in female external genital development, challenging the widely held view that female external genital development is passive because it can occur in the absence of fetal gonadal hormones" (p. 692).

33. Greene's results showing estrogen's potential to actively feminize male embryos rankled. Jost continued to note the need for further experimentation to resolve such contradictory results. Slowly, however, references to Greene's work and calls for further experimentation disappeared from Jost's writing. By 1965, the mono-hormonic theory appeared in Jost's writing as fully proven fact, rather than tentative theory requiring further experimental verification. Although continuing to note that estrogens could feminize male embryos, he suggested that injected estrogen did not actively cause differentiation. Rather, it damaged the testes' ability to make testosterone, thus allowing the "natural" femininity of the embryo to emerge. In 1965, Jost still considered the presence/absence theory of male and female development to be "speculative." Although he could present a tidy-looking story, such a presentation "should not conceal the necessity of new crucial experiments" (Jost 1965, p. 614). but he never did perform all of the critical experiments suggested in is 1947 paper.

34. See notes 43 and 46 for evidence of this claim. In a 1999 debate about the concept of default development, one Loveweb member wrote: "Maybe the female program is also dependent on some hormone—all we know is that gonadal hormone isn't required. How about the 20–30 hormones that probably exist that we haven't discovered yet? The more I grow old and curmudgeonly, the less sense this default stuff makes. I don't think it means a da**ed thing, but merely poses as a phrase that means something." Evidence continues to emerge that suggests the importance of events in the ovary for regulating sexual differentiation (Vainio et al. 1999). It does seem likely, how-

ever, that in mice neither progesterone nor estrogen is a major actor in initial events (Smith, Boyd, et al. 1994; Lydon et al. 1995; Korach 1994).

35. This process is called primary sex determination.

36. Once a fetal gonad appears, it can produce hormones that induce secondary sexual development—the problem that researchers in the 1930s through the 1950s addressed, and to which I will return later in this chapter.

37. Schafer et al. 1995, p. 271; emphasis added.

38. Wolf 1995, p. 325; emphasis added.

39. Capel 1998, p. 499.

40. Angier 1999, p. 38.

41. See, for example, Mittwoch 1996.

42. The metaphor that promotes feminist glee can also fuel masculine oppression. "Western culture," writes the psychologist Helen Haste, "has a strong tradition of rationality overcoming the forces of chaos that is closely interwoven with masculine versus feminine. . . . One pole is not only antithetical to, it triumphs over, the other pole. Dark forces must be challenged and conquered" (Haste 1994, p. 12). In a similar vein, the feminist historian Ludmilla Jordanova notes how the Enlightenment brought us word pairs such as nature/culture, woman/man, physical/mental, mothering/thinking, feeling and superstition/abstract knowledge and thought, darkness/light, nature/science and civilization (Jordanova 1980 and 1989).

43. Wolf 1995, p. 325. At least one scientist I have corresponded with disputes this claim, but I believe it is justifiable. Many embryology texts have a section entitled "sex determination" that discusses only male development. For example, Carlson considers the topic of "the genetic determination of gender." He first notes that females develop in the absence of a Y chromosome, then spends the entire section discussing male development. Figure 15–22 in his book illustrates a complex and detailed account of the mechanisms of male development, but there is no analogous illustration of the mechanisms of female development (Carlson 1999, pp. 375–76). The only modern textbook that treats male and female development in an evenhanded manner is by Scott Gilbert (Gilbert 1997). And it is no accident that one of Gilbert's public hats is that of a feminist historian of science. See also Swain et al. 1998; Haqq et al. 1994; and McElreavey et al. 1993.

44. Fausto-Sterling 1989.

45. Eicher and Washburn 1986, pp. 328–29.

46. Wolf acknowledges that "female development is undoubtedly not spontaneous" (p. 325), but does not otherwise discuss female development. Two articles by Sinclair discuss the testis-determining pathway, and although acknowledging that there is complexity underlying both ovarian and testicular determination, never hypothesizes an ovarian determining pathway (Sinclair 1995, 1998). Capel writes that the default terminology "may be mis-

leading because it suggests that the female pathway is not an active, genetically controlled process" (1998, p. 499). Hunter gives a paragraph to Eicher and Washburn's hypothesis, but then spends the rest of a sixty-six-page chapter (entitled "Mechanisms of Sex Determination") discussing genes for testis determination (Hunter 1995). Swain et al. write: "ovary differentiation is unlikely to be passive as there are changes in gene expression that occur very early in XX genital ridge development" (1998, p. 761).

Only three current papers picture genes active in female development. Such accounts of "sex differentiation" (as opposed to male differentiation) are still in the minority (Werner et al. 1996; Jiménez and Burgos 1998; Schafer and Goodfellow 1996).

47. The "master" gene hypothesis weighs heavily in this story. Most current work on primary sex determination considers that the Y chromosome contains a "master gene," a switch that starts the development ball rolling. It takes, according to this model, only one gene to determine male development. Others argue that development is a process for which many genes are critical, as is getting the timing of gene action right. On the latter viewpoint, see Mittwoch 1989, 1992, and 1996.

48. Milton Diamond writes: "As a graduate student my first thesis attempt in this vein was to see if estrogens could feminize male fetuses as androgens masculinized females. My injections of estrogens into pregnant guinea pigs invariably resulted in fetal death. This was a great disappointment to me since it's hard to study behavior that way" (Diamond 1997a, p. 100). Another researcher wrote me that the effects of estrogen on animal behavior were small and hard to measure. "That doesn't mean that they are unimportant, of course, but if you were an Assistant Professor and you wanted to be productive, I hope you'd choose to study robust effects and not subtle ones" (anonymous, personal communication).

49. For Jost's description of meeting Wilkins, see Jost 1972, pp. 38–39.

50. Frank Beach writes: "The importance of support distributed by this committee to development of hormone behavior research has never been adequately recognized . . . the decision of the Committee for Research in Problems of Sex to encourage investigations of copulation in rats . . . , or frequency of orgasm in married women . . . , was a courageous one that eventually opened the way for general expansion of research on effects of hormones on a very important category of behavior" (Beach 1981, p. 354).

The work on hormones and animal behavior that evolved from the late 1930s through the 1960s built directly and consciously on the issues addressed by early hormone researchers. Beach cites Lillie, Moore, Marshall, Heape, and many others as early contributors to the field (Beach 1981).

Beach's Ph.D. mentor at the University of Chicago was Karl S. Lashley (1890–1958). Lashley's work on brain mechanisms and intelligence emphasized a holistic view of brain function, and his views are clearly reflected in

Beach's work and manner of thinking. For more on Lashley, see Weidman, 1999.

Beach discussed his results on brain-injured rats with an endocrinologist who suggested that brain injury could disturb pituitary secretion and thus affect gonadal hormone secretion. Beach wrote of this encounter: "I hadn't the faintest understanding of what he was talking about; but after reading a bit of endocrinology I decided to inject some of my brain-operated, de-sexed males with testosterone just to see what would happen . . . lo and behold! The injected rats regained their libido; and I thought I was on the way to a Nobel Prize" (Beach 1985, p. 7.).

In the United States, the field of animal psychology was known as comparative psychology. In Europe, a related but distinct tradition was known as ethology. Only during the 1950s did European ethology strongly influence American comparative psychologists. For a historical treatment of comparative psychology, see Dewsbury 1989 and 1984.

51. As one researcher wrote me, "For the behaviorist, that is the beauty of it because there is so much that can be easily measured." Even closely related species differ in the details. Male guinea pigs, for example, resemble primates in the use of repetitive thrusts but a single intromission (anonymous, personal communication).

52. Behaviors such as nest building, maternal care, and aggression in territorial defense also defined masculinity and femininity in rats, but in this period, Beach focused primarily on figuring out the components of mating behaviors. For recent theories on hormones, experience, and parenting behavior, see Krasnegor and Bridges 1990.

53. For an overwrought account of the necessity of psychoanalysis for daily life, see Lundberg and Farnham 1947.

54. See, for example, Watson 1914 and Dewsbury 1984.

55. Beach was not enamored of Watson and the behaviorists. In 1961 he wrote: "It seems to me the time has come for a re-examination of these problems with great attention being given to genetically-influenced biologic factors which may contribute to some of these differences" between the sexes and between racial groups (Beach 1961, p. 160).

56. In a retrospective moment William C. Young wrote: "Research on the relationships between the hormones and sexual behavior has not been pursued with the vigor justified by the biological, medical, and sociological importance of the subject. Explanation may lie in the stigma any activity associated with sexual behavior has long borne. In our experience, restraint has been requested in the use of the word 'sex' in institutional records and in the title of research proposals. We vividly recollect that the propriety of presenting certain data at scientific meetings and seminars was questioned" (Young 1964, p. 212).

57. Beach 1942b, p. 173.

58. In 1947 he wrote: "*Importance of the holistic approach*: Physiological experiments designed to identify the nervous pathways involved in a particular genital reflex, or to measure the importance of secretions from a single gland to the occurrence of copulatory reactions, have contributed a great deal to our understanding of sexual behavior. It should be obvious, however, that the full significance of such findings becomes apparent only when they are viewed against the broader background of the total sexual pattern as it appears in the normal animal" (Beach 1947, p. 240).

59. "Individual differences in the ease with which various inexperienced males become sexually aroused constitute an important factor which must be taken into consideration in any attempt to define the adequate stimulus for mating behavior. A stimulus situation eliciting copulation in one male may fail to call forth the mating reactions of a less excitable individual of the same species" (Beach 1942c, p. 174).

60. "The appearance of the overt copulatory pattern depends jointly upon the male's sexual excitability, and the intensity of the stimulation afforded by the incentive animal. A highly excitable male may attempt copulation with an incentive animal of relatively low stimulus value. . . . A less excitable male fails to show mating reactions in response to all incentive animals other than the receptive female with which he will copulate. A male of low excitability may not be aroused to the point of copulation even when offered the receptive female" (Beach 1942e, p. 246). Beach and other researchers commented on the fact that there were always males and females in a colony that seemed to have no interest in mating. Eventually, it became common practice to eliminate such animals from tests of mating activity.

61. Beach 1942c.

62. Apparently animals could still mate, even with their cortex removed. See Beach 1942b,c, pp. 179–181; and Beach 1943.

63. Beach 1941.

64. Beach 1942a. Normal females did not require outside testosterone to show a male mating pattern. Beach and Priscilla Rasquin raised females in sexually segregated quarters and then tested them daily through four mating cycles. During the test, they allowed the female to adapt to the test cage, placed her with a receptive female for five minutes, and then with a sexually active male. They divided the female's masculine mating behaviors into three types: (1) mounting and embracing the mounted animal with her forepaws; (2) mounting, touching the mounted animal with her forepaws, and pelvic thrusting; and (3) mounting, touching, and "giving a final forceful thrust and dismounting with a pronounced backward lunge." Of 20 females, 18 exhibited the sexual clasp, 18 showed mounting, touching, and pelvic thrusting, and 5 engaged in the complete "male" copulation pattern. The masculine behaviors occurred whether or not the females were in heat.

Beach and Rasquin drew some startling conclusions: First, they noted that the majority of the female rats in their colony had the brain and muscular anatomy needed for a male mating pattern. Second, they concluded that the same stimulus—a female in heat—elicited this male pattern in both sexes. Finally, they noted that ovarian hormones did not control masculine mating in female rats (Beach and Rasquin 1942); see also Beach 1942a and f. Beach first reported on these cross-gendered behaviors in 1938. He quotes from his own lab journal, dated 1937, on Male No. 156 interacting with Female No. 192:

> 10:05 AM: Female dropped into observation cage containing male. . . .
> 10:15 AM: . . . Both animals display all signs of intense sexual excitement but the male never actually mounts and palpates the female. 10:16: Female whirls about, approaches male from the rear and mounts and palpates actively. The forepaws of the female clasp and palpate the male . . . and the female's pelvic region is moved in and out with the piston-like action characteristic of the copulating male. After this brief display of masculine activity the female dismounts, without the typical masculine lunge, and does not clean the genital region. 10:17: Female responds to male's investigatory activity by crouching, arching the back, and vibrating the ears rapidly.

Beach notes that this particular female mounted and palpated the male seven times in a fifteen-minute observation period. He emphasizes that she exhibits both masculine and feminine responses (Beach 1938, p. 332).

65. Beach 1942b, p. 183. To reinforce his point, Beach also cites Carl Moore's earlier debates with Steinach, especially Moore's insistence that individual rats varied too much to be used as an indicator of hormone presence or absence.

66. This mass effect is compatible with Lashley's approach to brain function.

67. Later he reported on experiments confirming this hunch. He continued to emphasize the holistic approach: "Evidence makes it plain that the effects of androgen are mediated by a complex combination of mechanisms, of which the supposed tactile functions of the glans are only one" (Beach and Levinson 1950, p. 168).

68. Beach 1947–1948, p. 276.

69. Beach 1965, p. vii.

70. Beach writes that certain statements in his text "are based upon data generously made available by Dr. A. C. Kinsey of Indiana University, whose extensive interview study of sexual behavior in more than 10,000 humans is to be published in the future (Beach 1947, p. 301). Kinsey and Beach were both funded by CRPS, a fact that Kinsey notes in the introduction to his 1948 study. They met and talked about their common interests.

71. Marc Breedlove, personal communication (May 1999). Kinsey used personal interviews to gather his data. He personally recruited and trained interviewers.

72. In Jones (1997) and Gasthorne-Hardy (1998) Beach discusses his friendship with Kinsey. Kinsey got his first CRPS grant in 1941 and received new funding yearly, in increasing amounts, through 1947 (Aberle and Corner 1953).

73. Kinsey et al. 1948, 1953. In the 1953 volume, Kinsey specifically thanks Beach for contributing information on animal behavior (p. ix).

74. See, for example, Bérubé 1990; Katz 1995.

75. For the many strands and complexities of this discussion, see Reumann 1998.

76. The architect of this new work had done many studies on individual variation and concluded with others that individuality emerged because each body—or, as the scientists call it, "substrate"—differed. He wrote: "it was clear that the central problem for the investigator interested in accounting for the great variability in patterns of mating behavior was to identify the factors which determine the character of the substrate on which the gonadal hormones act" (Young 1960, p. 202). This article brought the latest in rat research into the psychiatric community. The theory of organization and activation is only infrequently used to explain differences among individuals of the same species, even though this question originally stimulated experiments that led to the O/A theory.

77. For a complete bibliography of Young's publications and a brief biography, see Goy 1967. He was supported through money Lillie obtained from CRPS (Dempsey 1968); see also Roofe 1968. Although he worked on other animals, especially rats and monkeys, and some of his students focused especially on primates, the bulk of Young's publications were devoted to guinea pig behavior.

78. Quoted in Goy 1967, p. 7.

79. Young 1941, p. 141.

80. Young and Rundlett 1939, p. 449.

81. Young et al. 1939. They wrote: "in any measurement of sexual drive, mounting activity and receptivity should be regarded as separable components of a sexual behavior complex and measured directly by whatever means are considered most appropriate" (p. 65).

82. Young and Rundlett 1939.

83. In this cyclical dependence guinea pig females differ from rats. Young indicates the lingering confusion discussed in the previous chapter engendered by expectations for so-called male and female hormones: "Early in the work it was anticipated that estrogen-androgen rather than estrogen-progesterone action would stimulate mounting activity. The relative ineffectiveness of the androgens which have been employed is surprising, but their

ability to substitute for progesterone more efficiently in the induction of heat than in the induction of the male-like mounting activity is even more puzzling" (Young and Rundlett 1939, p. 459).

84. Young 1941, p. 311. Here we see the culture of scientific practice at work. To do science at all, some measurable starting point was needed. Young, like the others, needed steady results in order to obtain funding, train students, and continue his work. Successful scientific practice, in other words, does not necessarily lead to a balanced overview of organismal function. It does lead to carefully designed experiments of the sort that give specific results and pave the way for more carefully designed experiments.

85. They also included another category of mating response called "other" (Young and Grunt 1951).

86. "It is postulated . . . that much of the difference between individuals is attributable to the reactivity of the tissues rather than to differences in the amount of hormone" (Grunt and Young 1952, p. 247). See also Grunt and Young 1953 and Riss and Young 1954.

87. Valenstein et al. 1955, p. 402. The additional papers detailing the importance of genetic background and experience in males are Valenstein et al. 1954; Riss et al. 1955; Valenstein and Young 1955; and Valenstein and Goy 1957. Young's group began in this period to flirt more seriously with the distinction between early organization of neural patterns and their activation at a separate time by circulating hormones. In one paper they write: "The data suggest the role of t.p. [testosterone propionate] to be that of an activator rather than a direct organizer of sexual behavior. The organization is dependent on variables associated with the strains and upon opportunity to learn the techniques of mounting and maneuvering a female" (Riss et al. 1955, p. 144). At the time Young also felt that the organization of sexual behaviors in males "is not as sharply restricted to an early critical period as is" imprinting in birds (Young 1957, p. 88). After 1959, Young and others began to insist on the importance of a critical period, and once they had demonstrated a prenatal organizing effect of testosterone, they no longer wrote about the social isolation effects as "organizing." Robert Goy, whom Young trained, also found strain differences and experience important for the organization of female mating responses. These findings assume importance in view of the later focus on the role (or lack thereof) of prenatal estrogen in organizing female mating patterns. See Goy and Young 1956–57; Goy and Young 1957; Goy and Jakway 1959.

88. Phoenix et al. 1959.

89. Ibid., p. 370.

90. Ford and Beach 1951, p. 125; Hampson and Hampson 1961, p. 1,425. Although this paper appeared two years after that of Phoenix et al., Young edited the volume in which it was published. Thus he and his co-workers had read it and could refer to it "in press."

91. The dispute was complex. Hampson and Hampson, for example, wrote that their study "of human hermaphroditism points strongly to the tremendous influence of rearing and social learning in the establishment of normal gender role . . . and by analogy, disordered psychologic sex." At the same time they did not entirely rule out genetic or constitutional contributions. But they thought the "evidence militates too strongly against a theory of innate, preformed and inherited behavioral imperatives, hormonal or otherwise" (1961, p. 1,428). There were also debates within Young's lab about the meaning of the findings: "The younger members of the team were more convinced [than Young] that this was a direct brain effect. . . . This was a hotly debated issue in the lab while the paper was being written and the somewhat contradictory views finally presented reflect a balance between what they suspected had occurred and what they could actually demonstrate" (Kim Wallen, personal communication, July 11, 1997).

92. I discussed the technical details of this paper at some length in Fausto-Sterling 1995. I have been convinced by critics that some aspects of this earlier treatment were in error, especially my failure to give Young his full historical due and my assertion that Phoenix et al. claimed a brain effect, when in fact they were more cautious, claiming a central nervous system effect. But the paper is useful for showing how the O/A theory has been modified in fairly fundamental ways since its original publication, and I stand by my critique that the model leaves out experience and genetic and individual difference. It is not the sort of holistic model that Beach wanted, nor that I develop in this chapter and the next.

93. Phoenix al. 1959, p. 372. They performed four basic experiments: (1) they injected prenatally exposed females in adulthood with estradiol and progesterone and measured aspects of their mating responses, concluding that prenatal androgen exposure suppressed the lordosis response, but not male-like mounting; (2) they tested for "permanence" of the effects of prenatal androgen and found them present at 6–9 and then again at 11–12 months of age (guinea pigs live for 10–12 years), concluding that "the suppression of the capacity for displaying the feminine components of the sexual behavior pattern . . . appears to have been permanent" (p. 377); (3) they studied the effects of injecting adults who had been prenatally exposed to androgen with testosterone, finding such females more responsive (i.e., more likely to exhibit a masculine mating pattern) to testosterone than were untreated females and concluding that "the earlier appearance and greater strength of masculine behavior by the hermaphrodites given testosterone propionate are believed to be effects of the prenatally administered testosterone propionate on the tissues mediating masculine behavior and therefore to be expressions of its organizing action"; (4) they examined the behavior of adult male siblings—also exposed to androgen prenatally; here they found no apparent effect of prenatal testosterone treatment.

Here I discuss only mating behavior. The authors were well aware of other sex-differentiated behaviors (e.g., maternal behaviors, nest building, territorial aggression), but Young and Beach had spent decades defining mating behaviors in a manner that could be quantitatively measured and evaluated.

94. Grady and Phoenix 1963, p. 483. Rats began to be used for these studies because there is a biological difference of practical importance between rats and guinea pigs. The important anatomical and organizational events in guinea pigs take place in utero because guinea pigs are long-gestation animals. Rats, however, gestate for a shorter time and are born far more sexually undifferentiated. Young and colleagues never succeeded in doing prenatal castrations (in utero) in guinea pigs, but in rats they could work on individual newborns rather than do surgery on a pregnant female. Furthermore, they could directly treat test individuals with hormones rather than inject pregnant females (Grady et al. 1965).

95. Beach 1981. Beach discusses both Young's and his early work in Beach (1981). In an autobiographical piece Beach lists the organizational effects of hormones during early development under the topic "Discoveries I almost made." He also discusses his dog experiments in this context (Beach 1978, p. 30).

96. Phoenix et al. 1959, p. 381. The central nervous system refers to the brain and spinal cord. Although they suspected brain involvement, the authors were cautiously agnostic, since they did not have evidence to this effect.

97. Phoenix et al. 1959, p. 379.

98. Ibid., p. 380. It took less than a decade for Young to adopt the presence/absence language introduced by Jost. In 1967, he wrote: "Many of those traits which are sexually dimorphic . . . appear to be influenced in the masculine direction by appropriate treatment with androgen and in the feminine direction by the absence of early steroid hormones" (Young 1967, p. 180).

99. Phoenix et al. 1959, p. 380.

100. Young continued to debate this question with both Beach and the Hampsons during the early 1960s. In 1961 and 1962, CRPS hosted two conferences, the organization's last actions before going out of the sex-study business, work by then so fully supported by the National Science Foundation and the National Institute of Mental Health as to render CRPS obsolete. Following the conferences, CRPS "recommended to the Chairman of the Division of Medical Sciences that the Committee for Research in Problems of Sex be discharged when the book resulting from the Conference on Sex and Behavior has been prepared for publication" (Beach 1965, p. ix). Beach edited a volume that summarized the two meetings, and it is in this volume that we find Young and Hampson talking to each other, with Beach's editorial hand clearly egging on the debate. For example, Young addressed John Hampson's upcoming paper: "By 'bisexuality' I do not mean . . . that an individual can move equally well in one direction or the other" (here an asterix refers the reader to Hamp-

son's account of neutrality in the upcoming chapter). "I believe," Young continued, "that . . . the evidence in the clinical literature" and primates "will reveal a predominance of masculine characteristics in the genetic male, and a predominance of feminine characteristics in the female. . . . Even in human beings before the individual is born the stage" may be "set for selective responsiveness to experiential and psychologic factors" (Young 1965, p. 103). Young reiterates this point in Young 1967. Beach twice flagged John Hampson's rejection of the idea of "sex hormones as a single causal agent in the establishment of an individual's gender role and psychosexual orientation" (p. 115), referring the reader back to Young's discussion. Hampson concludes "that an individual's gender role and orientation as boy or girl, man or woman, does not have an innate, preformed instinctive basis. . . . Instead . . . psychologic sex is undifferentiated at birth—a sexual neutrality one might say—and . . . the individual becomes psychologically differentiated as masculine or feminine in the course of the many experiences of growing up" (Hampson 1965, p. 119).

101. "The possibility must be considered that the masculinity or femininity of an animal's behavior *beyond that which is purely sexual* has developed in response to certain hormonal substances within the embryo and fetus" (Phoenix et al. 1959, p. 381; emphasis added).

102. Ibid., p. 381. The possibility that fetal or perinatal estrogen plays a role in the developing female brain remains in dispute to this day. See Fitch and Denenberg 1998; Fitch et al. 1998; Etgen et al. 1990; Fadem 1995; and Ogawa et al. 1997.

103. Van den Wijngaard 1991b.

104. Beatty 1992.

105. By the late 1960s, John Money and Anke Ehrhardt had applied the paradigm to the study of CAH girls (chapter 3). In a popular account of their work, they introduced the idea that prenatal androgen exposure masculinized the brains of XX kids exposed to high levels of testosterone in utero. Just as with the guinea pigs and rats, Money and his colleagues argued that prenatal hormones induced such girls to engage in a more masculine style of play (Money and Ehrhardt 1972). Also in this period, the German endocrinologist Günther Dörner suggested that the new understandings proffered by the O/A theory might offer a cure for homosexuality. Citing experiments showing that perinatal castration seemed to prevent masculinization of a rat's brain, Dörner hoped that the same might be true for humans. "These results," he wrote, "suggest . . . that male homosexuality may be prevented by androgen administration during the critical period" (Dörner and Hinz 1968, p. 388).

106. Young 1961, p. 1,223. Young wrote of the role of genes on female behavior: "As in the male, differences were seen in every measure of behavior studied: responsiveness to [hormone] treatment . . . , duration of induced

heat . . . duration of maximal lordosis, and amount of male-like mounting" (Young 1961, p. 1,215).

In order to obtain usable data, scientists often made their experimental animals more uniform. In one sense, then, working scientists *produced* a typical account of sexual behaviors by systematically eliminating genetic diversity from their studies. A brief recent article on contemporary, commercially produced laboratory rats notes that commercial companies have selected them to breed as rapidly as possible (thus increasing profit margins). As a result, they now average almost double what they used to weigh twenty years ago, and they die much younger. There is little doubt that this selective breeding has changed the physiology of our "standard" laboratory rat to meet both commercial and experimental needs. Thus scientific theories based on these rats—especially, I suspect, ones having to do with energy metabolism—are peculiarly structured to the laboratory. In this sense, we have "created" biology—i.e., the facts from which we will generalize attempts to devise medicines, diet regimes, and theories of biology will come from a peculiar creature that is subject only to human selections, not natural selection (see Wassersug 1996; Clause 1993).

Young cited especially his experiments on social isolation. These showed that for one genetic strain the development of mounting, intromission, and ejaculatory behaviors depended "almost completely . . . on the contact [the animals] had with other young animals" (Young 1961, p. 1,218).

107. Young 1964, p. 217. Of course, some researchers continued to acknowledge the importance of social interactions and experience and to design experiments based on such acknowledgment. This was not, however, the reigning paradigm, and to many inside and outside the field, and to the general public, this other, more complex approach was indeed invisible.

108. Phoenix 1978, p. 30.

109. During the 1960s, Beach continued to challenge the O/A and insist on adult bisexuality. He explained the evidence on lordosis by calling on neuromuscular units developed before birth in both sexes: "They are present in both sexes and their organization during development is not dependent upon gonadal hormones" (Beach 1966, p. 532). As the male matures, the reflexes come under inhibitory influences that a variety of environmental circumstances can release.

110. Money and Ehrhardt (1972) were anxious about the judgment of women's liberationists, who, they noted, were not going to like all they had to say. Their book also has an odd index entry. Under "Women's Liberation: Quotable Material," they list the page locations of items that they apparently felt would bolster the feminist viewpoint (see p. 310). The psychologist Richard Doty wrote a paper in which he called on researchers to extend more "equal opportunity" to female rodents (Doty 1974, p. 169), while the psy-

chologist Richard Whalen expressed concern about whether his theories of gender formation in rodents were "sexist." See, e.g., Whalen 1974, p. 468. In a symposium held in 1976 in honor of Beach's sixty-fifth birthday, his student Leonore Tiefer infuriated Beach with a talk offering a feminist perspective on contemporary research. Later, when Beach read the piece, he apologized and suggested that her viewpoint was indeed worth listening to. See Tiefer 1978 and van den Wijngaard 1991.

111. During its first ten years of publication, *Hormones and Behavior* devoted fully 80 percent of its research articles to hormones and gendered behavior.

Supporters of the organizational theory, Beach suggested (1971), had gotten carried away with the embryological metaphor, but Young and his followers could not specify what, exactly, was being organized. He also found the notion that androgen organizes a brain (a male one, at that) problematic, suggesting that castration would thus *disorganize* the brain (and the female brain, at that). What, he wondered, could a disorganized brain imply? He pressed home his point with a doctored photo purporting to show disorganized neural pathways. He expressed concern about the loss of "hard-earned knowledge regarding relationships between gonadal hormones and behaviors. Many theorists are so sadly and seriously affected with neurophilia (which in its terminal phases inevitably develops into cerebromania) that they are able seriously to entertain only those interpretations of behavior couched in the vocabulary of the neurologist" (Beach 1971, p. 286).

The published work offered a concentrated dose of his famous acid wit. But rather than burning a hole into the heart of the organizational theory, his words fell, I gather (from corresponding with some who were there), on somewhat embarrassed ears. Beach understood what the reception would be. He wrote: "No one is more fully aware than I that many readers will feel that I am tilting windmills" (Beach 1971, p. 291).

112. In his own history of the field, Beach carefully works his way around his earlier objections without citing the Beach 1971 paper (Beach 1981). The remarkable nature of Beach's silence can be seen in McGill et al. 1978. This 436-page volume celebrating Beach's sixty-fifth birthday contained articles on the current research of at least seventeen of his former students. Only one even referred to Beach's critical article, and then only to mention a particular fact, not the critique itself.

There are, of course, microexplanations: (1) a new breed of biochemists was taking over, and Beach knew little of the molecular approach, so he was off base, but his respectful junior colleagues were too kind to tell him so in public; (2) his article was so intemperate that it exceeded acceptable norms of behavior, and people chose to turn the other cheek rather than return the insults.

In addition to attacking linguistic ambiguities, Beach considered alternate explanations for results of experiments on early hormone treatment. He looked particularly at the claim that testosterone organized male and female copulatory behavior. He noted that androgen strongly affected the postnatal growth of the penis. Thus males castrated in infancy might later fail to achieve intromission and ejaculation because their penises were too small, not because their brains had failed to be masculinized. For more on the penis-size debate, see Beach and Nucci 1970; Phoenix et al. 1976; and Grady et al. 1965. In general, he argued that many of the experimental results achieved could have resulted from effects on the peripheral nervous system or genitalia rather than on the central nervous system. See, for example, Beach and Nucci 1970. In 1968, the first evidence suggesting that the brain was at least one component of the central nervous system involved in organizing behavior was published by Nadler. During the 1970s and early 1980s, additional evidence accumulated on this point. See Christensen and Gorski 1978; Hamilton et al. 1981; and Arendash and Gorski 1982. (Thanks to Elizabeth Adkins-Regan for this chronology.)

Beach further insisted that whatever the effects of early hormones in males, they did not permanently wipe out the neural connections needed to express lordosis. Perhaps, as he had suggested earlier, prenatal hormones changed the level of sensitivity of nerve cells to later hormone stimulation. But the metaphor of mutually exclusive permanent electronic circuits (male or female) seemed untenable. Beach cited a study of male rats castrated as adults. According to the O/A theory, these males should not exhibit lordosis even when stimulated by estrus-inducing hormones because their brains had been properly masculinized in and around the time of birth. Indeed, normal quantities of estrogen did *not* elicit lordosis. However, a more prolonged series of injections induced these castrated males to exhibit lordosis almost as frequently as normal females in estrus. He wrote: "It becomes increasingly apparent that neural mechanisms capable of mediating lordosis and possibly ancillary receptive responses as well are organized in the central nervous system of male rats despite the presence of testis hormone during prenatal and early postnatal periods" (Beach 1971, p. 267).

113. Ibid., p. 270.

114. Beach 1976, p. 261.

115. Beach and Orndoff 1974; Beach 1976.

116. Hart (1972) concluded that manipulation of neonatal androgen affected both penile development and the central nervous system.

117. Raisman and Field 1973.

118. Goy and McEwen 1980, p. 18. The conference that led to this book took place in 1977.

119. Beach 1975.

1 2 0. Feder 1981, p. 141.

1 2 1. Evaluating Beach's critique in 1990, Michael Baum wrote:

Ironically, Beach's warning that we should resist the temptation to attribute all steroid-induced changes in behavioral potential to structural changes in the central nervous system still has some merit in the beginning of the 1990's. . . . While at present most workers would agree that the developmental effects of androgen on masculine coital responsiveness to adult steroids probably reflect a change in the nervous system, such behavioral changes cannot be localized in any of the rather limited current inventory of sexually dimorphic brain structures of the various mammalian species studied to date. Furthermore, some aspects of steroid-induced changes in mating potential may, as Beach predicted, result from the indirect perinatal action of androgens on the developing masculine genital organs." (Baum 1990, pp. 204–5)

Balthazart et al. echo Baum's point, writing, "in all model species . . . it is still impossible to identify satisfactorily brain characteristics that differentiate under early steroid action and explain the sex differences in behavioral activating effects of steroids" (1996, p. 627). Cooke et al. (1998) and Schlinger (1998) make similar points.

1 2 2. For a good overview of these changes, see Chafe 1991. For specific information on the history of the U.S. gay liberation movement, see D'Emilio 1983.

1 2 3. Money and Ehrhardt 1972, p. xi.

1 2 4. Doty 1974. Doty also noted that the sense of smell might be a key aspect of mating behavior totally unobserved by studies relying on visual components of behavior. One implication: some hormone effects might be mediated by changes in odor or odor responsiveness, rather than changes in the brain or central nervous system. This concern paralleled Beach's interest in hormonal effects on peripheral sensory systems.

1 2 5. Doty was not the first to develop such a critique. Whalen and Nadler, for example, had called for better experimental definition of female receptivity: "If receptivity is defined by the presence of spermatozoa in the vagina, some estrogen-treated females are receptive. If receptivity is defined by the rapid and easy elicitation of the lordosis response, spontaneous and hormone-induced receptivity is suppressed" (1965, p. 152). Whalen continued his methodological critiques during the 1970s. See, for example, Whalen 1976.

1 2 6. De Jonge 1995, p. 2. If a female is not in estrus, not even a much larger male can succeed in mating with her. Several researchers have emphasized to me that a rodent male cannot succeed in mating with an unwilling female and that in some species a female may attack and even kill an unwelcome suitor.

127. Clark 1993b, p. 37. In the wild, an unwilling female hides in her burrow, while the interested male tries to entice her to emerge. In her test cage, with no possible escape, a female may respond aggressively, screaming and biting the male (Calhoun 1962; de Jonge 1995).

128. Speaking at a symposium in honor of Young, held shortly after Young's death, Beach noted the difficulty of proving the absence of a particular neural representation (Beach 1968). This seems to be a good example of his point. Under some circumstances the lordosis response was absent and presumed missing because the neural substrate needed for it had been suppressed in early testosterone treatment. But under some experimental circumstances a positive result—frequent lordosis—appeared, thus suggesting that the neural substrate was there after all.

129. Gorski 1971, p. 251.

130. "The rapidly increasing precision and sophistication in endocrinological techniques," he wrote, "have not been accompanied by comparable advances in the definition and measurement of behavioral variables" (Beach 1976, p. 105).

131. More recent work shows quite clearly that proceptive and receptive behaviors respond to different activating hormones in adulthood (de Jonge 1986; Clark 1993).

132. In a later (1977) paper, Madlafousek and Hlinak offered a *thick description*—to borrow an anthropological term—of the various aspects of a female rat's behavior as she proceeded through estrus. (A "thick description" offers a lot of detail out of which a nuanced interpretation is thought to emerge.)

133. Whalen 1974; Davis et al. 1979.

134. Whalen and Johnson 1990.

135. Bem 1974. The parallel between the 1974 Bem and Whalen publications is striking: each noted the independence of masculinity and femininity. Whalen writes: "Bem and I had no contact about the ideas that we put forth at the time. The time must have been right" (personal communication, September 19, 1996). Sandra L. Bem writes: "I think the zeitgeist . . . is probably another hypothesis that must be considered in addition to direct contact. . . . I'm quite sure that I had never met or talked to Whalen in the time period you're asking about" (personal communication, September 28, 1996).

136. Goy and McEwen 1980, pp. 5, 6. They noted the new respectability afforded hormone research: "While there is still reasonable and serious dispute regarding the biological cause of different organizations of sexuality . . . hormonal hypotheses have earned a respectability that allows their inspection even for problems of human sexual behavior, a permission that was not readily granted by clinical workers a few decades ago."

137. Brain cells contain an enzyme called *aromatase*, which transforms testosterone into estrogen. Recent studies show that the hypothalamus of de-

veloping male mice contains higher activities of aromatase than does that of developing female brains. This implies that some masculine behaviors may result from higher concentrations of estrogen in male than in female brains! The aromatase enzyme system is not distributed uniformly throughout the brain, and the multiple and complex roles of the sex steroids in their various molecular incarnations, as well as the enzymes that transform them and the various brain regions that contribute to their synthesis, still awaits some uniform understanding or unifying hypothesis. See, for example, Naftolin et al. 1971; Naftolin et al. 1972; Naftolin and Ryan 1975; Naftolin and Brawer 1978; Naftolin and MacLusky 1984; and Hutchison et al. 1994.

While the conversion hypothesis produced a small tidal wave of research on estrogen production by various organs in the male, only a very small number of researchers seem to have noticed that the results ought also to call for a reevaluation of the presence/absence hypothesis of male and female development. In 1978 one researcher raised the question "Is female sexual differentiation hormone-mediated?" and again in 1984, another pointed out that "sexual differentiation in males *and* females is hormone dependent (Döhler 1976, 1978; Döhler et al. 1984; Toran-Allerand 1984; emphasis in original).

138. Bell et al. 1981.

139. See, for example, the mixture of articles in Young and Corner 1961 or de Vries et al. 1984.

140. Beach emphasized the normal status of female mounting and urged it be studied as a typical female behavior. He also reasoned that humans had the neural mechanisms needed for same-sex attraction, although he thought that exclusively homosexual attractions resulted from the complexities of culture and experience (Beach 1968).

141. Kinsey et al. write: "Several investigators (Ball, Beach, Stone, Young et al.) have shown that the injection of gonadal hormones may modify the frequency with which an animal shows an inversion of behavior. . . . Among many clinicians this work has been taken to mean that the sex hormones control the heterosexuality or homosexuality of an individual's behavior. This, of course, is a totally unwarranted interpretation" (Kinsey et al. 1948, p. 615).

142. This is a culturally specific attitude. In many Latin American cultures, for example, only the receptive male is understood to be homosexual.

143. Nothing stirred up this debate more than Simon LeVay's 1991 publication. See also LeVay 1991; Byne and Parsons 1993; Byne 1995.

144. Adkins-Regan 1988. She noted that this distinction was often lost on medical researchers applying animal results to humans, despite many animal researchers having clearly articulated it in the past. See esp. p. 336 for this discussion.

145. In one study, researchers removed the ovaries of adult females and then injected them with testosterone that had been chemically altered to prevent its conversion to estrogen, or progesterone. Female rats treated with

the altered testosterone preferred to mate with males, but had no lordosis response, while progesterone facilitated both receptive (lordosis) and proceptive (hopping and darting) behaviors, but did not induce male sexual preference. Thus in female rats, the mechanisms for sexual preference and actual mating behaviors differ. Furthermore, prenatal androgens seem to have no effect on the sexual orientation of female rats. Rather, the adult hormonal environment interacts with the rats' prior experience (de Jonge et al. 1986; de Jonge et al. 1988; Brand et al. 1991; Brand and Slob 1991a and 1991b).

146. Francien de Jonge and her co-workers removed the ovaries of adult female rats, some of which had had prior sexual experience and some of which had not. They then induced sexual behaviors by injecting testosterone (or, for controls, plain oil). Inexperienced females preferred the company of males when they got testosterone but showed no preference without it, while females with prior mount experience with other females continued to prefer females regardless of whether they received oil or testosterone. If, instead, their prior experience had been with males, they subsequently showed no particular sexual preference (de Jonge et al. 1986). Although adult hormones and prior experience seem to be the keys to female laboratory rat sexual preference, in male lab rats, prenatal hormones assume a greater importance. Julie Bakker completed a series of experiments showing that male rats for whom the conversion of testosterone into estrogen is blocked at birth later develop strongly bisexual or asexual potentials. If left intact and put on the right kind of light/dark cycle, they will run back and forth between test males and test females, exhibiting both altered mating behaviors and altered preferences. In adulthood, estrogen induces homosexual preferences in such males, while testosterone seems to permit greater bisexuality (Bakker 1996). Bakker also showed that, for males, social isolation from the moment of weaning to adulthood had no effect on sexual preference, although such isolation drastically impaired sexual performance. Adult social interactions, however, did affect male sexual preference. Aromatase inhibitor-treated rats required physical interactions with their potential partners in order to differentiate themselves from control males. Although I have primarily used Bakker's Ph.D. thesis to write this section, much of her work also appears in the following publications: Brand and Slob 1991a and 1991b; Brand et al. 1991; Bakker et al. 1995a; Bakker, Brand, et al. 1993; Bakker, van Ophemert, et al. 1993; Bakker, 1995; and Bakker et al. 1994.

147. See, for example, LeVay 1996.

148. Schlinger 1998.

149. Wallen 1996.

150. The psychologist Gilbert Gottlieb (1997) summarizes his lifetime of experiments on the development of bird behaviors such as imprinting and applies the tradition of systems theory to his results. It's a good read!

151. Ward 1992.

152. See, for example, Houtsmuller et al. 1994. There is a fairly large literature on the effects of location in the uterus on future behavior.

153. Gottlieb 1997.

154. Laviola and Alleva 1995.

155. Harris and Levine 1965.

156. De Jonge et al. 1988.

157. Harris and Levine 1965.

158. Feder 1981.

159. Gerall et al. 1967; Valenstein and Young 1955; Hard and Larsson 1968; Thor and Holloway 1984; and Birke 1989.

160. For example, when nonovulating female rats were housed with sexually experienced males, they would not mate. But after 3 months of continuous cohabitation, 18 out of 60 of these females responded to male mounting (Segal and Johnson, cited in Harris and Levine 1965).

161. Ward 1992.

162. Moore et al. 1992. Moore describes the effects of early testosterone treatment as either a web or a cascade. Her model has no linear connections. The number of affected organs grows as hormones influence the scent glands and the brain early in the process and subsequently alter liver physiology, genital anatomy, and muscle development. Finally maternal licking, overall body size, play, exploration, and self-grooming behaviors all interact with hormonal effects. Thus, behavior results from the intersection of links among physiology, anatomy, and behavior. For example, maternal licking causes and is caused by the interrelationships between pup odor, pup urine production and retention, pup leg-extension behavior, maternal water and salt balance related to lactation and attraction to pup odor. The relationships are complex and decentralized. Hormones become part of a web that includes—among other things—experience, the brain, peripheral muscles, and general physiology (Moore and Rogers 1984; Moore 1990).

163. Drickamer 1992.

164. Moore and Rogers 1984; Moore 1990.

165. Arnold and Breedlove 1985.

166. Breedlove 1997, p.801. There are other hormone effects as well. Prenatal or perinatal testosterone treatment lowers thyroid function, affects the liver, and causes a wide variety of reproductive system abnormalities (Moore and Rogers 1984; Moore 1990; Harris and Levine 1965; de Jonge et al. 1988; de Jonge 1986).

167. Södersten describes a strain of rats in which intact males exhibit significant levels of lordosis, often considered to be an exclusively female behavior, while van de Poll and colleagues report on one showing no hormonally induced alterations in aggressive behavior. Finally, Luttge and Hall and McGill and Haynes discuss strain differences in how mice respond to testosterone

treatment (van de Poll et al. 1981; Södersten 1976; McGill and Haynes 1973; Luttge and Hall 1973).

168. See, for example, Calhoun 1962; Berry and Bronson 1992; Smith, Hurst et al. 1994.

169. Gerall et al. 1973.

170. Södersten 1976.

171. Adkins-Regan et al. 1989.

172. De Jonge et al. 1988. This result is consistent with the report that an ovary present around puberty in either male or female rats facilitated the appearance of female behavior when the animals were examined as adults (Gerall et al. 1973).

173. Tobet and Fox 1992.

174. Toran-Allerand 1984, p. 63; emphasis added.

175. One correspondent who read this comment scoffed, suggesting it would be a waste of time to do long-term studies, since he was certain the outcome wouldn't change. Given the current explosion of information on neural plasticity, I believe that long-term studies that manipulate environmental variables are quite appropriate.

176. Brown-Grant 1974.

177. Beach 1971.

178. Feder 1981, p. 143.

179. Arnold and Breedlove 1985.

180. Thor and Holloway 1984 review work on social play in juvenile rats.

181. The pituitary of adult female rats, for example, controls the reproductive cycle with periodic or cyclical secretions. In contrast, the male rat pituitary controls reproduction with a constant flow of hormones. Perinatal testosterone seems to permanently suppresses cyclicity in treated females, while castration of newborn males results in adults with a cyclically functioning pituitary (Harris and Levine 1965). In primates, however, prenatal hormonal effects on pituitary function are not permanent. Thus the development of sex differences in pituitary physiology differs in rats and primates. In the latter group, functional modulation in adulthood is possible (Baum 1979).

182. Feder 1981; Adkins-Regan 1988.

Chapter 9: Gender Systems:
Toward a Theory of Human Sexuality

1. Sterling 1954, 1955. A number of scholars took the time to read and critique an earlier draft of this chapter. They of course bear no responsibility for its final condition, but they do deserve my heartfelt thanks: Liz Grosz, John Modell, Cynthia García-Coll, Robert Perlman, Lundy Braun, Peter Taylor, Roger Smith, and Susan Oyama.

2. Sterling 1970.

3. For example, perhaps her genetic makeup synchronized with her environment, and thus both pushed in the same direction. Or, what if she had wanted to dress in pink and hated the woods? Could any amount of maternal pressure have parted her from her Betsy Wetsy? Then again, what if she had grown up in New York City, born of parents who had little curiosity about how the natural world works? Would her inner scientist have suffered the fate of Shakespeare's sister, described with such sadness by Virginia Woolf in *A Room of One's Own*? There is no way to sort out these possibilities, and thus the speculation about origins always remains, as with the corpus callosum debate, as much in the political realm as in the scientific.

4. See, for example, Money and Ehrhardt 1972; Zucker and Bradley 1995.

5. Dewey and Bentley 1949, p. 69.

6. The philosopher Alfred North Whitehead writes: "the notion of 'organism' has two meanings . . . the microscopic meaning and the macroscopic meaning. The microscopic meaning is concerned with . . . a process of realizing an individual unity of experience. The macroscopic meaning is concerned with the givenness of the actual world . . . the stubborn fact which at once limits and provides opportunity for the actual occasion. . . . In our experience we essentially arise out of our bodies which are the stubborn facts of the immediate relevant past" (Whitehead 1929, p. 129). Like a number of biologists (Waddington 1975; Gottlieb 1997), I find Whitehead's process philosophy the most appropriate way to think about organisms. For more on Whitehead, see Kraus 1979.

7. Hubbard and Wald 1993; Lewontin et al. 1984; Lewontin 1992.

8. Crichton 1990.

9. Hubbard and Wald 1993.

10. Hamer et al. 1993, pp. 321, 326. Rice et al. (1999) have been unable to repeat the finding that places it among a large number of genetic claims about complex behavior that continue to be in dispute.

11. Pool 1993, p. 291.

12. Anonymous 1995a; Anonymous 1995b.

13. A workshop of behavioral scientists that focused on the question "How do genes set up behavior?" wrote that future work will lead to the conclusion that "gene products are but a minute fraction of the total number of behavioral determinants. A second, small fraction will be identifiable as relatively straightforward environmental factors. Most importantly, however, the vast majority of deterministic factors will reside in the multitude of as yet unpredictable interactions between genetic and environmental factors." While this group still uses the language of interactionism, their results and conclusions suggest strongly that dynamic systems will provide the better path

to understanding relationships between genes and behavior (Greenspan and Tully 1993, p. 79).

14. There are four kinds of bases that, when grouped together three at a time, can signal the cell to bring a particular amino acid to a structure called a ribosome, which is itself made up of several proteins and a different kind of gene product called ribosomal RNA. On the ribosome other molecules, RNAs, and proteins cooperate to link different amino acids into linear arrays called proteins. Protein assembly takes place in the cell but outside the nucleus.

15. Cohen and Stewart 1994; Ingber 1998.

16. See Stent 1981.

17. Brent 1999. Developmentalists are only now thinking about how to handle and analyze such complexity. Some have even reached for connectionist models! See, for example, Reinitz et al. 1992. Furthermore, geneticists have become increasingly aware of the complexity of expression even of genes usually trotted out as examples of a "pure" 1:1 relationship between genetic structure and phenotype (Scriver and Waters 1999).

18. Stent 1981, p. 189.

19. The ethical question of whether these children were "captured" or "rescued" is discussed in Noske 1989. See also Singh 1942; Gesell and Singh 1941.

20. Recent results on humans include Eriksson et al. 1998; Kemperman and Gage 1999. Recent results on other mammals include Barinaga 1998; Johansson et al. 1999; Wade 1999; Gould et al. 1999; Kemperman et al. 1998; and Gould et al. 1997.

21. Barinaga 1996; Yeh et al. 1996; Vaias et al. 1993; Moore et al. 1995. Dramatic examples come from fish that change sex depending on their social setting. See Grober 1997; see also Kolb and Whishaw 1998.

22. Examples of plasticity from nonhuman vertebrates have been accumulating for years. See, for example, Crair et al. 1998; Kolb 1995; Kirkwood et al. 1996; Kaas 1995; Singer 1995; Sugita 1996; and Wang et al. 1995. It is imperative to incorporate this work into theories of sexual development. It no longer seems acceptable to me to conclude—even tentatively—from consistent patterns emerging from, for example, studies of cognition in adult heterosexual males and females compared to gay male and lesbian adults that "prenatal sex hormones are critical determinants of a wide range of sex-typical characteristics" (Halpern and Crothers 1997, p. 197).

23. See White and Fernald 1997.

24. But remember how hard this turns out to be—the same genetic strain of mouse behaves differently in different laboratories (Crabbe et al. 1999).

25. See also Juraska and Meyer 1985. Morphological changes in the shape of individual nerve cells can happen very rapidly (within 30 minutes) after a

period of intense activity (Maletic-Savatic et al. 1999; Engert and Bonhoeffer 1999. Longer-term behavioral changes may involve changes in the structure and relationships of so-called neural assemblies—groups of interconnected cells. See Hammer and Menzel 1994.

Consider the dwarf Siberian hamster. Like many animals living in the wild, males develop mature testes and mate during certain seasons, but their gonads shrink and no longer make sperm during their "down time." While short day length can induce the regression of mature gonads, it can do so only if there are no receptive females and young in the vicinity. Diet can also affect the pattern. Day length, social cues, and diet are all environmental signals that directly affect the hypothalamus, a part of the brain involved in regulating hormonal signals that can affect behavior (Matt 1993). Similar stories can be told for birds, see Ball 1993.

The frequency of sex can also affect the nervous system. The psychologist Marc Breedlove studied spinal cord nerves in rats, focusing on specific nerves involved with erection and ejaculation. Sexually active male rats had smaller nerve cells in certain spinal cord nerves than did celibate ones. This observation is important when trying to interpret information such as that provided by LeVay's finding that gay and straight men had slightly different cell groupings in their hypothalamus. We have no way of knowing if the difference caused a behavior or vice versa. Given the complexity of human sexual desire, I suspect the latter is a more likely interpretation (Breedlove 1997; LeVay 1991).

26. Specifically, there was binding in the bed nucleus of the stria terminalis, the hippocampus, subiculum, lateral septal nuclei, entorhinal and piriform cortex, and medial preoptic area and arcuate nucleus of the hypothalamus. There was a decreased presence of estrogen receptor binding cells in the periventricular gray area of the midbrain (Ehret et al. 1993).

27. Blakeslee 1995; Zuger 1997.

28. Kolata 1998b.

29. Huttenlocher and Dabholkar 1997.

30. Another recent animal example: The neurobiologist Eric Knudsen provided young barn owls with prism glasses, thus distorting their early visual experiences. This led, in turn, to permanent adult changes in the visual fields of the treated owls. He writes that "the act of learning abnormal associations early in life leaves an enduring trace . . . that enables unusual functional connections to be reestablished as needed, in adulthood, even when the associations represented by these connections have not been used for an extended period of time." (Knudsen 1998, p. 1,531).

31. Benes et al. 1993; see also Paus et al. 1999. There are two caveats to this claim. First, the study only goes through the seventh decade of life. I predict that the finding of continued new myelination will be extended as our lifespan increases. Second, Benes et al. studied only one particular region of

the brain—a region of the hippocampus. Not all regions of the brain have the same developmental pattern, but I suspect that the general finding that brain development continues throughout life will become more and more supported by future studies on a variety of brain regions.

32. The study of neuroplasticity, especially in adult humans, is in its early days. I expect that additional mechanisms of neural plasticity will be found as studies continue. For a recent example, see Byrne 1997.

33. Kirkwood et al. 1996; Wang et al. 1995; Singer 1995; Sugita 1996.

34. This finding fits nicely with work showing a change in cortical representation of monkeys trained to repeatedly use the middle finger of one hand (Travis 1992; Elbert et al. 1995).

35. Cohen et al. 1997; Sterr et al. 1998.

36. Pons 1996; Sadato et al. 1996.

37. Baharloo et al. related the development of perfect pitch in musicians to early musical training (Baharloo et al. 1998).

38. For a discussion of how earlier physiologists interpreted the phenomenon, see Grosz 1994.

39. Aglioti et al. 1994; Yang et al. 1994; Elbert et al. 1997.

40. Elbert et al. 1994; Kaas 1998. The explanations of phantom limb pain are complicated. See Flor et al. 1995; Knecht et al. 1996; Montoya et al. 1997.

41. Such knowledge has stimulated the development of training programs for those who have lost the use of limbs due to stroke. Some programs include verbal as well as physical interventions, again suggesting that the world outside the body can help shape the body's interior (Taub et al. 1993; Taub et al. 1994).

42. Arnstein 1997, p. 179.

43. For analyses of embodiment during pregnancy and of the effects of new technologies of fetal visualization on the embodiment of pregnancy, see Young 1990, chapter 9, and Rapp 1997.

44. Elman et al. 1996, pp. 354, 365.

45. Elman and colleagues acknowledge their intellectual debt to other systems theorists. Clearly, thought has converged from many intellectual locations toward the idea of dynamic systems development.

These days some psychologists and many neurobiologists have collapsed the distinction between body and mind. One contributor to Loveweb writes: "The only reason we use psychological language intentions, goals, motives, plans) at all is that we don't know how to talk about these states in neurophysiological terms . . . Environmentalists and interactionists who believe that social/cultural/contextual influences cannot, in principle, be reduced to biological influences are using discourse that is incommensurate with science." Other psychologists disagree with such bio-imperialism. One respondent to this entry writes: "The key point about 'psychological language' is that it formalizes the way in which conscious humans have evolved to carve up the firm realities of the world of inner personal awareness and its imperfect) social exchange. . . . What we call objective 'scientific' observation and thought are parasitic on the capacity to share subjective experiences. . . . And it's only because we can eventually and appreciably relate physical descriptions of brains, genes, etc. back to experiential accounts that the former can tell us anything with human usefulness." For a feminist analysis of mind, body, and cognitive psychology, see Wilson 1998. In this chapter I use the words *psyche* and *mind* interchangeably. Traditionally, according to the OED (online), *psyche* has meant "the animating principle in man and other living beings . . . in distinction from its material vehicle, the soma or body"; in psychology the word has meant "the conscious and unconscious mind and emotion, esp. as influencing the whole person."

46. West and Fenstermaker 1995, p. 21.

47. West and Zimmerman 1987.

48. West and Fenstermaker 1995; Alarcón et al. 1998; Akiba et al. 1999; Hammonds 1994.

49. The study of human development over the entire life cycle has come into its own in the past twenty or so years. For a thorough review, see Elder 1998.

50. For more on the psychoanalytic approach, see Fast 1993; Magee and Miller 1997.

51. Jacklin and Reynolds 1993. Lott and Maluso write: "What appears to be central to all social learning perspectives, and the unifying factor in otherwise differing approaches, is the use of general learning principles to explain human social behavior" (Lott and Maluso 1993, p. 100). For a theory combining learning and cognitive approaches as well as emphasizing gender as a lifelong accomplishment, see Bussey and Bandura 1998.

52. Kessler and McKenna 1978.

53. One exception is the visionary work of Kessler and McKenna (1978), who provided a mature theory of gender construction at a time when thinking about the social construction of gender was in its infancy. See also Beall and Sternberg 1993; Gergen and Davis 1997.

54. Magee and Miller 1997, p. xiv.

55. The several process or systems approaches to the study of human development differ in detail, but none address gender at much length. See Grotevant 1987; Wapner and Demick 1998; and Gottlieb et al. 1998.

56. Fogel and Thelen 1987, p. 756.

57. Ibid., p. 757.

58. Ibid.

59. The psychologist Esther Thelen and her colleagues have applied these ideas to the development of basic motor skills in infants. Traditionally, psychologists believe that infants develop through a series of stages, in which

neuromuscular development precedes the acquisition of new abilities such as crawling or walking. Traditionalists presume that neuromuscular development proceeds according to a gene-driven developmental plan. In contrast, Thelen offers evidence that neuromuscular connections needed for walking are present at birth, but that infants don't walk because other aspects of their support structure—bone and muscle strength, for example—are not developed enough to support the body's weight. Infant crawling, for example, is not "an inevitable human stage" but "an ad hoc solution to the problem of getting desired distant objects discovered by individual infants, given a particular level of strength and postural control" (Thelen 1995, p. 91). Thelen does not find the emphasis on individuality at odds with species similarities. She writes: "Because humans also share anatomy and common biomechanical . . . constraints, solutions to common motor problems also converge. We all discover walking rather than hopping (although our gait styles are individual and unique)" (p. 91). These latter particularities have developed as part of the child's prior movements in interaction with the environment.

Thelen and her colleagues see developmental change "as a series of states of stability, instability and phase shifts" (p. 84). Knowing when such phase shifts or periods of instability are under way can be important for both physical and mental therapy, since these are periods when behaviors have a greater possibility of change. The technical term for such stabilization is *canalization*, a word C. H. Waddington first applied to embryological development, but a number of developmental psychologists now apply it to the development of behavior. Thelen uses a Waddington-style diagram of canalization to illustrate her point. See also Gottlieb 1991, 1997; Gottlieb et al. 1998; and Waddington 1957. Change can occur throughout a lifetime and is always accompanied by the destabilization of a current system, followed by a period of instability—a phase of exploration—and ultimately the settling in of a new pattern.

The infant lives in a rich environment, absorbing information from sight, sound, touch, taste, and muscle, joint, and skin receptors that register the constant changes imbibed by an active body. Along with a growing number of developmental psychologists, Thelen rejects a dualism between structure and function. Instead, "repeated cycles of perception and action give rise to new forms of behavior without preexisting mental or genetic structures" (p. 93). Thelen lists six goals for a developmental theory: "1. To understand the origins of novelty. 2. To reconcile global regularities with local variability, complexity, and context-specificity. 3. To integrate developmental data at many levels of explanation. 4. To provide a biologically plausible yet nonreductionist account of the development of behavior. 5. To understand how local processes lead to global outcomes. 6. To establish a theoretical basis for generating and interpreting empirical research" (Thelen and Smith 1994, p. xviii).

60. For an in-depth treatment, see Fogel et al. 1997. Other studies fit

well into Fogel's theories, theories that attract me because emotion can be seen to develop as a system that is at the same time physiological and relational. See, for example, Dawson et al. 1992. Jerome Kagan and his colleagues correlated individual differences in temperament found in very young infants with the subsequent development of childhood and adult personality traits. In their view, temperament emerges as a component of nervous activity that, just as with smile development, the child and its environment transform into a recognizable pattern of behavior. For example, Kagan proposes the temperamental category *inhibited,* which develops from "very low motor activity and minimal crying in response to unfamiliar events at four months and sociable, fearless behavior in response to discrepant events at one and two years of age" (Kagan 1994, p. 49). He believes that the motor activity of newborns is the product of complex genetic and environmental interactions. The terminology used here can very confusing. Researchers, reporters, and laypeople often confuse terms such as *genetic, biological,* and *inborn.* Technically, a genetic cause would be one form of biological difference. Something inborn could be inherited in the DNA, or it could result from something that affected the fetus in utero. The term *environment* could also refer to events in utero. For example, infection with the German measles virus can cause permanent damage to a developing fetus. This damage is environmental rather than genetic, but it is also biological, because it interferes with embryonic development. The term *environment* can also refer to postbirth effects resulting from parental reinforcement or modeling, peer interactions, and the like. "Development," he suggests, "is a cooperative mission, and no behavior is a first-order, direct product of genes" (Kagan 1994, p. 37).

Kagan offers a systematic account to what every mother claims to know: Children have different temperaments from the moment of birth. Individual personality traits develop and refine over the life cycle. Herein lie two important contributions to the study of human sexuality. First, individual variability is at least as important as belonging to a particular category such as male or female; and second, behavioral profiles (personalities) develop over the entire life cycle. A particular early pattern does not necessarily become a specific later one. The vast majority of researchers in this field study group differences; those critical of such an approach argue that group difference studies erase variability within groups, variability that is often as great or greater than between-group difference. Furthermore, such an approach fixes the categories. For example, the idea of "the woman" emerges rather than more differentiated categories, such as "the white, middle class woman in her fifth decade." See discussions by Lewis 1975; Hare-Mustin and Marecek 1994; Kitzinger 1994; James 1997; and Chodorow 1995. Lott and Maluso note that gender is a complex category because it is always part of a complex that includes race, class, and individual experiences (family, sibling order, etc.). This makes gender a fairly unreliable predictor of behavior. They write: "our gender prophecies based on stereotyped expressions often fail, particularly in situations/contexts where other social categories or personal attributes are more salient or relevant. Our social institutions continue, nevertheless, to strongly support the stereotypes and to generalize behavior, thereby maintaining gender inequities in power and privilege" (Lott and Maluso 1993, p. 100). See also Valsiner 1987 for a detailed evaluation of theories in developmental psychology.

Kagan does examine sex differences. He reported that about 15 percent of girls who were inhibited at nine and fourteen months became very fearful by twenty-one months of age, while very few low-reactive boys became more timid with time. He presumes (with some evidence) that minimal sex differences in personality became exaggerated over time because "parents unconsciously treat sons and daughters in different ways and produce the larger number of older fearful girls" (Kagan 1994, p. 263).

61. Of the psychologists cited in the coming paragraphs, Sandra Bem and Barrie Thorne are outspoken feminists. I do not know the political outlook of the other scholars whose work I use here.

62. Fagot et al. 1986.

63. Infants as young as nine months can perceive the difference between adult male and female faces, but their ability to label others or self does not develop until some time later (Fagot and Leinbach 1993). Fagot and Leinbach rated behaviors according to types of toys chosen (e.g., dolls vs. transportation toys), communication with adults, and levels of aggression. By the time the child reached 2.25 years, the parents of early and late labelers no longer differed in the frequency of positive and negative responses to sex-stereotyped play (Fagot and Leinbach 1989, p. 663). On sex-stereotyped parental responses to newborn children, see Karraker et al. 1995.

64. Fagot and Leinbach 1989, p. 672. Levy (1989) found that certain types of parental interactions correlated with greater gender schematization in children; girls with mothers who worked outside the home had greater gender flexibility, as did children with fewer siblings. Boys who watched entertainment TV had a greater knowledge of sex roles, while girls who watched educational television had greater gender role flexibility. Thus many factors contribute to the strength and rigidity of gender role schemas in young children aged 2.8 to 5 years old.

65. Developmental psychologists use the term *gender constancy* to describe a child's ability to tell a person's sex regardless of clues such as dress or hairstyle. There is dispute about when and how such gender constancy develops (Bem 1989).

66. Bem (1989) used photos of children with short hair, but gave them gender-appropriate wigs when she created the gender-typical photos. See also de Marneffe 1997.

67. Martin and Little 1990, pp. 1,436, 1,437; Martin 1994.

68. Martin et al. 1990. For additional interactions between cognitive maturation and socialization experiences in middle childhood, see Serbin et al. 1993.

69. Thorne 1993, pp. 3–4. In 1998, Judith Rich Harris's book caused a big media flap because she argued the importance of peer socialization. She makes an extreme statement of what Thorne and many other psychologists have known for years. See Harris 1998. The September 7, 1998, issue of *Newsweek* devoted its cover story to the book. For recent research on intrafamilial effects of sibling order, gender, and parental attitudes, see McHale et al. 1999.

70. Thorne is far from alone in questioning the utility of continued research on difference. See, e.g., James 1997.

71. García-Coll et al. (1997) suggest seven new research approaches: 1) "Focus on the social and psychological processes that become packaged as 'race,' ethnicity, social class and/or gender;" 2) "Examine how contexts shape children's understandings of social categories;" 3) "Examine the intersection and boundaries of social categories in children's lives;" 4) "Examine how children participate in constructing, using, and resisting social categories;" 5) "Examine how social identities influence children's goals, values, self-concepts, and behavioral engagement;" 6) "Study 'race,' ethnicity, social class and gender as developmental phenomena;" 7) "Study the categories themselves."

72. Lorber 1994, p. 32; emphasis in original. Lorber is also careful to point out that gender is not the only socially produced dichotomy; she focuses additionally on race and class. Presumably, subjective identities are not acquired additively, but gender comes to mean different things within the added matrices of race and class. Psychologists and sociologists concentrate on gender for two positive reasons: The gender dichotomy becomes established very early on, and it is a major component of the way many, if not all, cultures produce social organization. There are, of course, also negative reasons— racism and classism—for the relative lack of study of the development of race and class dichotomy in a society in which these aspects of human existence also loom large. See also West and Fenstermaker 1995.

73. See, for example, Epstein 1997; Lott 1997.

74. Lorber 1994; Fiske 1991; Bem 1993; Halley 1994; Jacklin 1989.

75. In a debate among feminist theorists, the political scientist Mary Hawkesworth wrote that "discussions of gender in history, language, literature and the arts, education, the media, politics, psychology, religion, medicine and science, society, law and the workplace have become staples of contemporary feminist scholarship" (Hawkesworth 1997). I agree that all of these intellectual arenas have the potential to contribute to the project of understanding the body as a biosociocultural system. Here I draw examples from the fields of sociology and history.

76. From Katherine B. Davis's work on women in prison (see chapter 6),

to present-day studies on the frequency of homosexual interactions in urban and rural settings, social scientists have wanted information with which to guide important social policy decisions. Are crime and sex related? Can we obtain realistic models of sexual activities and networks that can help us stop the spread of AIDS and other sexually transmitted diseases? Is teenage pregnancy really on the rise, and if so, why? Getting answers to these questions is not easy, and whatever conclusions we *can* reach are always qualified by the limits on information gained through mass survey methods (di Mauro 1995, Ericksen 1999).

77. Hacking 1986.

78. Delaney 1991. Or what about men who will not use the word *sex* to describe homosexual encounters? Instead they have sex with their wives and "fool around" with men (Cotton 1994).

79. Garber (1995) discusses bisexuality. Other discussions of problems with using oversimplified categories of sexual preference may be found in (Rothblatt 1995; Burke 1996).

80. Diamond 1993, p. 298. Such homosexuality is not necessarily "displacement activity." One need only read in the genre of prison biography to find men who genuinely fall in love in prison, but who have a heterosexual love life on the outside. For a moving account of falling in love with other men in prison, see Berkman 1912. Berkman, Emma Goldman's longtime lover, writes of his deep feelings developed on two occasions while in prison. It is hard to interpret these as merely a sexual outlet. For a more modern account, see Puig 1991.

81. The fear that naming categories and asking people whether they fit in them will actually *create* the behaviors in question lies at the root of the political difficulties that sexologists (here I speak primarily of sociologists and psychologists who study human sexual behavior) encounter in obtaining funding to do such studies (Fausto-Sterling 1992a; Laumann, Michael, et al. 1994). Mainstream scholars as well as politicians view the study of human sexual behavior with more than a little suspicion. In the 1960s no academic journal would publish Masters and Johnson's original work on the physiology of the human sexual response (Masters and Johnson 1966). More recently, Cynthia Jayne, a clinical psychologist in private practice, could not convince a major psychology journal to accept her study on female orgasm and sexual satisfaction although a sexology journal took it right away. Since their work is often attacked as scandalous, sex researchers have adopted a defensive posture. This fact has contributed significantly to the intellectual shape of the field. As Jayne writes: "There then exists a narrow path which sex researchers must navigate between responding to inappropriate criticism and generating the critiques that ensure the health and continued professional growth of the field" (Jayne 1986, p. 2). See also Irvine 1990a, 1990b.

82. Elder 1998, p. 969.

83. Weeks 1981b. Weeks does not claim these as the only categories, but thinks of them more as a set of guidelines.

84. Evans (1993) writes that "state penetration of civil society in consumer capitalism means that instead of capital domination being grounded in a civil society colonised to the ends of reproducing labour, now civil society is colonised by the state to the ends of reproducing consumers, 'men and women whose needs are permanently redirected to fit the needs of the market', in their obsessive pursuit of sexuality, 'the medium through which they seek to define their personalities and to be conscious of themselves" (p. 64).

85. Weeks 1981b, p. 14.

86. For a detailed historical account of the making of gay male private spaces and culture in New York City, see Chauncey 1994.

87. See, for example, Kates 1995. Leslie Feinberg presents a fascinating history of people who cross-dressed and assumed cross-gendered identities, pointing out that in more than a few cases, individuals who transgressed gender divides also engaged in other revolutionary actions: peasant revolts, religious rebellions, and more. Her book breaks new ground, painstakingly stitching together fragments of history. Although in the genre of "recovered history" typical of the beginning of new social movements, it presents a challenge to historians to look more deeply into the cases she brings to light (Feinberg 1996).

88. For the importance of technology in the emergence of transsexualism and contemporary definitions of gender, see Hausman 1995. For the history of cosmetic surgery more generally, consult Haiken 1997. Both books illustrate the importance of technology in the processes of producing sex and gender.

89. The medical anthropologist Margaret Lock concurs with this point when she writes that most accounts of the body in culture do not "take into account the powerful transformations of the material brought about by technoscience or consider the impact this has on subjectivity, representation and the politics of everyday life" (Lock 1997, p. 269).

90. My attempt to provide a visual map of systems of human sexual development was inspired by the work of the science studies scholar Peter J. Taylor. The first working principle is that social and natural processes cannot be separated. The second is that quite different modes of inquiry offer important insight into complex puzzles. Taylor applies a systems approach to two different examples, one involving ecosystems and the other a mental illness—severe depression. Consider the process of soil erosion in a Mexican village. Taylor says it can be understood only by the simultaneous consideration of the region's social and political history, the character of agriculture and ecology ("natural" factors such as rainfall, soil structure, etc.), the nature of local social and economic institutions, and regional demographic changes. Traditionally, scholars study each of these factors as if they were independent enti-

ties. Taylor, however, represents them as horizontal parallel lines crisscrossed by vertical hen tracks. The hen tracks represent events such as regulation of goat grazing or the use of terracing, which change the nature of the parallel lines. An accurate picture of the current situation can be grasped only by looking at all four lines and their interconnections (Taylor 1995, 1997, 1998a, and 1998b).

91. Although he did not use the stacking-doll metaphor, many years ago the embryologist Paul Weiss used a diagram of development that resembles a cross section of a Russian doll. He included more of the organismal layers than I do, but the idea is quite similar (Weiss 1959). Others have used more complex diagrams to visualize human development. See, for example, Wapner and Demick 1998, fig. 13.1. They use Dewey and Bentley's notion of transaction to describe the "organism in environment" system, which they characterize in terms of levels of integration. These range from activities within the individual organism to what Wapner and Demick call the "person in the world system" (p. 767).

92. Dewey and Bentley use the words *extradermal* and *intradermal* to communicate this idea. They also are very wary of the idea of "the mind." They write: "The 'mind' as 'actor,' still in use in present-day psychologies and sociologies, is the old self-acting 'soul' with its immortality stripped off, grown dessicated and crotchety. 'Mind' or 'mental' as a preliminary word in casual phrasing is a sound word to indicate a region or at least a general locality in need of investigation; as such it is unobjectionable. 'Mind,' 'faculty,' 'I.Q.' or what not as an actor in charge of behavior is a charlatan, and 'brain' as a substitute for such a 'mind' is worse. Such words insert a name in place of a problem" (Dewey and Bentley 1949, pp. 131–32). I use the idea of mind or psyche as a placeholder for processes we can examine, but not as descriptions of a mechanism.

93. Of course there are smaller units within the cells—organelles, molecules, etc. But the cell is the last of the independently functioning unit systems. A nucleus and its genes cannot create an organism outside a cell.

94. Harding 1995.

95. This is a paraphrase of "Primatology Is Politics by Other Means," Haraway 1986, p. 77.

BIBLIOGRAPHY

1935. Report of the second conference on the standardisation of sex hormones. *Quarterly Bulletin of the Health Organization*: 618–30.

1992. IAAF joins critics of Olympic sex testing. *Atlanta Constitution*, p. G2. Feb. 12.

1992. Science: Sexing the sportswomen. *Daily Telegraph* (London), July 20.

1993. Five failed controversial Olympics sex test. *Science* 261 (July 2): 27.

1993. Five female athletes had male genes. *The Herald* (Glasgow), p. 4. June 18.

1994. American Council on Surgery training tape number 1613. Surgical reconstruction of ambiguous genitalia in female children.

1999. Kuwaiti women likely to get the vote. *Providence Journal* (Providence, RI), p. A12. July 5.

Aaronson, I. A., M. A. Cakmak, et al. 1997. Defects of the testosterone biosynthetic pathway in boys with hypospadias. *Journal of Urology* 157 (May): 1884–88.

Abdullah, M. A., S. Katugampola, et al. 1991. Ambiguous genitalia: Medical, socio-cultural and religious factors affecting management in Saudi Arabia. *Annals of Tropical Paediatrics* 11: 343–48.

Aberle, S., and G. W. Corner 1953 . *Twenty-five years of sex research: History of the National Research Council Committee for Research in Problems of Sex, 1922–1947.* Philadelphia: W. B. Saunders.

Abir-Am, P. 1982. The discourse of physical power and biological knowledge in the 1930's: A reappraisal of the Rockefeller Foundation's 'policy' in molecular biology. *Social Studies of Science* 12: 341–82.

Aboitiz, F. 1998. To normalize or not to normalize overall size? *Behavioral and Brain Sciences* 21(3): 327–28.

Aboitiz, F., E. Rodriguez, et al. 1996. Age-related changes in the fibre composition of the human corpus callosum: Sex differences. *NeuroReport* 7: 1761–64.

Aboitiz, F., A. B. Scheibel, et al. 1992a. Individual differences in brain asymmetries and fiber composition in the human corpus callosum. *Brain Research* 598: 154–61 .

———. 1992b. Morphometry of the sylvian fissure and the corpus callosum, with emphasis on sex differences. *Brain* 115: 1521–41.

Abramovich, D. R., I. A. Davidson, A. Longstaff, and C. K. Pearson. 1987. Sexual differentiation of the human midtrimester brain. *European Journal of Obstetrics, Gynecology, and Reproductive Biology* 25: 7–14.

Abu-Arafeh, W., B. Chertin, et al. 1998. One-stage repair of hypospadias—experience with 856 cases. *European Journal of Urology* 34(4): 365–7.

Adkins, R. 1999. Where sex is born(e): Intersexed births and the social urgency of heterosexuality. *Journal of Medical Humanities* 20: 117–30.

Adkins-Regan, E. 1988. Sex hormones and sexual orientation in animals. *Psychobiology* 16(4): 335–47.

Adkins-Regan, E., O. Orgeur, et al. 1989. Sexual differentiation of reproductive behavior in pigs: Defeminizing effects of prepubertal estradiol. *Hormones and Behavior* 23: 290–303.

Aglioti, S., A. Bonazzi, et al. 1994. Phantom lower limbs as a perceptual marker of neural plasticity in the mature human brain. *Proceedings of the Royal Society of London Series B* 255(1344): 273–78.

Akiba, D., N. Gardner, et al. 1999. Children of color and children from immigrant families: The development of social identities, school engagement and interethnic social attribution during middle childhood. Southwest Regional Conference on Child Development, Albuquerque.

Alarcón, O., L. A. Szalacha, et al. 1998. The color of my skin: An index to measure children's awareness of and satisfaction with their skin color. Wellesley, MA: Wellesley College.

Alberch, P. 1989. The logic of monsters: Evidence for internal constraint in development and evolution. *Geobios* 12 (memoire special): 21–57.

Alizai, N. K., D. F. M. Thomas, R. I. Lilford, et al. 1999. Feminizing genitoplasty for congenital adrenal hyperplasia: What happens at puberty? *The Journal of Urology* 161, 1588–91.

Allen, B., J. Qin, et al. 1994. Persuasive communities: A longitudinal analysis of references in the Philosophical Transactions of the Royal Society, 1665–1990. *Social Studies of Science* 24(2): 279–310.

Allen, E., C. H. Danforth, et al. 1939. *Sex and internal secretions.* Baltimore, MD: Williams and Wilkins.

Allen, E., and E. A. Doisey. 1923. An ovarian hormone: Preliminary report on its localization, extraction, and partial purification and action in test animals. *Journal of the American Medical Association* 81(10): 819–21.

Allen, G. E. 1975. *Life science in the twentieth century.* New York: Wiley.

———. 1978. *Thomas Hunt Morgan: The man and his science.* Princeton, NJ: Princeton University Press.

Allen, L. E., B. E. Hardy, et al. 1982. The surgical management of the enlarged clitoris. *Journal of Urology* 128: 351–54.

Allen, L. S., M. F. Richey, et al. 1991. Sex differences in the corpus callosum of the living human being. *Journal of Neuroscience* 11(4): 933–42.

Amandusson, Å., O. Hermanson, et al. 1995. Estrogen receptor-like immunoreactivity in the medullary and spinal dorsal horn of the female rat. *Neuroscience Letters* 196: 25–28.

Ammini, A. C., J. Pandey, et al. 1994. Human female phenotypic development:

Role of fetal ovaries. *Journal of Clinical Endocrinology and Metabolism* 79(2): 604–8.

Anderson, C. 1992. Tests on athletes can't always find line between males and females. *Washington Post*, January 6, A3.

Anderson, S. C. 1996. Otto Weininger's masculine utopia. *German Studies Review* 19(3): 433–53.

Andrews, H. O., R. Nauth-Misir, et al. 1998. Iatrogenic hypospadias—a preventable injury? *Spinal Cord* 36(3): 177–80.

Angier, N. 1994. Male hormone molds women, too, in mind and body. *New York Times*, May 3, C1, C13 .

———. 1997a. New respect for estrogen's influence. *New York Times*, June 24, C1ff.

———. 1997b. Sexual identity not pliable after all, report says. *New York Times*, March 14, 1ff.

———. 1999. *Woman, an intimate geography.* New York: Houghton Mifflin.

Anonymous. 1917. The internal secretion of the reproductive glands. *The Lancet* (November 3): 687.

———. 1994a. Be open and honest with sufferers. *British Medical Journal*: 1041–42.

———. 1994b. Once a dark secret. *British Medical Journal* 305: 542.

———. 1995a. "Gay gene" research links homosexuality in males with heredity. *Providence Journal*, October 31, (Providence, RI), A8.

———. 1995b. Schizophrenia gene search getting closer, say studies. *Providence Journal* (Providence, RI), A8.

Arai, C., Y. Murakami, et al. 1994. Androgen enhances degeneration in the developing preoptic area: Apoptosis in the anteroventral periventricular nucleus. *Hormones and Behavior* 28(4): 313–19.

Arendash, G. W., and R. A. Gorski 1982. Enhancement of sexual behavior in female rats by neonatal transplantation of brain tissue from males. *Science* 217: 1276–78.

Armstrong, C. N. 1966. Treatment of wrongly assigned sex. *British Medical Journal* 2: 1255–56.

Arnold, A. P., and M. Breedlove. 1985. Organizational and activational effects of sex steroids on brain and behaviors: A reanalysis. *Hormones and Behavior* 19: 469–98.

Arnstein, P. M. 1997. The neuroplastic phenomenon: A physiologic link between chronic pain and learning. *Journal of Neuroscience Nursing* 29(3): 179–86.

Ascheim, S., and B. Zondek. 1927. Hypophsenvorderlappenhormon und Ovarialhormon in Harn von Schwangeren. *Klinische Wochenschrift* 6: 1322.

Asopa, H. S. 1998. Newer concepts in the management of hypospadias and its complications. *Annals of the Royal College of Surgeons of England* 80(3): 161–8.

Atkins, D., ed. 1998. *Looking queer: Body image and identity in lesbian, bisexual, gay and transgender communities.* New York: Harrington Park Press (Haworth Press).

Azziz, R., R. Mulaikal, et al. 1986. Congenital adrenal hyperplasia: Long-term results following vaginal reconstruction. *Fertility and Sterility* 46(6): 1011–14.

Baharloo, S., P. A. Johnston, et al. 1998. Absolute pitch: An approach for identification of genetic and nongenetic components. *American Journal of Human Genetics* 62: 224–31.

Bailey, J. M., and R. C. Pillard. 1991. A genetic study of male sexual orientation. *Archives of General Psychiatry* 48 (December): 1089–96.

Bailey, J. M., R. C. Pillard, et al. 1993. Heritable factors influence sexual orientation in women. *Archives of General Psychiatry* 50 (March): 217–23.

Bailez, M. M., J. P. Gearheart, et al. 1992. Vaginal reconstruction after initial construction of the external genitalia in girls with salt-wasting adrenal hyperplasia. *Journal of Urology* 148: 680–84 .

Bain, J., E. S. E. Hafez, et al., eds. 1978. *Andrology: Basic and clinical aspects of male reproduction and infertility. Progress in Reproductive Biology.* Basel, Switz.: S. Karger.

Baker, L. D. 1994. The location of Franz Boas within the African-American struggle. *Critique of Anthropology* 14(2): 199–217.

Baker, S. 1981. Psychological management of intersex children. *Pediatric and Adolescent Endocrinology* 8: 261–69.

Bakker, J. 1996. Sexual differentiation of the brain and partner preference in the male rat. *Endocrinology and Reproduction*. Rotterdam, Erasmus University of Rotterdam: 251.

Bakker, J., T. Brand, et al. 1993. Hormonal regulation of adult partner preference behavior in neonatally ATD-treated male rats. *Behavioral Neuroscience* 107(3): 480–87.

Bakker, J., J. van Ophemert, et al. 1993. Organization of partner preference and sexual behavior and its nocturnal rhythmicity in male rats. *Behavioral Neuroscience* 107(6): 1049–59.

———. 1994. A semiautomated test apparatus for studying partner preference behavior in the rat. *Psychoneuroendocrinology* 56(3): 597–601.

———. 1995a. Endogenous reproductive hormones and nocturnal rhythms in partner preference and sexual behavior of ATD-treated male rats. *Behavioral Neuroendocrinology* 62: 396–405.

———. 1995b. Postweaning housing conditions and partner preference and sexual behavior of neonatally ATD-treated male rats. *Psychoneuroendocrinology* 20(3): 299–310.

Ball, G. F. 1993. The neural integration of environmental information by seasonally breeding birds. *American Zoologist* 33: 185–200.

Balmer, B. 1996. The political cartography of the human genome project. *Social Studies of Science* 4(3): 249–82.

Balthazart, J., O. Tlemçani, et al. 1996. Do sex differences in the brain explain sex differences in hormonal induction of reproductive behavior? What 25 years of research on the Japanese quail tells us. *Hormones and Behavior* 30: 627–61.

Barad, K. 1996. Meeting the universe halfway: Realism and social constructivism without contradiction. In *Feminism, science and the philosophy of science*, ed. L. H.

Nelson and J. Nelson. Dordrecht: Netherlands. Kluwer Academic Publishers, pp. 161–94.

Bardin, W. C., and J. F. Catterall. 1981. Testosterone: a major determinant of extragenital sexual dimorphism. *Science* 211: 1285–94.

Barinaga, M. 1996. Social status sculpts activity of crayfish neurons. *Science* 271 (January 19): 290–91.

———. 1998. No-New-Neurons Dogma Loses Ground. *Science* 279 (March 27): 2041–42.

Baum, M. J. 1979. Differentiation of coital behavior in mammals: A comparative analysis. *Neuroscience and Behavioral Reviews* 3: 265–84.

———. 1990. Frank Beach's research on the sexual differentiation of behavior and his struggle with the organizational hypothesis. *Neuroscience and Biobehavioral Reviews* 14: 201–6.

Beach, F. A. 1938. Sex reversals in the mating pattern of the rat. *Journal of Genetic Psychology* 53: 329–34.

———. 1941. Female mating behavior shown by male rats after administration of testosterone proprionate. *Endocrinology* 29: 409–12.

———. 1942a. Execution of the complete masculine copulatory pattern by sexually receptive female rats. *Journal of Genetic Psychology* 60: 137–142.

———. 1942b. Analysis of factors involved in the arousal, maintenance and manifestation of sexual excitement in male animals. *Psychosomatic Medicine* 4: 173–98.

———. 1942c. Analysis of the stimuli adequate to elicit mating behavior in the sexually inexperienced rat. *Journal of Comparative Psychology* 33(2): 163–208.

———. 1942d. Comparison of copulatory behavior of male rats raised in isolation, cohabitation and segregation. *Journal of Genetic Psychology* 60: 121–36.

———. 1942e. Effects of testosterone propionate upon the copulatory behavior of sexually inexperienced male rats. *Journal of Comparative Psychology* 33(2): 227–48.

———. 1942f. Male and female mating behavior in prepuberally castrated female rats treated with androgens. *Endocrinology* 31: 73–678.

———. 1943. Effects of injury to the cerebral cortex upon the display of masculine and feminine mating behavior in female rats. *Journal of Comparative Psychology* 36(3): 169–200.

———. 1947. A review of physiolgical and psychological studies of sexual behaviors in mammals. *Physiological Reviews* 27: 240–307.

———. 1947–48. Sexual behavior in animals and man. *Harvey Lectures* 43: 254–80.

———. 1961. Sex differences in the physiological bases of mating behavior in mammals. In *The Physiology of the Emotions*, ed. A. Simon, C. Herbert, and R. Straus. Springfield, IL: Charles Thomas, 151–62.

———. 1965. Preface. In *Sex and Behavior*, ed. F. A. Beach. New York: Wiley.

———. 1966. Ontogeny of coitus-related reflexes in the female guinea pig. *Proceedings of the National Academy of Science* 56: 526–33.

————. 1968. The control of mounting behavior. In *Reproduction and Sexual Behavior*, ed. M. Diamond. Bloomington: Indiana University Press, 83–131.

————. 1971. Hormonal factors controlling the differentiation, development, and display of copulatory behavior in the ramstergig and related species. In *The Biopsychology of Development*, ed. E. Tobach, L. R. Aronson, and E. Shaw. New York: Academic Press, pp. 249–96.

————. 1975. Behavioral endocrinology: An emerging discipline. *American Scientist* 63: 178–87.

————. 1976a. Sexual attractivity, proceptivity, and receptivity in female mammals. *Hormones and Behavior* 7: 105–38.

————. 1976b. Hormonal control of sex-related behavior. In *Human sexuality in four perspectives*, ed. F. A. Beach. Baltimore: Johns Hopkins University Press, 247–67.

————. 1976c. Prolonged hormone deprivation and pretest cage adaptation as factors affecting the display of lordosis by female rats. *Physiology and Behavior* 16: 807–8.

————. 1978. Confessions of an imposter. In *Pioneers in Neuroendocrinology II*, ed. J. Meites, B. T. Donovan, and S. M. McCann. New York: Plenum Press, 17–37.

————. 1981. Historical origins of modern research on hormones and behavior. *Hormones and Behavior* 15: 325–76.

————. 1985. Conceptual issues in behavioral endocrinology. In *Autobiographies in Experimental Psychology*, ed. R. Gandelman. Hillsdale, NJ: Lawrence Erlbaum, 5–17.

Beach, F. A., and G. Levinson. 1950. Effects of androgen on the glans penis and mating behavior of castrated male rats. *Journal of Experimental Zoology* 114: 159–71.

Beach, F. A., and L. P. Nucci. 1970. Long-term effects of testosterone phenylacetate on sexual morphology and behavior in castrated male rats. *Hormones and Behavior* 1: 223–34.

Beach, F. A., and R. K. Orndoff. 1974. Variation in responsiveness of female rats to ovarian hormones as a function of preceding hormone deprivation. *Hormones and Behavior* 5(3): 201–5.

Beach, F., and P. Rasquin. 1942. Masculine copulatory behavior in intact and castrated female rats. *Endocrinology* 31(4): 393–409.

Beall, A. E., and R. J. Sternberg, eds. 1993. *The psychology of gender.* New York: Guilford Press.

Bean, R. B. 1906. Some racial peculiarities of the negro brain. *American Journal of Anatomy* 5: 353–415 .

Beatty, W. W., ed. 1992. Gonadal hormones and sex differences in nonreproductive behaviors. *Handbook of Behavioral Neurobiology.* New York: Plenum Press, pp. 85–117.

Begley, S. 1995. Gray Matters. *Newsweek*, March 27, 48–54.

Beheshti, M., B. E. Hardy, et al. 1983. Gender assignment in male pseudoher-maphrodite children. *Urology* 22(6): 604–7.

Bell, A. D., and S. Variend. 1985. Failure to demonstrate sexual dimorphism of the corpus callosum in childhood. *Journal of Anatomy* 143: 143–47.

Bell, A. P., M. S. Weinberg, et al. 1981. *Sexual preference: its development in men and women*. Bloomington: Indiana University Press.

Bell, B. W. 1916. *The sex-complex: A study of the relationships of the internal secretions to the female characteristics and functions in health and disease*. New York: William Wood and Company.

Bellinger, M. F. 1993. Subtotal de-epithelialization and partial concealment of the glans clitoris: a modification to improve the cosmetic results of feminizing genitoplasty. *Journal of Urology* 150: 651–53.

Bem, S. L. 1974. The measurement of psychological androgeny. *Journal of Consulting and Clinical Psychology* 42(2): 155–62.

———. 1989. Genital knowledge and gender constancy. *Child Development* 60: 649–62.

———. 1993. *The lenses of gender: Transforming the debate on sexual inequality*. New Haven: Yale University Press.

Benbow, C. P., and D. Lubinski. 1993. *Psychological profiles of the mathematically talented: Some sex differences and evidence supporting their biological basis*. Chichester, U.K.: Wiley, pp. 44–78.

———. 1997. Psychological profiles of the mathematically talented: some sex differences and evidence supporting their biological basis. In *Women, men and gender: Ongoing debates*, ed. M. R. Walsh. New Haven: Yale University Press, 274–82.

Bender, B. G., R. J. Harmon, et al. 1995. Psychosocial adaptation of 39 adolescents with sex chromosome abnormalities. *Pediatrics* 96(2): 302–8.

Benes, F. M., M. Turtle, et al. 1993. Myelination of a key relay zone in the hippo-campal formation occurs in the human brain during childhood, adolescence and adulthood. *Archives of General Psychiatry* 51 (June): 477–84.

Benjamin, H. 1945. Eugen Steinach, 1861–1944: A life of research. *Scientific Monthly* 61: 427–42.

Ben-lih, L., and L. Kai. 1953. True hermaphroditism: Report of two cases. *Chinese Medical Journal* 71: 148–54.

Ben-lih, L., H. Shu-Chieh, et al. 1959. True hermaphroditism: A case report. *Chinese Medical Journal* 78: 449–51.

Benson, K. R., J. Maienschein, et al., eds. 1991. *The expansion of American biology*. New Brunswick, NJ: Rutgers University Press.

Berenbaum, S. A., and M. Hines. 1992. Early androgens are related to childhood sex-typed toy preferences. *Psychological Science* 3(3): 203–6.

Berenbaum, S. A., and S. M. Resnick. 1997. Early androgen effects on aggression in children and adults with congenital adrenal hyperplasia. *Psychoneuroendocrinology* 22(7): 505–15.

Berenson, A., A. Heger, et al. 1991. Appearance of the hymen in newborns. *Pediatrics* 87(4): 458–65.

———. 1992. Appearance of the hymen in prepubertal girls. *Pediatrics* 89(3): 387–94.

Berg, I. 1963. Change of assigned sex at puberty. *The Lancet* 2: 1216–17.

Berg, R., and G. Berg. 1983. Penile malformation, gender identity and sexual orientation. *Acta psychiatrica scandinavia* 68: 154–66.

Berkman, A. 1912. *Prison memoirs of an anarchist.* New York: Mother Earth.

Berman, L. 1921. *The glands regulating physiology.* New York: Macmillan.

Berry, R. J., and F. H. Bronson. 1992. Life history and bioeconomy of the house mouse. *Biological Reviews* 67: 519–50.

Berthold, A. A. 1849. Transplanation der Hoden. *Archiv für Anatomie und Physiologie* 42.

Bérubé, A. 1990. *Coming out under fire: A history of gay men and women in World War Two.* New York: Free Press.

Besa, E. C. 1994. Hematologic effects of androgens revisited—An alternative therapy in various hematologic conditions. *Seminars in Hematology* 31(2): 134–45.

Besnier, N. 1994. *Polynesian gender liminality through time and space.* In *Third sex third gender: beyond sexual dimorphism in culture and history,* ed. G. Herdt. New York: Zone Books, pp. 285–328.

Bin-Abbas, B., F. A. Conte, et al. 1999. Congenital hypogonadotropic hypogonadism and micropenis: Effect of testosterone treatment on adult penile size— Why sex reversal is not indicated. *Journal of Pediatrics* 134 (May): 579–83.

Birke, L. 1989. How do gender differences in behavior develop? A reanalysis of the role of early experience. *Perspectives in Ethology* 8: 215–42.

———. In press. *Feminism and the biological body.* Edinburgh: Edinburgh University Press.

Birken, L. 1988. *Consuming desire: Sexual science and the emergence of a culture of abundance.* Ithaca: Cornell University Press.

Bishop, K. M., and D. Wahlsten. 1997. Sex differences in the human corpus callosum: Myth or reality. *Neuroscience and Biobehavioral Reviews* 12: 581–601.

Bisiacchi, P., C. A. Marzi, et al. 1994. Left-right asymmetry of callosal transfer in normal human subjects. *Behavioural Brain Research* 64: 173–78.

Black, M. 1992. Mind over gender. *Elle:* 158–62.

Blackless, M., A. Charuvastra, et al. 1999. How sexually dimorphic are we? A review article. *American Journal of Human Biology* (in press).

Blakeslee, S. 1995. In brain's early growth, timetable may be crucial. *New York Times,* August 29, C1–C3.

———. 1999. New theories of depression focus on brain's two sides. *New York Times,* January 19, D2.

Bleier, R. 1984. *Science and gender: A critique of biology and its theories on women.* New York: Pergamon.

Bloom, A. 1994. The body lies. *The New Yorker* 70: 38–49.

Bly, R. 1992. *Iron John.* New York: Vintage.

Bock, G. R., and K. Ackrill, eds. 1993. *The origins and development of high ability.* Ciba Foundation Symposium. New York: Wiley.

Bohan, J. S. 1997. Regarding gender: Essentialism, constructionism, and feminist psychology. In *Toward a new psychology of gender: A reader,* ed. M. M. Gergen and S. N. Davis. New York: Routledge, pp. 31–48.

Bolin, A. 1994. Transcending and transgendering: Male-to-female transsexuals, dichotomy and diversity. In *Third sex third gender: Beyond sexual dimorphism in culture and history,* ed. G. Herdt. New York: Zone Books, pp. 447–86.

Boman, U. W., A. Möller, et al. 1998. Psychological aspects of Turner Syndrome. *Journal of Psychosomatic Obstetrics and Gynaecology* 19(1): 1–18.

Bordo, S. 1993. *Unbearable weight: Feminism, western culture, and the body.* Berkeley: University of California Press.

Borell, M. 1976. Brown-Séquard's organotherapy and its appearance in America at the end of the nineteenth century. *Bulletin of the History of Medicine* 50(3): 309–20.

———. 1978. Setting the standards for a new science: Edward Schäfer and endocrinology. *Medical History* 22: 282–90.

———. 1985. Organotherapy and the emergence of reproductive endocrinology. *Journal of the History of Biology* 18(1): 1–30.

———. 1987. Biologists and the promotion of birth control research, 1918–1938. *Journal of the History of Biology* 20(1): 51–87.

Bornstein, K. 1994. *Gender outlaw: On men, women and the rest of us.* London: Routledge.

Boswell, J. 1990. Sexual and ethical categories in premodern Europe. In *Homosexuality/heterosexuality: Concepts of sexual orientation,* ed. D. P. McWhirter, S. A. Sanders, and J. M. Reinisch. New York: Oxford University Press, 15–31.

———. 1995. *Same-sex unions in premodern Europe.* New York: Villard Books.

Bradley, S. J., G. D. Oliver, et al. 1998. Experiment of nurture: Ablatio penis at 2 months, sex reassignment at 7 months and a psychosexual follow-up in young adulthood. *Pediatrics* 102(1): e9.

Brand, T., J. Kroonen, et al. 1991. Adult partner preference and sexual behavior of male rats affected by perinatal endocrine manipulations. *Hormones and Behavior* 25: 323–41.

Brand, T., and A. K. Slob. 1991a. Neonatal organization of adult partner preference behavior in male rats. *Physiology and Behavior* 49: 107–11.

———. 1991b. On the organization of partner preference behavior in female Wistar rats. *Physiology and Behavior* 49: 549–55.

Bray, A. 1982. *Homosexuality in Renaissance England.* London: Gay Men's Press.

Brecher, E. M., and J. Brecher. 1986. Extracting valid sexological findings from severely flawed and biased population samples. *Journal of Sex Research* 22(1): 6–20.

Breedlove, S. M. 1997. Sex on the brain. *Nature* 389 (October 23): 801.

Breines, W. 1992. *Young, white and miserable: Growing up female in the fifties.* Boston: Beacon Press.

Brent, R. 1999. Functional genomics: Learning to think about gene expression data. *Current Biology* 9: 338–41.

Brewer, J. I., H. O. Jones, et al. 1952. True hermaphroditism. *Journal of the American Medical Association* 148: 431–35.

Brooten, B. J. 1996. *Love between women: Early Christian responses to female homoeroticism.* Chicago: University of Chicago Press.

Brown, C., T. J. Adler, et al. 1994. Androgen treatment decreases estrogen receptor binding in the ventromedial nucleus of the rat brain: A quantitative in vitro autoradiographic analysis. *Molecular and Cellular Neurosciences* 5(6): 549–55.

Brown, J. B., and M. P. Fryer. 1957. Hypospadias—complete construction of penis, with establishment of proper sex status after 13 years of mistaken female identity. *Postgraduate Medicine*: 489–91.

Brown-Grant, K. 1974. On "critical periods" during post-natal development of the rat. In *Endocrinologie sexuelle de la période périnatale*, ed. Forest and J. Bertrand. Paris: INSERM.

Bryden, M. P., and M. B. Bulman-Fleming. 1994. Laterality effects in normal subjects: Evidence for interhemispheric interactions. *Behavioural Brain Research* 64: 119–29.

Bryden, M. P., I. C. McManus, et al. 1994. Evaluating the empirical support for the Geschwind-Behan-Galaburda model of cerebral lateralization. *Brain and Cognition* 26: 103–67.

Buhrich, N., J. M. Bailey, et al. 1991. Sexual orientation, sexual identity and sex-dimorphic behaviors in male twins. *Behavior Genetics* 21(1): 75–96.

Bullough, V. L. 1988. Katherine Bement Davis, sex research and the Rockefeller Foundation. *Bulletin of the History of Medicine* 62: 74–89.

———. 1994. *Science in the bedroom: A history of sex research.* New York: Basic Books.

Bullough, V. L., and J. A. Brundage, eds. 1996. *Handbook of medieval sexuality.* New York: Garland Publishing.

Burke, P. 1996. *Gender shock: Exploding the myths of male and female.* New York: Doubleday.

Bussey, K., and A. Bandura. 1998. Social cognitive theory of gender development and differentiation. Manuscript.

Butler, J. 1993. *Bodies that matter: On the discursive limits of sex.* New York: Routledge.

Byne, W. 1995. Science and belief: Psychological research on sexual orientation. *Journal of Homosexuality* 28(3–4): 303–44.

Byne, W., R. Bleier, et al. 1988. Variations in human corpus callosum do not predict gender: A study using magnetic resonance imaging. *Behavioral Neuroscience* 102(2): 222–27.

Byne, W., and B. Parsons. 1993. Human sexual orientation: The biologic theories reappraised. *Archives of General Psychiatry* 50 (March): 228–39.

Byrne, J. H. 1997. Plastic plasticity. *Nature* 389 (October 23): 791–92.

Cadden, J. 1993. *Meanings of sex difference in the Middle Ages: Medicine, science and culture.* New York: Cambridge University Press.

Cahn, S. K. 1994. *Coming on strong: Gender and sexuality in 20th century women's sports.* Cambridge: Harvard.

Caldamone, A. A., L. E. Edstrom, et al. 1998. Buccal mucosal grafts for urethral reconstruction. *Urology* 51 (5A Suppl): 15–9.

Calhoun, J. B. 1962. The ecology and sociology of the Norway rat. Bethesda, MD: U.S. Department of Health, Education and Welfare.

Callegari, C., S. Everett, et al. 1987. Anogenital ratio: Measure of fetal virilization in premature and full-term newborn infants. *Journal of Pediatrics* 111(2): 240–43.

Candland, D. K. 1993. *Feral children and clever animals.* New York: Oxford University Press.

Canty, T. G. 1977. The child with ambiguous genitalia: A neonatal surgical emergency. *Annals of Surgery*: 272–81.

Capel, B. 1998. Sex in the 90s: SRY and the switch to the male pathway. *Annual Review of Physiology* 60: 497–523.

Caplan, P. J., and J. B. Caplan. 1997. Do sex-related cognitive differences exist and why do people seek them out? In *Gender differences in human cognition*, ed. J. T. E. Richardson. Oxford, U. K.: Oxford University Press.

Capon, A. W. 1955. A case of true hermaphroditism. *The Lancet*, I: 563–65.

Carlson, A. 1991. When is a woman not a woman? *Women's Sports and Fitness* 13: 24–29.

Carlson, B. M. 1999. *Human embryology and developmental biology.* St. Louis: Mosby.

Carpenter, E. 1909. *The intermediate sex: A study of some transitional types of men and women.* New York: Mitchell Kennerly.

Case, M. A. C. 1995. Disaggregating gender from sex and sexual orientation: The effeminate man in the law and feminist jurisprudence. *Yale Law Journal* 105: 1–105.

Catlin, A. J. 1998. Ethical commentary on gender reassignment: A complex and provocative modern issue. *Pediatric Nursing* 24(1): 63ff.

Chafe, W. H. 1991. *The Unfinished Journey: America Since World War II.* New York: Oxford University Press.

Chase, C. 1995. Re: Measurement of pudendal evoked potentials during feminizing genitoplasty: Technique and applications. *Journal of Urology* 153: 1139–40.

———. 1998a. Hermaphrodites with attitude: Mapping the emergence of intersex political activism. *GLQ: A Journal of Lesbian and Gay Studies* 4(2): 189–211.

———. 1998b. Surgical progress is not the answer to intersexuality. *Journal of Clinical Ethics* 9(4): 385–92.

—————. 1999. Rethinking treatment for ambiguous genitalia. *Pediatric Nursing* 25: 451–55.

Chauncey, G., Jr. 1985. Christian brotherhood or sexual perversion? Homosexual identities and the construction of sexual boundaries in the World War I era. *Journal of Social History* 19: 189–212.

—————. 1989. From sexual inversion to homosexuality: The changing medical conceptualization of female "deviance." In *Passion and power: Sexuality in history*, ed. K. Peiss and C. Simmons. Philadelphia: Temple University Press, 87–117.

—————. 1994. *Gay New York: Gender, urban culture and the making of the gay male world, 1890–1940.* New York: Basic Books.

Cheek, A. O., and J. A. McLachlan. 1998. Environmental hormones and the male reproductive system. *Journal of Andrology* 19(1): 5–10.

Council on Pharmacy and Chemistry. 1928. Ovarialhormon, folliculin, menoformon. *Journal of the American Medical Association* 91(16): 1193.

—————. 1936. The nomenclature of estrus-producing compounds. *Journal of the American Medical Association* 107(15): 1221–23.

Chen, T.-S., M.-L. Doong, et al. 1995. Effects of sex steroid hormones on gastric emptying and gastrointestinal transit in rats. *American Journal of Physiology* 31(1): G171–76.

Chiarello, C. 1980. A house divided? Cognitive functioning with callosal agenesis. *Brain and Language* 11: 128–58.

Chodorow, N. J. 1995. Gender as a personal and cultural construction. *Signs* 20(3): 516–44.

Christensen, L. W., and R. A. Gorski. 1978. Independent masculinization of neuroendocrine systems by intracerebral implants of testosterone or estradiol in the neonatal female rat. *Brain Research* 146: 325–40.

Chung, Y. B., and M. Katayama. 1996. Assessment of sexual orientation in lesbian/gay/bisexual studies. *Journal of Homosexuality* 30(4): 49–62.

Clark, E. J., D. O. Norris, et al. 1998. Interactions of gonadal steroids and pesticides DDT, DDE on gonaduct growth in larval tiger salamanders, Ambystoma tigrinum. *General Comparative Endocrinology* 109(1): 94–105.

Clark, J. T. 1993. Analysis of female sexual behavior: Proceptivity, receptivity, and rejection. *Methods in Neuroscience* 14: 54–75.

—————. 1993. Component analysis of male sexual behavior. *Methods in Neuroscience* 14: 32–53.

Clarke, A. 1990a. A social worlds research adventure: The case of reproductive science. In *Theories of science in society*, ed. S. E. Cozzens and T. F. Gieryn. Bloomington: Indiana University Press: 23–50.

—————. 1990b. Controversy and the development of reproductive sciences. *Social Problems* 37(1): 18–37.

—————. 1991. Embryology and the rise of American reproductive sciences, circa 1920s–1950. *The expansion of American biology*, ed. K. R. Benson, J. Maienschein, and R. Rainger. New Brunswick, NJ: Rutgers University Press, 107–32.

————. 1993. Money, sex and legitimacy at Chicago, circa 1892–1940: Lillie's Center of Reproductive Biology. *Perspectives on Science* 1(3): 367–415.

————. 1995. Research materials and reproductive science in the United States, 1910–1940 with epilogue: Research materials (re)visited. In *Ecologies of knowledge: New directions in sociology of science and technology*, ed. S. L. Star. Albany: State University Press of New York.

————. 1998. *Disciplining reproduction: Modernity, American life sciences and the "problems of sex."* Berkeley: University of California Press.

Clarke, A. E., and J. Fujimura, eds. 1992. *The right tools for the job: At work in twentieth-century life sciences*. Princeton, Princeton University Press.

Clarke, E. H. 1873. *Sex in education; Or, a fair chance for the girls*. Boston: James R. Osgood.

Clarke, J. M., and R. B. Lufkin. 1993. Corpus callosum morphometry and dichotic listening performance: Individual differences in functional interhemispheric inhibition? *Neuropsychologia* 31(6): 547–57.

Clarke, J. M., and E. Zaidel. 1994. Anatomical-behavioral relationships: Corpus callosum morphometry and hemispheric specialization. *Behavioural Brain Research* 64: 185–202.

Clarke, S., R. Kraftsik, et al. 1989. Forms and measures of adult and developing human corpus callosum: Is there a sexual dimorphism? *Journal of Comparative Neurology* 280: 213–30.

Clause, B. T. 1993. The Wistar rat as the right choice: Establishing mammalian standards and the ideal of a standardized mammal. *Journal of the History of Biology* 26(2): 329–49.

Cohen, J., and I. Stewart. 1994. Our genes aren't us. *Discover* (April): 78–84.

Cohen, L. G., P. Celnik, et al. 1997. Functional relevance of cross-modal plasticity in blind humans. *Nature* 389 (September 11): 180–82.

Cohn, C. 1987. Sex and death in the rational world of defense intellectuals. *Signs* 12(4): 687–718.

Colapinto, J. 1997. The true story of John Joan. *Rolling Stone*, December 11, 54ff.

Coleman, W. 1971. *Biology in the 19th century: Problems of form, function and transformation*. New York: Wiley.

Constant, D., and H. Ruther. 1996. Sexual dimorphism in the human corpus callosum? A comparison of methodologies. *Brain Research* 727: 99–106.

Constantinople, A. 1973. Masculinity-femininity: An exception to a famous dictum? *Psychological Bulletin* 80(5): 389–407.

Conte, F. A., and M. A. Grumbach. 1989. Pathogenesis, classification, diagnosis, and treatment of anomalies of sex. *Endocrinology*, ed. L. De Groot, NY: Saunders, 1810–47.

Cooke, B., C. D. Hegstrom, et al. 1998. Sexual differentiation of the vertebrate brain: Principles and mechanisms. *Frontiers in Neuroendocrinology* 19: 323–62.

Corballis, M. C. 1994. Split decisions: Problems in the interpretation of results from commissurotomized subjects. *Behavioural Brain Research* 64: 163–72.

Corner, G. W. 1964. *A history of the Rockefeller Institute: 1901–1953*. New York: Rockefeller Institute Press.

———. 1965. The early history of oestrogenic hormones. *Journal of Endocrinology* 31: iii–xvii.

Costa, E. M., B. B. Mendonca, et al. 1997. Management of ambiguous genitalia in pseudohermaphrodites: New perspectives on vaginal dilation. *Fertility and Sterility* 67(2): 229–32.

Cott, N. 1987. *The grounding of modern feminism*. New Haven: Yale University Press.

Cotton, P. 1994. How "definitive" is new sex survey? Answers vary. *Journal of the American Medical Association* 272(22): 1727–30.

Cowell, P. E., A. Kertesz, et al. 1993. Multiple dimensions of handedness and the human corpus callosum. *Neurology* 43: 2353–57.

Cowley, G. 1996. Attention: Aging men. *Newsweek*, September 16, 68–75.

Crabbe, J. C., D. Wahlsten, et al. 1999. Genetics of mouse behavior: Interactions with laboratory environment. *Science* 284 (June 4): 1670–72.

Crair, M. C., D. C. Gillespie, et al. 1998. The role of visual experience in the development of columns in cat visual cortex. *Science* 279 (January 23): 566–70.

Crawford, M., and R. Chaffin. 1997. The meanings of difference: Cognition in social and cultural context. In *Gender differences in human cognition*, ed. J. T. E. Richardson. Oxford, U.K.: Oxford University Press.

Crew, F. A. E. 1933. Ten years of sex research. *Journal of Heredity* 24(6): 249–51.

Crichton, M. 1990. *Jurassic Park*. New York: Knopf.

Culianu, J. P. 1991. A corpus for the body. *Journal of Modern History* 63: 61–80 .

Cunniff, C., S. J. Hassed, et al. 1995. Health care utilization and perceptions of health among adolescents and adults with Turner syndrome. *Clinical Genetics* 48: 17–22.

Dale, H. H. 1932. Conference on the standardization of sex hormones. *Quarterly Bulletin of the Health Organization League of Nations* 3(1934): 121–27.

Dally, A. 1991. *Women under the knife: A history of surgery*. New York: Routledge.

Danziger, K. 1990. *Constructing the subject: Historical origins of psychological research*. Cambridge, U.K.: Cambridge University Press.

Daston, L. 1992. The naturalized female intellect. *Science in Context* 5(2): 209–35.

Daston, L., and K. Park. 1985. Hermaphrodites in Renaissance France. *Critical Matrix* 1(5): 1–19.

———. 1998. *Wonders and the order of nature, 1150–1750*. New York: Zone Books.

Davatzikos, C., and S. M. Resnick. 1998. Sex differences in anatomic measures of interhemispheric connectivity: Correlations with cognition in women but not in men. *Cerebral Cortex* 8: 635–40.

David, K., J. Freud, et al. 1934. 184. Conditions of hypertrophy of seminal vesicles in rats II. the effect of derivatives of oestrone (menoformon). *Biochemical Journal* 28(2): 1360–67.

Davidson, R. J., and K. Hugdahl, eds. 1995. *Brain asymmetry.* Cambridge: MIT Press.

Davis, D. L., and R. G. Whitten. 1987. The cross-cultural study of human sexuality. *Annual Review of Anthropology* 16: 69–98.

Davis, K. B. 1929. *Factors in the sex life of twenty-two hundred women.* New York: Harper and Bros.

Davis, P. G., C. V. Chaptal, et al. 1979. Independence of the differentiation of masculine and feminine sexual behavior in rats. *Hormones and Behavior* 12: 12–19.

Dawson, G., L. G. Klinger, et al. 1992. Frontal lobe activity and affective behavior of infants of mothers with depressive symptoms. *Child Development* 63: 725–37.

de Beauvoir, S. 1949. *The second sex.* New York: Vintage.

De Grazia, E., R. M. Cigna, et al. 1998. Modified-Mathieu's technique: A variation of the classic procedure for hypospadias surgical repair. *European Journal of Pediatric Surgery* 8(2): 98–99.

de Jonge, F. 1986. Sexual and aggressive behavior in female rats: Psychological and endocrine factors. *Nederlands Institut voor Hersenonderzoek.* Amsterdam: University of Utrecht, 201.

———. 1995. A sex bias in the study of oestrus behavior of rats and swine. Unpublished manuscript.

de Jonge, F., E. M. J. Eerland, et al. 1986. The influence of estrogen, testosterone, and progesterone on partner preference, receptivity and proceptivity. *Physiology and Behavior* 37: 885–92.

de Jonge, F., J. W. Muntjewerff, et al. 1988. Sexual behavior and sexual orientation of the female rat after hormonal treatment during various stages of development. *Hormones and Behavior* 22: 100–15.

de Kruif, P. 1926. *Microbe hunters.* New York: Blue Ribbon Books.

———. 1945. *The male hormone.* New York: Harcourt, Brace.

de la Chapelle, A. 1986. The use and misuse of sex chromatin screening for "gender identification" of female athletes. *Journal of the American Medical Association* 256(14): 1920–23.

de Lacoste, C., J. B. Kirkpatrick, et al. 1985. Topography of the human corpus callosum. *Journal of Neuropathology and Experimental Neurology* 44(6): 578–91.

de Lacoste, M. C., R. L. Holloway, et al. 1986. Sex differences in the fetal human corpus callosum. *Human Neurobiology* 5: 93–96 .

de Lacoste-Utamsing, C., and R. L. Holloway. 1982. Sexual dimorphism in the human corpus callosum. *Science* 216: 1431–32.

de Marneffe, D. 1997. Bodies and words: A study of young children's genital and gender knowledge. *Gender and Psychoanalysis* 2(1): 3–33.

de Vries, G. J., J. P. C. deBruin, et al., eds. 1984. *Sex differences in the brain: The relation between structure and function. Progress in Brain Research.* Amsterdam: Elsevier.

Deanesly, R., and A. S. Parkes. 1936. Oestrogenic action of compounds of the androsterone-testosterone series. *British Medical Journal* 1 (Feb. 8): 257–58.

Delaney, S. R. 1991. Street talk/straight talk. *Differences* 3(2): 21–38.

Demeter, S., J. L. Ringo, et al. 1988. Morphometric analysis of the human corpus callosum and anterior commissure. *Human Neurobiology* 6: 219–26.

D'Emilio, J. 1983. *Sexual politics, sexual communities: The making of a homosexual minority in the United States: 1940–1970*. Chicago: University of Chicago Press.

———. 1993. Capitalism and gay identity. In *The lesbian and gay studies reader*, ed. H. Abelove, M. A. Barale, and D. M. Halperin. New York: Routledge, 467–76.

D'Emilio, J., and E. B. Freedman. 1988. *Intimate matters: A history of sexuality in America*. New York: Harper & Row.

Dempsey, E. W. 1968. William Caldwell Young: An appreciation. In *Reproduction and sexual behavior*, ed. M. Diamond. Bloomington: Indiana University Press, 453–58.

Denenberg, V. H., A. Kertesz, et al. 1991. A factor analysis of the human's corpus callosum. *Brain Research* 548: 126–32.

Devesa, R., A. Munoz, et al. 1998. Prenatal diagnosis of isolated hypospadias. *Prenatal Diagnosis* 18(8): 779–88.

Devor, H. 1997. *FTM: Female to male transsexuals in society*. Bloomington: Indiana University Press.

Dewey, J., and A. F. Bentley. 1949. *Knowing and the known*. Boston: Beacon Press.

Dewhurst, C. J., and R. R. Gordon. 1963. Change of sex. *The Lancet* 2: 1213–16.

———. 1969. *The intersexual disorders*. London: Bailliere, Tindall & Cassell.

Dewsbury, D. A. 1984. *Comparative psychology in the twentieth century*. Stroudsburg: Hutchinson Ross.

———. 1989. A brief history of the study of animal behavior in North America. *Perspectives in Ethology*. 8: 85–122.

di Clemente, N., S. Ghaffari, et al. 1992. A quantitative and interspecific test for biological activity of anti-Müllerian hormone: The fetal ovary aromatase assay. *Development* 114: 721–27.

di Mauro, D. 1995. *Sexuality research in the United States: An assessment of the social and behavioral sciences*. New York: Social Science Research Council.

Diamond, M. 1965. A critical evaluation of the ontogeny of human sexual behavior. *Quarterly Review of Biology* 40: 147–75.

———. 1982. Sexual identity, monozygotic twins reared in discordant sex roles and a BBC follow-up. *Archives of Sexual Behavior* 11(2): 181–86.

———. 1993. Homosexuality and bisexuality in different populations. *Archives of Sexual Behavior* 22(4): 291–310.

———. 1996. Gender identity: More options than "man" or "woman." *Honolulu Advertiser*, June 30, B1–4.

———. 1997a. The road to paradise. In *How I Got into Sex*, ed. B. Bullough, V. L. Bullough, M. Fithian, W. E. Hartman, and R. S. Klein. Buffalo, NY: Prometheus.

————. 1997b. Sexual identity and sexual orientation in children with trauma-tized or ambiguous genitalia. *Journal of Sex Research* 34(2): 199–211.

Diamond, M., and K. Sigmundson. 1997a. Management of intersexuality: Guidelines for dealing with persons of ambiguous genitalia. *Archives of Pediatric and Adolescent Medicine* 151 (October): 1046–50.

————. 1997b. Sex reassignment at birth: Long-term review and clinical impli-cations. *Archives of Pediatric and Adolescent Medicine* 151 (March): 298–304.

Dickinson, R. L. 1949. *Human sex anatomy.* Baltimore: Williams and Wilkins.

Dicks, G. H., and A. T. Childers. 1934. The social transformation of a boy who had lived his first fourteen years as a girl: A case history. *American Journal of Orthopsychiatry* 4: 508–17.

Diedrich, A. 1994. Deconstructing gender dichotomies: Conceptualizing the Native American berdache. *InterSections: An Interdisciplinary Journal* 2(1): 14–24.

Dittmann, R. W., M. H. Kappes, et al. 1990a. Congenital adrenal hyperplasia I: Gender-related behavior and attitides in female patients and sisters. *Psychoneuro-endocrinology* (15)5&6: 401–20.

————. 1990b. Congenital adrenal hyperplasia II: Gender-related behavior and attitudes in female salt-wasting and simple-virilizing patients. *Psychoneuroendo-crinology* (15)5&6: 421–34.

————. 1992. Sexual behavior in adolescent and adult females with congenital adrenal hyperplasia. *Psychoneuroendocrinology* 17(2–3): 153–70.

Döhler, K. D. 1978. Is female sexual differentiation hormone-mediated? *Trends in Neuroscience* 1 (November): 138–40.

Döhler, K. D., J. L. Hancke, et al. 1984. Participation of estrogens in female sex-ual differentiation of the brain; neuroanatomical, neuroendocrine and behav-ioral evidence. In *Progress in brain research: Sex differences in the brain*, ed. G. J. de Vries, J. P. C. de Bruin, H. B. M. Uylings, and M. A. Corner. Amsterdam, Elsevier, 61.

Doisy, E. A. 1939. Biochemistry of the estrogenic compounds. In *Sex and internal secretions*, ed. E. Allen, Charles H. Danforth, and Edward A. Doisy. Baltimore: Williams and Wilkins, 846–76.

Dolk, H. 1998. Rise in prevalence of hypospadias. *The Lancet* 351(9105): 770.

Dolk, H., M. Vrijheid, et al. 1998. Risk of congenital anomalies near hazardous-waste landfill sites in Europe: The EUROHAZCON study. *The Lancet* 352(9126): 423–27.

Donahoe, P. K., and W. H. Hendren III. 1984. Perineal reconstruction in ambig-uous genitalia in infants raised as females. *Annals of Surgery* 200(3): 363–71.

Donahoe, P. K., and M. M. Lee. 1988. Ambiguous genitalia. In *Current therapy in endocrinology and metabolism*, ed. B. C. Wayne. St. Louis: Mosby.

Donahoe, P. K., D. M. Powell, et al. 1991. Clinical management of intersex ab-normalities. *Current Problems in Surgery* 28(8): 513–70 .

Donahue, P. 1985. *The human animal.* New York: Simon & Schuster.

Dörner, G., and G. Hinz. 1968. Induction and prevention of male homosexuality by androgen. *Journal of Endocrinology* 40: 386–88.

Dorsey, G. A. 1925. *Why we behave like human beings.* New York: Harper and Bros.

Doty, R. L. 1974. A cry for the liberation of the female rodent: Courtship and copulation in rodentia. *Psychological Bulletin* 81(3): 159–72.

Downey, G. L., and J. Dumit, eds. 1997. *Cyborgs and citadels: Anthropological interventions in emerging sciences and technologies.* Santa Fe: School of American Research Press.

Dreger, A. D. 1993. Doubtful sex and doubtful status: Hermaphrodites and medical doctors in Victorian England. Unpublished manuscript, 1–41.

———. 1998a. Ambiguous sex—or ambivalent medicine? Ethical issues in the treatment of intersexuality. *Hastings Center Report* (May–June): 24–35.

———. 1998b. *Hermaphrodites and the medical invention of sex.* Cambridge: Harvard University Press.

———. 1998c. The history of intersexuality from the age of gonads to the age of consent. *Journal of Clinical Ethics* 9(4): 345–56.

Drickamer, L. C. 1992. Behavioral selection of odor cues by young female mice affects age of puberty. *Developmental Psychobiology* 25(6): 461–70.

Driesen, N. R., and N. Raz 1995. The influence of sex, age and handedness on corpus callosum morphology: A meta-analysis. *Psychobiology* 23(3): 240–47.

Dubbert, J. L. 1980. Progressivism and the masculinity crisis. In *The American Man,* ed. E. Pleck and J. Pleck. New York: Prentice-Hall, 303–20.

Duberman, M. 1991. *Cures: A gay man's odyssey.* New York: Dutton.

Dubois, E., and L. Gordon. 1983. Seeking ecstasy on the battlefield: Danger and pleasure in 19th-century feminist sexual thought. *Feminist Studies* 9(1): 7–25.

Duckett, J. W. 1993. Editorial comment. *Journal of Urology* 150: 1477.

———. 1996. Editorial comment. *Journal of Urology* 155 (January): 134.

Duckett, J. W., and H. M. I. Snyder. 1992. Meatal advancement and glanuloplasty hypospadias repair after 1,000 cases of meatal stenosis and regression. *Journal of Urology* 147 (March): 665–69.

Duden, B. 1991. *The woman beneath the skin.* Cambridge: Harvard University Press.

Duel, B. P., J. S. Barthold, et al. 1998. Management of urethral strictures after hypospadias repair. *Journal of Urology* 160(1): 170–71.

Duggan, L. 1990. Review essay: From instincts to politics: Writing the history of sexuality in the U.S. *Journal of Sex Research* 27(1): 95–109.

———. 1993. The trials of Alice Mitchell: Sensationalism, sexology, and the lesbian subject in turn-of-the-century America. *Signs* 18(4): 791–814.

Dumit, J. 1997. A digital image of the category of the person: PET scanning and objective self-fashioning. In *Cyborgs and citadels: Anthropological interventions in emerging sciences, technologies and medicines,* ed. G. L. Downey and J. Dumit. Santa Fe: School of American Research Press, pp. 83–102.

———. 1999. Objective brains, prejudicial images. Unpublished manuscript.

———. 1999. When explanations rest: Good-enough brain science and the new sociomedical disorders. Unpublished manuscript.

Dupré, J. 1993. *The disorder of things: Metaphysical foundations of the disunity of science.* Cambridge: Harvard University Press.

Dynes, W. R., and S. Donaldson, eds. 1992a. *Asian homosexuality.* New York: Garland Publishing.

———. 1992b. *Ethnographic studies of homosexuality.* New York: Garland Publishing.

Eberle, J., S. Uberreiter, et al. 1993. Posterior hypospadias: Long-term follow-up after reconstructive surgery in the male direction. *Journal of Urology* 150: 1474–77.

Edwards, C. H. C. 1959. Recent developments concerning the criteria of sex and possible legal implications. *Manitoba Bar News* 31: 115–28.

Efron, R. 1990. *The decline and fall of hemispheric specialization.* Hillsdale, NJ: Lawrence Erlbaum.

Ehrenreich, B. 1983. *The Hearts of Men: American Dreams and the Flight from Commitment.* New York: Doubleday.

Ehrenreich, B., and D. English. 1973. *Complaints and Disorders: The Sexual Politics of Sickness.* New York: Feminist Press.

Ehret, G., A., Jurgens, et al. 1993. Oestrogen receptor occurrence in the male mouse brain—modulation by paternal experience. *Neuroreport* 4(11): 1247–50.

Ehrhardt, A., K. Evers, et al. 1968. Influence of androgen and some aspects of sexually dimorphic behavior in women with the late-treated adrenogenital syndrome. *Johns Hopkins Medical Journal* 123: 115–22.

Ehrlich, R. M., and G. Alter. 1996. Split-thickness skin graft urethroplasty and tunica vaginalis flaps for failed hypospadias repairs. *Journal of Urology* 155 (January): 131–34.

Eicher, E., and L. L. Washburn. 1986. Genetic control of primary sex determination in mice. *Annual Review of Genetics* 20: 327–60.

Ekins, R., and D. King. 1997. Blending genders: Contributions to the emerging field of transgender studies. *International Journal of Transgenderism* 1(1): electronic journal: http://www.symposion.com/ijt/ijtco101.htm.

Elbert, T., H. Flor, et al. 1994. Extensive reorganization of the somatosensory cortex in adult humans after nervous system injury. *Neuroreport* 5(18): 2593–97.

Elbert, T., C. Pantev, et al. 1995. Increased cortical representation of the fingers of the left hand in string players. *Science* 270 (October 13): 305–7.

Elbert, T., A. Sterr, et al. 1997. Input-increase and input-decrease types of cortical reorganization after upper extremity amputation in humans. *Experimental Brain Research* 117(1): 161–64.

Elder, G. H. 1998. The life course and human development. In *Theoretical models of human development,* ed. R. M. Lerner. New York: Wiley. 1: 939–91.

Elger, W., K.-J. Gräf, et al. 1974. Hormonal control of sexual development. In *Advances in the biosciences: Hormones and embryonic development,* ed. G. Raspée. Oxford, U.K.: Pergamon. 13: 41–69.

Elias, S., and G. J. Annas. 1988. Commentary. *Hastings Center Report* 18 (October/November): 34–35.

Ellis, A. 1945. The sexual psychology of human hermaphrodites. *Psychosomatic Medicine* 7: 108–25.

Ellis, H. 1928. *Studies in the psychology of sex Vol. II: Sexual Inversion*. Philadelphia: P. A. Davis.

Elliston, D. A. 1995. Erotic anthropology: "Ritualized homosexuality" in Melanesia and beyond. *American Ethnologist* 22(4): 848–67.

Elman, J. L., E. A. Bates, et al. 1996. *Rethinking innateness: A connectionist perspective on development*. Cambridge: MIT Press.

Elster, A. D., D. A. DiPersio, et al. 1990. Sexual dimorphism of the human corpus callosum studied by magnetic resonance imaging: Fact, fallacy and statistical confidence. *Brain and Development* 12(3): 321–25.

Emans, S. J. 1992. Sexual abuse in girls: What have we learned about genital anatomy? *Journal of Pediatrics* 120 (no. 2, p. 1): 258–60.

Emory, L. E., D. H. Williams, et al. 1991. Anatomic variation of the corpus callosum in persons with gender dysphoria. *Archives of Sexual Behavior* 20(4): 409–17.

Engert, F., and T. Bonhoeffer. 1999. Dendritic spine changes associated with hippocampal long-term synaptic plasticity. *Nature* 399 (May 6): 66–70.

Epple, C. 1998. Coming to terms with Navajo Nádleehí: A critique of berdache, gay, alternate gender and two-spirit. *American Ethnologist* 25: 267–90.

Epstein, C. F. 1997. The multiple realities of sameness and difference: Ideology and practice. *Journal of Social Issues* 53(2): 259–78.

Epstein, J. 1990. Either/or—Neither/both: Sexual ambiguity and the ideology of gender. *Genders* 7: 99–142 .

Epstein, J., and K. Straub 1991. Introduction: The guarded body. In *Bodyguards: The cultural politics of gender ambiguity*, ed. J. Epstein and K. Straub. New York: Routledge, pp. 1–28.

Epstein, J., and K. Straub, ed. 1991. *Body Guards: The cultural politics of gender and gender ambiguity*. New York: Routledge.

Ericksen, J. A. 1999. *Kiss and tell: Surveying sex in the twentieth century*. Cambridge: Harvard University Press.

Eriksson, P. S., E. Perfilieva, et al. 1998. Neurogenesis in the adult human hippocampus. *Nature Medicine* 4(11): 1313–17.

Escoffier, J., R. Kunzel, et al., eds. 1995. The queer issue: New visions of America's lesbian and gay past. *Radical History Review* 62.

Etgen, A. M., I. Vathy, et al. 1990. Ovarian steroids, female reproductive behavior and norepinephrine neurotransmission in the hypothalamus. *Comparative Physiology* 9: 116–28.

Evans, D. T. 1993. *Sexual citizenship: The material construction of sexualities*. London: Routledge.

Evans, H. M. 1939. Endocrine glands: Gonads, pituitary, and adrenals. *Annual Review of Physiology* 1: 577–652.

Exner, M. J. 1915. *Problems and principles of sex education: A study of 948 college men.* New York: Association Press.

Fadem, B. 1995. The effects of neonatal treatment with tamoxifen on sexually dimorphic behavior and morphology in gray short-tailed opossums (*Monodelphis domestica*). *Hormones and Behavior* 29: 296–311.

Faderman, L. 1982. *Surpassing the love of men.* New York: William Morrow.

Fagot, B. I., and M. D. Leinbach 1989. The young child's gender schema: Environmental input, internal organization. *Child Development* 60: 663–72.

———. 1993. Gender-role development in young children: From discrimination to labeling. *Developmental Review* 13: 205–24.

Fagot, B. I., M. D. Leinbach, et al. 1986. Gender labeling and the adoption of sex-typed behaviors. *Developmental Psychology* 224: 440–43.

Fairbairn, D. J. 1997. Allometry for sexual size dimorphism: Pattern and process in the coevolution of body size in males and females. *Annual Review of Ecology and Systematics* 28: 659–87.

Fast, I. 1993. Aspects of early gender development: A psychodynamic approach. In *The psychology of gender*, ed. A. E. Beall and R. J. Sternberg. New York: Guilford, 173–93.

Fausto-Sterling, A. 1987. Society writes biology, biology constructs gender. *Daedalus* 116: 61–76.

———. 1989. Life in the XY corral. *Women's Studies International Forum* 12 (3): 319–31.

———. 1992a. Why do we know so little about human sex? *Discover*: 13: 6, 28–30.

———. 1992b. *Myths of gender: Biological theories about women and men.* New York: Basic Books.

———. 1993a. The five sexes: Why male and female are not enough. *The Sciences* (March-April): 20–24.

———. 1993b. Sex, race, brains and calipers. *Discover* 14: 32–37.

———. 1993c. Changing life in the new world dis/order: I. Replacements of organisms and bodies. Paper delivered to the International Society for the History, Philosophy and Social Studies of Biology; Brandeis University.

———. 1993. How many sexes are there? *New York Times*, March 12, A29.

———. 1995. Animal models for the development of human sexuality: A critical evaluation. *Journal of Homosexuality* 283/4: 217–36.

———. 1997a. Beyond difference: A biologist's perspective. *Journal of Social Issues* 532: 233–58.

———. 1997b. Feminism and behavioral evolution: A taxonomy. In *Feminism and evolutionary biology*, ed. P. A. Gowaty. New York: Chapman and Hall, 42–60.

Fechner, P. Y., C. Rosenberg, et al. 1994. Nonrandom inactivation for the Y-bearing X chromosome in a 46,XX individual: Evidence for the etiology of 46, XX true hermaphroditism. *Cytogenetics and Cell Genetics* 66: 22–26.

Feder, H. H. 1981. Perinatal hormones and their role in the development of sexually dimorphic behaviors. In *Neuroendocrinology of reproduction: Physiology and behavior*, ed. N. T. Adler. New York: Plenum Press, pp. 127–58.

Federman, D. D. 1967. *Abnormal sexual development: A genetic and endocrine approach to differential diagnosis*. Philadelphia: W. B. Saunders.

Feinberg, L. 1996. *Transgender warriors*. Boston: Beacon Press.

———. 1998. *Trans liberation: Beyond pink or blue*. Boston: Beacon Press.

Ferguson-Smith, M. A., A. Carlson, et al. 1992. Olympic row over sex testing. *Nature* 355: 10.

Ferrario, V. F., C. Sforza, et al. 1996. Shape of the human corpus callosum in childhood: Elliptic Fourier analysis on midsaggital magnetic resonance scans. *Investigative Radiology* 311: 1–5.

Fichtner, J., D. Filipas, et al. 1995. Analysis of meatal location in 500 men: Wide variation questions need for meatal advancement in all pediatric anterior hypospadias cases. *Journal of Urology* 154: 833–34.

Fichtner, J., M. Fisch, et al. 1998. Refinements in buccal mucosal grafts urethroplasty for hypospadias repair. *World Journal of Urology* 163: 192–94.

Figlio, K. M. 1976. The metaphor of organization: An historiographical perspective on the bio-medical sciences of the early 19th century. *History of Science* 14: 17–53.

Figueroa, T. E., and K. J. Fitzpatrick 1998. Transverse preputial flap for ventral penile skin coverage in hypospadias surgery. *Techniques in Urology* 42: 83–86.

Finkelstein, M. 1966. Professor Bernhard Zondek: An interview. *Journal of Reproduction and Fertility* 12: 3–19.

Fischer, R. 1990. Why the mind is not in the head but in the society's connectionist network. *Diogenes* 151 Fall: 1–28.

Fiske, S. T., Donald N. Bersoff, Eugene Borgida, Kay Deaux, and Madeline E. Heilman, 1991. Social science research on trial: Use of sex stereotyping research in Price Waterhouse v. Hopkins. *American Psychologist* 4610: 1049–60.

Fitch, R. H., P. E. Cowell, et al. 1998. The female phenotype: Nature's default? *Developmental Neuropsychology* 142/3: 213–31.

Fitch, R. H., and V. H. Denenberg 1998. A role for ovarian hormones in sexual differentiation of the brain. *Behavioral and Brain Sciences* 21: 311–52.

Fitzpatrick, E. 1990. *Endless crusade: Women social scientists and progressive reform*. New York: Oxford University Press.

Flatau, E., Z. Josefsberg, et al. 1975. Penis size in the newborn infant. *Journal of Pediatrics* 874: 663–64.

Fliegner, J. R. 1996. Long-term satisfaction with Sheares vaginoplasty for congenital absence of the vagina. *Australian and New Zealand Journal of Obstetrics and Gynecology* 362: 202–04.

Flor, H., T. Elbert, et al. 1995. Phantom limb pain as a perceptual correlate of cortical reorganization following arm amputation. *Nature* 375 (June 8): 482–84.

Fogel, A., L. Dickson, et al. 1997. Communication of smiling and laughter in mother-infant play: Research on emotion from a dynamic systems perspective. *New Directions in Child Development* 77 (Fall): 5–24.

Fogel, A., and E. Thelen 1987. Development of early expressive and communicative action: Reinterpreting the evidence from a dynamic systems perspective. *Developmental Psychology* 236: 747–61.

Fonkalsrun, E. W., S. Kaplan, et al. 1977. Experience with reduction clitoroplasty for clitoral hypertrophy. *Annals of Surgery* 186: 221–26.

Ford, C. S., and F. A. Beach. 1951. *Patterns of sexual behavior.* New York: Harper and Bros.

Forel, A. 1905. *La question sexuelle.* Lausanne, Switz.: Edwin Frankfurter.

Foreman, J. 1994. Brainpower's sliding scale. *Boston Globe*, May 16, 25, 29.

Forest, M. G. 1981. Inborn errors of testosterone biosynthesis. *Pediatric and Adolescent Endocrinology* 8: 133–55.

Foucault M. 1970. *The order of things: An Archeology of the human sciences.* New York: Random House.

———. 1978. *The history of sexuality.* New York: Pantheon.

———. 1979. *Discipline and Punish.* New York: Random House.

———. 1980. Two lectures. In *Power/knowledge: Selected interviews and other writings 1972–1977 by Michel Foucault*, ed. C. Gordon. New York: Pantheon, pp. 78–108.

———. 1990. *The use of pleasure: The history of sexuality.* New York: Vintage Books.

France, D. 1999. Testosterone, the rogue hormone, is getting a makeover. *New York Times*, Feb. 17, 3.

Frank, J. D. 1997. Editorial comment. *British Journal of Urology* 79: 789.

Frank, R. T. 1929. *The female sex hormone.* London: Bailliere, Tindall and Cox.

Frank, R. T., and M. A. Goldberger. 1931. Channels of excretion of the female sex hormone. *Proceedings of the second International congress for sex research*, London 1930, ed. A. W. Greenwood. Edinburgh: Oliver and Boyd, 378–87.

Fu, D. D., and C. A. Hornick. 1995. Modulation of lipid metabolism at rat hepatic subcellular sites by female sex hormones. *Biochimica et Biophysica Acta—Lipids and Lipid Metabolism* 12543: 267–73.

Fujimura, J. H. 1987. Constructing "Do-able" problems in cancer research: Articulating alignment. *Social Studies of Science* 17: 257–93.

———. 1997. "Canons and purity control in science: The howl of the Boeotians." 119th Annual Meeting of the American Ethnological Society, Seattle, Washington.

Fuss, D. 1993. Freud's fallen women: Identification, desire, and a case of homosexuality in a woman. *Cultural Politics* 6: 42–68.

Gallagher, C., and T. Laqueur, eds. 1987. *The making of the modern body.* Berkeley: University of California Press.

Gallagher, T. F., and F. C. Koch 1929. The testicular hormone. *Journal of Biological Chemistry* (2): 495–500.

———. 1931. Studies on the quantitative assay of the testicular hormone and on its purification and properties. *Proceedings of the second international congress for sex research, London 1930*, ed. A. W. Greenwood. Edinburgh: Oliver and Boyd, p. 312–21.

Galton, F. 1892. *Hereditary genius*. London: Watts and Company.

Garber, M. 1995. *Vice versa: Bisexuality and the eroticism of everyday life*. New York: Simon & Schuster.

García-Coll, C. T., B. Thorne, et al. 1997. *Beyond social categories: "Race," ethnicity, social class, gender and developmental research*. Washington, D.C.: Society for Research on Child Development.

Gardner, J. J. 1992. Descriptive study of genital variation in healthy, nonabused premenarchal girls. *Journal of Pediatrics* 120 (no. 2, pt. 1): 251–57.

Garrety, K. 1997. Social worlds, actor-networks and controversy: The case of cholesterol, dietary fat and heart disease. *Social Studies of Science* 27: 727–73.

Gasperino, J. 1995. Androgenic regulation of bone mass in women. *Clinical Orthopaedics and Related Research* 311: 278–86.

Gasthorne-Hardy, Jonathan. 1998. *Alfred Kinsey: Sex the measure of all things*. London: Chatto and Windus.

Gautier, R. 1935. The health organization and biological standardization. *League of Nations Quarterly Bulletin of the Health Organization* 4(3): 497–554.

Gearhart, J. P., and R. N. Borland. 1992. Onlay island flap urethroplasty: Variation on a theme. *Journal of Urology* 148 (November): 1507–09.

Gearhart, J. P., A. Burnett, et al. 1995. Measurement of pudendal evoked potentials during feminizing genitoplasty: Technique and applications. *Journal of Urology* 153 (February): 486–87.

Geddes, P., and J. A. Thomson. 1895. *The evolution of sex*. London: Walter Scott.

Gelman, D. 1992. Born or bred. *Newsweek*, Feb. 24, 46–52.

George, F. W., L. Milewich, et al. 1978. Oestrogen content of the embryonic rabbit ovary. *Nature* 274 (July 13): 172–73.

Gerall, A. A., J. L. Dunlap, et al. 1973. Effect of ovarian secretions on female behavioral potentiality in the rat. *Journal of Comparative and Physiological Psychology* 82: 449–65.

Gerall, H. D., I. Ward, et al. 1967. Disruption of the male rat's sexual behavior induced by social isolation. *Animal Behavior* 15: 54–58.

Gergen, M. M., and S. N. Davis, eds. 1997. *Toward a new psychology of gender: A reader*. New York: Routledge.

Gerson, E. M. 1983. Scientific work and social worlds. *Knowledge: Creation, Diffusion, Utilization* 4 (3): 357–77.

Gesell, A., and J. A. Singh. 1941. *Wolf child and human child: Being a narrative interpretation of the life history of Kamala, the wolf girl; based on the diary account of a child who was reared by a wolf and who then lived for nine years in the orphanage of Midnapore, in the province of Bengal, India*. New York: Harper and Bros.

Gigerenzer, G., Z. Swijtink, et al. 1989. *The empire of chance*. Cambridge, U. K.: Cambridge University Press.

Gilbert, D. A., G. H. Jordan, et al. 1993. Phallic reconstruction in prepubertal and adolescent boys. *Journal of Urology* 149: 1521–26.

Gilbert, S. 1997. *Developmental biology.* Sunderland, Ma.: Sinauer Associates.

Gilgenkrantz, S. 1987. Hermaphrodisme vrai et double fécondation. *Journal Génétique Humaine* 35 (2–3): 105–18.

Gilman, S. 1994. Sigmund Freud and the sexologists: A second reading. In *Sexual knowledge, sexual science,* ed. R. Porter and M. Teich. Cambridge, U.K.: Cambridge University Press, 323–49.

Gitterman, M. R., and L. F. Sies. 1992. Nonbiological determinants of the organization of language in the brain: A comment on Hu, Qiou and Zhong. *Brain and Language* 43: 162–65.

Gittes, G. K., C. L. Snyder, et al. 1998. Glans approximation procedure urethroplasty for the wide, deep meatus. *Urology* 523: 499–500.

Glassberg, Kenneth I. "Editorial: Gender assignment and the pediatric urologist." *Journal of Urology* 161: 1308–10.

Glen, J. E. 1957. Female pseudohermaphroditism: A case presenting unusual problems. *Journal of Urology* 78 (2): 169–72 .

Going, J. J., and A. Dixson. 1990. Morphometry of the adult human corpus callosum: Lack of sexual dimorphism. *Journal of Anatomy* 171: 163–67.

Goldberg, E., R. Harner, et al. 1994. Cognitive bias, functional cortical geometry, and the frontal lobes: Laterality sex and handedness. *Journal of Cognitive Neuroscience* 6 (3): 276–96.

Goldberg, S. 1973. *The inevitability of patriarchy.* New York: William Morrow.

Golden, R. J., K. L. Noller, et al. 1998. Environmental endocrine modulators and human health: an assessment of the biological evidence. *Critical Review of Toxicology* 28 (2): 109–227.

Goodall, J. 1991. Helping a child to understand her own testicular feminization. *The Lancet* 337 (January 5): 33–35.

Goodwin, B., and P. Saunders, eds. 1989. *Theoretical biology: Epigenetic and evolutionary order from complex systems.* Baltimore: Johns Hopkins University Press.

Gooren, L., and P. T. Cohen-Kettenis. 1991. Development of male gender identity/role and a sexual orientation towards women in a 46, XY subject with an incomplete form of the androgen insensitivity syndrome. *Archives of Sexual Behavior* 205: 459–70.

Gordon, L. 1976. *Woman's body, woman's right: A social history of birth control in America.* New York: Grossman.

Gorman, C. 1992. Sizing up the sexes. *Time,* January 20: 42–51.

Gorski, R. A. 1971. Gonadal hormones and the prenatal development of neuroendocrine function. *Frontiers in Neuroendocrinology* 3: 237–89.

Gottlieb, G. 1991. Experiential canalization of behavioral development: Theory. *Developmental Psychology* 27 (1): 4–13.

———. 1997. *Synthesizing nature-nurture: Prenatal roots of instinctive behavior.* Mahwah, N.J.: Lawrence Erlbaum.

Gottlieb, G., D. Wahlsten, et al. 1998. The significance of biology for human development: A developmental psychobiological systems view. In *Handbook of Child Psychology*, ed. W. Damon. New York: Wiley, 233–73.

Gould, E., A. Beylin, et al. 1999. Learning enhances adult neurogenesis in the hippocampal formation. *Nature Neuroscience* 2 (3): 260–70.

Gould, E., B. S. McEwen, et al. 1997. Neurogenesis in the dentate gyrus of the adult tree shrew is regulated by psychosocial stress and NMDA receptor activation. *Journal of Neuroscience* 17 (7): 2492–98.

Gould, S. J. 1981. *The mismeasure of man*. New York: Norton.

Gowan, J. C. 1985. Spatial ability and testosterone. *Journal of Creative Behavior* 18: 187–90.

Goy, R. W. 1967. William Caldwell Young, September 8, 1899 to August 30, 1965. *Anatomical Record* 157: 3–12.

Goy, R. W., F. B. Bercovitch, et al. 1988. Behavioral masculinization is independent of genital masculinization in prenatally female Rhesus monkeys. *Hormones and Behavior* 22: 552–71.

Goy, R. W., and J. S. Jakway. 1959. The inheritance of patterns of sexual behaviour in female guinea pigs. *Animal Behavior* 7: 142–49.

Goy, R. W., and B. S. McEwen. 1980. *Sexual differentiation of the brain*. Cambridge: MIT Press.

Goy, R., and W. C. Young. 1956–57. Strain differences in the behavioral responses of female guinea pigs to alpha-estradiol benzoate and progesterone. *Behavior* 10 (3–4): 340–353.

————. 1957. Somatic basis of sexual behavior patterns in guinea pigs. *Psychosomatic Medicine* 19: 144–51.

Grady, D. 1992. Sex test. *Discover*, June, 78–82.

Grady, K. L., and C. Phoenix. 1963. Hormonal determinants of mating behavior: The display of feminine behavior by adult male rats castrated neonatally motion picture. *American Zoologist* 3: 482–83 (abstract).

Grady, K. L., C. H. Phoenix, et al. 1965. Role of the developing rat testis in differentiation of the neural tissues mediating mating behavior. *Journal of Comparative and Physiological Psychology* 59 (2): 176–82.

Gray, R. 1992. Death of the gene: Developmental systems strike back. In *Trees of Life*, ed. P. Griffiths. Dordrecht, The Netherlands: Kluwer Academic Publishers, 165–207.

————. 1997. In the belly of the monster: Feminism, developmental systems and evolutionary explanations. In *Feminism and evolutionary biology*, ed. P. A. Gowaty. New York: Chapman and Hall.

Greenberg, Julie. 1999. "Defining male and female: Intersexuality and the collision between law and biology." *Arizona Law Review* 41: 265–328.

Greene, R. R., M. W. Burrill, et al. 1940a. Experimental intersexuality: The effect of antenatal androgens on sexual development of female rats. *American Journal of Anatomy* 65 (3): 416–69.

————. 1940b. Experimental intersexuality: The effects of estrogens on the antenatal sexual development of the rat. *American Journal of Anatomy* 67: 305–45.

Greenspan, R. J., and T. Tully. 1993. Group report: How do genes set up behavior? In *Flexibility and constraint in behavioral systems*, ed. R. J. Greenspan and C. P. Kyriacou. New York: Wiley, 65–80.

Griffin, J. E., and J. D. Wilson. 1989. The androgen resistance syndromes: 5-alpha reductase deficiency, testicular feminization and related disorders. In *The metabolic basis of inherited disease*, ed. C. R. Scriver, A. L. Beaudet, W. S. Sly, and D. Valle. New York: McGraw Hill.

Griffiths, P. E., and R. D. Gray. 1994. Developmental systems and evolutionary explanation. *Journal of Philosophy* 91 (6): 277–304.

———. 1994b. Replicators and vehicles? Or developmental systems? *Behavioral and Brain Sciences* 17 (4): 623–24.

Grober, M. S. 1997. Neuroendocrine foundations of diverse sexual phenotypes in fish. In *Sexual orientation: Toward a biological understanding*, ed. L. Ellis and L. Ebertz. Westport, CT: Praeger, 3–20.

Groneman, C. 1994. Nymphomania: The historical construction of female sexuality. *Signs* 19 (2): 337–67.

Gross, R. E., and I. A. Meeker, Jr. 1955. Abnormalities of sexual development: Observations from 75 cases. *Pediatrics* 16: 303–24.

Gross, R. E., J. G. Randolf, et al. 1966. Clitorectomy for sexual abnormalities: Indications and technique. *Surgery* 59: 300–08.

Grosz, E. 1966. Intolerable ambiguity: Freaks as/at the limit. In *Freakery: Cultural spectacles of the extraordinary body*, ed. R. G. Thomson. New York: New York University Press, 55–66.

———. 1994. *Volatile bodies: Towards a corporeal feminism*. Bloomington: Indiana University Press.

———. 1995. *Space, time and perversion*. New York: Routledge.

Grotevant, H. D. 1987. Toward a process model of identity formation. *Journal of Adolescent Research* 23: 203–22.

Groveman, S. 1996. Letter. *Canadian Medical Association Journal* 154 (12): 1829–30.

Grunt, J. A., and W. C. Young. 1952. Differential reactivity of individuals and the response of the male guinea pig to testosterone propionate. *Endocrinology* 513: 237–48.

———. 1953. Consistency of sexual behavior patterns in individual male guinea pigs following castration and androgen therapy. *Journal of Comparative and Physiological Psychology* 46: 138–44.

Guinet, P., and J. Decourt. 1969. True hermaphroditism. In *Selected topics on genital anomalies and related subjects*, ed. M. N. Rashad and W. R. M. Morton. Springfield, IL: Charles C. Thomas, pp. 553–83.

Gustafson, M. L., and P. K. Donahoe. 1994. Male sex determination: Current concepts of male sexual differentiation. *Annual Review of Medicine* 45: 505–24.

Gustafsson, J. 1994. Regulation of sexual dimorphism in rat liver. In *The differences between the sexes*, ed. R. V. Short and E. Balaban. Cambridge, U.K.: Cambridge University Press, 231–41.

Gustavson, R. G. 1939. Bioassay of androgens and estrogens. In *Sex and internal secretions*, ed. Charles H. Allen, and Edward A. Doisy. Baltimore: Williams and Wilkins, 877–900.

Habib, M., D. Gayraud, et al. 1991. Effects of handedness and sex on the morphology of the corpus callosum: A study with brain magnetic resonance imaging. *Brain and Cognition* 16: 41–61.

Hacking, I. 1982. Biopower and the avalanche of printed numbers. *Humanities in Society* 53/4: 279–95.

———. 1983. *Representing and intervening: Introductory topics in the philosophy of science.* Cambridge, U.K.: Cambridge University Press.

———. 1986. Making up people. In *Reconstructing Individualism: Autonomy, individuality and the self in Western thought*, ed. T. C. Heller, Morton Sosna, and David E. Wellbery. Stanford, CA: Stanford University Press, 222–36.

———. 1990. *The taming of chance.* Cambridge, U.K.: Cambridge University Press.

———. 1991. How should we do the history of statistics? In *The Foucault effect: Studies in governmentality*, ed. G. Burchell, C. Gordon, and P. Miller. Chicago: University of Chicago Press.

———. 1992. World-making by kind making: Child abuse for example. In *How classification works: Nelson Goodman among the social sciences*, ed. M. Douglas and D. Hull. Edinburgh: Edinburgh University Press, pp. 180–238.

———. 1995. *Rewriting the soul: Multiple personality and the sciences of memory.* Princeton: Princeton University Press.

Haffner, S. M., and R. A. Valdez. 1995. Endogenous sex hormones: Impact on lipids, lipoproteins, and insulin. *American Journal of Medicine* 98 (suppl. 1A): S40–47.

Haiken, E. 1997. *Venus envy: A history of cosmetic surgery.* Baltimore: Johns Hopkins University Press.

Halberstam, J. 1998. *Female masculinity.* Durham, NC: Duke University Press.

Hall, D. L. 1976. Biology, sex hormones and sexism in the 1920's. In *Women and philosophy: Toward a theory of liberation*, ed. C. K. Gould and W. Marx. New York: Putnam, 81–96.

Hall, J. A. Y., and D. Kimura. 1995. Sexual orientation and performance on sexually dimorphic motor tasks. *Archives of Sexual Behavior* 24 (4): 395–407.

Hall, R. 1928. *The Well of Loneliness.* London: Cape.

Haller, K. B. 1998. When John became Joan. *Journal of Obstetric, Gynecologic and Neonatal Nursing* 27 (1): 11.

Halley, J. 1991. Misreading sodomy: A critique of the classification of homosexuals in federal equal protection law. In *Bodyguards: the cultural politics of gender ambiguity*, ed. J. Epstein and K. Straub. New York: Routledge, 351–77.

Halley, J. E. 1993. The construction of heterosexuality. In *Fear of a queer planet: Queer politics and social theory*, ed. M. Warner. Minneapolis: University of Minnesota Press, 82–102.

————. 1994. Sexual orientation and the politics of biology: A critique of the argument from immutability. *Stanford Law Review* 46 (3): 503–68.

Halperin, D. A. 1993. Is there a history of sexuality? In *The lesbian and gay reader*, ed. H. Abelove, M. A. Barale, and D. A. Halperin. New York: Routledge, 416–31.

Halperin, D. M. 1990. *One hundred years of homosexuality and other essays on Greek love.* New York: Routledge.

Halpern, D. F. 1997. Sex differences in intelligence: Implications for education. *American Psychologist* 52 (10): 1091–1102.

————. 1998. Recipe for a sexually dimorphic brain: Ingredients include ovarian and testicular hormones. *Behavioral and Brain Sciences* 21 (3): 330–31.

Halpern, D. F., and M. Crothers. 1997. Sex, sexual orientation and cognition. In *Sexual orientation: Toward a biological understanding*, ed. L. Ellis and L. Ebertz. Westport, CT: Praeger, 181–97.

Halwani, R. 1998. Essentialism, social constructionism and the history of homosexuality. *Journal of Homosexuality* 35 (1): 25–51.

Hamblen, E. C. 1957. The assignment of sex to an individual: Some enigmas and some practical clinical criteria. *American Journal of Obstetrics and Gynecology* 74 (6): 1228–40.

Hamer, D., S. Hu, et al. 1993. Linkage between DNA markers on the X chromosome and male sexual orientation. *Science* 261: 321–25.

Hamilton, M. A., A. J. Vomachka, et al. 1981. Effect of neonatal intrahypothalamic testosterone implants on cyclicity and adult sexual behavior in the female hamster. *Neuroendocrinology* 32: 234–41.

Hammer, M., and R. Menzel. 1994. Neuromodulation, instruction and behavioral plasticity. In *Flexibility and constraint in behavioral systems*, ed. R. J. Greenspan and C. P. Kyriacou. New York: Wiley, 109–18.

Hammonds, E. 1994. Black (w)holes and the geometry of black female sexuality. *Differences* 6 (2&3): 126–45.

Hampson, E., J. F. Rovet, et al. 1998. Spatial reasoning in children with congenital adrenal hyperplasia due to 21-hydroxylase deficiency. *Developmental Neuropsychology* 14 (2): 299–320.

Hampson, J. 1955. Hermaphroditic genital appearance, rearing and eroticism in hyperadrenocorticism. *Bulletin of the Johns Hopkins Hospital* 96: 265–73.

Hampson, J. C., and J. Money. 1955. Idiopathic sexual precocity in the female. *Psychosomatic Medicine* 17 (1): 16–35.

Hampson, J. L. 1965. Determinants of psychosexual orientation. In *Sex and behavior*, ed. F. A. Beach. New York: Wiley, 108–32.

Hampson, J. L., and J. G. Hampson. 1961. The ontogenesis of sexual behavior in man. In *Sex and internal secretions*, ed. W. C. Young and G. W. Corner, Baltimore: Williams and Wilkins, 1401–32.

Hanley, D. F. 1983. Drug and sex testing: Regulations for international competition. *Clinics in Sports Medicine* 2: 13–17.

Hansen, B. 1989. American physicians' earliest writings about homosexuals, 1880–1900. *Milbank Quarterly* 67 (suppl. 1): 92–108.

———. 1992. American physicians' discovery of homosexuals, 1880–1900: A new diagnosis in a changing society. In *Framing disease*, ed. C. Rosenberg and J. Golden. New Brunswick, NJ: Rutgers University Press, 104–33.

Haqq, C. M., C.-Y. King, et al. 1994. Molecular basis of mammalian sexual determination: Activation of Müllerian inhibiting substance gene expression by Sry. *Science* 266 (December 2): 1494–1500.

Haraway, D. 1986. Primatology is politics by other means. In *Feminist approaches to science*, ed. Ruth Bleir. New York: Pergamon Press, pp. 77–118.

———. 1989. *Primate visions.* New York: Routledge.

———. 1991. *Simians, cyborgs and women: The reinvention of nature.* New York: Routledge.

———. 1997. *Modest_witness@second_millennium.femaleman_meets_oncomouse*[tm]. New York: Routledge.

Hard, E., and K. Larsson. 1968. Dependence of mating behavior in male rats on the presence of littermates in infancy. *Brain and Behavioral Evolution* 1: 405–19.

Harding, S. 1992. After the neutrality ideal: Science, politics, and strong objectivity. *Social Research* 59 (3): 567–87.

———. 1995. Strong objectivity: A response to the new objectivity question. *Synthèse* 104 (3): 1–19.

Hare-Mustin, R. T., and J. Marecek. 1994. Asking the right questions: Feminist psychology and sex differences. *Feminism and Psychology* 4 (4): 531–37.

Harmon-Smith, H. 1998. Ten commandments of treating hermaphrodites and the family. *Journal of Clinical Ethics* 9 (4): 371.

Harrington, A. 1985. Nineteenth-century ideas on hemisphere differences and duality of mind. *Behavioral and Brain Sciences* 8: 617–60.

———. 1987. *Medicine, mind and the double brain.* Princeton: Princeton University Press.

Harris, G. W., and S. Levine. 1965. Sexual differentiation of the brain and its experimental control. *Journal of Physiology* 181: 379–400.

Harris, J. R. 1998. *The nurture assumption.* New York: Free Press.

Hart, B. L. 1972. Manipulation of neonatal androgen: Effects on sexual responses and penile development in male rats. *Physiology and Behavior* 8: 841–45.

Harwood, J. 1993. *Styles of scientific thought: The German genetics community 1900–1933.* Chicago: University of Chicago Press.

Haste, H. 1994. *The sexual metaphor.* Cambridge: Harvard University Press.

Hausman, B. L. 1992. Demanding subjectivity: Transsexualism, medicine and the technologies of gender. *Journal of the History of Sexuality* 3 (2): 270–302.

———. 1995. *Changing sex: Transsexualism, technology and the idea of gender in the 20th century.* Durham, NC: Duke University Press.

Hawkesworth, M. A. 1997. Confounding gender. *Signs* 223: 649–85.

Hayashi, Y., T. Maruyama, et al. 1998. [Operative methods for severe hypospadias]. *Nippon Hinyokika Gakkai Zasshi* 89 (7): 635–40.

Hayashi, Y., M. Mogami, et al. 1998. Results of closure of urethrocutaneous fistulas after hypospadias repair. *International Journal of Urology* 5 (2): 167–69.

Heape, W. 1913. *Sex antagonism*. New York: Putnam.

———. 1914. *Preparation for marriage*. London: Cassell and Company.

Hecker, B. R., and L. S. McGuire. 1977. Pyschosocial function in women treated for vaginal agenesis. *American Journal of Obstetrics and Gynecology* 129 (5): 543–47.

Held, L. I. 1994. *Models for embryonic periodicity*. Basel, Switz.: Karger.

Hellige, J. B. 1993. *Hemispheric asymmetry: What's right and what's left?* Cambridge: Harvard University Press.

Hellige, J. B., K. B. Taylor, et al. 1998. Relationships between brain morphology and behavioral measures of hemispheric asymmetry and interhemispheric interaction. *Brain Cognition* 26 (2): 158–92.

Hendren, H., and J. D. Crawford. 1969. Adrenogenital syndrome: The anatomy of the anomaly and its repair. Some new concepts. *Journal of Pediatric Surgery* 4 (1): 49–58.

Hendricks, M. 1993. Is it a boy or a girl? *Johns Hopkins Magazine*, 45 no. 6: 10–16.

Hendriks-Jansen, H. 1996. *Catching ourselves in the act: Situated activity, interactive emergence, evolution, and human thought*. Cambridge: MIT Press.

Herdt, G. 1990a. Developmental discontinuities and sexual orientation across cultures. In *Homosexuality/heterosexuality: Concepts of sexual orientation*, ed. D. P. McWhirter, S. Sanders, and J. M. Reinisch. New York: Oxford University Press, pp. 208–36.

———. 1990b. Mistaken gender: 5-alpha reductase hermaphroditism and biological reductionism in sexual identity reconsidered. *American Anthropologist* 92: 433–46.

———. 1994a. Mistaken sex: Culture, biology and the third sex in New Guinea. In *Third sex third gender: Beyond sexual dimorphism in culture and history*, ed. G. Herdt. New York: Zone Books, 419–46.

———. 1994b. Third sexes and third genders. In *Third sex third gender: Beyond sexual dimorphism in culture and history*, ed. G. Herdt. New York: Zone Books: 21–84.

Herdt, G. H., and J. Davidson. 1988. The Sambia Turnim-man: Sociocultural and clinical aspects of gender formation in male pseudohermaphrodites with 5 alpha-reductase deficiency in Papua New Guinea. *Archives of Sexual Behavior* 17 (1): 33–56.

Heriot, A. 1975. *The castrati in opera*. New York: Da Capo Press.

Herrn, R. 1995. On the history of biological theories of homosexuality. *Journal of Homosexuality* 28 (1 and 2): 31–56.

Herschberger, R. 1948. *Adam's Rib*. New York: Pellegrini and Cudahy.

Hess, D. J. 1997. *Science studies: An advanced introduction*. New York: New York University Press.

Hess, R. A., D. Bunick, et al. 1997. A role for oestrogens in the male reproductive system. *Nature* 390 (December 4): 509–12.

Hill, R. T. 1937*a*. Ovaries secrete male hormone I. Restoration of the castrate type of seminal vesicle and prostate glands to normal by grafts of ovaries in mice. *Endocrinology* 21: 495–502.

———. 1937*b*. Ovaries secrete male hormone III. Temperature control of male hormone output by grafted ovaries. *Endocrinology* 21: 633–36.

Hines, M. 1990. Gonadal hormones and human cognitive development. *Comparative Physiology* 8: 51–63.

Hines, M., L. Chiu, et al. 1992. Cognition and the corpus callosum: Verbal fluency, visuospatial ability, and language lateralization related to midsagittal surface areas of callosal subregions. *Behavioral Neuroscience* 106 (1): 3–14.

Hines, M., and M. L. Collaer. 1993. Gonadal hormones and sexual differentiation of human behavior: Developments from research on endocrine syndromes and studies of brain structure. *Annual Review of Sex Research* 4: 1–48.

Ho, M.-W. 1989. A structuralism of process: Towards a post-Darwinian rational morphology. In *Dynamic Structures in Biology*, ed. B. Goodwin, A. Sibatani, and G. Webster. Edinburgh: Edinburgh University Press, 31–48.

Ho, M.-W., and S. W. Fox. 1988. Processes and metaphors in evolution. In *Evolutionary processes and metaphors*, ed. M.-W. Ho and S. W. Fox. Chichester, U.K.: Wiley, 1–16.

Ho, M.-W., A. Matheson, et al. 1987. Ether-induced segmentation disturbances in Drosophila melanogaster. *Roux's Archives for Developmental Biology* 196: 511–21.

Hoebeke, P., E. V. Van Laecke, et al. 1997. Current trends in the treatment of hypospadias. *Acta Urologica Belgica* 65 (4): 17–23.

Holden, C. 1992. Experts slam Olympic gene test. *Science* 255 (5048): 1073.

Holloway, R. L. 1998. Relative size of the human corpus callosum redux: statistical smoke and mirrors? *Behavioral and Brain Sciences* 21 (3): 333–35.

Holloway, R. L., P. J. Anderson, et al. 1993. Sexual dimorphism in the human corpus callosum from three independent samples: Relative size of the corpus callosum. *American Journal of Physical Anthropology* 92: 481–98.

Holloway, R. L., and M. C. de Lacoste. 1986. Sexual dimorphism in the human corpus callosum: An extension and replication study. *Human Neurobiology* 5: 87–91.

Holmes, M. 1994. Medical politics and cultural imperatives: Intersexuality beyond pathology and erasure. Master's thesis, Interdisciplinary Studies, York University.

Holmes, S. A. V., J. M. W. Kirk, et al. 1992. Surgical reinforcement of gender identity in adolescent intersex patients. *Urologia Internationalis* 48: 430–33.

Hornstein, G. 1988. Quantifying psychological phenomena: Debates, dilemmas, and implications. In *The rise of experimentation in American psychology*, ed. J. G. Morawski. New Haven: Yale University Press, 1–34.

Hornstein, G., and S. L. Star. 1994. Universality biases: How theories about human nature succeed. *Philosophy of the Social Sciences* 20 (4): 421–36.

Horowitz, I. L. 1995. The Rushton file: Racial comparisons and median passions. *Society* 32: 7ff.

Hoshino, S., S. Inoue, et al. 1996. Demonstration of isoforms of the estrogen receptor in the bone tissue of osteoblastic cells. *Calcified Tissue International* 57 (6): 466–68.

Houtsmuller, E. J., J. Juranek, et al. 1994. Males located caudally in the uterus affect sexual behavior of male rats in adulthood. *Behavioral Brain Research* 62 (2): 119–225.

Howe, J. W., ed. 1874. *Sex and education: A reply to Dr. E. Clarke's "Sex in education."* Boston: Roberts Brothers.

Hubbard, R. 1990. *The politics of women's biology.* New York: Routledge.

Hubbard, R., and E. Wald. 1993. *Exploding the gene myth: How genetic information is produced and manipulated by scientists, physicians, employers, insurance companies, educators and law enforcers.* Boston: Beacon Press.

Hughes, W., C. C. Erickson, et al. 1958. True hermaphroditism: Report of a case. *Journal of Pediatrics* 52: 662–69.

Hunt, M. M. 1997. *How science takes stock: The story of meta-analysis.* New York: Russell Sage Foundation.

Hunter, R. H. F. 1995. *Sex determination, differentiation and intersexuality in placental mammals.* Cambridge, U.K.: Cambridge University Press.

Hurtig, A. L., J. Radhakrishnan, et al. 1983. Psychological evaluation of treated females with virilizing congenital adrenal hyperplasia. *Journal of Pediatric Surgery* 18 (6): 887–93.

Hutchison, J. B., C. Beyer, et al. 1994. Brain formation of oestrogen in the mouse: Sex dimorphism in aromatase development. *Journal of Steroid Biochemistry and Molecular Biology* 49 (4–6): 407–15.

Hutson, J. 1992. Clitoral hypertrophy and other forms of ambiguous genitalia in the labor ward. *Australia and New Zealand Journal of Obstetrics and Gynecology* 32(3): 238–39.

Huttenlocher, P. R., and A. S. Dabholkar. 1997. Regional differences in synaptogenesis in human cerebral cortex. *Journal of Comparative Neurology* 387: 167–78.

Huussen, A. H. J. 1987. Sodomy in the Dutch Republic during the eighteenth century. In *'Tis nature's fault: Unauthorized sexuality during the enlightenment,* ed. R. P. Maccubbin. Cambridge, U. K.: Cambridge University Press: 169–78.

Hyde, J. S. 1997. Gender differences in math performance: Not big, not biological. In *Women, men and gender: Ongoing debates,* ed. M. R. Walsh. New Haven: Yale University Press, 283–87.

Hyde, J. S., and N. M. McKinley. 1997. Gender differences in cognition: Results from meta-analyses. In *Gender differences in human cognition,* ed. J. T. E. Richardson. Oxford, U.K.: Oxford University Press.

Hynd, G., J. Hall, et al. 1995. Dyslexia and corpus callosum morphology. *Archives of Neurology* 52: 32–38.

Ingber, D. E. 1998. The architecture of life. *Scientific American* (January): 48–57.

Ingelman-Sundberg, A. 1997. The anterior vaginal wall as an organ for the transmission of active forces to the urethra and the clitoris. *International Urogynecol Journal of Pelvic Floor Dysfunction* 8 (1): 50–51.

Innes-Williams, D. 1981. Masculinizing genitoplasty. *Pediatric and Adolescent Endocrinology* 8: 237–46.

Irvine, J. M. 1990a. *Disorders of desire: Sex and gender in modern American sexology.* Philadelphia: Temple University Press.

————. 1990b. From different to sameness: Gender ideology in sexual science. *Journal of Sex Research* 27 (1): 7–24.

Issa, M. M., and J. P. Gearhart. 1989. The failed MAGPI: Management and prevention. *British Journal of Urology* 64: 169–71.

Jacklin, C. N. 1989. Female and male: Issues of gender. *American Psychologist* 44 (2): 127–33.

Jacklin, C. N., and C. Reynolds. 1993. Gender and childhood socialization. In *The Psychology of gender,* ed. A. E. Beall and R. J. Sternberg. New York: Guilford Press, 197–214.

Jackson, M. 1987. "Facts of life" or the eroticization of women's oppression? Sexology and the social construction of heterosexuality. In *The cultural construction of sexuality,* ed. P. Caplan. London: Tavistock Publications, 52–81.

Jacobs, P., P. Dalton, et al. 1997. Turner Syndrome: A cytogenetic and molecular study. *Annals of Human Genetics* 61: 471–83.

Jacobs, S.-E., W. Thomas, et al., eds. 1997. *Two-spirit people: Native American gender identity, sexuality and spirituality.* Urbana: University of Illinois Press.

James, J. B., ed. 1997. *The significance of gender: Theory and research about difference.* Boston: Blackwell.

Jäncke, L., H. Steinmetz, et al. 1992. Dichotic listening: What does it measure? *Neuropsychologia* 30 (11): 941–50.

Jayanthi, V. R., G. A. McLorie, et al. 1994. Can previously relocated penile skin be successfully used for salvage hypospadias repair? *Journal of Urology* 152 (August): 740–43.

Jayne, C. E. 1986. Methodology in sex research in 1986: An editor's commentary. *Journal of Sex Research* 22 (1): 1–5.

Jeffreys, S. 1985. *The spinster and her enemies: Feminism and sexuality 1880–1930.* London: Pandora.

Jilka, R. L., G. Hangoc, et al. 1992. Increased osteoclast development after estrogen loss: Mediation by interleukin-6. *Science* 257: 88–91.

Jiménez, R., and M. Burgos. 1998. Mammalian sex determination: Joining pieces of the genetic puzzle. *BioEssays* 209: 696–99.

Johansson, C. B., S. Momma, et al. 1999. Identification of a neural stem cell in the adult mammalian central nervous system. *Cell* 96: 25–34.

Johnson, D., and D. J. Coleman. 1998. The selective use of a single-stage and a two-stage technique for hypospadias correction in 157 consecutive cases with the aim of normal appearance and function. *British Journal of Plastic Surgery* 51 (3): 195–201.

Johnson, S. C., T. Farnworth, et al. 1944. Corpus callosum surface area across the human adult life span: Effect of age and gender. *Brain Research Bulletin* 35 (4): 373–77.

Johnson, S. C., J. B. Pinkston, et al. 1996. Corpus callosum morphology in normal controls and traumatic brain injury: Sex differences, mechanisms of injury and neurophysiological correlates. *Neurophysiology* 10 (3): 408–15.

Johnston, T. D. 1987. The persistence of dichotomies in the study of behavioral development. *Developmental Review* 7: 149–82.

Johnston, T. D., and G. Gottlieb. 1990. Neophenogenesis: A developmental theory of phenotypic evolution. *Journal of Theoretical Biology* 147: 471–96.

Jones, A. R., and P. Stallybrass. 1991. Fetishizing gender: Constructing the hermaphrodite in Renaissance Europe. In *Bodyguards: The cultural politics of gender ambiguity*, ed. J. Epstein. New York: Routledge, 80–111.

Jones, H. W., and L. Wilkins. 1961. Gynecological operations in 94 patients with intersexuality. *American Journal of Obstetrics and Gynecology* 82: 1142–53.

Jones, James H. 1997. *Alfred Kinsey: A public/private life.* New York: Norton.

Jordanova, L. J. 1980. Natural facts: A historical perspective on science and sexuality. In *Nature, culture and gender*, ed. C. P. MacCormack and M. Strathern. Cambridge, U.K.: Cambridge University Press.

———. 1989. *Sexual visions: Images of gender in science and medicine between the 18th and 20th century.* Madison: University of Wisconsin Press, pp. 42–69.

Joseph, V. T. 1997. Pudendal-thigh flap vaginoplasty in the reconstruction of genital anomalies. *Journal of Pediatric Surgery* 32 (1): 62–65.

Jost, A. 1946*a*. Recherches sur la différenciation sexuelle de l'embryon de lapin: Action des androgènes de synthèse sur l'histogenèse génitale. *Archives d'Anatomie Microscopique* 36 (3): 242–70.

———. 1946*b*. Recherches sur la différenciation sexuelle de l'embryon de lapin: Introduction et embryologie génitale normale. *Archives d'Anatomie Microscopique* 36 (2): 151–200.

———. 1946*c*. Recherches sur la différenciation sexuelle de l'embryon de lapin: Rôle des gonades foetales dans la différenciation sexuelle somatique. *Archives d'Anatomie Microscopique* 36 (4): 271–315.

———. 1947. Sur les effets de la castration précoce de l'embryon mâle de lapin. *Comptes Rendus des Séances de la Société de Biologie* 141 (3–4): 126–29.

———. 1953. Problems of fetal endocrinology. In *Recent progress in hormone research*, ed. G. Pincus. New York: Academic Press, VIII: 379–419.

———. 1954. Modalities in the action of gonadal and gonad-stimulating hormones in the foetus. *Memoirs of the Society for Endocrinology* 4 (pt. 1): 237–48.

———. 1960. Hormonal influences in the sex development of bird and mammalian embryos. *Memoirs of the Society for Endocrinology* 7: 49–62.

———. 1965. Gonadal hormones in the sex differentiation of the mammalian fetus. In *Organogenesis*, ed. R. L. DeHaan and H. Ursprung. New York: Holt, Rinehart and Winston.

———. 1972. A new look at the mechanisms controlling sex differentiation in mammals. *Johns Hopkins Medical Journal* 130 (January): 38–53.

Jost, A., and Y. Bergerard. 1949. Culture in vitro d'ébauches du tractus génital du foetus de rat. *Comptes Rendus des Séances de la Société de Biologie* 144 (9–10): 608–9.

Jost, A., and B. Bozic. 1951. Donnés sur la différenciation des conduits génitaux du foetus de rat, étudiée in vitro. *Comptes Rendus des Séances de la Société de Biologie* 145 (9–10): 647–50.

Jost, A., B. Vigier, et al. 1973. Studies on sex differentiation in mammals. Recent *Progress in Hormone Research*, ed. R. O. Greep. 29: 1–41.

Juhn, M., F. E. D'Amour, et al. 1931. Effect of the female hormone oestrin upon the sex type of the feathers of brown leghorns. *Proceedings of the second international congress for sex research, London 1930*, ed. A. W. Greenwood. Edinburgh: Oliver and Boyd, 388–95.

Juraska, J. M., and M. Meyer. 1985. Environmental, but not sex, differences exist in the gross size of the rat corpus callosum. *Society for Neurosciences Abstracts* 11: 528.

Kaas, J. H. 1995. How the cortex reorganizes. *Nature* 375 (June 29): 735–36.

———. 1998. Phantoms of the brain. *Nature* 391 (January 22): 331–32.

Kagan, J. 1994. *Galen's prophecy: Temperament in human nature.* New York: Basic Books.

Kahnt, L. C., and E. A. Doisy. 1928. The vaginal smear method of assay of the ovarian hormone. *Endocrinology* 12: 760–68.

Kalaitzoglou, G., and M. I. New. 1993. Congenital adrenal hyperplasia: Molecular insights learned from patients. *Receptor* 3(3): 211–22.

Kalloo, N. B., J. P. Gearhart, et al. 1993. Sexually dimorphic expression of estrogen receptors, but not of androgen receptors in human fetal external genitalia. *Journal of Clinical Endocrinology and Metabolism* 77 (3): 692–98.

Kammerer, P. 1923. *Rejuvenation and the prolongation of human efficiency: Experiences with the Steinach-Operation on man and animals.* New York: Boni and Liveright.

Karaviti, L. P., A. B. Mercado, et al. 1992. Prenatal diagnosis/treatment in families at risk for infants with steroid 21-hydroxylase deficiency congenital adrenal hyperplasia. *Journal of Steroid Biochemistry and Molecular Biology* 41 (3–8): 445–51.

Karkare, S., T. R. Kelly, et al. 1995. Morphological aspects of female Syrian hamster gallbladder induced by one-month sex steroid treatment. *Journal of Submicroscopic Cytology and Pathology* 27 (1): 35–52.

Karraker, K., D. A. Vogel, et al. 1995. Parents' gender-stereotyped perceptions of newborns: The eye of the beholder revisited. *Sex Roles* 33 (9–10): 687–701.

Kates, G. 1995. *Monsieur d'Eon is a woman: A tale of political intrigue and sexual masquerade.* New York: Basic Books.

Katz, J. 1976. *Gay American history: Lesbians and gay men in the USA: A documentary history.* New York: Crowell.

———. 1990. The invention of heterosexuality. *Socialist Review* 20: 7–34.

———. 1995. *The invention of heterosexuality.* New York: Dutton.

Kay, L. E. 1993. *The molecular vision of life: Caltech, the Rockefeller Foundation and the rise of the new biology*. New York: Oxford University Press.

Keller, E. F. 1985. *Reflections on gender and science*. New Haven: Yale University Press.

Keller, E. F., and J. Ahouse. 1997. Writing and reading about Dolly. *BioEssays* 19 (8): 741–42.

Kellogg, N. D., and J. M. Parra. 1991. Linea vestibularis: A previously undescribed normal genital structure in female neonates. *Pediatrics* 87 (6): 926–29.

Kemperman, G., and F. H. Gage. 1999. New nerve cells for the adult brain. *Scientific American* (May): 48–53.

Kemperman, G., H. G. Kuhn, et al. 1998. Experience-induced neurogenesis in the senescent dentate gyrus. *Journal of Neuroscience* 18 (9): 3206–12.

Kennedy, E. L., and M. D. Davis. 1993. *Boots of leather, slippers of gold: The history of a lesbian community*. New York: Routledge.

Kertesz, A., M. Polk, et al. 1987. Cerebral dominiance, sex, and callosal size in MRI. *Neurology* 37: 1385–88.

Kessler, S. J. 1990. The medical construction of gender: Case management of intersexed infants. *Signs* 16 (1): 3–26.

———. 1998. *Lessons from the intersexed*. New Brunswick, NJ: Rutgers University Press.

Kessler, S. J., and W. McKenna. 1978. *Gender: An ethnomethodological approach*. New York: Wiley.

Kevles, D. J. 1968. Testing the army's intelligence. *Journal of American History* 55(3): 565–81.

———. 1985. *In the name of eugenics: Genetics and the uses of human heredity*. New York: Knopf.

Kim, J. H. Y., A. Ellman, et al. 1996. A re-examination of sex differences in axon density and number in the splenium of the rat corpus callosum. *Brain Research* 740: 47–56.

Kinsey, A. C., W. B. Pomeroy, et al. 1948. *Sexual behavior in the human male*. Philadelphia: Saunders.

———. 1953. *Sexual behavior in the human female*. Philadelphia: Saunders.

Kinsman, G. 1987. *The regulation of desire: Sexuality in Canada*. Montreal: Black Rose Books.

Kipnis, K., and M. Diamond. 1998. Pediatric ethics and the surgical assignment of sex. *Journal of Clinical Ethics* 9 (4): 398–410.

Kirkwood, A., M. G. Rioult, et al. 1996. Experience-dependent modification of synaptic plasticity in visual cortex. *Nature* 381 (June 6): 526–28.

Kitzinger, C. 1994. Should psychologists study sex differences? *Feminism and Psychology* 44 (4): 501–6.

Klein, F. 1990. The need to view sexual orientation as a multivariable dynamic process: A theoretical perspective. In *Homosexuality / heterosexuality: Concepts of sexual orientation*, ed. D. P. McWhirter, S. A. Sanders, and J. M. Reinisch. New York: Oxford University Press, 277–82.

Klein, M., and A. S. Parkes. 1937. The progesterone-like action of testosterone and certain related compounds. *Proceedings of the Royal Society of London B* 3: 574–79.

Knecht, S., H. Henningsen, et al. 1996. Reorganizational and perceptional changes after amputation. *Brain* 119 (4): 1213–19.

Knudsen, E. I. 1998. Capacity for plasticity in the adult owl auditory system expanded by juvenile experience. *Science* 279 (March 6): 1531–33.

Koch, F. C. 1931a. Biochemical studies on the testicular hormone. In *Proceedings of the second international congress for sex research*, ed. A. W. Greenwood. Edinburgh: Oliver and Boyd, 322–28.

———. 1931b. The extraction, distribution and action of testicular hormones. *Journal of the American Medical Association* 96 (12): 937–39.

———. 1939. Biochemistry of androgens. In *Sex and internal secretions*, ed. E. Allen, C. H. Danforth, and E. A. Doisy. Baltimore: Williams and Wilkins, 807–45.

Koenig, H. L., M. Schumacher, et al. 1995. Progesterone synthesis and myelin formation by Schwann cells. *Science* 268 (June 9): 1500–03.

Koertge, N. 1990. Constructing concepts of sexuality: A philosophical commentary. In *Homosexuality/heterosexuality: Concepts of sexual orientation*, ed. D. McWhirter, S. A. Sanders, and J. M. Reinisch. New York: Oxford University Press, pp. 387–98.

Kohler, R. E. 1976. The management of science: The experience of Warren Weaver and the Rockefeller Foundation programme in molecular biology. *Minerva* 14 (3): 279–99.

———. 1994. *Lords of the fly: Drosophila genetics and the experimental life*. Chicago: University of Chicago Press.

Kojima, Y., Y. Hayashi, et al. 1998. [A case of successful hypospadias repair without infection using recombinant human granulocyte-colony stimulating factor rhG-CSF for idiopathic neutropenia]. *Hinyokika Kiyo* 44 (6): 419–21.

Kolata, G. 1992. Who is female? Science can't say. *New York Times*, Feb. 16, Section 4, p. 6.

———. 1998a. Researchers report success in method to pick baby's sex. *New York Times*, September 9, A1ff.

———. 1998b. Studies find brain grows new cells. *New York Times*, March 17, C1ff.

Kolb, B. 1995. *Brain plasticity and behavior*. Mahwah, NJ: Lawrence Erlbaum Associates.

Kolb, B., and I. Q. Whishaw. 1998. Brain plasticity and behavior. *Annual Review of Psychology* 49: 43–64.

Korach, K. S. 1994. Insights from the study of animals lacking functional estrogen receptor. *Science* 266 (December 2): 1524–27.

Korenchevsky, V., M. Dennison, et al. 1932. 249. The rat unit of testicular hormone. *Biochemical Journal* 262: 2097–2107.

————. 1937. 103. The action of testosterone proprionate on normal adult female rats. *Biochemical Journal* 31 (1): 780–85.

Korenchevsky, V., and K. Hall. 1937. The bisexual and co-operative properties of the sex hormones as shown by the histological investigation of the sex organs of female rats treated with these hormones. *Journal of Pathology and Bacteriology* 45: 681–708.

————. 1938. Manifold effects of male and female sex hormones in both sexes. *Nature* 142: 998.

Koyanagi, T., K. Nonomura, et al. 1994. One-stage repair of hypospaias: Is there no simple method universally applicable to all types of hypospadias? *Journal of Urology* 152 (October): 1232–37.

Krafft-Ebing, R. V. 1892. *Psychopathia sexualis, with especial reference to contrary sexual instinct: A medico-legal study.* Philadelphia: F. A. Davis.

Krasnegor, N. A., and R. S. Bridges, eds. 1990. *Mammalian parenting.* New York: Oxford University Press.

Kraus, E. M. 1979. *The metaphysics of experience: A companion to Whitehead's process and philosophy.* New York: Fordham University Press.

Kropfl, D., A. Tucak, et al. 1998. Using buccal mucosa for urethral reconstruction in primary and re-operative surgery. *European Journal of Urology* 34 (3): 216–20.

Kuhnle, U., H. P. Schwartz, et al. 1994. Familial true hermaphroditism—paternal and maternal transmission of true hermaphroditism 46, XX and XX maleness in the absence of Y-chromosomal sequences. *Human Genetics* 92 (6): 571–76.

Kumar, H., J. H. Kiefer, et al. 1974. Clitoroplasty: Experience during a 19-year period. *Journal of Urology* 111: 81–84.

Kunitz, S. J., and H. Haycraft, eds. 1942. *Twentieth century authors: A biographical dictionary of modern literature.* New York: H. W. Wilson.

Kupfer, S. R., C. A. Quigley, et al. 1992. Male pseudohermaphroditism. *Seminars in Perinatology* 16 (5): 319–31.

Lajic, S., A. Wedell, et al. 1998. Long-term somatic follow-up of prenatally treated children with congenital adrenal hyperplasia. *Journal of Clinical Endocrinology and Metabolics* 83 (11): 3872–80.

Lander, Eric S., and J. N. Schork. 1994. Genetic dissection of complex traits. *Science* 265: 2037–48.

Landrigan, P. J., J. E. Carlson, et al. 1998. Children's health and the environment: A new agenda for prevention research. *Environmental Health Perspectives* 106 (suppl 3): 787–94.

Laqueur, E., and S. E. de Jongh. 1928. A female (sexual) hormone. *Journal of the American Medical Association* 91 (16): 1169–72.

Laqueur, T. 1990. *Making sex: Body and gender from the Greeks to Freud.* Cambridge: Harvard University Press.

————. 1992. Sexual desire and the market economy during the industrial revolution. In *Discourses of sexuality*, ed. D. C. Stanton. Ann Arbor: University of Michigan Press.

Larosa, J. C. 1995. Androgens and women's health: Genetic and epidemiological aspects of lipid metabolism. *American Journal of Medicine* 98 (suppl. 1A): S22–26.

Latour, B. 1983. Give me a laboratory and I will raise the world. In *Science Observed*, ed. K. Knorr-Cetina and M. Mulkay. London: Sage, pp. 141–70.

———. 1987. *Science in action*. Milton Keynes, U.K.: Open University Press.

———. 1988. *The Pasteurization of France*. Cambridge: Harvard University Press.

———. 1990. Drawing things together. In *Representation in Scientific Practice*, ed. Lynch M., and S. Woolgar. Cambridge: MIT Press, 19–68.

———. 1993. *We have never been modern*. Cambridge: Harvard University Press.

Lattimer, J. K. 1961. Relocation and recession of the enlarged clitoris with preservation of the glans: An alternative to amputation. *Journal of Urology* 86 (1).

Laue, L., and O. M. Rennert. 1995. Congenital adrenal hyperplasia: Molecular genetics and alternative approaches to treatment. *Advances in Pediatrics* 42: 113–43.

Laumann, E. O., J. H. Gagnon, et al. 1994. *The social organization of sexuality: Sexual practices in the United States*. Chicago: University of Chicago Press.

Laumann, E. O., R. T. Michael, et al. 1994. A political history of the national sex survey of adults. *Family Planning Perspectives* 26 (1): 34–38.

Laviola, G., and E. Alleva. 1995. Sibling effects on the behavior of infant mouse litters Mus domesticus. *Journal of Comparative Psychology* 109 (1): 68–75.

Laycock, H. T., and D. V. Davies. 1953. A case of true hermaphroditism. *British Journal of Surgery* 41: 79–82.

Le Fanu, J. 1992. Olympic chiefs urged to drop sex test. *Sunday Telegraph*, Feb. 2 (London), 2.

Lee, E. H.-J. 1994. Producing sex: An interdisciplinary perspective on sex assignment decisions for intersexuals. Senior thesis, Brown University.

Lee, P. A., T. Mazur, et al. 1980. Micropenis. I. Criteria, etiologies and classification. *Johns Hopkins Medical Journal* 146: 156–63.

Lee, P., and P. Gruppuso. 1999. Should cosmetic surgery be performed on the genitals of children born with ambiguous genitals? *Physicians Weekly* 16, no. 31 (electronic version).

Leland, J., and M. Miller. 1998. Can gays "convert"? *Newsweek*, August 17, 46–50.

LeVay, S. 1991. A difference in hypothalamic structure between heterosexual and homosexual men. *Science* 253: 1034–37.

———. 1996. *Queer science: The use and abuse of research on homosexuality*. Cambridge: MIT Press.

Leveroni, C. L., and S. A. Berenbaum. 1998. Early androgen effects on interest in infants: Evidence from children with congenital adrenal hyperplasia. *Developmental Neuropsychology* 14 (2–3): 321–40.

Levy, G. D. 1989. Relations among aspects of children's social environments, gender schematization, gender role knowledge and flexibility. *Sex Roles* 21 (11–12): 803–23.

Lewin, M. 1984. Rather worse than folly? Psychology measures femininity and masculinity, 1. From Terman and Miles to the Guilfords. In *In the Shadow of the past: Psychology portrays the sexes: A social and intellectual history*, ed. M. Lewin. New York: Columbia University Press, 155–78.

Lewis, D. W. 1971. Katherine Bement Davis. In *Notable American Women, 1607–1950; A biographical dictionary*, ed. J. W. James and P. S. Boyer. Cambridge: Harvard University Press.

Lewis, M. 1975. Early sex differences in the human: Studies of socioemotional development. *Archives of sexual behavior* 4 (4): 329–35.

Lewis, S. 1925. *Arrowsmith*. New York: P. F. Collier.

Lewontin, R., and R. Levins. 1985. *The dialectical biologist*. Cambridge: Harvard University Press.

Lewontin, R. C. 1974. The analysis of variance and the analysis of causes. *American Journal of Human Genetics* 26: 400–11.

————. 1992. *Biology as ideology*. New York: HarperCollins.

Lewontin, R. C., S. Rose, et al. 1984. *Not in our genes*. New York: Pantheon.

Lillie, F. R. 1916. The theory of the free-martin. *Science* 43: 39–53.

————. 1917. The Free-Martin: A study of the action of sex hormones in the foetal life of cattle. *Journal of Experimental Zoology* 23 (2): 371–423.

————. 1939. General biological introduction. In *Sex and Internal Secretions*, ed. E. Allen. Baltimore: Williams and Wilkins, 3–14.

Lindgren, B. W., E. F. Reda, et al. 1998. Single and multiple dermal grafts for the management of severe penile curvature. *Journal of Urology* 160 (3 pt. 2): 1128–30.

Litteria, M. 1994. Long-term effects of neonatal ovariectomy on cerebellar development in the rat: A histological and morphometric study. *Developmental Brain Research* 811: 113–20.

Lobe, T. E., D. L. Woodall, et al. 1987. The complications of surgery for intersex: Changing patterns over two decades. *Journal of Pediatric Surgery* 22 (7): 651–52.

Lock, M. 1997. Decentering the natural body: Making difference matter. *Configurations* 5 (2): 267–92.

Lombroso, C., and W. Ferrero. 1895. *The female offender*. London: T. Fisher Unwin.

Longino, H. 1990. *Science as social knowledge: Values and objectivity in scientific inquiry*. Princeton: Princeton University Press.

Lorber, J. 1993. Believing is seeing: Biology as ideology. *Gender and Society* 7 (4): 568–81.

————. 1994. *Paradoxes of gender*. New Haven: Yale University Press.

Lorenz, K. Z. 1952. *King Solomon's ring*. New York: Crowell.

Lott, B. 1997. The personal and social correlates of a gender difference ideology. *Journal of Social Issues* 53 (2): 279–98.

Lott, B., and D. Maluso. 1993. The social learning of gender. In *The Psychology of Gender*, ed. A. E. Beall and R. J. Sternberg. New York: Guilford Press, 99–123.

Lowry, T. P., and T. S. Lowry, eds. 1976. *The clitoris*. St. Louis: Warren H. Green.

Lubs, H. A., O. Vilar, et al. 1959. Familial male pseudohermaphrodism with labial testes and partial feminization: Endocrine studies and genetic aspects. *Journal of Clinical Endocrinology and Metabolism* 19: 1110–20.

Lunbeck, E. 1994. *The psychiatric persuasion: Knowledge, gender, and power in modern America*. Princeton: Princeton University Press.

Lundberg, F., and M. F. Farnham. 1947. *Modern woman: The lost sex*. New York: Harper and Bros.

Luttge, W. G., and N. R. Hall. 1973. Differential effectiveness of testosterone and its metabolites in the induction of male sexual behavior in two strains of albino mice. *Hormones and Behavior* 4 (1–2): 31–44.

Lydon, J. P., F. DeMayo, et al. 1995. Mice lacking progesterone receptor exhibit pleiotropic reproductive abnormalities. *Genes and Development* 9: 2266–78.

Lynch, M. 1990. The externalized retina: Selection and mathematization in the visual documentation of objects in the life sciences. In *Representation in scientific practice*, ed. M. Lynch and Steven Woolgar. Cambridge: MIT Press, 153–86.

McCann, J., R. Wells, et al. 1990. Genital findings in prepubertal girls selected for nonabuse: A descriptive study. *Pediatrics* 86(3): 428–39.

McCauley, E., and A. J. Urquiza. 1988. *Endocrine influences on human sexual behavior*. Amsterdam: Elsevier.

McClanahan, E. T. 1995. The "five-sex follies," and all that. *Providence Journal*, August 31. Providence, RI: B6.

McCormick, C. M., S. Witelson, et al. 1990. Left-handedness in homosexual men and women: neuroendocrine implications. *Psychoneuroendocrinology* 15: 69–76.

McElreavey, K., E. Vilain, et al. 1993. A regulatory cascade hypothesis for mammalian sex determination: SRY represses a negative regulator of male development. *Proceedings of the National Academy of Science, USA* 90(April): 3368–72.

McEwen, B., H. Cameron, et al. 1994. Resolving a mystery: Progress in understanding the function of adrenal steroid receptors in hippocampus. *Progress in Brain Research* 100: 149–55.

McGill, T. E., D. A. Dewsbury, et al., eds. 1978. *Sex and behavior: Status and Prospectus*. New York: Plenum Press.

McGill, T. E., and C. M. Haynes. 1973. Heterozygosity and retention of ejaculatory reflex after castration in male mice. *Journal of Comparative Physiology and Psychology* 84: 423.

McHale, S. M., A. C. Crouter, et al. 1999. Family context and gender role socialization in middle childhood: Comparing girls to boys and sisters to brothers. *Child Development* 70(4): 990–1004.

McIntosh, M. 1968. The Homosexual Role. *Social Problems* 16: 182–92.

Mackenzie, D. A. 1981. *Statistics in Britain: 1865–1930: The social construction of scientific knowledge*. Edinburgh, Edinburgh University Press.

MacLusky, C., N. J. Walters, et al. 1994. Aromatase in the cerebral cortex, hippocampus and mid-brain: Ontogeny and developmental implications. *Molecular and Cellular Neurosciences* 56: 691–698.

McNay, L. 1993. *Foucault and feminism*. Boston: Northeastern University Press.

Madlafousek, J., and Z. Hlinak. 1977. Sexual behavior in the female laboratory rat: Inventory, patterning and measurement. *Behavior* 63: 129–174.

Madsen, P. O. 1963. Familial female pseudohermaphroditism with hypertension and penile urethra. *Journal of Urology* 90(4): 466–69.

Magee, M., and D. C. Miller. 1997. *Lesbian lives: Psychoanalytic narratives old and new*. Hillsdale, N.J.: Analytic Press.

Magid, B. 1993. A young woman's homosexuality reconsidered: Freud's "The psychogenesis of a case of homosexuality in a woman." *Journal of the American Academy of Psychoanalysis* 21(3): 421–32.

Maienschein, J. 1991. *Transforming traditions in American biology, 1880–1915*. Baltimore: Johns Hopkins University Press.

Maletic-Savatic, M., R. Malinow, et al. 1999. Rapid dentritic morphogenesis in CA1 hippocampal dendrites induced by synaptic activity. *Science* 283(March 19): 1924–26.

Mall, F. P. 1909. On several anatomical characteristics of the human brain, said to vary according to race and sex, with special reference to the frontal lobe. *American Journal of Anatomy* 9: 1–32.

Malson, L., and J. M. G. Itard. 1972. *Wolf children and the problem of human nature and the wild boy of Aveyron*. New York: Monthly Review Press.

Mann, C. C. 1994. Can meta-analysis make policy? *Science* 266: 960–62.

Manning, K. R. 1983. *Black Apollo of science: The life of Ernest Everett Just*. New York: Oxford University Press.

Marcus, E. 1992. *Making history: The struggle for gay and lesbian equal rights*. New York: HarperCollins.

Marks, J. 1994. *Human biodiversity: Genes, race and history*. New York: Aldine de Gruyter.

Marshall, F. H. A. 1910. *The physiology of reproduction*. New York: Longmans, Green.

———. 1929. Walter Heape, F. R. S. *Nature* 124(3128): 588–89.

Marshall, F. H. A., and W. A. Jolly. 1907. Results of removal and transplantation of ovaries. *Transactions of the Royal Society of Edinburgh* 45(no. 21, p. 3): 589–99.

Martin, C. L. 1994. Cognitive influences on the development and maintenance of gender segregation. *New Directions for Child Development* 65(Fall): 35–51.

Martin, C. L., and J. K. Little. 1990. The relation of gender understanding to children's sex-typed preferences and gender stereotypes. *Child Development* 61: 1427–39.

Martin, C. L., C. H. Wood, et al. 1990. The development of gender stereotype components. *Child Development* 61: 1891–1904.

Martin, J. B. 1993. Molecular genetics of neurological diseases. *Science* 262: 674–75.

Martin, J. R. 1994. Methodological essentialism, false difference, and other dangerous traps. *Signs* 19(3): 630–57.

Masters, W. H., and V. E. Johnson. 1966. *Human sexual response.* Boston: Little, Brown.

Matt, K. S. 1993. Neuroendocrine mechanisms of environmental integration. *American Zoologist* 33:266–74.

Matthews, G. T., ed. 1959. 259. A Lansquenet bears a child. News and Rumor. In *Renaissance Europe (The Fugger Newsletters)*. New York: Capricorn Books.

Maxted, W., R. Baker, et al. 1965. Complete masculinization of the external genitalia in congenital adrenocortical hyperplasia: Presentation of two cases. *Journal of Urology* 94: 266–70.

May, E. T. 1988. *Homeward bound: American families in the cold war.* New York: Basic Books.

May, E. T. 1995. *Barren in the promised land: Childless Americans and the pursuit of happiness.* New York: Basic Books.

Mercado, A., R. C. Wilson, et al. 1995. Extensive personal experience: Prenatal treatment and diagnosis of congenital adrenal hyperplasia owing to steroid 21-hydroxylase deficiency. *Journal of Clinical Endocrinology and Metabolism* 80(7): 2014–20.

Merleau-Ponty, M. 1962. *Phenomenology of perception.* New York: Humanities Press.

Meyer-Bahlburg, H. F. L. 1998. Gender assignment in intersexuality. *Journal of Psychology and Human Sexuality* 10(2): 1–21.

Meyer-Bahlburg, H., R. S. Gruen, et al. 1996. Gender change from female to male in classical congenital adrenal hyperplasia. *Hormones and Behavior* 30: 319–32.

Miettinen, R. 1998. Object construction and networks in research work: The case of research on cellulose-degrading enzymes. *Social Studies of Science* 283: 423–63.

Miller, M. A. W., and D. B. Grant. 1997. Severe hypospadias with genital ambiguity: adult outcome after staged hypospadias repair. *British Journal of Urology* 80: 485–88.

Miller, W. G. 1993. *The work of human hands: Hardy Hendren and surgical wonder at Children's Hospital.* New York: Random House.

Milletti, N. 1994. Tribadi, saffiste, invertite e omosessuali: Categorie e sistemi sesso/genere nella rivista de anthropologia criminali fondata da Cesare Lombroso 1880–1949. *DWF* 4(24): 50–122.

Mininberg, D. T. 1982. Phalloplasty in congenital adrenal hyperplasia. *Journal of Urology* 128: 355–56.

Minton, H. 1996. Community empowerment and the medicalization of homosexuality: Constructing sexual identities in the 1930's. *Journal of the History of Sexuality* 6(3): 435–58.

Mitman, G. 1992. *The state of nature: Ecology, community and American social thought, 1900–1950*. Chicago: University of Chicago Press.

Mitman, G., and A. Fausto-Sterling. 1992. Whatever happened to Planaria? C. M. Child and the physiology of inheritance. In *The right tools for the job: At work in twentieth century biology*, ed. A. E. Clarke and J. H. Fujimura. Princeton: Princeton University Press, pp. 172–97.

Mittwoch, U. 1989. Sex differentiation in mammals and tempo of growth: Probabilities vs. switches. *Journal of Theoretical Biology* 137: 445–55.

———. 1992. Sex determination and sex reversal: Genotype, phenotype, dogma and semantics. *Human Genetics* 89: 467–79.

———. 1996. Sex-determining mechanisms in animals. *Trends in Ecology and Evolution* 11(2): 63–67.

Moffat, S. D., E. Hampson, et al. 1998. Morphology of the planum temporale and corpus callosum in left handers with evidence of left and right hemisphere speech representation. *Brain* 121: 2369–79.

Money, J. 1952. Hermaphroditism: An inquiry into the nature of a human paradox. *Social Sciences*. Cambridge: Harvard University, Ph.D. Thesis.

———. 1955. Hermaphroditism, gender and precocity in hyperadrenocorticism: Psychological findings. *Johns Hopkins Medical Journal* 96: 253–64.

———. 1956. *Hermaphroditism, gender and precocity in hyperadrenocorticism: Psychologic findings*. New York: Grune and Stratton.

———. 1961. Components of eroticism in man: II. The orgasm and genital somesthesia. *Journal of Nervous and Mental Disease* 132: 289–97.

———. 1968. *Sex errors of the body*. Baltimore: Johns Hopkins University Press.

———. 1970. Critique of Dr. Zuger's manuscript. *Psychosomatic Medicine* 32(5): 463–67.

———. 1994. *Sex errors of the body and related syndromes: A guide to counseling children, adolescents and their families*. Baltimore: Paul H. Brookes.

———. 1998. Case consultation: Ablatio penis. *Medicine and Law* 1: 113–23.

Money, J., and J. Dalèry. 1976. Iatrogenic homosexuality: Gender identity in seven 46,XX chromosomal females with hyperadrenocortical hermaphroditism born with a penis, three reared as boys, four reared as girls. *Journal of Homosexuality* 1(4): 357–71.

Money, J., and A. A. Ehrhardt. 1972. *Man and woman, boy and girl*. Baltimore: Johns Hopkins University Press.

Money, J., and J. G. Hampson. 1955. Idiopathic sexual precocity in the male. *Psychosomatic Medicine* 171: 2–15.

Money, J., J. G. Hampson, et al. 1955a. An examination of some basic sexual concepts: The evidence of human hermaphroditism. *Bulletin Johns Hopkins Hospital* 97: 301–19.

———. 1955b. Hermaphroditism: Recommendations concerning assignment of sex, change of sex, and psychologic management. *Bulletin Johns Hopkins Hospital* 97: 284–300.

———. 1956. Sexual incongruities and psychopathology: The evidence of human hermaphrodites. *Bulletin Johns Hopkins Hospital* 98: 43–57.

———. 1957. Imprinting and the establishment of gender role. *American Medical Association Archives of Neurology and Psychiatry* 77: 333–36.

Money, J., and M. Lamacz. 1987. Genital examination and exposure experienced as nosocomial sexual abuse in childhood. *Journal of Nervous and Mental Disease* 175(12): 713–21.

Montoya, B., W. Larbig, et al. 1997. The relationship of phantom limb pain to other phantom limb phenomena in upper extremity amputees. *Pain* 72: 87–93.

Moore, A. J., N. L. Reagan, et al. 1995. Conditional signaling strategies: Effects of ontogeny, social experience and social status on the pheromonal signal of male cockroaches. *Animal Behavior* 50: 191–202.

Moore, C. 1990. Comparative development of vertebrate sexual behavior; levels, cascades and webs. In *Issues in Comparative Psychology*, ed. D. A. Dewsbury. New York: Sinauer, 278–99.

Moore, C. L., H. Dou, et al. 1992. Maternal stimulation affects the number of motor neurons in a sexually dimorphic nucleus of the lumbar spinal cord. *Brain Research* 572: 52–56.

Moore, C. L., and S. Rogers. 1984. Contributions of self-grooming to onset of puberty in male rats. *Developmental Psychobiology* 17: 243–53.

Moore, C. R. 1919. On the physiological properties of the gonads as controllers of somatic and psychical characteristics I. The rat. *Journal of Experimental Zoology* 28: 137–60.

———. 1920. The production of artificial hermaphrodites in mammals. *Science* 52: 179–82.

———. 1921a. A critique of sex hormone antagonism. *Proceedings of the second international congress for sex research*, ed. A. W. Greenwood. London: Oliver and Boyd.

———. 1921b. On the physiological properties of the gonads as controllers of somatic and psychical characteristics III. Artificial hermaphroditism in rats. *Journal of Experimental Zoology* 333: 129–71.

———. 1921c. On the physiological properties of the gonads as controllers of somatic and psychical characteristics IV. Gonad transplantation in the guinea pig. *Journal of Experimental Zoology* 33:365–89.

———. 1922. On the physiological properties of the gonads as controllers of somatic and psychical characteristics: V. The effects of gonadectomy in the guinea pig on growth, bone lengths, and weight of organs of internal secretion. *Biological Bulletin* 43: 285–312.

Moore, C. R., and D. Price. 1930. The question of sex hormone antagonism. *Proceedings of the Society for Experimental Biology and Medicine* 28: 38–40.

———. 1932. Gonad hormone functions, and the reciprocal influence between gonads and hypophysis with its bearing on the problem of sex hormone antagonism. *American Journal of Anatomy* 50(1): 13–71.

Moore, H. L. 1994. *A passion for difference: Essays in anthropology and gender.* Bloomington: Indiana University Press.

Moore, K. L. 1977. *The developing human: clinically oriented embryology,* 2nd edition, Philadelphia: W. B. Saunders.

Moore, L. J., and A. E. Clarke. 1995. Clitoral conventions and transgressions: Graphic representations in anatomy texts, c1900–1991. *Feminist Studies* 21(2): 255–301.

Moreno, A. 1998. Am I a man or a woman? *Mademoiselle,* March 1998. 178ff.

Morin, A. 1996. La tératologie de Geoffroy Saint-Hilaire à nos jours. *Bulletin de l'Association des Anatomistes* 80(248): 17–31.

Morris, R. C. 1995. All made up—Performance theory and the new anthropology of sex and gender. *Annual Review of Anthropology* 24: 567–92.

Mort, F. 1987. *Dangerous sexualities: Medico-moral politics in England since 1830.* New York: Routledge.

Moscucci, O. 1990. *The science of woman: Gynaecology and gender in England 1800–1929.* Cambridge, U.K.: Cambridge University Press.

Mulaikal, R. M., C. J. Migeon, et al. 1987. Fertility rates in female patients with congenital adrenal hyperplasia due to 21-hydroxylase deficiency. *New England Journal of Medicine* 316(4): 178–82.

Mureau, M. 1997. De psychoseksuele en psychosociale ontwikkeling van patiënten met hypospadie. *Nederlands Tijdschrift Geneeskunde* 25(4) [January 25]: 188–91.

Mureau, M. A. M., F. M. E. Slijper, et al. 1995a. Genital perception of children, adolescents and adults operated on for hypospadias: A comparative study. *Journal of Sex Research* 32(4): 289–98.

———. 1995b. Psychosexual adjustment of children and adolescents after different types of hypospadias surgery: A norm-related study. *Journal of Urology* 154:1902–07.

———. 1995c. Psychosexual adjustment of men who underwent hypospadias repair: A norm-related study. *Journal of Urology* 154 (October): 1351–55.

———. 1997. Psychosocial functioning of children, adolescents and adults following hypospadias surgery: A comparative study. *Journal of Pediatric Psychology* 22(3): 371–87.

Murray, J. 1991. Agnolo Firenzuola on female sexuality and women's equality. *Sixteenth Century Journal* 22(2): 199–213.

Murray, S. O., ed. 1992. *Oceanic homosexualities.* New York: Garland.

Nadler, R. D. 1968. Masculinization of female rats by intracranial implantation of androgen in infancy. *Journal of Comparative and Physiological Psychology* 66:157–67.

Naftolin, F., and J. R. Brawer. 1978. The effect of estrogens on hypothalamic structure and function. *American Journal of Obstetrics and Gynecology* (December 1): 758–65.

Naftolin, F., and N. MacLusky. 1984. Aromatization hypothesis revisited. In *Sex-*

ual Differentiation: Basic and clinical aspects, ed. M. Serio, M. Motta, M. Zanisi, and L. Martini. New York: Raven Press, 79–91.

Naftolin, F., and K. J. Ryan. 1975. The metabolism of androgens in central neuroendocrine tissues. *Journal of Steroid Biochemistry* 6: 993–97.

Naftolin, F., K. J. Ryan, et al. 1971. Aromatization of androstenedione by the diencephalon. *Journal of Clinical Endocrinology and Metabolism* 33(2): 368–70.

————. 1972. Aromatization of adrostenedione by the anterior hypothalamus of adult male and female rats. *Endocrinology* 90: 295–98.

Nanda, S. 1986. The Hijras of India: cultural and individual dimensions of an institutionalized third gender role. *Journal of Homosexuality* 11(3–4): 35–54.

————. 1989. *Neither man nor woman: The Hijras of India*. Belmont, MA: Wadsworth.

————. 1994. Hijras: An alternative sex and gender role in India. In *Third sex third gender: Beyond sexual dimorphism in culture and history*, ed. G. Herdt. New York: Zone Books, 373–418.

Natarajan, A. 1996. Medical ethics and truth telling in the case of androgen insensitivity syndrome. *Canadian Medical Association Journal* 154(4): 568–70.

Nelson, L. H., and J. Nelson, eds. 1996. *Feminism, science, and the philosophy of science*. Boston: Kluwer Academic.

Nelson, W. O., and C. Merckel. 1937. Effects of androgenic substances in the female rat. *Society for Experimental Biology and Medicine* 36: 823–35.

New, M. I. 1998. Diagnosis and management of congenital adrenal hyperplasia. *Annual Review of Medicine* 49: 311–28.

New, M. I., P. C. White, et al. 1989. The adrenal hyperplasias. In *The metabolic basis of inherited disease*, ed. C. R. Scriver, A. L. Beaudet, W. S. Sly, and D. Valle. New York: McGraw-Hill, 1881–1917.

New, M. L., and L. S. Levine. 1981. Adrenal hyperplasia in intersex states. *Pediatric and Adolescent Endocrinology* 8: 51–64.

Newman, K., J. Randolf, et al. 1992a. The survival management of infants and children with ambiguous genitalia: lessons learned from 25 years. *Annals of Surgery* 215(6): 644–53.

————. 1992b. Functional results in young women having clitoral reconstruction as infants. *Journal of Pediatric Surgery* 27(2): 180–84.

Newman, L. M., ed. 1985. *Men's ideas, women's realities: Popular science, 1870–1915*. New York: Pergamon Press.

Newsom, B. 1994. Hugh Hampton Young, M.D., 1870–1945. *Journal of the South Carolina Medical Association* 90(5): 254.

Niemi, M. 1987. Andrology as a specialty: Its origin. *Journal of Andrology* 8 (July/August): 201–02.

Nihoul-Fekete, C. 1981. Feminizing genitoplasty in the intersex child. *Pediatric and Adolescent Endocrinology* 8: 247–60.

Nihoul-Fekete, C., F. Phillipe, et al. 1982. Résultats à moyen et long terme de la chirurgie reparatrice des organes génitaux chez les filles atteintes d'hyperplasie congénitale virilisante des surrenales. *Archives Francaises de Pediatrie* 39: 13–16.

Nikolaenko, N. N., and A. Y. Egorov. 1998. Types of interhemispheric relations in man. *Brain Cognition* 37(1): 116–19.

Njinou, B., Terryn, F., et al. 1998. [Correction of severe median hypospadias. Review of 77 cases treated by the onlay island flap technique]. *Acta Urologica Belgica* 66(1): 7–11.

Noble, D. F. 1977. *America by design: Science, technology and the rise of corporate capitalism*. New York: Knopf.

Nogales, F., E. Villar, et al. 1956. Zwei fälle echten Hermaphroditismus. *Geburtshilfe und Frauenheilkunde* 9: 774–69.

Nonomura, K., H. Kakizaki, et al. 1998. Surgical repair of anterior hypospadias with fish-mouth meatus and intact prepuce based on anatomical characteristics. *Eur Urol* 34(4): 368–71.

Norris, A. S., and W. C. Keettel. 1962. Change of sex during adolescence. *American Journal of Obstetrics and Gynecology* 84(6): 719–21.

Norton, M. 1996. *Founding mothers and fathers: Gendered power and the formation of American society*. New York: Knopf.

Noske, B. 1989. *Humans and other animals: Beyond the boundaries of anthropology*. London: Pluto Press.

Nussbaum, E. 1999. The sex that dare not speak its name. *Lingua Franca* (May-June): 42–51.

Nye, R. A. 1998. Introduction. In *Oxford readers: Sexuality*, ed. R. A. Nye. Oxford, U.K.: Oxford University Press, 3–15.

Nyhart, L. 1995. *Biology takes form: Animal morphology and the German universities, 1800–1900*. Chicago: University of Chicago Press.

Oberfield, S. E., A. Mondok, et al. 1989. Clitoral size in full-term infants. *American Journal of Perinatology* 6(4): 453–54.

O'Connell, H. E., J. M. Hutson, et al. 1998. Anatomical relationship between urethra and clitoris. *Journal of Urology* 159 (June): 1892–97.

O'Donovan, K. 1985. Transsexual troubles: The discrepancy between legal and social categories. In *Gender, sex and the law*, ed. S. Edwards. London: Croom Helm, 9–27.

Oesterling, J. E., J. P. Gearhart, et al. 1987. A unified approach to early reconstructive surgery of the child with ambiguous genitalia. *Journal of Urology* 138: 1079–84.

Ogawa, S., D. B. Lubahn, et al. 1997. Behavioral effects of estrogen receptor gene disruption in male mice. *Proceedings of the National Academy of Science* 94: 1476–81.

Ogilvie, M. 1986. *Women in science: Antiquity through the nineteenth century*. Cambridge: MIT Press.

O'Kusky, J., E. Strauss, et al. 1988. The corpus callosum is larger with right-hemisphere cerebral speech dominance. *Annals of Neurology* 24(3): 379–83.

Olsen, G. W., F. D. Gilliland, et al. 1998. An epidemiologic investigation of reproductive hormones in men with occupational exposure to perfluorooctanoic acid. *Journal of Occupational and Environmental Medicine* 40(7): 614–22.

Oppenheim, J. S., A. B. Benjamin, et al. 1987. No sex-related differences in human corpus callosum based on magnetic resonance imagery. *Annals of Neurology* 21: 604–6.

O'Rahilly, R., and F. Müller. 1996. *Human embryology and teratology, 2nd ed.* New York: Wiley-Liss.

O'Rand, A. 1989. Scientific thought style and the construction of gender. In *Women and a new academy: Gender and cultural contexts*, ed. J. F. O'Barr. Madison: University of Wisconsin Press, 103–21.

Ormrod, R. 1992. The medico-legal aspects of sex determination. *Medico-Legal Journal*: 78–88.

Ortner, S. B. 1996. *Making gender: The politics and erotics of culture.* Boston: Beacon Press.

Oudshoorn, N. 1990. Endocrinologists and the conceptualization of sex, 1920–1940. *Journal of the History of Biology* 23(2): 42–83.

———. 1994. *Beyond the natural body: An archeology of sex hormones.* London: Routledge.

Overzier, C. 1963. True hermaphroditism. In *Intersexuality*, ed. C. Overzier. London: Academic Press, 182–234.

Oyama, S. 1985. *The ontogeny of information.* Cambridge, U. K.: Cambridge University Press.

———. 1989. Ontogeny and the central dogma: Do we need the concept of genetic programming in order to have an evolutionary perspective? In *Systems and Development*, ed. M. R. Gunnar and E. Thelen. Hillsdale, N.J.: Lawrence Erlbaum, 22.

———. 1992a. Ontogeny and phylogeny: A case of metarecapitulation? In *Trees of Life*, ed. P. Griffiths. Dordstadt, Kluwer, Netherlands, 211–39.

———. 1992b. Transmission and construction: Levels and the problem of heredity. In *Levels of social behavior: Evolutionary and genetic aspects*, ed. E. Tobach and G. Greenberg. Wichita: T. C. Schnierla Research Fund, 51–60.

———. 1993. How shall I name thee? The construction of natural selves. *Frontiers of Developmental Theory and Psychology* 3:471–96.

Oyewumi, O. 1997. *The invention of women: Making an African sense of Western gender discourses.* Minneapolis: University of Minnesota Press.

———. 1998. De-confounding gender: Feminist theorizing and Western culture, a comment on Hawkesworth's "Confounding Gender." *Signs* 23(4): 1049–62.

Ozbey, H. 1998. Gender assignment in female congenital adrenal hyperplasia. *British Journal of Urology* 81: 180.

Padgug, R. 1979. Sexual matters: On conceptualizing sexuality in history. *Radical History Review* 20: 3–23.

Pang, S. 1994. Congenital adrenal hyperplasia. *Current Therapy in Endocrinology and Metabolism* 5: 157–66.

Park, K. 1990. Hermaphrodites and lesbians: Sexual anxiety and French medicine, 1570–1621. Talk given at Annual Meeting of the History of Science Society, 1–19.

Parker, L. A. 1998. Ambiguous genitalia: Etiology, treatment, and nursing implications. *Journal of Obstetric, Gynecologic, and Neonatal Nursing* 27(1): 15–22.

Parkes, A. S. 1938. Terminology of sex hormones. *Nature* 141: 36.

———. 1966a. The rise of reproductive endocrinology, 1926–1940. *Journal of Endocrinology* 34(3): 20–32.

———. 1966b. *Sex, science and society: Addresses, lectures and articles.* London: Oriel Press.

Pattatucci, A. M. 1998. Molecular investigation into complex behavior: Lessons from sexual orientation studies. *Human Biology* 70(2): 367–86.

Pattatucci, A. M. L., and D. H. Hamer. 1995. Development and familiality of sexual orientation in females. *Behavior Genetics* 25(5): 407–20.

Paul, D. 1995. *Controlling human heredity.* Highlands, N.J.: Atlantic Humanities Press.

———. 1998. *The politics of heredity: Essays on eugenics, biomedicine and the nature-nurture debate.* Albany: State University of New York Press.

Pauly, P. J. 1987. *Controlling life: Jacques Loeb and the engineering ideal in biology.* New York: Oxford University Press.

———. 1988. Summer resort and scientific discipline: Woods Hole and the structure of American biology. In *The American Development of Biology,* ed. R. Rainger, K. R. Benson, and J. Maienschein. Philadelphia: University of Pennsylvania Press, pp. 121–50.

Paus, T., A. Zijdenbos, et al. 1999. Structural maturation of neural pathways in children and adolescents: In vivo study. *Science* 283 March 19: 1908–11.

Payer, P. J. 1993. *The bridling of desire: Views of sex in the later middle ages.* Toronto: University of Toronto Press.

Pennisi, E. 1997. Differing roles found for estrogen's two receptors. *Science* 277 (September 5): 1439.

Peris, L. A. 1960. Congenital adrenal hyperplasia producing female hermaphroditism with phallic urethra. *Obstetrics and Gynecology* 16(2): 156–66.

Perovic, S. V. 1998. The penile disassembly technique in hypospadias repair [letter; comment]. *British Journal of Urology* 81(4): 658.

Perovic, S. V., and M. L. Djordjevic, 1998. A new approach in hypospadias repair. *World Journal of Urology* 16(3): 195–9.

Perovic, S. V., M. L. Djordjevic, et al. 1998. A new approach to the treatment of penile curvature. *Journal of Urology* 160 (3, pt. 2): 1123–127.

Perovic, S. V., V. Vukadinovic, et al. 1998. The penile disassembly technique in hypospadias repair [see comments]. *British Journal of Urology* 81(3): 479–87.

Peters, M. 1988. The size of the corpus callosum in males and females: The implications of a lack of allometry. *Canadian Journal of Psychology* 42(3): 313–24.

Phillip, M., C. De Boer, et al. 1996. Clitoral and penile sizes of full term newborns in two different ethnic groups. *Journal of Pediatric Endocrinology and Metabolism* 9(2): 175–79.

Phoenix, C. 1978. Prenatal testosterone in the nonhuman primate and its consequences for behavior. In *Sex differences in behavior*, ed. R. C. Friedman, R. M. Richart, and R. L. Van de Wiele. Huntington, N.J.: Robert E. Krieger Publishing Company, 19–32.

Phoenix, C. H., K. H. Copenhaver, et al. 1976. Scanning electron microscopy of penile papillae in intact and castrated rats. *Hormones and Behavior* 7(212–27).

Phoenix, C. H., R. W. Goy, et al. 1959. Organizing action of prenatally administered testosterone propionate on the tissues mediating mating behavior in the female guinea pig. *Endocrinology.* 65: 369–82.

Phornphutkul, C., A. Fausto-Sterling, et al. 1999. Gender self-reassignment in an XY adolescent male born with ambiguous genitalia. *Pediatrics* in press.

Pinker, S. 1997. *How the mind works.* New York: Norton.

Pintér, A., and G. Kosztolányi. 1990. Surgical management of neonates and children with ambiguous genitalia. *Acta Paediatrica Hungarica* 30(1): 111–21.

Piro, C., M. de Diego, et al. 1998. [Autologous buccal mucosal graft for urethral reconstruction]. *Cirugia Pediatrica (Barcelona)* 11(2): 71–72.

Plumwood, V. 1993. *Feminism and the mastery of nature.* New York: Routledge.

Pons, T. 1996. Novel sensations in the congenitally blind. *Nature* 380 (April 11): 479–80.

Pool, R. 1993. Evidence for homosexuality gene. *Science* 261 (July 16): 291–92.

———. 1994. *Eve's rib: The biological roots of difference.* New York: Crown Publishers.

Poovey, M. 1993. Figures of arithmetic, figures of speech: The discourse of statistics in the 1830's. *Critical Inquiry* 19 (Winter): 256–76.

———. 1995. *Making a social body: British cultural formation, 1830–1864.* Chicago: University of Chicago Press.

Porter, R., and L. Hall. 1995. *The facts of life: The creation of sexual knowledge in Britain, 1650–1950.* New Haven: Yale University Press.

Porter, R., and T. Mikuláš, eds. 1994. *Sexual knowledge, sexual science: The history of attitudes to sexuality.* Cambridge, U.K.: Cambridge University Press.

Porter, T. M. 1986. *The rise of statistical thinking, 1820–1900.* Princeton: Princeton University Press.

———. 1992. Quantification and the accounting ideal in science. *Social Studies of Science* 22: 633–52.

———. 1995. *Trust in numbers: The pursuit of objectivity in science and public life.* Princeton: Princeton University Press.

———. 1997. The management of society by numbers. In *Science in the Twentieth Century*, ed. J. Krige and D. Pestre. Australia: Harwood Academic Publishers, 97–110.

Potter, E. 1989. Modeling gender politics in science. In *Feminism and Science*, ed. N. Tuana. Bloomington: Indiana University Press, 132–46.

Pratt, J. P. 1939. *Sex functions in man.* In *Sex and internal secretions*, ed. Charles H. Allen and Edward A. Doisy. Baltimore: Williams and Wilkins, 1263–1334.

Press, A. 1998. Jury gives $2.9 million to transvestite's mother. *New York Times*, 39.

Preves, S. 1999. For the sake of the children: Destigmatizing intersexuality. In *Intersex in the age of ethics*, ed. Alice D. Dreger. Hagerstown: University Publishing Group, 51–58.

Price, D. 1972. Mammalian conception, sex differentiation, and hermaphroditism as viewed in historical perspective. *American Zoologist* 12: 179–91.

———. 1974. Carl Richard Moore, December 5, 1892-October 16, 1955. *Biographical Memoirs of the National Academy of Sciences* 45: 384–412.

Prokop, V. A., M. Oehmichen, et al. 1990. Geschlechtsdimporphismus des Corpus callosum? *Beitrage zur Gerichtlichen Medizin* 48: 263–70.

Puig, M. 1991. *Kiss of the Spiderwoman*. New York: Vintage.

Quercia, N., D. Chitayat, et al. 1998. Normal external genitalia in a female with classical congenital adrenal hyperplasia who was not treated during embryogenesis. *Prenatal Diagnosis* 18(1): 83–85.

Quetelet, M. A. 1842. *A treatise on man and the development of his faculties*. New York: Burt Franklin.

Quigley, C. A., A. Debellis, et al. 1995. Androgen receptor defects: Historical, clinical and molecular perspectives. *Endocrine Reviews* 16(3): 271–321.

Raboch, J., J. Kobilková, et al. 1987. Sexual development and life of women with gonadal dysgenesis. *Journal of Sex and Marital Therapy* 13(2): 117–27.

Rainger, R., K. Benson, et al., eds. 1988. *The American development of biology*. Philadelphia: University of Pennsylvania Press.

Raisman, G., and P. M. Field. 1973. Sexual dimorphism in the neuropil of the preoptic area of the rat and its dependence on neonatal androgen. *Brain Research* 54: 1–29.

Rajfer, J., R. M. Ehrlich, et al. 1982. Reduction clitoroplasty via ventral approach. *Journal of Urology* 128 (August): 341–43.

Randolf, J. G., and W. Hung. 1970. Reduction clitoroplasty in females with hypertrophied clitoris. *Journal of Pediatric Surgery* 5(2): 224–31.

Randolf, J., W. Hung, et al. 1981. Clitoroplasty for females born with ambiguous genitalia: a long-term study. *Journal of Pediatric Surgery* 16(6): 882–87.

Rapp, R. 1997. Real-time fetus: The role of the sonogram in the age of monitored reproduction. In *Cyborgs and Citadels*, ed. G. L. Downey and J. Dumit. Santa Fe: School of American Research Press, 31–48.

Rauch, R. A., and R. J. Jinkins. 1994. Analysis of cross-sectional area measurements of the corpus callosum adjusted for brain size in male and female subjects from childhood to adulthood. *Behavioural Brain Research* 64: 65–78.

Raynaud, A., and M. Frilley. 1947. Destruction des glades génitales de l'embryon de souris, par une irradiation au moyen des rayons X, a l'age de treize jours. *Annales d'endocrinologie* 8(5): 400–419.

Rechter, J. E. 1997. The glands of destiny: A history of popular, medical and scientific views of the sex hormones in 1920's America. History Dept. Berkeley: University of California. Ph.D. thesis.

Reilly, J. M., and C. R. J. Woodhouse. 1989. Small penis and the male sexual role. *Journal of Urology* 142 (August): 569–71.

Reinarz, S. J., C. E. Coffman, et al. 1988. MR imaging of the corpus callosum: Normal and pathologic findings and correlation with CT. *American Journal of Radiology* 151: 791–98.

Reiner, W. 1996. Case study: Sex reassignment in a teenage girl. *Journal of the American Academy of Child and Adolescent Psychiatry* 35(6): 799–803.

———. 1997a. Sex assignment in the neonate with intersex or inadequate genitalia. *Archives of Pediatric and Adolescent Medicine* 151 (October): 1044–45.

———. 1997b. To be male or female—That is the question. *Archives of Pediatric and Adolescent Medicine* 151 (March): 1997.

Reinitz, J., E. Mjoisness, et al. 1992. A connectionist model of the Drosophila blastoderm. In *Principles of organization in organisms*, ed. J. Mittenthal and A. Baskin. New York: Addison-Wesley, 109–18.

Reiss, I. 1995. Is this the definitive sex survey? *Journal of Sex Research* 32(1): 77–91.

Renard, E., J. Bringer, et al. 1993. Steroides sexuels: Effets sur le metabolisme hydrocarbone avant et après la menopause. *La Presse Médicale* 22(9): 431–35.

Retik, A. B., and J. G. Borer. 1998. Primary and reoperative hypospadias repair with the Snodgrass technique. *World Journal of Urology* 16(3): 186–91.

Reumann, M. 1998. The Kinsey reports and American sexual character, 1946–1964. American Civilization. Providence: Brown University. Ph.D. thesis.

Rey, M. 1987. Parisian homosexuals create a lifestyle, 1700–1750: The police archives. In *'Tis nature's fault: Unauthorized sexuality during the enlightenment*, ed. R. P. Maccubbin. Cambridge, U.K.: Cambridge University Press, 179–91.

Reyes, F. I., R. S. Boroditsky, et al. 1974. Studies on human sexual development II. Fetal and maternal serum gonadotropin and sex steroid concentrations. *Journal of Clinical Endocrinology and Metabolism* 38 (January–June): 612–17.

Ribot, C., and F. Tremollieres. 1995. Sexual steroids and bone tissue. *Endocrinology and Metabolism* 56(1): 49–55.

Rice, G., C. Anderson, et al. 1999. Male homosexuality: Absence of linkage to microsatellite markers at Xq28. *Science* 284 (April 23): 665–67.

Richardson, J. T. E. 1997. Introduction to the study of gender differences in cognition. In *Gender differences in human cognition*, ed. J. T. E. Richardson. Oxford, U.K.: Oxford University Press.

Richardson, S. 1994. The brain-boosting sex hormone. *Discover* (April): 30–32.

Catholic League for Religious and Civil Rights. 1995. The holy see: Voice of sanity in a sea of madness. *New York Times*, September 3, advertisement, section 4, p. 11.

Riley, W. J., and A. L. Rosenbloom. 1980. Clitoral size in infancy. *Journal of Pediatrics* 96(5): 918–19.

Rink, R. C., and M. C. Adams. 1998. Feminizing genitoplasty: State of the art. *World Journal of Urology* 16(3): 212–18.

Riss, W., E. S. Valenstein, et al. 1955. Development of sexual behavior in male guinea pigs from genetically different stocks under controlled conditions of androgen treatment and caging. *Endocrinology* 57(2): 139–46.

Riss, W., and W. C. Young. 1954. The failure of large quantities of testosterone propionate to activate low drive male guinea pigs. *Endocrinology* 54(2): 232–35.

Robinson, P. 1976. *The modernization of sex: Havelock Ellis, Alfred Kinsey, William Masters and Virginia Johnson.* Ithaca: Cornell University Press.

Roofe, P. G. 1968. William Caldwell Young. In *Reproduction and sexual behavior,* ed. M. Diamond. Bloomington: Indiana University Press, 449–52.

Rosario, V., ed. 1997. *Science and homosexualities.* New York: Routledge.

Roscoe, W. 1991. *The Zuni man-woman.* Albuquerque: University of New Mexico Press.

———. 1994. How to become a berdache: Toward a unified analysis of gender diversity. In *Third sex third gender: Beyond sexual dimorphism in culture and history,* ed. G. Herdt. New York: Zone Books, 329–72.

Rose, H. 1994. *Love, power, and knowledge: Towards a feminist transformation of the sciences.* Bloomington: Indiana University Press.

Rose, S. 1998. *Lifelines: Biology beyond determinism.* Oxford, U.K.: Oxford University Press.

Rosenberg, R. 1982. *Beyond separate spheres: Intellectual roots of modern feminism.* New Haven: Yale University Press.

Rosenbloom, A. L. 1998. Evaluation of severe hypospadias [letter; comment]. *Journal of Pediatrics* 133(1): 169–70.

Rosenwald, A. K., J. H. Handlon, et al. 1958. Psychologic studies before and after clitoridectomy in female pseudohermaphroditism caused by congenital virilizing adrenal hyperplasia. *Pediatrics* 21: 832–39.

Rossiter, K., and S. Diehl. 1998. Gender reassignment in children: Ethical conflicts about surrogate decision making. *Pediatric Nursing* 24(1): 59–62.

Rossiter, M. W. 1982. *Women scientists in America: Struggles and strategies to 1940.* Baltimore: Johns Hopkins University Press.

———. 1995. *Women scientists in America: Before affirmative action.* Baltimore: Johns Hopkins University Press.

Rothblatt, M. 1995. *The apartheid of sex: A manifesto on the freedom of gender.* New York: Crown.

Roubertoux, P., and M. Carlier. 1978. Intelligence: Différence individuelles, facteurs génétiques, facteurs d'environnement et interaction entre génotype et environnement. *Annales Biologique Clinique* 36: 101–12.

Rubin, G. 1975. The traffic in women: Notes on the "political economy" of sex. In *Toward an anthropology of women,* ed. R. R. Reiter. New York: Monthly Review Press, 157–210.

———. 1984. Thinking sex: Notes for a radical theory of the politics of sexuality. In *Pleasure and Danger: Exploring female sexuality,* ed. C. S. Vance. Boston: Routledge & Kegan Paul.

Rushton, H. G., and A. B. Belman. 1998. The split prepuce in situ onlay hypospadias repair. *Journal of Urology.* 160 (3 pt. 2): 1134–36; discussion 1137.

Russett, C. E. 1989. *Sexual science: The Victorian construction of womanhood*. Cambridge: Harvard University Press.

Sadato, N., A. Pascual-Leone, et al. 1996. Activation of the primary visual cortex by Braille reading in blind subjects. *Nature* 380 (April 11): 526–28.

Sagehashi, N. 1993. Clitoroplasty for clitoromegaly due to adrenogenital syndrome without loss of sensitivity. *Plastic and Reconstructive Surgery* 91(5): 950–56.

Sakemi, T., H. Toyoshima, et al. 1995. Estrogen attenuates progressive glomerular injury in hypercholesterolemic male Imai rats. *Nephron* 69(2): 159–65.

Salat, D., A. Ward, et al. 1996. Sex differences in the corpus callosum with aging. *Neurobiology of Aging* 18(2): 191–97.

Sand, K. 1919. Experiments on the internal secretion of the sexual glands, especially on experimental hermaphroditism. *Journal of Physiology* 53: 257–63.

Sandberg, D. E., and H. F. L. Meyer-Bahlburg. 1995. Gender development in boys born with hypospadias. *Psychoneuroendocrinology* 20(7): 693–709.

Sane, K., and O. H. Pescovitz. 1992. The clitoral index: A determination of clitoral size in normal girls and in girls with abnormal sexual development. *Journal of Pediatrics* 120(2): 264–66.

Santti, R., S. Makela, et al. 1998. Phytoestrogens: Potential endocrine disruptors in males. *Toxicol Ind Health* 14(1–2): 223–37.

Sapolsky, R. 1997. A gene for nothing. *Discover*. 18: 40–46.

Sawicki, J. 1991. *Disciplining Foucault*. New York: Routledge.

Schafer, A. J., M. A. Dominguez-Steglich, et al. 1995. The role of SOX9 in autosomal sex reversal and campomelic dysplasia. *Philosophical Transactions of the Royal Society of London B* 350: 271–78.

Schafer, A. J., and P. N. Goodfellow. 1996. Sex determination in humans. *BioEssays* 18(12): 955–64.

Schiebinger, L. 1992. The gendered brain: Some historical perspectives. In *So human a brain: Knowledge and values in the neuroscience*, ed. A. Harrington. Boston: Birkauser, 110–20.

———. 1993a. Why mammals are called mammals: Gender politics in eighteenth-century natural history. *American Historical Review* 98(2): 382–411.

———. 1993b. *Nature's body: Gender in the making of modern science*. Boston: Beacon Press.

Schilder, P. 1950. *The image and appearance of the human body: Studies in the constructive energies of the psyche*. New York: International Universities Press.

Schlaug, G., L. Jäncke, et al. 1995. Increased corpus callosum size in musicians. *Neuropsychologia* 33(8): 1047–55.

Schlesinger, A. J. 1958. The crisis of American masculinity. *Esquire* 50: 63–65.

Schlinger, B. 1998. Sexual differentiation of avian brain and behavior: Current views on gonadal hormone-dependent and independent mechanisms. *Annual Review of Physiology* 60: 407–29.

Schlinger, B. A., and A. P. Arnold. 1991. Brain is the major site of estrogen synthesis in the male songbird. *Proceedings of the National Academy of Science*: 4191–94.

Schmidt, F. L. 1992. What do data really mean? Research findings, meta-analysis and cumulative knowledge in psychology. *American Psychologist* 47(10): 1173–81.

Schmidt, G. 1984. Allies and persecutors: Science and medicine in the homosexuality issue. *Journal of Homosexuality* 88(10)(3–4): 127–40.

Schober, J. M. 1998. Feminizing genitoplasty for intersex. In *Pediatric surgery and urology: Long term outcomes*, ed. M. D. Stringer, K. T. Oldham, P. D. E. Mouriquand, and E. R. Howard. London: Saunders, 549–58.

Schreiner, O. 1911. *Woman and labor*. New York: Frederick Stokes.

Schutte, H., and J. R. Herman. 1975. Eugen Steinach, 1861–1944. *Investigative Urology* 12(4): 330–31.

Scott, J. 1993. The evidence of experience. In *The lesbian and gay studies reader*, ed. H. Abelove, M. A. Barale, and D. M. Halperin. New York: Routledge.

Scott, J. W. 1988. *Gender and the politics of history*. New York: Columbia University Press.

Scott, M. 1995. *Shadow man*. New York: Tom Doherty Associates.

Scriver, C. R., and P. J. Waters. 1999. Monogenic traits are not simple: Lessons from phenylketonuria. *Trends in Genetics* 15(7): 267–72.

Seckl, J. R., and W. L. Miller. 1997. How safe is long-term prenatal glucocorticoid treatment? [see comments]. *Journal of the American Medical Association* 277(13): 1077–79.

Sengoopta, C. 1992. Science, sexuality and gender in the fin de siècle: Otto Weininger as Baedeker. *History of Science* 30: 249–79.

———. 1993. Rejuvenation and the prolongation of life: Science or quackery? *Perspectives in Biology and Medicine* 37(1): 55–65.

———. 1996. The unknown Weininger: Science, philosophy and cultural politics in fin-de-siècle Vienna. *Central European History* 29(4): 453–94.

———. 1998. Glandular politics: Experimental biology, clinical medicine, and homosexual emancipation in fin-de-siècle Central Europe. *Isis* 89: 445–73.

Serbin, L. A., K. K. Powlishta, et al. 1993. *The development of sex typing in middle childhood*. Chicago: University of Chicago Press.

Serrat, A., and A. Garcia de Herreros. 1993. Determination of genetic sex by PCR amplification of Y-chromosome-specific sequences. *The Lancet* 341: 1593.

Several. 1997. The pediatric forum: Sex reassessment at birth. *Archives of Pediatric and Adolescent Medicine* 151 (October): 1062–64.

Shapin, S. 1994. *A social history of truth: Civility and science in seventeenth-century England*. Chicago: University of Chicago Press.

Sharp, R. J., T. M. Holder, et al. 1987. Neonatal genital reconstruction. *Journal of Pediatric Surgery* 2(22): 168–71.

Sharpe, R. M. 1997. Do males rely on female hormones? *Nature* 390 (December 4): 447–48.

Silverman, K. 1992. *Male subjectivity at the margins*. New York: Routledge.

Simpson, J. L. 1986. Gender testing in the Olympics. *Journal of the American Medical Association* 256(14): 1938.

Sinclair, A. H. 1995. New genes for boys. *American Journal of Human Genetics* 57: 998–1001.

————. 1998. Human sex determination. *Journal of Experimental Zoology* 281: 501–5.

Sinforiani, E., C. Livieri, et al. 1994. Cognitive and neuroradiological findings in congenital adrenal hyperplasia. *Psychoneuroendocrinology* 19(1): 55–54.

Singer, W. 1995. Development and plasticity of cortical processing architectures. *Science* 270 (November 3): 758–64.

Singh, J. A. L. 1942. *Wolf-children and feral man.* New York: Harper.

Sitruk-Ware, R. 1995. Cardiovascular risk at the menopause—Role of sexual steroids. *Hormone Research* 43: 58–63 .

Skakkebaek, N. E., E. Rajpert-De Meyts, et al. 1998. Germ cell cancer and disorders of spermatogenesis: An environmental connection? *Apmis* 106(1): 3–11; discussion 12.

Slijper, F. M. E., S. L. S. Drop, et al. 1994. Neonates with abnormal genital development assigned the female sex: Parent counseling. *Journal of Sex Education and Therapy* 20(1): 9–17.

————. 1998. Long-term psychological evaluation of intersex children. *Archives of Sexual Behavior* 27(2): 125–44.

Slootweg, M. C., A. G. H. Ederveen, et al. 1992. Oestrogen and progestogen synergistically stimulate human and rat osteoblast proliferation. *Journal of Endocrinology* 133: R5–R8.

Smart, C. 1992. Disruptive bodies and unruly sex: The regulation of reproduction and sexuality in the 19th century. In *Regulating womanhood,* ed. C. Smart. New York: Routledge.

Smith, E. D. 1997. The history of hypospadias. *Pediatric Surgery International* 12: 81–85.

Smith, E. P., J. Boyd, et al. 1994. Estrogen resistance caused by a mutation in the estrogen receptor gene in a man. *New England Journal of Medicine* 331(16): 1056–61.

Smith, J., J. L. Hurst, et al. 1994. Comparing behaviour in wild and laboratory strains of the house mouse: Levels of comparison and functional inference. *Behavioural Processes* 32: 79–86.

Snarch, B. 1992. Neither man nor woman: Berdache—A case for non-dichotomous gender construction. *Anthropologia* 34: 105–21.

Snodgrass, W., M. Koyle, et al. 1998. Tubularized incised plate hypospadias repair for proximal hypospadias. *Journal of Urology* 159(6): 2129–31.

Södersten, P. 1976. Lordosis behavior in male, female and androgenized female rats. *Journal of Endocrinology* 70: 409–20.

Sotiropoulos, A., A. Morishima, et al. 1976. Long-term assessment of genital reconstruction in female pseudohermaphrodites. *Journal of Urology* 115: 599–601.

Speiser, P. W., J. Dupont, et al. 1992. Disease expression and molecular genotype in congenital adrenal hyperplasia due to 21-hydroxylase deficiency. *Journal of Clinical Investigation* 90: 584–95.

Speiser, P. W., and M. I. New. 1994*a*. Prenatal diagnosis and treatment of congenital adrenal hyperplasia. *Clinical Perinatology* 21(3): 631–45.

———. 1994*b*. Prenatal diagnosis and treatment of congenital adrenal hyperplasia. *Journal of Pediatric Endocrinology* 7(3): 183–91.

Spelman, E. 1988. *Inessential woman: Problems of exclusion in feminist thought*. Boston: Beacon Press.

Spence, J. T. 1984. Masculinity, femininity, and gender-related traits: A conceptual analysis and critique of current research. *Progress in Experimental Personality Research* 13: 1–97.

———. 1985. Gender identity and its implications for the concepts of masculinity and femininity. *Nebraska Symposium on Motivation* 32: 59–95.

Squier, S. 1999. From Omega to Mr. Adam: The importance of literature for feminist science studies. *Science, Technology and Human Values* 24(1): 132–58.

Sripathi, V., S. Ahmed, et al. 1997. Gender reversal in 47,XX congenital virilizing adrenal hyperplasia. *British Journal of Urology* 79: 785–89.

Stanley, J. C. 1993. Boys and girls who reason well mathematically. In *The origins and development of high ability*, ed. G. R. Bock and K. Ackrill. Chichester: Wiley, 119–38.

Star, S. L. 1983. Simplification in scientific work: An example from neuroscience research. *Social Studies of Science* 13: 205–28.

———. 1992. The skin, the skull and the self: Toward a sociology of the brain. In *So human a brain: Knowledge and values in the neurosciences*, ed. A. Harrington. Boston: Birkhauser, 204–28.

Star, S. L., and J. R. Griesemer. 1989. Institutional ecology, "translations" and boundary objects: Amateurs and professionals in Berkeley's Museum of Vertebrate Zoology, 1907–1939. *Social Studies of Science* 19: 387–420.

———. 1999. Male, female hormone treatment can help revive interest in sex. *Providence Journal*, Jan. 1:L10.

Stecker, J. F., C. Horton, E., et al. 1981. Hypospadias cripples. *Urologic Clinics of North America* 8(3): 539–44.

Stein, E. 1998. Review of queer science: The use and abuse of research on homosexuality. *Journal of Homosexuality* 35(2): 107–17.

———. 1999. *The mismeasure of desire: The science, theory and ethics of sexual orientation*. Oxford, U.K.: Oxford University Press.

Steinach, E. 1910. Geschlechtstrieb und echt sekundäre Geschlechtsmerkmale als Folge der innersekretorischen Funktion der Keimdrüse. *Zentralblatt für Physiologie* 24(13): 551–66.

———. 1912. Willkürliche Umwandlung von Säugertier-Männchen in Tiere mit ausgeprägt weiblichen Geschletscharakteren und weiblicher Psyche. *Pflüger's Archiv für Physiologie* 144: 71–108.

————. 1913. Pubertätsdrüsen und Zwitterbildung. Roux's *Archiv für Entwicklungsmechanik* 42: 307–32.

————. 1913. Feminierung von Mannchen und maskulierung von Weibchen. *Zentralblatt fur Physiologie* 27(14): 717–23.

————. 1940. *Sex and life: Forty years of biological and medical experiments*. New York: Viking Press.

Steinach, E., and H. Kun. 1926. Antagonistische Wirkungen der Keimdrüsen-Hormone. *Biologia Generalis* 2: 815–34.

Steinmetz, H., L. Jäncke, et al. 1992. Sex but no hand difference in the isthmus of the corpus callosum. *Neurology* 42: 749–52.

Steinmetz, H., J. F. Staiger, et al. 1995. Corpus callosum and brain volume in women and men. *NeuroReport* 6: 1002–4.

Stent, G. S. 1981. Strength and weakness of the genetic approach to the development of the nervous system. *Annual Review of Neuroscience* 4: 163–94.

Sterling, D. 1954. *The story of mosses, ferns and mushrooms*. New York: Doubleday.

————. 1955. *Insects and the homes they build*. New York: Doubleday.

————. 1979. *Black foremothers: Three lives*. Old Westbury, NY: The Feminist Press.

————. 1991. *Ahead of her time: Abby Kelley and the politics of antislavery*. New York: Norton.

Sterling, P. 1970. *Sea and earth: The life of Rachel Carson*. New York: Crowell.

Sterr, A., M. M. Müller, et al. 1998. Changed perceptions in Braille readers. *Nature* 391 (January 1998): 134–35.

Stigler, S. M. 1986. *The history of statistics: The measurement of uncertainty before 1900*. Cambridge: Harvard University Press.

Stockard, C. N., and G. N. Papanicolaou. 1917. The existence of a typical oestrus cycle in the guinea pig, with a study of its histological and physiological changes. *American Journal of Anatomy* 22: 225–65.

Stocking, G. 1987. *Victorian anthropology*. New York: Free Press.

Stocking, G. W., ed. 1988. *Bones, bodies, behavior: Essays on biological anthropology*. Madison: University of Wisconsin Press.

Stone, C. P. 1939. Sex drive. In *Sex and internal secretions*, ed. E. Allen, C. H. Danforth, and E. A. Doisy. Baltimore: Williams and Wilkins, 1213–62.

Strain, L., J. Dean, et al. 1998. A true hermaphrodite chimera resulting from embryo amalgamation after in vitro fertilization. *New England Journal of Medicine* 338(3): 166–69.

Strauss, A. 1978. A social worlds perspective. *Studies in Symbolic Interaction* 1: 199–228.

Strock, C. 1998. *Married women who love women*. New York: Doubleday.

Sugita, Y. 1996. Global plasticity in adult visual cortex following reversal of visual input. *Nature* 180 (April 11): 523–26.

Swain, A., V. Narvaez, et al. 1998. Dax1 antagonizes Sry action in mammalian sex determination. *Nature* 391 (February 19): 761–67.

Sylven, L., K. Hagenfeldt, et al. 1993. Life with Turner's syndrome—A psychosocial report from 22 middle-aged women. *Acta Endocrinologica* 129: 188–94.

Symons, D. 1979. *The evolution of human sexuality.* Oxford, U.K.: Oxford University Press.

Tagatz, G. E., R. A. Kopher, et al. 1979. The clitoral index: A bioassay of androgenic stimulation. *Obstetrics and Gynecology* 54: 562–64.

Taub, E., J. E. Crago, et al. 1994. An operant approach to rehabilitation medicine: Overcoming learned nonuse by shaping. *Journal of Experimental Analysis of Behavior* 61(2): 281–93.

Taub, E., N. E. Miller, T. A. Novack, et al. 1993. Technique to improve chronic motor deficit after stroke. *Archives of Physical and Medical Rehabilitation* 74(4): 347–54.

Taylor, P. J. 1995. Building on construction: An exploration of heterogeneous constructionism, using an analogy from psychology and a sketch from socioeconomic modeling. *Perspectives on Science* 3(1): 66–98.

———. 1997. Appearances notwithstanding, we are all doing something like political ecology. *Social Epistemology* 11(1): 111–27.

———. 1998a. Natural selection: A heavy hand in biological and social thought. *Science as Culture* 7(1): 5–32.

———. 1998b. Inseparable and distributed complexity: Three projects for mapping and negotiating social-natural processes. Unpublished manuscript.

Teague, J. L., D. R. Roth, et al. 1994. Repair of hypospadias complications using the metal-based flap urethroplasty. *Journal of Urology* 151 (February): 470–72.

ten Berge, B. S. 1960. True hermaphroditism with female chromatic pattern: Marriage between partners of the same sex. *Gynaecologia* 149: 112–18.

Tessitore, L., E. Sesca, et al. 1995. Sexual dimorphism of cell turnover during liver hyperplasia. *Chemico-Biological Interactions* 97(1): 1–10.

Thelen, E. 1995. Motor development: A new synthesis. *American Psychologist* 50(2): 79–95.

Thelen, E., and L. B. Smith. 1994. *A dynamic systems approach to the development of cognition and action.* Cambridge: MIT Press.

Thomas, W. I. 1907. *Sex and society: Studies in the social psychology of sex.* Chicago: University of Chicago Press.

Thomson, R. G., ed. 1996. *Freakery: Cultural spectacles of the extraordinary body.* New York: New York University Press.

Thönnessen, W. 1969. *The emancipation of women: The rise and decline of the women's movement in German social democracy, 1863–1933.* London: Pluto Press.

Thor, D. H., and W. R. Holloway. 1984. Social play in juvenile rats: A decade of methodological and experimental research. *Neuroscience and Biobehavioral Reviews* 8: 455–64.

Thorne, B. 1993. *Gender play: Girls and boys in school.* New Brunswick, NJ: Rutgers University Press.

Tiefer, L. 1978. The context and consequences of contemporary sex research: A feminist perspective. In *Sex and behavior: Status and prospectus*, ed. T. E. McGill, D. A. Dewsbury, and B. D. Sachs. New York: Plenum Press, 363–86.

———. 1994a. The medicalization of impotence: Normalizing phallocentrism. *Gender and Society* 8(3): 363–77.

———. 1994b. Might premature ejaculation be organic? The perfect penis takes a giant step forward. *Journal of Sex Education and Therapy* 20(1): 7–8.

Titley, O. G., and A. Bracka. 1998. A 5-year audit of trainees experience and outcomes with two-stage hypospadias surgery. *British Journal of Plastic Surgery* 51(5): 370–75.

Tobet, S. A., and T. O. Fox. 1992. Sex differences in neuronal morphology influenced hormonally throughout life. In *Handbook of Neurobiology*, ed. A. A. Gerall, H. Moltz, and I. I. Ward. New York: Plenum Press, 41–82.

Tolmein, O., and A. Bergling. 1999. Intersexuell. *Die Zeit* 5: 12-15.

Toran-Allerand, C. D. 1984. On the genesis of sexual differentiation of the central nervous system: Morphogenetic consequences of steroidal exposure and possible role of alpha-fetoprotein. *Progress in Brain Research* 61: 63–97.

Toublanc, J. E., E. Thibaud, et al. 1997. Enquête sur l'avenir socio-psycho-affectif des femmes atteintes du syndrome de Turner. *Contraception Fertilité Sexualité* 25(7–8): 633–38.

Trautman, P. D., H. F. Meyer-Bahlburg, et al. 1995. Effects of early prenatal dexamethasone on the cognitive and behavioral development of young children: Results of a pilot study. *Psychoneuroendocrinology* 20(4): 439–49.

———. 1996. Mothers' reactions to prenatal diagnostic procedures and dexamethasone treatment of congenital adrenal hyperplasia. *Journal of Psychosomatic Obstetric Gynaecology* 17(3): 175–81.

Travis, J. 1992. The brain remaps its own contours. *Science* 258 (October 9): 216–20.

Trope, E., P. Rozin, et al. 1992. Information processing in the separated hemispheres of callosotomy patients: Does the analytic-holistic dichotomy hold? *Brain and Cognition* 19: 123–47.

Trumbach, R. 1987. Sodomitical subcultures, sodomitical roles, and the gender revolution of the eighteenth century: The recent historiography. In *'Tis nature's fault: Unauthorized sexuality during the Enlightenment*, ed. R. P. Maccubbin. Cambridge, U.K.: Cambridge University Press, 109–21.

———. 1989. Gender and the homosexual role in modern western culture: The 18th and 19th centuries compared. In *Homosexuality, which Homosexuality?*, ed. D. Altman. Amsterdam: An Dekker/Schorer, 149–69.

———. 1991a. London's Sapphists: From three sexes to four genders in the making of modern culture. In *Bodyguards: The cultural politics of gender ambiguity*, ed. J. Epstein and K. Straub. New York: Routledge, 112–41.

———. 1991b. Sex, gender, and sexual identity in modern culture: Male sodomy and female prostitution in Enlightenment London. *Journal of the History of Sexuality* 2(2): 186–203.

————. 1998. *Sex and the gender revolution: Heterosexuality and the third gender in Enlightenment London.* Chicago: University of Chicago Press.

Tsuruo, Y., K. Ishimura, et al. 1996. Immunohistochemical localization of estrogen receptors within aromatase-immunoreactive neurons in the fetal and neonatal rat brain. *Anatomy and Embryology* 193(2): 113–21.

Tuladhar, R., P. G. Davis, et al. 1998. Establishment of a normal range of penile length in preterm infants. *Journal of Paediatric Child Health* 34(5): 471–73.

Turkle, S. 1995. *Life on the screen.* New York: Simon & Schuster.

Tyler, C. R., S. Jobling, et al. 1998. Endocrine disruption in wildlife: A critical review of the evidence. *Critical Reviews of Toxicology* 28(4): 319–61.

Uecker, A., and J. E. Obrzut. 1994. Hemisphere and gender differences in mental rotation. *Brain and Cognition* 22: 42–50.

Unsigned. 1921a. Disappointments of endocrinology. *Journal of the American Medical Association* 76(24): 1685–86.

————. 1921b. The endocrine glands—A caution. *Journal of the American Medical Association* 76(22): 1500–1501.

————. 1928. Ovarian hormones and ovarian organotherapy. *Journal of the American Medical Association* 91(16): 1194–95.

————. 1992. Homosexuality and cognition. *Science* 255: 539.

————. 1993. Five failed controversial Olympics sex test. *Science* 261: 27.

Vaias, L. J., L. M. Napolitano, et al. 1993. Identification of stimuli that mediate experience-dependent modification of homosexual courtship in Drosophila melanogaster. *Behavior Genetics* 23(1): 91–97.

Vainio, S., M. Heikkilä, et al. 1999. Female development in mammals is regulated by Wnt-4 signaling. *Nature* 397 (February 4): 405–9.

Valenstein, E. S., and R. W. Goy. 1957. Further studies of the organization and display of sexual behavior in male guinea pigs. *Journal of Comparative and Physiological Psychology* 50(2): 115–19.

Valenstein, E. S., W. Riss, et al. 1955. Experiential and genetic factors in the organization of sexual behavior in male guinea pigs. *Journal of Comparative and Physiological Psychology* 48: 397–403.

Valenstein, E. S., R. Walter, et al. 1954. Sex drive in genetically heterogeneous and highly inbred strains of male guinea pigs. *Journal of Comparative and Physiological Psychology* 47: 162–65.

Valenstein, E. S., and W. C. Young. 1955. An experiential factor influencing the effectiveness of testosterone propionate in eliciting sexual behavior in guinea pigs. *Endocrinology* 56: 173–77.

Valian, V. 1998a. Running in place. *The Sciences* (January/February): 18–23.

————. 1998b. *Why so slow? The advancement of women.* Cambridge: MIT Press.

Valsiner, J. 1987. Culture and the development of children's action: A cultural-historical theory of developmental psychology. New York: Wiley.

van de Poll, N. E., F. H. de Jonge, et al. 1981. Failure to find sex differences in testosterone activated aggressive behavior in two strains of rats. *Hormones and Behavior* 15: 94–105.

Van den Wijngaard, M. 1991*a*. The acceptance of scientific theories and images of masculinity and femininity. *Journal of the History of Biology* 24(1): 19–49.

————. 1991*b*. *Reinventing the sexes: Feminism and biomedical construction of femininity and masculinity 1959–1958*. Amsterdam: University of Amsterdam, 187.

van der Kamp, H. J., F. M. E. Slijper, et al. 1992. Evaluation of young women with congenital adrenal hyperplasia: A pilot study. *Hormone Research* 37 (suppl. 3): 45–49.

van Seters, A. P., and A. K. Slob. 1988. Mutually gratifying heterosexual relationship with micropenis of husband. *Journal of Sex and Marital Therapy* 14(2): 98–107.

Van Wyk, J. J. 1999. Should boys with micropenis be reared as girls? *Journal of Pediatrics* 134 (May): 537–38.

Vance, C. S. 1991. Anthropology rediscovers sexuality: A theoretical comment. *Social Science and Medicine* 33(8): 875–84.

Vandersteen, D. R., and D. A. Husmann. 1998. Late onset recurrent penile chordee after successful correction at hypospadias repair. *Journal of Urology* 160 (3 pt. 2): 1131–33; discussion 1137.

Velidedeoglu, H. V., O. K. Coskunfirat, et al. 1997. The surgical management of incomplete testicular feminization syndrome in three sisters. *British Journal of Plastic Surgery* 50: 212–16.

Velut, S., C. Destrieux, et al. 1998. Anatomie morphologique du corps calleux. *Neurochirurgie* 44 (suppl. 1): 17–30.

Verbrugge, M. H. 1997. Recreating the body: Women's physical education and the science of sex differences in America, 1900–1940. *Bulletin of the History of Medicine* 71(2): 273–304.

Vicinus, M. 1989. "They wonder to which sex I belong": The historical roots of the modern lesbian identity. In *Homosexuality, which homosexuality?*, ed. D. Altman. Amsterdam: An Dekker/Schorer, 171–198.

Vines, G. 1992. Last Olympics for the sex test? *New Scientist* 135(1828): 39–42.

vos Savant, M. 1996. Ask Marilyn. *Parade Magazine*, August 4, 6.

Voyer, D. 1998. On the reliability and validity of noninvasive laterality measures. *Brain and Cognition* 36: 209–36.

Voyer, D., S. Voyer, et al. 1995. Magnitude of sex differences in spatial abilities: A meta-analysis and consideration of critical variables. *Psychological Bulletin* 117(2): 250–70.

Waddington, C. H. 1957. *The strategy of the genes*. London: Allen and Unwin.

————. 1975. *The evolution of an evolutionist*. Ithaca, N.Y.: Cornell University Press.

Wade, N. 1994. Method and madness: How men and women think. *New York Times Magazine*, July 12, 32.

————. 1999. Parent cells found in brain may be key to nerve repair. *New York Times*, January 8, A12.

Wahlsten, D. 1990. Insensitivity of the analysis of variance to heredity-environment interaction. *Behavior and Brain Sciences* 13: 109–161.

————. 1994. The intelligence of heritability. *Canadian Psychology* 35: 244–60.

Wahlsten, D., and K. M. Bishop. 1998. Effect sizes and meta-analysis indicate no sex dimorphism in the human or rodent corpus callosum. *Behavioral and Brain Sciences* 21(3): 338–39.

Wallen, K. 1996. Nature needs nurture: The interaction of hormonal and social influences on the development of behavioral sex differences in Rhesus monkeys. *Hormones and Behavior* 30: 364–78.

Wang, X., M. M. Merzenich, et al. 1995. Remodeling of hand representation in adult cortex determined by timing of tactile stimulation. *Nature* 378 (November 2): 71–75.

Wapner, S., and J. Demick. 1998. Developmental analysis: A holistic, developmental, systems oriented perspective. New York: Wiley.

Ward, I. L. 1992. Sexual behavior: The product of perinatal hormonal and prepubertal social factors. In *Handbook of Behavioral Neurobiology*, ed. A. Gerall, M. Howard, and I. L. Ward. New York: Plenum Press, 157–80.

Wassersug, R. 1996. Fat rats in the lab of luxury. *Natural History* 6: 18–19.

Watson, J. B. 1914. *Behavior: An introduction to comparative psychology*. New York: Holt.

Wavell, S., and A. Alderson. 1992. Row looms over Olympic sex test. *Sunday New York Times*, Overseas News, January 26.

Wedell, A. 1998. Molecular genetics of congenital adrenal hyperplasia 21-hydroxylase deficiency: Implications for diagnosis, prognosis and treatment. *Acta Paediatrica* 87: 159–64.

Weeks, J. 1981a. Discourse, desire and sexual deviance: Some problems in a history of homosexuality. In *The making of the modern homosexual*, ed. K. Plummer. London: Hutchinson, 76–111.

————. 1981b. *Sex, politics and society: The regulation of sexuality since 1800*. London: Longman.

Weidman, N. M. 1999. *Constructing scientific psychology: Karl Lashley's mind-brain debates*. Cambridge, U.K.: Cambridge University Press, 618.

Weidensall, J. 1916. *The mentality of the criminal woman*. Baltimore: Warwick and York.

Weinrich, J. D. 1987. *Sexual landscapes: Why we are what we are; why we love whom we love*. New York: Scribner.

Weir, J. J. 1895. The effect of female suffrage on posterity. *The American Naturalist* 29: 815–25.

Weis, S., G. Weber, et al. 1988. The human corpus callosum and the controversy about a sexual dimorphism. *Psychobiology* 16(4): 411–15.

Weisman, Y., F. Cassorla, et al. 1993. Sex-specific response of bone cells to gonadal steroids—modulation in perinatally androgenized females and in testicular feminized male rats. *Steroids* 58(3): 126–33.

Weiss, P. 1959. Cellular dynamics. *Reviews of Modern Physics* 31: 11–20.

Weiss, S., G. Weber, et al. 1989. The controversy about a sexual dimorphism of the human corpus callosum. *International Journal of Neuroscience* 47: 169–73.

Werner, M. H., J. R. Huth, et al. 1996. Molecular determinants of mammalian sex. *Trends in Biochemical Sciences* 21(8): 302–8.

West, C., and S. Fenstermaker. 1995. Doing difference. *Gender and Society* 9(1): 8–37.

West, C., and D. H. Zimmerman. 1987. Doing gender. *Gender and Society* 1(2): 125–51.

Weston, K. 1993. Lesbian and gay studies in the house of anthropology. *Annual Review of Anthropology* 22: 339–67.

Whalen, R. E. 1974. Sexual differentiation: Models, methods and mechanisms. In *Sex Differences in Behavior*, ed. R. C. Friedman, R. M. Richart, and R. L. Van de Wiele. Huntington, N.Y.: Robert E. Krieger, 467–81.

Whalen, R. E., and F. Johnson. 1990. To fight or not to fight: The question is "whom"? *Comparative Physiology* 9: 301–12.

Whalen, R. E., and R. D. Nadler. 1965. Modification of spontaneous and hormone-induced sexual behavior by estrogen administered to neonatal female rats. *Journal of Comparative Psychology* 60: 150–52.

Whitacre, C. C., S. C. Reingold, et al. 1999. A gender gap in auto-immunity. *Science* 283 (February 26): 1277–88.

Whitam, F. L., M. Diamond, et al. 1993. Homosexual orientation in twins: A report on 61 pairs and three triplet sets. *Archives of Sexual Behavior* 33(3): 187–206.

White, S. A., and R. D. Fernald. 1997. Changing through doing: Behavioral influences on the brain. *Recent Progress in Hormone Research* 52: 455–74.

Whitehead, A. N. 1929. *Process and reality: An essay in cosmology.* New York: Macmillan.

Wickelgren, I. 1997. Estrogen stakes claim to cognition. *Science* 276 (May 2): 675–78.

Wiesner, B. P. 1935. The post-natal development of the genital organs in the albino rat VI. Effects of sex hormones in the heteronomous sex. *Journal of Obstetrics and Gynaecology* 42: 8–78.

Williams, S. J., and G. Bendelow. 1998. *The lived body: Sociological themes, embodied issues.* London: Routledge.

Williams-Ashman, H. G., and A. H. Reddi. 1971. Actions of vertebrate sex hormones. *Annual Review of Physiology* 33: 31–82.

Williamson, S., and R. Nowak. 1998. The truth about women. *New Scientist* 21(45): 34–35.

Wilson, B., and W. G. Reiner. 1998. Management of intersex: A shifting paradigm. *Journal of Clinical Ethics* 9(4): 360–70.

Wilson, E. 1998. *Neural geographies: Feminism and the microstructure of cognition.* New York: Routledge.

Wilson, E. O. 1978. *On human nature.* Cambridge: Harvard University Press.

Wilson, R. A. 1966. *Feminine forever.* New York: M. Evans.

Wilson, R. C., A. B. Mercado, et al. 1995. Steroid 21-hydroxylase deficiency:

Genotype may not predict phenotype. *Journal of Clinical Endocrinology and Metabolism* 80(8): 2322–29.

Wise, M. N., ed. 1995. *The values of precision*. Princeton: Princeton University Press.

Wishart, J. M., A. G. Need, et al. 1995. Effect of age on bone density and bone turnover in men. *Endocrinology and Metabolism* 42(2): 141–46.

Wisniewski, A. B. 1998. Sexually dimorphic patterns of cortical asymmetry, and the role for sex steroid hormones in determining cortical patterns of lateralization. *Psychoneuroendocrinology* 23(5): 519–47.

Archiv für sexual wissenschaft. 1999. Robert Koch Institut.

Witelson, S. 1985. The brain connection: The corpus callosum is larger in left-handers. *Science* 229: 665–68.

———. 1989. Hand and sex differences in the isthmus and genu of the human corpus callosum. *Brain* 112: 799–835.

———. 1991a. Sex differences in neuroanatomical changes with aging. *New England Journal of Medicine* 325(3): 211–12.

———. 1991b. Neural sexual mosaicism: Sexual differentiation of the human temporo-parietal region for functional asymmetry. *Psychoneuroendocrinology* 16: 131–53.

Witelson, S. F., and C. F. Goldsmith. 1991. The relationship of hand preference to anatomy of the corpus callosum in men. *Brain Research* 545: 175–82.

Witschi, E., and W. F. Mengert. 1942. Endocrine studies on human hermaphrodites and their bearing on the interpretation of homosexuality. *Journal of Clinical Endocrinology* 2(5): 279–86.

Wolf, U. 1995. The molecular genetics of human sex determination. *Journal of Molecular Medicine* 73: 325–31.

Womack, E. B., and F. C. Koch. 1932. The testicular hormone content of human urine. *Endocrinology* 16: 273–77.

Wood, R. I., and W. S. Newman. 1995. Androgen and estrogen receptors coexist within individual neurons in the brain of the Syrian hamster. *Neuroendocrinology* 62: 487–97.

Woodhouse, C. R. J. 1994. The sexual and reproductive consequences of congenital genitourinary anomalies. *Journal of Urology* 152: 645–51.

Wright, R. 1994. *The moral animal*. New York: Pantheon.

Wright, T. 1999. A one-number census: Some related history. *Science* 283: 491.

Yang, T. T., C. C. Gallen, et al. 1994. Noninvasive detection of cerebral plasticity in adult human somatosensory cortex. *NeuroReport* 5: 701–4.

Yavuzer, R., C. Baran, et al. 1998. Vascularized double-sided preputial island flap with W flap glanuloplasty for hypospadias repair. *Plastic and Reconstructive Surgery* 101(3): 751–15.

Yazgan, M. Y., B. E. Wexler, et al. 1995. Functional significance of individual variations in callosal area. *Neuropsychologia* 33(6): 769–79.

Yeh, S.-R., R. A. Fricke, et al. 1996. The effect of social experience on serotonergic modulation of the escape circuit of crayfish. *Science* 271 (January 19): 366–69.

Young, H. H. 1937. *Genital abnormalities, hermaphroditism and related adrenal diseases.* Baltimore: Williams and Wilkins.

Young, I. M. 1990. *Throwing like a girl and other essays in feminist philosophy and social theory.* Bloomington: Indiana University Press.

Young, W. C. 1941. Observations and experiments on mating behavior in female mammals. *Quarterly Review of Biology* 16(2): 135–56.

———. 1957. Genetic and psychological determinants of sexual behavior patterns. In *Hormones, brain function and behavior*, ed. H. Hoagland. New York: Academic Press.

———. 1960. A hormonal action participating in the patterning of sexual behavior in the guinea pig. In *Recent advances in biological psychiatry*, ed. J. Wortis. New York: Grune and Stratton, 200–209.

———. 1961. The hormones and mating behavior. In *Sex and internal secretions*, ed. W. C. Young and G. W. Corner. Baltimore: Waverly Press, 1173–1239.

———. 1964. Hormones and sexual behavior. *Science* 143: 212–18.

———. 1965. The organization of sexual behavior by hormonal action during the prenatal and larval periods in vertebrates. In *Sex and Behavior*, ed. F. A. Beach. New York: Wiley, 89–107.

———. 1967. Prenatal gonadal hormones and behavior in the adult. In *Comparative psychopathology: Animal and human*, ed. J. Zubin and H. F. Hunt. New York: Grune and Stratton.

Young, W. C., and G. W. Corner, eds. 1961. *Sex and internal secretions.* Baltimore: Williams and Wilkins.

Young, W. C., E. W. Dempsey, et al. 1939. Sexual behavior and sexual receptivity in the female guinea pig. *Journal of Comparative Psychology* 27(1): 49–68.

Young, W. C., and J. A. Grunt. 1951. The pattern and measurement of sexual behavior in the male guinea pig. *Journal of Comparative and Physiological Psychology* 44(5): 492–500.

Young, W. C., and B. Rundlett. 1939. The hormonal induction of homosexual behavior in the spayed female guinea pig. *Psychosomatic Medicine* 1(4): 449–60.

Zachariae, Z. 1955. A case of true hermaphroditism. *Acta Endocrinologica* 20: 331–37.

Zita, J. N. 1992. Male lesbians and the postmodernist body. *Hypatia* 7(4): 106–27.

Zondek, B. 1934. Mass excretion of oestrogenic hormone in the urine of the stallion. *Nature* 133: 209–10.

Zucker, K. J. 1996. Commentary on Diamond's "Prenatal predisposition and the clinical management of some pediatric conditions." *Journal of Sex and Marital Therapy* 22(3): 148–60.

Zucker, K. J., and S. J. Bradley. 1995. *Gender identity disorder and psychosexual problems in children and adolescents.* New York: Guilford Press.

Zucker, K. J., S. J. Bradley, et al. 1996. Psychosexual development of women with congenital adrenal hyperplasia. *Hormones and Behavior* 30: 300–318.

Zuger, A. 1997. Removing half of brain improves young epileptics' lives. *New York Times*, August 19, C4.

Zuger, B. 1970. Gender role determination: A critical review of the evidence from hermaphroditism. *Psychosomatic Medicine* 32(5): 449–63.

INDEX